## Praise for Gail Collins

"In a deft and entertaining work of historical [...]
erature of American women's history to we [...]
of women's experiences, one that challenges [...]
forces readers to think in new ways not just [...]
tion and how we came to be."

"What a pageant! Gail Collins's *America's Women* sweeps across four centuries of the history of women in America in one seamless take. Collins has gathered material from scholars and writers in an ambitious . . . and highly readable volume."
—Bettyann Holtzmann Kelves, *Los Angeles Times*

"With *America's Women* Gail Collins has changed the face and gender of American history. From the colonial women to the suffragettes to the modern feminists, it is rare to come across a book that is this expansive, important, and a joy to read. *America's Women* is a major achievement."
—Wendy Wasserstein

"Collins has a genius for identifying fascinating, provocative facts that help us imagine the daily lives of women in the past."
—*New York Newsday*

"This is an astonishing book. Like every other son, husband, and father, I thought I knew about women. Turns out I didn't. There is the shock of belated recognition on every page."
—Richard Reeves

"A fascinating compendium."
—*O, The Oprah Magazine*

"*America's Women* is a one-stop account of the lives and times of the second sex in the U.S. . . . There's a wealth of information. . . . Collins's accessible, entertaining style makes it a brisk, enjoyable read."
—*Business Week*

"At last the perfect American Herstory, or herstories. Gail Collins has followed the trail from Eleanor Dare's voyage to Virginia to Betty Friedan's march down Fifth Avenue, stopping along the way to talk about suffrage and fashion, birth control and corsets. It's a treasure."
—Ellen Goodman

"Written in the same lively prose that characterized Collins's work as a columnist for *New York Newsday* and the *New York Times* before her 2001 promotion, *America's Women* stands out from other historical surveys."
—*Time Out* (New York)

"*America's Women* is the product of a powerful and consistent intelligence and trenchant wit. Collins has created a remarkable history. . . . A triumphant, kaleidoscopic self-definition of American women through their actions and achievements."
—*Book* magazine

"Written in a lively, readable style, *America's Women* is an enthralling social history woven around profiles of women you've heard of and women you haven't."
—*St. Louis Post-Dispatch*

"Enormously entertaining and illuminating."
—*Boston Globe*

*New York Times*

---

## *About the Author*

---

GAIL COLLINS is the editorial page editor at the *New York Times*—
the first woman to hold this position. Prior to that, she was a columnist
for the paper's op-ed page, a member of the editorial board, and a
columnist for the *New York Daily News* and *New York Newsday*. She is
the author of *Scorpion Tongues: Gossip, Celebrity, and American Politics*.

ALSO BY GAIL COLLINS

*Scorpion Tongues: Gossip, Celebrity, and American Politics*

*The Millennium Book* (with Dan Collins)

FOUR HUNDRED YEARS

OF DOLLS,

DRUDGES,

HELPMATES,

AND

HEROINES

# AMERICA'S
# WOMEN

## Gail Collins

Perennial

*An Imprint of* HarperCollins*Publishers*

A hardcover edition of this book was published in 2003 by William Morrow, an imprint of HarperCollins Publishers.

HarperCollins books may be purchased for educational, business, or sales promotional use. For information please write: Special Markets Department, HarperCollins Publishers Inc., 10 East 53rd Street, New York, NY 10022.

First Perennial edition published 2004.

*Designed by Betty Lew*

The Library of Congress has catalogued the hardcover edition as follows:
Collins, Gail.
    America's women / Gail Collins—1st ed.
        p.  cm.
    Includes bibliographical references and index.
    ISBN 0-06-018510-4
    1. Women—United States—History. 1. Title.
HQ1410.C588  2003
305.4'0973—dc21                                                2003051011

ISBN 0-06-095981-9 (pbk.)

04 05 06 07 08 ❖/RRD 10 9 8 7 6 5 4 3 2 1

*To my mother*

*When I was young if a girl married poor,*
*she became a housekeeper and a drudge.*
*If she married wealthy, she became a pet and a doll.*

—Susan B. Anthony

*A smart woman can do very well in this country.*

—A young woman in nineteenth-century California

# CONTENTS

# INTRODUCTION

When I look back through all of American history, the one moment that stays with me is the image of women standing on the deck of the *Mayflower,* staring out at a whole continent of dense forest. On the trip over, they must have been fixated on simply getting to land. They could never have imagined how wild it would seem, how big and empty of everything they knew. Plenty of male Europeans had made the same voyage before them, but they were explorers or traders or fishermen, out to get what they needed and return home. For the women, this was going to be the only home they would ever know again. The real job of settling was theirs. Most of them would die before they could put down real roots, but those who survived generally went on to have big families, whose descendants took special pride in knowing they shared the DNA of those simple, scared, determined women.

The history of American women is all about leaving home—crossing oceans and continents, or getting jobs and living on their own. Some of our national heroines were defined by the fact that they never nested—they were peripatetic crusaders like Susan B. Anthony, Clara Barton, Sojourner Truth, Dorothea Dix. The center of our story is the tension between the yearning to create a home and the urge to get out of it.

I started thinking about American women when I was doing my last book, *Scorpion Tongues*, and stumbled across Louisa Adams, the wife of the sixth president of the United States and daughter-in-law of the formidable Abigail. As First Lady, Louisa was so miserable she spent much of her time eating chocolate and writing memoirs she called *Adventures of a Nobody*. But she had been a diplomat's wife who traveled in midwinter from Russia, crossing the icy and corpse-laden fields of Europe in the middle of the Napoleonic War, alone in a carriage with her small son. She was a hostess so skilled that her party-giving helped propel her distinctly unlovable husband into the presidency. You've got to take note of that kind of duality; it crops up all along our history. This was a country, after all, where some nineteenth-century females became famous for writing books about why women had to stay out of the public eye, while others traveled all around the country lecturing on how women should never leave home. In World War II, women pilots risked their lives pulling targets so that inexperienced gunners could practice firing at them. And women pilots were arrested if they left the air base wearing slacks after dark.

The history of American women is about the fight for freedom, but it's less a war against oppressive men than a struggle to straighten out the perpetually mixed message about women's role that was accepted by almost everybody of both genders. Southern matriarchs aspired to be the image of the helpless female, then ran the plantations while their husbands went to Congress—or luxuriated at a spa. Pioneer women rode sidesaddle and wore gloves to protect their soft hands, then crawled up the side of mountains with a newborn baby in one arm. Everyone believed that married women were obliged to stay home with their children, while everyone bought factory goods produced by poor working mothers, made from cotton picked by female slaves. When slavery ended, nothing irritated white Southerners—or visiting Northerners—more than the idea that ex-slave women wanted to stop working and become homemakers.

Writing *America's Women* gave me the opportunity to read hundreds of books about the women of this country, which was a joy. We live in a great age for women's history, one that makes it easy to forget that only a few decades ago college professors were discouraged from teaching the subject because people believed that there wasn't enough material to fill up an entire semester. I hope reading this book leads others back through the tracks of the writers I've followed. From everything I've learned, I've tried to spin a story that's about both what women did and what it felt like for them to do it. Everything they achieved through the Victorian age was accomplished in very long dresses and, generally, tight corsets. This is the story of the woman who saved Washington's army by setting fire to New York, and the mystery of what pioneers on the wagon trains did about menstruation and wet diapers. I tried to see the nineteenth century as an era when women first demanded the right to vote, but also as the time when they were medicating themselves into mercury poisoning and making their first cautious commitment to regular bathing. That period ended with the Gilded Age, when the suffrage movement went into a funk, when women first began earning a living behind a typewriter, and when the most glamorous chorus girls were the ones with huge thighs.

The middle of *America's Women* is about the Civil War, and how women, black and white, confronted slavery and abolition. As in every other period of crisis, the rules of sexual decorum were suspended due to emergency. The chaos of the battlefield turned out to be the ideal ground for female initiative—disorganized and desperately in need of people who would work for nothing and do any task required. That pattern repeats itself throughout this story. It took our entire history to actually change the rules of proper female behavior. But those rules were temporarily abandoned whenever the country needed women to do something they weren't supposed to do. And even in circumstances less critical, women were almost always welcomed in new enterprises that hadn't yet become either prestigious or profitable—whether it was early radio or early cattle drives.

The Great Depression unleashed a national war against working women, followed by World War II, when there was a national crusade to get women to take jobs. Our own era began with the late 1960s and early 1970s, when everything changed so fast the country was banning job discrimination against women while they still couldn't serve on juries in some states, and nonvirgins weren't allowed to bring rape charges in others.

Everyone can choose their own heroines in this story; I have a particularly soft spot for the eccentric, heroic Grimke sisters, who braved violent mobs to speak out against slavery, and demonstrated, to the utter delight of the other female reformers, that it was possible to believe in women's rights and still find a husband. One of the tricks to being a great historical figure is to leave behind as much information as possible. We talk a lot more about the Pilgrims than Eleanor Dare of Virginia; she came first but vanished before history got a chance to know her. New England spinsters get way more than their share of attention because of their winning habit of keeping diaries. Native American women who had no written language left behind almost nothing of their voices. It's absolutely impossible to write this kind of book without wanting to apologize for the failure to give them their due.

The first women in America whose names we know actually came half a millennium before Eleanor Dare. Gudrid and Freydis were Vikings, relatives of Leif Eriksson, and they sailed with their men on missions of trade and exploration. Gudrid gave birth to the first European child in the New World, in what is now Canada, and was known for her ability to get along with the strange people the Vikings encountered in their travels. Freydis organized a massacre of her business partners, finishing off the wives and female servants herself.

That, at least, was the tale the Vikings told, and there's a good-or-bad plot that fits the image of women throughout our history— virtuous wives on one hand, and on the other, the women who stepped outside their appointed roles, causing disaster. Gudrid actually did some amazing things, making her a pretty good prototype for the traditional American woman. She is said to have traveled on the Hudson River and visited Greenland, Norway, and Italy, outliving several husbands before ending her life as a nun in Iceland. Freydis, for her part, turned out to be a handy person to have around in a pinch. When the Viking camp was attacked by Indians, causing the male defenders to flee, a pregnant Freydis grabbed a handy weapon, took out her swollen breasts, "and whetted the sword upon them" according to a Viking chronicler. The sight of her so unnerved the war party they "became afraid and ran away."

That's pretty much our story: Melanie and Scarlett, Annie Oakley and Calamity Jane, the soccer moms and the vampire slayers. All of them are more complicated than they let on. The Gudrids embraced their humble identity and hid their moments of endurance or courage or innovation under the all-purpose excuse of emergency. The Freydises were sometimes less rebels than victims of their own naïveté about the way the world worked. But as you read through history you always wait for them to appear—standing in a clearing, beating a sword against a naked breast.

# AMERICA'S
# WOMEN

# The First Colonists:
# Voluntary and Otherwise

### THE EXTREMELY BRIEF STORY OF VIRGINIA DARE

Eleanor Dare must have been either extraordinarily adventurous or easily led. In 1587, when she was pregnant with her first child, she set sail across the Atlantic, headed for a continent where no woman of her kind had ever lived, let alone given birth. The only English-speaking residents of the New World at the time were a handful of men who had been left behind during an earlier, unsuccessful attempt at settlement on Roanoke Island, off what is now the coast of North Carolina. Eleanor's father, John White, was to become governor of the new colony. Her husband, Ananias, a bricklayer, was one of his assistants.

Under the best of circumstances, a boat took about two months to get from England to the New World, and there were plenty of reasons to avoid the trip. Passengers generally slept on the floor, on damp straw, living off salted pork and beef, dried peas and beans. They suffered from seasickness, dysentery, typhoid, and cholera. Their ship could sink, or be taken by privateers, or run aground at the wrong place. Even if it stayed afloat, it might be buffeted around for so long that the provisions would run out before the travelers reached land. Later would-be colonists sometimes starved to death en route. (The inaptly named *Love* took a year to make the trip, and at the end of the voyage rats and mice were being sold as food.) Some women considered the odds and decided to stay on dry land. The wife of John Dunton, a colonial minister, wrote to him that she would rather be "a living wife in England than a dead one at sea."

But if Eleanor Dare had any objections, they were never recorded. She and sixteen other women settlers, along with ninety-one men and nine children, encountered no serious problems until they stopped to pick up the men who had been left at Roanoke. When they went ashore to look for them, all they found were the bones of a single Englishman. The uncooperative ship's captain refused to take them farther, and they were forced to settle on the same unlucky site.

Try to imagine what Eleanor Dare must have thought when she walked, heavy with child, through the houses of the earlier settlers, now standing empty, "overgrown with Melons of divers sortes, and Deere within them, feeding," as her father later recorded. Eleanor was a member of the English gentry, hardly bred for tilling fields and fighting Indians. Was she confident that her husband the bricklayer and her father the bureaucrat could keep her and her baby alive, or was she beginning to blame them for getting her into this extremely unpromising situation? All we know is that on August 18, the first English child was born in America and christened Virginia Dare—named, like the colony, in honor of the Virgin Queen who ruled back home. A few days later her grandfather boarded the boat with its cranky captain and sailed back to England for more supplies, leaving Eleanor and the other settlers to make homes out of the ghost village. It was nearly three years before White could get passage back to Roanoke, and when he arrived he discovered the village once again abandoned, with no trace of any human being, living or dead. No one knows what happened to Eleanor and the other lost colonists. They might have been killed by Indians or gone to live with the local Croatoan tribe when they ran out of food. They were swallowed up by the land, and by history.

The Dares and other English colonists who we call the first settlers were, of course, nothing of the sort. People had lived in North America for perhaps twenty millennia, and the early colonists who did survive lasted only because friendly natives were willing to give them enough food to prevent starvation. In most cases, that food was produced by native women. Among the eastern tribes, men were generally responsible for hunting and making war while the women did the farming. In some areas they had as many as 2,000 acres under cultivation. Former Indian captives reported that the women seemed to enjoy their work, tilling the fields in groups that set their own pace, looking after one another's youngsters. Control of the food brought power, and the tribes whose women played a dominant role in growing and harvesting food were the ones in which women had the highest status and greatest authority. Perhaps that's why the later colonists kept trying to foist spinning wheels off on the Indians, to encourage what they regarded as a more wholesome division of labor. At any rate, it's nice to think that Eleanor Dare might have made a new life for herself with the Croatoans and spent the rest of her life working companionably with other women in the fields, keeping an eye out for her daughter and gossiping about the unreliable men.

## "FEDD UPON HER TILL HE HAD CLEAN DEVOURED ALL HER PARTES"

Jamestown was founded in 1607 by English investors hoping to make a profit on the fur and timber and precious ore they thought they were going to find. Its first residents were an ill-equipped crew of young men, many of them the youngest sons of good families, with no money but a vast sense of entitlement. The early colonists included a large number of gentlemen's valets, but almost no farmers. They regarded food as something that arrived in the supply ship, and nobody seemed to have any interest in learning how to grow his own. (Sir Thomas Dale, who arrived in 1611 after two long winters of starvation, said he found the surviving colonists at "their daily and usuall workes, bowling in the streetes.") The first women to arrive were the wife of one Thomas Forrest and her maid, Anne Burras. They came in 1608, the only women in a colony of around 200 misfits and mercenaries. The Jamestown that greeted them was a fort, about an acre in size, with a shopping district composed of one storehouse and a church that looked "like a barne," according to Captain John Smith. The homes were tumbledown shacks that one visitor said were inferior to the lowest cottage he had ever seen back in England.

There is no record of Mrs. Forrest's first name, or what she thought when she discovered that she was marooned in what must have seemed like a long, rowdy fraternity party, minus food. All we hear is a report that she had a baby during the "Starving Time" of 1609–10, which killed all but about 60 of the settlers out of a population of 20 women and 470 men. People gnawed on "Dogges & horses . . . together with Rates, mice, snakes," and one unnamed colonist killed his wife and turned her into dinner. He "fedd upon her till he had clean devoured all her partes," wrote another colonist, who added that the man was "burned for his horrible villany."

We don't know if Mrs. Forrest and her baby survived the winter, but her former maid, Anne Burras, did. Anne, who was only fourteen when she arrived, soon married a twenty-eight-year-old laborer in Virginia's first wedding ceremony and gave birth to a daughter— another Virginia—who also lived through the famine. So did Temperance Flowerdew, a young woman who had arrived in Virginia in 1609, after surviving a hurricane at sea. The storm hit a small fleet of boats destined for the colony. One, the *Sea Venture,* was destroyed, her passengers shipwrecked in an uninhabited part of Bermuda for nearly a year, while the crew turned the wreckage into two smaller boats. The marooned men and women weathered their ordeal on a warm island filled with food, while Temperance and the other émigrés who made it to Virginia were foraging for scraps and cooking rats. But after that unpromising beginning, a number of the women did very well. Temperance was the wife of two of the colony's governors. The first, Captain George Yeardley, was knighted in 1618 and became one of the richest men in Virginia, with several plantations. He named one of them Flowerdew in honor of Lady Yeardley. After his death, Temperance, then about forty-two, married Captain Francis West, one of his successors. Joan Pierce and her young daughter, Jane, endured the long, hungry winter in Jamestown on their own while her husband,

William, was stranded with the passengers on the *Sea Venture*. But after William finally made his way to the colony, he quickly became a wealthy planter. When Joan returned to England for a visit in 1629, she spent much of her time bragging about her garden in Jamestown and how she could "keep a better house in Virginia for 3 or 4 hundred pounds than in London." Her daughter Jane grew up to marry John Rolfe after the death of his wife, Pocahontas.

Pocahontas was the one Native American woman who had a starring role in the colonists' version of seventeenth-century history, although she suffers from having had her story told only from the point of view of Englishmen. Captain John Smith and the other early Virginia settlers tended to look upon her as a sort of colonial groupie, eager to befriend the Europeans and to become as much like them as possible. But they may have misread her entirely. Pocahontas was a member of her people's nobility, and while she obviously enjoyed the company of the new white-skinned arrivals, her actions may have been dictated more by diplomacy than affection. Her father, Powhatan, was a powerful chief of a confederacy of Algonquin tribes, an aggressive warrior who was one of the suspects in the destruction of Roanoke. Pocahontas was his favorite daughter. She first visited Jamestown when she was ten, and she became a familiar figure in the tiny, struggling colony. She was certainly a good and useful friend. Her help in getting the Indians to provide food to the starving and feckless colonists was, Smith wrote, the salvation of the settlement. When Powhatan ordered Smith beheaded for venturing too far into his territory, Pocahontas raced in and put her head next to his on the chopping block and successfully begged for mercy.

The young Indian girl may have done all this simply because she liked Smith and the other Englishmen, or it may have all been part of Powhatan's attempts to control the relationship between his tribe and the newcomers. Some historians think the beheading drama was staged to put Smith in Powhatan's debt. Certainly Pocahontas understood the frictions between the whites and her own people—at one point, the English seized her and held her as hostage. Her marriage to the English leader John Rolfe cemented peace between the colonists and Powhatan's confederacy for the rest of her life. Both husband and wife may have seen their union as diplomatic, rather than romantic. Rolfe wrote a letter to his superiors justifying the marriage "for the good of this plantation." The bride-to-be did not confide her own feelings to anyone who had the power to write them down, but she was said to have already been married to a man from her own tribe. Later, she went with Rolfe and their young son to England in what we would today call a public relations tour, aimed at encouraging more investment in Virginia. She had her portrait painted wearing English clothes, satisfied all the nobility's curiosity to see a "noble savage," and was presented at court and reunited with her old friend John Smith. Before she could return home she died, probably of pneumonia. She was only about twenty years old.

## "IT IS NOT KNOWEN WHETHER MAN OR WOMAN BE THE MOST NECESSARY"

Almost every unmarried Englishwoman who emigrated to the Chesapeake must have dreamed of duplicating Temperance Flowerdew's or Joan Pierce's luck. There wasn't much prospect of finding a good, upwardly mobile mate back home, where England was changing from a rather backward agricultural country to a mercantile giant and dislocating hundreds of thousands of rural workers in the process. Very few available men could support a family. In fact, there seemed to be very few men around, period—the country was still recovering from a plague that had mysteriously killed far more men than women. Of the many sales pitches offered by the colonies, none struck home with women more than the prospects of finding a suitable spouse. "If any Maid or single Woman have a desire to go over, they will think themselves in the Golden Age, when Men paid a Dowry for their Wives; for if they be but civil, and under 50 years of Age, some honest Man or other will purchase them for their Wives," promised one promoter. (An even more enthusiastic propagandist announced that the women of North Carolina were terrifically fertile "and many Women from other Places who have been long Married and without Children, have remov'd to Carolina, and become joyfull Mothers.")

The recruiters preferred not to mention certain details. Even after the food shortages ended, the Chesapeake was a death trap. The brackish water, mosquito-laden swamps, and steamy weather killed most people during their first year. Those who survived often suffered from weakness or periodic fits as an aftermath of their exposure to malaria. At least 6,000 people came to Virginia between 1607 and 1624; by 1625, only 1,200 survivors were still there. But the colonies' sponsors were desperate to get females, by hook or by crook—their ventures were in danger of being wrecked on the shoals of dissolute, irresponsible young manhood. In 1619, the Virginia House of Burgesses, petitioning that wives as well as husbands be eligible for grants of free land, argued that in a new plantation, "it is not knowen whether man or woman be the most necessary." London recruiters began searching for marriageable women, offering free passage and trousseaus for girls of good reputation and a sense of adventure. When they married, their new husbands had to reimburse the company with 120 pounds of good leaf tobacco. The first shipment of ninety "tobacco brides" arrived in Jamestown in the spring of 1620. The youngest, Jane Dier, was fifteen or sixteen when she left England. Allice Burges, at twenty-eight, was one of the oldest and said to be skillful in the art of brewing beer— important in a place where the water was generally undrinkable. Cicely Bray was from one of the best families, of a rank that required her to be addressed as "Mistress" rather than the more plebian "goodwife." But all the brides were respectable women, mostly the offspring of middle-class tradesmen who had died, leaving them with no male protectors. All of them provided references, attesting to their honesty, sobriety, and past behavior. Anne Richards was "a woman of an honest [life] and conversation . . . and so is and ever hathe bynne esteemed," wrote one of her parish elders.

We don't know which tobacco brides won the golden ring and became a contented farm wife or a prosperous plantation mistress. Only a few of their disasters made it into history. Some of the women, including Cicely Bray, were killed in an Indian attack in 1622, when 347 settlers lost their lives. Examining the site of that massacre, modern archaeologists were puzzled to discover the skeleton of one woman with an iron band around her head that apparently had protected her from scalping. Women in England, they later deduced, used those bands to fasten a roll of cloth under their hair, to make their hairdo look fuller. Perhaps she was a tobacco bride, still trying to maintain her old standards of fashion.

Some British contractors, hired to provide the colonies with wives and female servants, simply went out and grabbed whatever warm bodies they could find, shoved them into a boat and set sail. In October 1618, a warrant was issued in England for one Owen Evans, who was kidnapping young women from their villages and sending them off to be sold in Bermuda and Virginia as indentured servants. "His undue proceedings breed such terror to the poor maidens as 40 of them fled out of one parish into such obscure and remote places as their parents and masters can yet have no news what is become of them," reported a correspondent to King James I. The danger of being dragged off to America against one's will figured prominently in the popular literature of seventeenth-century England—playwrights found the shanghai artists, or "spirits," a handy deus ex machina for eliminating characters midplot. Parents sometimes pursued the spirits' vessels down the Thames, where they ransomed their kidnapped children before they disappeared forever. The law didn't seem to do much to dissuade the abductions. In 1680, a woman named Ann Servant confessed to attacking Alice Flax, a young maiden, putting her on board a ship and selling her in Virginia. Servant was fined a little over 13 shillings. In the coinage of the era, that was enough to buy a dozen lobsters or pints of ale, but hardly the value Alice Flax would have put on her liberty.

Besides wanting to populate the new colonies, the English government was also eager to get rid of its more undesirable citizens, who were overloading the urban jails. Some convicts were involuntarily deported; others were given the choice between a long jail term and life as an indentured servant across the ocean. Sarah Wilson, a former lady's maid in the court of Queen Charlotte, was found guilty of stealing a jewel in the royal palace. She was undoubtedly relieved when her death sentence was reduced to transportation to Maryland.

There, she escaped from her masters and made her way to South Carolina where she introduced herself as Queen Charlotte's sister, Princess Susanna Carolina Matilda. Wilson happily sold royal preferments to the gullible colonists until she was undone by advertisements by her Maryland master, seeking the return of his runaway servant.

France sent a raft of convicts to its colony in Louisiana, some of them women who shared Sarah Wilson's spirit. "The wenches in crossing Paris sang as though without care, and hailed passers-by, inviting them to come along on a voyage to the Mississippi," wrote a French diarist who watched 300 female prisoners, each with a yellow bow in her hair, riding off to the port. The French female convicts were all expected to enthusiastically embrace careers as farmwives in the rough, steamy colony, a transmutation that was easier said than done. Even the women who arrived in New Orleans as the French equivalent of tobacco brides were unhappy and demanded to go home. (Good Parisians, they complained endlessly about the quality of the local food.) One of the commissioners of the colony in the 1720s, after listing the problems the women had caused him, hopefully suggested that they might be shipped off to marry into the hostile Indian tribes.

→ Most of the single women who came to the southern colonies, however, voluntarily sold themselves as indentured servants. They paid the cost of their passage with a term of four or five years in service. At the end, they were supposed to receive food, clothing, and tools to give them a start in life, then emerge into a world filled with wife-hungry young men and take their pick. That really did happen in many cases. Some women were even luckier and married their employers, or they met men with enough resources to purchase their freedom for them. But many others had fatally bad luck. A quarter of the indentured servants died before they gained their freedom. Those who lived often got pregnant before their term of service was up—a study in one Maryland county showed that 20 percent of the women who arrived as servants during the second half of the seventeenth century wound up in court for bearing illegitimate children. Some of them must have been seduced or raped by the master of the house, but they were still punished as if they had chosen freely. Their service was extended to repay their master for the labor lost to childbearing, and if a mother was still under indenture by the time the baby was weaned, her child was bound out as a servant, even though still a toddler. The legislature reasoned that servants who were impregnated by their employers could not be allowed to go free because "it might probably induce such loose persons to lay all their bastards to their masters."

The court records reveal terrible stories of women found "beaten to a jelly" or infected with fatal cases of syphilis by rapacious masters. A Maryland couple, Captain and Mistress Bradnox, were infamous for their treatment of servants. When one of them, Thomas Watson, died from an apparent beating, another servant, Sarah Taylor, testified in court that she had seen Thomas confined without food and water and forced to drink his own urine. Sarah's outspokenness did not endear her to the Bradnoxes, who beat her with a knotted rope. When she ran away and took shelter with a sympathetic local planter, the county commissioners made her benefactor ask Captain Bradnox's forgiveness in open court, and Sarah was required to apologize to her master and mistress on her knees. But Sarah's story went on, through more beatings and assaults, until she finally appeared in court, asking for protection and showing the commissioners her scars. A witness testified he had seen the captain hit Sarah with a stool when he found her reading, crying, "You dissembling jade, what do you with a book in your hand?" The court decided to free Sarah from service for her own safety. We can only hope she cleared out of the county fast, because Mrs. Bradnox contested the decision to the governor, who compelled each of the merciful justices to pay her 220 pounds of tobacco. It's not likely they showed similar charity in the future.

An indentured servant's fortune depended very much on who her master and mistress were, and canny émigrés opted for a system that allowed them to travel to America first and then barter with prospective employers for a contract that would repay the ship's captain for their passage. But even women who managed to avoid getting tied to psychopaths or sex criminals must have found the work harder than they anticipated. "What we unfortunat English People suffer here is beyond the probability of you in England to Conceive," moaned Elizabeth Springs, one of the few indentured servants who was able to read and write, in a letter to her family. "Let it suffice that I one of the unhappy Number, am toiling almost Day and Night . . . what rest we get is to rap ourselves up in a Blanket and ly upon the Ground, this is the deplorable Condition your poor Betty endures."

## "PERFORM THE MOST MANFUL
## EXERCISES AS WELL AS MOST MEN"

The women who did survive in the early southern colonies found themselves in a place where the old gender rules had been, if not abolished, at least temporarily suspended due to emergency conditions. It was a raw country, and the first generations of colonial women did things that their granddaughters would have found unthinkable. A "modest Gentlewoman" named Alice Proctor ignored officials' urging that she abandon her home during Indian raids and move to the safety of Jamestown. She stuck to her farmhouse until worried neighbors threatened to burn the place down. Well-born women labored like field hands and made their way through the roadless countryside on horseback or by waterway. "Many of the Women are very handy in Canoes, and will manage them with great Dexterity and Skill, which they become accustomed to in this watry Country," reported a traveler in 1700. William Byrd described an acquaintance who lived on the Virginia frontier as "a very civil woman" who could nonetheless "carry a gunn in the woods and kill deer, turkeys . . . shoot down wild cattle, catch and tye hoggs . . . and perform the most manful exercises as well as most men in these parts."

Almost everyone lived on a farm—the whole point of the colonial dream was to get your own land and grow a profitable cash crop like tobacco. The English believed that fieldwork was a man's task, but the colonies were desperately short on labor, and young planters expected their wives to labor alongside them in the fields. The farms were almost all isolated, surrounded by endless forests, down winding waterways without any real roads to connect them. Plantation owners

were forced to be away from home for long periods of time on business, and they often depended on their wives, or even daughters, to
drain swamps, tend cattle, cultivate the tobacco, and otherwise manage
things while they were gone.

The dissolution of the normal boundaries between women's work
and men's allowed some women to operate with an independence the
nation would never really see again until the twentieth century. One of
the most spectacular examples was Margaret Brent, who virtually ran
the colony of Maryland during a period of crisis. Margaret, her sister
Mary, and two brothers arrived in Maryland in 1638. The still-tiny
colony was a haven for Catholics, the Brents' religion. It's possible
that Margaret and Mary had embraced some form of lay sisterhood.
They never married, which was practically unheard of in a land of
woman-starved bachelors.

→ Virtually all the colonial women wanted to marry, but when they
did, they were automatically stripped of their legal rights. A wife's
possessions became her husband's, and she was unable to do business
on her own, sue, borrow money, or sign contracts. ("The husband and
wife are one, and the husband is that one," said Sir William Black-
stone, the eminent English jurist.) But as unmarried women, the Brent
sisters could own and manage their own property. Margaret had a letter from Lord Baltimore, the proprietor of the colony, granting them
land in their own names. They established a home on a seventy-acre
plot they named Sisters' Freehold in what is now southern Maryland,
next to the estate of their brother Giles. The colony was still very
young, with about 400 settlers, most of them tenant farmers or laborers who worked on the estates of a few wealthy landowners like the
Brents.

Margaret became an active businesswoman, who specialized in
lending money to newly arrived settlers. When her debtors failed to
meet their obligations, she was quick to go to court to demand payment. Between 1642 and 1650, she was recorded as a party in 134 suits,
mainly as plaintiff—representing herself in court and winning most of
her cases. She became a close friend of Governor Leonard Calvert,

the brother of Lord Baltimore, and the two became coguardians of the young daughter of the chief of the Piscataway Indians. Margaret later permitted her brother Giles to marry the girl, who was only eleven years old, an act that made Giles's political opponents wary, and which certainly raises questions about whether Margaret was really looking after her ward's best interests.

Nothing Margaret wrote has survived, and we have no portraits of her. (Her contemporaries remembered her as a large woman with red hair.) Her great moment in American history came in 1645, when Maryland was drawn into the civil war being carried out in England between the forces of Charles I and the Puritan Parliament. Protestant mercenaries raided the lands of the Catholic settlers, and one of them sailed off to London with Giles Brent as a prisoner. It must have been a traumatic time for Margaret and Mary—their brother had been kidnapped and Governor Calvert eventually fled, leaving the remaining settlers at the mercy of the mercenaries. The colonists who stayed behind called it the "plundering time." The European population of Maryland dropped to under 100.

Governor Calvert finally returned in late 1646 at the head of a small band of soldiers and restored order. But he died in June 1647, while his restless army was still waiting to be paid for its services. There was a very real threat that if the money was not forthcoming, the soldiers would try to take it out of the hides of the colonists. On his deathbed, Calvert appointed Margaret Brent the executor of his estate, instructing her to "Take all and pay all." He had pledged his estate and that of his brother, Lord Baltimore, to satisfy the soldiers, but his own assets were far too insignificant to cover the costs. Margaret held the soldiers off, selling her own cattle to feed them and maneuvering to try to get money either from the colonial government or Lord Baltimore's estate. On January 21, 1648, she appeared before the Maryland Assembly and demanded two votes—one for herself and one as Lord Baltimore's representative. The Assembly declined to give her even one, and Margaret departed after lodging a protest against "all proceedings . . . unlesse shee may be present and have vote as aforesaid." Besides being regarded as the nation's first female lawyer, Margaret was the first colonial woman to demand the right to vote.

Margaret did accomplish her critical objective of getting power to sell some of Lord Baltimore's cattle to pay off the soldiers, who then left peaceably. Lord Baltimore, however, was furious at the loss of part of his estate. The Maryland Assembly defended her, writing their proprietor that his affairs were better left "at that time in her hands than in any mans . . . for the soldiers would never have treated any other with . . . Civility and respect." Margaret, they concluded "rather deserved favour and thanks from your Honor" than "bitter invectives." But Lord Baltimore was not appeased. Rather than continue living under the authority of an implacable enemy, the Brents moved away. Margaret had saved Maryland, and its status as a bastion of religious toleration, but she could never again live there herself. The family relocated to Virginia, which seemed willing to drop its opposition to Catholicism in order to nab such high-status residents. Until her death in 1671, Margaret lived on her new plantation, which she had named "Peace"—something she probably felt she deserved a little of.


## "CONTRACTING HERSELF TO . . . SEVERAL MEN AT ONE TIME"

Some women came to the new world to get away from a man, in the form of a harsh master or unsatisfactory lover. (The niece of the novelist Daniel Defoe, plagued by a suitor she detested, fled England for the colonies and sold herself as an indentured servant in Maryland.) Women who were independent enough to sail to America by themselves were also inclined to take matters into their own hands if they got stuck in unhappy marriages after they arrived. In the early eighteenth century, a minister described North Carolina as "a nest of the most notorious profligates on earth . . . Women forsake their husbands come here and live with other men." Early southern newspapers carried as many advertisements from husbands renouncing their runaway wives as owners seeking their runaway slaves.

It was virtually impossible to get a divorce, but thanks to the malar-

ial swamps, few people wound up married for life. The average union
ended with the death of one partner within about seven years. During
the first half of the seventeenth century the mortality rate in the
Chesapeake was about 80 percent. It created patchwork families made
up of widows, widowers, and several degrees of stepchildren. People
developed new terms for their father's "now-wife" or their "new husband's children"—like Eskimos with their many words for snow. Men
who made it through their first year in the Chesapeake could claim the
title of "seasoned," but their life expectancy was still only about forty-
five years. Women's life expectancy was even lower, but since they
married so young—almost as soon as they hit puberty—they still
often outlived their husbands. The colonies were crowded with widows, many of them managing large estates. Historians who studied the
wills in Maryland found that most men named their wives as executor,
something that was highly unusual back in England. In some cases,
this was a matter of pure affection. "All I have I leave her, and if I had
more she should enjoy it," wrote John Smithson of Maryland in his
will. But often, the wife was chosen as executor out of sheer practical-
ity. In the seventeenth-century South, many people had no close relatives in America, or near neighbors who could be trusted to oversee an
estate.

Few women stayed single long in the South; some went through
five or six husbands. (One minister sued a newly married couple for
his fee—for performing both the marriage service and the funeral of
the bride's first husband a few days earlier.) Some women built large
estates through their serial marriages, moving up in the world with
every widowhood. Sarah Offley of Virginia married Adam Thorowgood, a former servant, in 1627. He left her a comfortable inheritance
when he died in 1640. Sarah then married Captain John Gookin, the
son of a wealthy planter, and when he, too, passed away about three
years later, the now-wealthy widow married Francis Yeardley, the son
of the famous Temperance Flowerdew. It was natural for a woman to
seek a new partner to help her care for her family and property. But all
newly empowered widows weren't willing to give up control in order
to acquire a helpmeet. Some married only when they had received

legal assurances that they could determine the disposition of their estates. Others took lovers, preferring to live in sin rather than risk the transfer of power that came with matrimony.

Over a quarter of the early male settlers in the Chesapeake never managed to find a wife, and women were very aware of the advantage the skewed gender ratio gave them. Men complained bitterly about hard-hearted and evasive women, and Virginia passed a law prohibiting women from promising themselves to more than one suitor. In 1624, Eleanor Spragg was sentenced to apologize before her church congregation for the "offence in contracting herself to . . . several men at one time." In 1687, William Rascow was so insecure about his fiancée, Sarah Harrison, that he got her to sign an oath promising not to marry anybody else. Oath notwithstanding, Sarah dumped Rascow for James Blair, who she married in a ceremony that did not include the promise to "obey."

The people who colonized the South didn't develop any new philosophies about the proper role of women in society—they just didn't have the resources to enforce the old rules that most of them still adhered to in theory. Back in England, young women were expected to consult their fathers and the other male authority figures in their lives before choosing a husband—particularly if they were young women of property. But in the South, there was an excellent chance that a girl's father had died before she became of marriageable age. Nearly a third of the children in the Chesapeake region lost at least one parent by the age of nine, and a quarter were completely orphaned by the time they reached eighteen. Chastity was still regarded as the most important female virtue, but girls were less likely to protect their virginity when they had no parents to supervise them. (In some areas, a third of all brides were already pregnant.) And unlike the unfortunate indentured servants, free women who had sex before marriage were unlikely to pay much of a price. When men outnumbered women six to one, they couldn't really afford to be too picky about a prospective wife's past history or object to a stepchild or two in the package. There were plenty of pregnant brides, but outside the servant class, very few unmarried mothers. Despite the wild and

wooly ambience of the early southern colonial towns, there is virtually no record of organized prostitution; women apparently found too
many other opportunities. A woman's reputation was important—
women frequently sued neighbors who had been overheard referring
to them as "whore." But unmarried men, too, found they had to protect themselves from gossip in a hypercompetitive marriage market. In
Maryland, men sometimes filed suit against people who said they were
abusive to women, on the grounds that the stories might harm their
ability to find a wife.

What we know about the behavior of early southern women settlers is skewed toward the outrageous, since so many of the surviving
records are court documents. But there are enough cases of women
physically assaulting their enemies, turning their husbands out of their
homes, leading religious dissent, and criticizing public officials to
make it clear that there were plenty of female émigrés who knew what
they wanted and weren't shy in making their feelings known. Ann
Fowler was sentenced to twenty lashes in 1637 for defaming a county
justice, Adam Thorowgood, with the somewhat undeferential suggestion that Captain Thorowgood could "Kiss my arse." The Virginia
General Assembly, which had originally held a husband responsible
for damages caused by outspoken wives, ruled in 1662 that the wives
could pay the penalty themselves, by submitting to a ducking in the
river—a de facto acknowledgment that the colony's husbands could
not always control the behavior of their women.

## "WHITE PEOPLE . . . ARE ENTIRELY RUINED AND RENDERED MISERABLE"

Mary Johnson may have been the first African American woman. She
arrived sometime before 1620 as the maid of a Virginia planter. Like
white women, the black residents of the early southern colonies found
opportunities in the general chaos around them. Johnson and her husband were indentured servants, and once they earned their freedom,
they acquired a 250-acre farm and five indentured servants of their
own. By the mid–seventeenth century, a free black population had

begun to emerge in both the North and the South. African American women, who weren't bound by the same social constraints as white women, frequently set up their own businesses, running boarding-houses, hair salons, or restaurants. Catering was a particularly popular career, as was trading.

In Charleston, South Carolina, black women took over the local market, selling vegetables, chickens, and other produce they acquired from the growing population of slaves, who generally had small plots beside their cabins. The city came to depend on the women for its sup-ply of fresh food, and whites complained long and loud about the power and independence of the trading women. In 1686, South Car-olina passed a law prohibiting the purchase of goods from slaves, but it had little effect. A half century later, Charleston officials were still complaining about the "exorbitant price" that black women charged for "many articles necessary for the support of the inhabitants." The trading women had sharp tongues, which they used to good effect. The clerk of the market claimed that the "insolent and abusive Manner" of the slave women made him "afraid to say or do Any-thing." It's hard to believe the marketers, some of whom were slaves, were as outspoken as their clientele made them out to be, but the war between the black female traders and their customers continued on into the nineteenth century. (One petition in 1747 said that because of the market "white people . . . are entirely ruined and rendered miser-able.")

The relative openness of life for African Americans only lasted while the black population was small—in the mid-seventeenth cen-tury, about 300 black Virginians lived among 15,000 whites. As the number of slaves grew, white Americans began self-consciously marking the differences between the races. White servants complained about being forced to work with blacks, and legislatures passed laws making it more difficult for them to gain their freedom, acquire prop-erty, or intermarry. Blacks and whites had married legally in many of the early settlements, and interracial love affairs were common. In Virginia, officials began requiring any white woman who had an ille-gitimate child "by a Negro" to pay a fine of 15 pounds or spend five years in indentured service. In 1662, Virginia legislators gave white masters free rein to molest their female slaves by declaring that children of slave women were slaves for life, no matter who their fathers were.

## "I FEAR THE POWER OF ENGLAND NO MORE THAN A BROKEN STRAW"

Although women were prohibited from voting or holding office, in the South they did play an active part in the raw politics of early colonial life. The most dramatic example was Bacon's Rebellion in 1676. The uprising began with a split between the people who lived on the Virginia frontier and the ruling oligarchy headquartered in Jamestown, led by the governor, William Berkeley. By the 1670s almost everything about Virginia society had been rigged to favor the wealthy. The frontier farmers were paying enormous taxes, and getting almost nothing in return because the money quickly went into the hands of a few politically connected families. The rebels, who came to include a number of black Virginians, were generally the more sympathetic figures in this conflict—unless you happened to be an Indian. One of the frontier families' most bitter complaints was that the governor, who engaged in profitable fur trade with the local tribes, did not share their enthusiasm for a genocidal war against the natives.

The frontier wives, who were frequently left alone in their remote homesteads, were the most outspoken members of the kill-the-Indians faction. When Nathaniel Bacon began a rebellion aimed at overthrowing Berkeley's government, the women spread the word about his victories and about the governor's unwillingness to defend the colonial households. A Mrs. Haviland was a particularly "excellent divulger of news" who directed her friends to go "Up and downe the Country as Bacon's Emissary to Carry his declarations and papers." Women also seemed to have taken part in the councils of war and strategy planning. Sarah Drummond, the wife of one of Bacon's advisers, was a landowner in her own right and an important member of the leadership. When the rebels' resolve seemed to flag, she picked up a twig and snapped it in two. "I fear the power of England no more than a broken straw," she said stoutly. Governor Berkeley's particular bête noire was Sarah Grendon, who he described as the "first great incourager and setter on of the ignorant vulger." In the great seventeenth-century Virginia tradition, Mrs. Grendon was already on her third husband when the rebellion broke out. Both of her first two husbands left her generous gifts, and she was probably a fairly wealthy woman. The governor never forgot her offenses, and when the rebellion failed, Mrs. Grendon was the only woman he refused to pardon.

The Baconites did not discriminate much between the sexes, either in their leadership or when they were on the attack. Landowners loyal to the governor left their wives behind to guard their estates under the theory that a lady's sex would be her best protection against raiders. But the rebels readily took the houses and beat the wives just as they would have the men. When Bacon stormed Jamestown, he sent his troops to round up the wives of the most prominent local men, including one of his own relatives. To buy time for the rebels to strengthen their position, Bacon placed the women along the top of a small fortification he had constructed, to stop the government authorities from rushing the encampment. "The poor Gentlewomen were mightily astonished at this project; neither were their husbands voide of amazements. . . . This action was a method in war, that they were not well acquainted with . . . that before they could com to pearce their enemies sides, they must be obliged to dart their weapons through their wives brest," wrote one annalist. The government forces held their fire.

The female captives went down in history as the "white aprons," and although they later became the stars of some very melodramatic Victorian fiction, in reality their role, and that of most other loyalist wives, was essentially passive. The governor's wife, Lady Frances Berkeley, was a very active exception. Sir William's critics claimed his much-younger spouse had tormented him with her sexual demands, forcing him to raise money to buy her luxuries to make up for his inadequacies in bed. That sort of theory has been popular throughout history when men try to explain the political activities of strong women. But whatever their private relationship, it was clear that during the uprising Sir William was an increasingly tired old man, while Frances had enough energy for an army. She fled to London when the rebellion began and lobbied vigorously at court to gain support for her husband's faction. She returned, seemingly triumphant, in the company of one of the royal commissioners and a thousand troops. But once order was restored—a challenge made much simpler by Bacon's death—Lady Berkeley responded bitterly to efforts by the king's representatives to limit her husband's authority. She may have been particularly angry when the commissioners refused to see the female rebels as anything more than hapless housewives led astray. To show her displeasure, she arranged to have the local hangman drive the commissioners' carriage, creating an enormous scandal. When Sir William died in 1677, his wife inherited all his estates and went on to beat Temperance Flowerdew's record by marrying three governors.

After Bacon's defeat, Governor Berkeley's partisans rode through the farms of their former enemies, evicting families and confiscating everything they owned. Sarah Grendon somehow managed to persuade the men to leave her alone in return for whatever goods they could carry off. But she was eventually charged with treason, a capital crime. Her husband, Thomas, acting on her behalf, approached the royal commissioners and petitioned them to try her themselves rather than leaving her to the mercy of the Berkeley regime. Mrs. Grendon then admitted that "being an Ignorant woman" she had spoken "some foolish and indiscreete words reflecting upon the sloe prosecution of the Indian warr," and said she was "most heartily sorrowfull for the same." The commissioners dismissed the charges. Thomas Grendon died several years later, leaving her yet another large bequest, and Sarah went on to marry a fourth husband.

Sarah Drummond's husband was hung as a traitor and his estate confiscated. But like Mrs. Grendon, she successfully took refuge in her identity as a powerless woman. She humbly begged the government to restore their property lest her "five poor children" starve. She also began lobbying London, and her protests reached as far as King Charles II, who not only granted her petition but also condemned

Governor Berkeley and put a halt to the wave of reprisals. "As I live, the old fool has put to death more people in that naked country than I did in England for the murder of my father," the king said angrily.

Lydia Chisman, another leading Baconite, took a different approach. When Governor Berkeley asked Edmund Chisman why he had supported the rebels, his wife stepped up "and tould his honour that it was her provocations that made her Husband joyne in the Cause that Bacon contended for," wrote a witness. Mrs. Chisman added that "if he had not bin influenc'd by her instigations, he had never don that which he had don." On bended knees, she begged Berkeley to pardon Edmund and hang her instead. The governor, who had referred to Mrs. Chisman as a "whore" during the trial, was unmoved. Edmund Chisman was condemned to hang, though he died in prison before the sentence could be carried out. Lydia, who was not charged, was later able to regain her husband's estate. And she married again.

# The Women of New England: Goodwives, Heretics, Indian Captives, and Witches

## "HIS DEAREST CONSORT, ACCIDENTALLY FALLING OVERBOARD"

When the *Mayflower* first sighted land off Cape Cod in November 1620, its 102 passengers had been at sea for ten weeks. The trip had been rough—so much so that the crew had considered turning back midvoyage. The would-be colonists had been seasick so often that one sailor had cursed the ship's passengers, telling them he looked forward to dumping half of them overboard. (William Bradford, the Pilgrim leader who reported the story, happily added that the sailor himself was the *Mayflower*'s first fatality.) There were nineteen adult women on board, all but one married, along with seven young girls and a handful of small children. Most of them were crammed in the area below the main deck, which must have reeked of seasick passengers who wore the same clothes, day and night, for the entire trip. In bad weather, when the hatch was closed, the room would have been dark except for an oil lamp or candle, the air cold and the floor wet from the seawater leaking in.

Looking out at the endless, bleak wilderness of North America, the Pilgrims must have wondered if their little group would be lost forever, another Roanoke. Later on, they would discover that fishermen had visited the area and taught English to some of the local Indians. But at the time they landed, they probably feared they would never have anyone to talk to again except the few dozen families in their party, some of whom had already grown to loathe one another. They had only a small store of provisions—one trunk per family. It was possible they would never again see a clock or a cat or eat an apple. If their few scrawny goats died—and the livestock on board was starting to die at a rapid rate—they would lose their only source of milk. There were no spinning wheels aboard, or other implements the women had used in Europe to make the things they could not buy at market. If they ruined a dress or broke a plate, it couldn't be replaced.

After they landed, the men went off to explore, leaving the women waiting on the *Mayflower* with the children and a skeleton crew. They had been remarkably lucky in surviving the voyage, but almost as soon as the ship was anchored, people began to get fatally ill from what was probably a form of pneumonia or typhus. None of the women on the *Mayflower* ever recorded their emotions as their ship bobbed up and down in the harbor and they stared at the unyielding forest, wondering whether their husbands would even return from their exploration. All we know is that one of them, Bradford's wife, Dorothy May, gave it all up and threw herself to her death in the water. The Pilgrims never acknowledged it was suicide, and they officially recorded that Dorothy May—who had managed to survive ten weeks in high seas—had failed to keep her footing while the ship lay at anchor. "His dearest consort, accidentally falling overboard, was drowned in the harbor," wrote Bradford's biographer, Cotton Mather. Dorothy May Bradford, the twenty-two-year-old mother of a small son left behind in England, slipped out of history. Her family and friends could not afford to mourn for long, or even acknowledge her despair. And her husband soon married again.

By the next spring, almost all the women who stood with Dorothy May looking over the side of the *Mayflower* were dead as well. The illness that became known as the General Sickness took about half the party, and it hit hardest among the wives. All but four of them died. They may have killed themselves caring for their families, tending their ailing spouses and children until they succumbed from exhaustion. Certainly, their high fatality rate was not due to the weakness of their sex, since the unmarried girls among the passengers survived. And although the *Mayflower*, when it set sail to return to England, offered free passage to any woman who wanted to leave, nobody accepted.

Most of the girls who survived the first winter went on to live long lives and produce flocks of little colonists. Mary Chilton, a thirteen-year-old whose parents both died in the winter infections, was, according to tradition, the first woman to step onto Plymouth Rock. She married a man who came over on the next boatful of settlers and they had ten children. Priscilla Mullins was orphaned by the General Sickness and married John Alden, the barrel maker, who was said by Bradford to be "much desired" as a potential husband. The legend that Alden came to ask for her hand on behalf of Miles Standish and that the clever Priscilla said "Speak for yourself, John" comes from a poem written in 1672 and retold in the nineteenth century. One of their eleven children, Captain John Alden, became an important participant in two of seventeenth-century New England's great crises—first, as hero in the Indian wars, and later, as an accused warlock during the Salem witch-hunt.

## "NOT SO HUMBLE AND HEAVENLY AS IS DESIRED"

Most of the early Massachusetts settlers whose boats came after the *Mayflower* were Puritans fleeing from religious persecution in England. Unlike the southern colonists, the Puritans never allowed things to become so disorderly that the normal lines of male dominance got blurred. The Puritans were very orderly indeed, and they believed that the husband represented God's authority in the household. A woman had a right to the love and support of her spouse, but she did not have a right to question his judgment. She was a daughter of Eve, morally weak and easily led into error. The Massachusetts authorities enforced both civil and religious law, and they took their lead from the Bible—particularly St. Paul, who had told the Corinthians, "Let your women keep silence in the Churches. . . . And if they will learn any thing, let them ask their husbands at home. . . ." In church, the women sat apart from men, entering through a separate door. They were not permitted to speak during services, and they had no formal say in the selection of a minister or any other community matters. "Touching our government, you are mistaken if you think we admit women . . . for they are excluded, as both reason and nature teacheth they should be," wrote Bradford in 1623. The Puritans back in Europe must have been gossiping that their friends in the American wilderness had adopted savage practices, like female suffrage.

But the Puritan women had crossed a large ocean in very small ships to get to America, and many of them were not feeling particularly deferential. When the residents of Chebacco, a town near Gloucester, decided they wanted to build their own meetinghouse, the men went off to Boston to petition the local authorities for permission. While they were gone, the women built the meetinghouse themselves. In Maine, tax collectors ran into irate housewives threatening to scald them with boiling water. The court records are full of examples of women who gave as good as they got in a verbal—or even physical—battle, and male Puritans sometimes complained about their bad attitudes. In 1644, a settler named John Brock noted that his own sister was "not so humble and heavenly as is desired." By the middle of the century Massachusetts teenagers were forming what the authorities regarded as gangs, and young women were sneaking off to attend coed parties or getting together with their girlfriends and singing bawdy songs.

As the colonies became larger and more commercial, they also attracted more non-Puritan residents who didn't share the early settlers' worldview. Even a virtuous matron walking the streets of Boston or Salem in the later seventeenth century had to make her way past the catcalls of sailors and fishermen lounging around the town. Loose women drank with men in the taverns and walked about with their breasts exposed. Between 1671 and 1687, the Boston selectmen drove forty-six women out of town for bad behavior. Several women wound up in trouble with the law for wearing trousers—one, who disguised herself as a sailor, was discovered by her fellow shipmates and tarred and feathered. Another, Dorothy Hoyt, was ordered whipped by the Essex County magistrate in 1677 for wearing men's clothing. But rather than reform, she simply fled the colony.

Although women were not supposed to hold positions that properly belonged to the head of the household, they frequently did the work anyway. Mary Starbuck, who moved to Nantucket in the 1660s, found the isolated community ready to accept her as a preacher and civic leader. "Little of moment was done without her," reported one visitor. Single women and widows had the legal ability to conduct business, and by 1687, more than 10 percent of the people involved in trade in Boston were female—most of them widows. Massachusetts also had its equivalent of Margaret Brent in a superachieving spinster named Elizabeth Poole, who purchased lands in Plymouth Colony from the Indians in 1637 and moved there with only her cattle for company. Besides founding the settlement of Taunton, Poole also became a major stockholder in the ironworks that was established there after iron ore was discovered on the banks of the local river.

Many businesses that were theoretically operated by men were actually conducted by their wives while they were at sea, or traveling, or engaged in some other commercial pursuit. Pennsylvania eventually gave women who were left in charge of their husbands' businesses the right to establish credit on their own, sue, and sign contracts. (The intent was not to make the women more independent, but to protect their creditors in case the traveling husbands abandoned them.) These wives were accepted as merchants, farmers, printers, or store managers, as long as they didn't take the title. A few jobs, like tavern and innkeeping, were seen as a natural extension of a housewife's hospitality. Midwives were, of course, almost universally women, and about a quarter of the doctors in seventeenth-century America were women as well. One Mistress Allyn served as an army surgeon during King Philip's War. She was paid 20 pounds for her effort, making her the only well-paid female physician of the century. But even at that, her salary was only about two-thirds of a male practitioner's.

## "PREACHES BETTER GOSPELL
## THAN ANY OF YOUR BLACK-COATES"

The church was everything in early New England—the organizing principle around which the government, the community, and the individual households revolved. So it's not really surprising that when women attempted to assert themselves, they did it through theology. Except for Roger Williams, the most famous dissident in early colonial history was Anne Hutchinson. Her father, a clergyman in England, educated Anne well beyond the level of most women—or men—of her day, and encouraged her to debate theological issues with him. When she was twenty-one, she married William Hutchinson, a successful merchant who always gave his "dear saint" the strongest possible support. No matter what else Anne was doing, she always seemed to be pregnant or nursing a baby—she eventually had fifteen children. She was forty-three and very much her own person when her family emigrated to Massachusetts in 1634, following their minister, John Cotton. Boston was still a very small place, with less than a thousand inhabitants. William quickly became an important member of the political elite and Anne, who was skilled in the "healing arts," became part of the community of women who helped one another at times of childbirth and illness. The conversations over the birthing bed drifted to Anne's religious philosophy—that the gift of heaven was freely bestowed by God and was attained through a direct relationship with the Almighty. To the gloomy Puritan community, obsessed with the concept of sin and perpetually worried that they might not turn out to be among those predestined for salvation, the idea of a personal, joyous relationship between believer and Deity must have been seductive. At some point Anne shifted from casual conversations among the women in the delivery room to more formal discussions in her own home. She soon began to attract what were, for the tiny colony, enormous crowds of up to eighty people. Most shockingly, some of the listeners were men.

Within a year of her arrival, Anne was the talk of the Massachusetts Bay Colony. Edward Johnson, a newcomer to Boston, reported that when he arrived in town he was approached by "a little nimble tongued Woman" who urged him to visit "one of her own Sex" and who "Preaches better Gospell than any of your black-coates that have been at the Ninneversity." Some historians believe that Anne's battles with the establishment were not, at bottom, about religion at all, but a larger struggle between the merchant class the Hutchinsons represented and the Puritan authorities, who feared the more open and diverse society that commerce required. At any rate, Governor Winthrop, whose own wife had the becoming habit of expressing her concern that she was not worthy of him, found Mrs. Hutchinson unbearably opinionated, "a woman of haughty and fierce carriage, of a nimble wit and active spirit, a very voluble tongue, more bold than a man," he wrote disapprovingly.

John Cotton, Anne's mentor, was worked upon by the other local clergy and finally joined in their consensus that she had to be brought under control. That was the way the men of Boston almost always resolved their disagreements. A small and fragile colony could tolerate only so much dissension, and once most of the male authority figures came down on one side of an argument, the minority took it as a sign that it was time to concede. Because women had never been allowed to take part in public affairs, they did not always understand the system. Anne Hutchinson was not the only strong-minded woman who would come to grief because she could not, or would not, accept the masculine approach to settling public disputes.

The ministers, among them John Cotton, passed a series of resolutions aimed at curbing dissidence, including a direct condemnation of the meetings at the Hutchinson home. In the fall of 1637, Anne was summoned before the General Court, with the governor presiding. She stood alone, facing a panel of men. The meeting room doors were held open so the crowd of eager bystanders could hear. For a long time she did very well, matching Governor Winthrop Bible citation for Bible citation. But she was doomed to lose eventually. Emboldened by her success, she began to instruct the members of the panel as she had her audiences at home, and her fate was sealed. She was banished, and Reverend Cotton urged the other women in his congregation to remember that although Anne had led them in many edifying conversations, "she is but a Woman and many unsound and dayngerous principles are held by her."

Once exiled, Anne moved with her family and a few followers to Rhode Island—a place so sparsely populated that she must indeed have felt like a voice crying out in the wilderness. She suffered either a miscarriage or from something called a hydatiform mole—a cluster of cysts that develop in the womb in place of an embryo. Word quickly spread that Anne Hutchinson had given birth to a mutant—with one lump for each of her heresies—and that one of her strongest supporters, Mary Dyer, had borne some sort of demon-child as well. The Reverend Thomas Weld claimed Hutchinson had delivered "30 monstrous births . . . none at all of them . . . of humane shape." Winthrop outdid himself in his attempt to describe the "beast" Mary Dyer delivered, which he claimed had a face and ears growing on its shoulders, three clawed feet, and four horns. People in England reported a rumor that Henry Vane, an ex-governor of the colony who had been one of Anne's supporters, had sailed across the Atlantic with Anne and Mary and had "debauched both, and both were delivered of monsters."

After her beloved husband died, Anne and her youngest children moved to an area of New York that is now part of the Bronx, where they were killed in an Indian attack. But her unhappy fate didn't deter other women from religious rebellion. Mary Oliver of Salem was said to outstrip even Hutchinson "for ability of speech, and appearance of zeal and devotion." Winthrop wrote that she might have been a real danger to the establishment if she had higher social status—Oliver was the wife of a poor workman. She was summoned before the magistrates six times for challenging church authority, jailed, forced to sit on public display in the stocks, and beaten. But she was apparently unbowed. Once, when a Salem official put her in the stocks without a trial, she sued him and collected damages of 10 shillings.

Anne Eaton, the wife of Winthrop's successor, was excommunicated in 1641 for her position on infant baptism. Her fall from grace, the authorities decided, was due to her failure to seek her husband's guidance. Lydia Wardwell of Hampton, summoned by the church elders to explain why she failed to show up for Sunday services, appeared before them in the nude. She told them she wanted to get their attention so she could point out the error of their ways. She got their notice all right, but she also got a lashing, and her husband was beaten, too, for defending his wife's right to protest. The Puritan establishment must have felt surrounded by outrageous women, challenging both their authority and their most sacred teachings. They had particular problems with the Quaker missionaries, like Mary Dyer, who had gone to England and become a Quaker after Hutchinson's expulsion. Puritan officials simply wanted to make Dyer go away, but she seemed drawn by the lure of martyrdom, returning to Boston over and over again. In 1660 she finally achieved her goal and was executed.

The Quakers gave women an active role in church affairs, although it was generally limited to the regulation and guidance of other women. But in a time when women were normally denied any chance to speak in public or assume roles of leadership, those opportunities were important. A Quaker woman from a humble family could rise in the community's esteem under her own power if she developed a reputation for saintliness and good sense within the meetings. She could even win a wealthy husband—a religious version of Cinderella. Susanna Hudson was a servant in Northern Ireland who married a poor weaver named Joseph Hatton. She became a minister at the local Quaker meetings and was so respected that when the family decided to emigrate to America, the community basically bribed them to stay put, paying apprenticeship fees for her boys. But in 1759 Joseph died, and Susanna, who had been left a small inheritance by another Quaker, used the money to visit Pennsylvania. Thomas Lightfoot, one of the wealthiest Quaker farmers in the colony, met her and was so moved by her testimony at the Quaker meeting that he followed her to Ireland, proposed, and brought her back to America as his wife.

If a colonial woman who wasn't a Quaker wanted to have a public voice and survive the experience, her best bet was to go to the frontier, like Mary Starbuck the Nantucket preacher. But Anne Bradstreet, who lived on the coast and maintained her social standing, still managed to write what the poet Adrienne Rich has called "the first good poems in

America." Like her contemporary, Anne Hutchinson, Bradstreet was reared in England by a father who believed girls should be educated, and she came to the New World as part of the Puritan elite—both her father and her husband, Simon, served as governor of the Massachusetts Bay Colony. She was a busy housewife, mother of four sons and four daughters, but turned to writing as an outlet for her active mind and troubled soul. Her poems were circulated only among her friends and family until 1650, when her brother-in-law had them published in London under the title *The Tenth Muse, lately sprung up in America . . . By a Gentlewoman in those parts.* Anne celebrated with a wry, self-deprecatory poem that did not quite conceal her pride. Her earlier work was self-conscious, but later she developed the confidence to write more naturally and directly, about the wild New England countryside, her struggles to come to grips with her faith, about the death of infant grandchildren, and her happy marriage. ("If ever two were one than surely we / If ever man were loved by wife, then thee.") She died an early colonial success story, a woman who made her mark not only through the children she bore but also through her art and intellect. But she always knew how skeptically the world would regard a female poet. "I am obnoxious to each carping tongue / Who says my hand a needle better fits," she wrote, adding that if the poems proved pleasing, "it won't advance / They'll say it's stol'n. or else it was by chance."

## "CHOPPED INTO THE HEAD
## WITH A HATCHET AND STRIPP'D NAKED"

A better-known homegrown colonial celebrity was Hannah Dustan, a farmer's wife in Haverhill, Massachusetts. In 1697, Indians attacked the town, burning about a half dozen homes and killing a number of citizens. Hannah's husband and seven oldest children escaped safely, but forty-year-old Hannah, who had just given birth, was taken captive, along with her nurse, Mary Neff, and newborn baby. "E'er they had gone many Steps, they dash'd out the Brains of the Infant against a Tree; and several of the other Captives, as they began to Tire in their sad Journey . . . the Salvages would presently Bury their Hatchets in their Brains and leave their Carcasses on the Ground for Birds and Beasts to Feed upon," recounted Cotton Mather, the famed Massachusetts preacher, who always had a sense for the finer detail.

Despite her weakened condition, Hannah managed to survive the hundred-mile march through the wilderness with her captors. She, Neff, and an English boy named Samuel Leonardson were given as prisoners to an Indian family. While the Indians were sleeping, the captives killed ten people, six of them children, cut off their scalps, and paddled off in a stolen canoe. They returned home to great acclaim, most of it heaped upon Hannah. Mather delivered a sermon in her honor. The General Court awarded her a generous bounty for the scalps—a reward she probably had in mind when she took time during her escape to slice off the tops of her captors' heads.

Another era would have viewed Dustan's conduct as unladylike, to say the least. ("Would that the bloody old hag had been drowned," wrote Nathaniel Hawthorne in 1836.) But when it came to fighting Indians, colonial society was willing to drop its normal criteria for feminine behavior. The early, harmonious relationship between the Pilgrims and the Native Americans had deteriorated as the colonists became more numerous and more pushy, leading to King Philip's War in 1675. More than half the towns in New England were attacked and a decade later, a new series of violent uprisings began. The frontier areas were particularly hard hit, and many of the residents there must have contemplated a retreat to safer and more populated areas. But the rest of the colonies needed the settlers to stay put and hold the perimeter against the enemy. That eagerness to make the frontier families feel empowered probably inspired colonial leaders to eulogize Hannah Dustan and other female Indian fighters. There are some vague reports about women learning to handle firearms, but they would not have found seventeenth-century guns user-friendly—they were heavy, unwieldy, and generally inaccurate. Instead, the colonists told stories about clever women who drove off Indians by throwing hot lye or burning coals on their attackers. Others were said to have tricked Indians by making a lot of noise and convincing them the settlement was defended by troops. Elizabeth Tozier of Salmon Falls dressed in men's clothes and stood guard over the fields while the men worked. Later it was reported that she had beaten back Indian attackers by throwing boiling soap on them, and survived being captured three times.

In 1682, Mary Rowlandson, the wife of a Massachusetts minister, published her account of her ordeal during King Philip's War, and it became a huge best-seller by the standards of the times. (In those days of small population and few books, a very popular volume sold perhaps 1,000 copies.) Although it's unlikely Mrs. Rowlandson ever actually handled firearms, the cover of the book sensationally showed her shooting at her attackers like a colonial Annie Oakley. The settlers wanted assurance there was life after an Indian attack, and that's what they got from Rowlandson's happy ending—she and her children all eventually got home. But her story was also a ripping tale, and the minister's wife didn't scrimp on the colorful details—like the colonist who was "chopped into the Head with a Hatchet and stripp'd naked." The author, who credited God's plan for everything, saw part of her ordeal as a divine method of convincing her to stop smoking tobacco.

When Rowlandson was captive she was forced to work as a servant to Wetamo, the female sachem, or leader, of a group of Wampanoag Indians. Wetamo commanded about 300 warriors, but Rowlandson's description of her is rather short on statecraft and long on clothing and cosmetics. Unsurprisingly, she also regarded Wetamo as proud and severe. Although in many of the eastern tribes the power of women was fading, as the whites encouraged male activities, like trapping and hunting, the Wampanoags were led by several female sachems. Wetamo was most famous, perhaps because she was sister-in-law to the Philip of King Philip's War. But she had reason to dislike the English herself, since her husband had died mysteriously while in colonial custody. Her army fought bravely against the settlers, until the war came to its inevitable end and Wetamo was killed, her head displayed on a pole for the edification of the English. Another female sachem, Awashonks, managed to steer a safe diplomatic course between the suspicious colonists and the angry Indians in Philip's army. The colonial historians regarded her as a dithering female trying to please both her warlike kinsmen and an English lover. But at a time when happy endings for Indians were in short supply, Awashonks managed to obtain one for her people.

## ᔓ SALEM ᔒ

### "BY MY OWN INNOCENCE
### I KNOW YOU ARE IN THE WRONG WAY"

The American colonists would have rated such crises as Bacon's Rebellion or King Philip's War as much more significant than the Salem witch-hunts. But there's something about the story of Salem that makes it a Rorschach test for our own vision of history. Some people look back on it as a story about repressed sexual hysteria. Some think it was all about the tensions between the settlers and the Indians. Others see slightly subliminal class warfare. Whatever happened, it was soaked in issues of gender. Women were the beginning and end of the Salem witch-hunt, the first accusers and the bulk of the accused. If seventeenth-century New England was a place full of women with personalities that were stronger than the society around them was prepared to accept, the witch craze can easily be interpreted as a story that began with teenage girls in crisis who stumbled on a very bad but effective way of trying to take control of their unhappy environment.

The trouble began during the long winter of 1691–92, with adolescents, worried about their future, experimenting with "little sorceries." With the help of Tituba, a twenty-five-year-old slave from Barbados, a small circle of Salem village girls tried to determine whom they would marry by dropping an egg white into water. Nothing was more critical for a New England woman than finding a suitable mate, and by the end of the seventeenth century, the options were becoming narrower. Prospective brides no longer enjoyed a seller's market. The ratio of men to women was evening out, and as the land along the coast became scarcer, many of the young single males were striking out for the frontier, leaving a surplus of girls behind. The shape of the egg white in the water was supposed to tell Tituba's audience what occupation their husbands would follow. But as it took form, the girls felt they saw the outline of a coffin. Good Puritans, they must have felt guilty already about dabbling in magic. The coffin probably made them feel they were looking into the face of their own doom.

Not long afterward, some of the girls who witnessed the experiment began to behave very peculiarly. Some of the descriptions of their condition sound as though they suffered the torments of the damned. One observer reported that the girls appeared to be "bitten and pinched by invisible agents. Their arms, necks and backs turned this way and that way, and returned back again, so as it was impossible for them to do so themselves, and beyond the power of any epileptic fits or natural disease to effect." But others described what sounded like children acting out, "getting into holes and creeping under chairs and stools," making "antic gestures" and "ridiculous speeches."

The girls knew the signs of possession. Cotton Mather had published a description of the affliction that supposedly befell the children of John Goodwin, an upstanding Boston resident in 1688. Sometimes, Mather wrote, the children were deaf "sometimes dumb and sometimes blind and often all this at once. . . . They would make most piteous outcries, that they were cut with knives, and struck with blows that they could not bear . . . they would roar exceedingly." Mather wasn't a reliable reporter—at one point, the minister had the children flying around the room "like geese." But the other Puritans believed him, and the case was known throughout the colonies.

Whether the Salem girls were suffering hysterical fits, or just playacting to cover up their psychic unease, they soon had the very unusual experience of being the center of attention. Adolescent girls were the least powerful people in a New England community. Their education was usually limited to learning enough to read the Bible. Many of them, even those from well-to-do families, were sent away from home to work as servants, to learn domestic skills and the proper spirit of obedience. (Six of the eight who would become the core of the witch-hunt accusers did not live with their own families.) But suddenly, important adults were trooping to their homes to see them and talk with them. Everything they said was taken very seriously.

These particular girls had unusually glo[...]
Puritans. Some had survived Indian attack[...]
members were slaughtered. The "victims" [...]
from two exceedingly unhappy families. N[...]
was the daughter of Samuel Parris, the Sa[...]
mother was an invalid, who probably left Betty unsupervised or in the
care of Tituba, their slave. Parris, a failed businessman attempting to
start a new career as a clergyman, had been involved in a long struggle
to keep his position, fighting a faction of the local power structure that
continually withheld his salary. He seems to have been a troubled and
troubling personality, both grasping and paranoid. In the small, dark
house, Betty was most likely exposed to her father's grievances, and
given a keen sense of who the family friends and enemies were in the
fractious village. She probably followed her father's lead in identifying
his enemies with the forces of Satan. Abigail Williams, her eleven-
year-old cousin, was an orphan who lived with the family.

The other earliest accuser was twelve-year-old Ann Putnam, the
daughter of Thomas and Ann Putnam. The Putnams were one of the
major families in the village, but for years their fortunes had been
ebbing, while their rivals became wealthier and more powerful.
Thomas and Ann had entered marriage confident that they would
come into large inheritances from their respective parents. But in both
cases, their stepmothers redirected the money to children of their
own. Ann Sr. suffered not only from thwarted expectations, but also
from poor health and the loss of several babies. Her sister Mary had
died after a series of unsuccessful pregnancies, and Ann was plagued
by dreams of Mary and the lost children. Ann Jr. became the leader of
the girls when the finger-pointing began, and soon her mother joined
in, too. Some students of the Salem saga believe that at some point
along the way, the Putnams actually took control of the accusations
and deliberately directed them toward their local enemies. Eventually
eight members of the Putnam family wound up accusing forty-six different people of witchcraft.

Although the Puritan leaders always referred to the accusers as
"the children," by the time the executions began many of the early

nts had dropped out, from guilt or exhaustion, and been
ed by older women with less innocent histories. (Betty Parris
s sent away by her parents, and eventually her signs of possession
stopped. Abigail Williams, her orphaned cousin, remained in Salem
and continued to see witches.) And the girls did not begin accusing
people spontaneously. They were pestered by their parents, and by
neighbors who swarmed in to see the young women and their dramatic fits. In other towns, clergymen had kept a lid on witch hysteria
by ignoring the accusers' more outrageous claims. But in Salem, visiting ministers and Betty's own father demanded that they name their
persecutors. The girls eventually identified three local women—
Tituba; Sarah Good, a homeless beggar; and Sarah Osborne, a sickly
middle-aged woman who had been involved in a legal battle with the
Putnams. Under normal circumstances, their arrest would have
ended the saga. But the male authority figures in the colony continued to follow the girls' lead, taking their most bizarre allegations at
face value, and holding trials in which the alleged witches were prodded to confess, while the girls shrieked that they were being tortured.
By September, 20 people had been executed as witches and over 150
others sent to jail, where four adults and one woman's newborn
infant died.

To the first Americans, witches were as real as wolves or Indians.
They flew on brooms or stools to special meeting places, where they
signed Satan's book of souls and got their marching orders. Then they
used their powers to bring down misfortune on their neighbors, killing
cows, ruining crops, and causing healthy babies to suddenly sicken
and die. Less than fifty years before the Salem crisis, several hundred
people were executed in England for witchcraft, about 90 percent of
them women. The definitive works on witchery by medieval Europeans all carefully explained that "more women than men are ministers
of the devil" because of their intellectual and moral inferiority. But if
most Americans believed in witches, only New Englanders seemed
particularly interested in ferreting them out. There were virtually no
witch trials in any colonies but Massachusetts and Connecticut. Even
there, the trials were generally isolated events, involving one or two

suspects. More people were charged and executed for witchcraft during the Salem crisis than over the rest of American history.

As in Europe, the typical American witch-suspect was a woman, frequently middle-aged with few or no children and a reputation as a difficult personality. But the rest of the profile had mutated in the new world. In the colonies, accused witches were not necessarily poor outsiders. Many of them, in fact, had either inherited or were likely to inherit property. A famous example was Ann Hibbens, a well-to-do Boston widow who was executed in 1656. Hibbens, the wife of a magistrate, had always been regarded as hard to deal with by some of her neighbors. The case that sealed her doom began when some carpenters came to her home and did some work that Hibbens regarded as poor in quality. Complaining she was overcharged, she took her grievance all the way to the governor without receiving satisfaction. Hibbens never backed down, although she was excommunicated, in part for serving as an "evil example" to "diverse other wives." But she was protected by the position of her husband, who seemed to care for her even if he could not entirely control her. When he died, charges of witchcraft were raised for the first time, and Hibbens's fate was sealed. One minister claimed she was sent to the gallows "only for having more wit than her neighbors," but to the Boston populace, she was yet another dangerous woman, a deadly combination of being different and powerful.

The first Salem women to be accused were more along the old stereotype of hapless outsiders. Sarah Good was a beggar who had been reared in more prosperous circumstances and showed her dissatisfaction with misfortune by cursing the people whom she petitioned for food and money. When she was brought to the Salem meetinghouse, her own husband testified that she was an awful wife and "an enemy to all good." Both the accused Sarahs denied being witches. But Tituba attempted to protect herself by saying what her questioners wanted to hear—a tactic that ultimately saved her life but gave the Salem authorities the ammunition they needed to keep the hunt going. She said a tall man from Boston with white hair had both tempted and threatened her, promising to kill the Parris children and herself as well if she refused to serve him. The accusers quickly picked up on Tituba's story. The slave described a creature like a cat, with two legs, wings, and a woman's head. Abigail Williams, Minister Parris's niece, announced that she had seen just such a being, and it had turned into Sarah Osborne.

Sarah Osborne died before she could be brought to trial. Good and Tituba were kept incarcerated, held in leg irons to make sure they did not fly away before they could be judged. The girls pressed further, naming Martha Corey, a respectable but outspoken middle-aged member of the community, who had made it clear she thought the entire witch business was so much hogwash. She was brought to the Putnam home to confront young Ann, who had accused her. As soon as she arrived, the girl fell into a fit and complained of being choked by an invisible specter. The Puritans believed witches often worked with "familiars"—beasts sent by the Devil to do his bidding—who nursed at "witch's teats" concealed on the guilty party's body. Ann Putnam claimed she saw a yellow bird nursing in the space between two of Martha Corey's fingers. When the older woman tried to show the girl that there was nothing between her fingers, Ann cried out that she had been struck blind. Then she screamed that she saw Corey roasting a man on a spit in the family fireplace.

The accused witches were helpless. Hauled into the Salem meetinghouse, they were confronted by outrageous charges—that they had killed babies, drowned sailors, flown through the air to demonic gatherings where they plotted the downfall of the community of the godly. When they attempted to defend themselves—pointing out that they had been in another town when some disaster occurred—the accusers simply said that the witch had sent her "specter" to do her bidding for her. The whole proceedings took place through a din of screaming and thrashing as the girls responded to any resistance by going into fits and claiming that the witch had sent a specter to pinch or smother them. The judges, who sometimes seemed as frightened of the girls as they were of witches, rarely asked the accused any questions except why they were torturing the children.

Besides the marginal characters like Sarah Good, most of the people the girls accused were either citizens who had expressed doubts about their credibility, or those who had in the past taken sides against the Putnams in the town's endless series of feuds and lawsuits. Virtually every Salem resident who was named as a witch came from the prosperous, commercial side of town, while the accusers who joined with the girls in identifying new suspects almost all came from the more remote agricultural end. The two sides had been divided over Reverend Parris's appointment, as well as dozens of other disputes involving property boundaries, inheritances, and local government. The girls may have fallen under the sway of older women, like Mrs. Putnam, who joined in the denunciations. Or they may have simply been acting out the emotional dramas they heard rehearsed over the living room fire by their bitter parents.

One of the most pathetic victims was Rebecca Nurse, a seventy-one-year-old Puritan matriarch whose family opposed the Putnams in a number of local battles. Ann Putnam Sr. was her main accuser, and some historians have suggested she may have seen Nurse as a surrogate for her husband's elderly stepmother, a powerful woman who was in the process of disinheriting Ann's family in favor of her own son. Ann, who claimed she had been suffering at the hands of the jailed Martha Corey, told the authorities that Martha was accompanied in her evil visits by Rebecca Nurse. Local officials visited the old woman, who was hard of hearing and ailing, at her home, where she was bedridden. She asked after the troubled girls, offered words of sympathy for Minister Parris and his family, but expressed the opinion that some of those who had been accused were "innocent as she." When told that she, too, was a suspect, Nurse sat silent for a minute, perhaps stunned. "As to this thing, I am innocent as the child unborn; But surely, what sin hath God found out in me unrepented of that he should lay such an affliction upon me in my old age?" she asked.

Dragged off to the meetinghouse, Nurse was forced to confront her accusers, who instantly fell to the ground, writhing in pain and crying that she was attacking them. The elder Ann Putnam claimed that she was being visited by the children of her sister, who reported that Rebecca Nurse had caused their deaths. The old woman, asked to explain all these bizarre occurrences, naturally had no good answer. "I cannot tell what to think," she said. She pointed out that during the time she was supposed to have been tormenting the girls, she was confined to her bed with illness. That denial simply caused the victims to howl louder. "Oh Lord help me," Nurse exclaimed. Eventually, two of her sisters, Sarah Cloyce and Mary Easty, were also charged with witchcraft.

The accused were confined in jails that resembled medieval dungeons—dark, cold, and frequented by rats. They were chained to the walls, the better to keep their specters under control. One of the prisoners was Dorcas Good, the four-year-old daughter of Sarah, who had probably expressed some bitterness at the people who had caused her mother to be dragged away. The girls claimed Dorcas's specter had been biting them. At her hearing, whenever the little girl looked at her accusers, they screamed and displayed bite marks on their arms. Dorcas was carted off to jail, where she was kept in heavy leg irons for nine months. The girl was eventually freed but remained mentally disturbed for the rest of her life.

As news of the Salem witches spread, women in other towns began to experience the symptoms of possession. Men almost never felt they were possessed, but they came up with charges of their own—sickness or agricultural disasters that could only have been caused by an unnatural evil—or reported nighttime visitations that tormented their sleep. The out-of-towners brought their cases to Salem and asked the girls who was responsible. The girls were always willing to comply, although sometimes, when they confronted the people they had named in court, they were unable to identify them.

When Rebecca Nurse was tried in Boston, her accusers screamed and cried out that they were being pinched by an invisible hand. Rebecca's daughter, Sarah, demonstrated that one of the girls had pulled pins out of her clothing and inflicted the pain on herself. Perhaps influenced by that discovery, or Nurse's virtuous history, the jury returned a verdict of not guilty. The girls shrieked and fell into fits, creating an uproar that terrified the courtroom. The chief justice asked the jury to go back and reconsider. The jurors obediently returned with a finding of guilty. The Massachusetts governor, William Phipps, then reviewed the case at the request of Nurse's family and issued a reprieve. But as soon as the old woman was released, the girls again fell into what looked like mortal illness and it was made clear that if any of them died, the governor would be held accountable. Phipps retracted his reprieve and Nurse was hanged along with four other women on July 19. It was the first mass execution of witches in American history. Later, Rebecca's sister, the gentle Mary Easty, was hanged too, after releasing a plea to the judges "that no more innocent blood be shed."

"By my own innocence I know you are in the wrong way," she wrote.

The girls began naming more and more powerful members of the community, including a number of men. George Burroughs, one of the former ministers at Salem village church, was hauled back from a parish in Maine and hanged as the witches' ringleader. George Jacobs, a feisty eighty-year-old Salemite who had also been allied against the Putnams, was accused by one of his servants. ("You tax me for a wizard, you may as well tax me for a buzzard," the old man said when he was arrested.) The servant, Sarah Churchill, later recanted and said she had been forced by the other girls to testify or risk being charged herself. Jacobs's granddaughter Margaret, who had also been charged, then accused her grandfather, possibly in an attempt to save her own life. But she later retracted her statements and begged her grandfather's forgiveness. Margaret's father, George Jacobs Jr., was accused next and fled to Canada. Her mother, Rebecca, who apparently had always been somewhat demented, was dragged off to jail.

Many of the people accused of witchcraft saved themselves by confessing. The authorities probably intended to punish them later anyway, but the ploy worked, and all the alleged witches who admitted their pact with Satan were able to remain alive until the trials came to an end, and they recanted their confessions. It seems surprising, in a way, that twenty people chose to insist on their innocence and face death. But they were Puritans who believed that claiming untruthfully to be a witch was as bad as embracing Satan himself, and they died for their religion. When a minister urged her to make a last-minute confession, the uncowable Sarah Good cried back from the scaffold: "I am no more a witch than you are a wizard, and if you take away my life, God will give you blood to drink."

The roster of accused witches became a cross section of seventeenth-century New England womanhood—pious matrons, sullen servants, homeless outcasts, canny businesswomen, feisty goodwives. Elizabeth Proctor, wife of one of the most prominent men in Salem, ran the family tavern while her husband looked after his other businesses. Twenty-two-year-old Abigail Hobbs was a wild child who roamed around at will, sleeping in the forest when the mood struck her, saying what she thought and running totally out of her parents' control. Mary English was married to the richest man in Salem and believed to be something of a snob. Bridget Bishop had been married three times and was frequently in court for fighting with her latest husband. Most of the men named were husbands of women who had already been accused. Giles Corey, the cranky eighty-year-old husband of Martha, refused to speak at his trial and was punished by being pressed to death under rocks, the only person in American history to be executed in that grisly manner. Elizabeth Proctor's husband, John, was hanged. (His name was used by Arthur Miller for the hero in his fictionalized play about the witch-hunts, *The Crucible*.) Mary English's husband was arrested, as was John Alden, a hero of the French and Indian Wars and the son of the famous Priscilla and John. "He lies with the Indian squaws and has Indian papooses," one girl cried as he was brought before them. The accusers were originally unable to pick Alden out from a crowd of other men, but the judges gave them a second chance, moving them outside so they would have better light to make their identification. Like the Englishes, Alden decided that flight was the better part of valor and escaped from jail, probably by bribing the eminently bribable wardens. He remained out of sight until the hysteria died away.

The backlash began with a ghost. On the day Mary Easty was hanged, a seventeen-year-old girl named Mary Herrick who lived in a town just outside Salem reported that Easty had appeared to her and declared her innocence. Meanwhile, some of the accused witches in prison who had confessed began to issue retractions. Increase Mather, one of Massachusetts's most important citizens, preached a sermon in which he argued that "it were better that ten suspected witches should escape than that one innocent person should be condemned." Critics who had long been unhappy with the hunt became more outspoken. Never before, they noted, had New England courts convicted people of witchcraft purely on the testimony of witnesses whose proof was visions nobody else could see. The prisons were overflowing with suspected witches, some as young as eight years old. The economy was suffering, as farms went untended while families struggled to cope with the imprisonment of their relatives. Children whose parents had been taken away were left to neighbors' charity.

Cotton Mather, one of the leading voices behind the prosecutions, was embarrassed by his father Increase's defection. But he was far more humiliated when an opponent of the trials published an eyewitness account of Mather's handling of another "bewitched" woman, Margaret Rule, with an emphasis on the clergyman's attempts to calm the girl by rubbing her naked breasts and belly. Governor Phipps, who had avoided the witch problem by going off to fight the Indians, returned to discover that his own wife had been accused. In October, he announced that he was forbidding any more imprisonments or trials. In January 1693, a year after the witch-hunt began, and after two dozen people had already died, a special court met to consider charges against fifty-two of the remaining prisoners and rapidly dismissed almost all the cases. Governor Phipps began signing reprieves for those who had already been convicted or confessed, and he later issued a general pardon. That didn't necessarily mean the accused witches could go home. Massachusetts required that prisoners pay for the cost of their room and board before they could leave jail, and some of those who had been incarcerated could not settle their bills. Young Margaret Jacobs had no one to pay for her release. Her father had fled the country; her mother, although free, was penniless and deranged; and her grandfather had been hanged. A local fisherman heard her sad story and finally put up the money, then later sued Margaret to recover his investment.

No one involved in the Salem saga got to enjoy a really happy ending. Minister Parris found many of his parishioners had turned against him—he seemed disturbed, and even surprised, that the family of Rebecca Nurse no longer wanted to be in the congregation. By 1695, he had been removed from the pulpit, but in typical Salem fashion it took several years before the competing factions in the community could actually agree it was time to go. Parris's wife died, his son became insane, and Betty married and faded into obscurity. The next pastor, a younger and far sunnier character, gradually reconciled the community and revoked the excommunications of Rebecca Nurse and Martha Corey.

Like Betty Parris, most of the other young girls who were involved in the trials grew up and married without making any further mark on history. The only witness who actually recanted was young Ann Putnam. In 1706 she confessed that she had been deluded. Satan, she told the Salem congregation, "deceived me in that sad time. I did it not out of any anger, malice or ill will." She expressed particular sorrow about her role in accusing Rebecca Nurse and her two sisters. The congregation, which apparently blamed Ann's already-dead mother for her behavior, forgave her. She died at the age of thirty-seven, never having married. In her case, at least, Tituba's magic proved accurate.

# Daily Life in the Colonies: Housekeeping, Children, and Sex

## "MY BASON OF WATER FROZE ON THE HEARTH"

If the Salem witch-craft "victims" were faking their attacks, they had the advantage of performing under the cover of half-darkness. Almost everything that the colonists did indoors occurred in dim light, or flickering shadows. The houses in which the women spent so much of their lives were generally extremely primitive—settlers in parts of Pennsylvania actually lived in caves. There was little in the way of windows, and for a long time there was no window glass; the colonists covered whatever small openings they made in the walls with oiled paper. Candles were expensive, and even at the beginning of the nineteenth century, most houses had only one or two candlesticks. What light there was generally came from the fireplace, although in some parts of the country splinters of pine were used as minitorches. Whatever the source of illumination, it was hard on the eyes. People who read by candle sometimes singed their books while trying to get the page close enough to the light. During the day, women who wanted to sew worked next to the window—an uncomfortable location in the winter.

During winter in the northern colonies, people must have felt cold all the time. Even the fireplace was limited help in a drafty, uninsulated house. To take advantage of the heat, you had to stand so close as to risk incineration. Harriet Beecher Stowe described a New England housewife "Standing with her back so near the blaze as to be uncomfortably warm" while her dishtowel was "freezing in her hand." Anna Green Winslow, a Revolutionary War–era schoolgirl, gave thanks in her diary for living in a warm house, then added that "my bason of water froze on the hearth with as good a fire as we could make in the chimney."

The fireplaces were huge—big enough to walk around in, and the scene of perpetual hazard. Children fell into the flames, and embers rolled out and burned down houses. What little furniture the houses had was not designed for comfort. Feather beds, the closest thing the colonists had to luxury, looked more appealing than they felt. They were dreadfully uncomfortable in hot weather and so high that people needed bed steps to get on top. "Night and morning were made fearful to me by the prospect of having to climb up and down," a Massachusetts woman recalled. Unless she managed to land right in the middle, she added, "I passed my night in rolling down hill, or in vain efforts to scramble up to the top, to avoid falling out on the floor."

Women could live out their entire lives without ever feeling back support. The churches, where they spent hours listening to sermons, offered only benches. At home they sat on stools. There was at most only one real chair in the average seventeenth-century American home, and it was reserved for the head of the household; hence, the word *chairman*. (When the elders of Boston started bearing down on Anne Hutchinson, one of the things they noted with alarm was that in meetings with both male and female followers, she was the one who got the best seat.) Indoors was a spare and grim place, but the average female settler wanted very much to be there. Recruiting pamphlets always made it a point to claim that women in the American colonies spent all their time at housework. In reality, few of the early farmers could afford to pass up the chance to use their wives as field hands. But it was what the Englishwoman wanted to hear; her goal was not to work side by side with her spouse, but to be in charge of her own domestic establishment.

Women didn't shun outdoor labor because they feared the work. Their domestic duties were actually harder, with no downtime and less variety. Field tasks changed with the seasons—once the planting was done, the farmer knew he would never have to look at another seed for eleven months. The homemaker was trapped in an endless cycle of cooking, cleaning up, and then getting ready for the next meal. "This day is forty years since I left my father's house and come here, and here have I seene littel els but harde labour and sorrow," wrote Mary Cooper, a housewife who lived on a farm in Long Island in the years before the Revolutionary War. Of all the American women who wrote diaries in the eighteenth century, Mary is unique in that she constantly complained. Colonists were a stoic lot, experts at repressing emotion or throwing all their woes into the lap of a hopefully benevolent Deity. But Mary didn't withhold. "O I am tired almost to death," was one of her favorite refrains.

In the seventeenth century, even wealthy colonial women worked like demons. In the frontier towns, the wives of the leading citizens were responsible for sheltering the rest of the community when Indians threatened. The visitors were called "garrison crowds," and they sometimes stayed long past their natural welcome. Elizabeth Saltonstall of Haverill, Massachusetts, entertained sixty guests for months on end during the Indian alerts of 1694. One of her sons, writing to a sister from his college, reported gingerly that their family in Haverill was "all Well in health, but much thronged with Children and Lice; which discourages our taking a Journey thither."

## "FOR SHE HAS BEEN AND IS A GOOD WIFE TO ME"

The house was the one place where a colonial housewife could be in charge, the chief executive and artisan of a little factory producing the items the family needed to survive. Elizabeth Buffum Chace said that besides the ordinary housework and the care of fourteen children, her colonial great-grandmother engaged in "candle making, soap making, butter and cheese making, spinning, weaving, dyeing and of course all the knitting and sewing and dressmaking and tailoring and probably the shoe making and the millinery of this large household." The most time-consuming chore was the making of cloth, and it was also one of the most critical. Early on, fabric was in such short supply in America that there are records of court suits fought over a missing handkerchief or a hole burned in a blanket. The colonists regarded the production of new cloth as crucial to their survival, and in 1656, the New England General Court ordered "all hands not necessarily employed on other occasions, as women, Girles and Boyes" be required to spin three pounds of thread a week for at least thirty weeks a year. This was basically a tax on women, who must have felt the officials had their nerve in presuming they were not "employed."

Colonial clothes were made from wool or flax. Turning the flax into linen thread was an excruciating process in which the stalks were dried, combed, softened, cleaned, dried again, then "broken" to separate the fibers, pounded, cleaned, and pounded again. The little mass of fiber that emerged from all this was spun into thread on a small wheel with a hand pedal. The thread then had to be treated with repeated washing, rinsing, bleaching, and beating before it was ready for the loom. With wool, the women used a much larger wheel and stood to do the work. They performed a sort of graceful dance, gliding backward to draw out the newly spun yarn, then coming forward to let it wind onto the spindle. In a full day of spinning, a woman could walk over twenty miles.

Spinning was one of the jobs housewives most eagerly foisted off on their daughters or servants. Cooking was another duty they found particularly burdensome—it was both repetitive and difficult to do well because the temperature of the fire could not be controlled. (Roasting was occasionally facilitated by "turnspit dogs" who ran on a revolving cylinder that kept the meat turning over the fire, but that novelty appeared mainly at commercial inns.) Women might have found their seasonal duties more interesting. In the autumn, they made apple butter and cider. When the pigs were butchered, they cleaned the intestines for sausage casing and stuffed them with meat scraps and herbs. They collected the fat to mix with lye for soap making—a long and arduous process that probably never ranked high on anyone's list of favorite chores. The grease and lye were boiled together, outdoors, in a huge pot over an open fire. It took about six bushels of ashes and 24 pounds of grease to make one barrel of soap, which was soft, like clear jelly.

In the cold weather, the women made candles and brewed beer. In the spring, they planted their kitchen gardens. Martha Ballard, a Maine midwife, grew beans, cabbage, lettuce, parsnips, carrots, turnips, beets, cucumbers, radishes, onions, garlic, peppers, squash, peas, muskmelon, watermelon, pumpkins, and a variety of herbs both for cooking and medicinal purposes. Cheese making started in early summer. The dairywoman slowly heated several gallons of milk with rennet—the dried lining of an animal's stomach. In an hour or two, the curd formed and she worked in some butter, packed the mixture into a mold, and put it in a wooden press for an hour or so, changing and washing the cheesecloths as the whey dripped out. A housewife who could make good clean butter and cheese was a real boon to her family, creating a product that was not only valuable at home but in the marketplace. To be a good dairywoman was a fine art and hard work. Turning milk into butter required an hour or so at the churn followed by kneading and pressing with the hands or wooden paddles.

Obviously most women weren't able to do all the housewifely tasks well. Someone who was good at cheese making might trade her wheels of cheese for cloth or meat or candles. A midwife or dressmaker might be paid for her services with a brace of geese or tub of sweet butter. Martha Ballard, who worked as a midwife in the late eighteenth century, was still collecting payment for her services in coffee, candles, unwashed wool, and even shingles. (Mrs. Ballard's midwife business was no minor sideline. During one three-week period in August, while supervising her large and active household, she recorded four deliveries, one false alarm, sixteen medical calls, and preparing three bodies for burial.) The community of women was both an informal barter economy and a network of mutual assistance. Women dropped in on one another freely, picking up some household duty like shelling peas as they sat and gossiped or consulted with one another about recent events. A Maine author remembered seeing a woman going to visit a neighbor on baking day, carrying her dough along with her. Daughters were regularly "lent out" by their mothers to help a neighbor with the spinning or harvest or nursing. "The women in families took care of their own sick by day and depended on their neighbors for watchers at night," wrote Elizabeth Buffum Chace. "I began to go out 'watching' when I was fourteen years old. We girls often went, two of us together, on such service. We had a good supper spread for us to eat in the night, and very sick patients were often left to our unskilled care."

Colonial women reached the height of their powers in middle age, when they were no longer burdened by continual pregnancy and had daughters old enough to help with the domestic enterprises. (The birth of a daughter was not unwelcome in most colonial families. The parents needed sons to help in the fields, but they also wanted girls to assist their mothers inside.) Although a prosperous matron had absolutely no voice in the public arena, she was expected to take a leading part in the parallel universe that was the world of women. Older women were the advisers, counselors, and judges of the younger. Male officials seemed to acknowledge their status. In 1664, Elizabeth Perkins and Agnes Ewens of Topsfield were summoned to court to testify in a case involving a young woman they both knew. The goodwives successfully invoked a kind of professional immunity. They had spoken to the woman, they said, as counselors, and because she had lived properly since their intervention, they preferred not to break her confidence.

A competent housewife also earned the respect of her husband, who could see firsthand the value of her labors. The farmer who slaughtered a pig needed his wife to make the sausages, process the bacon, and preserve the pork. As he sat by the fireside at night, mending his fishing net or fixing his tools, he could watch her turning the flax he had harvested and the wool he had sheared into the family's clothes. The candle that lit their way to bed came from her hand, as did the vegetables, eggs, cheese, and chickens they ate and the beer or cider they drank. They were very much partners in the family business, and if the man was at all sensible he understood how critical his wife was to their mutual success. When Ensign Hewlett, a seventeenth-century Ipswich man, needed cash for a new enterprise, he borrowed it from his wife, a successful poultrywoman. A friend wondered why Hewlett didn't just claim the money as his own, but the husband replied: "I meddle not with the geese nor the turkeys for they are hers. For she has been and is a good wife to me."

## "WOMEN CHOOSE RATHER TO HAVE A THING DONE WELL THAN HAVE IT OFTEN"

Cotton Mather urged Puritan women to take as their model Herpine, who in her eagerness to serve her ailing husband "bore him on her Back, a thousand and three Hundred English Miles to Bath." It's an interesting image, which endows the wife with a combination of terrific power and terrific deference. But if court records are any indication, New England women were much less submissive to the man of the house than Mather wanted. A third of the accused spouse-beaters were women, and there are plenty of cases in which the goodwife seemed to be getting the best of her husband when their dispute was hauled off to court. Still, in several critical areas, a married woman was virtually powerless. All her property was under her husband's control, and he had complete legal sway over the children. His character determined how far she could rise in life. A hardworking woman could pull up a less-than-ambitious spouse, but she could not triumph over a dissolute one. Divorce was rarely an option—New England courts sometimes allowed a couple to separate, but they hardly ever dissolved a union. Unhappy southern wives could at least hope for early widowhood, but those in the North were yoked for what would probably be a long life. New Englanders who survived childhood could expect to live to their sixties, and a quarter made it into their eighties. If childbirth didn't kill you, you could wind up a very old woman, still married to your original husband.

Husbands' obligations to their wives included being affectionate, a good provider, and a good example. (The male colonists tended to regard women as frail creatures who were likely to stray from the path of godliness unless wiser, stronger males continually herded them in the right direction.) The Puritans disapproved of wife beating, and in early New England towns, families lived so close to each other that the howls of an abused spouse would bring a delegation of concerned church members to the door. But a man who was indifferent to his neighbors' bad opinion could discipline his wife as harshly as he liked without risking serious punishment. Daniel Ela, who defended himself in a wife-beating case by arguing that she was "his servant and his slave," was not prosecuted further. One man who had beaten his wife, kicked her, hit her on the head, and threatened to slit her throat and burn her was sentenced to be lashed but was granted a reprieve when he promised to reform.

In New England, it was against the law for a couple to have sex before they were married. (Cynics might argue it was against the law to do practically anything.) If a first child arrived before a marriage was nine months old, the couple could be hauled into court and charged with fornication and punished with nine lashes "upon the Naked back" or a steep fine. But as time went on, fewer and fewer women saved themselves for their wedding night. In Bristol, Rhode Island, none of the couples that married at the end of the seventeenth century had a child less than nine months after the ceremony. But between 1720 and 1740, 10 percent had babies whose early arrival gave evidence of premarital intercourse, and by 1760 to 1780, it was 44 percent. In other parts of the country, premarital sex was taken for granted. A visitor to New York in 1695 reported that "commonly, enjoyment precedes the marriage, to which they seldom come till a great belly puts it so forward, that they must either submit to that, or to shame and disgrace."

Adultery was a more serious matter. The Puritans defined adultery as sex between a married woman and any man other than her husband. (A married man who strayed was only guilty of fornication.) Adultery was theoretically a capital offense, although like most of the early colonists' capital offenses, it generally carried a less drastic punishment. Still, at least three married women in New England were hanged for sleeping around. The most notorious, Mary Latham of

Boston, had married an older man and then took a dislike to him, "setting a knife to his breast and threatening to kill him, calling him old rogue and cuckold." She admitted committing adultery with twelve different men.

Women were expected to enjoy sex—indeed, the colonists felt it was critical. Most people believed conception could occur only if a woman reached orgasm. New Haven justices dismissed a young woman's claim that she had been impregnated while in "a fit of swooning" by arguing that "no woman can be gotten with child without some knowledge, consent & delight in the acting thereof." Men who read books about sex, like the popular *Aristotle's Master Piece,* got tips on how to arouse their sexual partners. ("Women choose rather to have a thing done well than have it often.") Colonial women were seen as flawed, but not particularly fragile creatures. One of their great failings, in fact, was believed to be their lustiness.

Many couples believed that when they made love, the man and the woman each emitted a "seed" and that conception occurred when the two seeds mixed. Others thought that a woman's womb contained seven sacs, three on each side and one in the center. The ones on the right produced boys, the ones on the left girls, and the one in the center, hermaphrodites. After sex, a woman was advised to lie on her right or left side, depending on which sex baby she hoped to bear. The colonists were more romantic than history gives them credit for, but having sex too often, they believed, "gluts the Womb and renders it unfit for its office."

## "THIS MIGHT POSSIBLY BE THE LAST TRIAL OF THIS SORT"

Childbearing dominated the lives of early female settlers. The average woman in New England married before her twentieth birthday and gave birth to about seven children. She nursed each baby for twelve to eighteen months. Nursing, which suppresses ovulation, served as a rough form of birth control. Elizabeth Drinker, a Philadelphia Quaker whose thirty-eight-year-old daughter had just given birth, wrote expressing her hope that "this might possibly be the last trial of this sort, if she could suckle her baby for 2 years to come."

In the malaria-ridden early South, a multitude of pregnancies produced a tragically small number of adults—half the children born in the Chesapeake area died before reaching adulthood. In New England, however, the fatality rate was much lower and people had very large families. Ten or more children were not at all uncommon. Benjamin Franklin was one of seventeen children. Sir William Phipps was said to be one of twenty-six, all from the same mother. In the eighteenth century, when colonists had learned how to survive the climate, the size of southern families boomed—a visitor to Charlestown reported that most of the households there had ten or twelve children. Southern women became obsessed with having babies, to the point where some announced their pregnancies in the newspaper. They also frequently took advantage of a happy superstition that held mothers-to-be would miscarry if they were denied anything they yearned for.

Childbirth was a communal affair, the great moment for the gathering of neighborhood women while their men waited on the other side of the door, passive outsiders. The early stages of labor were partylike, as was the celebration at the end of a successful delivery. Samuel Sewall of Boston recorded that after his wife gave birth to their twelfth child, he found the women who had helped her dining on "rost Beef and minc'd Pyes, good Cheese and Tarts." When she began to deliver, the mother-to-be might squat over a low open-seated stool or sit in another woman's lap. If there was a lactating woman in the group—and there almost always was—she nursed the baby first because a new mother's milk was believed to be impure. During very difficult childbirths, the woman in labor was urged to drink another woman's milk. When the crisis was over, there were generally bawdy jokes about the umbilical cord. (A long one for a boy meant he would grow a sizable member. A girl's was supposed to be cut short or she would become immodest.) Eventually, the husband was allowed to reenter the room, and the world of women gave way to the patriarchal family.

Midwives were a critical resource in colonial communities—the normally apolitical matrons of Boston went on a virtual strike when their favorite midwife came under attack by the church elders. Several New England towns provided a rent-free house for their midwife and in New Amsterdam, midwives were actually public servants who received rather large salaries. The support of the midwife and female neighbors during delivery was the emotional center of women's community, but it was also a matter of life and death. About a fifth of the pregnant women in New England died giving birth, and the figures were much higher in the South. Cotton Mather, ever one to look on the bright side, advised pregnant women that "PREPARATION FOR DEATH is that most Reasonable and Seasonable thing, to which you must now apply yourself." Wealthy women had special sets of childbed linens, which they put on their beds after delivery was completed. If tragedy occurred, the linens became the woman's shroud. In an era in which masculine bravery was celebrated, it was the women who actually dared to stare down death on a regular basis.

Since they were almost always either pregnant or nursing an infant, colonial women spent their lives in a continual balancing act, in which the dangers of overexertion had to be weighed against the simple necessity of getting through the day. The 40-pound pots had to be lifted on and off the fire, no matter what the mother's condition. Colonial-era Americans harbored many theories about the delicacy of expectant mothers, and the danger to the fetus if she should be surprised or confronted with an unpleasant object. (A woman who saw a deformed beggar in the street, they believed, might give birth to a deformed baby.) However, these were yet another series of rules that could be suspended whenever necessary. If a wife's services were needed in an area that was replete with alarming surprises—say, working in the fields of a frontier farm while under threat of Indian attack—she was expected to do her job, pregnancy or no.

Women traveled while they were pregnant, but once a baby was born, they tended to stay close to home while nursing. Some women took "weaning trips" when the baby was in its first year to make the withdrawal of the maternal breast easier—on the mother, at least. In a crisis, a friend might provide "courtesy nursing" to a mother in need of help. Sometimes her own mother could do the favor. In a culture in which women began to have children very young, and continued until rather late in life, it wasn't at all unusual for mother and daughter to be pregnant at the same time. Given the amount of suckling that went on, there was obviously a lot of concern about how to treat sore breasts. One popular physician recommended a poultice: "take new Milk and grate white bread into it, then take Mallows and Red Rose Leaves, 1 handful of each then chop them small and boyl them together till it be thick, then put some honey and turpentine mix them, then spread it on a cloth and apply it."

## "IF I ONLY KNIT MY BROW SHE WILL CRY"

All sorts of perils lay in wait for colonial children. Samuel Sewall, in his diary, constantly records accidents that befell youngsters in Boston—accidentally shot, dragged to death by a galloping horse, fallen through the ice while skating, scalded to death by boiling home-made beer. The Puritans regarded such incidents as a just God's pun-ishment for the sins of the parents—Sewall felt that two of his young children died because he participated as a judge in the Salem witch tri-als. People seemed resigned, to some extent, that their offspring sim-ply had to take their chances. Their greatest fear was infectious disease, which could sweep off entire families. In 1740, a virulent strain of diphtheria claimed as many as half the children in some New England towns.

Mothers didn't dote. They seemed to feel a generalized concern for the whole tribe of youngsters under their care (many of the servants were children themselves) rather than a concentrated devotion on a few individuals. In a large household community of children, ser-vants, visiting friends, and relatives, the smaller children were often tended by people other than their mothers, and child care doesn't seem to have ranked as a true domestic duty. Women's advice books, which said a great deal about cooking and household management, hardly mentioned children. The diaries of colonial housewives, which are mainly lists of chores and duties accomplished, do not generally refer to children except when one is being born or dying. Babies were called "it"—possibly because the parents wanted to make sure an infant had a good chance of survival before they began to bond.

If colonial parents followed the practices of Britain—as they did in most things—they bound their newborns, sometimes wrapping them against a board to straighten their backs. The tight binding tended to slow down the baby's metabolism, so that it cried less. Fanny Kemble, the British actress who spent a long unhappy period at her husband's American plantation in the nineteenth century, noted that the slaves had adopted a custom that had only recently been abandoned among white colonists and "pin up the lower part of their infants, bodies, legs, and all, in red flannel as soon as they are born and keep them in the selfsame envelope till it literally falls off."

New Englanders believed in early discipline. The Puritan minister John Robinson had famously advised that "there is in all children . . . a stubbornness, and stoutness of mind arising from natural pride, which must, in the first place, be broken and beaten down." Esther Burr, the wife of the president of Princeton, wrote to her best friend in 1754 that she had "begun to govourn Sally," her firstborn. "She has been Whip'd once . . . and she knows the differance between a Smile and a frown as well as I do. When She has done anything that She Suspects is wrong, will look with concern to See what Mamma says, and if I only knit my brow She will cry till I Smile." Sally was not yet ten months old.

The colonies lacked an orderly progression to maturity, with certain achievements earmarked for certain ages. It was not unknown for ten- and eleven-year-old boys to enter Harvard, or for near infants of two or three years of age to be bound out as indentured servants. A Madam Coleman wrote about her problems with her eight-year-old granddaughter Sally, who was sent from Barbados to live in Boston in 1719. The little girl arrived with her maid and, offended that her grandmother made her drink water with her meals, decamped on her own and moved into a boardinghouse. Her brother wrote demanding that Sally return to her grandmother's home. But Mrs. Coleman reported that Sally had said that "her Brother has nothing to do with her as long as her father is alive," and sent word that she needed a new muff.

Girls who were neither wealthy nor indigent were still given what we would regard as extraordinary responsibilities. Susan Blunt recalled that when she was ten she was sent to keep house "for a week" for a man who left her in charge of his twin little girls and an elderly father. Her duties began at 5:00 A.M., when she toted water in from a distant well, then made everyone a breakfast of boiled potatoes, fried pork, and coffee. She tended the old man, baked biscuits and beans for dinner, cleaned and mended. As her reward, she received enough money to buy a new apron.

Girls generally didn't receive much schooling in the colonial period. "Female education in the best families went no farther than writing and arithmetic and in some few rare instances, music and dancing," wrote Abigail Adams, the wife of the second president. Few towns permitted girls to be educated past the "dames schools" which were closer to day care centers than actual institutions of learning. (There's a pathetic story about a little girl in western Massachusetts who sat outside the schoolhouse door every day, trying to learn what she could from listening to the boys recite their lessons.) The women who ran dames schools were the only female teachers in America during the pre-Revolutionary period and their pay reflected the community's estimate of the value of education imparted by a female. In Woburn, Massachusetts, in 1641, a respected local widow named Mrs. Walker established a school. Her salary for the first year, after deductions, was 1 shilling and 3 pence.

In the North, Puritan and Quaker families wanted their daughters to learn their letters well enough to read the Bible, if not necessarily to write. In the South, most women were totally illiterate in the seventeenth century. In Virginia, only one in three could sign her name, compared to three in five men. Wealthier young women were prepared for a good marriage, and too much learning was regarded as a defect in an attractive woman. Caroline Howard Gilman recalled that when the family tutor proposed teaching her the same lessons as her brother, her father worried that "the girl would consider herself more learned than her father," and finally reluctantly agreed, saying: "Well, well, only do not spoil her eyes and shoulders."

## "NOT HAVING BEEN WETT ALL OVER ATT ONCE, FOR 28 YEARS PAST"

Cleanliness was not high on the colonists' list of priorities. Virtually no one took baths—there were no bathrooms, and whatever bathing was done usually occurred from a basin, in the presence of other people. Most people simply scrubbed their faces with cold water. In 1798, Elizabeth Drinker, a highly respected sixty-five-year-old Quaker matron in Philadelphia, bathed in a shower box that her husband set up in the backyard of their house. "I bore it better than I expected, not having been wett all over att once, for 28 years past," she wrote in her diary. The baths in Elizabeth's life seem to have been infrequent enough to be recorded as milestones. The incident twenty-eight years before the momentous shower had taken place on the Delaware River, where she and her husband were spending seven weeks at what was the colonial equivalent of a spa. Elizabeth and some of her friends went to the baths, where she "found the shock much greater than expected." Although she returned the next day, she "had not courage to go in."

These baths would have been immersions in mineral water for the sake of health or sociability. The concept of giving oneself a good scrub seemed unknown. The soft soap that women made themselves was used for washing clothes, not people. At the beginning of the nineteenth century, innkeepers were still surprised when European travelers asked for a bar of soap with which to wash. If a woman's hair was dirty or greasy, she could conceal it under a linen cap, which was worn indoors and out. It was harder to hide the evidence of a lack of toothbrushes. Visitors remarked about the poor condition of colonial teeth. "The women are pitifully tooth-shaken, whether through the coldness of the climate, or by sweet-meats, of which they have a score, I am not able to affirm," said a visitor.

One of the great mysteries of colonial women's lives is what they did about menstruation. They didn't wear underpants, and while later settlers may have used rags, the early colonials probably would have been reluctant to waste precious cloth. Neither their diaries nor the midwives' manuals say a word about what women used as seventeenth- and eighteenth-century versions of sanitary napkins. Talking about menstruation seems to have been the ultimate taboo—child molestation was written about more freely. In Northampton in the late seventeenth century, Hannah Clark and a friend were stopped on the street by one Oliver Warner, who asked them, "When will the moon change?" and hinted that he knew they were having their periods: "I believe you have circles round your Eyes—I believe it runs." Their minister, the famous Jonathan Edwards, decided this sort of behavior was the result of young men reading midwifery books for titillation and launched a campaign against the practice.

Given how often they were pregnant or nursing, colonial women did not spend nearly as much time in normal menstrual cycles as modern women. When they did have their periods, their scanty diets probably restricted the amount of bleeding. Perhaps poor women allowed the blood to flow and cleaned up as best they could. (Moreau de St. Mèry, a French traveler after the Revolutionary War, said that for servants, the only protection during menstruation "is a skirt of bunting which they wear next to the skin, and which they use until its old age forces them to take another.") But middle-class and wealthy women certainly used some kind of protection. Those living along the coast may have used sponges, and some colonial women may have emulated the Indians and used moss or grass or leaves. But chances are most created a sort of makeshift diaper out of linen homespun.

The colonists were not as sensitive to smells and the sight of dirt as modern Americans. The farmers' homes and yards were filled with offal, debris, and garbage. People were less likely to use an outhouse than to take to the bushes. Clothes were washed infrequently—many women did the laundry only once a month, and on the frontier, never.

Washing clothes was an arduous process that began very early in the morning, when water was carried in from the well, then heated to a boil over those troublesome fireplaces. The laundress scrubbed and pounded the clothes in the tubs, working up to her elbows in hot water, sometimes for hours on end. When she was done, she spread the clothes out to dry on bushes—clotheslines didn't seem to come along until later. A truly dedicated housewife might then iron her husband's shirts and her aprons. The irons had their own heaters, which had to be filled with coals from the fire. The laundress always used two, so clothes didn't dry out while she was reheating her iron.

Given the amount of effort laundering required, it's unlikely that many women actually washed their babies' diapers. Most simply left the wet napkin by the fire to dry, then put it back on. It was a practice Dr. William Dewees, an early-nineteenth-century expert on obstetric issues, was still thundering against. "It is much better that it be without a diaper from time to time than have those returned to it stiffened with salts and reeking with offensive odor," he wrote. The entire issue of colonial diapering practices doesn't bear close examination by those with delicate sensibilities. Some women actually regarded wet diapers as a wholesome device for hardening the baby's constitution— another "monstrous error" Dr. Dewees was still decrying in the 1800s. In some households, the family dog was encouraged to lick the baby clean. And many women solved the diaper issue by toilet training their babies very early—sometimes beginning within a few weeks of birth. To train an infant to have its bowel movements at regular times, the mother used the equivalent of a suppository, made of a quill covered with lubricated cloth.

People who lived in towns maintained a higher level of cleanliness than those in the country, but by modern standards they would have seemed pretty gamy. The fireplace, dirt roads, and summer flies brought far more filth into the house than housewives could possibly drive away. When a room seemed to need freshening, they simply sprinkled around a little vinegar. Animals were everywhere—dogs and cats walked freely through houses, churches, taverns, even courthouses. There was no system of garbage disposal, and housewives generally threw things they were through with out the window. Chamber pots were often just dumped onto the street. (Lewis Miller, writing about York, Pennsylvania, in 1801, reported the unfortunate story of a woman on her way to a wedding whose silk dress was ruined when a man poured his chamber pot from an upper window.) Some of the historians who've studied the diaries of Mary Cooper, that Long Island farm wife who kept complaining about how exhausted she was, theorized that she was so fatigued because she was one of the few women of her era who actually attempted to keep things clean.

## "STRANGERS ARE SOUGHT AFTER WITH GREEDINESS"

Unlike the women in the North, the white women of the South had little opportunity to create a community of their own. Things were too spread out—a whole county might contain only a couple thousand people. Southern hospitality was to a great extent the creation of a desperately lonely people. George Washington used to post a slave at the crossroads near his plantation to invite any passerby to dinner. "Strangers are sought after with Greediness," wrote an observer. A circuit judge in North Carolina in the Revolutionary War era stopped at the home of some well-to-do newlyweds who were living on the husband's farm, eighteen miles from the nearest neighbor. He wrote that when a male visitor told the young bride he would bring his own wife to visit her, she wept with gratitude. But a good hostess had no control over when the blessing of company would arrive, or for how long. Friends, family, and unknown passersby felt free to drop in by the wagonful without notice, and they expected to be fed and lodged when they arrived. Neighbors who came together for balls, weddings, or even dancing lessons often stayed on for several days.

Church was an important social event for southerners, who didn't take their religion quite as seriously as the colonists up north. Visitors were scandalized to see southern women joining the men as they

smoked after church. Inside during services, it was the general custom for the women and lower classes to take their seats on time, and
for the wealthy men to arrive a half hour into the proceedings, the
better to display their fine clothes. The less prosperous families in
rural areas also came together for communal events like barn raisings
and husking frolics that might attract thirty to fifty people. These
combinations of neighborly helpfulness and socializing were popular
in the rural North, too. Women must have approached them with
mixed emotions. They were a chance to see neighbors, but they were
often alcohol fueled and violent. As time went on, farmers began to
question whether their half-drunk neighbors were really doing a very
good job of husking the corn or building the house, and the tradition
died out.

Southern women weren't expected to pursue the finer household
crafts, like butter making or even spinning. They were needed in the
fields, and back home they spent much of their time grinding corn—a
pastime that made spinning look like a picnic. As they gained wealth,
the most prosperous families graduated their daughters directly into
the world of fine needlepoint and dance lessons. Carving became a
major domestic art, and some wealthy young women took training
from a special carving master. The hostess was responsible for cutting
up the meat and making sure that each honored guest had the appropriate tasty bits. It was a chore so demanding that some women dined
before their dinner parties in order to be able to devote complete con-
centration to the job. There was a different term for cutting up different types of bird—theoretically, at least, one would "break" a goose,
"thrust" a chicken, "spoil" a hen, and "pierce" a plover.

The wild and wooly era of early colonial settlement in the South
had faded by the end of the seventeenth century. People were no
longer dying off so quickly—thanks in part to the new apple orchards
that had been planted, providing juice that displaced the brackish
water. The male-female sex ratio began to even out, and families were
no longer necessarily the collection of offspring from widows' and
widowers' former marriages. Men had male relatives they could rely

on to handle their estates in case they died, as well as lawyers to take care of plantation business in their absence. More men lived to see their children grow up, and they were able to leave their estates directly to their adult sons. Meanwhile, the windows of opportunity for independent women were beginning to close.

# 4

# Toward the Revolutionary War

## "TO SPEND . . . WHAT OTHERS GET"

Sixteen-year-old Hetty Shepard came from the country to visit a friend in Boston in 1676 and was thunderstruck by how much *stuff* was available in the stores. "Through all my life I have never seen such an array of fashion and splendor," she wrote. "Silken hoods, scarlet petticoats, with silver lace, white . . . plaited gowns, bone lace and silken scarves. The men with periwigs, ruffles and ribbons." America was undergoing the first of what would become a long line of consumer revolutions. Soon, even humble families began to acquire something more than the bare necessities—a teapot or a painted dish might brighten up a housewife's dark cabin. Wealthier colonial families began importing books, pictures, and rich clothing from Europe and installing real glass in their windows. Most homes were still very simple, with no carpets or curtains and minimal lighting. But families were dining off individual plates, drinking from their own cups, and sitting in their own chairs. By 1700, most women were no longer confined to benches and stools—although the backs on the newly available chairs were, unfortunately, very hard and straight.

On the frontier, life was pretty much the same as it had been in the early 1600s. While he was traveling through the Shenandoah Valley in

1748, George Washington spent the night with a family that had not
yet acquired the luxury of beds. He "lay down before the fire upon a
little hay, straw, fodder or bearskin . . . with man, wife, and children,
like a parcel of dogs and cats." But the settled parts of the country
were becoming more civilized, and in many ways, things were getting
easier. Even farm families could acquire bolts of cloth from the nearest store, freeing housewives from the tyranny of the spinning wheel.
Everyday necessities like candles and soap, which had to be manufactured at home in the seventeenth century, could be purchased in the
eighteenth. American women would have regarded this as a definite
improvement, but the change also seems to have contributed to a slip-
page in their status. The housewife's contribution to the family started
to be described in terms of emotional support, not the kind of economic partnership that had led Ensign Hewlitt to honor his wife's
right to do what she wanted with the profits from her turkeys and
geese. Some newspapers started ridiculing housewives as spongers,
lazy and trivial. Women, Cotton Mather told his female readers, "have
little more Worldly Business, than to spend . . . what others Get."

Most women actually performed as much labor as they had a generation earlier. Although they may have done less spinning, higher
standards of cleanliness dictated that they do much more washing and
sweeping and polishing. But their husbands hardly noticed their
efforts and found it hard to connect them with the support of the family. On the farm, instead of planting flax that their wives turned into
linen, men planted cash crops that they sold, and bought cloth with the
profit. The women seemed to be out of the loop entirely. The era of
barter economy, in which they had played such an important part, was
closing. And in some places, their exclusion from the world of commerce was much starker. In New Amsterdam, the Dutch had followed
the traditions of their mother country and encouraged female entrepreneurs, training both their young men and women to enter business
careers. Dutch women could maintain a separate civil identity after
marriage, buy and sell goods and property, contract debt, and determine who would inherit their property. But when the English took
over in 1664, turning New Amsterdam into New York, the women's

rights began to erode. Dutch farmers in New York stopped leaving their estates equally to all their children and started giving their land to their sons while daughters got a cash bequest. By 1700 there was not a single woman trader left in Albany, and the number in New York City dropped from 134 in 1653 to 43 in 1774.

Just as women were losing their status as household producers, they were gaining respect as mothers. This was a new idea—to the degree that seventeenth-century opinion makers ever thought of child rearing at all, it was in terms of the father's role. Women, who were supposed to be less intelligent, less self-controlled, and even a little silly, were hard for their sons to take seriously. (A well-known Puritan writer in England, who was also read in America, counseled boys that their duty to honor their mother was "the truest triall" of childhood.) But as fathers absented themselves from the home, mothers became the main nurturers of the next generation. Women were also beginning to get a much larger role in religion, particularly in New England. Church membership, which had been so central to the life of every community in the seventeenth century, began to decline, and women began to outnumber men in most congregations. The conflict between religious values and sharp business practices that had tormented the early Puritans was resolved tidily by putting the men in charge of business and the women, under the minister's leadership, in charge of church.

## "LEFT TO PONDER ON A STRIP OF CARPET"

Women's economic power was narrowing even faster in the pre-Revolutionary South, but the region still continued to produce some remarkable women, worthy successors to the pioneers who dared malaria and shipwreck to seek their fortunes. Eliza Lucas was fifteen years old when her father moved the family to South Carolina in 1738, settling on a plantation seventeen miles from Charleston. George Lucas was called back to military duty the next year, and he left Eliza in charge of the plantation, as well as her invalid mother and younger sister. He knew what he was doing—Eliza not only kept her father's properties running in his absence, she began experimenting with ways to diversify the area's rice-based farm economy. She focused on indigo, a plant that was valued for the blue dye it produced, even though it was difficult to cultivate. By 1744—despite attempts at sabotage by the indigo expert her father had dispatched to help her—Eliza had successfully raised a crop of good commercial-grade dye and given away parcels of the seed to her neighbors. That was imaginative generosity, for it created enough supply to make it worthwhile for merchants to include South Carolina in their indigo trade. When she wasn't busy revolutionizing the colony's agriculture, Eliza found time to instruct her younger sister in French, set up a plantation school for the slave children, see to her father's other business affairs, carry on an extensive correspondence, practice handicrafts, and teach herself shorthand. She eventually married the attorney Charles Pinckney, a widower much her senior. After his sudden death, she ran several plantations he had left in her care and reared her three formidable children. Her daughter managed her own husband's plantations and both of her sons served as governor.

But most southern women weren't given that kind of independence. Slavery was gradually dominating the culture of the South and there was little about the role of southern women that was not defined by the "peculiar institution." By the time of the Revolutionary War, prosperous white women shunned almost every kind of physical labor, and they were dependent on slaves to do their housework—nearly a fifth of the workforce on some Virginia plantations was involved in household duties, and even a middle-class farmer might have two or three female slaves dedicated to chores like clothmaking or cooking. The self-sufficient Eliza Pinckney, living alone in old age in Charleston, still required six servants to run her household.

Wealthy southern families were beginning their experiment with the sort of cultivated lifestyle that we associate with the *Gone with the Wind* era. But the real life on the plantations, at least during the colonial era, was a peculiar combination of gentility and disorder. Just as the theoretically tidy Yankee farm families lived in yards full of garbage, the plantation hospitality had a wild edge that unnerved outsiders. The slaves were often the children of African parents, given neither the training nor the incentive to turn themselves into efficient butlers or maids. So meals were served several hours after the appointed time and the process of carrying the dishes from the cookhouse—always located away from the mansion—left much of the food overcooked and underheated. The plantations didn't invest much in clothing for the slaves, either. "I have frequently seen in Virginia, on visits to gentlemen's houses . . . young negroes from sixteen to twenty years old, with not an article of clothing, but a loose shirt, descending half way down their thighs, waiting at table where were ladies," wrote one Revolutionary-era visitor.

Once southern agriculture had become dependent on slave labor, it became necessary to raise upper-class southern men to dominate, to control large numbers of potentially rebellious slaves, and impose their will upon them. The wives inevitably got the spillover. Southern white womanhood was supposed to be submissive, as well as frail and chaste, the better to contrast with black women who were thought of as sturdy and sexually promiscuous. Caroline Gilman, a lively southern matron who wrote a memoir of her life in South Carolina, described her internal battle to mold herself into a proper wife: "To repress a harsh answer, to confess a fault, and to stop (right or wrong) in the midst of self-defense, in gentle submission, sometimes requires a struggle like life and death; but these *three* efforts are the golden threads with which domestic happiness is woven." She praised her husband as one of the rare men in South Carolina who included women in his conversation. None of the other men in the neighborhood, however, were interested in hearing anything she had to say and when male guests came to call, "after the ordinary questions were answered, I was usually left to ponder on the strip of carpet before the hearth, and wonder why it did not come up to the chairs" while the men talked over her, as if she was not in the room.

## "THEY LACED HER UP, THEY STARVED HER DOWN"

In both the North and South, the daughters of the wealthy urban gentry were becoming the nation's first leisure class. The girls learned fancy stitching, dancing, and music and spent a great deal of time worrying about their figures, which were supposed to be very slender and straight-backed. Elegant bearing was regarded as a critical accomplishment, and many young women spent their adolescence wearing harnesses or strapped to backboards in order to improve their posture. One Revolutionary physician recalled in verse:

> *They braced my aunt against a board,*
> *To make her straight and tall*
> *They laced her up, they starved her down*
> *To make her light and small.*

The "pretty gentlewoman" replaced the fecund workhorse as the colonial female ideal. When upper-class family matrons began sitting for their portraits, historian Laurel Ulrich has noted, the artists were encouraged to depict them not as the middle-aged mothers they were in real life but as "tiny-waisted, full-bosomed, raven-haired creatures." Nicholas Culpeper, that best-selling author of medical advice books, offered a remedy to make matronly figures look more youthful: "Take hemlocks, shred them and boyl them in white-wine, then make plaster of them and apply them to the breasts."

Visiting was the main occupation of many young women, and sometimes even their mothers. They traveled from one friend's home to another, for stays of a few days or a few months, amusing themselves and exposing marriageable daughters to the widest possible array of suitors. Lucinda Lee, a wealthy Virginian, kept a diary of her two-month round of visits in the Revolutionary War era, and it depicts a life that would be regarded today as either extremely carefree or extremely useless. Lucinda and her friends read novels, entertained young men, played cards, fixed each other's hair, went dancing and riding, and drove around in a carriage. She did note that she spent one morning "putting my clothes to rights—a dreadful task."

As so often happened in American history, society was sending young women two completely opposite signals. They were expected to become wives who could perform an enormous number of tasks so skillfully that their husbands never noticed that they were busy. But they prepared for married life by spending their youth in leisure that was supposed to be so refined as to leave them almost immobile. (Dr. William Buchan, a popular writer on medical issues, advised that the only proper activities for young women were "playing on some musical instrument, singing and reading aloud delightful pieces of poetry or eloquence.") Well-bred American girls were also getting a raft of advice about how to conceal their intelligence. A young woman's literary magazine featured in its first issue the sad tale of one Amelia, a clergyman's daughter who was taught Latin and Greek, and as a result became "negligent in her dress" and filled with "pride and pedantry." In his popular *A Father's Legacy to His Daughters,* John Gregory urgently advised young women to refrain from displaying their good sense in public: "If you happen to have any learning, keep it a profound secret, especially from the men, who generally look with a jealous and malignant eye on a woman of great parts, and a cultivated understanding." Dr. Gregory, who had a habit of giving with one hand and then taking away with another, admitted that "a man of real genius and candor" would rise above such meanness. But he added that it was unlikely such a paragon would appear.

Fashion began to get very complicated in the eighteenth century. Most women continued to wear the loose skirts and smocks that farm wives had worn for generations. But upper-class wives and daughters tried to outdo one another in the most uncomfortable getups imaginable. Skirts acquired hoop petticoats so huge that ladies had trouble getting into carriages or walking two abreast on the streets. At one point the hoops were six feet in diameter, and wags reported that ministers of well-to-do congregations despaired of finding adequate seats for all those billowing churchgoers. Women also wore extremely tight corsets that covered much of the body, and shoes with very high heels, usually made of wood. When they were outdoors, they balanced their shoes on pattens—leather or iron or wooden clogs mounted on rings of iron. The pattens kept the thin-soled shoes out of the mud, but they made a stroll down the street as challenging as stilt-walking. When women went outside in daylight, they also wore masks to protect their complexion, as well as gloves to keep their hands smooth. (It's hard to imagine how someone encumbered with a body-length corset and huge hoop skirt would be able to get involved in any activity conducive to nail breakage, let alone chapping.) Well-born little girls wore the same clothes as their mothers. Their stiffness in colonial portraits may reflect the fact that they had already been bound up in corsets.

The most spectacular eighteenth-century fashion was the tower hairdo, in which the hair was piled on top of the head in stiff poufs and topped by a wire frame covered with ribbons, beads, jewels, and feathers. The women must have looked like floats in a parade, but the towers went in and out of style several times over the 1700s. "Some of the ladies appear sensible and dress neat," wrote John May after a visit to Philadelphia in 1788, "and some appear by their garb to be fools. I have seen a headdress in this city at least three feet across." In 1782, a minister described Mrs. Henry Knox, the wife of the secretary of war, as "very gross . . . her hair in front is craped at least a foot high much in the form of a churn bottom upward and topped off with a wire skeleton in the same form covered with black gauze which hangs in streamers down her back. Her hair behind is in a large braid, turned up and confined with a monstrous crooked comb."

Very few women in the colonies had either the money to buy these getups or the leisure to be immobilized by them. Nevertheless, the obsession with shopping and display must have seemed like the end of the world to ministers who believed that the colonies were supposed to represent the kingdom of God on Earth. They were shocked by women's revealing fashions—a Boston journal in 1755 suggested that if current trends continued, women would soon be completely nude. And the ministers were horrified when people started dancing with the opposite sex. Previously, those who dared to dance at all generally performed the contradance, in which men and women faced each other from opposing lines. The new style, in which couples danced in pairs, was called "gynecandrical" or "promiscuous" by the scandalized arbiters of morality. Cotton Mather, naturally, had something to say about it:

*Because the daughters of Zion are haughty,*
*and walk with outstretched necks.*
*Glancing wantonly with their eyes,*
*Mincing along as they go,*
*tinkling with their feet;*
*The Lord will smite with a scab*
*the heads of the daughters of Zion*
*and the Lord will lay bare their private parts.*

Prenuptial pregnancy went through the roof during the eighteenth century, and the authorities gave up trying to mete out punishments, concentrating instead on identifying the fathers of illegitimate children and forcing them to support their offspring. But while young women seemed to become more sexually active, particularly with men they expected to marry, American society was developing ideals of courtship in which the woman was supposed to play a passive, virtually hostile role. A truly ladylike female rejected a suitor on first proposal, even if she intended to accept him eventually. And she never felt the surges of something as tawdry as sexual attraction, or even romantic love. "A man of taste and delicacy marries a woman because he loves her more than any other," wrote Dr. Gregory. "A woman of equal taste and delicacy marries him because she esteems him and because he gives her that preference."

## "MISERABLE OLD AGE AND HELPLESS INFANCY"

The number of really poor people grew in eighteenth-century America, and as now, the most distressed segment of the population was single women with children. In the colonists' case, they were mainly widows, whose numbers had exploded as a result of the British wars against the French in North America. In 1742 there were 1,200 widows in Boston alone—nearly a third of all the women in the town who had ever been married. Those with young children tried to stay afloat by taking in piecework, wet-nursing other women's babies, or doing laundry in their homes. Those with older children often bound them out, or placed their daughters in domestic service.

Widows who inherited establishments from their husbands sometimes did very well. They ran taverns and stores and printing shops, a business that for some reason seemed particularly well suited to colonial women's talents. But any female who worked for wages was poor. The maximum weekly rate paid for women in domestic service in New England around the time of the Revolution was the same as the maximum *daily* rate for male farm laborers. Even women who worked as tailors, one of the few crafts open to them, made only about a third of what men made.

Some colonies had a rough welfare system, but it was very unpleasant. In parts of Pennsylvania, a woman on the dole had to wear a red P, for pauper, on her upper sleeve, along with the first letter of the county providing the support. Massachusetts established almshouses for the indigent, but only the most pathetic and infirm were willing to be institutionalized in return for bread-and-water diets and employment at the looms. Judith Stevens, who visited an almshouse in 1775, was shocked by what she saw. The inmates, she said, were "occupied by unsuccessful industry, destitute vice, miserable Old Age and helpless infancy. . . . I passed through many divisions of this abode of wretchedness." If an impoverished mother died, many communities accepted responsibility for her children. But they showed little appetite for the job and bound their young wards out as indentured servants as soon as possible. There are records of girls being bound out as early as two years of age.

In 1748, Boston came up with a new plan—a factory, sponsored by public subscription, which employed widows and orphaned children in the manufacture of linen cloth. But despite the urgings of the minister of the Brattle Street Church that factory employment would add to "the innocent Gaiety and Sprightliness of Childhood," mothers were reluctant to enlist their offspring in an army of infant textile workers. Nor were the women themselves much more eager for work that took them out of their homes and separated them from their children. The factory closed without ever making a profit, and meanwhile the French and Indian War was creating yet a new generation of widows and fatherless children.

## "A VERY EXTRAORDINARY FEMALE SLAVE"

Phillis Wheatley was born in Senegal and arrived in America on a slave ship around 1761, when she was seven or eight years old, and was purchased in Boston by John Wheatley, who wanted a personal servant for his wife, Susanna. When the Wheatleys' daughter saw Phillis trying to make letters with chalk on the wall, she taught her to read. Within a year and a half, Phillis was fluent in English and had also begun to study Latin. By the time she was thirteen she was writing poetry. Her work began appearing in New England newspapers, and she became a regional celebrity. Like Anne Bradstreet, she had found a way out of the normal restrictions of her assigned role in life through verse.

Treated more as a daughter than a servant by the Wheatley family, Phillis became known for her poise and conversation as well as her writing. In Britain, the Countess of Huntingdon admired one of her poems, and arranged the publication of a book by "a very Extraordinary female Slave." The high point of Phillis Wheatley's life came in 1773, when she traveled to England, where she was taken up by the literary celebrities of the day and invited to be presented at court. But the illness of Susanna Wheatley cut short her visit, and Phillis returned to Boston, where her mistress died and John Wheatley officially freed her.

Her renown far outstripped Anne Bradstreet's, and she was the first American writer to achieve international fame. Benjamin Franklin read her work, which sometimes compared the experience of a slave to that of an American colonist under the yoke of British tyranny. George Washington invited her to visit him at his camp during the Revolutionary War. Some admirers credit her with Washington's decision to allow black men to serve in the Continental Army. "I, young in life, by seeming cruel fate," she wrote, "Was snatch'd from *Afric's* fancy'd happy seat . . . Such, such my case. And can I then but pray / Others may never feel tyrannic sway?"

Wow   Poet

Phillis Wheatley found no happiness in her own liberty. She continued living with her old master until his death, but the intelligentsia of Boston had much less interest in her as a free black woman than they did when she was the beloved slave of a prominent white family. She married John Peters, a free black man who turned out to be a poor provider and who eventually abandoned her. None of her three children lived past infancy, and she was working as a servant in a cheap tavern when she died at the age of thirty-one.

## "WHAT HAVE I TO DO WITH POLITICKS?"

The struggle for independence was going to be one of the many, many moments in American history when the country found it necessary to do a sudden about-face on the conventional wisdom of what women were really like. The late-eighteenth-century feminine ideal was fragile, fair, not particularly bright, and certainly not interested in public affairs. But if the colonies were going to succeed in their fight for self-determination, women needed to become political, very fast. In the years leading up to the Declaration of Independence, resistance to the British was expressed mainly in boycotts of imported products. For the boycotts to work, women would have to step into the breach and provide the cloth and foodstuffs that could no longer be brought in from overseas. The housewives were also the family shoppers, and they were asked to shun all the "taxables"—items that the British imposed levies on without the colonials' consent. Getting the cooperation of the women was the critical challenge "without which 'tis impossible to succeed," said the South Carolina patriot Christopher Gadsden in 1769. Tea was, of course, a very important battleground. It was an extremely popular drink in colonial America—half of all homes had tea sets. Women patriots joined enthusiastically in the boycott, and those who found some particularly splashy way to express their determination became national heroines. Nine-year-old Susan Boudinot was invited to a tea party hosted by the governor of New Jersey, a Tory. She took her cup of tea, raised it to her lips, then threw it out the window. Only moments earlier, in the historical sense of time, Americans had been subscribing to the theory that women were supposed to be demure and deferential. Now they celebrated the defiance of a little girl who insulted a governor in a manner that would normally have earned her a spanking.

In 1774, fifty-one women in Edenton, North Carolina, issued a public statement endorsing the boycott, much to the amusement of British journalists and cartoonists, who depicted them as bad mothers, harlots, and heavy drinkers. But they were praised as patriots back home. Southern ladies wore dresses made of homespun cloth to their fancy balls, and they joined their husbands and fathers in making political toasts and singing patriotic songs. The northern women organized spinning bees and were honored for their production of homemade material, which they proudly presented to local officials. A much-quoted poem addressed to the "Daughters of Liberty" in 1768 derided men for allowing themselves to be stripped of their rights and urged:

> Let the Daughters of Liberty, nobly arise,
> And tho' we've no Voice, but a negative here,
> The use of the Taxables, let us forbear,
> Stand firmly resolved and bid Grenville to see
> That rather than Freedom, we'll part with our Tea.

As much as the male rebels wanted to encourage their wives and daughters in defiance, they still liked to picture patriotic women engaged in safe, feminine forms of protest. The *Virginia Gazette* announced approvingly that the young women of Amelia County had "entered into a resolution not to permit the addresses of any person . . . unless he has served in the American armies to prove, by his valour, that he is deserving of their love." But the women were actually required to do far more than boycott tea and vet their boyfriends for political correctness. If men were going to have to fight, women were going to have to take over their farms and businesses, and in some parts of the country, endure life under an army of occupation. Eliza Pinckney, who was not generally given to complaint, described

her situation in South Carolina to a friend: "my property pulled to
pieces, burnt and destroyed; my money of no value, my Children sick
and prisoners." Some women were raped by Tory soldiers, but many
victims kept it secret rather than bear the stigma. "Against both Justice
and Reason we Despise these Poor Innocent Sufferers," admitted a
New Jersey man. A North Carolina man recalled his widowed mother
being "tied up and whipped by the Tories, her house burned and property all destroyed" while he was away with the militia.

"We are in no ways dispiritted here," wrote Abigail Adams, who
was holding down the fort at the family farm in Massachusetts. "We
possess a Spirit that will not be conquerd. If our Men are all drawn off
and we should be attacked, you would find a Race of Amazons in
America." Abigail spent much of her married life as a veritable widow
to the Revolution—her husband John was always off serving his
country as a statesman or diplomat. Now, she was sheltering soldiers
and refugees from the conflict, and as the war approached Boston, she
made contingency plans for grabbing her children and fleeing into the
woods. When dysentery struck the area, her home became a hospital.
"And such is the distress of the neighbourhood that I can scarcely find
a well person to assist me in looking after the sick," she wrote. She
raised their five children, managed their finances, ran their farm, and
kept the house throughout the war. The Revolution not only deprived
her of her helpmate, but of a companion she dearly loved. Still, in her
letters, she urged him on. In November 1775, she reported to John that
when their minister had prayed for a reconciliation between the
colonies and the mother country, "I could not join." England, she
wrote, was "no longer parent State but tyrant State. . . . Let us separate. . . . Let us renounce them."

In the summer of 1777, more than 100 Boston housewives gathered
in front of the store of one Thomas Boylston. They were, one
observer reported, "reputable Clean drest Women Some of them with
Silk gownes on," and they were angry about Boylston's extortionate
wartime prices. They were prepared to boycott tea, but not to let a
merchant gouge them for coffee. Abigail Adams wrote to her husband
that the women "assembled with a cart and trucks, marched down to

the Ware House and demanded the keys, which he refused to deliver, upon which one of them seazd him by his Neck and tossd him into the cart." Boylston gave up his keys, and the women opened the warehouse, took out the coffee they required, and drove away. "A large concourse of Men stood amazd silent Spectators of the whole transaction," Abigail reported gleefully.

The women sometimes took a more aggressive part in the war— one South Carolina man claimed the women in his state "talk as familiarly of shedding blood and destroying the Tories as the men do." In Massachusetts, a group of women disguised in their husbands' clothes intercepted a Tory captain en route to Boston, took the important papers he was carrying, and escorted him to the Groton jail. In 1776, when the British troops took control of New York, the city was suddenly engulfed in fire, which protected the retreating Americans. Edmund Burke told the British House of Commons that the blaze had been started by "one miserable woman, who . . . arrested your progress in the moment of your success." The female rebel, he said, had been found in a cellar "with her visage besmeared and smutted over, with every mark of rage, despair, resolution and the most exalted heroism, buried in the ashes   she was brought forth, and knowing that she would be condemned to die, upon being asked her purpose said 'to fire the city!' and was determined to omit no opportunity for doing what her country called for."

A few women donned male clothing and fought with the Revolutionary Army. Deborah Sampson Gannett fought for more than two years before being discovered, and her husband was later granted a pension as the widower of a Revolutionary soldier. Far more women traveled with their soldier husbands, cooking, washing, mending, and sometimes replacing them in the lines. The legendary "Molly Pitcher" who took her wounded husband's place loading a cannon at a critical moment during the battle of Monmouth may have actually been a camp follower named Mary Ludwig Hays, but whoever she was, she was representative of dozens of women who shared their mates' lives in the field and sometimes the dangers of battle as well. Margaret Corbin stepped in for her slain husband at the Battle of Fort Washington and was severely wounded, losing the use of one arm. The Continental Congress awarded her a pension and she was eventually buried at the West Point cemetery.

Some women appeared to get a new sense of purpose from their responsibilities as patriots and stand-ins for their husbands at home. Letters to husbands away at war gradually took on a more confident tone, and farms and crops that had been referred to as "your" when the war began, became "our" as time went on. Nevertheless, they were still tentative about expressing political opinions. Ann Gwinnett, widow of the president of Georgia, wrote to the Continental Congress to warn that the officer corps in her colony was full of Tory sympathizers. "These things (tho from a Woman, & it is not our sphere, yet I cannot help it) are all true," she penned. Another wrote, "Tho a female, I was born a patriot and cant help it if I would." The deeply political Sarah Jay stopped in a letter on the events of the day to protest wryly: "But whither, my pen, are you hurrying me? What have I to do with politicks? Am I not a woman, and writing to Ladies? Come then, the fashions to my assistance." When the federal Constitution was being debated in Philadelphia, Thomas Jefferson wrote to Angelica Church, who had apparently solicited his opinions about political developments, that "the tender breasts of ladies were not formed for political convulsion." (Admirers of Jefferson might best be advised to skip everything he ever wrote about women and restrict their attention to the Declaration of Independence.)

No matter what the ladies' contribution, the Revolution was not fought to prove that all women were created equal. One of the era's most quoted letters was written by Abigail Adams to her husband when the Continental Congress was meeting to draw up the Declaration of Independence: "In the new Code of Laws which I suppose it will be necessary for you to make I desire you would Remember the Ladies, and be more generous and favorable to them than your ancestors. Do not put such unlimited power into the hands of the Husbands. . . . That your Sex are Naturally Tyrannical is a Truth so thoroughly established as to admit of no dispute, but such of you as wish to be happy willingly give up the harsh title of Master for the more tender and endearing one of Friend. Why then, not put it out of the power of the vicious and the Lawless to use us with cruelty and indignity and impunity. Men of Sense in all Ages abhor those customs which treat us only as the vassals of your Sex."

Adams's response, which is less well known, wounded his wife deeply: "As to your extraordinary code of laws," he wrote, "I cannot but laugh."

## "WE MAY SHORTLY EXPECT TO SEE THEM TAKE THE HELM—OF GOVERNMENT"

The only colony that permitted women to vote after the Revolutionary War was New Jersey. Possibly due to pressure from Quakers who lived in the southern part of the state, it awarded the franchise to "all free inhabitants" who owned a certain amount of property. That seemed to apply to at least a limited number of widows and single women, as well as a few free black residents.

In 1797, during a hard-fought election for the state legislature in Essex County, about seventy-five women turned out to vote—most of them in favor of William Crane, the Federalist candidate who lost to John Condict of Newark. In 1800, a larger number of women showed up at the polls, including some who probably didn't qualify under a strict interpretation of the property requirements. (Well into the twentieth century, New Jersey had a reputation both for vigorous political campaigns and a lack of regard for the finer points of election law.) People began to complain and predict dire consequences if the women weren't curbed. Before you knew it, critics argued, "we may shortly expect to see them take the helm—of government."

The fatal blow was struck in 1806, when the state decided to build a new courthouse in Essex County and left it up to the voters to decide whether to place it in Elizabeth or Newark. Local sentiment was so aroused that it became dangerous for residents of Elizabeth to be seen on the streets of Newark, and vice versa. On election day, men and boys skipped from one polling place to another, voting repeatedly. Outsiders were carted in to increase the local turnout. Women and girls, black and white, joined in the excitement, and when the balloting was over, nearly 14,000 votes had been cast in an area where the previous record turnout had been about 4,500. Unsurprisingly, the vote in Elizabeth was almost unanimously for building the courthouse in Elizabeth. But Newark was even more successful in marshalling people for the Newark site.

"A more wicked and corrupt scene was never exhibited," one Elizabethtown writer described it. The people of Newark were too busy celebrating to be shocked. But eventually, the whole episode was sent to the state legislature for consideration. The legislature decided to reform the election law, and the head of the committee charged with proposing changes was none other than John Condict. His suggested reforms included the end to female suffrage. When a motion was made to strike out that clause, Mr. Condict rose to his feet and eloquently defended the limitation of the franchise to "free, white, male citizens."

The legislature voted to stop women from voting in the one state where their rights as citizens had been acknowledged. Mr. Condict had his revenge, and women lost their official voice in American politics for the next century.

# 5

# 1800–1860: True Women, Separate Spheres, and Many Emergencies

## "MAN IS STRONG—WOMAN IS BEAUTIFUL"

In the first half of the nineteenth century, American women changed from colonial goodwives to people with more modern concerns. They went to school, and they knew a great deal more about what was going on in the world outside their own neighborhoods. They were still religious, but they wanted to be happy in this earthly life as well as in the next. They thought about marriage in terms of romance and companionship rather than a simple economic partnership. They believed their children were special individuals, in need of constant care and supervision, and they hoped to see them rise higher in the world than their parents did. They wanted their homes to be attractive, and comfort was becoming an important priority.

No one understood all this better than Sarah Josepha Hale, the powerful editor of *Godey's Lady's Book*. Hale was a mother of five who was widowed young—she wore black for fifty-four years in memory of her departed husband. Pregnant with her last child and nearly forty years old when he died, she first tried to feed her brood by selling hats, and then by writing, entering essay contests with ferocious energy. She churned out poems (including the one about Mary's little lamb) and published a novel, which she assured her followers had been written "not to win fame, but support for my little children." In 1827, a Boston minister offered her a job running *Ladies' Magazine,* a new publication that became the first magazine edited by a woman, for women.

The development of the publishing industry offered women one of the first opportunities to exercise their clout as the nation's premier consumers. In the years after the Revolutionary War, girls were taught to read and write almost as a matter of course, the better to prepare them for their role as mothers of the next generation of citizens. These literate women became the nation's first mass book-buyers. (Light reading was presumed to be of little interest to the male half of the population since it was not a profit-making activity.) In the pre–Civil War era, *Harper's Magazine* estimated that four-fifths of the reading public was female.

Until Hale came along, American magazines were generally collections of work bootlegged from English periodicals. But the frantically prolific Sarah (who later wrote a nine-hundred-page book called *Sketches of All Distinguished Women from the Creation to 1851*) made sure her copy was original, even if she had to write most of it herself, including the letters to the editor. In 1836, she was hired to take over *Godey's Lady's Book,* a popular periodical that was famous for its colored pictures of women's fashions. By 1860, under her continued direction, the magazine had 160,000 subscribers—a huge number for that era. Its publisher boasted that "from Maine to the Rocky Mountains, there is scarcely a hamlet, however inconsiderable, where it is not received and read." Mill girls passed it around the Massachusetts textile factories, and in New York Irish immigrant servants copied the dresses they saw in *Godey's* in cheaper, brighter fabrics, much to the horror of their mistresses. Although the serious-minded Hale had always decried the rule of fashion, she kept the illustrations of elegant wardrobes and added sections on interior decoration, "How to Make Wax Flowers and Fruit," recipes and patterns. But she also told her readers how to view their role in society. She lectured them about the importance of sticking to home and hearth, and she promised them that if they performed their role well, they would be able to influence, and ennoble, the entire world. "Our men are sufficiently money-making. Let us keep our women and children from contagion as long as possible," she wrote.

It would be hard to find a more perfect example of the contradictions of nineteenth-century womanhood than the workaholic editor continually reminding her readers how lucky they were to be presiding over the hearth rather than engaging in "the silly struggle for honor and preferment" in the outside world. The period before the Civil War was, for women, both a time of liberation and new restrictions. Teaching became a respectable career, giving middle-class girls an option in life beyond marriage or dependent spinsterhood. Working-class girls entered the factories. (When Mrs. Hale noticed that *Godey's* fashion plates were being tinted by an army of female workers, she announced that any job done indoors qualified as a domestic occupation.) A few female pioneers fought their way into the professions and became doctors or ministers or journalists; others entered the public world as reformers or lecturers. But at the same time, Americans of both sexes were setting the most rigid rules for proper womanly behavior in the country's history. Writers loved to list the qualities of the True Woman, and they were always the opposite of the virtues of the true man. "Man is strong—woman is beautiful. Man is daring and confident—woman is diffident and unassuming. Man is great in action—woman in suffering," explained *Ladies Museum* magazine. Men were lustful, so it stood to reason that women—contrary to the theories of the colonial era—were chaste and possibly passionless. "The majority of women (happily for them) are not much troubled by sexual feeling of any kind," wrote the popular lecturer and reformer William Acton.

This vision of virtuous, sexless womanhood was actually a sign of higher status—before, women were viewed as the morally unreliable descendants of the sinful Eve. But it was still as restrictive as the corsets that immobilized them from girlhood. "True feminine genius," wrote the popular novelist Grace Greenwood, "is ever timid, doubtful and clingingly dependent, a perpetual childhood." From a very early age, girls were taught to restrain themselves physically and emotionally. A story in *Godey's Lady's Book* told about a tomboy named Ellen, who insisted on playing rough sports outdoors. When Ellen refused to heed her aunts' warnings about appropriate womanly behavior, she was thrown from her horse and crippled for life. It was a familiar plot theme, including the paralysis, and the happy ending always came when the immobilized heroine realized this was God's way of teaching her how to act like a lady. The term "tomboy," one nineteenth-century author recalled, looking back at the pre–Civil War era, "was applied to all little girls who showed the least tendency toward thinking and acting for themselves."

The colonial housewife had contributed to the family with her chickens and butter money, but the True Woman that Sarah Hale helped popularize relied totally on her husband for emotional and financial support. Her only resources were spiritual. If her husband stopped loving her, she had to suffer in silence and, as *Ladies' Magazine* recommended, try to win him back "by increased anxiety to please."

The law of the True Woman was attractive to many Americans in the pre–Civil War era because it emphasized safety and control. The new industrial economy was creating unheard-of opportunities for making money, but it was unstable, with booms and panics and get-rich-quick schemes and bankruptcies. In the bust of 1818, land values fell as much as 75 percent almost overnight, and when the panic of 1837 hit New York, more than a third of the city's workers lost their jobs. Nervous businessmen embraced the idea of the family as a little nest detached from the outside world. The whole country was like the nation's transportation system, which had improved so fast that it was possible for people to travel to places they would not have dreamed of a few decades earlier—but at a price. The railroads kept having wrecks and the steamships blew up—there were at least 150 major explosions between 1825 and 1850. It was a giddy, frightening time, and many women liked the idea of being protected by strict boundaries.

## "IN DANGER OF BECOMING
## PERFECT RECLUSES"

Men's and women's lives operated on separate tracks, even in society. At many dinner parties, the sexes were actually seated at opposite ends of the table. After they had finished eating, the men always left the ladies and retired to smoke and drink brandy. In the business districts, men lived in a growing alternate universe of restaurants and clubs and theaters, while women kept to their parlors and sewing rooms. Frances Trollope reported from Cincinnati that husbands even did the marketing. If it weren't for church services, she said, "all the ladies . . . would be in danger of becoming perfect recluses." Women were so cut out of the public life that even the holidays went on without them. The Fourth of July, with its military maneuvers and all-male parades, was the biggest occasion of the year. "Staid in all day and saw the procession and all there was to be seen from my window," wrote a San Francisco housewife. As the nation got closer to midcentury, women gradually became the audience, clustering in yards and balconies to wave handkerchiefs, or perhaps sitting on special stands along the parade route. (Young ladies were promoted even further, to decorations on the floats.) Women's main response to being excluded was not to demand a chance to march, but to create entirely new holidays, which people celebrated by staying home. Sarah Hale led the effort to get Abraham Lincoln to proclaim Thanksgiving a national holiday. The novelist Catherine Maria Sedgwick popularized the Christmas tree in one of her stories.

The male view of why women had to be kept out of the public world was basically that they just weren't up to it. "She has a head almost too small for intellect and just big enough for love," said Dr. Charles Meigs of Jefferson Medical College in Philadelphia, in a famous speech on the "Distinctive Characteristics of the Female," which he delivered to a class of male gynecology students in 1847. "The great administrative faculties are not hers. She plans no sublime campaign, leads no great armies to battle nor fleets to victory. . . . Do you think that Woman . . . could have developed, in the tender soil of her intellect, the strong idea of a Hamlet, or a Macbeth? Such is not woman's province, nature, power or mission. She reigns in the heart . . . the household altar is her place of worship and service."

Even if women had a higher opinion of their own capabilities, they were not all that attracted to the outside world. The streets were full of mud and garbage, and many cities had yet to evict the local livestock. (Complaining about the constant presence of pigs in Cincinnati, Frances Trollope claimed that when she walked across Main Street "the chances were five hundred to one against my reaching the shady side without brushing by a snout.") After dark, the streets in most cities were lit only by the moon, and a woman walking unescorted risked robbery, assault, or at the least, getting lost in black twisting alleys. "This darkness, this stillness is so great that I almost felt it awful," said Mrs. Trollope, after coming out of a Philadelphia theater.

Last but most definitely not least, men chewed and spit tobacco everywhere. "I hardly know any annoyance so deeply repugnant to English feelings as the incessant, remorseless, spitting of Americans," said Mrs. Trollope, who found that words failed her when she attempted to describe the condition of the carpet in the gentleman's lounge of a steamship. Women who ventured out of their homes in their long skirts were continually at risk. A Mrs. Hall, reporting on a dance in Washington, said she was walking upstairs to waltz when she heard her partner clearing his throat in an ominous manner. "I said to myself 'surely he will turn his head to the other side,' " she wrote a friend. "The gentleman, however, had no such thought but deliberately shot across me." If fancy-dress balls were not expectorant-free zones, theaters were worse. Men not only felt free to spit, they drank, threw food at the stage, and generally behaved as if they were relaxing in a tavern. Mrs. Trollope attended a performance in Washington where one patron began vomiting, to the general amusement of his fellow playgoers. And the upper tiers were packed with prostitutes, who got free tickets from the management eager to attract male clientele and who occasionally serviced their customers in the hallways. In women's magazines like *Godey's* the outside world was depicted as a dangerous and mysterious place, where men pursued incomprehensi-

ble occupations. The magazines never attempted to educate their readers about "business," although they occasionally tried to make it relevant by blaming all financial failures on thoughtless wives who
insisted on spending the family fortune on social climbing and fancy
dresses.

## "INITIATED INTO THE ARTS AND
## MYSTERIES OF THE WASH TUB"

Lydia Maria Child had a particular depth of experience in the economic uncertainties of the pre–Civil War era. Her husband, David,
was a political reformer of great energy but negative moneymaking
capacity. ("Oh, if we only could have ever so small a house where you
could be contented, and have no dreams of Congress," she mourned.)
Both Lydia and her friends had expected her to have a career as a serious writer. But in 1829 she was thinking only about paying the rent
when she threw together a collection of household hints and recipes,
which were published as *The American Frugal Housewife*. "Dedicated
to those who are not ashamed of economy," Child's book was nothing
if not down-to-earth, full of tips on how to remove inkspots, stew
prunes, and, of course, save money. ("Keep a bag for odd pieces of
tape and strings; they will come in use.") She put in a good word for
pig's head ("It is despised because it is cheap; but when well cooked it
is delicious") and gave advice on how to salvage practically anything,
from a moldy feather bed to "injured" meat. Critics pointed out that
Child's wedding cake recipe called for 4 pounds of flour, 3 pounds of
butter, 3 pounds of sugar, 4 pounds of currants, 2 pounds of raisins, 24
eggs, and a pint of brandy. But it was, after all, for a special occasion.

    The book became one of the publishing phenomena of the first
half of the nineteenth century, even though an unenthusiastic Sarah
Hale regarded *Frugal Housewife* as rather ungenteel. (Child's emphasis on frugality, Hale felt, was so excessive as to encroach into the masculine world of finance.) Some of Child's former friends, including an
ex-suitor, Nathaniel Willis, snorted that the book was "written for the
lower classes." But Lydia Maria Child became the first in a line of

domestic gurus of the pre–Civil War era, when women book-buyers turned the art of housekeeping into a national obsession.

In 1841, Child's book was displaced by Catharine Beecher's *A Treatise on Domestic Economy*, which combined a celebration of woman's role as goddess of the hearth ("extending over the world those blessed influences . . . to renovate degraded man") with practical tips on how to destroy bedbugs or build a privy. Beecher was part of a remarkable family—the great American women of the early nineteenth century seem to have been born in clumps, two or three to a household. One of Beecher's sisters, Harriet, wrote *Uncle Tom's Cabin;* another, Isabella, became a prominent suffragist. Their brothers were almost all well-known ministers and one, Henry Ward Beecher, became the most celebrated preacher of his era and the star of one of the century's biggest sex trials. (How-to manuals for women were so much in demand that even Henry Ward's famously miserable wife, Eunice, wrote one called *All Around the House; or How to Make the Home Happy.*)

Catharine never married—she was officially in mourning for a fiancé drowned at sea—and she seldom kept house after she left her father's residence to make a living as an educator. Her nesting instinct was so lightly developed that Harriet referred to her as "wandering like a trunk without a label." Yet she fought all her life to elevate women's position by raising the stature of housework. She argued that the wives who were charged with educating the nation's children and elevating degraded men had to be prepared for the job—preferably in an excellent boarding school that taught philosophy, chemistry, astronomy, botany, geology, mineralogy, and moral philosophy in the afternoon and washing, sewing, and cooking in the morning. (When a girl was taught to launder her clothes, Beecher referred to it as being "initiated into the arts and mysteries of the wash tub.") When these well-educated young ladies married, they would not become mere housewives, but some combination of domestic scientist and goddess of the hearth. Like Sarah Hale, Beecher believed that women could develop a parlor-based culture that would spread their influence over the entire nation. Any woman who strove to establish a niche in the public male-dominated world was a traitor who endangered this division of power.

All this discussion about women's role was directed at a minority of the American households—most wives and daughters were still on the farm, doing the same rough chores their grandmothers had performed. As late as 1840, only one in nine Americans lived in a town with 2,500 or more people, and many urban women were too poor to contemplate their appropriate role in society. Still, thanks to the publishing industry, housewives in raw settlements and isolated farms devoured magazines that lectured to them about their rights and duties as True Women, along with hints on how to decorate an elegant parlor and raise a decorous child.

## "HOW COULD *I* TELL
## SHE WAS GOING TO BE SO FAMOUS!"

During the first part of the nineteenth century, America became crammed with what Nathaniel Hawthorne bitterly called "a d—d mob of scribbling women" who supported themselves with their pens. Although most made little or no money, some of the women novelists, essayists, poets, and short-story writers did actually become rich— Harriet Beecher Stowe, who hoped *Uncle Tom's Cabin* would make enough for her to buy a new dress, wound up with a mansion and a Florida orange plantation. Hawthorne's irritation had a great deal to do with the fact that *The Lamplighter*, the novel by twenty-seven-year-old Maria Cummins that inspired his outburst, sold four times as many copies in the first month as *The Scarlet Letter* sold in Hawthorne's lifetime.

The scribbling women performed a delicate balancing act, creating careers while disdaining ambition. Harriet Beecher Stowe, whose writings forthrightly exposed the sexual exploitation of female slaves and the grisly tortures undergone by African Americans in the South, tried hard to present herself as "a little bit of a woman" who never intended to achieve international fame. "I have been forced into it, contrary to my natural modesty," she assured a fan. Sarah Hale always said the need to support her fatherless children forced her to become an extraordinarily successful editor and writer, despite her wishes to the contrary. Cynics might have noted that her family emergency lasted until she retired at age ninety, when her youngest child was fifty-five.

The most popular novels often involved heroines who, like Hale, had emergencies. The stories pledged allegiance to the woman's place being in the home, and the importance of showing deference to male authority figures. But fathers, brothers, and husbands always seemed to be conveniently absent when the curtain went up, and the heroines were forced to travel, pursue careers, and do any number of other exciting things that they would have been expected to avoid under normal circumstances.

*St. Elmo*, by Augusta Evans, one of the best-selling novels of the century, told the story of Edna, an orphan adopted by a kindly widow. St. Elmo—men in that era were sometimes named after saints—was the widow's embittered son, who was attracted to Edna despite his contempt for educated women. ("I should really enjoy seeing them tied down to their spinning wheels and gagged in their own books, magazines and lectures.") Edna went off to become an internationally acclaimed philosopher, albeit one who believed woman suffrage was "the most loathsome of political leprosies." Eventually, St. Elmo calmed down, became a minister, and married her. *The Deserted Wife*, by E.D.E.N. (Emma Dorothy Eliza Nevitte) Southworth, starred Hagar, an orphan who is abandoned by her husband and becomes an internationally famous singer to support her family. *Ruth Hall*'s title character was a widow—and an orphan—who is forced to become a wildly successful writer in order to support her children. Although Ruth never remarries, the reader does get to enjoy a happy ending in which her selfish relatives get their comeuppance. ("How could *I* tell she was going to be so famous!")

Although most of the successful women writers were rather obviously fibbing about hating the limelight, almost all of them really were desperate for money. Fanny Fern, the author of *Ruth Hall*, and E.D.E.N. Southworth were single mothers. Augusta Jane Evans was saddled with a wastrel father. So was Susan Warner, whose book *The Wide, Wide World* may have been the nation's first real best-seller. (An extremely long saga about an abandoned, and eventually orphaned, girl, it was estimated to have "245 tear flows" in 574 pages.) Their successes were also advertisements for the fact that in a society that celebrated sheltered, protected wives and daughters, many husbands and fathers were not holding up their end of the cultural bargain.

Hawthorne was not the only man of letters who decried the feminization of American fiction. Nathaniel Willis, the influential editor of *Home Journal,* denounced the "universality of cheap and trashy novels" and the oversentimentality of women writers. Willis may be remembered as the ex-suitor of Lydia Child who made vicious fun of *Frugal Housewife.* He cruelly discouraged his own sister's literary ambitions. (Under the pen name Fanny Fern, she got revenge by depicting Ruth Hall's brother as a snobby editor who spends $100 on a vase while his sister is starving.) The men were right, however, that a lot of the women's literature of the era was pretty dreadful. There were gift books full of short stories with names like *Shy Peeps into the Heart Feminine* and poetry by people like Lydia Sigourney, "the Sweet Singer of Hartford," whose dying words were said to be "I love everybody." Even the best of the novels tended to have villains so madly evil they made Cinderella's stepsisters look like social workers. When the heroine of *Ruth Hall* was starving in a garret with her children, her wealthy aunt refused to offer assistance, protesting, "Are we *not* doing something for her? I allow Ruth to do her washing in our kitchen every week, providing she finds her own soap."

Some people blamed this soppiness on Charles Dickens, America's most popular writer, whose most bathetic characters were saintly, precocious infants and perfect "little" women. ("I observe that feminine virtue is invariably below medium height," commented novelist Bret Harte.) The other British writer whose work obsessed American women was Charlotte Brontë. "My mother, then a loom-tender in Lowell, has told me how 'Jane Erie' as her companions pronounced it, ran through the mill-girl community like an epidemic," wrote the author R. L. Pattee. *Jane Eyre* was a brilliant expression of the Victorian woman's romantic vision of sexual struggle. A great powerful lover tries to dominate Jane in part one, but the intervention of the mad wife in the attic and the terrible fire leave him chastened, blind, and broken. American women purchased one novel after another in which difficult men were brought to heel by spunky heroines. But unlike Jane, most of the women in American novels happily crawled under their lover's thumb just as the curtain fell. In the extremely popular *Beulah*, the groom, Guy, demands: "Do you belong to that tyrant ambition or do you belong to that tyrant Guy Hartwell?" And the bride (an orphan who became a famous writer) happily chooses the latter.

## "INTEMPERANCE AMONG THE MEN AND LOVE OF DRESS AMONG THE WOMEN"

Women who weren't completely fulfilled as wives and mothers gravitated toward reform movements—almost all of which were viewed as the natural outgrowth of maternal concern. Women conducted prayer meetings in front of bordellos in the name of motherhood, expeditions that *The Advocate of Female Reform* called "thrilling." They expressed their motherly instincts by marching for temperance and sometimes by breaking up saloons. When a young man was killed in a bar in Greenfield, Ohio, in the 1860s, his family could get no satisfaction from the law. "But a large number of the respectable ladies of the town, after some secret counsels, accompanied by the bereaved mother, proceeded to the saloon and with axes and other weapons knocked in the heads of barrels and casks, and demolished bottles and fixtures," reported Mother Stewart, a temperance crusader.

Helping strangers was a relatively new concept in America. Before the Revolutionary War, communities tended to limit their charitable responsibilities to loving their literal neighbors. In the early nineteenth century, most of women's philanthropic ventures involved raising money for missionary activities among the urban poor or western Indians or sewing clothes for the needy. The more daring got together to discuss strategies for combating "vice"—a catchall that usually referred to prostitution. A handful of women ventured into direct action, like visiting the poor in their urban ghettoes or marching on saloons or bordellos. A few organizations hired surrogates to do it for them, paying outreach workers like Louisa May Alcott. For $500 a year, the future author of *Little Women* collected clothing for a Boston mission, conducted sewing classes, ran schools for black children, and distributed food for immigrants.

The bulk of women's reform activities may have been more important for the way they affected the respectable ladies who took part in them than for anything they did for the unfortunate. Many of the moral improvement projects of the period showed a lack of appreciation for human nature. A refuge for prostitutes in New York required the residents to rise at 5 A.M., go to sleep at 8:30 in the evening, and remain inside the asylum until their betters deemed them sufficiently reformed to venture outdoors. It was eventually closed for lack of clientele. One member of the Society for the Relief of Poor Widows with Small Children wrote that the principal causes of poverty were "intemperance among the Men and the love of dress among the Women." Some charities refused to aid Catholics, unless they converted, or to assist women who lived on particularly disreputable streets or who worked at jobs that were considered unladylike, like street vending. Maria Burley, who appeared at the Asylum for Lying-In Women nine months pregnant, "shivering with cold, without comfortable apparel," was sent back out onto the streets to obtain letters of reference. "It is painful to relate that after a walk of two miles in this extreme cold she was obliged to seek refuge for the night in an open garret with only one quilt for covering and before morning and alone she was delivered of a female infant, which when she was found by two men was frozen to her clothing and with great difficulty restored to life," reported the ladies. They admitted Mrs. Burley the next day—after they had checked her references.

But while their accomplishments were mixed, the benevolent organizations did give their members experience in leadership and organizing, in running fund-raising drives and keeping financial records. And doing good almost inevitably led to political activities, no matter how hard women tried to regard their work as simply heavy-duty influencing. "You cannot imagine the labor of converting and convincing. Some evenings I had at once twenty gentlemen for three hours' steady conversation," wrote Dorthea Dix as she worked to convince legislators to build an insane asylum in New Jersey. As their goals grew more ambitious and urgent, they tended to become more frustrated by their restrictions, and in the 1840s and 1850s, organizations of temperance advocates and slavery opponents repeatedly splintered over the issue of allowing female delegates to speak before audiences that included men.

## "STANDING UP WITH BARE-FACED IMPUDENCE"

Most women who managed to achieve fame in the years before the Civil War were careful to behave like discreet housewives in public. When Harriet Beecher Stowe made her triumphant tour of England after the publication of *Uncle Tom's Cabin* in 1852, she sat silently in the "women's gallery" of the crowded auditoriums, while her husband read her speech from the stage. Actresses, who could not pretend that they abhorred attention, were almost always ostracized by polite society. (Mary Ann Duff, the first great American tragedienne, was buried in 1857 in a grave that only bore the words "My Mother and Grandmother" in order to conceal the fact that a former actress was in the coffin.) Many Americans, who seemed to be terrified by pleasure of almost any sort, regarded plays as not only immoral but potentially addictive. Although the theatrical community was in general well behaved and hardworking, ministers made it clear that any decent man would rather see his sister in the grave than in a play. William Wood, a theatrical manager, was outraged in 1816 when a Baltimore clergyman publicly denounced his latest production and its leading lady—who was both Wood's wife and one of the clergyman's parishioners.

Given the demands of constant travel, not to mention the behavior of those theater audiences, acting was a profession for the dedicated or the desperate. (Wood's wife survived not only the embarrassment of hearing herself attacked during a Sunday sermon, but also the effects of being hit by a musket ball that was thrown by an overly excited member of the audience.) Still, it was one of the very few lines of work in which women could hope to get salaries equal to their male peers. In 1840, when factory girls made an average of 33 cents a day in New York, the very lowest-ranked stage extra got 25 to 50 cents a night for far less arduous work. A domestic servant made $6 to $7 a month; an experienced actress could make $40 a week.

Lectures, which carried an aura of self-improvement the theater did not, became very popular in the nineteenth century. The first woman who broke the sexual barrier on the lecture circuit was probably Fanny Wright, an Englishwoman and heiress who immigrated in 1825. Attractive, energetic, and possessed of an extremely impractical form of intelligence, she made a disastrous attempt to found a utopian community that would demonstrate how slaves could be educated and freed. Her friend Frances Trollope was stunned when the place Wright had been describing as a paradise turned out to be three roofless log cabins in a swamp, inhabited by a few of her followers and a small and bewildered colony of slaves.

In 1828, Wright was the main speaker at an Independence Day celebration at New Harmony, Indiana—possibly the first time a woman addressed a mixed audience at a public gathering in America. (Characteristically, she devoted her breakthrough Fourth of July talk to an attack on "all ideas of military glory," including parades.) She turned out to have a gift for speaking, and she embarked on a tour, drawing huge crowds who wanted, at least in part, simply to have a look at the lecturing lady. It was a phenomenon only slightly less surprising than a talking dog. Naturally, Catharine Beecher was appalled. "Who can look without disgust and abhorrence upon such an one as Fanny Wright, with her great masculine person, her loud voice, her untasteful attire, going about unprotected and feeling no need of protection, mingling with men in stormy debate and standing up with bare-faced impudence to lecture to a public assembly?" she demanded.

Catharine Beecher was a public woman herself, although she

would have denied it. She traveled all around the country, raising funds for projects, founding schools, writing about all the great issues of the day. She took part, with her pen, in all the great debates. She testified before Congress. But because she was arguing against a public role for women, she presumably felt her activities didn't count. Fanny Wright had no cover. She was a radical, an abolitionist, a suffragist, and an enemy of organized religion. When her utopian community failed, a few of her followers wrote about the very active sex life at the settlement, and Fanny was branded "The Great Red Harlot." Wright never spoke about sex in her lectures—Mrs. Trollope said her most outrageous comment was a statement that "Washington was not a Christian." Nevertheless, America identified her with free love, and she became the most controversial woman of her era, her name a byword for irresponsible radicalism.

Although Fanny didn't get any benefit, the taboo against women speaking in public, which had lasted for so many centuries, fell rather quickly. The Grimke sisters, daughters of a Southern slave owner, began giving antislavery lectures in the North shortly after Wright's brief career sputtered out; they found the American mood slightly more accepting. Fifteen years later, Antoinette Brown prepared for her work as a minister by spending several seasons lecturing on temperance and women's rights to mixed audiences, and her talks often received positive reviews in local newspapers. (One of Brown's biographers noted that the reviewers were so surprised that a woman could speak so well they forgot to mention anything she said.) By 1872, Harriet Beecher Stowe would be undertaking lecture tours to promote her books.

## "OUR SIS CAME OFF WITH FLYING COLOURS"

The number of American women who stepped out of their assigned sexual roles and became public figures in the pre–Civil War era probably numbered only in the dozens. But other women knew they were out there. In Lancaster, Pennsylvania, the overseer of a poorhouse asked Dorothea Dix to write an article for the local paper, telling her: "Every man and woman in Lancaster, if not in our state, knows who you are." Dix was one of the most remarkable self-starters of the age. She had been an anonymous Massachusetts spinster living on a small inheritance and plagued by ill health when, in 1841, a friend asked her to teach a Sunday school class for female inmates in a local jail. Along with the lawbreakers she found a number of mentally ill women who had simply been stashed away in cold, unfurnished cells. Dix became obsessed with the plight of these forgotten people. In the years that followed, she visited every state but California, looking for the out-of-the-way cells, cages, closets, and barns where local officials kept the helpless people they called lunatics. She then used her shocking reports to lobby state legislators to build modern mental hospitals.

Dix spent much of her time sitting up on wooden benches in cold, empty railroad stations and took coaches and lumber wagons through the mud to the towns where the trains could not go. She reached one destination in Pennsylvania via a trip downstream with "an old waterman astride upon a drift log half under water," followed by a ride in which four separate carriages broke down and a five-mile hike. She was on board a stagecoach in Kentucky when it was stopped by a robber; he let the passengers go unscathed when he recognized Dix as the teacher of his old prison Bible class.

Margaret Fuller was another member of this small cadre of female superstars. ("Humanity is divided into three classes: Men, women and Margaret Fuller," wrote Edgar Allan Poe.) Fuller was the one female writer of the period who declared war on the idea that women's place was in the home. "Let them be sea captains if they will," she urged in her most famous work, *Women in the Nineteenth Century*. To supplement her writing income, Fuller organized a series of "conversations" in which groups of up to thirty-five women paid to have her lead them in a night of intellectual inquiry, on topics from Greek mythology to the difference between the sexes. She went to Europe as a foreign correspondent for Horace Greeley's *New York Tribune*, married a young Roman nobleman, and joined him in the fight for a new Roman republic.

When their cause failed, Margaret and her husband and young son sailed for New York. Their ship ran aground on a sandbar just off-shore, and the three of them were drowned. Henry David Thoreau spent days unsuccessfully searching for her body and the lost manu-script of her book on the Italian revolution.

It's hard to imagine how women made the leap into professions for which they had no role models, no invitation, and very little encour-agement. Antoinette Brown ignored her weeping parents and went off to Oberlin College determined to become the nation's first ordained female minister, even though the faculty assured her it would never happen. (Oberlin did allow her to take theology classes and publish an essay in its *Quarterly Review* in which she reinterpreted that directive of St. Paul's to "let your women keep quiet in church," which had tor-tured American women with an interest in theology from the days of Anne Hutchinson.) Brown was not permitted to graduate, but she eventually found a progressive parish in New York where she was ordained and made pastor.

Elizabeth Blackwell, the first woman to graduate from an Ameri-can medical school, claimed she was inspired to go into medicine by a friend in Cincinnati who was dying of uterine cancer and, like so many women, had been unable to discuss her medical problems freely with a male physician. "If I could have been treated by a lady doctor, my worst sufferings would have been spared me," the woman said. Blackwell may also have been spurred on by her upbringing as the daughter of a freethinking British sugar refiner who emigrated to the United States with his wife, a large brood of children, and four single aunts. Certainly there was something about the family that nurtured pioneering women. Two of the Blackwell daughters became physi-cians, and one of Elizabeth's brothers eventually married the Rev-erend Antoinette Brown.

But probably most important, Blackwell had a taste for combat. "The idea of winning a doctor's degree gradually assumed the aspect of a great moral struggle, and the moral fight possessed immense attraction for me," she wrote. Dozens of medical schools turned down her application. (A few helpful faculty members suggested she disguise herself as a man and try Paris.) Finally, she was accepted by Geneva College, a small medical school in upstate New York. The faculty had put the question of admitting a woman up to a vote of the student body, and the students, in a particularly rowdy mood, voted unanimously to have women. Some of them apparently thought the application was a joke perpetrated by a rival college. The men were in a more subdued mood when Elizabeth actually arrived on campus. "A hush fell over the class as if each member had been stricken by paralysis," recalled one of the students at her first lecture. However, she went on to graduate first in her class and later to found both the New York Infirmary and a medical college for women. "Our sis came off with flying colours," reported Henry Blackwell, who had accompanied Elizabeth to her graduation and who later expressed the family genes by marrying Lucy Stone, the pioneer feminist.

The first few women struggling to establish themselves in professional careers immediately ran into problems over how to balance the demands of career and the desire for a family. Elizabeth Blackwell, who decided that medicine and marriage would not mix, eventually adopted a homeless Irish girl. "Who will ever guess the restorative support which that poor little orphan has been to me?" she wrote in her journal. Her sister Emily, who also became a doctor, set up what seemed to be a happy home life with an adopted daughter and another female physician. The image of domestic life with a grateful orphan, sensible companions, and no demanding males seems to have been seductive for the Blackwells' set. Before she married, Antoinette Brown wrote to Lucy Stone, proposing they adopt some "ragged" children and create a domestic nest for themselves without the interference of husbands. "I need a pleasant happy home to rest in and some pleasant happy children there to keep me from being a misanthrope," she wrote. Brown, who traveled continually in her ministry, seemed to have thought the home and orphans would be cared for by servants. She learned about reality later, when she had seven very real children of her own.

## "APPEAR TO BE AVERSE
## TO WHAT SHE INWARDLY DESIRES"

Trials of the century, which seemed to happen about once a decade, often gave women a good lesson in the true balance of power between the sexes. Just before the nineteenth century opened, Henry Bedlow, a wealthy rake from a good New York family, went on trial for the rape of Lanah Sawyer, a seventeen-year-old daughter of a local sea captain. It was the first of the great American sex scandals in which the double standard went on trial with the defendant. The basic facts weren't in dispute. Bedlow had met Lanah, a seamstress, when she was out walking. He introduced himself as "Lawyer Smith" and escorted her home, asking permission to see her again. On their third outing, he lured her into a bordello, where he forced himself on her.

The question for the all-male jury was, in effect, whether Lanah had asked for it. Bedlow's lawyers demanded to know how a seamstress could have believed that a lawyer was interested in her for anything but sex. Why had she been out on the streets at night without an escort anyway? And while the girl might have put up a struggle, she was only going through the motions, like those middle-class girls who refused their suitor's first proposal of marriage in the full expectation that he'd ask again. "Some degree of force possibly might have been used by the Prisoner at the Bar; but it was a force only to save the delicacy and feelings of the Prosecutrix," said the defense. "Any woman who is not an abandoned Prostitute will appear to be averse to what she inwardly desires."

Rape was a capital crime, and the defense reminded the men in the jury that if Bedlow was found guilty, the lives of all male citizens would be put "in the hands of a woman, to be disposed of almost at her will and pleasure." It took the jury only fifteen minutes to agree on an acquittal. But the story didn't end quite there. Although Bedlow's lawyer had referred to Lanah's family as "an obscure set of people, perhaps of no character themselves," they were not obscure within the working-class community of Manhattan. The neighborhood rioted, and for three days afterward crowds roamed the city's red-light district, known as the Holy Ground, looting bordellos and burning down the one where Lanah had been attacked. The working-class men were rebelling—if not against the double standard, at least against the upper-class men's appropriation of their women.

Decades later, the nation had another trial that homed in on the sexual rules for men and women when Daniel Sickles, a New York congressman, fatally shot Phillip Barton Key, a Washington, D.C., district attorney who had been having an affair with Sickles's wife, Teresa. Representative Sickles himself had a terrific reputation for dissipation—as a state legislator, he had been censured for bringing his mistress Fanny White onto the floor of the Assembly. After he married Teresa, he left her at home and took Fanny on a trip to England. But the prosecutor chose not to mention Sickles's own infidelities, and while the defendant sat in the courtroom sobbing loudly, his lawyers referred to Teresa as a "prostitute" and argued that their client had been maddened by grief. Sickles became the first person to be found not guilty of murder by reason of insanity in an American trial. He marched out to cheering crowds while his wife entered a life of disgrace, shunned by everyone from her old friends to the corner grocer. When her husband offered to take her back, she quickly agreed.

But the stain of marital infidelity in a woman was too terrible to be overlooked, and the same people who had ignored Sickles's own adulteries and forgiven him for killing an unarmed man were outraged when he forgave his wife. "His warmest personal and political friends bitterly denounce this course," wrote the *New York Dispatch*. Almost every paper in New York felt compelled to editorialize on the subject and only Horace Greeley applauded the idea of the Sickles' reunion. When Congress reconvened, Sickles was treated "as if he had the smallpox," wrote a woman from Washington. The Civil War saved his reputation, and after being hailed as a hero of the Battle of Gettysburg he was appointed ambassador to Spain. He left Teresa behind in New York. She died, a virtual prisoner in her home, at age thirty-one.

## "THE CHANCE THAT IN MARRIAGE
## SHE WILL DRAW A BLOCKHEAD"

Virtually all nineteenth-century opinion makers and upwardly mobile families agreed that education was important for girls. Women had won the right to schooling during the Revolutionary War when they were given the responsibility of raising the republican citizens of the future. Thomas Jefferson, no great fan of learned women, said he had his daughter Martha well taught because "The chance that in marriage she will draw a blockhead I calculate at about fourteen to one, and . . . the education of her family will probably rest on her own ideas and directions without assistance." Martha wound up having twelve children, and a husband who became mentally disturbed.

As young people began choosing their own spouses, and marriage became more a matter of romance and companionship, parents came to believe that their girls needed some education in order to be interesting mates for well-bred husbands. Sarah Hale enthusiastically championed the cause of women's schooling, although she warned that "we should solicit education as a favor, not exact it as a right." In a demonstration of Hale's commitment, an 1846 issue of *Godey's* featured a story in which a young man named Ernest expresses a negative opinion of learned females. His cousin Alice points out that their aunt Barbara, a writer, is nevertheless a model of "the spirit of feminine gentleness." Ernest is forced to agree, recalling that when he had a cold "she not only made me a bottle of cough syrup, but when I complained of nothing new to read, set to work and wrote some twenty stanzas on consumption."

When public schools first began opening to girls, the curriculum was mainly based on memorization and beatings. Elizabeth Buffum Chace, who attended school in Connecticut in 1816, remembered that by the time she was twelve "I had recited *Murray's Grammar* through perhaps over a dozen times without a word of explanation or application from the book or the teacher." Still, Chace wrote, "for that time it was a good school." Teachers in the middle and southern states were so frequently drunkards that the alcoholic schoolteacher became a stereotype.

As the demand for public schools increased, it became very clear that there were not going to be enough male schoolteachers to go around—in 1833 the estimated teacher shortage was more than 30,000. Thomas Gallaudet, the educator, warned that it would always be difficult to find good male candidates "as there are so many other avenues open in our country to the accumulation of property and the attaining of distinction." Officials were reluctant to hire women, partly out of concern over whether middle-class females should work outside the home, and partly because they believed that the only way to control older boys was by beating them. One superintendent wrote that a woman teacher was inappropriate "for the same reason that she cannot so well manage a vicious horse or other animal, as a man may do."

But as always happened in American history, the dogma of appropriate gender roles gave way to necessity. There simply weren't enough men available to staff the public schools, while the pool of available educated women was huge. And the price was right. In 1838, Connecticut paid $14.50 a month to male teachers and $5.75 a month to women. In Ohio, the Superintendent of Common Schools enthused that his districts "are able to do twice as much with the same money as is done in those counties where female teachers are almost excluded." By 1870, of the 200,000 primary and secondary school teachers in America, more than half were women. The question of whether it was appropriate to have women working was taken care of by the ever-popular excuse of maternal feeling. "They are the natural guardians of the young," announced Governor William Seward of New York.

Many of the first generations of women teachers were products of the Female Seminary Movement, which began around 1815 under the leadership of women like Catharine Beecher, Mary Lyon—the founder of Mt. Holyoke College—and Emma Willard, who founded the Troy Female Seminary in 1821 with the intention of offering women the same kind of intellectually rigorous education that boys received. ("They'll be educating the cows next," remarked a critic when Willard announced she was offering geometry to her girls in Troy.) Among her students were the daughters of Sarah Hale, one of whom became a career teacher herself.

It became a matter of status for prosperous parents to send their daughters off to boarding school, where they received both advanced instruction and socially desirable lessons in dancing, music, and the arts. It's not clear how much actual education most of them got there, or indeed how much their mentors felt was appropriate. (Although there have been "women whose minds have been equal to any human undertaking," *The Young Lady's Companion* opined, "happily the giants of their kind are rare.") Very young teachers were not uncommon. Jane Cannon Swisshelm, the future journalist, became a teacher when she was fourteen years old. The Beechers' friend Delia Bacon began teaching at fifteen, after only a year of formal schooling in Hartford, and she founded her own school when she was seventeen. At eighteen, Harriet Beecher was virtually running her sister's school in Catharine's absence.

Margaret Fuller, who was disappointed in her own schooling, concluded that girls covered even more subjects than boys did, but "without being really taught anything." Certainly parents seemed to expect a wide array of classes for their tuition money. In Petersburg, Virginia, a girl's academy opened in 1817 with the intention of taking its students through "orthography (spelling), reading, writing, grammar, composition, belles-lettres, geography, natural history, history of nations, chronology, natural philosophy and chemistry." Catharine Beecher's first class of fifteen girls learned geography, grammar, and rhetoric, but parental demand convinced Beecher to add philosophy, chemistry, ancient and modern history, arithmetic, algebra, geometry, moral philosophy, natural theology, and Latin. "Dear Madam," began a parody in *Godey's,*

> *I've called for the purpose of placing my daughter at school.*
> *She's only thirteen I assure you,*
> *And remarkably easy to rule.*
> *I'd have her learn painting and music*
> *Gymnastics and dancing pray do,*
> *Philosophy, grammar and logic,*
> *You'll teach her to read of course, too.*

## "THEY WEAR OUT FASTER
## THAN ANY OTHER CLASS OF PEOPLE"

Women's arrival in the public schools was an enormous change—both for the schools and the women, who finally could train for a respectable profession that would make them self-supporting. Although the percentile of women working as teachers at any given time was tiny, a much larger number had the experience at some point in their lives. A quarter of the native-born women in pre–Civil War Massachusetts were current or former schoolteachers. Thanks to teaching, a large minority of American women knew what it was like to have earned their own bread.

It was a difficult job. Maria Waterbury, a teacher who went to a "water cure" resort in Elmira, New York, to recover her health, reported that the physician who greeted her said he was used to seeing members of her profession: "We have the most trouble with teachers of any class of patients. They are worn out. They wear out faster than any other class of people." Female teachers proved able to maintain discipline in the classroom without violence, but they still had the challenge of trying to instruct up to sixty children in what was usually an uncomfortable one-room schoolhouse. A special commission in Connecticut reported in 1830 that out of forty schoolhouses in one county, only one had any ventilation. The average size of a building was 18½ feet by 7½ feet, and 7 feet high. A later report, in 1848, found that only about half of the schoolhouses in the state offered the luxury of an outhouse. When Elizabeth Blackwell taught early in her career, she wrote that her school in Kentucky was so cold she wound up teaching in gloves and blanket shawl, with a hood around her head. Conditions were, unsurprisingly, even worse on the frontier. "Went over to make my fire, and the wood was all wet and unchopped except a couple of sticks which lay under the stove," wrote a young teacher in Des Moines. "And as I puffed away to make the wet mass burn I found myself all at once crying like a child."

Southern women, who had been taught to regard any sort of paid work as unladylike, seldom became teachers except under extreme duress. "Teaching before dependence, death before teaching," vowed one Louisiana woman. Before the Civil War less than 8 percent of the teachers in North Carolina were female, and that was the highest percentage in the South. In the West, the extreme shortage of teachers drew eastern women who were eager for adventures. A would-be teacher named Martha Rogers rode in a stagecoach for three days, followed by a trek in a lumber wagon to get to her job in Missouri. When she arrived, sick from exhaustion, she discovered that the school had given her job to someone else. Another young teacher, Annie Perry, was in a steamboat wreck on the Ohio River.

The frontier teachers had wildly mixed classrooms—Ellen Lee, aged twenty, found herself in a log schoolhouse facing fifty pupils, aged fourteen to twenty-two. Fanny Warner, who brought a globe with her, discovered her rural Wisconsin students thought the world was "round like a wheel rather than an orange." Even given extremely modest standards of living, some of the teachers found it impossible to survive on their salaries. "Expect when I get what clothes worn out that I brought with me I shall be obliged to wear a blanket," wrote Arozina Perkins, who was eventually forced to leave her job in Des Moines to look for better-paying work.

Most of the teachers lived with local families, a situation that was almost never completely comfortable. Mahala Drake wrote back from Iowa that her landlady expected her to do the sewing and take care of the baby after school. Another teacher in rural Indiana said her room was so small and cold she could not sit in it, and that the house itself lacked even the most primitive toilet facilities. Elizabeth Blackwell was forced to share a bedroom with three members of her host's family. Augusta Hubbell boarded with an Iowa couple and wound up having to flee home when the wife became jealous of her. The teachers were all single—well into the twentieth century, school systems required women to resign when they married. Many school boards prohibited their teachers from anything they regarded as a potential impropriety, ranging from riding in a carriage with a man to being out after 8 P.M. In the South during the Civil War, one sixteen-year-old teacher was told that she was required to stay inside the schoolhouse during daylight hours and then go directly to her quarters to shut herself up for the night. She was forbidden, the school officials added unnecessarily, to do anything that might "create talk."

## "I AM LIVING ON NO ONE"

Just as the school boards came to like female teachers, the nation's infant factory system was taken with the idea of mill girls. American employers were worried about creating a permanent class of rough, hard-to-handle industrial workers, like the ones who were causing so much trouble in England. Girls did not usually stay long enough to become troublemakers—after a few years, most left to get married. In the meantime they were cheaper than male workers, and easier to control. By the 1820s, New England was full of textile factories where virtually all the workers were women, each making $2 or $3 a week. (The supervisors, who were men, got $12.) At first, they lived in paternalistic, company-owned boardinghouses, where they were barred from staying out late, and required to attend Sunday services. The girls, who had probably expected to stay home or go into domestic service until they married, seemed pleased that they could make enough money to accumulate a trousseau, or help their families, or simply support themselves. "Don't I feel independent!" wrote Anne Appleton to her sister. "The thought that I am living on no one is a happy one indeed to me." Harriet Hanson, who entered the mills at age ten, said she wanted "to earn *money* like the other little girls," and she may have been telling the truth. Her mother ran a boardinghouse, and until little Harriet entered the factory, her job was to wash the dishes for forty-five people, three times a day.

Life in places like Lowell, Massachusetts, during the textile industry's earliest days sounded rather idyllic to outsiders. In 1833, when President Jackson visited Lowell, he was greeted by mill girls who "walked in procession, like troops of liveried angels, clothed in white (with green-fringed parasols). . . ." The girls contributed essays to a literary magazine, *The Lowell Offering,* and formed their own "improvement circles" in which they read and criticized each other's stories and poetry. A third of the female workers went to night school, and some went on to become teachers, artists, librarians, and missionaries.

But when the panic of 1837 hit, the mills' management became less paternalistic and more tightfisted. Within a short time, the mill girls were on strike against speedups and wage cutbacks. Much of their dissatisfaction focused on the length of the workday. It had always been long—in 1834 it stretched from eleven to twelve hours—but by 1850 women were working thirteen-and-a-half-hour days, and at a much faster pace. In 1845, millworker Eliza Hemingway testified before the Massachusetts House of Representatives that in the summer she worked from 5 A.M. to 7 P.M. with two breaks for meals. "She thought there was a general desire among the females to work but ten hours, regardless of pay," reported a newspaper account. Many of the native-born mill girls were replaced by immigrants of both sexes, who were desperate enough to accept starvation wages.

In the period before the Civil War, there were only a handful of ways respectable women could earn their own living, and teaching and millwork were two of them. Some women kept boarders—88 of the 150 boardinghouses in 1800 New York were run by women, though it's doubtful most of them made enough to support a family. The bookbinding and typesetting trades accepted a select number of female applicants. Otherwise, women were limited to needlework—which often meant piecework sewing in their homes—or domestic service. They were bleak options. (A survey of New York City prostitutes in the 1850s showed that a quarter of the women had previously been in the sewing trade, and half in service.) In 1845, the New York *Daily Tribune* estimated that twice as many women were seeking jobs as seamstresses as there were jobs available. Everybody wanted to avoid domestic service, both because the pay was poor and because most women disliked being so directly under the supervision of a demanding housewife. Millworker Mary Paul said most of the girls she knew "would live on 25 cents per week at sewing or school teaching rather than work at housework. . . . This all comes from the way servants are *treated*." Many Northern women seemed to expect that their domestic servants would develop a loyalty to their "family," just as southerners imagined such devotion from their slaves. The wealthy housewife Elizabeth Sullivan Stuart, growing irritated with the revolving door of Irish servants in the 1850s, exclaimed in outrage: "I believe nothing will bind them but dollars and cents."

## "OH LIZZIE! THOU WILL MAKE US RIDICULOUS!"

In 1840 in London, the World Anti-Slavery Convention refused to let the women delegates speak, and an outraged Lucretia Mott was relegated to the gallery—much as Harriet Beecher Stowe was voluntarily stashed away during her *Uncle Tom* tour. Steaming, she began talking with young Elizabeth Cady Stanton, another American, who was there with her new husband, Henry. We'd have long since forgotten the convention otherwise. "As Mrs. Mott and I walked home, arm in arm, commenting on the incidents of the day, we resolved to hold a convention as soon as we returned home, and form a society to advocate the rights of women," Stanton recalled.

It was eight years coming. Stanton had spent her early married life happily in Boston, in a charming house surrounded by sympathetic friends and assisted by two hardworking servants. She couldn't understand why every woman didn't love housework. "There is such a struggle among women to become artists that I really wish some of their gifts could be illustrated in clean, orderly, beautiful homes," she sniffed. She gave the man who delivered her firewood a tip to pile the logs with the smooth ends outward.

Then Henry Stanton moved the family to Seneca Falls in upstate New York, a distinctly unromantic mill town where the house was isolated, the servants untrained, and the neighbors not particularly sympathetic. While her husband traveled, Elizabeth was left alone with three small sons who were extremely active whenever they weren't extremely sick. She discovered that "the novelty of housekeeping had passed away." Lucretia Mott popped up visiting relatives at nearby Waterloo, and Stanton went to see her, pouring out her complaints "with such vehemence and indignation that I stirred myself, as well as the rest of the party, to do and dare anything."

They wrote up a newspaper announcement calling for a women's rights convention five days later, drafted a "Womanifesto" modeled after the Declaration of Independence, and found a Methodist church where the sessions could be held. On the appointed day, to everyone's surprise, the roads to the church were crowded with wagons and carriages. When forty men turned up, the organizers decided to drop their plan to exclude males. In fact, out of deference to the sensibilities of the time, they asked Mott's husband, James, to preside.

Stanton spoke for the first time in public—too quietly, people complained, to make herself heard. But she defied even Lucretia Mott with her call for the right for women to vote. "Oh Lizzie!" the Quaker cried. "If thou demands that, thou will make us ridiculous! We must go slowly." Henry Stanton left town when he discovered his wife planned to demand the "elective franchise." Her father—who had rushed over to check for signs of insanity in his daughter—found her mentally sound and threatened to disinherit her. The convention got national newspaper coverage, most of it scornful, and the popular reaction was so negative that most of the women who had signed the Declaration of Rights withdrew their names.

But two weeks later, a different cadre of Quakers, freethinkers, and restless housewives held a second convention in Rochester. Stanton managed to attend, even though she had trouble getting a baby-sitter, and embarrassed herself by fearfully refusing to support a motion that a woman actually chair the women's rights convention. "My only excuse is that woman has been so little accustomed to act in a public capacity that she does not always know what is due," she wrote a friend later.

Like everybody else, she would be learning as she went along.

# 6

# Life Before the Civil War:
# Cleanliness and Corsetry

## "A TERRIBLE DECAY OF FEMALE HEALTH ALL OVER THE LAND"

There was a virtual consensus in the first half of the nineteenth century that American women—at least the ones society worried about—were very sickly. By some estimates, a quarter of the female members of the middle and upper classes were laid up. They kept to their rooms, or lay on the couch weakly receiving visitors, or traveled from one health spa to another, seeking treatment. Catharine Beecher was convinced there was "a terrible decay of female health all over the land." She conducted an unscientific but much-quoted survey of women in 200 towns and found only two communities in which a majority felt well.

There was certainly a lot of illness going around—malaria in the South, consumption in the North, and typhoid and cholera epidemics in the cities, where rain mixed with garbage and animal droppings in the street, creating stagnant pools of fetid water. But Americans were not any more prone to disease than the rest of the world; in areas like the rural Northeast, people probably lived longer on average than anywhere else on the planet. And except for childbearing, women did not seem to be in greater peril than men—by 1840, their life expectancy was actually higher. It's possible that they gave the impression of increased sickliness because they felt freer to complain about the disorders they had always endured. The nineteenth century was the first time in American history that ill health was not taken as a given. Until then people were routinely in constant pain. The number of doctors increased four times as fast as the population in the first half of the century, and it was in their economic interest to make people believe they were entitled to feel well, while finding as many illnesses as possible—particularly among women, who were their most faithful customers.

Some of the newly discovered maladies seemed psychological. "Hysteria" was a nervous disorder with symptoms not unlike the ones the Salem witchcraft accusers displayed. "Let the reader imagine the patient writhing like a serpent upon the floor, rending her garments to tatters, plucking out handsful of hair and striking her person with violence—with contorted and swollen countenance and fixed eyes resisting every effort of bystanders to control her," said a physician in 1840. Hysteria struck women in the prime of their lives and afflicted them with nervousness, depression, fatigue, and general weepiness. Most physicians found hysteria impossible to treat, because the symptoms were so obscure and variable. (Health reformers who advocated the "water cure" treated hysteria by pouring a jug of cold water over the victim's head.) It was regarded as an upper-class disorder, but physicians who bothered to examine immigrant women in their tenement houses found cases there, too.

Just being female made women candidates for perpetual medical care, because doctors began treating all the normal passages of their lives—puberty, menstruation, childbirth, and menopause—as illnesses. Menstruation in particular was seen as dangerous—"an internal wound, the real cause of all this tragedy," said one physician. Many doctors believed that during their periods, women were deprived of blood to the brain, leaving them "idiotic" or temporarily insane. Early onset of menstruation was regarded as a sign a girl might be oversexed, and some doctors encouraged parents to keep prepubescent daughters on a vegetarian diet, since meat was seen as sexually "stimulating." No matter what a woman's complaint, doctors diagnosed a problem in the womb. Everything from a backache to hysteria was traced back to the childbearing organs. One professor of medicine thought that it was "as if the Almighty, in creating the female sex, had taken a uterus and built a woman around it."

But a great many of the female invalids of the early nineteenth century were suffering from tangible physical problems. Tuberculosis, or consumption, accounted for one out of every four American deaths in the 1830s, and young women were the prime victims. It was a lingering disease, and a woman could live with it, in varying degrees of distress, for decades. TB sufferers grew pale and delicate, their cheeks frequently flushed with fever. "Such complexions are generally esteemed handsome, but to the experienced eye, it is a beauty fraught with . . . mournful associations," said the American doctor William Sweetser. It was, as diseases go, a romantic affliction, and many perfectly healthy women seemed eager to mimic the fragile, pink-and-ivory quality that consumption imparted. Tuberculosis was novelists' favored method of sending the tender child-heroines of the era off into the happier world of heaven. The saintly little Eva in *Uncle Tom's Cabin* faded away from consumption, as did countless lesser-known characters.

The victims, of course, knew its other side. Unlike the serene Eva, many were tortured by night-sweats and diarrhea, stomach pain, and a "graveyard" cough. "How is your cough," Deborah Fiske of Amherst wrote to her fellow consumptive, Harriet Fowler. "Mine sounds now very much like yours—deep and hoarse and I am obliged to keep an old cup and expectorate, no matter if [my husband] is disturbed by it." The daughter of a consumptive, Fiske had lived with the classic medical regimen of leeches, blistering, and opium for so long that she learned to treat herself, and even raised her own leeches. (Handling leeches—bloodsucking worms that were attached to various parts of the body until they dropped off, gorged—was one of women's domestic duties. In *The Young Lady's Friend*, future wives were advised to regard them as rather adorable: "their ornamental stripes should recommend them even to the eye, and their valuable services to our feelings.") Childbirth increased the danger of tuberculosis, but doctors didn't counsel their patients to avoid pregnancy. Deborah Fiske never recovered from the birth of her fourth child.

Many of the mysterious invalids of the era had probably suffered damage during childbirth that the physicians weren't skilled enough to repair. Sometimes the uterus descended from its normal position, creating an uncomfortable, dragging sensation that made moving around difficult, if not impossible. There are grisly reports of midwives who, in a misguided attempt to remove the afterbirth, tugged on the uterus until they dragged it out of the body. Prolapsed uterus was common enough that doctors and mail-order houses invented plugs and other devices that were supposed to hold the womb in place. Most of them must have been extremely uncomfortable—one was so large it had to be worn under a skirt with an enormous hoop.

Other invalids suffered from an awful malady called vesico-vaginal fistula. During childbirth, the wall between their vagina and the bladder or rectum ripped, leaving them unable to control the leakage of urine or feces through the vagina. The condition had been recognized for centuries, but some historians believe that it increased when doctors began delivering babies and inserting their instruments into the womb. The nineteenth-century German surgeon Johann Friedrich Dieffenbach called it "the greatest misfortune that can happen to a woman, and the more so because she is condemned to live with it without the hope [of dying] from it. The skin . . . becomes inflamed and covered by pustulous eruption. An unsupportable itching and burning sensation tortures the patient, so much so that she scratches the skin to bleeding. . . . The comfort of a clean bed, that grave for all sorrows and afflictions, is not their lot, for it will soon be drenched with urine. Many of the wealthier classes are, therefore, condemned forever to the straw. The air of the room of the unfortunate woman nauseates the visitor, and drives him off. The husband has an aversion from his own wife, a tender mother is exiled from the circle of her own children. She sits, solitary and alone in the cold, on a perforated chair. This is not fiction but naked truth, and the cure for such an evil is the prize for which we all labor."

J. Marion Sims, an Alabama physician, devised an operation that successfully closed the fistulas and let these tormented women resume their lives. But the discovery came at a horrifying cost. Sims was a surgeon in Montgomery in 1845 when he was called, within a few weeks' time, to see three different slave women who had lost control of their bladders after childbirth. He experimented with surgical techniques while the women balanced on their knees and elbows, in order to give him a better view of what he was doing. "The first patient I operated on was Lucy," Dr. Sims wrote later. "That was before the days of anaesthetics, and the poor girl, on her knees, bore the operation with great heroism and bravery." There were many more procedures to come. Four years later, he finally succeeded in repairing the fistula of a slave named Anarcha, who had been with him since she was seventeen years old. It was Anarcha's thirtieth operation, all of them performed without anesthetics.

Sims claimed the women had begged him to keep trying his experiments and it's possible that was true—returning home without a cure may have seemed like a worse fate than the continuing torment of the operations. They might also have become addicted to the opium he gave them for their pain. But they were still slaves, with no real option to say no, and Sims chose to work on them in part because he believed white women could not endure the kind of pain he was inflicting. There is a statue in honor of Dr. Sims in New York City, where he did most of his later work, and another in South Carolina, where he was born. But there are no monuments to Anarcha or the other slave women, who slipped out of history as soon as he had finished with them.

Doctors in the first half of the nineteenth century had begun to come up with surgical techniques to cure some of the conditions that could ruin women's lives, but they did not yet have the skill to make the procedures safe, or the anesthetic to make them bearable. In 1809, Jane Todd Crawford of Kentucky—whose cousin Mary would later marry Abraham Lincoln—discovered that what she thought was her fifth pregnancy was in fact a huge ovarian cyst. No American doctor had ever successfully removed such a tumor, and Mrs. Crawford

appeared doomed to a life of hidden-away invalidism. A visiting surgeon, who had been trained at the University of Edinburgh, said he
would try to operate if only someone could find a way to transport her
to his office, which was sixty miles away over rough, roadless territory. A few days later, Mrs. Crawford arrived at his door, having ridden on horseback, supporting her swollen belly on the horn of her
saddle. He gave her a mixture of opium and alcohol to ease the pain
and removed the tumor. A month later she rode home, cured. Legend
has it that an angry crowd surrounded the doctor's home while he was
treating Mrs. Crawford, threatening to kill him for his outrageous
assault on a female body.

But few doctors had the surgical skills necessary to perform that sort
of operation. They were imperfectly trained, often in fly-by-night medical schools. Their arsenal of treatments included bleeding, blistering,
and cleaning out the system by purging or inducing the patient to vomit.
A favorite all-purpose remedy, calomel, was actually mercurous chlo-
ride, and many Americans' ruined gums and teeth showed the effect of
constant dosing. Both Harriet Beecher Stowe and Catharine Beecher
suffered from mysterious complaints involving headaches and loss of
control of the hands that were probably signs of mercury poisoning.
One of Harriet's biographers suggested that her notoriously disorganized household management might have been another symptom.

To cure nervous complaints, doctors injected water, milk, and lin-
seed into the uterus. For infections, they cauterized it with silver
nitrate, or even a hot iron. They put leeches on the vagina, and even
on the rectum. (A famous English gynecologist, whose work was
studied by American doctors, advocated placing leeches right on the
neck of the uterus, but he cautioned his readers not to let the leeches
wander off into the organ itself. "I think I have scarcely ever seen
more acute pain than that experienced by several of my patients under
these circumstances," he wrote.) Leeches were actually a moderate
approach compared with doctors who tried to bring down a patient's
temperature by opening a vein and drawing blood. Salmon P. Chase,
Lincoln's secretary of the treasury, watched doctors take 50 ounces of
blood from his fever-stricken wife before she died.

It's no wonder that alternative treatment systems began to blossom in the nineteenth century, some of them bearing names we now associate with items in the kitchen cupboard—Sylvester Graham, John Harvey Kellogg. Hydropaths believed in the curative powers of water. Homeopaths stressed natural remedies, and the administration of very tiny bits of medicine, diluted in great amounts of water. The Botanical Movement, which taught that laypeople could treat themselves better than physicians, was founded by Samuel Thomson after six doctors called in to help his seriously ill wife prescribed six different treatments. All the movements celebrated healthy, robust womanhood and decried the "silly fashion of appearing frail even to the point of invalidism." They stressed exercise, sunlight, temperance, and sensible dress. William Alcott, a well-known reformer who advocated a diet restricted to vegetables and water, urged women to found anticorset societies. The health reformers did share the traditional doctors' belief that people had only a finite amount of "vital force" or energy, and most of them promoted celibacy, or at least a restricted sex life. (Sylvester Graham claimed that engaging in sexual intercourse more than once a month would endanger a man's health.) These theories might have been eccentric, but they often helped women convince their husbands to limit the size of their families.

Many prominent American women reported being relieved of chronic illness by taking "the cure" in the many retreats that the health reform movements set up around the country. Catharine Beecher and Harriet Beecher Stowe both favored the hydropaths, who had their visitors soaking in hot tubs, leaping into cold ones, and being massaged in a "wave-bath" that must have been something like a Jacuzzi. It may have been the healthful lifestyle of the resorts that rejuvenated the patients, or simply the chance to get away from home. Harriet Beecher Stowe spent ten months at a cure in 1847, while her husband Calvin tended their large brood of children. "I wish you could be with me in Brattleboro, and coast down hill on a sled, go sliding and snowballing by moonlight!" she wrote her husband, who undoubtedly wished the same thing. When she returned home, Calvin came down with ailments that required a fifteen-month stay at the spa.

## "AFRAID OF NOTHING SO MUCH
## AS GROWING STOUT"

Everyone commented about American women's failure to exercise. William Baxter, a visitor from England, noted that at vacation resorts and country inns, all the women did was sit in rocking chairs. "They would regard anyone who proposed vigorous physical exercise as a madman," he said. There was actually an excellent reason why they didn't move around more—they were immobilized by their clothes. Women were encased in rigid, ribbed underwear and restricted by dresses with arms that were either long and tight or huge and full of flounces. They were also half-blinded by extended bonnets and caps that eliminated all side vision and weighted down by floor-length skirts made of heavy fabrics, over multitudinous petticoats. Harriet Beecher Stowe theorized that women's skirts were intended to trail along the ground as a way of demonstrating by their clean hems that the wearers never had to walk anywhere.

For a while, women wore stiff petticoats made from horsehair to give their skirts volume, but eventually those gave way to "cages" made of hoops of increasing diameter. Over the cages, skirts swung gracefully as their wearers walked, sometimes revealing ankles that had not been displayed for decades and, inadvertently, some fancy underdrawers. Their lightness must have been a relief after the petticoats, but they were unwieldy. They got stuck in carriages, caught on fire, and even, it was alleged, blew their owners off cliffs.

Worst of all was the corset, which was worn everywhere from the breakfast table to the ballroom in the perpetual and generally hopeless pursuit of the ideal 20-inch waist. Preadolescent girls wore corsets and old women wore corsets, and mothers-to-be wore corsets even in the advanced stages of pregnancy. Women's tiny waists defined them as members of the leisure class—wives and daughters so well taken care of that they were never required to take a deep breath. But the industrial revolution made corsets affordable for almost everyone, and factory girls and servants also began wearing undergarments that were as tight as their occupations allowed. Young women of courting age were laced to rib-cracking tightness. One commentator claimed that it was not unusual to see "a mother lay her daughter down upon the carpet, and placing her foot on her back, break half a dozen laces in tightening her stays." Comparisons to Chinese footbinding were rife, and stories were passed around about deformed babies born with corset lines imprinted in their flesh. Virtually every clergyman, doctor, and magazine editor decried the custom of tight corsetry. In an age when medical experts found everything from education to meat-eating dangerous to the delicate female sensibility, the corset was blamed both for problems it really did cause, like shortness of breath or miscarriages, and those that it didn't, like curvature of the spine and cancer.

While virtually everything women read told them that corsets were bad, everything they saw stressed how essential they were. Magazines pictured women with tiny waists and dresses that sported long, tight sleeves; heavy fabrics; and huge skirts. Fathers sometimes urged their daughters to consider their health before appearance, but mothers often sided with the forces of fashion. A southern woman wrote to her daughter in 1818, noting with alarm that she had heard rumors the girl had made her undergarments large enough to slip on and off without the trouble of lacing. "If you love me, alter these corsets before I see you," she urged.

This was one of many eras in American history when young women were at war with their bodies. "We in America have got so far out of the way of a womanhood that has any vigor of outline or opulence of physical proportion that, when we see a woman made as a woman ought to be, she strikes us as a monster," wrote Harriet Beecher Stowe. "Our willowy girls are afraid of nothing so much as growing stout. . . ." Girls starved themselves to win the ultimate compliment of "fairylike." Warm clothing was not fairylike, and fashionable women wore only shawls for protection in the winter. Although shoemakers were finally learning how to differentiate between left and right feet, women of fashion didn't seem to make fit a priority. "They never wear muffs or boots, and appear extremely shocked at the sight of comfortable walking shoes and cotton stockings," wrote Frances Trollope. Tanned skin was also unacceptable, particularly in the South.

"Remember . . . not to go out without your bonnet because it will make you very ugly and then we should not love you so much," wrote Thomas Jefferson, demonstrating once again that he could always find just the wrong thing to say to a devoted daughter.

Everybody talked about fashion reform, but anyone who actually tried it ran the risk of universal ridicule. Elizabeth Cady Stanton fell in love with what would come to be known as the bloomer dress—a short skirt over full Turkish-style trousers. But she found, as did many of her friends, that no amount of comfort was worth constantly being jeered at by little boys on the street, snubbed by old acquaintances, and hollered at by male authority figures. No matter how you got around it, the things on bloomer-wearers' legs were a form of pants, and critics, citing Deuteronomy's prohibition of cross-dressing, claimed that the Bible was antibloomer. The dress reformers fought on for some time, but even the health journals had correspondents who wrote in arguing that when ridicule became overwhelming, it was time to abandon dress reform. Perhaps the bloomers would have done better if they had been more flattering. Cady Stanton, whose figure was by no means fairylike, admitted the outfit really required "a perfection of form, limb and feet such as few possessed."

## "ONE OF THE BEST OBSTETRICIANS OF HIS TIME WAS BLIND"

One of the early casualties of the nineteenth century was the tradition of female neighbors assisting in the delivery of babies. Poor and rural families continued to use midwives, but in the cities, middle-class women began calling in male doctors, who quickly cleared the room of female friends and relatives. Childbirth occurred in privacy, with only the mother and the physician present for the great drama.

The best-trained doctors had some potentially lifesaving skills. Forceps, which had been popularized in England, allowed them to dislodge babies who were stuck in the birth canal. If midwives were unable to turn the infant with their hands, they were forced to dismember it to save the mother. But the real cause of the change was the growing population of doctors and their desire to acquire the mid-wives' clientele. The doctors won rather quickly. In Philadelphia, twenty-one women listed their professions as midwife in the 1815 city directory; by 1824, there were only six.

For the mothers-to-be, the change was not necessarily an improve-ment. The vast majority of births were not problematic, and a skilled midwife believed in letting nature take its course. That was better by far for both mother and child, since the medical profession had yet to embrace the concept of sterility. Anytime a hand or instrument was inserted into a woman's body, she was in danger of becoming infected, with fatal results. Childbed, or puerperal, fever became epidemic at times in the nineteenth century, particularly in hospitals, where a sin-gle doctor could carry infection from one patient to the next. Hospitals were the delivery rooms for the urban poor, and in 1840 at Bellevue in New York, almost half the women giving birth during the first six months of the year contracted the fever. Eighty percent of them died.

Doctors charged much more than midwives, and they wanted to look as if they were making an effort. They sometimes used forceps to speed deliveries, risking both tearing the mother and hurting the baby. A physician might also make use of one of the "heroic" remedies of the day, like bloodletting. William Dewees, who taught at the Univer-sity of Pennsylvania, wrote proudly that in one protracted labor he took "upwards of two quarts" of blood from a woman while she was standing up. The woman, unsurprisingly, fainted, and after that, the doctor said, "everything appeared better." Bleeding women until they swooned stopped them from crying out, which must have been a relief for the doctor and the family members waiting nearby.

In 1833 in Boston, a woman who was eight months pregnant went into convulsions. The doctors took 8 ounces of blood and gave her a purgative to empty her bowels. The next day, when she had more con-vulsions, they took 40 ounces of blood and gave her emetics to induce vomiting and put ice on her head and burning mustard plasters on her feet. A few hours later, when she had more convulsions, they took another 12 ounces of blood, and then 6 ounces more. The woman, who had now lost two-fifths of her blood over two days, lapsed into a coma as she began to deliver. The doctors gave her ergot, a dangerous fungus found on rye grain that was believed to hurry contractions. When the woman went into convulsions again, they gave her another emetic and calomel to again purge her system. The child was stillborn but the woman eventually recovered, and the doctors regarded their treatment as relatively conservative, because they hadn't used forceps or otherwise intruded on the uterus.

To protect their patients' delicate sensibilities, most male physicians delivered babies without ever looking between the mother's legs. Doctors were constrained both by women's sense of modesty and the strong public suspicion that seeing a half-naked woman in labor would provoke sexual excitement in any man. (A Virginia doctor, Thomas Ewell, claimed that he knew for a fact that doctors who assisted in childbirth became "inflamed with the thoughts of well-shaped bodies of the women they have delivered" and were driven to "adultery and madness.") Male doctors worked by sense of touch on women who were fully clothed, or covered by a sheet. A famous illustration from the period shows a doctor kneeling next to a standing patient, his face averted and his hand up her skirt. (Dr. Thomas Denman told his readers in 1848 that "Degorges, one of the best obstetricians of his time, was blind.") Medical students were not permitted to watch actual deliveries and learned what they could from manikins and textbooks. When the choice was between modesty and safety, decorum trumped good medicine every time. "I confess I am proud to say that, in this country . . . there are women who prefer to suffer the extremity of danger and pain rather than waive those scruples of delicacy which prevent their maladies from being fully exposed," said Dr. Meigs, who had made the famous speech about the nature of women to his gynecology students. But even he admitted that a little more candor might be helpful.

The concern for modesty caused some cultural conservatives, including Sarah Hale, to champion female doctors. But male physicians resisted this, occasionally arguing that menstruation made women too mentally unstable for such responsibilities. Although the Blackwell sisters and others broke the barrier, the medical profession never willingly opened its doors to women in the nineteenth century. When Dr. Oliver Wendell Holmes got the Harvard medical school to admit a female student, the move was revoked after protests from undergraduates who wrote, to national acclaim, "we are not opposed to allowing woman her rights, but we do protest against her appearing in places where her presence is calculated to destroy our respect for the modesty and delicacy of her sex."

## "MARRIED PERSONS WILL READILY UNDERSTAND THE NATURE OF THE TOPICS"

During the colonial period, the average woman gave birth to seven children, and visitors wrote home in amazement about the size of the families. But beginning around 1800, American households began shrinking steadily—by the end of the nineteenth century, the birth rate had been cut in half and was lower than any European nation except France. Obviously, people were practicing birth control. Women relied mainly on their mothers' methods, the most venerable of which was nursing one baby to stave off the chances of getting pregnant with another. In 1840, Priscilla Cooper Tyler, a young matron, wrote to her sister pointing out the dangers that even the Queen of England might face if she decided to forgo the tradition. "I suppose you have heard that Victoria is expecting again. Poor thing! So much for not nursing." Breastfeeding reduces the chance of conception, but it certainly doesn't eliminate it. Abstinence does, and given women's new status as the moral center of the home, along with the health reform movement's enthusiasm for celibacy, many American couples were probably convinced to forgo intercourse altogether.

Beginning around 1830, a great deal of literature about birth control began floating around the country. Robert Dale Owen's well-read *Moral Physiology* recommended coitus interruptus, or withdrawal. *The Fruits of Philosophy*, by Dr. Charles Knowlton, urged women to douche—to wash their private parts right after intercourse with water and a spermicide like alcohol or vinegar. Dr. Knowlton seemed to feel he had invented the technique and attempted to sue another birth control advocate for copyright infringement. But early American recipe books already contained directions for making "preventative lotion." (A mixture of bichloride of mercury, milk of almonds, and rosewater was deemed "infallible if used in proper time.") Douching was far from foolproof, but like breastfeeding, it cut down on the chances of conception and may have been effective enough for couples who were simply hoping to keep the number of pregnancies down to a manageable level.

Thanks to an increasingly efficient mail system, Americans could send away for birth control pamphlets, medical devices like diaphragms and syringes, condoms, spermicides for douching, and pills that promised to induce abortions. Ads for condoms, cures for venereal disease, aphrodisiacs, and abortion services were an economic mainstay of the urban newspapers. Agents distributed ads for birth control devices on street corners and mailed them to newlyweds. "French" was a code word for a contraceptive, and "Portuguese" for something that induced abortion ("The Portuguese Female Pills always give Immediate Relief "). One New York firm advertised 201 styles of douching syringes; National Syringes unveiled a model with changeable nozzles that could be used for both birth control and watering houseplants. Diaphragms, called pessaries or "womb veils," were also popular and easy to obtain. They were used to correct problems with the uterus as well as for birth control, and some women never took them out—there are records of people keeping them in for thirty or forty years.

Dozens, perhaps hundreds, of itinerate lecturers specialized in sexual topics, giving anatomy lessons, recipes for marital happiness, and explaining about birth control. Frederick Hollick, one of the best known, exhibited life-size papier-mâché models of the human body. "The conviction that they are natural is at first so strong that many have even *fainted away* at first view, from the impression that they were viewing a live body," he bragged. Hollick gave lectures on female anatomy and women's diseases to women-only audiences, but he discussed reproductive control in front of mixed groups. His ad in Boston in 1849 announced a new series of lectures for "married per-

sons [who] will readily understand the nature of the topics to be introduced and will see their importance especially to them. The want of
such information, at a timely period, is the cause of incalculable suffering and unhappiness."

Availability of information was less of a problem than accuracy.
Merchants frequently made up wild claims for pills and potions that
were nothing more than alcohol and flavored water, and there was no
way a befuddled young couple could tell which advertisements were
reliable. Advocates of the rhythm method offered completely different estimates on what part of a woman's cycle was the safest, with
some recommending what was actually the period of maximum fertility. Lester and Lizzie Ward, who married right before the Civil War,
wanted to continue their educations and remain childless. Over the
early years of their marriage, Lester's diary recounts one abortion,
rejection of mail-order contraceptive pills, use of an "instrument" that
failed, and then the purchase of "a fine syringe with India rubber
tube." The Wards seemed to have run the gamut of options, yet Lizzie
became pregnant at least twice.

Like Lizzie Ward, many women resorted to abortion when other
methods failed. Even doctors who didn't perform abortions reported
that they were routinely asked to do so by their patients. Midwives
hung flags in their window to signal that they provided abortion services. Although far from socially acceptable, abortions performed
early in a pregnancy were generally regarded as a form of contraception. Most people held to the tradition that the fetus was not a human
being until the "quickening," when it began to move around in the
womb. The churches, including the Catholic clergy, generally seem to
have had the same attitude.

Many of the abortions were performed by women—Elizabeth
Blackwell had trouble renting office space in New York because land-
lords presumed that "female physician" meant abortionist. Madame
Restell, who made a fortune in New York City in the pre–Civil War
era, advertised herself as a former "Female Physician in the two principal female hospitals in Europe—those of Vienna and Paris—where,
favored by her great experience and opportunities, she attained that

celebrity in those great discoveries in medical science so specially adapted to the female frame." In real life, Madame Restell was Ann Lohman, a seamstress married to a newspaper compositor with pretensions to medical expertise. Although she became infamous as an abortionist, she did most of her business selling contraceptive devices and running a confidential maternity hospital. If a pregnancy was past the quickening stage, she preferred to arrange for a clandestine adoption. She was a constant target of angry editorials in the city newspapers (which nevertheless took her advertising), and a public shunning so complete that the houses on either side of her Fifth Avenue brownstone were empty. After a young woman from upstate New York died from an abortion, Madame Restell was sentenced to a year in prison on Blackwell's Island, where the warden was eventually fired for giving her special treatment. When her stepdaughter married, Madame presented the newlyweds with $50,000 and a European honeymoon.

### "TOO SPARING IN THEIR USE OF WATER"

One of the things that separated nineteenth-century women from their colonial forebears was their belief that bathing is a good idea. Middle-class Americans became attached to the idea of personal hygiene even before they acquired running water or central heating. Lucy Larcom, the mill girl turned author, remembered watching her sister in 1835 taking a full bath before going to work, "even though the water was chiefly broken ice. . . . It required both nerve and will to do this at five o'clock on a zero morning in a room without a fire."

Cleanliness, like most of the transformations of the pre–Civil War period, was mainly a phenomenon of the larger towns and cities. William Alcott, the health reformer, estimated in 1850 that a quarter of New England's population bathed their whole bodies less than once a year, and the numbers of unwashed Americans in the South and western states must have been staggering. (The girls at the Euphradian Academy in Rockingham, North Carolina, had to get special permission from their parents to take a full bath.) But the people setting the pace—the prosperous urban families—had decided that cleanliness was, if not next to godliness, at least a sign of gentility. By midcentury, every middle-class bedroom had a water pitcher and washbasin.

Still, the concept of real head-to-toe bathing was slow to catch on. By 1860 there were only about 4,000 bathtubs in Boston, which had a population of 178,000. Washing generally didn't include soap; people stood in tubs and rubbed themselves with a wet sponge, followed by a brisk toweling. Some women boasted that they could take a complete bath in a carpeted room without spilling a drop. "Females, with all their scrupulous attention to cleanliness, are . . . too sparing in their use of water," advised *The American Lady's Medical Pocket-Book*. "Many ridiculously suppose that its free and repeated application to the skin gives it a disagreeable roughness, and otherwise injures its beauty." The idea of washing one's body was still so novel that people believed in waiting two hours after eating for even a sponge bath.

Women were also being counseled to keep their hair clean, but shampoo was still in the future. Health and beauty books were full of recommendations about what to use when washing your hair: a beaten egg yolk, cold tea, castor oil mixed with brandy and bay rum, or olive oil in which flowers had been allowed to stand. Although magazines urged readers to brush their teeth, visitors from abroad still commented on the poor quality of American dental care and many women became toothless very young. "The loss of my teeth has been the severest mortification to which my vanity has ever been subjected," wrote Sarah Gayle, the wife of the future governor of Alabama. Gayle was one of the rare Americans who consulted a dentist, but her efforts weren't rewarded. The dentist not only subjected her to "unspeakable" pain, he eventually gave her a fatal case of tetanus.

What nineteenth-century women did about menstruation was still shrouded in secrecy, although the problem must have cropped up much more frequently than in the colonial era, due to better diet and fewer pregnancies. *The American Lady's Medical Pocket-Book* urged girls to exercise when they were having their periods but said absolutely not one word about what to wear to absorb the blood. It's easy to imagine the strategies they used at home. The most important function of the household "rag bag" was to provide pieces of cotton or linen that women could put "between the limbs" during their periods, wash, and then use again. But in the decades before the Civil War, despite the cult of domesticity, women were traveling and working outside the home more than ever before. They took steamboat trips that lasted five or six days, stayed at hotels, and waited overnight for connections at railroad stations. Teachers and mill girls spent long days at work with no chance to return home and clean up. All these women were wearing long dresses, often with petticoats and corsets. Each one of them must have had a personal strategy for making napkins, keeping them secure, disposing of them, and replacing them. Did some of them invent makeshift tampons? Did they simply throw the used linens away, or did they retain them in some way for washing? It was a topic that was simply not discussed in polite society, and the women themselves are utterly silent, even in letters to friends and private journals. At the very end of the nineteenth century, fifteen-year-old Lou Henry, the future wife of President Herbert Hoover, wrote in her diary that she had been excused from gym class that day "for reasons best known to myself."

## "BEAT IT THREE QUARTERS OF AN HOUR"

By 1850, the vast majority of homes in the settled parts of the country used stoves for both heating and cooking. Traditionalists bemoaned the loss of the blazing fireplace and questioned whether their forefathers would have fought the Revolutionary War for a hearthless homestead. Nostalgic writers claimed cooking always tasted better when it was done over a fireplace. "To be sweet, nutritious and delightful to the palate, a roast must be cooked in the open air," claimed the author of *Eighty Years of Progress in the United States* in 1861. But coal-burning stoves definitely made life easier for the men of the house, who were beginning to have trouble finding firewood in the areas around long-settled communities. The entire family benefited from heat that actually circulated through the room, instead of simply singeing the person closest to the blaze.

However, the stoves actually compounded the housewife's cooking chores. Women who were used to preparing dinner by hanging a single pot over the hearth now had an oven and as many as six or ten plates on the top for boiling, simmering, and frying. Their families eventually came to expect five or six different dishes at dinner, and more if guests dropped by. In her recipe book, Catharine Beecher described a dinner that an American housewife might whip up for ten to twelve people: soup, fish, a boiled ham, a boiled turkey with oyster sauce, three roasted ducks, scalloped oysters, potatoes, parsnips, turnips, and celery. And for dessert: pudding, pastry, fruit, and coffee. The days when a housewife could set up her kitchen with a few pans and a spit were long gone. Now there were corers and seeders for different types of vegetables and fruits, and special kettles just for making farina or porridge. In 1850, a Philadelphia hardware store stocked 250 kitchen tools. Each one seemed to introduce a new species of chore.

Baking was a special challenge. At a time when the eggbeater and baking powder had yet to arrive on the scene, when sugar was sold in loaves, confections required an enormous amount of effort to give them volume. "Take eight eggs, yolks and whites," instructed one recipe for a basic cake, "beat and strain them and put to them a pound of sugar beaten and sifted; beat it three quarters of an hour together." For much of this period, women did their beating with a simple fork or whisk. The arrival of the manual eggbeater must have been cause for national rejoicing.

The cast-iron stove, which made these recipes possible, was very temperamental. Martha Coffin Wright told a correspondent that she was finishing her letter when "whack! Went the stove equal to a cannon and now both windows are open to let out the smoke . . . Bang! Goes the *blamed* stove again. I had got all the smoke out and closed the windows and then raised the door to get the stove hot again—before it was too hot I shut it nearly down and it *chose* to puff." Stoves were hard to light, but for all their noise and smokiness, surprisingly delicate. They had to be cleaned every night and coated regularly with a black, waxy polish to keep them from rusting. Many of the most genteel families felt wrestling with the stove was a servant's job; the mistress of the house was perfectly helpless when left alone in the kitchen.

By 1830, about a quarter of all homes had parlor carpets. About one in five had a painting or engraving, and by the 1840s, when cheap lithographs became available, even poor people had pictures on the wall. Decorated pottery, too, became so inexpensive that almost anyone could acquire a few pieces of dinnerware with views of the Alps or the Roman Forum. A chair could be purchased for as little as 30 cents, which meant that humble families could entertain a number of friends at one time. By the 1830s, upholstered furniture started showing up in prosperous parlors, along with books, vases, plant stands, and pillows. All those extra obstacles to foot traffic may have increased the desire for better lighting; people were getting tired of stumbling around in the near dark. Most middle-class housewives were beginning to use oil lamps, which were cheaper than candles but got dirty quickly and had to be cleaned daily. Like the stove, they could be fragile and cranky. "Who has not, after long deliberation, purchased a set of expensive lamps only to suffocate himself or his friends with smoke?" asked Clarissa Packard in *Recollections of a Housekeeper*. "Who has not heard his glass shades pop one after another, with a report as harassing as the small arms of an enemy?" By the 1830s, a few big cities had introduced gas service to residential areas, and although it was far too expensive for poor families, the affluent began putting in fixtures immediately. That was a huge transformation. With gas lights, families could sit together and read or work without straining their eyes. There was less danger of people setting fire to themselves while reading in bed.

But the brighter light made it easier to see household dirt, and things got dirty very fast in the nineteenth century—with soot from the fireplaces and stoves, and mud that arrived from the unpaved streets. ("It is all shoreless tideless hopeless unmitigated mud here," Harriet Beecher Stowe wrote from Cincinnati in the spring of 1849. "Mud without hope or end—dreadful to look upon & like the Egyptian frogs it comes into our houses to our bed chambers & kneading troughs.") Insects swarmed in during warm weather—the window screen was another household necessity that was still waiting to be invented. Women who wanted to keep bugs off the food when they served dinner had to cover each dish. Writing to her sister-in-law from Detroit in 1853, Lavinia Stuart said the flies had driven her almost mad, and her face felt "as if some unseen spirit was sticking needles into it."

Cleanliness was a sign not only of good housekeeping but also of social status, and women became somewhat fanatic about it. The first brooms were sold commercially in 1798, and by 1840 Americans were buying two million of them every year. In the spring, ambitious housewives embarked on the annual big cleaning, which sometimes took a month or more. They took up the carpets and beat them, then mended the worn spots. They polished glasses—the invention of molded glass had made glassware cheap for the first time. They aired out rooms, scrubbed down floors, and dusted the books and artifacts. Nobody seemed to enjoy spring cleaning, or any other part of house-work, very much. Everyone complained about inept servants; the brides of the era often had very little in the way of domestic skills. Young couples sometimes avoided housekeeping by moving into a residential hotel. In Chicago in 1844, one person in six listed in the city directory was living in a hotel, and another one in four in a boarding-house.

## "CHILDREN ARE KILLED BY THE MANNER IN WHICH THEY ARE DRESSED"

One theme that showed up perpetually in the women's literature of the nineteenth century was infant death. Fanny Fern's *Fern Leaves from Fanny's Portfolio* had twelve different children dying off in twelve different short stories, and of the six stories in Lydia Sigourney's *The Young Lady's Offering,* five closed with a funeral procession. Magazines were packed with stories like "Agnes and the Key of Her Little Coffin," or "The Empty Crib," in which saintly children die in the most inspiring manner conceivable. When she was five, Helen Hunt, the future novelist, received a gift subscription to *Youth's Companion,* a magazine that included in every issue at least one story about the death of a small child, who departed this vale of tears in greatest piety.

Although Americans were more likely to live to adulthood than ever before, childhood death was still common, and people found comfort in the thought that it was actually a triumphant passage into a better life in heaven. (Harriet Beecher Stowe had been mourning the death of her own small son from cholera when she created the ultimate saintly dying child, Little Eva.) Medicine was not much further along than it had been in the colonial era. The difference was that now it was the mother, not God, who society held accountable if anything happened to the baby. One physician announced that most infant mortality stemmed from "ignorance and false pride of the mothers. Children are killed by the manner in which they are dressed, and by the food that is given them as much as any other cause." It must have been terrifying for young wives who lived in the mobile, urban society that didn't provide them with neighborhood women to turn to in time of trouble. Their husbands were gone most of the time, and they didn't have telephones to connect them with the rest of the world. Everybody knew dozens of stories of infants who died, suddenly and mysteriously, or thriving toddlers who woke up with a fever and passed away before nightfall. The mother had no clear weapons against the danger except her manuals, the leeches, and the newer medical potions that probably did more harm than good.

One happy result was a new concern for keeping youngsters clean. The habit of letting wet diapers dry without washing them faded away. Swaddling was also abolished in favor of clean, loose clothes that the modern mother could wash. But some Puritan childrearing influences were slow to die. The influential Dr. William Dewees, in his 1826 *Treatise on the Physical and Medical Treatment of Children,* set a goal of toilet training by one month. And parents were increasingly likely to drug their children. An 1833 guide used by southern women suggested daily doses of laudanum, an opium derivative—four drops for a nine-month-old and five to six drops for a toddler.

Motherhood was not only woman's highest calling, it was an obsession in a period that was trying to redefine the relationship between parent and child, rejecting the Calvinist theories about babies being born sinful and in need of correction. People began to believe that children were born unsullied innocents. And since they spent their formative years under maternal supervision, it was probably the mother's fault if they went astray. Women's magazines made a fetish of celebrating George Washington's mother, who had managed to produce the perfect American son. It was an ironic choice, since Washington had found her a most unsatisfactory parent and avoided visiting her whenever possible.

## "FADED AT TWENTY-THREE"

Visitors to America were struck by how quickly women seemed to age. "As the principal cause of the sudden decline, some allege the climate," wrote a visitor. "But I ascribe it more willingly to the great assiduity with which American ladies discharge their duties as mothers. No sooner are they married than they begin to lead a life of comparative seclusion, and once mothers, they are buried from the world."

If American mothers failed to force their daughters to learn the domestic skills they'd need as wives, it was probably because they understood how very sweet, and short, the life of an unmarried young woman could be. Daughters, who had the least status and freedom of any family member during most of the colonial period, were liberated in the nineteenth century. A Spaniard, Domingo Sarmiento, wrote in 1847 that Americans had developed methods of treating well-bred young girls "which have no parallel and which are unprecedented on this earth. The unmarried woman . . . is as free as a butterfly until marriage. She travels alone, wanders about the streets of the city, carries on several chaste and public love affairs under the indifferent eyes of her parents, receives visits from persons who have not been presented to her family, and returns home from a dance at two o'clock in the morning accompanied by the young man with whom she has waltzed or polkaed exclusively all night."

Alexis De Toqueville, who felt that "nowhere are young women surrendered so early or so completely to their own guidance," was also astounded at how fast the door shut after marriage. "In America, the independence of women is irrecoverably lost in the bonds of matrimony," he wrote. "If an unmarried woman is less constrained there than elsewhere, a wife is subjected to strict obligations. The former makes her father's house an abode of freedom and pleasure; the latter lives in the home of her husband as if it were a cloister." Another visitor, Moreau de St. Mèry, who found American women "charming and adorable at fifteen . . . faded at twenty-three, old at thirty-five, decrepit at forty," was amazed by women's "universal eagerness to be married, to become wives who will for the most part be nothing but housekeepers."

The thought was occurring to a number of American women, too. The percentage of nonimmigrant women who never married was beginning to rise, and although it would get much higher later in the century, women were no longer all seeing spinsterhood as the worst possible fate. In the 1840s, the Young Ladies Association of Oberlin College conducted debates on the topic "Is married life more conducive to a woman's happiness than single?" Magazines urged women not to marry for money or social position, and they depicted maiden ladies positively, although perhaps somewhat depressingly, as unselfish beings who dedicated their lives to others. "Better single than miserably married" was one of the aphorisms of the era, and heroines in novels declared they would remain alone rather than marry a man they didn't love and respect. But as a reward for their solid values, the right suitor always showed up in the end.

Some places seemed to produce bumper crops of spinsters. An estimated 40 percent of the Quaker women in pre–Civil War Philadelphia never married, and one western New York city in 1855 had a 17 percent rate of spinsterhood. Massachusetts had almost twice as many unwed women as the nation in general. In 1850, the governor of Massachusetts worried about the 30,000 "surplus" women in his state and suggested shipping them to Oregon or California, where there were plenty of bachelors. But the legislature disagreed, citing the economic impact: "The whirring music of millions of spindles would be silent as a sepulcher, while the mistresses of more than 100,000 dwellings would be in consternation from the catastrophe of such a withdrawal of 1, 2, or 3 or more domestics from their premises."

# African American Women:
# Life in Bondage

### "THE WOMEN WERE THE PLUCKIEST"

Most American slaves came from West Africa, where women frequently worked as both farmers and merchants. In fact, outsiders had the impression that the women did pretty much everything that needed to be done. "They are the ones who work the fields, and plant the crops, and the houses in which they live, even though small, are clean and bright," wrote a Portuguese man who lived in West Africa in the late seventeenth century. Perhaps their usefulness was one of the reasons that white slave traders found it easier to acquire male captives. "Women are scarce," reported the English captain of a slave ship that arrived in the colonies with three men for every woman.

A slave ship took anywhere from three weeks to three months to cross the Atlantic from West Africa. By various estimates, somewhere between one-sixth and two-thirds of the Africans died along the way. Suicides were common. One ship, acquiring slaves in Angola, was preparing for departure when eighteen of the women flung themselves into the ocean. The men spent the voyage chained together in the hold, packed so tight they could not sit upright, lying in their own body wastes. Sometimes the women fared better and were allowed to spend time on deck with the children. Occasionally, they used their liberty to help stage rebellions. In 1721, an African woman stole weapons and served as lookout for two male slaves who attempted to take over the slave ship *Robert*. On another boat in 1785, the captain said he had been attacked by a group of women who tried to toss him overboard. When they were overpowered, some of the women threw themselves to their death down the hatchway, and others starved themselves. Edward Manning, a sailor on an American slave ship, had a low opinion of the male Africans his ship picked up. "The women were the pluckiest," he said, "and had they all been of that sex we should probably have had a mutiny on board before the ship had been at sea two weeks."

When the slave ships arrived in America, the new country seemed so strange to the captives that some were convinced they had been taken by cannibals and were doomed to be eaten. Most of the early slaves faced lives of terrible isolation—only one in ten wound up in households with other Africans to talk to. Some embarked on a lifetime of passive resistance. Samuel Hall, a former slave, remembered that his mother, who had been captured in Liberia, "would never work after she was sold into slavery but pined away, never even learning the language of the people of this country."

## "I NEVER SEE HOW MY MAMMY STAND SUCH HARD WORK"

The first African Americans were free, and there were always sizable communities of free blacks in towns along the Atlantic seaboard. By the late 1700s in the North, black women had begun starting schools and organizing clubs that sponsored social welfare programs. Katy Ferguson, who became the nation's first black female educator, was herself illiterate but possessed a determination to help New York City's poor children. Ferguson, a slave whose own children had died in infancy, purchased her freedom in 1793. She used the money she made by catering parties for wealthy white families to establish New York's first Sunday school and classes in reading and writing. She also offered adoption services for homeless children, white and black, taking forty-eight of those waifs into her own home.

But soon the bulk of the American black population was composed of slaves in the southern states. By the mid-nineteenth century, there were nearly 4 million. The vast majority, including about 80 percent of the women, worked in the fields, plowing, hoeing, planting and picking crops. They worked up to fourteen hours a day, and perhaps sixteen hours at harvest time. The women did the same jobs as the men, using heavy iron tools to hoe and in some cases steering the bulky wooden plows, controlling the mules or oxen that pulled them. The elderly, children, and pregnant women were put on "trash gangs" that did weeding and cleaning chores. Those were the only work units that female slaves were ever chosen to lead.

Slave owners expected women to do three-quarters of the fieldwork a man could do, but some did much more. At a time when a reasonably productive male slave picked about 200 pounds of cotton a day, Susan Mabry of Virginia could pick 400 to 500. Some plantation records list a female slave as the best picker. But even though both sexes worked together in the fields, the men did not share much in the family housework. "The women plowed just like the men," remembered former slave Henry Baker. "On Wednesday night they had to wash and after they washed they had to cook supper. The next morning they would get up with the men and they had to cook breakfast before they went to the field and had to cook [the noon meal] at the same time and take it with them." Men hunted for game and tilled the family garden, but even small boys were generally excused from cooking, cleaning, or washing chores.

In addition to the fieldwork, many planters required women to do a quota of spinning or weaving before they went to bed. They worked as a group, with the children helping to card the wool. Bob Ellis, whose mother was head spinner on a Virginia plantation, said that as the other slaves worked, she walked around checking progress, singing "Keep your eyes on the sun. See how she run. Don't let her catch you with your work undone." The point, Ellis said, was to make the women finish before dark because it was "mighty hard handling that cotton thread by firelight." Fannie Moore held the light for her mother to see while she made quilts. Sometimes, she said, her mother sewed through the night: "I never see how my mammy stand such hard work."

During her working life, a female slave spent much of her time pregnant, and most owners put a high value on good "breeders." Thomas Jefferson wrote: "A child raised every two years is of more profit than the crop of the best laboring man . . . what she produces is an addition to capital." The *Plantation Manual* advised readers to encourage reproduction by giving every woman "with six children alive" all their Saturdays off. Major Wallon, a plantation owner, offered every new mother a calico dress and a silver dollar. More important than the presents to many young women was the fact that if they became pregnant, they were much less likely to be sold away from their husbands and relatives.

## "I WANT TO BE IN HEAVEN SITTING DOWN"

On large plantations, only a small percentage of slaves worked as house servants. Although those jobs seemed on the surface to be more pleasant and higher in prestige, many women tried to avoid them, and some deliberately failed at their house chores in order to get back into the fields. Their impulses were similar to the ones that made young white women prefer even the more unpleasant types of factory work to domestic service. Housework meant being under the close watch of a mistress who had high expectations when it came to her family's comfort, and who might not know how to give clear directions. House slaves had no downtime—even their meals had to be grabbed on the run. When white people were in the room, they had to remain standing. (A spiritual from the era says, "I want to be in heaven sitting down.") Residents of the Big House even expected slaves to sleep at the foot of their beds, in case they wanted something during the night. Angelina Grimke said she knew of a black woman who had been married eleven years "and yet has never been allowed to sleep out of her mistress's chamber." The image of the slave lying at the foot of the bed like a dog sometimes was extended further. Some slaves reported that, as children, they were encouraged to sit under the table during dinner and beg scraps from their mistress.

Slaves were not permitted to learn to read or write. "If Marse catch a paper in your hand he sure whip you," recalled Ellen Betts, a former slave in Louisiana. "Marse don't allow no bright niggers around. If they act bright he sure sell them quick. He always say: 'Book learning don't raise no good sugarcane.' " Owners also feared, with some justi-fication, that slaves who became literate would forge passes that allowed their friends and relatives to escape. But despite all the obsta-cles, about 5 percent of the slaves learned how to read anyway. Some were taught by their owners. Others simply listened while their mas-ter's children learned their ABCs, and taught themselves. The idea of educating African Americans was so threatening in the South that even white women who taught free black children were sometimes arrested and a literate slave caught teaching others would generally be sold as punishment. Milla Granson learned to read from her master's children in Kentucky and then instructed other slaves. When she was sold to Mississippi, she taught in the middle of the night, and slaves who had worked all day in the field—and, if they were women, spent several more hours spinning thread—sat up half the night, struggling to learn.

## "IT WAS FREEDOM BEFORE
## SHE COME OUT OF THAT CAVE"

When female slaves were whipped, they were often stripped to the waist and tied to a tree, or from a rafter in the barn. Pregnant women were beaten, too. "They'd dig a hole in the ground and put their stom-ach in the hole and then beat them," recounted Anne Clark, a former slave. A woman's husband and children were helpless. "Husbands always went to the woods when they know the wives was due for a whipping," remembered Jordan Johnson. "But in the field they dare not leave. Had to stay there, not daring even [to] look like they didn't like it." Once, Johnson said, a slave named Annie Jones was working

in the same field with her husband while she was far along in a pregnancy. When she made a mistake and chopped down some young cotton plants, the overseer beat her until she fell to the ground screaming.
"And Charlie he just stood there hearing his wife scream and staring at
the sky, not daring to look at her or even say a word."

Leah Garrett remembered one man who hid his wife in the woods
when she was threatened with a beating. "He carried her to a cave and
hauled pine straw and put [it] in there for her to sleep on," she said.
"He fixed that cave up just like a house for her, put a stove in there and
run the pipe out through the ground into a swamp. . . . He sealed the
house with pine logs, made beds and tables out of pine poles, and they
lived in this cave seven years. During this time they had three children . . . and they was wild." Her husband, who stayed on the plantation, brought the woman food, Garrett said, and "it was freedom
before she come out of that cave for good."

That kind of active resistance was rare. Slaves who endured
repeated beatings often responded much like battered wives or abused
children. They lost confidence, became dependent on the judgments
of others, and sometimes identified with the very people who abused
them. Salomon Oliver, whose mother was beaten to death by white
overseers, concluded that she might have deserved it: "I guess sometimes she took advantage and tried to do things that maybe wasn't
right."


## "WE MADE THE GALS HOOPS OUT OF GRAPEVINES"

In the 1930s, Violet Guntharpe, an elderly South Carolinian, remembered being courted by her future husband when she was a fifteen-
year-old slave. "I glance at him one day at the pigpen when I was
slopping the hogs. I say, 'Mr. Guntharpe, you follows me night and
morning to this pigpen; do you happen to be in love with one of those
pigs?' . . . Thad didn't say nothing but just grin. Him took the slop
bucket out of my hand and look at it, all round it, put it upside down
on the ground, and set me on it. . . . Us carry on foolishness about the
little boar shoat pig and the little sow pig, then I squeal with laughter.

The slop bucket tipple over and I lost my seat. That ever remain the happiest minute of my eighty-two years."

Under slavery, African Americans led desperately constricted and frequently brutal existences. But ordinary life went on as well. For most, the average day was filled with couplings and quarreling, friendship and feuds, moments of silliness, acts of selfishness, and gestures of incredible kindness. They carved out their own worlds as best they could.

Plantation slaves typically lived in one-room cabins. Some were substantial, with plank floors raised well above the ground and solid chimneys. But many were as small as ten feet square, with dirt floors and no windows. Although some former slaves reminisced about the sturdy furniture their fathers made for the cabins, and visitors sometimes reported seeing homes that were well appointed and decorated with painted china or wall hangings, most had little but mattresses made of straw or moss, and some pots for cooking. Slaves often had plots of land where they gardened, although the work had to be done, as one recalled, "on moonlight nights and on a Saturday evening." Although visitors to Southern plantations often commented on the unwashed bodies and soiled clothes of the house servants, Southerners seldom said anything about their slaves' hygiene, and they may have regarded cleanliness as something reserved to the upper class. (When Fanny Kemble urged her husband's slaves to tidy their houses, they protested—probably with some accuracy—that they were already as clean as poor white households.) Certainly a woman who had spent twelve hours in the field and a few more spinning thread wouldn't want to do much heavy-duty scrubbing. But according to the oral histories taken from ex-slaves in the 1930s, many mothers struggled to wash the family clothes every weekend, and women told how, as young girls, they kept their best dress pressed with flowers and herbs so it would smell nice. A white Georgian recalled seeing, on Saturday nights, the roads filled with male slaves on their way to visit wives on other plantations, "each pedestrian or horseman bearing his bag of soiled clothes."

Women often obtained calico to make a special dress for parties and church—some owners doled out calico dresses to reward good performance, and it was one of the first things slave women bought if they made money by selling garden produce. Red, which was reserved for royalty in some parts of Africa, was a favorite color. "Sunday clothes was dyed red for the gals. . . . We made the gals hoops out of grapevines. They give us a dime, if they had one, for a set of hoops," recalled Gus Feaster of South Carolina. To stiffen their petticoats, girls starched them with hominy and water. Slaves tended to dress more carefully for church than the poor whites, and if they had to walk a long way to service, they carried their shoes to keep them clean.

Half the Southern slaves worked for small farmers, who lived in houses only slightly more impressive than the slave cabins on large plantations. White women on small Southern farms worked exceedingly hard, and when a farmer became prosperous enough to acquire a slave, his first purchase was often a woman to help his wife. "That sure was hard living there," recalled Mary Lindsay, who was the only slave of a poor white blacksmith. "I have to get up at three o'clock sometimes so I have time to water the horses and slop the hogs and feed the chickens and milk the cows, and then get back to the house and get the breakfast." A former slave in Nashville whose master hired her out to a working-class family said that she was required "to nurse, cook, chop in the fields, chop wood, bring water, wash, iron and in general just do everything." She was six years old at the time.

Besides the multitudinous chores, the lone slave was cut off from the community that was the one great source of comfort and support in a world where she was regarded as something less than fully human by the whites. Katie Phoenix, who was sold as a little girl to a solitary woman who had no other slaves, said she had no idea that she was a child until her mistress's granddaughter came for a visit. "I thought I was just littler, but as old as grown-ups. I didn't know people had grown up from children," she said.

Christmas was the biggest holiday of the year. "Slaves lived just for Christmas to come round," said Fannie Berry. "Start getting ready the first snowfall. Commence to saving nuts and apples, fixing up party clothes, snitching lace and beads from the big house. General celebrating time, you see, because husbands is coming home and families is getting united again. Husbands hurry on home to see the new babies. Everybody happy." On regular Saturday nights there were dances in the slave quarters or gatherings of young people who played kissing games. "Used to go over to the Saunders place for dancing," said Fannie Berry. "Must have been a hundred slaves over there, and they always had the best dances. . . . Gals always tried to fix up for partying, even if they ain't got nothing but a piece of ribbon to tie in their hair." Courtship rituals were much like those of other working-class Americans. Girls concerned themselves with their hair and dresses. "All week they wear the hair rolled up with cotton," said Amos Lincoln of Charleston. "Sunday come, they comb the hair out fine." Like white girls of the era, the young slaves felt eating in public was unladylike, and they ate at home before they went out to dinner. Men initiated a romantic pursuit, but the chain of approval necessary for courting a slave girl was more arduous than that of an upper-class heiress. "Couldn't spring up, grab a mule and ride to the next plantation without a pass," explained Andy Marion, a former slave who remembered the difficulties for men who couldn't find a desirable partner on their own plantation. "Suppose you get your master's consent to go? Look here, the girl's master's got to consent, the gal got to consent, the gal's daddy got to consent, the gal's mammy got to consent. It was a hell of a way!"

## "A CHANCE HERE THAT WOMEN HAVE NOWHERE ELSE"

It was not unusual for unwed girls to get pregnant, but they generally were married soon after, frequently to their child's father. Most slave communities did not think that premarital sex was immoral, although they vigorously disapproved of adultery. Slave women, the well-to-do Virginian Mary Chesnut wrote somewhat enviously, "have a chance here that women have nowhere else. They can redeem themselves—the 'impropers' can. They can marry decently and nothing is remembered against these colored ladies." This attitude toward premarital sex was probably carried from Africa, where a woman who had demonstrated her fertility was seen as a more valuable marriage partner than an untested virgin. But as African Americans converted to Christianity, the standards for sexual behavior changed in some communities. Priscilla McCullough, who had been a slave in Darien, Georgia, said that sexually active girls were sometimes "put on the banjo. . . . When they play that night they sing about that girl and they tell all about her. That's putting on the banjo. Then everybody know and that girl she better change."

Slaves were not allowed to marry legally, but they almost always celebrated their union with a ceremony. Many preferred religious services—as many as two-fifths of the Episcopalian weddings in the Confederate states in the year before the war involved slaves. But the ministers never said "what God has joined together, let no man put asunder." The white owner could sunder a marriage with the wave of a pen, and in the eyes of the law, slaves could no more marry than they could go to court, own property, or control their children's fate. One black preacher in Kentucky, in a stroke of realism, told his brides and grooms that they were married "until death or distance do you part."

Sometimes an owner underwrote the wedding of a favored slave, including a feast for the entire plantation. "We was married on the front porch of the big house," recalled Temple Durham, a former slave in North Carolina. ". . . Miss Betsy had Georgianna, the cook, to bake a big wedding cake all iced up white as snow with a bride and groom standing in the middle holding hands. . . . I had on a white dress, white shoes and long white gloves that come to my elbow, and Miss Betsy done made me a wedding veil out of a white net window curtain. When she played the wedding march on the piano, me and Exter marched down the walk and up on the porch to the altar Miss Betsy done fixed. . . . Exter done made me a wedding ring. He made it out of a big red button with his pocket knife. He done cut it so round and polished it so smooth that it looked like a red satin ribbon tied around my finger." Temple and her husband retired to a cabin that had been fixed up for the wedding night, but the next day he had to return to his own plantation. "But he come back every Saturday night," she said. "We had 11 children."

On plantations where the white people were not interested in their slaves' personal affairs, the bride and groom could seek out a wise elder, usually a woman, to perform the ceremony. Often, husband and wife sealed their union by jumping over a broomstick—a ritual that some poor southern whites followed as well. "Didn't have to ask Marsa or nothing," said Caroline Johnson Harris. "Just go to Aunt Sue and tell her you want to get married." When Harris and her intended went, Aunt Sue sent them home to think hard about it. "After two days Mose and I went back and say we done thought about it and still want to get married. Then she called all the slaves after tasks to pray for the union that God was gonna make. Pray we stay together and have lots of children and none of them get sold away from the parents. Then she lay a broomstick across the sill of the house we gonna live in and join our hands together. Before we step over it she asked us once more if we was sure we wanted to get married. Of course we say yes. Then she say, 'In the eyes of Jesus step into Holy land of matrimony.' When we step across the broomstick, we was married."

Most slaves married and stayed married to the same person all their lives. But husbands were often a fleeting presence, living on another plantation, arriving on Saturday night and leaving the next evening. Hannah Chapman remembered that her father sometimes snuck an extra visit during the week. "Us would gather round him and crawl up in his lap, tickled slap to death, but he give us these pleasures at a painful risk," she said. Sometimes her father was discovered by the "patrollers"—working-class whites who made extra money watching for slaves who were out at night without permission. When the patrollers caught her father, Chapman said, "us would track him the next day by the blood stains." In a sense, slave families were matriarchies in which the women were the only stable element. But fathers often made heroic efforts to stay involved in their children's lives. Mattie Jackson, a slave raised in Georgia, said her father and mother originally lived on neighboring plantations. When her mother's owner moved twenty miles away, her father continued his weekly visits "walking the distance every Saturday evening and returning Sunday evening." Charles Ingram ran away from his master and was living and working as a free man when his wife died and his sons were sold to Texas. Ingram gave himself up and voluntarily resumed life as a slave in order to take care of them.

## "THE GREATEST ORATOR I EVER HEARD WAS A WOMAN"

The threat of being sold hung over every family. On well-run plantations, slaves sometimes lived in housing that was better than the cabins of poor Southern whites or the tenements of Northern factory workers. And they probably had more food as well. But poor white Americans did not have to fear that their spouses, or children, would be taken away forever. Cornelius Garner, who had been a slave on a Virginia plantation, remembered times when the children would make too much noise on Sunday and disturb the people in the big house. "Finally, Old Master come clumping down to the quarters, pick out the family that got the most children and say: 'For God, nigger, I'm going to sell all them children of yours less you keep them quiet.' Everybody sure keep quiet after that." One historian estimated that over a typical slave woman's thirty-five-year life, she had a fifty-fifty chance of being sold at least once and would likely see the sale of several members of her immediate family. " 'Oh my mother! My mother!' I kept saying to myself. 'Oh my mammy and my sisters and my brothers, shall I never see you again!' " wrote Mary Prince, a former slave recalling the day she was sold away from her family. Sojourner Truth's parents woke up one morning to find their owners bundling their five-year-old son and three-year-old daughter into a sleigh and driving them off to sale. The boy attempted to escape by hiding under his parents' bed, but their owner dragged him out while his mother and father stood by, helpless. The episode haunted Truth's childhood. Years later she discovered that she and her lost sister Nancy had been attending the same church in New York City. But Nancy died before they could be reunited.

Slaves who were being separated from their families begged their new owners to purchase their spouse or children as well. John Randolph, the Virginia politician who had known all the Founding Fathers, was once asked to name the most moving speaker he had ever known. "The greatest orator I ever heard was a woman," he said. "She was a slave and a mother and her rostrum was an auction block." When Delcia Patterson of Missouri was fifteen years old, she was brought to the local courthouse to be sold. When a man she recognized as one of the cruelest owners in the county bid on her, "I spoke right out on the auction block and told him 'Old Judge Miller don't you bid for me, because if you do, I would not live on your plantation. I will take a knife and cut my own throat from ear to ear before I would be owned by you.' " She was successful in discouraging Judge Miller, but she also undid a plan of her father's, who had convinced his own master to bid on his daughter. "When father's owner heard what I said to Judge Miller, he told my father he would not buy me because I was sassy and he never owned a sassy nigger and did not want one that was sassy. That broke my father's heart."

Many slave owners disapproved of breaking up families, and some went to great lengths to keep them intact. William Massie of Virginia, who fell into financial difficulties, chose to sell his most cherished property rather than any of his slaves. "To know that my little family, white and *black*, is to be fixed permanently together would be as near that thing happiness as I ever expect to get," he wrote. "Elizabeth has raised and taught most of them, and having no children, like every other woman under like circumstances, has tender feelings toward them." But the death of a "good" master or mistress often broke up an estate and led to the sale of the human property. Wills ordering that families be left intact, or freed, were routinely ignored. Southern widows often discovered that their husbands had left them deeply in debt, forcing them to sell their slaves to pay creditors. On some plantations, when the owner died, it was the custom for his children to put the names of the slaves in a hat and draw for them.

As the younger sons of Southern planters moved west, they took their share of the family slaves with them. "One morning we is all herded up and mammy am crying and say they going to Texas but can't take papa," recalled Josephine Howard, whose father was owned by a different family. "That the lastest time we ever seed Pappa." Laura Clark remembered being taken off to the frontier by her master when she was a small girl and seeing her mother run after the wagon, fall down, and "roll over on the ground, just acryin'."

During the Civil War, when slaves began escaping behind Union lines, nearly 20 percent said they had lost a husband or wife by "force." Many went searching for their spouses, but the few who were successful often discovered that their old mate had remarried. "I love you just as well as I did the last time I saw you, and it will not do for you and I to meet. I am married and my wife have two children, and if you and I meets it would make a very dissatisfied family," wrote Laura Spicer's former husband in an anguished letter in which he begged her to find a new mate. In 1863, an ex-slave from Virginia who had been separated from her husband met him by accident in Norfolk. Both had remarried. "Twas like a stroke of death to me," she told a Yankee teacher. "We threw ourselves into each other's arms and cried. . . . White folks got a heap to answer for the way they've done to colored folks."

## "I WAS TOO YOUNG TO UNDERSTAND RIGHTLY MY CONDITION"

Slave women were actually less likely to die in childbirth than their mistresses—probably because they got a lot of exercise, did not wear corsets, and were spared the services of nineteenth-century physicians. But their infants died at twice the rate of white babies because of poor prenatal care and bad nutrition. More than a third died before age ten. Nursing mothers were usually sent back to the fields and allowed to leave a few times a day to tend their babies. The process of dashing back and forth was so exhausting that many infants were weaned prematurely. While their parents were in the field, slave children were tended by their siblings or elderly "grannies," who might be in charge of a dozen or more very small youngsters. Mothers sometimes came back to find their babies left lying in the sun, covered with flies or ants. The older children were cared for like a herd of livestock. Octavia

George, who had been a slave in Mississippi, said that while the mothers were in the field, children were "fed in boxes and troughs, under the house. They were fed corn meal mush and beans. When this was poured into their box they would gather around it the same as we see pigs, horses and cattle gather around troughs today."

Small boys and girls frequently played with white children, unaware of their different status. "This was the happiest period of my life; for I was too young to understand rightly my condition as a slave," wrote Mary Price. They played marbles, skipped rope, and pitched horseshoes. One ex-slave remembered holding make-believe auctions in which the children "sold" each other, taking pride in the high prices they imagined they might bring. But when white children began to learn to read, the black children went to work. Girls put on skirts and learned to light bedroom fires in the morning, make beds, polish shoes and silver, and carry food from the kitchen—which was usually separated from the house—to the dining room. They washed dishes, gathered eggs, and "minded flies" by brushing them from the white folk. Slave girls were sometimes assigned, at remarkably young ages, to care for white infants. Ellen Betts said that when she was a small eight-year-old, she was put in charge of babies "so big and fat I had to tote the feet while another girl tote the head." Leah Garrett said one of her relatives was forced to tend the master's grandchildren when she was very small. "The front steps was real high and one day this poor child fell down these steps with the baby," she said. When the master came home and heard what had happened, "he picked up a board and hit this poor child across the head and killed her right there."

Angelina Grimke remembered seeing slave children "kept the whole winter's evening, sitting on the stair-case in a cold entry, just to be at hand to snuff candles or hand a tumbler of water from the sideboard." Small children who tried to light fires, carry heavy loads down stairs, or peel vegetables with sharp knives were often injured. Even more frequently, they were beaten for falling asleep or stealing food. Young Henrietta King's face was crushed when her mistress stuck her head under a rocker as a punishment for stealing a piece of candy.

"She rock forward so as to hold my head and whip me some more," King told a historian decades later. "Seems like that rocker pressing on my young bones had crushed them all to a soft pulp. . . . And I ain't never growed no more teeth on that side. Ain't never been able to chew nothing good since. Don't even remember what it is to chew. Been eating liquid, stews and soup ever since that day, and that was 86 years ago."

## "A SAD EPOCH IN THE LIFE OF A SLAVE GIRL"

Fannie Berry treasured the memory of Sukie, a slave who worked in Petersburg, Virginia, as a cook. Sukie was making soap when her owner, a Mr. Abbott, tried to rape her. "She took and punched old marsa and made him break loose and then she gave him a shove and push his hindparts down in a hot pot of soap," Berry recalled. "Soap was near to boiling and it burned him near to death. He got up holding his hindparts and ran from the kitchen, not daring to yell because he didn't want [his wife] to know about it." Even though the story ends with Sukie being sold, it's hard not to wonder whether her perfect revenge actually happened, or whether the story really expresses what female slaves wished they could do to white men who forced their attentions on them.

Next to the sale of their children or spouse, rape was perhaps the worst nightmare of slavery. We have no way of knowing how often it happened. At the end of the Civil War, somewhere between 10 and 20 percent of the slaves were believed to be part white, but how many of those mixed bloodlines resulted from voluntary couplings, and how many women were assaulted without becoming pregnant is impossible to calculate. We do know that white women were haunted by the fear that their husbands, fathers, or sons were having sex with their slaves. And we know that black mothers nervously watched their daughters to protect them from dangers they could not understand. Harriet Jacobs, who was sexually harassed by her master, called puberty "a sad epoch in the life of a slave girl." Rather than warning their daughters against dangers they could not really avoid, mothers apparently preferred to shield girls from learning anything about sex at all for as long as possible. Anne Broome, a former slave from South Carolina, said she was ridiculed by her white playmates because she believed her mother's story that she had been delivered by a railroad train. "People was very particular in them days. They wouldn't let children know anything like they do now," said another.

A woman who tried to repulse her master risked a beating, but one who gave in risked antagonizing the mistress of the household. One ex-slave told the story of a white woman who "slipped in a colored gal's room and cut her baby's head clean off because it belonged to her husband." The white community tended to believe that every African American woman yearned "to bring a little mulatto into the world," but in fact many slave communities resented the half-white children who reminded them that black men were unable to protect their wives and daughters. Masters seldom acknowledged their illegitimate children. Annie Burton, an ex-slave, said that her mistress often told her that her father was a planter who owned a nearby estate. "Whenever my mistress saw him going by she would take me by the hand and run out upon the piazza and exclaim 'Stop there I say! Don't you want to see and speak to and caress your darling child?' " Her father would then "whip up his horse and get out of sight and hearing as quickly as possible."

A few white men stayed true to the slaves they had seduced. Thomas Foster, a married planter in Mississippi, had an affair with Susy, one of his slaves. When his wife tried to sell her off the estate, he abandoned his family and took Susy away. When Senator Richard Johnson of Kentucky was nominated to run as vice president in 1836, Southern delegates refused to ratify his selection because the unmarried Johnson lived openly with a slave named Julia, by whom he had two daughters. (Johnson's critics were less concerned about the liaison than about the rumors that Johnson had attempted to take the girls into society as if they were white.) But very few of these stories ended happily. In Mississippi shortly before the war, a Mr. Carter attempted to provide in his will for Harriet, his daughter by the family house slave. The girl was given over to the care of a neighbor who was paid to treat her "as a free white person." But Carter's heirs objected, and a judge ruled that Harriet should be sold along with the other slaves. The judge wrote: "The example of a Negro, or mulatto, brought up in the . . . style specified . . . would necessarily exert a most baleful influence upon the surrounding Negro population."

New Orleans had a "fancy girl" market in which young and beautiful—and light-skinned—female slaves were sold for very fancy prices. Simon Northrup, who wrote an account of his experiences as a slave, told a terrible story of meeting a woman named Eliza. She had been the concubine of a planter, who promised to free her and their son and daughter. He took them to New Orleans where Eliza believed the papers were to be executed. But instead, she and her children were sold—the small daughter to a man who predicted that in a few years someone would pay five thousand dollars "for such an extra, handsome, fancy piece as Emily would be."

## "IT'S ME, HARRIET. IT'S TIME TO GO NORTH."

Slave women were much less likely to run away than men. Black men who escaped from their masters in the colonial era often ran away to sea, where most ships had mixed-race crews and captains were not too careful about checking the background of a potential seaman. But that was not open to women. Later on, when slavery was abolished in northern states, men were usually the ones who attempted to make their way north to freedom while women stayed behind, unwilling to leave their families.

The most famous runaway slave, however, was a woman. Harriet Tubman, the granddaughter of Africans, was born on a plantation in Maryland where she worked in both the fields and house, although she preferred the relative freedom of fieldwork. When she was about thirteen, an impatient overseer accidentally fractured her skull with a heavy weight, leaving her subject to fits of narcolepsy throughout her life. But she developed unusual strength and stamina. In 1849, when she was about thirty years old, she heard rumors that she was about to be sold and escaped. Making her way to Philadelphia, she cleaned houses until she had enough saved to finance a return trip.

A year after her escape, a slave at her old plantation heard a noise at his cabin and saw a figure dressed like a man. "It's me, Harriet," the figure said. "It's time to go North." All in all, she made as many as nineteen trips over the border. In one, using a hired wagon, she retrieved her elderly parents. In another, she led eleven slaves to freedom. She continued going back to Maryland and shepherded more friends and relatives to the North—only her own husband, who had remarried, refused the offer of escape. She was expert at disguises, appearing as an old woman or a vagabond, or a mentally disturbed man. She carried paregoric to quiet crying babies, and if anyone showed signs of panicking, she ominously fingered the revolver she always carried. Maryland slaveholders offered a bounty of $40,000 for her capture.

Tubman was extraordinarily cool in a crisis. On one occasion, when she saw a former owner coming toward her, she turned loose several chickens at a market and pretended to be chasing after them as she scurried by unnoticed. Another time, when she realized she had been tracked to a railroad station, she calmly boarded a southbound train, guessing correctly that no one would suspect a black woman traveling deeper into slave territory. She usually began her expeditions on Saturday night, giving her an extra day before the aggrieved owner could advertise his loss in the Monday papers. "I was the conductor of the underground railroad for eight years and I can say what most conductors can't say—I never ran my train off the track and I never lost a passenger," she said.

When the Civil War began, Tubman left her home in Auburn, New York, and served as a spy and a scout for the Union Army, bringing back reports from black informants on the other side of the Confederate lines. "Col. Montgomery and his gallant band of 300 black soldiers, under the guidance of a black woman, dashed into the enemy's country, struck a bold and effective blow, destroying commissary, stores, cotton and lordly dwellings," stated a report at the time. After the war she married a Union veteran and lived on her

Auburn farm, where she took in orphans and old people who had no other homes. Harriet was "a woman of no pretensions, indeed a more ordinary specimen of humanity could hardly be found among the most unfortunate-looking farm hands of the South," wrote William Still, an African American leader in Philadelphia. "Yet in point of courage, shrewdness and disinterested exertions to rescue her fellow-man, she was without equal."

## "STOMP DOWN FREEDOM TODAY"

The slaves who lived closest to the battle lines during the Civil War were the most keenly aware of what was at stake. "The news went from plantation to plantation and while the slaves acted natural and some even more polite than usual they prayed for freedom," said Mary Anderson of North Carolina. "In a day or two every body on the plantation seemed to be disturbed and master and missus were crying. Master ordered all the slaves to come to the great house at nine o'clock. Nobody was working and slaves were walking over the grove in every direction. At nine o'clock all the slaves gathered at the great house and master and missus came out on the porch and stood side by side. You could hear a pin drop everything was so quiet. . . . Then master said, 'Men, women and children, you are free. You are no longer my slaves. The Yankees will be here soon.' "

After emancipation actually occurred, many slave communities took some time to come to grips with what had happened. "I remember the first Sunday of freedom," said Charlotte Brown. "We was all sitting around resting and trying to think what freedom meant and everybody was quiet and peaceful. All at once old Sister Carrie who was near about a hundred started in to talking:

> *'Taint no more sellin' today*
> *Taint no more hirin' today*
> *Taint no pullin' off shirts today,*
> *It's stomp down Freedom today.*
> *Stomp it down!'*

"And when she says 'Stomp it down' all the slaves commence to shouting with her:

> *'Stomp down Freedom today—*
> *Stomp it down,*
> *Stomp down Freedom today.'*

"Wasn't no more peace that Sunday. Everybody started in to sing and shout once more. First thing you know they done made up music to Sister Carrie's stomp song and sang and shouted that song all the rest of the day. Child, that was one glorious time!"

# 8

# Women and Abolition:
# White and Black, North and South

## ॐ THE NORTH ॐ

### "THEN LET IT SINK. I WILL NOT DISMISS HER."

Prudence Crandall came to Canterbury, Connecticut, as a career move. In 1831, the twenty-seven-year-old teacher was working in the town of Plainfield when the more upscale residents of Canterbury invited her to start a school for their daughters. Owning a school for young ladies of means was just about the pinnacle of achievement and financial security for a single woman in Crandall's class. She invested what money she had in a large, handsome house in the center of town and soon her "genteel female seminary" was an established success.

At that point, Sarah Harris applied. "A colored girl of respectability . . . called on me some time during the month of September and said, in a very earnest manner, 'Miss Crandall, I want to get a little more learning, enough if possible to teach colored children, and if you will admit me to your school, I shall be under the greatest obligation to you,' " the teacher remembered later. The girl's father, a farmer, was active in the antislavery movement, and she probably had a pretty well-informed idea of what local reaction to her enrollment might be.

"If you think it will be the means of injuring you," Sarah added, "I will not insist on the favor."

Crandall was a Quaker, who opposed slavery and believed in educating freed blacks. She was also capable of being extremely hard-headed—when the Canterbury proposal first came up, her brother worried how long Prudence could manage to stay on the good side of her students' self-important parents. But the school was her home and her income, and she hesitated for a while before finally agreeing.

Sarah Harris had gone to the local public school and had attended classes there with some of the students in Crandall's much superior establishment. She probably hoped that as a known quantity, she would be accepted without much fuss. "There could not have been a more unexceptionable person than Sarah Harris, save her complexion," wrote Samuel Joseph May, one of Crandall's loyal supporters. But once word spread, it became obvious that people weren't going to cooperate. A delegation of women, led by the Episcopalian minister's wife, warned that unless the black girl was sent away, the school would be ruined. "Then let it sink. I will not dismiss her," Prudence retorted. Pressed against the wall, her response was true to type and bore out all her brother's worries about her stubbornness. When the white students threatened to leave, she decided to start a school for African American girls—or, as she advertised in *The Liberator,* "for young Ladies and little Misses of color." The curriculum would be the same as before, including the teas and piano recitals.

The idea of young black women being educated in a manner appropriate for upper-class whites enraged people further. Catharine Beecher thought it was terrible and the *Norwich Republican* accused Crandall of trying "to foist upon the community a new species of gentility, in the shape of sable belles . . . to cook up a palatable morsel for our white bachelors. . . . In a word, they hope to force the two races to amalgamate." The fear of mixed marriages was the greatest of white anxieties, but when one of her neighbors brought it up to Crandall, she retorted: "Moses had a black wife."

A town meeting, led by Andrew Judson, a lawyer, politician, and Crandall's next-door neighbor, warned the school would "collect

within the town of Canterbury large numbers of persons from other
States whose characters and habits might be various and unknown to
us, thereby rendering insecure the persons, property and reputation of
our citizens." As a woman, Crandall was not permitted to attend the
gathering. Her male representatives, who came bearing an offer to
move the school to a less conspicuous spot in town, were not allowed
to speak and were met with "fists doubled in our faces."

Meanwhile, fifteen very brave African American students arrived
in April 1833. They came from Philadelphia and New York and
Boston as well as Connecticut. Some were the daughters of slaves.
One, whose mother was too poor to pay the $25-per-quarter tuition,
was supported by another woman, a childless ex-slave who had saved
up the money by working as a servant. The ride in on the stagecoach
gave the girls some idea of what they would be up against. One was
dumped off at a town six miles from Canterbury. She shouldered her
baggage and walked.

The local shops refused to sell food to the school. The village doctor and druggist boycotted Crandall's students. Someone threw
manure into the well and smashed the school windows. When the girls
went out to take their daily walk, people blew horns, fired pistols, and
threw chicken heads at them. Town officials arrested a seventeen-year-
old student from out of state on vagrancy laws and were threatening
to whip her "on the naked body" when supporters arrived to put up
bond for her release. On May 24, the Connecticut state legislature
passed a "Black Law" making it illegal to establish a school for the
instruction of out-of-state black children. "Joy and exultation ran wild
in Canterbury," wrote one of Crandall's students. "The bell rang and
a cannon was fired for half an hour. Where is the justice? In the midst
of all this Miss Crandall is unmoved."

A month later, Prudence Crandall was arrested. "I am only afraid
they will not put me in jail," she told her supporters. She slept in a cell
whose former occupant had been a murderer before she would allow
her supporters to post bail. She went on trial in August, with the prosecution led by her neighbor Andrew Judson. Despite the judge's obvious
prejudice against the school, the jury could not reach an agreement.

But a second panel, after having been instructed by the judge that free African Americans were not actually citizens, convicted her of violating the Black Law. While Crandall appealed, her school went on. Abolitionists from around the world began visiting Canterbury to deliver presents and support.

But there were signs that the Quaker schoolmistress was beginning to falter. Most notably, she became engaged to a visiting minister who her friends regarded as dubious husband material. She may have realized, deep down, that her position was hopeless and reached out to matrimony as a lifeline. After an appeals court threw out her conviction on technical grounds, Canterbury citizens slit the neck of a cat and hung it on the school gate, then tried to set the building on fire. In the middle of the night on September 9, 1834, men smashed the school's downstairs windows with clubs and iron bars. While the girls huddled upstairs in terror, the mob destroyed the house beneath them. Crandall's own wavering confidence infected the students, who already had good reason to wish they were someplace else. They returned to their homes, and the school was closed for good.

The short-term finale to Crandall's story is not particularly cheerful. She had, indeed, married the wrong man. Much later, she said he "would not let me read the books that he himself read." (Prudence-like, she read them anyway.) When he died, she moved to Kansas where her brother had a farm. A regiment of black Union soldiers discovered her living in poverty and raised a fund to present to her. "My whole life has been one of opposition," she told an interviewer in 1886. "I never could find anyone near me to agree with me."

But over the long run, there was a happy ending. Sarah Harris did become a teacher, as did some of the other girls who endured that traumatic time in Canterbury. After the war, Connecticut voted to give its black citizens the right to vote, with Canterbury's Windham County leading the way. Crandall had not been able to carry through her plan to educate young black women, but as her old friend Samuel May said, she had been successful in teaching her neighbors. The state legislature repealed the Black Law and voted to give Crandall a pension for life, "mindful of the dark blot that rests upon our fair fame and name, for the cruel outrages inflicted upon a former citizen of our Commonwealth." One of the first signatures on the resolution was that of Andrew Judson's nephew. While her opponents have faded into total obscurity, remembered only in their role of villains in this story, Prudence Crandall is one of the heroes of Connecticut history. And the big house in the middle of Canterbury is now a museum and a National Historic Landmark.

## "WE ABOLITION WOMEN ARE TURNING THE WORLD UPSIDE DOWN"

Slavery became the all-consuming political question between 1830 and the Civil War. But it was a moral issue, too, and a number of Northern women felt they had an obligation to fight an institution that broke up families and subjected young women to sexual molestation. Abolition of slavery was different from other reform movements, partly because it drew women so clearly into politics, and partly because it drew them so near to genuine violence. Between 1834 and 1837, there were at least 157 anti-abolition mob actions in the North, and Prudence Crandall was far from the only stubborn woman who stood up against her angry neighbors. Speaking against slavery in a Maine church, Ellen Smith encountered an audience that responded by "howling, stamping, kicking, slamming . . . pew doors, and pounding . . . the pews with their fists." Boys threw hymn books at her. When the abolitionist William Lloyd Garrison—always a lightning rod—attempted to speak before a racially mixed group of women in Boston, the mayor begged the audience to disperse rather than incite a riot. The ladies declined. "If this is the last bulwark of freedom, we may as well die here as anywhere," said Maria Weston Chapman, the wife of a wealthy merchant. She eventually led the audience out through the angry mob, in pairs, black and white together.

The antislavery movement did a lot to liberate its female members as well as the slaves. (One Boston volunteer called the times "distressing and exciting.") Northern society was still deep in the era of Catharine Beecher and the cult of domesticity, yet abolitionist women were not only signing petitions and going to political meetings, they also began speaking in public, to mixed audiences.

"Confusion has seized us and all things go wrong," wrote Maria Chapman mischievously.

> *The women have leaped from "their spheres."*
> *And instead of fixed stars, shoot as comets along,*
> *And are setting the world by the ears!*
> *. . . . . . . . . . . . . . . . .*
> *They've taken the notion to speak for themselves,*
> *And are wielding the tongue and the pen;*
> *They've mounted the rostrum, the termagent elves!*
> *And—oh horrid!—are talking to men!*

The first female antislavery lecturers were Angelina and Sarah Grimke of South Carolina. Their family was part of the slaveholding elite, and even though many of its members were high achievers, it's still a mystery how the Grimkes produced such a unique pair of women. Virtually everything the sisters did was a first, unprecedented. Yet they seemed utterly unself-conscious, almost oblivious to their notoriety. Sarah, the older, was four when she accidentally witnessed the whipping of a slave, and the sight upset her so much that her nurse found her on the wharves, asking a ship's captain to take her to a place where such things never happened. "Slavery was a millstone around my neck," Sarah wrote later, "and marred my comfort from the time I can remember." After her father died she flouted every convention of the South, where it was unacceptable for women to even travel alone, and moved to Philadelphia to live independently. Her family tried to avoid gossip by announcing they were sending Sarah on a trip for her health.

In an age when women were supposed to be hypersensitive to the demands of social decorum, the Grimkes, earnest, humorless, and kindly, always seemed able to follow their own stars. In 1834, Angelina, who had followed her sister north, published *Appeal to the Christian Women of the Southern States*. In it, she urged Southern women to persuade their husbands and fathers "that slavery is a crime against God and man," and to free, or at least educate, any slaves they owned. It was the only such document a white Southern woman would ever write, but its intended audience probably never saw it, since it was burned whenever it reached a Southern post office and Angelina was barred from ever returning to Charleston.

Sarah and Angelina had been conducting "parlor talks" with Northern women interested in the slavery issue, and the American Anti-Slavery Society offered them jobs as the first female abolitionist lecturers in the United States. Soon they began speaking in churches, although friends warned them that lecturing before large groups would be seen as a "Fanny Wright affair." But the Grimkes managed much better than Wright, possibly because of their impeccable personal lives and their high moral tone. Both men and women wanted to hear the Southern slaveholders turned abolitionists, so the organizers began opening the meetings to everyone. Angelina was the more gifted speaker, and Sarah, who tended to be rather flat and to lose track of the time while she was talking, adopted the role of helper and backup. The sisters spoke at five to six meetings a week, each in a different town, traveling by stage, horseback, or wagon. They frequently had to skip meals and take their nourishment at the tea parties their admirers expected them to attend at every stop. The halls were almost always stuffy, and very crowded. At Worcester, they lectured to more than 1,000 people while hundreds of others stood outside. In Woonsocket Falls, the beams of the gallery began to crack under the crowd, and when no one would leave, Sarah had to close the meeting.

The speaking tour ended when Angelina contracted typhoid fever. During her recovery, she fell in love with Theodore Weld, a dashing antislavery lecturer who had encouraged her speaking career. Friends did not expect much from the relationship, since Weld had pledged not to marry until slavery was abolished. But after a long, intellectual correspondence that dwelt mainly on things like religion and the importance of logical inquiry, Weld suddenly declared that "for a long time you *have had my whole heart.*" Angelina responded characteristically, in a letter that first rapturously announced they were "two bodies animated by one soul" and then swerved into a discussion of her plans to address the Massachusetts state legislature. In February 1838, Angelina submitted antislavery petitions to the Massachusetts House committee, and became the first woman ever to speak before a legislative hearing. She talked for two hours and then returned two days later to continue her remarks. At the second appearance, the room was so packed that she was asked to stand at the Speaker of the House's lectern so the crowd could have a better look at her. Sarah, meanwhile, was seated in the Speaker's chair. "We abolition women are turning the world upside down," Angelina told her.

Three months later, the first American woman to address a legislative body became the first American advocate of women's rights to marry. Angelina had become as vocal about the subjugation of women as she was about slaves, and her supporters were thrilled by this demonstration that a woman who believed in female equality could nonetheless find a husband. The day after the wedding ceremony—at which nobody promised to obey and Theodore denounced the laws that gave husbands control over their wives' property—they went to Pennsylvania Hall for the Women's Anti-Slavery Convention.

Pennsylvania Hall was a handsome new building the Philadelphia reformers had built at great expense to make sure they would have a place for their lectures and meetings. That evening, William Lloyd Garrison spoke to 3,000 abolitionists while a large, noisy crowd milled around outside. As Angelina was introduced, bricks crashed through the windows. Nevertheless, the new bride lectured for over an hour through the noise and the shower of stones and glass. The abolitionists survived their encounter with the Philadelphia mob, but their proud new meeting hall didn't. The rioters burned it to the ground.

Angelina and her husband invited Sarah to live with them, and the Grimke sisters settled down to housekeeping, determined to show that women with "well regulated minds" were not "ruined as domestic characters." Still, it was a good thing that Weld was as committed to Spartan living and good works as his wife and sister-in-law. Angelina and Sarah were fervent believers in the health reform movements of the era and adopted the diet of Sylvester Graham, which prohibited meat, butter, and cheese. They also continued to boycott slave-labor products like sugar, tea, coffee, and spices. They cooked hot food only once a week and served their bemused guests rice and molasses for dinner, and breakfasts of raw apples and cold water. Angelina gave birth to the first of three children in 1839 and was ever after something of an invalid. Sarah told a friend that her sister's problem was a fallen uterus, so severe that it sometimes protruded from her body, causing great pain.

The sisters and Theodore founded a progressive boarding school, where gray-haired Angelina, clad in her bloomer costume, served meals in the chilly community hall. Despite their meager income, they entertained an exhaustive number of guests. They also supported a swarm of relatives and some ex-Grimke slaves, one of whom was afflicted with fits and a bad temper. In 1868, the sisters discovered they had black nephews, the sons of their brother Henry, who as a widower had been engaged in a long secret relationship with a slave named Nancy. (When he died, Henry directed his son and heir, Montague, to care for Nancy and her children as members of the family. Montague ignored the will and appropriated the boys—his half-brothers—as his servants.) Sarah and Angelina welcomed the young men into the family and paid for their college education. With their aunts' help, Archibald Henry Grimke graduated from Harvard Law School and became a leader in the National Association for the Advancement of Colored People, while Francis James Grimke graduated from Princeton Theological Seminary and became a prominent Washington minister.

The Graham diet must have worked, for the Grimke sisters lived on far beyond the Civil War era. At age seventy-nine, Sarah was still marching up and down the countryside, selling copies of John Stuart Mill's *Subjection of Women.* In March 1870, an election day, suffrage supporters decided that a few brave women would attempt to vote, in the first of what would later become many thousands of such demonstrations. A fierce snowstorm arrived with the election, but forty-two women and their male escorts formed a procession and marched to the polling place amid jeers of the townspeople. At the head of the procession, first of the first pioneers, were Angelina and Sarah Grimke.

## "PUTTING THEM ON AN EQUALITY
## WITH OURSELVES"

In 1833, Lydia Maria Child, of frugal-housewife fame, wrote *An Appeal in Favor of That Class of Americans Called Africans*. One of the first antislavery books to be published in America, it was also one of the boldest, arguing that the races should be able to mix freely when traveling, at the theater, in church, and when choosing marital partners. It shocked her traditional readers, and while she continued to write, the general public never again snapped up her books as they had before. "Her fine genius, her soul's wealth has been wasted," mourned Sarah Hale of *Godey's*. (Hale's magazine managed to ignore not only the abolition issue but also the entire Civil War.)

Child, along with the Grimke sisters, was unusual even among abolitionists in her belief in integration and the equality of the races. The Northern women who worked for abolition were generally not free of racial prejudice—many female abolition societies refused to allow black members. In Fall River, Elizabeth and Lucy Buffum found that the other white women in their antislavery group were willing to let "respectable" black women attend the meetings but "did not think it was at all proper to invite them to join the society, thus putting them on an equality with ourselves." (The Buffum sisters were always ahead of their time. As a child, Elizabeth recalled listening to her older sister Sarah read a futuristic essay she had written about twentieth-century America in which "she pictured the Negroes as in possession of the government and at the head of society" and "great consternation existed at the capital because the daughter of the President of the United States had married a white man." Some of their friends, Elizabeth added, "did not like the paper very well.")

Middle-class black women in the North were almost all deeply involved in antislavery work. The vast majority of African American families, however, were poor, and had neither the leisure nor the income to participate in outside activities. Still, some poor women made heroic efforts to contribute to the cause. Hannah Austin of Hartford, for instance, supported an invalid husband and four children by taking in washing, but she still managed to stay active in a local abolitionist society.

## "THE MOST ODIOUS OF TASKS"

In the early 1830s, when the abolition movement was just beginning, the male leaders presumed that women would take part just as they had in the Revolutionary War—by rearing abolitionist children and by leading the boycott of slave-produced products. "How can you eat how can you drink," asked an anonymous poet in *The Liberator*:

> *How wear your finery, and ne'er think*
> *Of those poor souls in bondage held,*
> *Whose painful labor is compelled?*

But boycotting had been easier in an era when housewives could make most of their own food. The difficulties and deprivations that came with avoiding slave-labor goods were so great, only the Grimkes seemed capable of sticking to their principles. The boycott, one ardent abolitionist admitted, banned from the dinner table "almost everything good." But women found other ways of getting involved. They went to lectures and joined sewing circles where people made items for fund-raising fairs while listening to one member read from an antislavery tract. The issue of whether something as unserious as refreshments should be featured at these gatherings sometimes took on epic proportions. The Dover Anti-Slavery Sewing Circle approved a motion to "retain the good old custom of having a social cup of tea," and the next retracted it. At another point the members voted to fine anyone who served more than "one kind of cake."

Women also began circulating abolition petitions, which they forwarded to John Quincy Adams, the crusty ex-president who had returned to Congress as an outspoken opponent of slavery. The petitions infuriated Southern legislators. The female petitioner was "the instrument of destroying our political paradise," hyperventilated John Tyler of Virginia, the future president, "a fiend to rejoice over the conflagration of our dwellings and the murder of our people." Collecting signatures involved braving slammed doors and racial slurs, and it was an enormous psychological strain for middle-class women, particularly since the job was never-ending. (Having collected signatures for the banning of slavery in Texas, the women would be sent out again to Washington, D.C., or Missouri.) Even the unstoppable Lydia Child called petitioning "the most odious of tasks." But it was a powerful force in politicizing Northern womanhood. In 1836, 20 percent of the adult women in Lowell and 38 percent in Lynn, Massachusetts, signed antislavery petitions.

The abolition movement came to rely heavily on the money raised by women. Maria Weston Chapman, the merchant's wife from Boston, was a particular genius at fund-raising and began what became a national phenomenon—antislavery fairs. Women made fancy scarves and doilies with antislave messages. They sold penwipers demanding their users "wipe out the blot of slavery" and needlework bags depicting a black man under the lash. Lydia Child made a cradle quilt for one fair that was embroidered with the words: "Think of the Negro-mother when *her* child is torn away." Embroidered linens boasted mottos like "May the points of our needles prick the slaveholders' consciences."

Maria Chapman was also the editor of antislavery magazines and newspapers, and such a fierce behind-the-scenes organizer that many regarded her as William Lloyd Garrison's chief lieutenant. (Lewis Tappan, Garrison's opponent in the battle for control of the abolitionist movement, called her "a talented woman with the disposition of a fiend.") Chapman, who spent her life within the large circle of prosperous abolitionists in Boston, was never ostracized socially because of her activities. But she still felt uncertain, in private, about whether she was betraying her femininity or shortchanging her family. "How heretical, harsh, fanatical, moon-struck, unsexed I am," she wrote a friend. She worked on, while raising three children. Her husband, who suffered from tuberculosis, gave her his full support. He died in 1842, whispering, "I leave you to the cause."

The hyperpolitical atmosphere of the era also drew many women into traditional politics, especially in 1856 when John Charles Fremont became the first Republican presidential candidate. Many female veterans of the abolition movement were particularly enraptured with Fremont's wife, Jessie, the daughter of Senator Thomas Hart Benton and a partner in all her husband's activities. His supporters cried for "Fremont and our Jessie," and women's enthusiasm for the ticket was so intense that traditionalists worried they were going overboard. Julia Lovejoy, a Kansas minister's wife, tried to deflect "little Misses and young ladies" into appropriately feminine modes of political expression, proposing that they sew "ornamental work for the parlor" with "the names of 'Fremont and Jessie' wrought in choicest colors." Older women, Lovejoy suggested, might retire to the dairy room and "make a mammoth 'Fremont cheese.' "

## "I AM TRYING TO GET UNCLE TOM OUT OF THE WAY"

In 1850, Congress passed the Fugitive Slave Law. The act made it easy for Southerners to reclaim former slaves who had fled to the North, or even kidnap free black people and drag them back across the border. It struck terror into the Northern black community. "Many families who had lived in [New York City] for twenty years, fled from it now," wrote Harriet Jacobs. "Many a poor washerwoman who, by hard labor, had made herself a comfortable home, was obliged to sacrifice her furniture, bid a hurried farewell to friends and seek her fortune among strangers in Canada." Although only a few hundred black people actually wound up being transported back to slavery under the law, those who did were given names and faces. The newspapers were full of stories about African Americans living in the North who had suddenly been wrested away from their homes and jobs and dragged down south by people who claimed to be their former masters. The stories were so pathetic that even Catharine Beecher was whipped into righteous wrath. "It did my heart good to find somebody in as indignant a state as I am about this miserable wicked fugitive slave business," Harriet wrote to her sister. "Why I have felt almost choked sometimes with pent up wrath that does no good." Another Beecher sister, Isabella, was equally roused. "Now Hattie," she wrote. "If I could use a pen as you can, I would write something that would make this whole nation feel what an accursed thing slavery is."

The Fugitive Slave Law helped bring forth *Uncle Tom's Cabin*, which did more than any other piece of literature to mobilize Northern sentiment against slavery. It was Stowe's first novel, and it took several Beecher siblings to get it written. Catharine moved into Harriet's home to take care of the children while Isabella copied the manuscript. (Calvin Stowe, although extremely supportive, doesn't seem to have been much practical help.) "I am trying to get Uncle Tom out of the way," Catharine wrote from the Stowe household. "At 8 oclock we are thro' with breakfast & prayers & then we send off Mr. Stowe & Harriet both to his room at the college. There was no other way to keep her out of family cares & quietly at work & since this plan is adopted she goes along finely."

*Uncle Tom's Cabin* was an extraordinarily powerful book. After decades of fiction about brave but deferential orphans whose fine character wins them a good husband, Beecher's novel practically exploded with energy and passion. The characters were one-dimensional, but its depiction of the "peculiar institution" is still affecting. It tells the story of Tom, the faithful and religious slave, who is sold down the river by an impecunious owner and passes through the home of the saintly, doomed Little Eva and on to the plantation of the villainous Simon Legree. It was a woman's book that saw slavery chiefly as a threat to families. When her master tries to sell her child, the slave Eliza is forced to flee across the Ohio River, leaping from ice floe to ice floe, in a scene that made theatrical productions of *Uncle Tom's Cabin* a favorite for generations.

The book became the most popular novel of the nineteenth century. Its sequel, *Dred*, sold over 100,000 copies in a single month—the equivalent of perhaps a million today, given the difference in population. "Mrs. Stowe, who was before unknown, is as familiar a name in all parts of the civilized world as that of Homer or Shakespeare," wrote *Putnam's Magazine* in 1853. It may have been only a legend that Abraham Lincoln called her "the little woman who wrote the book that made this great war." But she was definitely the little woman who mobilized the antislavery sentiments of average Americans, particularly other women. On New Year's Day in 1863, when abolitionists gathered at Boston Music Hall to celebrate the issuance of the Emancipation Proclamation, the crowd chanted "Harriet Beecher Stowe! Harriet Beecher Stowe!" until Mrs. Stowe stood up, with tears in her eyes, and acknowledged their cries.

### "I CRAWLED ABOUT MY DEN FOR EXERCISE"

Stowe had almost no firsthand knowledge of slavery, but she had access to plenty of abolitionist reports, including one in an antislavery magazine about a woman named Eliza, who carried her daughter to freedom across the frigid Ohio River. The real Eliza had six children. When she learned that she was about to be sold, she took her youngest girl and escaped in midwinter, crossing the Ohio by leaping from one ice floe to the next. Miraculously arriving at the other side, she was sheltered at the home of the Rankin family, one of the most active stations on the Underground Railroad that aided fugitive slaves. Cutting her hair to disguise herself and her daughter as boys, she made her way to Canada. But the following year, she reappeared at the Rankins', once again disguised as a man and determined to rescue the rest of her family. She made her way back to the old plantation and returned to the river with her five children. They stood in the shallows all day to throw the bloodhounds off the scent. At twilight Mr. Rankin, disguised in women's clothing, distracted the slave catchers. Eliza and her children were ferried across the river and made their way back to Canada.

Perhaps because stories of female slaves who ran to freedom were relatively rare, they captured the imagination of the public. Ellen Craft, a light-skinned slave in Georgia, became a celebrity in the North when she escaped with her husband, William, by disguising herself as a young white man who was traveling north with his slave. Ellen bandaged her right hand so that hotel registrars couldn't tell she was unable to write, and pretended to be deaf to avoid long conversations. She wrapped her head, as if she had a toothache, to cover her beardless chin, and donned green glasses. After a series of close calls they arrived in Philadelphia in 1848, where abolitionists sheltered them, and Ellen recovered from a near breakdown resulting from the stress of the trip. Meanwhile, people flocked to shake the hands of the couple who had pulled off such a dramatic flight. When the Fugitive Slave Law was passed, the Crafts feared they might be recaptured, and their friends helped them make their way to England, where they went to school and raised a family. After the Civil War they returned to Georgia, purchased a plantation, and established a school for black children.

Lydia Maria Child helped an escaped slave named Harriet Jacobs turn her experiences into one of the frankest and most astonishing memoirs of African American life in bondage. Jacobs was the granddaughter of a free black woman who made a modest living selling baked goods to her neighbors. Harriet's owner refused to let her grandmother purchase her freedom, but her mistress did teach the girl to read, and Harriet believed she would be set free her in her mistress's will. Instead, Jacobs was bequeathed to a three-year-old niece, along with a bureau and worktable. Jacobs, who was sexually harassed by the little girl's father, eventually ran away. But she was unable to get out of the area and wound up hiding for seven years in an attic in her grandmother's home. "The garret was only nine feet long and seven feet wide," she wrote. "The highest part was three feet high, and sloped down abruptly to the loose board floor. There was no admission for either light or air. . . . It was impossible for me to move in an erect position, but I crawled about my den for exercise." Finally, she had an opportunity to escape to the North.

Jacobs's story, like most of the fugitive slave memoirs, was directed at the female heart, which responded to the mother torn from her children, the young girl sullied by a lecherous old man. Child, the editor, wrote that she hoped it would rouse Northern women "to the sense of their duty in the exertion of moral influence on the question of slavery." Not every writer was as generous with her assistance as Lydia Child. Harriet Beecher Stowe, who Jacobs first approached for help with her story, not only ignored the plea but sent Jacobs's letter to her former employer, asking for corroboration so Stowe could include it in her own upcoming book.

## "WHY CAN'T SHE HAVE HER LITTLE PINT FULL?"

As the nineteenth century wore on, women took to the podium more and more frequently, and for young women reared in reform circles, lecturing began to seem like a perfectly feasible, and exciting, career. "See if Im not a speaker some day," fifteen-year-old Ellen Wright wrote to a friend in 1855. "See if I dont rouse the people." Audiences were particularly eager to hear about slavery from black people who they assumed had the inside story. Frances Ellen Watkins Harper, a member of a prominent free black family, was employed by the Maine Anti-Slavery Society as a traveling lecturer and attracted large audiences even though her experiences with slavery were almost as remote as Harriet Beecher Stowe's. Male ex-slaves were common on the lecture trail, and Harriet Tubman made occasional speeches. But Sojourner Truth was the only female ex-slave who pursued a career as a public speaker. Perhaps she was the only American strong enough to overcome the combined insecurities that came with being a woman and being a slave.

Sojourner Truth was born Isabella Van Wagenen, in New York's Hudson Valley. She was sold for the first time when she was nine, winding up with a farm family named Dumont. She looked upon her master "as a *God*," Truth said later, even though he beat her regularly. She ran away from the family shortly before New York abolished slavery. But over the years she sometimes slipped into the kind of dependency and acceptance of abuse common among battered women. At one point she fell in with a religious charlatan named the Prophet Matthias, whom she joined in a bizarre commune that included a fanatic who called himself "the Tishbite," and a wealthy man whose wife was promptly appropriated by Matthias as his "match spirit." Isabella, the only African American in the commune, stayed with the group until it broke up and even afterward continued to send Matthias money.

Eventually, Isabella found strength in her own form of religion, which involved the traditional solace of a loving God but also added a sense of strength and specialness. She regularly saw visions and heard voices telling her she had a mission. That sort of thing was not unusual—in the nineteenth century, many women trying to gather the strength to leap over social boundaries were helped along by mystical experiences. Isabella's visions helped her remake herself into Sojourner Truth, a woman selected by God to travel and preach. Tall, with a low, powerful voice, she became celebrated for her direct and colorful language. Addressing a women's rights convention in Ohio, she said: "I have heard much about the sexes being equal; I can carry as much as any man, and can eat as much too, if I can get it. I am as strong as any man that is now. As for intellect, all I can say is, if a woman have a pint and man a quart—why can't she have her little pint full?" In a famous encounter in Indiana, pro-slavery hecklers claimed Truth was really a man—an accusation frequently thrown at women who spoke in public. The hecklers insisted that Truth show her breasts to the women in the audience. Instead, she bared her breasts to the entire room, and, according to the *Boston Liberator,* told the men that she "had suckled many a white babe, to the exclusion of her own offspring . . . and she quietly asked them, as she disrobed her bosom, if they, too, wished to suck!" She went to Indiana to hold rallies when a law forbade blacks from entering the state, and when rebel sympathizers threatened to burn down the hall where she was to appear, Truth said, "Then I will speak upon the ashes."

Truth was one of the few public women of her day who did not pick favorites when it came to the claims of race and sex. "If colored men get their rights and not colored women theirs, you see the colored men will be masters over the women, and it will be just as bad as it was before," she said. Not all black women agreed with her. Frances Watkins Harper decided that the women's rights movement was a luxury reserved for the white and prosperous. "I tell you that if there is any class of people who need to be lifted out of their airy nothings and selfishness, it is the white women of America," she said.

## "DOES SHE BELONG TO YOU?"

Elizabeth Jennings was born in New York, the daughter of a free African American tailor. One of her brothers was a businessman in Boston, another a dentist in New Orleans. Elizabeth was a teacher and an organist at the First Colored American Congregational Church. In 1854, she was twenty-four years old and unmarried. On Sunday, July 16, she was rushing to play the organ in church. She and her friend, Sarah Adams, saw a horse-drawn trolley car and held up their hand to stop it. "We were starting to get on board," Elizabeth said later, "when the conductor told us to wait for the next car." The one they had stopped did not bear the sign "Colored People Allowed."

"I told him that I could not wait . . . he then told me that the other car had my people in it . . . I then told him I had no people . . . I wished to go to church as I had been going for the last six months and I did not wish to be detained." The conductor finally said she could enter, "but remember, if the passengers raise any objections, you shall go out."

"I answered again and told him I was a respectable person, born and raised in New York, did not know where he was born, that I had never been insulted before while going to church, and that he was a good for nothing impudent fellow for insulting decent persons while on their way to church," she recounted. "He then said I should come out or he would put me out." The conductor tried to pull Jennings off the car while she hung on to the window. He and the driver grabbed hold of her arms and dragged her "flat down on the bottom of the platform, so that my feet hung one way and my head the other, nearly on the ground. I screamed murder with all my voice." As soon as the driver let go to return to his horses, Jennings made another dash into the car. The driver then drove the entire trolley to the nearest station house.

A police officer removed Jennings from the car "and tauntingly told me to get redress if I could." She took him at his word. A public protest was held the next day, and Frederick Douglass wrote about her case in his newspaper. Supporters hired a young attorney named Chester A. Arthur to represent Jennings in court. Arthur, who later became president of the United States, had been admitted to the bar only two months before. On his advice, she filed suit for $500. The jury awarded her $225—a large sum in that era. "Railroads, steamboats, omnibuses, and ferry boats will be admonished from this, as to the rights of respectable colored people," wrote the *New York Daily Tribune,* overoptimistically.

A century before Rosa Parks made history, black women in America repeatedly stood their ground against conductors, ticket-takers, and cabdrivers who tried to turn them into second-class citizens. Frances Watkins Harper had a series of bruising fights on the Pennsylvania trains. Sarah Walker Fossett, a well-known hairdresser in Cincinnati, went to court when a conductor shoved her back on the street as she tried to board a streetcar. Mary Green, the secretary of the Lynn Female Anti-Slavery Society, refused to get off a white car in Lynn and was "dragged out . . . in a very indecent manner with an infant in her arms, and then struck and thrown to the ground. Her husband when he arrived on the scene, was also beaten for daring to interfere for her protection."

The battles went on after the Civil War. In 1865, Harriet Tubman was injured in New Jersey by a railroad conductor who dragged her out of her seat and threw her into the baggage car. At about the same time, Sojourner Truth, working in the Freedmen's Hospital in Washington, had several run-ins with streetcar conductors who refused to allow her to ride with whites. Truth fought back ferociously, had one conductor fired, and had another arrested for assault and battery. Before her campaign was over, she reported, "the inside of those cars looked like salt and pepper" and conductors were urging black women to "walk in, ladies." But Truth was painting the brightest picture possible. She had been seriously injured by the row with the conductor, and at seventy years old, she needed a long time to recover. It must have taken her at least as long to get over hearing the conductor demand of her white colleague, "Does she belong to you?"

## "IT IS PLEASANT TO LOOK AT—
## ALTHOUGH IT IS BLACK"

The emotional burdens on middle-class black women in the nine-teenth century were stupendous. The barrier of prejudice separated them from white people of similar taste and education, and they had almost nothing in common with the vast majority of other African Americans, who were still unschooled and rough. They felt compelled to behave with perfect decorum at all times, and it's no wonder that many of them suffered from migraines. Black women who had the advantage of a good education were expected to use it to improve the race, to teach even if they hated the classroom. Charlotte Forten, a member of one of the nation's wealthiest black clans, wrote that teaching children made her feel "*desperate.* . . . This constant *warfare* is *crushing,* killing me." But she kept at it, eventually traveling south to work with newly freed slaves.

Forten's story was an excellent example of the pressures that con-founded young black women who were financially and educationally among the most fortunate African Americans in the nineteenth century. Her family had been free Americans since long before the Revolution-ary War; their lifestyle was described as "uncommonly rich and ele-gant." But her father found the racism in American society unbearable and emigrated to England after his wife died, leaving his daughter with her grandparents and aunts and uncles. She was tutored at home because the schools available to blacks were inferior. When she was fourteen years old, she was sent to an integrated school in Salem, where she met all the celebrities of the antislavery movement, including William Lloyd Garrison, Lydia Maria Child, and Maria Chapman. But she felt abandoned by her father and isolated. She referred to her books as her "closest friends" and strove desperately for self-improvement. (One evening, after teaching all day, she "Translated several passages from 'Commentaries' and finished the 'Conquest of Mexico.' ") But she was dogged by a sense of failure. Although she bitterly resented the racism she encountered in middle-class white people, she had imbibed enough of their attitudes to look on most other black people with disdain. "He has such a good honest face," she wrote of a wounded soldier she had met. "It is pleasant to look at—although it is black."

When she traveled to the Sea Islands in South Carolina to teach freed black people during the Civil War, at first her students did not know how to treat someone who seemed neither to deserve the deference they gave to white people nor the friendly familiarity with which they treated other African Americans. She eventually won them over with her piano playing, and her work with the ex-slaves seemed to give her the professional fulfillment she always sought. Personally, she was still lonely. She developed a friendship with David Thorpe, a Rhode Islander who was running a local plantation, and the local residents began to gossip about the white Yankee and the black teacher. "Rumor says he more than likes me," she wrote bleakly in her journal. "But I *know* it is not so. Although he is very good and liberal he is still an *American* and w'ld of course never be so insane as to love one of the proscribed race."

Charlotte Forten must have told herself that marriage was virtually out of the question for her. But when she was forty, she met Francis Grimke, the ex-slave nephew of Angelina and Sarah who the sisters had sent to Princeton. Grimke, a minister, was twelve years younger than Charlotte, but they shared the same intellectual interests and dedication to the service of African Americans. As the son of a white man and black woman, Grimke must also have shared her feeling of not quite belonging to either race. They worked and wrote together, enjoyed the intellectual discussions they had each longed for, and lived happily ever after until Charlotte died in 1914, at age seventy-six.

## ঽৈ THE SOUTH ৶ৎ

### "KEPT MOIST AND BRIGHT
### WITH THE OIL OF KINDNESS"

Harriet Beecher Stowe insisted all her life that *Uncle Tom's Cabin* was not an attack on Southerners—after all, Simon Legree was a transplanted Yankee. But Southerners failed to appreciate the distinction.

"Mrs. Stowe betrays a malignity so remarkable that the petticoat lifts of itself, and we see the hoof of the beast under the table," wrote one critic. Caroline Lee Hentz, a Southern writer, produced a series of novels defending slavery even though her dialogue suggested she had never talked to a black person in her life. In the great tradition of the pro-slavery novel, her books were populated with African Americans who had no desire whatsoever to be free. "It is true they were slaves but their chains never clanked," she wrote in *Marcus Warland*. "Each separate link was kept moist and bright with the oil of kindness."

In the pre–Civil War era, only about 5 percent of white Southern women actually lived on plantations and about half the Southern households owned no slaves at all. Still, slavery defined everything about life in the South, including the status of white women. Southern culture orbited around the strong father figure, simultaneously ruling and caring for his dependents—Mary Hamilton Campbell was struck when her servant Eliza referred to Campbell's husband as "our master." Black and white women never seemed to develop any sense of common cause, but every Southern female from the plantation wife to the field slave was assigned a role that involved powerlessness and the need of a white man's constant guidance. A Southern slave owner named George Balcombe advised a friend to "Let women and Negroes alone. Leave them in their humility, their grateful affection, their self-renouncing loyalty, their subordination of the heart, and let it be your study to become worthy to be the object of their sentiments."

## "THERE IS MANY THINGS TO DO ABOUT A PLACE THAT YOU MEN DON'T THINK OF"

Southerners compared themselves to the ancient Romans, another proud race of slave owners. Dipping back two millennia, they gave their slaves names like Cato and Cicero and celebrated a culture in which families were strong, men were in charge, and slaves did the physical labor. Women were expected to follow the lead of the Roman matron, who presided over the hearth, took care of the children, and entertained her husband's guests. Poor women, of course, did not get to stay home—they worked as seamstresses and washerwomen, often to support a family in which the man had run away or failed in his duties as a breadwinner. Slave women were expected to labor with their men in the fields. But plantation wives, who set the tone for Southern culture despite their small numbers, did not do physical housework. Their letters, which are full of reports about gardening, smoking of meat, cooking, and sewing, actually referred to work done by slaves, which the white mistress supervised.

The overwhelming impression of the lives of most plantation wives is of isolation. When Anne Nichols moved to her husband's Virginia estate, she wrote that she was "absolutely as far removed from every thing . . . as if I was in a solitary tomb." Houses were far apart, and Southern mores prohibited ladies from traveling alone, or even with another woman. "It is quite out of our power to travel any distance this summer as we have no gentleman to go with us," wrote a stranded plantation mistress. Considering how fragile women were presumed to be, planters left them alone on remote farms among hundreds of slaves with stunning impunity. "I presume you have planted all the crop. I have only to add that I wish you good luck and good speed," wrote one husband in 1790. John Steele, who had been away in Washington for years while his wife ran the plantation, responded to her complaints by writing, "I know you will live disagreeably, the Negroes will be disobedient, the overseer drunken and foolish, but I must rely on your good management." These casual demands were sometimes interspersed with reminders about the importance of maintaining the standards of Southern femininity, which the wives must have found maddening. "I would willingly follow your advice and not go in the sun if I could avoid it, but there is many things to do about a place that you men don't think of," wrote a Louisiana woman to the husband who had left her in charge. The husbands' absences were not always compulsory. Southern men went to spas to "take the waters" about five times more frequently than women.

## "I WOULD NOT CARE IF THEY ALL DID GO"

For all their indignation about Northern abolitionists, Southern women were distinctly less enthusiastic than men about the institution of slavery. Charles Eliot Norton, a Northerner who visited Charleston in 1855, wrote home of the strangeness of hearing principled Southern men defend slavery. "It is very different with the women," he added. "Their eyes fill with tears when you talk with them about it." It could be that Norton's hostesses were simply trying to be accommodating and sympathize with their guest's harangue. But in their journals and letters, the plantation wives frequently recorded opinions about slaveholding that were at best mixed. "In all my life I have only met one or two womenfolk who were not abolitionists in their hearts—and hot ones, too," an overseer told Mary Chesnut, a wealthy Carolinian. Although only a handful of Southern women ever spoke out publicly against slavery, there were a number of instances in which women surreptitiously helped their own family slaves escape. A New Orleans slave, who was being sold to Georgia traders, was freed from his handcuffs by his young mistress, who pointed out the North Star to him and told him to follow it. When a Maryland plantation owner died and the slaves were scheduled for sale to pay his debts, the dead man's granddaughter visited the slave quarters and helped them get away. In Mississippi, a fugitive slave who sought refuge with his former owner was warned by the man's wife that her husband was planning to turn him in. She gave him money and directions that led him to the North. There is also some evidence that women who owned slaves were more likely to regard them as human beings. They emancipated favored slaves in their wills more frequently than men did and seemed more sensitive to the breaking up of slave families. When they wrote to relatives who had relocated on the frontier, women often inquired by name about the slaves who had been taken west with the settlers, something their husbands and sons almost never did. Some white women developed deep and lasting friendships with female slaves, most often the nurse who had been the family "mammy." (Susan

Davis Hutchinson reported paying a condolence call on a friend upon the death of a slave "who had been more of a mother than a servant to her.")

But in general, women seemed to dislike slavery mainly because they found it so difficult to handle the slaves. "I sometimes think I would not care if they all did go, they are so much trouble to me," wrote one Southern housewife in a typical outburst. Sarah Gayle, the wife of an Alabama governor, berated herself for losing her temper with the slaves and wrote in her journal, "I would be willing to spend the rest of my life at the North, where I never should see the face of another Negro." Just as Northern women complained about the difficulty in getting good servants, the Southern women complained bitterly about their slaves. Absent the incentive of wages, slaves were motivated mainly by the fear of punishment, and although some white women did whip their servants, most did not really have the power to instill physical fear. Mistresses who actually hurt slaves generally did it in the heat of anger, grabbing whatever was available—knitting needles, kitchen knife, fork, or boiling water—and sometimes permanently maiming them.

Southern women constantly pointed out that unlike Northern women, they were responsible for housing and clothing their servants and tending them when they were sick. They frequently described themselves as the real slaves. Caroline Merrick, who admitted that much of the comfort of her life was due to her servants, nonetheless felt the "common idea of tyranny and ill-usage of slaves was often reversed," and claimed to have been "subject at times to exactions and dictations of the black people . . . which now seem almost too extraordinary to relate." Southern women felt they had to go to a great deal of trouble to look after slaves, who did not go to a great deal of trouble for them. But their claims that they wanted to see an end to the system were mostly imaginary, as demonstrated by how miserable they were when the slaves actually left. The housewives did not want to do the work themselves—they simply wanted the people who did it for them to work harder.

If Southern women ever really hated slavery, it was because they feared it was sexually corrupting their men. "Slavery degrades the white man more than the Negro and oh exerts a most deleterious effect upon our children," wrote Gertrude Thomas of Georgia, who suspected that both her father and husband had black mistresses. Catherine Hammond, who remained loyal to her philandering husband during a scandal involving his conduct with his nieces—her dead sister's children—did leave him in 1850 because he refused to give up his slave mistress. In an indication of what a Southern male who had been taught to dominate could be like, Hammond blamed the rupture on the "utter want of refinement and tone" in his wife's family.

"God forgive us, but ours is a monstrous system," wrote Mary Chesnut. Like many of her fellow Southerners, she disliked the institution yet wanted the service. But on the subject of sex, her intense feeling was uncomplicated. The most famous remark in her diaries was that every Southern lady "tells you who is the father of all the mulatto children in everybody's household, but those in her own she seems to think drop from the clouds, or pretends so to think."

# 9

# The Civil War: Nurses, Wives, Spies, and Secret Soldiers

## "MY STATE IS OUT OF THE UNION"

For Southern women, the beginning of the Civil War offered an unusual opportunity to get involved in public life. "Politics engrosses my every thought," wrote Amanda Sims. In this crisis, showing a deep interest in masculine concerns was not considered unfeminine. Keziah Brevard, a fifty-eight-year-old widow, said she was so emotionally involved in the political drama that if she awoke in the middle of the night "my first thought is 'my state is out of the union.'" There were the usual wartime stories of young women who refused to allow draft dodgers to pay them court. (Girls in Texas were alleged to be handing out bonnets and hoopskirts to men who failed to enlist.) But this early-stage patriotism came easy: most Americans, North and South, believed the war would be resolved very quickly, perhaps even before any blood was actually shed. When their husbands actually saddled up and rode off to battle, a number of women began questioning whether there was any cause they'd be willing to sacrifice their loved ones for. "Charlie is dearer to me than my country," admitted Kate Rowland of Georgia.

The women left behind knew they would have a new role to play, although they weren't particularly clear what it would entail. Writing to her local paper, one Confederate urged her fellow Southern females to "hurl the destructive novel in the fire and turn our poodles out of doors, and convert our pianos into spinning wheels." Young women wrote in their diaries that they wished they were men. Feeling both useless and anxious, they embroidered razor kits, formed relief committees to sew clothing for the troops, and held benefits to raise money for the war effort. But unlike their Revolutionary era ancestors, the Southern elite refused to wear homemade clothing as a badge of patriotic fervor. According to the *Southern Illustrated News,* "Not five out of five hundred ladies would be caught in the street in a homespun dress."

## "DOES SHE MEAN TO TAKE CARE OF ME— OR TO MURDER ME?"

Confederate women became keenly aware that they were alone on remote farms with slaves who believed they might soon be freed. Keziah Brevard, who woke up in the middle of the night to thoughts of secession at the onset of the war, found that as the months rolled by, the thing keeping her awake was the possibility of a slave uprising. A middle-aged widow, Brevard was used to living alone on her plantation with a great many slaves, but by 1861, she was writing that "we know not what moment we may be hacked to death in the most cruel manner." There were indeed a few spectacular murders, and everyone had heard about them. Lewis B. Norwood, a wealthy North Carolina planter, was killed by two of his slaves. A husband and wife, they held him down, shoved a funnel into his mouth, and poured scalding water down his throat. (Norwood had just sold the couple's baby and was preparing to sell the wife.) The wealthy Mary Chesnut, who bragged in her diary about her lack of fear, may have thought twice after her elderly cousin, Betsey Witherspoon ("a saint on earth"), was smothered by one of her servants. As Chesnut discussed the tragedy with her sister Kate, a maid came in and announced that she intended to sleep in Kate's room in order to protect her. "For the life of me, I cannot make up my mind. Does she mean to take care of me—or to murder me?" Kate asked her sister.

Plantation mistresses had been left alone a great deal before the war. But then their slaves were not expecting to be freed any minute, and white male neighbors were normally nearby. During the war, the women were truly alone, and very few of them seem to have welcomed an opportunity to demonstrate their leadership skills. They began to flood the Confederate government with petitions asking that their men be exempted from duty in order to defend the lives and chastity of their wives and daughters from the local slaves. In fact, as civil rights leaders pointed out after the war, there were far fewer instances of rape or assault than anyone might have expected. The women's far more realistic worry was that they might wake up one morning and find that their servants had simply taken off. "I dread our house servants going and having to do their work," wrote Mary Lee, a Virginia woman whose male slaves ran away in 1862, with the females threatening to follow. One Georgia slave-owning family was so determined to keep their prized cook that they chained her to the kitchen— the Union Army found her with "heavy iron shackles put on her feet so she could not run off." Women from prosperous Southern families had been raised to regard physical work as degrading, and having slaves do it for them was a very deep-rooted part of their identity as Southern ladies. Many well-to-do women had no idea how to do household chores, and when they learned, they didn't much like it. Kate Foster of Mississippi was forced to do the laundry when the house servants ran off, and she reported she "came near ruining myself for life as I was too delicately raised for such hard work." There were reports of women who "fainted dead away" while washing windows or who took to their beds after a bout of floor scrubbing.

## "THE WOMEN ARE AS BAD AS MEN DOWN HERE"

The Confederate Army began to draft soldiers in the spring of 1862, during planting time, and the sight of women behind plows became common. As the war dragged on, the towns became virtually all-female worlds, stripped of able-bodied men who could help with the local defense, run local businesses, or even lift heavy furniture.

In New Bern, North Carolina, only 20 of the 250 white residents were male, and most of those were old or on the verge of being inducted. Inflation became a terrible problem in the South. A soldier's pay was $11 a month, and at wartime prices in some areas that was not enough to feed a family of four on grain alone. Many men, meanwhile, still managed to maintain a mythical image of what their wives were doing at home. "I do not like the idea of your weaving. It is mortifying to me. I wish you would not do it," wrote Will Neblett to his wife, Lizzie, who really had no other way to clothe her family and eleven slaves.

Women got increasingly surly and started food riots, attacking merchants and army agents, raiding grain warehouses, mills, and stores. In areas where the farms were small and people had never owned many slaves to begin with, enthusiasm for the war burned out rather quickly, and wives pestered their husbands to come home and help feed their families. When the men complied, they camped out in the woods while the women supplied them with food and blankets. Some women physically attacked Confederate officers who were trying to reclaim their male relatives. "The women are as bad as men down here," complained a militia officer in North Carolina. Militias sometimes tortured women in order to locate their sons and husbands. One deserter's wife had her hands placed under a fence rail while a soldier sat on it. Another woman was suspended from a cord tied to her two thumbs behind her back.

Newspapers began commenting disapprovingly about women's lack of support for the cause. "The self-sacrifice has vanished, wives and maidens now labor only to exempt husbands and lovers from the perils of service," mourned the *Montgomery Daily Advertiser* in 1864. In the larger cities, elite women consoled themselves for their troubles with a round of social activity. This was particularly true in Richmond, where during the last winter of the war Mrs. Robert Stannard was said to have spent more than $30,000 on entertainment.

### "WATCH OVER THEIR DAUGHTERS
### AS WELL AS THEIR SONS"

When the war began, Northern women responded the same way as in the South. They held meetings—generally chaired by men—in which they pledged their patriotism and vowed to fold bandages or sew clothing for the soldiers at the front. But the Northern women's relief efforts soon became a national organization, the United States Sanitary Commission, which performed a critical role in providing food and medical services for the soldiers. Although men still occupied the top jobs in the commission, women had a great many managerial duties, and as time went on, middle-class matrons began to praise each other for having "executive talents." The necessary supplies "were almost universally collected, assorted, and dispatched, and re-collected, re-assorted, and re-dispatched, by women, representing with great impartiality, every grade of society in the Republic," said Alfred Bloor of the Sanitary Commission. The women had taken over, he said, after the men were discouraged when it became clear the war was not going to be short-lived after all.

Working-class urban women were less enthusiastic about supporting the war effort. They saw the family breadwinners being forced to fight while wealthier men were able to buy their way out of service. In 1863, when Irish New Yorkers rioted to protest losing their young men to the draft, the *New York Herald* blamed women for starting the trouble. "The female relatives of the conscripts mingled their wildest denunciations against the conscription law, and thus gave the people a . . . motive to enact the terrible scenes," the paper thundered. The archbishop of New York warned Catholic parents to "watch over their daughters as well as their sons" during the riots "and keep them at home."

The Draft Riots were more brutal than any mob action that occurred in the South. The rioters, mainly poor immigrants, burned down the Colored Orphan Asylum, set fire to houses, and killed people who got in their way. A Colonel O'Brien, who had ordered his men to fire on the mob, was beaten to death. Angry women, a report stated, "committed the most atrocious violence on the body." A small black child was thrown from a fourth-story window of the orphanage; a black woman was beaten with her newborn baby in her arms. The female rioters also assaulted members of their own sex who had married black men, and a tavern owner named Black Sue whose establishment had separated many sons and husbands from their paychecks.

At her infirmary, Dr. Elizabeth Blackwell and her sister spent three days and nights tending the sick while the city rocked with riots. They ignored demands by their white patients that sick black men and women should be expelled before the mob discovered them. When the houses next to the infirmary were set on fire, the women blocked the view from their patients. The infirmary survived, and Blackwell never even mentioned the incident in her autobiography.

## "WERE THEY THE SAME SCHOOL GIRLS OF 1861?"

An estimated 400 women disguised themselves as men to fight in the Civil War. Many were like Amy Clarke, who enlisted so she could remain with her husband when he joined the Confederate Army. Amy continued to fight after he was killed, and she was wounded herself and taken prisoner. Women also served as spies, much to the joy of newspapers that delighted in reporting their adventures. The Confederacy seemed to attract the most colorful Mata Haris. Rose O'Neal Greenhow, "The Rebel Rose," was a Washington society hostess who was arrested as a Southern spy in 1861 and imprisoned with her eight-year-old daughter. Released a year later, she ran the Union blockade and sailed to Europe, put her daughter in a French convent, published her prison memoirs, and became the toast of London and Paris. Returning home to confer with Confederate leaders, she attempted to evade the blockade in a small boat. When it overturned, Mrs. Greenhow drowned, weighed down by her book royalties—a purse full of heavy gold coins.

The most famous Southern spy was Belle Boyd. Her talent for self-promotion was demonstrated early in life when, angry at being excluded from a party for adults, she rode her horse into the living room. Taking advantage of Union soldiers' gallantry toward a beautiful teenage girl, she served as a courier for the Confederate intelligence service and delivered information on troop size and placement she had picked up from her admirers. On her final mission, Belle sailed to England carrying Confederate dispatches and was captured by a Union blockade. She later married the Union officer who had taken command of her captured steamer. She was only twenty-one years old when the war ended, already a widow with a small child, and she turned to the theater and lecture circuit, where real-life celebrities were always welcome.

Belle was one of the very few Southern women for whom the war was a glamorous adventure. For many it was a nightmare. Their neighborhoods were shelled, their farms commandeered by the military, their cities put under siege. More than 250,000 people, most of them women and children, were forced to leave their homes. As the Union forces moved into the South and conditions became more desperate, families began living in boxcars or tents. Others fled into caves, which they attempted to furnish with rugs or stuffed chairs. Three-fourths of Columbia, South Carolina, was burned down in a single night. In Vicksburg, the citizens had been given so many warnings of imminent attack that many people failed to flee when the Yankees actually did arrive in 1862. Those who were trapped in the city during the ensuing siege wound up desperate for food, eating rats and mules. An Atlanta resident regarded her friends and asked, "were these the same people—these haggard, wrinkled women, bowed with care and trouble, sorrow and unusual toil . . . were they the same school girls of 1861?"

Black women, who often fled toward the Union Army, found little welcome when they got there. At Camp Nelson, Kentucky, soldiers razed a shantytown, leaving 400 women and children homeless in the cold. While marching to Savannah, Sherman's troops dismantled a pontoon bridge before black refugees could get across, leaving them to the oncoming Confederates. Former slaves who joined the Union forces were promised pay and rations for their families, but it didn't always arrive. Emma Steward, left behind with the children in Florida

when her husband, Solomon, joined the First South Carolina Volunteers regiment of ex-slaves, wrote to him in February 1864 that an

> *angel Has Come and borne My Dear Little babe to Join*
> *with Them. My babe only Live one day. It was a Little Girl.*
> *Her name Is alice Gurtrude steward. I am now sick in bed*
> *and have Got nothing To Live on. The Rashion That They*
> *Give for six days I Can Make It Last but 2 days. They don't*
> *send Me any wood. I don't Get any Light at all. You Must*
> *see To That as soon as possible for I am In want of some*
> *Thing to eat.*
>
> *All the family send thair love to you. No more at pressant*
> *Emma Steward.*

## "THE BEST THING
## THAT COULD HAVE TAKEN PLACE FOR ME"

Although many Southern women came to regard the war as a betrayal
by the men who were supposed to take care of them, some saw it as an
opportunity. In a gesture of liberation, they let down their hair and
took off their hooped skirts. "Nothing looks funnier than a woman
walking around with an immense hoop—barefooted," one said.
Amanda Worthington of Mississippi gave up the huge skirts in 1862,
when her worn hoop began to fall off during church services. By 1863,
she had constructed a "bloomer costume" so she could fish to help feed
her hungry household. Young women also began to cut their hair
short, much to their mothers' dismay, and even the more conservative
gave up elaborate hairstyles once they had no slaves to arrange them.

Southern women began to fill government clerical jobs, particularly in the Treasury Department, where each Confederate banknote
had to be signed individually. The job required good handwriting and
good political connections. Most of the women came from elite families and their pay reflected their status—while privates in the army
were getting $11 a month, female clerks got $65. Some of them regarded
it as a great adventure. "I am rarely ill now even with a headache,"

reported twenty-year-old Adelaide Stuart, who spent her days signing Treasury bills and her nights sampling the still-active Richmond social whirl. Being forced to take a job, she decided, was "the best thing that could have taken place for me—it is bringing into active service and strengthening all the best parts of my character and enabling me to root out all that was objectionable." Other women, however, were humiliated at being forced to work for pay, no matter how cushy the job and lucrative the check. "How mean I felt," wrote Mary Darby DeTreville, after she lined up for her wages.

Women from less influential backgrounds got jobs as well. Thousands took in piecework for the Confederate Clothing Bureau, sewing shirts for $1 apiece and coats for $4. Others packed cartridges at the arsenal for $1 a day. It was dangerous work—in 1863, fifty of the ordnance workers were killed in an explosion in Richmond. Their supporters bitterly asked why poor women working at such hazardous jobs got paid so little "when so many of the departments are filled with young ladies (not dependent on their pay) with nothing to do, at salaries equal to and in some cases better than the best male clerks?" The split consciousness that worshiped the image of a lady with soft hands and no occupation, while expecting most of Southern womanhood to spend their lives in hard labor, was still at work. In 1864, when the note signers were ordered to move from Richmond to Columbia if they wanted to keep their jobs, the women were treated like martyrs. But there was a limit to public sympathy. Late in the war, one Confederate congressman proposed that government vehicles be used to take the women to their offices when "their lives and health are jeopardized by the weather." The ensuing hilarity indicated that the women's pedestal had been trimmed to a more manageable height.

In the North, Francis Spinner, Abraham Lincoln's U.S. treasurer, was a fan of female clerical workers. He liked their efficiency and, not incidentally, the fact that they were much cheaper than men. Eventually, 447 women worked in the Treasury Department. They made $720 a year—a generous salary for female workers but barely a living wage in a time of high inflation. In 1865, women Treasury workers petitioned for a raise and got $900 a year. It was half the salary paid to men, and it was the last raise they'd get for twenty years.

If the female workers in the South were treated like fragile flowers, the Northern Patent Office women were viewed as a potential source of sin in the workplace. In 1864, Congressman James Brooks of New York, who was at odds with a Treasury official named Spencer Clark, claimed that Clark and the Treasury women were participating in "orgies and bacchanals." Brooks's target might have been Clark, but his victims were the girls accused of having relations with him. When one, Laura Duvall, died, Baker claimed she had succumbed from the aftereffects of an abortion. But an autopsy on her body—removed from the hearse on the way to the cemetery—found she was a virgin who had died of pneumonia. In the end, the investigations committee declared that Brooks had unjustly "compromised the reputation of three hundred females . . . wives or sisters of soldiers fallen in the field." But the Patent Office women had gotten a reputation that stuck long after Brooks and Clark had vanished from the scene.

## "ALMOST WILD ON THE SUBJECT OF HOSPITAL NURSING"

Until midcentury, nursing had been a job for men and lower-class women. Florence Nightingale made it respectable for ladies. She was a well-born Englishwoman who became an international heroine in 1855 when she reorganized the nursing care in the Crimean War, reducing the death rate in British field hospitals from 45 to 2 percent. When the Civil War began, one observer noted, there was "a perfect mania to act Florence Nightingale." At least 3,000 women held paid nursing positions in the North and South, and thousands of others worked as volunteers. "The war is certainly ours as well as men's," said Kate Cummings of Mobile, Alabama, who became the matron of a large Confederate hospital.

The Nightingale mania struck particularly hard in the North. "Our women appear to have become almost wild on the subject of hospital nursing," said a wartime correspondent for the *American Medical*

*Times.* When Elizabeth Blackwell called an emergency meeting at her infirmary to organize nursing aid for the war effort, 4,000 volunteers showed up. Not everyone was pleased. A wartime correspondent for the *American Medical Times* was disturbed by the image of "a delicate refined woman assisting a rough soldier to the close-stool or supplying him with a bedpan." He urged that women restrict themselves to "delicate soothing attentions, which are always so grateful to the sick." But public opinion once again chose necessity over proper standards of ladylike behavior. A Confederate congressional investigation discovered that the mortality rate among soldiers cared for by female nurses was only half that of those tended by men. "I will not agree to limit the class of persons who can affect such a savings of life as this," said a senator from Louisiana. Suddenly, people on both sides of the Mason-Dixon line switched from regarding nursing as an inappropriate job for well-bred women to seeing it as one for which they were uniquely qualified.

Still, authorities were wary of putting young girls in intimate contact with bedridden soldiers. Dorothea Dix, when she was appointed superintendent of Union nurses, set a minimum age of thirty for her volunteers and demanded they be "plain looking women." As the war went on and the need for medical assistance became more desperate, Dix ignored her own regulations. But she was firm in the beginning. One young woman from Auburn, New York, was told that she could volunteer only if the elderly family physician agreed to accompany her. She wrote a friend that if she ever became a nurse, it would be in an "Old Maid's Hospital." Elida Rumsey Fowle was rejected because she was only nineteen years old and instead became a sort of early era USO. She entertained the patients with songs and stories, giving more than 200 performances in a year, and established a soldier's library in Washington. Later she and her husband also collected medical supplies and delivered them to the front.

Fowle and the other volunteers who took care of the wounded during the early parts of the Civil War were basically on their own. They determined where the fighting was, wheedled their way through to the front, and did what they could to help. Neither the Union nor Confederate Army was in any way prepared to feed and clothe its soldiers, let alone care for them when they were injured. In the first terrible years of the war, wounded men died on the battlefield after lying there for days, untended, in the hot sun. There was no organized system of getting them to a field hospital. It took an enormous leap for well-bred women to enter the gory army hospitals to tend the wounded men, and it's hard to imagine the kind of daring they must have needed to get to the battlefield unescorted. Yet a number of them managed to do it, on their own.

## "I AM A U.S. SOLDIER . . . AND THEREFORE NOT SUPPOSED TO BE SUSCEPTIBLE TO FEAR"

Clara Barton was one of those restless New England spinsters of the nineteenth century who spent their lives going from place to place, living with friends and relatives, never finding a spot to settle in. She was intellectual, athletic, and afflicted with periodic bouts of depression. (She was also an advocate of free love, but if she ever acted on her beliefs, she was extremely discreet.) A talented teacher, she quit a good position in New Jersey when a man was appointed head of a public school system she had founded. She became one of the first Patent Office women in Washington and was, remarkably, paid the same salary as the male workers, although the Commissioner of Patents never dared include her on the official roll of employees he sent to Congress.

When the war began, one of the first New England volunteer regiments that traveled through Washington on its way to the South was the Sixth Massachusetts. Nearly forty of the men in the unit had been Barton's pupils, and the mothers of Clara's "boys" targeted her as a useful go-between in sending food and clothing to their sons. Soon her house was so crammed with boxes that she had to move. The turning point in Barton's life came when she realized that the lovingly packed gifts that piled up in her living quarters were not just special treats. The soap, fruits, and other presents were dire necessities for men serving in an army bereft of supplies. The medical situation was worst of all. There were not enough field hospitals, and those that existed sometimes lacked even bandages. There was not enough medicine and certainly not enough medical staff. Doctors operated with instruments that had not been disinfected, and they dosed the men with quinine and morphine, when they were lucky enough to have even that. Most of the wounded died—nine out of ten men with abdominal injuries failed to survive their treatment. When trains bearing the wounded arrived back from the front, they brought fallen soldiers who had not been given anything to eat or drink for days. Katherine Wormeley, a Union nurse, described the cargo of the trains as "a festering mass of dead and living together." Although the official recruitment of nurses went slowly, anyone who wanted to help out could find an open field of opportunity.

Barton began actively soliciting donations and supplies. The women she contacted responded with a flood of fruit preserves and soap and lemons to combat scurvy. Within six months Barton had filled three warehouses. She bought perishables like bread with her own scanty funds and distributed her wares at military hospitals. Once the hospitals were better organized and flooded with female volunteers eager to hand out food or wipe fevered brows, Barton began to meet the ships and trains carrying back wounded men from the front. The next obvious step was to get to the battlefield itself, and after months of bureaucratic wrangling, she got permission to pass through the lines with her wagons of supplies. It would be the last time she would bother to ask. The army became so grateful for her efforts that soon she began to get unofficial leaks directing her to the next site of the fighting.

After the war, Barton became famous as the organizer of the American Red Cross, but her finest hours came in those hectic, disorganized trauma centers of the Civil War's early years. Her face turned blue from the gunpowder, and her skirts were so heavy with blood that she had to wring them out before she could walk under their weight. Her courage under fire was legendary. Walking across a rickety bridge under heavy battery, she barely missed being killed by a shell that tore away a portion of her skirt. At Antietam, when doctors were not available, she removed a bullet from a soldier's face while another wounded man held his head still. Later, when the operating room came under fire and the male assistants fled, Barton stayed to hold down the table where a surgeon was operating. "I am a U.S. soldier you know and therefore not supposed to be susceptible to fear," she said. (Barton's critics noted later that she was definitely susceptible to the urge for self-promotion.)

Barton was not the only woman who assigned herself to organize health care on the battlefield. Mary Ann ("Mother") Bickerdyke first arrived at an army camp in Cairo, Illinois, to deliver a relief fund. Seeing the filthy, overcrowded hospital tents, she simply got to work cleaning and nursing, without asking anyone's permission. In her Quaker bonnet, she trotted across nineteen battlefields in four years, lantern in hand, searching for the wounded. She was famous for ordering everyone around, and her reputation gave her the clout to get away with it. An army surgeon who challenged one of her orders was told: "Mother Bickerdyke outranks everybody, even Lincoln." When a brigade marched past her, exhausted after a long day of rushing toward the front but forbidden by the officer in command to rest, Bickerdyke simply yelled "Halt!" and was able to distribute soup and coffee before the officer could get his men moving again.

## "A HOSPITAL HAS NONE
## OF THE COMFORTS OF HOME"

In the South, nurses had to deal with the irregularities created by a conflict carried out on home territory, where families were often close enough to help care for their wounded, or to get in the way of those who were trying to do so. Phoebe Yates Pember, a thirty-nine-year-old widow who became matron of Chimborazo Hospital in Richmond, had a patient whose wife came for a visit and stayed for weeks, giving birth to their daughter on his cot. Pember cared for the new baby, who was named Phoebe in her honor, and got the mother a ticket home. She then learned that the woman had abandoned her child at the station. Rousing the father, she discharged him and sent him home with little Phoebe. As in the North, the first female Confederate nurses were mainly women who simply started helping out. Mary Rutledge Fogg of Nashville was so appalled at watching wounded soldiers die in her own city that she raised money to recruit nurses. She then informed the government that her volunteers were on the way to the front lines in Virginia, whether anyone was ready to receive them or not. Women's organizations created wayside hospitals around the country that could aid wounded soldiers making their way home.

Some found a strange sense of liberation in their duties. "Nobody chided me then as unwomanly, when I went into a crowd and waited on suffering men," said Rebecca Latimer Felton. "No one said I was unladylike to climb into cattle cars and box cars to feed those who could not feed themselves." Still, Southern women did not flock to serve. "Are the women of the South going into the hospitals? I am afraid candor will compel me to say they are not! It is not respectable, and requires too much constant attention, and a hospital has none of the comforts of home," wrote Kate Cummings, who said she was very tired of hearing her female friends tell her what they would do if only they were men.

As the war went on, women on both sides volunteered to nurse in order to stay with their husbands. Others signed up after they learned their loved ones had died in battle. Whatever the impulse, they frequently wound up working under conditions that were not much less dangerous than those on the battle lines. They nursed under artillery fire or served in hospitals for soldiers with communicable diseases like smallpox. They worked themselves into a state of exhaustion that left them susceptible to typhoid or pneumonia. "I have had men die clutching my dress till it was almost impossible to loose their hold," said Lois Dunbar. During the battle of Pea Ridge, Mary Ellis remembered standing at the operating table for hours "with the hot blood steaming into my face, until nature rebelled against such horrible sights and I fainted, but as soon as possible I returned." Annie Etheridge was dressing the wound of a soldier when he was hit by a shell and torn to pieces. Delia Fay marched with her husband's regiment, carrying her own supplies as well as the load of any sick soldier she came upon.

Anna McMahon, who came down with a fatal case of measles, looked up at the doctor and asked: "Have I done my duty?" On being assured that she had, she sighed, "Good-bye, I will go to sleep," and died. Rebecca Wiswell volunteered to dress the wounds of men who had been shot through the bowels. "The worst case no doctor ever dressed but three times; then he was left in my care and I did it five months," she said later. And for some of them, it was the best part of their lives. "We all know in our hearts that this is thorough enjoyment to be here," wrote Katharine Wormeley from a Northern hospital ship.

But the number of women who wanted to give soldiers inspirational tracts or home-baked treats outstripped those who sought to be nurses. Southern hospital personnel passed around the stories of volunteers who killed dysentery patients by feeding them sweet delicacies. Francis Bacon, a Northern surgeon, complained of being "subjugated and crushed by a woman who sings the Star Spangled Banner copiously through all the wards of my hospital." Doctors on both sides of the conflict often preferred Catholic nuns as nurses because they were used to hard work and discipline and inclined to be deferential. Eventually 617 sisters from twenty-one different religious communities served in either Union or Confederate medical facilities. Nuns were not exempt from the anti-Catholic hysteria that was rampant in America at the time, and Dorothea Dix refused to appoint them as government nurses. But the army physicians, and the nuns, managed to work around her.

## "GIRLS HAVE MARRIED MEN THEY WOULD NEVER HAVE GIVEN A THOUGHT OF"

For all the reports of ladies living high in Richmond or shirking their nursing duties, the vast majority of Southern women suffered during the war, and they began to realize that they were going to suffer a great deal more when it was over. There was a sense of universal loss, which the postwar Southerners would soothe by creating a mythology of the glorious prewar South, like Scarlet O'Hara's Tara. "My happy life! I love to think of it now," wrote Sarah Morgan, a Louisiana girl, in her diary. "Until that dreary 1861, I had no idea of sorrow or grief." Some mothers had lost four, five, even seven sons in the war. Brides of less than a year were left widows. In what the whole South came to regard as an emblematic tragedy, the beautiful Hetty Cary of Richmond married a handsome Confederate general in one of the social highlights of the season, only to return to the church three weeks later to bury him. General Robert E. Lee wrote to his wife that he found the change in the young socialite's appearance shocking. There were 80,000 widows just in Alabama—three-quarters of them in dire distress.

Nearly a quarter of the men of military age in the South were killed, and perhaps another quarter returned home wounded. To make up to the men for what they had lost, Southern girls were urged to do their part by marrying handicapped veterans. "Girls have married men they would never have given a thought of had it not been thought a sacred duty," wrote a North Carolina woman whose daughter had just taken the plunge. "You would never believe how our public speakers . . . excite the crowd to this thing." While many men returned with an empty sleeve or ruined leg, ready to begin a new life, a good many others suffered from more complicated and destructive wounds. They were alcoholics, or depressives, or simply lost souls from the prewar era, unable to make a postwar life for themselves. It was a crisis that the narrow prewar life of wealthy Southern manhood had paved the way for. Sarah Morgan wrote that she intended to marry a man who had a profession because a rich man could lose his money "and Master is turned adrift on the tender mercies of the world, without the means to turn an honest penny, even if he had the inclination or energy, which most rich men do not . . . so he quietly settles down, and goes to the dogs, not forgetting you, but insisting on your company for the first time in your married life."

If Southern women felt a sense of betrayal when their men left them alone and went off to lose the war, their slaves, and their property, they must have felt even more aggrieved when those men failed to get hold of themselves once they returned. One newspaper concluded that Southern manhood, "the mighty oak," had been "hit by lightning" and depended on the "clinging vine" to hold it up. Jefferson Davis, the president of the Confederacy, might have represented his entire generation when he emerged from a Union prison ill, depressed, and never again able to find a career that could support his family. His wife, Varina, not only struggled to keep the family together and educate their children but also had to cope with the humiliation when Davis moved onto the estate of a wealthy and worshipful widow while Varina was in England recovering from a heart ailment. After they reconciled, she was still required to care for and support an ailing ex-hero who obsessively relived his wartime experiences.

Many single Southern women had to face the fact that the war had probably deprived them of any chance of getting married. Families who had allowed their daughters to work during the war expected to reel them in afterward. But some of the daughters had other ideas. "I will not be a dependent old maid at home with any allowance doled out to me while I could be made comfortable by my own exertions," replied Elizabeth Grimball when her family tried to make her give up her job at a private girls' school. By 1883, an Alabama official reported: "members of the most elegant and cultivated families in the State are engaged in teaching."

## "IF I STAY HERE I'LL NEVER KNOW I'M FREE"

After the war, the first thing freed slaves wanted to do was move around—from job to job, and from plantation to city. Patience, an ex-slave in South Carolina, passed up a profitable job cooking for her former owner. "I must go," she said. "If I stay here I'll never know I'm free." The black population of Atlanta, about 20 percent before the war, reached 46 percent by 1870. Most were women who got jobs as laundresses, frequently working in their own homes where they could watch their children while making some money. By the 1880s, nearly 98 percent of black women in the workforce were domestics. But they and their employers had different expectations about how hard their newly freed workers should have to labor, and at what tasks. Black household workers quit their jobs frequently—in what must have been a heady experience after slavery. In response to white complaints,

Southern state legislatures began passing laws that turned any worker who had quit her job into an automatic "vagrant." The Ku Klux Klan took a more direct route. "Many times, you know, a white lady has a colored lady for cook . . ." explained a state legislator in Georgia, Alfred Richardson. "They have a quarrel, and sometimes probably the colored woman gives the lady a little jaw. In a night or two a crowd will come in and take her out and whip her."

Part of the Klan's strategy for terrorizing the black population was sexual assault. In Georgia, Rhoda Ann Childs was taken from her home and beaten by eight white men. "(T)wo men stood upon my breast, while two others took hold of my feet and stretched my limbs as far apart as they could, while the man standing upon my breast applied the strap to my private parts until fatigued into stopping, and I was more dead than alive," she said. An ex-soldier then raped her. Although the South was obsessed with the idea of black men molesting white women, the real peril was for black women at the mercy of white men. "It is all on the other foot . . . colored women have a great deal more to fear from white men," acknowledged Z. B. Hargrave, a white attorney.

The Georgia legislature passed the Apprentice Act, allowing employers to get custody of black orphans, allegedly so they could teach them a trade. But it was actually a way for whites to get free labor. The American Missionary Association, which sent orphans to white households looking for domestic help, shipped off not only all the homeless black children that could be found but also a number who had families eager to take care of them. "Somehow these black people have the faculty of finding out where their children are," complained the matron of an orphanage from which children were recruited, after a few relatives had managed to retrieve nephews and nieces from the Association's clutches. (They did so at some risk. In South Carolina an ex-slave named Sue was beaten and then shot to death when she opposed her former owner's attempt to apprentice her nephew.)

White people—even those who did not go so far as to kidnap the children of ex-slaves—were irritated by the behavior of freed blacks, who wanted the things they had been deprived of, including pretty clothes. "Slavery to our Islanders meant field work, with no opportunity for the women and girls to dress as they chose and when they chose," said a teacher of ex-slaves in Georgia. Women who had spent their lives alternating between the two smocks they were given each Christmas by the master felt proud and independent walking down the street in colorful dresses and hats. Their husbands felt proud, too, because their wives' clothing showed the world that they were good providers. The whites concocted endless explanations for why that was inappropriate. "The airs which the Negroes assume often interfere with their efficiency as laborers," complained a South Carolinian.

Newly freed black families also wanted to keep the women at home. Mothers who had been forced to leave their children behind when they went out to the fields wanted to stay with them. Husbands reveled in the idea of having their wives devote all their time to cooking and keeping house. ("When I married my wife I married her to wait on me and she has got all she can do right here for me and the children," said an ex-slave who refused to send his spouse back into the fields.) Everyone wanted to protect their daughters from the clutches of rapacious employers. The white community, however, was horrified at the idea of black women becoming full-time housewives. They called it "acting the lady" and "the evil of female loaferism." Southern plantation owners were desperate for farm labor, and they regarded any woman who wanted her husband to "support her in idleness" as a threat to the agricultural economy. Northerners tended to side with the Southern elite on this issue. To be self-sustaining, they felt, black families needed income from all members. But the bottom line was that the sight of blacks behaving like whites in any way—by dress or manner or by keeping their wives at home—threatened the white sense of racial superiority. An agent for the Freedmen's Bureau in South Carolina, which existed to look after the interests of ex-slaves, complained that "myriads of women who once earned their own living now have aspirations to be like white ladies and, instead of using the hoe, pass the days in dawdling over their trivial housework or gossiping among their neighbors."

# Women Go West: Pioneers, Homesteaders, and the Fair but Frail

## "I THOUGHT WHERE HE COULD GO I COULD GO"

In 1841, when Nancy Kelsey was seventeen years old, she became the first woman to travel to California on a wagon train, in a party that included her husband, their infant daughter, and about thirty other men. They left Missouri with great expectations and a stunning lack of preparation. The group had no guides or maps or particularly clear idea about how one got to California. It was a wonder they made it to Wyoming before they got lost, but once they did, they wandered around so long they were forced to abandon their wagons and try to outrun the winter weather. Nancy celebrated her eighteenth birthday on the summit of the Sierra Nevadas, worrying about snow and Indians. Several of the pack animals fell over a cliff, and when the last of the cattle had been killed, the party continued on without any food. "My husband came very near dying with the cramps and it was suggested to leave him but I said I would never do that," Nancy told a reporter in her old age. Amazingly, she and the others all made it to California. Of Nancy, a fellow emigrant said, "She bore the fatigues of the journey with so much heroism, patience and kindness that there still exists a warmth in every heart for the mother and the child." Baby Ann, the others noted, was never sick a day during the trip. After the

Kelseys arrived in California, Nancy rested only a few months before her husband, who was obviously all pioneer and no settler, decided to try Oregon. She followed him from place to place throughout the West, giving birth to eleven children. Looking back, she remembered the adventures. "I have enjoyed riches and suffered the pangs of poverty," she said. "I have seen U.S. Grant when he was little known. I have baked bread for General Fremont and talked to Kit Carson. I have run from bear and killed most all other kinds of smaller game."

Americans had been going west—or dreaming about it—since the early colonial days, with the definition of "west" changing in each era. But it was not until the 1840s that American families began emigrating to the actual West Coast, heading for California or the rich, heavily timbered land of the Pacific Northwest. They studied manuals like *The National Wagon Road Guide*, which provided detailed but optimistic descriptions of what the trip would entail—the books generally estimated it would take three months, when in real life the trip was at least six. (The *Daily Missouri Republican* advised readers that the trek west would be "little else than a pleasure excursion.") The manuals suggested what to pack, what livestock to buy, and how to organize a wagon train. But they said little or nothing about how to cook dinner over a campfire, what to do about diapers for the babies, or how to keep small children occupied for ten hours a day in a crowded, jolting wagon.

The idea of going west almost always seemed to come from husbands, and although wives were consulted, not many had actual veto power. In their diaries and letters, when pioneer women describe arguments with their spouses about migration, they were generally fighting to be included on a trip the man was planning to make solo. "I would not be left behind," wrote Luzena Wilson. "I thought where he could go I could go, and where I went I could take my two little toddling babies. . . . I little realized then the task I had undertaken." Wilson wound up gaining and losing several small fortunes in the West, where her skills as a cook turned out to be much more valuable than her husband's talent as a gold miner.

Although most of the women who went west came from farm families, they were not necessarily used to lives of great hardship. Poor people rarely migrated. Buying and outfitting a wagon cost between $600 and $1,000, at a time when a factory worker might make $300 a year, so pioneer wives were generally middle class. They certainly thought of themselves as ladies. Most rode sidesaddle during the trip, with one leg hooked over the pommel and their long skirts covering their legs. It might have been more decorous, but it was difficult to keep one's balance. (Bethenia Owens-Adair, one of the early female doctors in the West, expanded the crusade for simpler dress into a call for simpler saddles. She urged women to ride as men did, not with "the right limb twisted around a horn and the left foot in a stirrup 12 or 15 inches above where it ought to be.") Pioneer women urged their daughters to wear sunbonnets to protect their skin, and some prescribed gloves to keep the hands smooth and soft. If they did a great many things that would normally be considered unladylike, there is no evidence they were trying to break out of the Victorian female mold. They saw chores like pushing wagons out of the mire, driving teams of oxen, pitching tents, and even handling guns as temporary emergencies.

As usual, the emergency only worked one way. The wives and daughters took on new, masculine duties, but the husbands and sons saw no necessity to repay the favor. "Some women have very little help about the camp, being obliged to get the wood and water (as far as possible) make camp fires, unpack at night and pack up in the morning and . . . have the milking to do, if they are fortunate enough to have cows," wrote Helen Carpenter, who was grateful that her husband was among the minority who pitched in. Many women were pregnant, but they still yoked loaded wagons and coped with morning sickness during the jostling ride. They crossed raging rivers on rafts and helped drag their children up the sides of mountains. One pioneer recounted assisting in a birth during a thunderstorm when the pregnant woman was placed on two chairs in the leaky wagon, with "the nurses *wading* around" to assist in her delivery.

The wagons stopped only at nightfall and started rolling again at dawn, and women learned how to do their domestic chores on the move. Some could roll a piecrust on the wagon seat while driving a team of oxen. But there weren't many chances to do laundry, and families went for a month or longer between clean clothes. Diapers were a particular problem, and many women wound up scraping and drying the used diapers and putting them back on the baby. One wrote that she washed the diapers out every night and made her husband hold them over the campfire until they dried. Nobody discussed menstruation, but if the women relied on rags, keeping them laundered must have been extremely difficult. Perhaps some of them followed the Indian custom of using grass or moss.

As the trains moved into the plains, where there were few trees and no firewood, the only fuel for the campfires was buffalo chips—the dried dung left behind by the herds, which the more playful pioneers referred to as "meadow muffins." Except for the smell, the chips made relatively good fires. But some wives never got used to the idea of cooking over dried manure and worried that the smoke was contaminating the food. Others had trouble learning how to make meals over an open fire. But most adapted. James Clyman wrote that he had watched a woman cooking next to a wagon on a rainy night in 1844: "After having kneaded her dough she watched and nursed the fire and held an umbrella over the fire and her skillet with the greatest composure for near 2 hours and baked bread enough to give us a very plentiful supper."

The rigors of the trail convinced at least a few women to adopt the bloomer uniform. But most stuck to the traditional long skirts and aprons, even though they were always in danger of catching their clothes on fire during the dinner preparation. (One migrant near the end of her trip described her frequently seared skirt as "a piece of wide fringe hanging from belt to hem.") Finding a private place to answer the call of nature was a continuous problem. On the plains, where there was no brush to crouch behind, women sometimes stood in a circle, their skirts fanned out to shield the person in the middle. Frances Grummond was traveling with an army wagon train through hostile Sioux country when she went off to find a concealed place to relieve herself. When she came back, the column had gone on without

her. "In my haste to reach the road or trail I had the dreadful misfortune to run into a cactus clump," she recalled. "My cloth slippers were
instantly punctured with innumerable needles. There was no time to
stop even for an initial attempt to extricate them, as fear of some
unseen enemy possessed my mind as cactus needles possessed my
feet." She ran nearly a mile in that crippled state before she caught up
with the column.

### "WE SAW LONG BRAIDS OF GOLDEN HAIR"

The wagon trains left in the spring, so they could get across the Sier-
ras before snow fell. The early part of the trip was often marked by
drenching thunderstorms, with winds that tore through the canvas
and rain that soaked the wagon interiors. In their diaries, women
complained constantly that they had no time to dry out the bedding.
Then the wet springs gave way to hot, dry summers. "Very dusty
roads," reported Elizabeth Dixon Smith. "You in the states know
nothing about dust. It will fly so that you can hardly see the horns of
your [oxen]. It often seems the cattle must die for want of breath,
and then in our wagon such a spectacle—beds, clothes, victuals and
children all completely covered." When autumn arrived, the trains
were generally headed toward the mountains, where they were vulnerable to cold and snow. "I carry my babe and lead or rather carry
another through snow and mud and water almost to my knees," said
Smith. Two days later she wrote: "I froze or chilled my feet so that I
cannot wear a shoe so I have to go round in the cold water barefooted."

As the trail got tougher and the animals got weaker, many families
lightened their load and got rid of everything other than the most crucial possessions, leaving future pioneers to pass by their abandoned
furniture and precious keepsakes. "Boxes and trunks of clothing were
thrown out, chests of costly medicine . . . cooking utensils, cooking
stoves, vessels of every description . . . table ware of every description, and in fact you can name nothing that was not lost on this road,"
wrote one woman. To relieve the animals, people got out of the wag-

ons and walked. Toddlers invariably wandered off and headed straight into a patch of cactus. "Days passed before all could be picked out of the skin," wrote one mother. Inevitably, women wound up carrying the smaller children. Juliette Brier walked 100 miles through the sand and rocks when her wagon train was lost in Death Valley. She carried one child on her back and another in her arms, while she led the third by a hand. Mrs. Samuel Young, who had just given birth, climbed the cliffs of the Sierra Nevadas with her newborn baby in her arms.

The possibility of sudden death was omnipresent. Cholera struck wagon trains that left Missouri in 1849 and swiftly killed 5,000 people. Children fell into campfires, or under the wheels of the wagons; men drowned in the rivers. Travelers who were alive and laughing one moment were dead the next, from a horse's kick or a rattlesnake's bite. When the wagon train stopped for the night at an established campsite, the pioneers often saw the remains of someone who had died from disease or accident on an earlier train. "If there were any graves near camp we would visit them and read the inscriptions," said Martha Gay Masterson, who traveled west as a child. "Sometimes we would see where wolves had dug into the graves after the dead bodies, and we saw long braids of golden hair telling of some young girl's burying place." Eventually, the children became used to the skeletons. They wrote verses on the skulls and left them behind for other youngsters to read and add a line or two.

The trains also passed stranded families who had come to desperate straits, many because of the sudden loss of a father. One pioneer remembered seeing "an open bleak prairie, the cold wind howling overhead . . . a new-made grave, a woman and three children sitting near by, a girl of 14 summers walking round and round in a circle, wringing her hands and calling upon her dead parent." Janette Riker was only a young girl when she headed for Oregon with her father and two brothers in 1849. Late in September they camped in a valley in Montana, and the men went out to hunt. They never returned. While she waited, Janette built a small shelter, moved the wagon stove in with all the provisions and blankets, and hunkered down. She killed the fattest ox from her family's herd, salted down the meat, and lived alone through the winter, amid howling wolves and mountain lions. She was discovered in April by Indians who were so impressed by her story that they took her to a fort in Washington. She never found out what happened to her family.

### "HE WAS IN GREAT HASTE TO MARRY TO SAVE A HALF SECTION OF LAND"

Once they reached the West, the early female pioneers enjoyed all the advantages that come with being scarce. "Even I have had men come forty miles over the mountains just to look at me, and I never was called a handsome woman, in my best days, even by my most ardent admirers," said Luzena Wilson. Irwin, Colorado, had only one respectable unmarried woman in a town that was filled with ambitious young men. A mining engineer noted in his diary that forty men were paying court to the eligible female, the sister of Mrs. Reed, the camp doctor's wife. The Reeds set up a system, limiting the parlor to six callers at a time and the callers to a maximum of "4 minutes on sofa with girl."

Although the gender balance evened out fairly quickly, single women who were willing to get married remained in great demand. The wife of an army officer seeking a nurse for her children deliberately picked out a very homely candidate. But, she reported in despair, the girl "had not been in the fort three days before the man who laid our carpets proposed to her." The matches made under such circumstances tended to be more economic than romantic bargains. Martha Gay Masterson recalled that as soon as her family set up camp in Oregon, a well-dressed man galloped up and begged her father to present him to the oldest daughter. "He was in great haste to marry to save a half section of land, as the law stated that all married men were entitled to a certain amount of land if married before a set date," she said. Although Martha's father angrily announced that he had "no daughter to barter for land," the man found a willing girl before the deadline.

Despite the rough manners of the early western men, a woman

with any claim to respectability could expect to be treated with great deference, if not outright awe. (When Elizabeth Gunn went to church with her children in Sonora, the men sitting along the street stood up and saluted as she passed by.) But the women desperately missed female friendships, and having so many single men in one place inevitably led to the kind of behavior that they found unpleasant. They complained in their letters about widespread drinking, gambling, swearing, and violence. "In the short space of 24 days," wrote Louise Clappe, the wife of a mining camp doctor, to her sister, "we have had murders, fearful accidents, bloody deaths, a mob, whippings, a hanging, an attempted suicide and a fatal duel."

Before they went west, most pioneer women had lived in houses that had heat, soft beds, and other comforts. But in the crowded cities and gold mining camps of California, they slept in leaky tents, sat on crates, and cooked over campfires. They slogged through mud and dust to get to Sunday services and gave birth to their children alone. Nevertheless, a lot of them seemed to enjoy themselves. "I *like* this wild and barbarous life," wrote Louise Clappe, who on another occasion had told her sister, "everybody ought to go to the mines, just to see how little it takes to make people comfortable in the world."

## "MORE ACTIVE AND INDUSTRIOUS THAN THE MEN"

The women in the far West before the settlers arrived included both Native Americans and the Mexicans, who had been living in the area for centuries. White Americans generally had a low opinion of Mexicans—as they did about any people they were trying to displace. Nonetheless, they were impressed by the warmth of Mexican families. "Their manners toward one and another is engaging and that of the children and the parents most affectionate," wrote Frederick Olmstead. But Americans also believed that the men were indolent and the women made to do all the work. "Riding on horseback and lounging lazily is the gamut of their days and the women bear all the responsibility of the house," wrote another observer in 1828. "These beautiful creatures are without a doubt more active and industrious than the men."

Ironically, the Mexicans said the same thing about the Indians. Indian women, wrote one Mexican missionary in 1801, "are slaves to the men, obliged to maintain them with the sweat of their brow." (Visitors to frontier towns said the same thing about white men, who often went off hunting or drinking while the women stayed home and worked.) Once the Americans became a growing economic presence in the West, many wealthy Mexicans wanted their daughters to intermarry and extend the family's political influence. The children of these marriages tended to adopt the language and manners of Americans. If their skin was light and they were wealthy, they were accepted and thenceforth referred to as "Spanish." Otherwise, they were still subject to discrimination.

Both the Mexicans and white Americans saw the Indians as enemies or targets for conversion. When Mexican priests built a mission, there was always a dormitory for the unmarried Indian girls, where they were cloistered off under the guard of an elderly Indian matron. "She never let them out of her sight. In the afternoon, after dinner, she locked them up and gave the key to the Priest," said a woman who had been brought to a mission as a foundling. The girls must have been hot, uncomfortable, and bored, but shutting them away was not totally irrational. Mexican soldiers had no compunctions about raping native women, sometimes lassoing them like cattle and shooting any male Indian who tried to intervene. After the women were raped, they were often considered "contaminated" by their own people, and "every white child born among them for a long period was secretly strangled and buried," said a Scotsman who had married into an Indian family.

Neither the Mexican nor the American missionaries went to the trouble of trying to look at the world from the Indians' point of view. One of the first white women to reach Oregon was a missionary, Narcissa Prentiss Whitman, who came out with her doctor husband, Marcus, to work among the Cayuse tribe. The Indians were eager to hear about farming techniques, but they weren't interested in becoming

Christians. The Cayuse women didn't like the idea of giving up the status that came with farming so that they could emulate white housewives and stay indoors. Narcissa's opinion of the Indians went downhill rapidly, and she began worrying that her family might "suffer ourselves to sink down to their standards." The Cayuse, meanwhile, saw the number of white people moving into their territory and realized, far more clearly than the missionaries, what it would mean for their own futures. After an outbreak of measles killed their children while passing over those of the white interlopers, the Cayuse held the mission responsible and killed the Whitmans, along with a dozen others.

## "I WENT INTO THE SPORTING LIFE
## FOR BUSINESS REASONS"

*The Home Missionary,* which was published in early San Francisco, estimated that half the women in frontier California were of "the loose element." That may have been an exaggeration, but the anecdotal evidence suggested that prostitutes were extremely well represented among the white women who first settled in early western cities. The "fair but frail," as prostitutes were called, often chose their profession with their eyes open. "I went into the sporting life for business reasons and for no other," said Mattie Silks, a Denver madam. "It was a way in those days for a woman to make money and I made it." In addition to providing lonely men with company, western prostitutes allegedly made hygienic history by becoming the first American women to shave under their armpits. It was a way of demonstrating to their customers that they were free of lice.

Prostitution could certainly be profitable. A Frenchman named Albert Bernard was shocked to discover his countrywomen charged $16 an evening for simply sitting at a man's table. "Nearly all these women at home were streetwalkers of the cheapest sort," he complained. "But out here for only a few minutes, they ask a hundred times as much as they were used to getting in Paris." Still, prostitutes who made enough money to retire in comfort were probably about as common as miners who struck it rich and managed to hang on to the profits. The women who worked in high-end bordellos were perpetually in debt to the madam, who paid for their clothing, jewelry, and perfume. And few western prostitutes made it to a bordello. Almost every town had a "line"—a row of one-room wooden shacks or cribs, where the whores lived and plied their trade. These women covered the bottom half of their beds with oilcloth, to protect the blanket from men who never bothered to take off their dirty boots. On paydays, the demand was so heavy they sometimes serviced eighty men in a single night. An even lower step was one of the "hog ranches" operating along the trails where muleskinners, stagecoach drivers, and teamsters stopped briefly to take their pleasure. "In my experience I have never seen a lower, more beastly set of people of both sexes," wrote a soldier who visited one of these establishments.

The most desperate stories involved Chinese women, who were brought to California as virtual slaves. Some were recruited—or simply kidnapped—from the streets of Canton; others were deluded by men who pretended to marry them and promised to take them off to a better life in the West. Some were sold by their parents. Lilac Chen recalled bitterly that she was only six years old when "that worthless father, my own father, imagine . . . sold me on the ferry boat. Locked me in the cabin while he was negotiating my sale." Girls who were purchased for $50 in China were resold for $1,000 in San Francisco. In the American brothels, Chinese girls were famous for their cleanliness, shaving their bodies and bathing frequently. Almost all of them, however, contracted venereal diseases from their clients. Some girls were chained to their beds and drugged to keep them from lashing out at their customers. By the time they were twenty years old, most had died, committed suicide, or been murdered by their employers. Toward the end of the century, a twenty-five-year-old missionary named Donaldina Cameron began a crusade against the trade in Chinese women. Working on tips that often came from the prostitutes, she led the police to the cribs and opium dens, sometimes chopping down the doors herself. Many of the girls she rescued found jobs or married, and in 1928 one of them, Yoke Keen, became the first Chinese woman to graduate from Stanford University.

## "A SMART WOMAN CAN DO VERY WELL
## IN THIS COUNTRY"

Luzena Wilson was cooking biscuits for her family over a campfire in
a mining town near Sacramento when a man came up and offered her
five dollars for the food. When she stared at him in silence, he doubled
the offer and handed her a ten-dollar gold piece. Like many newly
arrived pioneer wives, Luzena suddenly realized that the household
skills that had been taken for granted in the East might win her a fortune in the West. While her husband, Mason, was off panning for
gold, Luzena bought two boards, made them into a table, "and when
my husband came back at night he found, mid the weird light of the
pine torches, 20 miners eating at my table. Each man as he rose put a
dollar in my hand and said I might count on him as a permanent customer." Within six months Luzena had made $20,000, which the
Wilsons invested in a wooden hotel and store. But the city caught fire,
and the family lost everything. They moved again and started a new
establishment with Mrs. Wilson serving dinner on her plank table
under a canvas roof, and the guests retiring for the night to a nearby
haystack.

For women, the gold in the California hills came from biscuits and
flapjacks. A woman wrote from California to a Boston newspaper,
reporting that in less than a year she had made $11,000 baking bread
and cakes "in one little iron skillet." Black women, who had a reputation for being good cooks, went west with the same dreams. One pioneer recalled seeing a crowd of people crossing the desert on foot
and noted that one of them was "a negro woman . . . carrying a
cast-iron bake oven on her head, with her provisions and blankets
piled on top—all she possessed in the world—bravely pushing on for
California."

With only a few dollars, grubstake, a woman could open a
makeshift boardinghouse and earn a comfortable income. It didn't
make sense to invest much in the houses, since the miners moved on at
the first news of a gold strike someplace else. Martha Gay Masterson,
who followed her husband through gold rush territory, moved twenty

times in twenty years, operating hotels, boardinghouses, grocery stores, and dry goods shops along the way. And though the men's standards were far from demanding, the boardinghouse owner's work was difficult, and full of unusual challenges. One woman was troubled by animals, which took advantage of the shortage of doors. "Sometimes I am up all night scaring the Hogs and mules out of the House," she said.

The labor shortage in the early West wiped out the normal rules about what jobs were appropriate for women. They worked as barbers and advertised their services as doctors, lawyers, and real estate agents. Nellie Pooler Chapman took over her husband's dental practice in Nevada City, California. Although a very small woman, Mrs. Chapman was apparently skilled in the era's dental arts, which leaned heavily in the direction of extraction. In Wyoming, Martha Maxwell supported herself and her daughter by working as a taxidermist. "A smart woman can do very well in this country," wrote one young woman to a friend back east. "It is the only country I was ever in where woman received anything like a just compensation for work."

Women also occasionally took up rough jobs like stagecoach driving, delivering the mail by pony express, and even, in a few cases, riding with outlaw gangs. Charley Parkhurst ran a stagecoach through dangerous territory for years and no one knew Charley was actually a woman until she died in 1879. "He was in his day one of the most dexterous and celebrated of the California drivers . . . and it was an honor to be striven for to occupy the spare end of the driver's seat when the fearless Charley Parkhurst held the reins," wrote the *San Francisco Morning Call* before Charley's sex was discovered.

Being a success as an entertainer was easy. An actress didn't need talent; she just needed to show up. The tolerance for any kind of performance by a female was so great that a girl of ten was said to have played Hamlet. Lotta Crabtree, who began her career as a child performer, made a fortune dancing and singing for the miners. She was the protégée of Lola Montez, who wowed western audiences with her "Spider Dance" in which she impersonated a woman trying to shake off tarantulas that are crawling around her underclothing. (The dance was a Spanish classic, but only Montez's version featured genuine fake spiders.) Legend has it that the first entertainer to appear in Virginia City, Nevada, was Antoinette Adams, a very tall, not very attractive blond who sang in a cracked voice to resounding cheers and a shower of silver dollars. The cheering covered up Antoinette's singing, and she left town with two sacks of money.

## "STANDING ERECT UPON THE BACK OF HER UNSADDLED HORSE"

Post–Civil War Americans were fascinated by cowboys and Indians, cattle drives and buffalo hunts. They loved western romances and adventure novels, and Wild West shows that reenacted runaway stagecoaches, Indian war dances, and pony express rides. It was hard to figure out exactly where women fit into the picture, except as victims in constant need of rescue. But gradually cowgirls were introduced to the eastern audiences through nineteenth-century pulp fiction. Hurricane Nell avenged her parents' death by disguising herself as a man and killing the villains. Wild Edna led a band of outlaws. Dauntless Dell of the Double D ranch amazed Buffalo Bill with her riding and shooting. These girls of the golden West existed mainly in books. But there were a few well-known real-life cowgirls, and the most famous by far were Annie Oakley and Calamity Jane. They were America's first action heroines, amalgams of femininity and fighting spirit. Not since Hannah Dustan scalped her Indian captors in 1697 had the country been so enamored with the idea of a woman warrior.

Far and away, Annie Oakley most successfully embodied the cowgirl myth, although she did not cross the Mississippi until 1885, when she joined Buffalo Bill's Wild West show. She was born Phoebe Ann Moses in Ohio in 1860. When she was six years old, her father, a postman, died of pneumonia, leaving a wife and seven small children. Annie taught herself to shoot her father's rifle and helped support the family by selling game to the Cincinnati hotels. Her birds were said to be particularly desirable because they were always neatly shot in the head. Frank Butler, a famous trick shot, arrived in town and met fifteen-year-old Annie at a shooting club, where she beat him in a match. They were married the next year, and she joined his act. She quickly became a sensation, and Butler, who taught his semi-illiterate wife to read and to speak like a lady, gradually became her manager rather than a costar. (The Butlers had what appeared to be an exceedingly successful marriage and partnership that lasted till their deaths a half century later. But movie versions of Annie's life always had to wrestle with the phenomenon of a man who put his wife's career ahead of his own. One had Frank losing his vision, and in the original *Annie Get Your Gun* the unbeatable Miss Oakley learns how to get a man when she realizes the importance of pretending to let Frank outshoot her.)

Unlike most touring sharpshooters, Annie never had to fake her act. She broke crockery, snuffed out candles, and drilled holes in playing cards with her rifle, standing, running, or riding at a gallop. In 1894 she starred in a ninety-second "movie" for Thomas Edison, and when it was released, crowds lined up in front of New York nickelodeons to watch her shatter glass balls with her shotgun. When she traveled with the Buffalo Bill show she became close to Sitting Bull, the Indian leader of the battle of Little Big Horn who had joined the troupe after his people were defeated and confined to a reservation. Annie was said to be the only person who could cheer him up during his frequent and understandable depressions. After his death, she was billed as "Sitting Bull's Adopted Daughter," and if that was hype, their regard for each other had been real.

Annie, with her tiny figure, long skirts, and gentle demeanor, embodied the kind of strong but feminine cowgirl easterners wanted to believe in. To maintain her image, she set firm boundaries. She refused to wear trousers and always rode sidesaddle. Frank told reporters that although Annie was able to hit targets while standing on her head, she considered it "not proper to do" in public. No one was permitted to curse or drink in her presence. She thought the idea of women voting was unladylike. At the turn of the century Oakley took to the stage, in plays that always featured her as the western cowgirl who defeats evil in a genteel manner. In the course of her long career, she made it acceptable for women to shoot, hunt, and even compete with men— as long as they kept both legs on the same side of the saddle.

Calamity Jane, unlike Annie, was a real westerner. She was born Martha Canary, the oldest child of an unsuccessful farmer and a mother who often rode into town to drink with men of questionable background. The family left their farm in Missouri during the Civil War to escape creditors and wound up in Montana, where her father became a gambler and her mother a prostitute, and the little girls were forced to beg for food. By the time she was a teenager, Martha's parents were dead, and she was homeless and illiterate. She may have turned to prostitution to support herself and her siblings. When the younger children were sent off to live with a Mormon couple in Salt Lake City, Martha struck out on her own, ending up in Piedmont, Wyoming, a small, wild railroad town where she was, at age thirteen, the only unattached female. Although nobody knows precisely what happened to her next, she most likely wound up in a brothel and may have made her way to the Dakotas as an army camp follower. By 1875, she had been dubbed Calamity Jane—"jane" was a western word for any female—and was known as a hard-drinking drifter who hung around with Wild Bill Hickok and his crowd. She seemed most comfortable wandering from one town to another, taking temporary lovers who she always referred to as "husbands" and occasionally running afoul of the law for stealing or getting drunk. Ultimately, she was a sad outsider, a woman who behaved like a man in places where men tended to behave very badly. But she was also well liked by people who could tolerate her antics. (Despite rumors that she and Hickok were married, he was not among her more patient acquaintances.) She was a good friend when she was sober, and a caring woman who reportedly dared to nurse smallpox victims during an outbreak in Deadwood, South Dakota, in 1878.

Calamity had a knack for telling tall tales, and she manufactured stories about having scouted for General Custer and ridden for the pony express that may have helped inspire her tabloid legends. But the real creator of the Calamity Jane known to most of America was Ned Wheeler, a writer of dime novels, a popular form of turn-of-the-century literature. Wheeler created a popular series of books featuring the ongoing adventures of Calamity Jane and her platonic friend, the totally fictional Deadwood Dick. The Jane in Wheeler's novels smoked cigars, wore buckskin trousers, and rode astride, but she never swore or drank. There were hints that she was the daughter of a good family who came west after she was betrayed in love. Above all she was beautiful, graceful, and daring. In one episode, intent on averting a mine explosion, Calamity "dashed madly down through the gulch, standing erect upon the back of her unsaddled horse and the animal running at the top of its speed. . . . her hair flowing wildly from beneath the brim of her slouch hat, her eyes dancing occasionally with excitement, every now and then her lips giving vent to a ringing whoop, which was creditable imitation . . . of a full-blown Comanche warrior."

The real Calamity, who was a great rider but neither beautiful nor particularly graceful, tried unsuccessfully on a few occasions to take advantage of her fame and published an extremely imaginative auto-biography. But she was no entertainer, and her attempts to perform in Wild West shows were failures. "Her sorrows seemed to need a good deal of drowning," Bill Cody told a Montana newspaper after Jane decamped from an exposition in Buffalo. She died in her forties, of the effects of drinking, hard living, and poverty.

## "SHE PUT HER ARMS AROUND A TREE
## AND HUGGED IT"

Most women who went west intended to be farm wives, not cowgirls. They rarely encountered cattle stampedes or mine explosions, but they did fight prairie fires, grasshopper invasions, tornadoes, and killer droughts. Their journeys west often ended not in California but Kansas or Nebraska, and the fact that the trip was shorter did not nec-essarily make it less grueling. Julia Lovejoy, traveling with two of her children to meet her minister husband in Kansas, took a riverboat to

Kansas City. Her small daughter, Edith, caught the measles on board, and when one of the male passengers offered Julia his cabin, she found it was so filthy that a dead cat was in one of the bureau drawers. After she cleaned the room as best she could, the original owner decided to reclaim it and evicted her and the children. After landing, they wound up staying in a falling-down shack, in the home of a woman who turned out to be a violent alcoholic, and later in a hotel where they had to pass dead bodies in the hallway to get to their room. When the little family finally got on the wagon to Lawrence, the driver, a "drunken rowdy," took four days to make the trip, instead of the usual two. There were no beds at night, and Edith slept moaning on the dirty floor of an Indian tepee. On the final night, the driver stole all their belongings, and Edith died.

Many settlers made their first homes in dugouts, glorified caves carved from the side of hills. One girl who lived in a dugout wrote that when it rained "we carried the water out with buckets, then waded around in the mud until it dried up. Then to keep us nerved up, sometimes the bull snakes would get in the roof and now and then one would lose his hold and fall down on the bed, and then off on the floor. Mother would grab the hoe and there was something doing and after the fight was over Mr. Bull Snake was dragged outside." Pioneer diaries mentioned snakes a lot, particularly the ones that fell from the ceiling into people's beds at night. One woman in Gaines County, Texas, reported killing 186 in one year. Julia Lovejoy found a rattlesnake under her bed, and another in a cupboard above her baby's cradle. "We have never enjoyed a walk in the garden, or gathering plums, or indeed sleeping in our unfinished cabin in warm weather on account of these intruders," she wrote.

The soddy, a somewhat superior shelter, was made out of bricks of sod, weighing up to 50 pounds apiece. It took an acre of prairie sod to build a one-room house. Soddies were sturdier than dugouts and many families lived in them for years. Wives may have yearned for a solid wood home, but if the family made money on the farm, the first priority for investment was to buy new equipment for the fields or better stock for the barn. One female pioneer said she and her neighbors grew so accustomed to gravel floors that they asked each other, "Have you done your house raking today?"

The flat, empty landscape of the prairies, the perpetual winds, and the dirt houses were enough to dispirit anyone, but some of the wives loved the challenge. "The wind whistled through the walls in winter and the dust blew in summer, but we papered the walls with newspapers and made rag carpets for the floor and thought we were living well, very enthusiastic over the new country we intended to conquer," said Lydia Lyons. But not every woman was that cheerful. "When our covered wagon drew up beside the door of the one-room sod house that father had provided, he helped mother down and I remember how her face looked as she gazed about that barren farm, then threw her arms around his neck and gave way to the only fit of weeping I ever remember seeing her indulge in," one girl recalled. Another woman begged her husband to take her along when he went to a town called Little River to purchase wood: "She hadn't seen a tree for two years, and when they arrived at Little River she put her arms around a tree and hugged it until she was hysterical."

Prairie fires were a threat from late summer through autumn, when a spark from lightning or a campfire could set the tall grass blazing. "Many a time my mother stayed up all night, watching the red glare of the prairie fires in more than one direction, in fear and trembling that they might come swooping down on us asleep in our little log cabin," said Lillian Smith. When that danger faded, the winter arrived, with winds reaching over fifty miles an hour. In a blizzard, a family could be cut off from the outside world for weeks, snowed in so effectively that they were unable to reach the woodpile. The wind was a force to be reckoned with year-round, shredding clothing on the line, blowing dust into houses through closed doors and windows.

One of the most bizarre and terrifying assaults of nature involved grasshoppers. Swarms would appear suddenly, in huge clouds, and devour everything in sight. "They commenced on a 40 acre field of corn about ten o'clock and before night there was not an ear of corn or green leaf to be seen," said Elizabeth Roe. Another woman remembered that the grasshoppers "struck the ground so hard it sounded almost like hail." If a housewife tried covering her garden with gunny-sacks, the bugs simply went under, or ate their way through them. They ate the peaches off the trees and left the pits hanging. After they ate the crops the grasshoppers moved into the barns and houses. They ate all the food, and some women said they devoured furniture, fence boards, and cabin siding. They ate the clothing and left window cur-tains hanging in shreds.

In the summer, flies or gnats swarmed over everything. In a des-perate attempt to drive away mosquitoes, plains women burned buf-falo chips—they could stand the smell longer than the bugs could. A visitor to frontier Illinois looked through a cabin window and saw a woman and her children dancing around in what he presumed was the ceremony of a religious cult. But on entering, he discovered "they were all busy in warring with the mosquitoes." In the Southwest, women were instructed to place their beds at least two feet away from the walls, lest they wake up covered with scorpions. Fleas were a terri-ble problem. Indian wives made houses that were easy to replace and simply burned them down when the fleas became too bothersome. But American settlers had a yen for permanence, and a sturdy house that lasted forever was also a permanent abode for vermin.

Most white women were terrified of Indians, even though rela-tively few settlers ever had a violent encounter with them. But they had read the captivity literature, which featured stories of gang rapes, mass murders, and disfigurements like that of Matilda Lockhart, who was taken by the Comanches and returned in 1840 with much of her nose burnt off—"all the fleshy end gone and a great scab formed on the end of the bone." George Custer instructed his men to shoot Mrs. Custer rather than let her be captured by hostile Indians. In reality, the range of experiences of women captives varied, depending on the tribe, the personality of the woman, and that of the Indian who claimed her. Some women were taken as slaves, others as wives. Susan Parrish, a pioneer, told the story of the Oatman family, who were attacked by Apaches while Mrs. Oatman was giving birth. The Indians murdered the parents and smaller children and carried away two older girls. Many years later one of the girls, Olive, was found by settlers while she was sitting on a riverbank, perhaps preparing to bathe. She had been sold to the Mohave Indians, and among them had married and raised a family. She desperately wished to return to them. "For four years she lived with us, but she was a grieving, unsatisfied woman who somehow shook one's belief in civilization," wrote Parrish.

While the white women were worried about Indians, the Indian women were absolutely frantic about the white settlers, and they often buried their babies in the dirt to conceal them from pale strangers. The Indians were incredulous at the disasters that the whites brought along with them, particularly the disease. The Lakota called 1844, the year of a measles epidemic, "The Rash Breaks Out on Babies Winter." In 1849, almost half the Cheyenne tribe died from cholera. By the time the first settlers made it to the West Coast, early contacts with whites had already left many of the California tribes well on the way to extinction. The Indians knew that white people were responsible for these terrible plagues and assumed, generally incorrectly, that the whites had done it deliberately.

But the whites *were* deliberately killing the buffalo. White women traveling across the plains saw buffalo hunting as merely something their men wasted time on when they should be pushing the train forward. However, Indian women were keenly aware the slaughter would doom their way of life. Pretty Shield, a Crow woman, said, "My heart fell down when I began to see dead buffalo all over our beautiful country, killed and skinned and left to rot by white men, many many hundred of buffalo." In the culture of the Plains Indians, women were responsible for butchering and drying meat after a buffalo hunt, processing and tanning the hides with a preparation made from the animal's brain and liver. It took about twenty-two hides to make a tepee, which the women sewed. They then owned the finished home. But as the buffalo vanished, the women's place in the tribe did, too.

Sarah Winnemucca, a Paiute who remembered being buried in the earth by her terrified mother when white men approached their camp, became a popular lecturer on the abuses suffered by her people. Winnemucca had great faith in women's capacity to bridge racial gulfs. "If women could go into your Congress," she wrote, "I think justice would soon be done to the Indians." Actually, white women had a range of emotions about Indians, many of them decidedly unsympathetic. A Mrs. Miller, writing from Oregon in 1852, explained cheerfully that the Indians were "dying here as elsewhere, where they are in contact with civilization. . . . I used to be sorry that there was so much prospect of their annihilation. . . . Now I do not think it is to be much regretted. If they all die, their place will be occupied by a superior race." Some white women did sometimes express pity for the Indians' plight, and a few developed friendships with Native American women. But almost no one expressed regret for taking their lands.

## "I CANNOT MAKE A FRIEND
## LIKE MOTHER OUT OF HENRY"

Life in the West was generally devoid of anything women regarded as fun. In Topeka in the 1890s, Martha Farnsworth, a young Kansas housewife, was so desperate for entertainment that she went to see the Wizard Oil Medicine show troupe thirteen times during its two-month run. In Wyoming, the chances for socializing were so rare that girls would ride forty miles on horseback to go to a dance. A Texas woman became so lonely she began going out to the watering hole to have conversations with the cattle. Women particularly missed talking with other women. "I have been very blue," wrote Nellie Wetherbee in her journal, "for I cannot make a friend like mother out of Henry." Margaret Armstrong, a teenager on the Texas frontier in 1872, wrote that she and her mother hardly saw an outsider once every six months. "If we did not have a lot of house work to do we would be at a loss how to kill time," she said. Armstrong, who clearly had a talent for seeing the glass half-full, eventually found happiness in marriage to a local teacher.

Women must have missed the company of their own sex most when they were pregnant. Annette Botkin said her mother, a Kansas pioneer, was expecting her third child and caring for toddlers four and eighteen months, when her husband left on a seventeen-mile journey to get wood. As soon as he was gone, she began feeling contractions.

She got the baby clothes together on a chair, along with scissors, drew a bucket of fresh water, made some bread-and-butter sandwiches, and set out milk for the babies. The family's faithful dog, which protected the children from snakes and other danger, was left on guard. When her husband arrived home, he discovered he had a baby boy. "My mother having fainted a number of times in her attempt to dress the baby, had succeeded at last; and when my father came in he found a very uncomfortable but brave and thankful mother."

Like the colonials, the pioneers lived in small, dark houses bereft of luxury. Jessie Hill Rowland of Kansas once told the story of the time her father, a justice of the peace, officiated at the wedding of a local farm family. Her parents were ushered into a dugout—one room, furnished with two chairs, a bed, a small table, a bench, and a stove. A small sheet had been stretched across one corner of the room, and the bride and groom stood behind it, attempting to look inconspicuous. The mother of the bride was grinding dried carrots for a kind of pseudo-coffee. She seated Rowland's parents on the two chairs until the neighbors arrived, and the couple emerged from behind the sheet to be officially married. "Soon after all sat down to the wedding supper. The sheet that hung across the corner of the room was taken down and spread over the table for a cloth." Besides the carrot coffee, the newlyweds served their guests bread and butter, fried pork, and sauces made out of wild plums. "After supper the bridegroom took my father to one side and asked him to accept some potatoes in payment for performing the ceremony. He readily consented and returned home."

Glass for windows was scarce, and many women had to do their chores by candlelight at noon. Susanna Townsend, the wife of a gold miner, theorized that the reason they didn't have windows was because the husbands were home only after sundown. When she finally set aside some money for glass, she wrote to her sister Fanny triumphantly, "I have a *window* in my house. . . . All the passers by stare and gaze at the wonderful phenomenon." Women tried to turn their surroundings into something pleasant. They papered the walls with newspapers and magazines, and a new tenant moving into a previously occupied house always got a kick out of "reading the walls." Bertha Anderson, a Danish immigrant, was determined to make her first home in Montana nice, even though it was a former chicken house, measuring about twelve by twelve, occupied by five children and three adults. She covered the log walls with newspaper, then whitewashed them, and spent one entire winter making rag rugs, which she put on the floor of the front room so her children could play without getting splinters from the rough planks. Her pride in her refurbished nest lasted about a week, until it rained hard and the roof began to leak. The muslin she had tacked on the ceiling hung heavy with mud, the beds were wet, and, Anderson reported sadly, "the poor carpet which was supposed to be striped had now faded and the colors had gone, so that it was a dirty mess."

The food was as spare as the land. At a luncheon at Fort Lincoln in the 1870s, the menu was tea, toasted hardtack, tart jelly made from buffalo berries, chokeberry pie, and lemonade. Elizabeth Custer said their post went so long without eggs, butter, and cream "the cook books were maddening to us." In California, new arrivals discovered that eggs, which had cost a few cents apiece back home, were a dollar, and chickens, which they remembered as costing a dime, were suddenly $10. Louise Clappe's remote mining village ran out of fresh meat over a long winter, and the residents were left with dried mackerel and "wagon loads of hard, dark hams . . . [that] nothing but the sharpest knife and stoutest heart can penetrate." On the plains, farm families just starting out often lived on nothing but corn and corn flour.

For clothes, most women made do with a couple of gingham or calico dresses, a sunbonnet, and an apron. The Sunday clothes were the same, only newer and cleaner. If they could not get cloth for sewing, some women wove their own. (One pioneer claimed his aunt used the fleece of wolves to spin into yarn.) Others ransacked the trunks they had brought with them, and used blankets, shawls, the canvas from the covered wagon, or heavy grain sacks. "Someone had said that the real pioneer in Kansas didn't wear any underwear, but this was not true of the Ellis County pioneer, and the clothes lines with undergarments advertising I. M. Yost's High Patent Flour were the best evidence," said one woman. Despite the sunbonnets, women's complexions often became weathered, and they complained that the alkali in the water made their hair dull and dry.

## "BESIEGED BY A CROWD OF MEN, ALL ANXIOUS TO EMPLOY HER"

In 1879, thousands of ex-slaves left the Deep South, intent on resettling in Kansas. They were fleeing post-Reconstruction Mississippi, Louisiana, and Tennessee, where the fury of ex-Confederates against the freed African Americans was bitter and frequently violent. They knew that if they could make their break from the South and farm 160 acres of Kansas land for five years, the law said it would be theirs. They were called Exodusters, and one of the main reasons for their migration was concern for the welfare of their women. "The white men here take our wives and daughters and serve them as they please, and we are shot if we say anything about it," one member wrote to the governor of Kansas. The wives and mothers prodded them along. "These sable workwomen claim they are exposed to robbery, murder, swindling and all the other foibles and pleasantries. They have organized an emigration society and say they propose to move," reported an unsympathetic white Tennessee paper. Thousands of African Americans took riverboats up the Mississippi or walked the Chisolm trail to Kansas. Armed whites, alarmed at losing their cheap labor, closed the Missisippi and threatened to sink boats that transported the Exodusters. The poorest ran out of money as they waited helpless on the riverbank for a boat with the courage to pick them up. Those who made it to Kansas arrived broke and exhausted. But within a few years most of the 15,000 Exodusters who stayed in Kansas were settled homeowners.

Black women who went west—particularly those who traveled on their own—were independent and fighters. They were usually better educated than the average white female pioneer, and less interested in farming. ("The scenery to me was not at all inviting and I began to cry," said Williana Hickman, a black woman who found herself living in a plains dugout in 1889.) Isolated communities and army outposts had very little discrimination because there were so few blacks—or people in general. "In the earliest days . . . each family was grateful for the help of each other family and we were all on a level. However later differences arose and sentiment against Negroes developed," recalled a black pioneer. Being the only black people in a thinly populated land was doubly lonely. "I ain't got nobody and there ain't no picnics nor church sociables nor buryings out here," moaned Eliza, a cook on a frontier outpost.

Black women in western towns could only find work as servants, although those jobs paid two or three times as much as they did in the East. Even the wealthiest black woman in California, Mary Ann Pleasant, always encouraged the impression that she was working as a domestic for the white men with whom she did business. Pleasant had, indeed, gotten her start working as a cook. When she arrived at the San Francisco wharf, she was by one account "besieged by a crowd of men, all anxious to employ her." She accepted one of the offers, for $500 a month, and invested her first earnings in an accounting firm.

Clara Brown, a freed slave, talked her way onto a wagon train to Pike's Peak by promising to do the cooking and washing for the would-be prospectors. In Cherry Creek, the future city of Denver, she made a good deal of money running a laundry and became a well-loved citizen who, in the words of a local paper, turned her house "into a hospital, a hotel, and a general refuge for those who were sick and in poverty." At the end of the Civil War, she took her savings and tried to find her husband and four children, who had been sold off to different owners before she was freed. Unsuccessful, she returned to Colorado instead with twenty-six former slaves, some of them orphaned, and helped them find homes and jobs. Her search for her family, her charity, and the duplicity of white businessmen drained her money. But thankfully, this story had a happy ending. In 1882, past eighty years old and impoverished, she received word from an old friend who had stumbled across Brown's daughter, Eliza Jane, a widow living in Iowa. With money donated by neighbors, Brown went by train to meet her daughter in Council Bluffs. She arrived in a rainstorm, and Eliza Jane slipped in the mud, but the two women embraced so joyfully they were oblivious to the wet. Clara brought her granddaughter Cindy back to Denver, where they continued her work and charitable efforts. When she died in 1885, the mayor and governor of Colorado were among the mourners and the minister eulogized "one of the most unselfish lives on record."

## "WE NOW EXPECT QUITE AN IMMIGRATION OF LADIES TO WYOMING"

In the summer of 1869, the suffragist Anna Dickinson was on her way to a speaking engagement in California when her train stopped briefly in Cheyenne, Wyoming. Venturing out on the platform for a breath of air, Dickinson was immediately surrounded by a crowd of local residents. When she retreated to the passenger car, they clustered around the windows, flattening their noses against the glass in an attempt to get a better look. It isn't entirely clear if they were drawn by Dickinson's celebrity, or simply her gender. (Wyoming was particularly short of women, with six adult men to every one female.) "Anna is good looking," reported the *Cheyenne Leader*, whose twenty-seven-year-old editor, Nathan Baker, expressed the hope that Dickinson would return and favor Cheyenne with her oratory.

Whether she found the residents of Cheyenne enthusiastic or simply alarming, Dickinson did indeed return in September, addressing a crowd of 250, including the governor and territorial secretary. There is no record of exactly what she said—the *Leader* remained fixated on her figure ("well formed"). But Wyoming, which was gearing up for the first election of a territorial legislature, was definitely aware of the suffrage issue. On the eve of the voting in 1869, Esther McQuigg Morris invited some of the most prominent citizens of her hometown of South Pass City to tea. The guests included local candidates for the state legislature, and the hostess asked each whether he would introduce a bill to give women the right to vote.

Morris was a large woman, nearly six feet tall, and she had been a milliner and a nurse in Oswego, New York. She came west with her husband, John, who was bent on prospecting. The family located in South Pass, which despite its small size was the largest town in Wyoming Territory, and Esther quickly became a popular citizen. She was a longtime supporter of the suffrage cause, and both candidates promised her they would support giving the vote to women. William Bright, the Democratic candidate who won, may already have been an advocate in his own right. He was a saloonkeeper whose young wife was as ardent about suffrage as Esther Morris. Legend had it that as he left for the legislature he told her: "You are a great deal better than I am; you know a great deal more and you would make a better member of the Assembly than I. I have made up my mind that I will do everything in my power to give you the ballot."

The Wyoming legislature, which had only twenty-one members in total, assembled for the first time on October 1, 1869, on the second floor of a dusty post office in Cheyenne. Bright was elected president of the all-Democratic Senate and proposed his suffrage bill, which some of his friends were convinced Mrs. Bright had written. "The favorite argument . . . and by far the most effective was this: it would prove a great advertisement, would make a great deal of talk and attract attention to the legislature, and the territory, more effectively than anything else," recalled one man. Other participants remembered that the whole issue was treated as a joke, but if so the legislature must have stayed in a frolicsome mood for a long time, because it also passed legislation to protect married women's property rights and require equal pay for female schoolteachers.

It made sense that a place like Wyoming would embrace women's rights. With very few women around, there was no danger that they could impose their will on the male majority. And the territory very much wanted to attract more women to come, so anything that served to distinguish Wyoming as a place that was friendly to feminine concerns was good. "We now expect quite an immigration of ladies to Wyoming," said the *Cheyenne Leader* after both the House and Senate voted in favor of the suffrage bill. Esther Morris's son, Robert, sent a report on the passage to *The Revolution,* a suffrage newspaper, that ended with a call for "the girls to come to this higher plain of Human Rights, as well as to have a home in our high, clear mountain atmosphere."

The bill was signed into law by Governor John Campbell on December 10, 1869. "Won't the irrepressible 'Anne D' come out here and make her home?" demanded the still-smitten *Leader*. "We'll even give her more than the right to vote—she can run for Congress." On September 6, 1870, led by Louisa Ann Swain, a seventy-year-old Laramie housewife, Wyoming women became the first ever to take part in a public election. "Many ladies have voted and without molestation or interference," the *Leader* reported that evening. Observers noted that the presence of women at the polls made election days far more decorous than had previously been the custom: "There was plenty of drinking and noise at the saloons, but the men would not remain, after voting, around the polls. It seemed more like Sunday than election day." Nevertheless, a Wyoming resident felt compelled to write to the *Ladies' Home Journal* and assure the nation that voting had not made the local women lose their femininity.

When Wyoming applied for statehood, members of the House of Representatives objected to women there having the ballot, and the territory delegate in Washington telegraphed home that it would be easier to get congressional approval if only men were permitted to vote. The state legislature telegraphed back: "We will remain out of the union a hundred years, rather than come in without our women." The statehood bill passed Congress by a narrow margin anyway. On July 23, 1890, Wyoming celebrated its official statehood in Cheyenne, with a two-mile-long parade. Mrs. Theresa Jenkins led off the speeches with a review of the struggle for suffrage. Her delivery was so forceful that her words could be heard at the back of the crowd, four blocks away. (Mrs. Jenkins had been practicing on an open prairie, orating while her husband rode farther and farther away in his buggy, shouting back, "Louder!") Esther Morris presented the governor with a new flag bearing forty-four stars. Back east, women who had been fighting for the ballot since before the Civil War gloried in the realization that they would live to see the day when at least some

American women would be able to vote for president. Suffragists, including Susan B. Anthony and Elizabeth Cady Stanton, made pilgrimages to Wyoming. "Neither is handsome," reported the disappointed editor of the *Cheyenne Leader*. Grace Greenwood, the famous writer, also arrived, expecting a great deal of the state capital. "I should rejoice to find it a very Eden, a vale of Cashmere—which it isn't," she reported.

The first dozen states to give women the right to vote were all in the West. Wyoming just managed to beat out Utah, which passed a suffrage law in February 1870. Colorado and Idaho followed suit before 1900. Westerners did not have any different ideology about women's role, but they had different needs. Wyoming was not the only state passing laws in hopes that more women might want to emigrate. When the California legislature was debating a married woman's property act, one bachelor argued that the proposal was "the very best provision to get us wives that we can introduce into the Constitution."

Not long after Wyoming gave women the right to vote and hold office, Esther Morris was appointed to fill out a vacated seat as justice of the peace, making her the first woman judge anywhere in the country. *Frank Leslie's Illustrated Newspaper* reported that on her first day in court, Morris "wore a calico gown, worsted breakfast-shawl, green ribbons in her hair and a green neck-tie." Despite the newspaper's amusement, and the fact that her predecessor refused to turn over his docket and records to a woman, she apparently fulfilled her duties firmly and impartially. Discussing her service later, she said she felt she had done a satisfactory job and that she had not neglected her family any more than if she had spent the time shopping.

# The Gilded Age:
# Stunts, Shorthand, and Study Clubs

## "THERE WAS PLENTY OF HER TO SEE"

In the decades after the Civil War, Americans began living large. Cornelius Vanderbilt II's new Fifth Avenue mansion had a forty-five-foot dining room with jewel-studded ceiling and oak beams inlaid with mother-of-pearl. A nation of newspaper readers devoured stories about fancy dinner parties where every guest got an oyster containing a black pearl, or a cigar wrapped in hundred-dollar bills. The Gilded Age, as it came to be known, was also perhaps the only era in the nation's history that favored large women. An Englishman reported that young American women appeared to be morbidly frightened of getting thin. "They are constantly having themselves weighed and every ounce of increase is hailed with delight, and talked about with the most dreadful plainness of speech," he reported. A "beautiful Connecticut girl," he added, told him proudly that she had "gained eighteen pounds in flesh since last April."

The great American beauty of the Gilded Age was the voluptuous Lillian Russell, famed singer, actress, and dining partner of Diamond Jim Brady. At her thinnest, the five-foot, five-inch Russell weighed about 140 pounds, but she frequently exceeded 160. She never attempted to conceal her love of food. Reporters covered her contests with Brady to determine who could eat the most corn on the cob. After one long battle, she revealed to the press that before dining she left her corset with the restaurant owner for safekeeping. "There was plenty of her to see," said Clarence Day, who was at Yale when Miss Russell made appearances in New Haven. "We liked that. Our tastes were not thin or ethereal."

Dance troupes from Europe that toured the United States featured chorus girls who were definitely Rubenesque, and American stage shows followed their lead. In the 1890s, *Metropolitan Magazine* claimed that the "regulation chorus girl type" had "thick ankles, ponderous calves and a waist laced so tight that the lines of the hips and bust were distorted into balloon-like curves." Perhaps fleshiness was appropriate in an era when Americans finally discovered the joys of appetite. Or perhaps it was a reaction against the morbid fragility of the "fairylike" women in the pre–Civil War era. Helen Hunt, a delicate widow who had gone west in 1872 to escape ill health and depression, wrote to her sickly friends proudly reporting that she now weighed 163 pounds.

Photography became common, and when women had their pictures taken they demanded that their cheeks look redder, their skin whiter, their hair brighter, until, one photographer complained, the subjects "looked like a ghastly mockery of the clown in a pantomime." It was only a small step from tinted photographs to tinted faces. Makeup was still considered the mark of a fast woman, but the late-nineteenth-century equivalent of the jet set used it anyway. "She is a compound frequently of false hair, false teeth, padding of various kinds, paint, powder and enamel . . . and she utterly destroys the health of her skin by her foolish use of cosmetics," complained one New York writer. Fashionable women used hot tongs to curl their hair into effortful coiffures, which were sprinkled with gold or silver dust for special occasions. They wore elaborate hats—huge affairs bearing flowers, lace, organdy, and every possible kind of feathers, from ostrich plumes to stuffed birds. Women wore the bodies of entire pheasants on their heads and one Chicago writer in 1900 wrote that he expected "to see life-sized turkeys . . . on fashionable bonnets before I die." The slaughter of wild birds for hat decorations finally reached such outrageous proportions that it led to the nation's first public environmental protests.

The rejection of the small, thin, and retiring female image came at a time when women were, in every way, becoming more visible. Wives completely took over the family shopping; the ones who had enough money turned that chore into a social pastime. And they were beginning to go out by themselves for amusement—to have lunch with friends or see a play at the theater. Women of all classes were experimenting with the pleasures of a night—or at least an afternoon—on the town.

Until the Gilded Age, nice restaurants generally did not serve women, and when couples went out to dinner, it was to the home of a friend. Men went to restaurants by themselves, to the theater by themselves, and even to the beach by themselves. It was only after the Civil War that people started to seriously explore the idea of entertainment that families could enjoy together. Summer vacations came into vogue and circuses became the most popular form of paid entertainment in the 1860s and 1870s. Small carnivals and stunt performers popped up everywhere. "I went down and saw Miss Ella LaRue walk a rope stretched from the brick building corner of D and Union streets to the balcony of the Opera House—about 160 feet," reported a man in Virginia City. "She was dressed in short frock, tights and trunks. . . . Great 'shape'—more of it than I ever saw in any female. Immense across the hips—huge thighs."

Theaters, once the preserve of rowdy young men and hardworking prostitutes, began to covet the family trade. In the 1870s, Broadway impresario Tony Pastor—the man who discovered Lillian Russell—sponsored "Ladies Night" when women got in free, and he offered door prizes he thought would appeal to housewives, such as dress patterns, coal, and flour. Amusement parks were a prime destination for city dwellers. In New York, one Coney Island attraction, Dream Land, bent so far over backward in search of a respectable audience that it included elevating exhibits such as "The End of the Earth," where patrons could see a vain young girl grabbed by two demons and thrown into a fiery pit. Dream Land, however, was never as popular as Steeplechase, featuring rides like the Barrel of Love and the parachute jump, which always seemed to either throw couples together or blow up the women's skirts.

The single most important new public amenity for women was the department store. A. T. Stewart led the way in 1862 when he opened his big emporium on the corner of Broadway and Chambers Street in Manhattan. It was five stories tall, with hydraulic elevators for ladies who wanted to avoid climbing the grand staircase. A rotunda soared from the first floor to the roof, and shoppers on the upper floors could peer down onto the action below. "Door boys" opened the heavy doors for customers from 7 A.M. to 7 P.M. and checked the patrons' umbrellas in stormy weather. The wide aisles were the promenades where women could shop and meet with friends, the ladies' room on the second floor a place for rest and refreshment. Outside of hotels, Stewart's rest room was one of the first acknowledgments that respectable women could be away from home long enough to need to go to the bathroom.

The department store was a revolution. Everything was on display, and there was no pressure to buy. The prices were fixed and the quality was standardized, reducing the risk in making a purchase. The department stores also imposed a new, very American kind of democracy, in which everyone was equal as long as they had the money to pay. (Marshall Field instructed his clerks to call all customers "ladies," no matter what their dress or manners.) Even poor women enjoyed the stores' big, carefully decorated windows, with displays that changed regularly. Mary Antin, a young immigrant girl, recalled Saturday nights in 1898 spent with her girlfriends, marching down Broadway "till all hours" looking at the windows and mentally taking "possession of all we saw." The department store was one of the signs that American women were beginning to develop the power of the prime family purchaser. Nathaniel Fowler, a pioneer in the advertising industry, advised his clients to target all their ads to women, even those for men's clothing. "Woman buys, or directs the buying, of everything from shoes to shingles," he decreed.

## "QUALITIES WHICH ALL SOUND-HEARTED MEN AND WOMEN ADMIRE"

The Gilded Age celebrated the outrageous, the splashy, and the out-spoken. Women—at least some of them—were allowed to attract attention, and they were rewarded if they did so with the proper panache. In the 1880s, Nellie Bly, a reporter for the New York *World*, was on the front page regularly with what the papers then called "stunt" journalism, an infant version of investigative reporting. Bly got herself committed to an insane asylum, posed as a homeless woman, and inserted herself into the New York demimonde as a way of exposing conditions in the city's jails and hospitals. In 1888, she became an international celebrity when she announced that she intended to become the first person to actually go around the world in eighty days. (Jules Verne, the futurist writer, had written a popular novel in which the male hero did just that.) Bly set off, carrying only one small bag crammed with underwear, writing equipment, and a large jar of cold cream. She sailed for England, raced through Europe, jumped off to Yemen, ricocheted through Hong Kong, and returned to San Francisco, where she was greeted like a conquering heroine before embarking on her cross-country train trip home. She arrived back at her starting point in seventy-eight days to hysterical acclaim, which the *World* decreed was a tribute to her "combination of superb qualities which all sound-hearted men and women admire." Nobody mentioned motherhood.

Women were also showing up at the workplace in less glamorous jobs than actress or journalist. These were not, for the most part, the professions pioneers like Elizabeth Blackwell and Antoinette Brown had been struggling so hard to break into before the Civil War. In 1870, the country had only five female lawyers, and Myra Bradwell, the founder and publisher of the extremely influential *Chicago Legal News*, was denied admission to the bar because she was a married woman. Out of 63,000 physicians, only 525 were women, and as the profession became more prestigious, men became even more resistant to letting them in. In 1869, a few women who had wrangled their way into the clinical lectures at Pennsylvania Hospital entered the amphitheater to hisses, yowls, mock applause, and "offensive remarks upon personal appearance." During the final hour of the lecture, a Philadelphia paper reported, "missiles of tinfoil . . . were thrown upon the ladies while some of the men defiled the dresses of the ladies near them with tobacco juice."

Thanks in large part to those department stores, 142,000 female salesclerks were hired before the end of the century—Lillian Russell's mother, in the days before her marriage, made news as the first female clerk in Buffalo. Clerking was more respectable than factory or domestic work, but it was still difficult. Department store saleswomen worked up to sixteen hours a day in the busy season, and although the stores made sure their patrons had comfortable rest rooms, the staff accommodations were dirty and depressing. Although they seldom got paid vacations, clerks were often required to go on unpaid leaves during slow seasons. Fines for lateness or infraction of other rules further reduced their pay. Some female department store workers actually rose to high positions, but most of the managerial jobs, including floorwalker, were reserved for men.

The work was hard but not necessarily grim. An in-house newspaper written by the workers at the Seigel-Cooper department store was crammed with stories about who was dating whom and comments on other workers' hairstyles and clothing, dancing ability, and general popularity. The men in the mail-order department accused the members of the Bachelor Girls Social Club of being "man haters," a charge the Bachelor Girls took up with umbrage. "No we are not married, neither are we man haters, but we believe in woman's rights, and we enjoy our independence and freedom notwithstanding the fact that if a fair offer came our way we might . . . consider it."

As the federal bureaucracy grew, it also found more openings for women, who occupied a third of all government jobs by 1900. The infant telephone industry decided that women were natural switchboard operators as soon as it discovered that men tended to talk back to the customers. Women were making rapid inroads into library work, where they were praised at the 1876 American Library Association meeting for being "the best of listeners." In 1891, the *Library Journal* published the first general discussion of women's place in library work. The author, Caroline Hewlins, estimated that women who worked as library assistants should expect to make $300 to $900 a year—about half of what men made—and be able to write steadily for six or seven hours a day. They should know half a dozen languages, Hewlins said, "understand the relation of all arts and sciences to each other and must have . . . a minute acquaintance with geography, history, art and literature." Women who aspired to be head librarians should expect to work ten hours a day, she continued, but "those who are paid the highest salaries give up all their evenings" as well. She added, perhaps unnecessarily, that librarians and their assistants "sometimes break down from overwork."

American business offices had always been relatively small and populated by men, but after the Civil War, the booming economy needed an army of clerical workers to process the paperwork. These were dead-end, relatively low-paying jobs that required a facility for spelling and grammar, good handwriting, and, later, skill with typewriters. Whenever there was a sudden demand for literate workers at low pay, women were usually the answer. The typewriter was a new invention in the 1880s, and it was quickly decided that women, with their smaller hands and nimble fingers, were particularly well suited to use it. The New York YWCA offered extremely popular typing courses in 1881, and generations of girls learned to type by practicing "Now is the time for all good men to come to the aid of the party," the slogan for the 1872 Republican presidential campaign. By 1880, 40 percent of the stenographers and typists were women, and by 1900, it was three-quarters. "Some females are doing more and better work for $900 per annum than many male clerks who were paid double that amount," enthused a government official in 1869. An ad in the *Nation* for Remington typewriters suggested that they made excellent Christmas gifts for ambitious young girls because "no invention has opened for women so broad and easy an avenue to profitable and suitable employment."

The first typists used the hunt-and-peck system, and when Mrs.

L. V. Longley of Cincinnati, a teacher of secretarial skills, proposed that it might be more efficient to use all the fingers, a typing trade magazine declared that "the best operators we know of use only the first two fingers of each hand." Only trained pianists, the magazine opined, should be expected to use more. A court stenographer from Salt Lake City invented the touch typing system and won a race against a two-finger opponent that set off a fad for typing speed contests that lasted through the Gilded Age.

The sexual revolution at the office went surprisingly peacefully, although some social commentators expressed concern that women's much-worried-about "nerves" could not stand the strain of pounding on the typewriter, and others claimed women weren't suited to such serious work. Marion Harland, in an essay called "The Incapacity of Business Women," compared the diligent office boy with a female typist or stenographer who "giggles" or has "tiffs" with the "old-maid" bookkeeper. Harland's essay inspired a rejoinder by Clara Lanza, who reported that she had interviewed the head of a large publishing house, who felt women clerical workers were "capable and industrious" while their male peers were "troublesome" and given to taking too many days off. As the need for women in office jobs increased, opinion makers inevitably started concluding that some experience in the business world would actually prepare women to be better wives and mothers.

If the first female office workers faced any problems, it was probably a Victorian version of sexual harassment. At the turn of the century, *Typewriter Trade Journal* reported that nine of ten employers wanted female secretaries and that requests were phrased in "most peculiar language," such as "a pretty blonde." In 1904, the organizer of the first secretarial union, Elise Diehl, said that "one of the main matters" her organization would undertake was to make clear that secretaries were offering "professional services, instead of 'companionship' in business offices."

Most female workers were single girls. Only in the African American community was it acceptable for a married woman to have a job, and in 1890, only 3 percent of white married women worked. But for the many women who had fallen through the cracks of the old Victorian theories about their proper role in life—abandoned wives, widowed mothers, single women on their own, or women whose husbands were unable to support their families—the change in opportunity was enormous. The old triumvirate of employment options— factories, teaching, and domestic work—had been cracked open.

## "WE HAD A LOVELY PICTURE OF HER
## WE GOT WITH COFFEE WRAPPERS"

The growth in the entertainment industry and the huge expansion in the number of popular newspapers created the nation's first celebrity culture, and whether or not it was respectable for a lady to have her name in the paper, the nation was learning that it certainly could be profitable. Nellie Bly had fame, success, and a popular board game that re-created her journey around the world. Lillian Russell was chosen to be the first person to use Alexander Graham Bell's new long-distance telephone service in 1890. She sang from her dressing room in New York to President Grover Cleveland in Washington.

The American public fell madly in love with Mrs. Cleveland, the beautiful twenty-one-year-old Frances Folsom, who married the forty-nine-year-old bachelor president in the White House in 1886. The idea of a glamorous First Lady was a new one for Americans— most presidents' wives, like most presidents, were middle-aged and dignified. Every time she appeared in public, Frances Cleveland caused riots of "Frankie-worshippers," even though she behaved like a decorous Victorian wife and never gave an interview or spoke to a reporter. Still, she could not have been a bigger celebrity if she had hired a press agent. Americans hung her pictures on their walls and pasted them among the actresses in their parlor albums. To the horror of the very traditional (and much less popular) president, advertisers shamelessly used Mrs. Cleveland's image to sell everything from soap to perfume to underwear. Women copied her hairstyle, and when two bored reporters made up a story that she had given up the bustle, it immediately went out of style. Far away in Colorado, young Anne

Ellis wrote that she "practiced being a lady" by imagining how Frances Cleveland would behave: "We had a lovely picture of her we got with coffee wrappers."

## "LURED WOMEN FROM THEIR DUTIES AS HOMEMAKERS"

Most women stayed out of the newspapers and devoted themselves to their families. But they were also reaching for something beyond the household. In an apparently spontaneous movement, women's study clubs started popping up all over the country. In cities, small towns, and even remote rural areas, middle-class housewives organized themselves into groups to study current affairs, world history, or English literature. By the turn of the century there were 5,000 local organizations in the General Federation of Women's Clubs, and that was only a tiny fraction of the total number of groups that were scattered around the United States. It was a sort of informal, do-it-yourself junior college system. The idea of doing something unrelated to their families was an enormous breakthrough for many members. Harriet Robinson, who joined the New England Women's Club in 1869, noted in her diary that the first meeting she attended was the first evening she had spent away from her husband in twenty years.

The first woman's club was probably Sorosis, which was organized in New York City in 1868 by Jane Cunningham Croly, a journalist who had been offended when she was excluded from an all-male New York Press Club dinner honoring Charles Dickens. Sorosis emphasized current events and had a membership list full of poets, artists, and educators; but most of the study clubs involved women who were not employed outside the home. They prepared and read papers and held group discussions. Charles Dickens was probably the favorite subject, followed by Shakespeare. Some clubs were extremely ambitious. The Lewiston Maine Reading Circle started off by reading *Intellectual History of Europe*. Groups tackled the Greek philosophers or began with ancient history, intent on making their way through to the modern era. Others had a tendency to skim effortlessly over vast chunks of human knowledge. They were satirized in Sinclair Lewis's *Main Street,* when a club member asks the heroine for help in preparing her report on "the English poets."

By the 1890s, women's reading clubs were a respected part of community life, their meetings regular grist for the women's pages in the local newspapers. But in the early years they were controversial. When the New England Women's Club was founded in 1868, the *Boston Transcript* predicted that "Homes will be ruined, children neglected, woman is straying from her sphere." In Greencastle, Indiana, a newspaper editorial attacked Elizabeth Ames, founder of a local women's club, claiming she had "lured women from their duties as homemakers" to join an "unspeakable menace." The social prejudice against "clubbers" was strongest in the South, and weakest in the West, where social divisions were vague. In Lemoore, California, where 600 residents were spread over a huge territory, humble farmers' wives and the spouses of the wealthiest professional men all belonged to the same club, which they often attended with babies in arm, driving in wagons from their far-flung households.

Black women were enthusiastic club members—they had been organizing societies since the Revolutionary War era, although most were directed toward mutual aid rather than intellectual improvement. Most white clubwomen were distinctly cool, if not hostile, to the idea that they should recognize African American women as peers, and the General Federation of Women's Clubs declined to accept black women's groups as members. In 1900, Josephine Ruffin, a prominent African American clubwoman from Massachusetts, was eligible to attend the Federation's national convention because of her membership in an integrated group. But when she made it clear she was also representing her own all-black New Era Club, the officers refused to accept her credentials, and one woman tried to rip off her badge. "It is the 'high-caste' Negroes who bring about all the ill-feeling," said a Georgia clubwoman. "The ordinary colored woman understands her position thoroughly."

## "WAS THAT CROQUET?"

Just as women were beginning to take part in urban public life, the new class of white-collar professional men began to move their families to suburbs in search of safety, quiet nights, trees, and good schools. Manhattan businessmen commuted by ferry from Brooklyn, a semibucolic place that New Yorkers called a "woman's town" because of its lack of a red-light district. Thanks to streetcar and railway service, there were thirty-one suburban cities and towns outside of Boston by 1900. In 1883, the travel writer Willard Glazer described the suburbs of Cincinnati as a "paradise of grass, gardens, lawns and tree-shaded roads." It was the beginning of a century of suburbanization that would offer women a trade-off of a better environment to raise children in return for isolation from the wider public world of the cities.

Having a yard was one of the great attractions of the suburbs. Greenery became extremely important as people's memories of rural life became more remote and more idealized. The farmer's wife in the early 1800s, who thought the yard was a good place to toss garbage, had been succeeded by a suburban matron who grew flowers along the borders of a carefully maintained lawn. The gender division of yard labor, in which the men mowed and the women planted, was born. A whole new generation of sports came into being, defined by the fact that they could be played by both sexes on lawns. Archery and lawn tennis were both popular. (In deference to the ladies' need to play in corsets and long skirts, lawn tennis did not involve any running for the ball—people just swatted it back and forth over the net.) Croquet was a universal favorite—people played croquet on the prairies of Kansas, and some sets were sold with candle sockets on the wickets for night playing. Young people, who had trouble finding places for physical interaction apart from the dance floor, were particularly enthusiastic.

> *I saw the scamp—it was light as day*
> *Put his arm around her waist in a loving way.*

*And he squeezed her hard.*
*Was that croquet?*


## "ZINC COFFINS"

The Gilded Age kitchen was full of new trinkets—parers, peelers, and pitters, each designed for one specific type of fruit. Yet the great leaps in technology that were transforming industry and transportation were not really doing much for the housewife. Women still performed their basic tasks the same way their grandmothers did. A study by the Boston School of Housekeeping determined that it took an hour a day to take care of even the most modern stove. Another study calculated that a woman with an eight-room house spent an average of eighteen hours a week just removing dust and tracked-in dirt. (Window screens became available for the first time after the Civil War, but for some reason, they were slow to catch on.) All in all, sweeping, dusting, cleaning lighting fixtures, washing windows, and maintaining the furnace and fireplaces took an estimated twenty-seven hours a week.

The greatest boon to the housewife was water. By the end of the century, close to half of the American population had access to public water of some kind. That didn't necessarily mean it came into the house, however. Women in urban tenements generally had to walk down several flights of stairs to get water from a public pump. Middle-class city dwellers began getting water pumped into their houses in the 1880s, and by 1890, a quarter of American homes had running water. For $48, a family could buy a Family Sunshine Range from Sears that included a boiler to force hot water into any part of the house where the primitive plumbing went. It must have been an incredible boon on washday, when homemakers were still struggling with hand-cranked washing machines, bars of soap that had to be scraped and boiled, and irons that had to be heated on the stove.

In many homes, the water went no farther than the kitchen, where it was pumped into a pan in the sink. Sewerage systems were much slower to arrive than town water, and in houses that had no drains,

women toted the dishwater and bathwater outside to a cesspool or gut-
ter. If they were careless enough or exhausted enough, they simply
tossed it out the nearest window. But wealthier families slowly acquired
complete plumbing systems. Real bathtubs, a rarity before the Civil
War, became more common, and in the 1870s the nation embarked on
a long debate about the benefits of baths as opposed to standing on an
oilcloth mat in front of a basin of water. Some experts decried the idea
of bodily immersion in "zinc coffins," but once Americans had the
chance to actually experience a hot bath, their cause was lost.

Even in houses with bathtubs and hot and cold running water, the
outdoor privy—or one connected to the far end of the house—was
still the rule. Many middle-class households installed water closets,
toilets with jerry-rigged waste disposal systems. The result was disaster. Cesspools leaked and poisoned well water, pipes eroded, sewage
backed up after rainfalls, and people worried about "sewer gas."
Catharine Beecher championed the earth closet—a commode that
dropped dirt on the human waste to eliminate odor and induce fer-
mentation. The earth closet never really caught on though, since all
the dirt had to be removed frequently and carted away.

The outhouse had few champions. Among its many other draw-
backs, it was beginning to be identified as a threat to women's health.
Experts worried that modest women delayed "their visits to the privy
until compelled by unbearable physical discomfort," allowing themselves "to become so constipated that days and sometimes weeks will
pass between stools." It's hard to believe women who were raised
using outdoor latrines suddenly found them too indelicate. But something was causing a near epidemic of constipation among nineteenth-
century women. It may have been the corsets, or the lack of exercise.
If modesty was the problem, the first flush toilets, which were noisy,
balky contraptions that tended to let the whole household know what
was going on in the bathroom, probably didn't help.

Few women had the luxury of fretting over such embarrassments.
In 1893 in New York, far and away the most advanced American city
when it came to sewage treatment, an estimated 53 percent of families
were still using outside privies; in other large cities, the figure was

70 percent or more. But middle-class Americans all knew what they wanted, and in Catharine Beecher's post–Civil War book *American Woman's Home,* the model house had complete indoor plumbing.

## "OH, DOCTOR, SHOOT ME, QUICK!"

One of the more grisly trends in the late nineteenth century was the removal of women's reproductive organs as a cure for their mental disorders. When the reformer and free love advocate Victoria Woodhull was bankrupt, under indictment, and being assailed by every newspaper in the country as a female Satan, she suffered a breakdown and was taken to a doctor. His diagnosis was that she suffered from "a female ailment, amenable to surgery." Woodhull managed to recover with her organs intact, but other, more tractable women offered themselves up to doctors, hoping that their antisocial behavior could be curbed by surgery. Removing the clitoris was prescribed for nymphomania and persistent masturbation. More common was ovariectomy, in which doctors effectively castrated their patients as a treatment for everything from painful menstruation to overeating. At the turn of the century, by one estimate 150,000 women had undergone the procedure. "Patients are improved, some of them cured . . . the moral sense of the patient is elevated . . . she becomes tractable, orderly, industrious and cleanly," said one enthusiast.

It's possible that a connection existed between the increasing independence of many women and the surgical assault on them. But it's even more likely that doctors started removing women's sexual organs simply because the arrival of anesthetics had made it safe to do so. Doctors had always regarded female reproductive organs as the source of all women's medical problems. The founders of Woman's Hospital in New York claimed "25 to 40 percent of all cases of insanity in women arise directly from organic female disease which, in most cases, might be remedied by appropriate and timely treatment."

Doctors were particularly likely to recommend removal of the ovaries for women who they regarded as oversexed. Dr. E. W. Cushing of Boston claimed that he had performed the operation on a woman who had sunk into depression because she masturbated, and that his grateful patient told him that "a window has been opened in heaven." It did not take much in the way of sexuality for a doctor to prescribe the knife. One doctor claimed to have treated a case of "virgin nymphomania." And physicians did not believe that even very young girls minded being deprived of their clitoris or ovaries. "We must not impute to a woman feelings in regard to the loss of her organs which are derived from what we as men would think of a similar operation on a man. A woman does not feel she is unsexed, and she is not unsexed," Dr. Cushing counseled his fellow physicians.

The aggressive use of new medical tools went beyond castration. Dr. Marion Sims discovered a condition called "vaginismus," in which a woman felt such pain from intercourse she was unable to bear penetration. He prescribed surgery, but another treatment was to put the woman under anesthesia so her husband was able to have sex with her. Sims described one case in which a physician had to visit the couple two or three times a week to anesthetize the woman before lovemaking.

Another new weapon in the doctor's arsenal was the hypodermic syringe, which arrived in America in 1856. Physicians quickly learned that by injecting their patients with opium or morphine, they could provide near-instantaneous relief from a wide range of symptoms. A report from the American Pharmaceutical Association noted that when a doctor was summoned to a prosperous home, he knew "a practice might be secured which would be valuable if he can only show his ability, and he does—there is not very much pain in the prick of a needle, and the result is so quick, so calming—wonderful man—the patient begins to improve at once." A doctor reported in an 1870 medical journal that one of his female patients always exclaimed when he entered her room, "Oh, doctor, shoot me, quick!"

Somewhere between 200,000 and 400,000 late-nineteenth-century Americans were addicted to drugs, and the typical addict was an older middle-class white woman, who was introduced to the habit by her doctor. When the playwright Eugene O'Neill was born in 1888, the doctor ordered morphine to ease Ella O'Neill's pain. She became

addicted, and her son, who came home from school when he was
twelve to find his mother giving herself an injection, described her as
"a walking twilight zone." Harriet Beecher Stowe's daughter Geor-
giania also became addicted to morphine. Jefferson Davis's female relatives all referred to it frequently in their diaries, as did Mary Chesnut.

Women had always relied on doctors more than men did, and they
were also particularly vulnerable to drugs that took the edge off reality. There were millions of farm wives in remote areas, and women
whose husbands traveled on business or spent their evenings at a club
or saloon. All of them sat alone in silent houses. A traveler who spent
time among the wives of seamen in Nantucket claimed the women had
a long-standing addiction to opium "and so deeply rooted is it that
they would be at a loss how to live without this indulgence." Women
were lonely, and they were often in pain from ailments that medicine
had not yet learned how to cure. They were not supposed to drink.
But they were given to "taking something" to ease their depression.
Laudanum, an opium derivative, was particularly common among
southern frontier wives. "When she first commenced the use of it to
relieve her mind after the loss of her son, little did she think future
existence and tolerable comfort would render its use absolute necessity," said one southern woman about a friend.

Drugs were generally legal and easy to get. In 1897, the Sears Roe-
buck catalog featured hypodermic kits, including carrying case, for
$1.50. Women who would never have thought of sending their chil-
dren to the corner saloon for a bottle of rum routinely sent them to the
druggist with a coin and a note for morphine. "No name is signed, no
questions asked. The bottle of morphine is wrapped up and passed to
the child over the counter," a Tennessee doctor wrote. Doctors and
pharmacists had little compunction about dispensing narcotics.
"Young women cannot go to a ball without taking a dose of morphine
to make them agreeable," a druggist said in 1876. A North Carolina
doctor claimed he had given one patient between 2,500 and 3,000 shots
over eighteen months "and so far see no signs of the opium habit."
Dr. Alexander Morgan, a physician in Chicago who had made extensive use of opium in his practice, died in 1872, leaving behind an

addicted widow. When her children and grandchildren got the local druggists to cut her off, she rode cable cars to faraway neighborhoods to get her fix.

The habit of "taking something" also extended to alcohol-laced patent medicines, which were enormously popular with women in the late nineteenth century. The most famous was Lydia Pinkham's Vegetable Compound, which was invented by a Massachusetts housewife whose face was on every bottle. The Pinkham family members were strict temperance advocates, and it apparently did not occur to them that there was anything wrong in the fact that Lydia's medicine contained more alcohol than the average table wine. Their advertising got increasingly expansive as time went on, promising to cure everything from painful menstruation to unhappy marriages. "I do wish that every woman who feels dissatisfied with her lot would realize that she is sick, and would take steps to make herself well. . . . Mrs. Pinkham's medicine will make a woman cheerful and happy, will make her more ready to meet the wishes of her husband . . ." the ad copy promised. Probably a bit more than three tablespoons of compound a day was required to produce all that good cheer and obliviousness.

American women of the late nineteenth century were drowning in drugs and alcohol that they ingested under the guise of medication. Colonel Hoestetters Stomach Bitters aided the digestion with a compound that was 44.3 percent alcohol—one tablespoon fed through a gas burner could maintain a bright flame for almost five minutes. Some of the alcohol-laced medicines were even recommended as cures for alcoholism.

## "THAT SO LITTLE SHOULD BE SAID ABOUT THEM SURPRISES ME FOR THEY ARE EVERYWHERE"

The post–Civil War generation had more women who never married than any other in American history. Of the women born in the United States between 1860 and 1880, more than 10 percent remained single. The changing economy made it easier for women to support themselves without a husband's help, and spinsterhood began to seem more acceptable. Suddenly, women were beginning to be celebrated for staying unattached and serving the community. In 1906, when a newspaper in Chicago ran a contest for "the best woman in Chicago" (Jane Addams won), the nominees were restricted to single women. "Unless the married woman ignores the wishes of her husband, it is difficult for her to achieve the same degree of goodness the unmarried woman does," the paper decreed.

Part of the reason so many women stayed single was the large number of men who had taken off to seek their fortunes in the West. In 1880, Massachusetts had 50,000 more women than men, and among the most marriageable age group, the odds were as bad as 86 men for every 100 women. The reformer Mary Livermore gave a popular speech around the country in the 1870s and 1880s that urged parents to train their daughters for self-support because their chances of getting a good husband were dwindling. Men were dying from alcohol, debauchery, or overwork, she said, and those who survived were still likely to be invalids or deserters, lazy or depraved.

Women in America had almost always found satisfaction in friendships with each other, and in the late nineteenth century, they had the option of stretching those friendships into something more akin to a marriage. The "Boston marriage," named in honor of that male-short city, was a permanent relationship between two women who lived together and supported one another. What was unstated was whether they shared sexual relations. Certainly many women of the era talked and wrote to each other in ways that suggested a physical relationship. "If only you were here so I could put my arm close around you and feel your heart beating against mine as in lang syne," wrote Antoinette Brown to Lucy Stone before the two young feminists married the Blackwell brothers. But the Victorian era was a determinedly innocent time, in which some sexual liaisons were so unthinkable they became relatively easy to carry out. The idea that respectable middle-class ladies could be lesbians was so far over the top that, with a little discretion, actually living as lesbians was no problem at all. Women had always slept together, the better to keep warm in unheated houses, and they had always been physically affectionate. On whatever terms the single women of the late nineteenth century shared their lives, many apparently found their situations more rewarding than life with men. "The loves of women for each other grow more numerous each day. . . . That so little should be said about them surprises me for they are everywhere," said Frances Willard, the head of the Women's Christian Temperance Union, in 1889.

# I 2

# Immigrants:
# Discovering the "Woman's Country"

In Europe, peasants wore shawls and only women of means wore hats. For poor women who immigrated to the United States in the nineteenth century, buying a hat was a big moment, when they left the old world behind and became Americans. "They say in this country you don't go to work without a hat," wrote Rose Pasternak, a newcomer whose brother greeted her at the boat and took her directly to a milliner. Neighbors jealously monitored the rate at which "greenhorn" women succumbed to American fashions. "In the old country she used to carry baskets of tomatoes on her head and now she carries a hat on it," they sniped.

Many older women kept to their shawls, remaining suspended between cultures, while their daughters created new selves in the new world. It took courage to make the change. Rose Cohen, who came to New York from Russia with her family, noticed her mother looked older than her father, who had begun cutting his beard like an American while his wife continued to wear the traditional scarf and wig, even indoors. One day, when Rose and her mother were alone, Rose persuaded her to uncover her head. She was surprised by how much prettier her mother looked. "She had never before in her married life had her hair uncovered before anyone," Cohen recalled in her autobiography. Sitting on her mother's lap, she pointed out that when women looked old-fashioned, "the husbands were often ashamed to go out with them." That must have done the trick, because Rose's father came home that night and found his wife bareheaded. "What! Already you are becoming an American lady?" he exclaimed. Rose's mother, with unexpected gumption, replied, "As you see, I am not staying far behind."

Beginning in the 1830s, immigrants poured into the United States, seeking opportunity—the chance to become, or help their daughters become, the kind of woman who wore a hat. Marie Prisland, a Slovenian immigrant, got her first surprise at the New York disembarking point. She and about 100 countrymen and women were waiting to be processed when someone asked a guard for a drink of water. When he returned with a pail, the men stepped forward, but the guard pushed them back, insisting "Ladies first." When "Ladies first" was translated into Slovenian, Prisland and her friends were stunned, "for in Slovenia, as in all Europe, women were second to men." As they mulled this over, an elderly lady stepped up, took a drink, and cried, in Slovenian, "Long live America, where women are first!"

Other women had heard rumors in Europe that their status might be higher in America, and that the balance of power between husband and wife might become more even after they emigrated. Word had gotten back to some villages that in America husbands helped with the housework and the children—a cataclysmic idea. Anyone who believed that particular story was probably disappointed. Although some social workers did notice out-of-work immigrant husbands doing the dishes while their wives sewed to make extra money, those sightings were rare. For the most part, immigrant wives were expected to take care of the house no matter how many extra duties they took on, and immigrant daughters were expected to help, even if they spent six days a week at a factory.

The immigrant women who arrived during the Gilded Age were much less inclined to write about themselves than those who came in the twentieth century. Two of the few who did were Rose Cohen and

Rosa Cavalleri, and the histories they left were both typical and unique, like every other woman who made that remarkable trip.

Rose Cohen was named Rahel Gollup when she came to the United States in 1892 at the age of twelve. She was sent to join her father, who had escaped earlier from a Russia that persecuted its Jewish families but would not permit them to leave legally. The wagon Rahel and her aunt were being smuggled in made it over the border, but another wagon in their party was discovered. "As we started off again I heard the crying of children in the distance and shooting," she wrote. In America, Rahel took the name Rose when someone warned her that "Rachel" was called out by the tough men who hung around the bars whenever a pretty Jewish girl passed by. She quickly went to work in the New York garment trade to help her father earn money for her mother's and siblings' passage. Her mother, brothers, and sister arrived safely, but without most of the family's belongings. Rose's mother had been assured at the boat that she could bring only the luggage she could carry. She discovered later it was a lie, told to her by a man who was eager to buy her possessions cheaply.

Rosa Cavalleri came to the United States in 1884 to join a husband she loathed, the product of an arranged marriage. An illegitimate child, abandoned at birth, she had grown up in a rural village in northern Italy and was married at age fourteen to a much older man. Unable to speak English and virtually illiterate, Cavalleri began her American life cooking for the Italian workers at a mining camp in Missouri. She ran away when her husband purchased a bordello where he attempted to make her work as the manager. She wound up living in Chicago, married to a second husband she chose for herself and trying to help support their children by working as a cleaning woman.

The immigrants who arrived on the East Coast between the Civil War and World War I were primarily from Europe. Germans, Irish, and Scandinavians came first. They were followed by Rose and Rosa's generation of refugees, who came from Eastern Europe and Italy. Most émigrés arrived at Ellis Island in New York, invariably confused and exhausted from an unpleasant and dangerous voyage. Health inspectors checked every immigrant, and while the inspections were not particularly rigid, people were routinely refused entry. Often it was a child, leaving the mother with a sort of Sophie's choice— whether to go back to Europe with the rejected son or daughter or stay with her husband and other children. "When they learned their fate, they were stunned," wrote Fiorello LaGuardia, who worked as an interpreter at Ellis Island when he was young. "They never felt ill . . . and they had no homes to return to."

The terrors and heartbreak at Ellis Island were minimal, however, compared with what Chinese immigrants were going through on the West Coast. An 1882 law made the Chinese the only ethnic group prohibited from coming to America, with a few narrow exceptions for diplomats, merchants, students, and their families. At Angel Island Immigration Station—their point of entry after 1910—one study found the Chinese immigrants were asked anywhere from several hundred to a thousand questions, many of them aimed at catching them in some minor lie or error that would disqualify them from entering. "It was like being in prison," said Law Shee Low, who was locked in a barracks with other women, waiting days, and sometimes weeks, to be interrogated.

## "AMERICA IS A WOMAN'S COUNTRY"

Every woman who came to America from another country wove her new life out of the strands of her own character, her family's support, and sheer luck. But the culture of the country she came from could also make a big difference. Irish women often came on their own, young and single, and as a group they were less focused on marriage than girls from other countries. (The Irish were the only ethnic group with a majority of female emigrants. At the other end were some of the Balkan areas, where only 10 percent of the immigrants were women.) Italian women came with their fathers or husbands. Often the men, like Rosa Cavalleri's first husband, emigrated first and sent for their families later. Most immigrant women spent their evenings at home while their husbands congregated in saloons or lodges with their fellow countrymen, but German wives often went with their husbands and children to beer gardens where they all sat together, listening to music, singing, and eating. Italian girls were kept close to home and were seldom allowed to go out without supervision. Jewish girls had more freedom, and their husbands and fathers were more likely to encourage them to take classes or go to settlement house lectures. The Jews tended to come to America as families, fleeing persecution and knowing they could never return to Europe. But Germans went back frequently, as did Italians. Overall, one in three immigrants returned permanently to their home countries.

No matter what their ethnicity, most immigrant women were the financial officers of their families. Their husbands turned over their pay, keeping only enough for carfare, lunch, and the great variable of "entertainment." The wife saved up and paid the rent, bought the food, and allocated money for other expenses. One of the great cost centers was sending money back home or putting aside funds to bring other relatives over. An immigrant mother proudly boasted that none of her children had ever opened their own pay envelope, and a "good" husband did the same. Even men who controlled the purse strings in the old country deferred to their wives once they reached America. Ukrainian men told an interviewer that they had given up their old tradition of handling the money. When asked why, they laughed and said, "America is a woman's country." An Italian immigrant said that when his father first came to America by himself, he gave his paycheck to a friend's wife, who kept his money until there was enough to pay for his family's passage.

But getting the family workers to turn over their pay was not always easy. Many men withheld money for drinking at a neighborhood saloon. A social worker described a man who "gave his wife five dollars on a Saturday night and when she said 'Is that all?' he put the five dollars back in his pocket." Girls tended to hand over their pay without a fight. "It was the respect to bring and give your mother the money," said an immigrant, Mollie Linker. Jane Addams surveyed 200 Chicago working girls and found that 62 percent gave their mothers every penny they earned. Only 5 percent really had full use of their salaries. Boys were more inclined to keep some money back for themselves or simply pay a given amount for board.

Handling the finances of a poor immigrant family was a tough job. When funds ran short, the wife had to placate creditors, scrounge money from friends and relatives, or talk storeowners into allowing her to run up a tab. In families unfamiliar with the concept of monthly rent, it was the wife who had to learn the discipline of putting something aside every week, no matter how urgent the family's other needs. The wife organized the children to go scrounging for bits of coal or wood for fires. She knit the family into a larger community of female neighbors who supported each other during all the crises of their crisis-packed lives.

The classic first home for a nineteenth-century immigrant family was a New York City tenement of three rooms, each perhaps ten feet square. The front room looked out on the street, the back room on an airshaft. The kitchen was in the middle, the better to heat the entire apartment, but it was almost completely dark and badly ventilated. To light the gas lamps, the tenant had to put a coin in a meter, but few immigrant families had coins to spare, so they used candles or kerosene. As time went on, the outdoor privy was replaced by a water closet in the hallway. But the plumbing was unreliable, and the frequently backed-up water closet was not necessarily a great improvement.

Running water —from a backyard pump or hallway faucet or even in the kitchen sink—was another matter. "Water . . . to my mother was one of the great wonders of America—water with just a twist of the handle and only a few paces from the kitchen. It took her a long time to get used to this luxury," said Leonard Covello. Nevertheless, for many, their first American home was less appealing than the place they had left behind. In the summer, tenement apartments were so hot the Boston Board of Health recommended that mothers take their babies to the rooftops at night. (Men and women regularly fell to their deaths when they rolled off a roof in their sleep.) In the winter, the tenements were so cold that people went to work even when they were sick just so they could get warm. The wives, who worked at home, had no escape. Women who had lived in the Italian or Russian or Irish countryside were crammed into neighborhoods where 30,000 people lived in an area equivalent to five or six city blocks. One tenement described by Jacob Riis had 170 children, and a 14-foot-square yard for them to play in.

No one in the tenements had any privacy—apartments looked into one another across the narrow airshafts, and women often carried on conversations with each other while working in their respective kitchens. A husband and wife knew that half the neighborhood could hear them arguing, or making love. A typical family might be composed of parents, who slept in the back room with the smallest child; a boarder, who claimed part or all of the front room for himself, and the other children, relatives, and visitors who slept on the floor, on chairs in the kitchen, or anywhere else they could fit. The barriers between inside and outside tended to blur. Children played in the streets, adults sat and talked in the hallways. Young women who wanted to visit with admirers regarded their front stoop as an extension of the house. "It was nothing unusual to receive 'company' on the street," said Rose Cohen.

Housewives were engaged in a constant struggle to keep their husbands home at night, and out of the saloons where each man felt compelled to "treat" his friends to a round of drinks. "A kind of obligation of honor was created which required the individual to continue drinking until everyone in the group he was part of had the opportunity to treat everybody else," said a reformer. The custom of treating—which must have been invented by a bartender—virtually guaranteed that any customer who walked into a saloon would walk out, at minimum, tipsy. Women hated it—partly because no one wanted to be confronted with a drunken husband late in the evening, but even more because it threatened the family future. Drinking cost money, and it made it less likely that the husband would get up in the morning and go off to a job that was probably both unpleasant and exhausting.

Despite the chaos and crowding, immigrant wives tried to create something that resembled a parlor, where their husbands and sons would want to sit and read or play cards or talk with friends. Most readily sent out for a pail of beer or bottle of wine if it kept their men at home rather than in the bar. The parlor was also a place to show off their acquisitions and demonstrate their status. "The walls are hung with gorgeous prints of many hued saints, their gilt frames often hanging edge to edge so that they form a continuous frieze around the walls," reported a visitor at the home of Slavic immigrants in Jersey City. "The mantel is covered with lace paper and decorated with bright colored plates and cups, and gorgeous bouquets of homemade paper flowers are massed wherever bureaus or shelves give space for vases."

## "I WORKED AND ROCKED THE BABY WITH MY FEET"

Immigrant families agreed with native-born whites that women should quit their jobs when they married and stay home to tend the house and children. If married women needed to find work in factories, they learned to hide their wedding rings, because employers shared the common prejudice. "The boss said that a woman that is married cannot keep her mind on the job," reported a bookkeeper. But the cultural ban was on working outside the home, not work itself. Many women were paid by the piece to sew garments in their apartments. That allowed them to stay with their children, but the working conditions could be even less pleasant than a factory because the tenements were so dark. Lighting was particularly important for garment workers who were expected to sew with a tiny backstitch; it took even an experienced needlewoman twelve hours to finish one shirt. And although the women were in the same place as their children, they were far from able to really mother them. "I used to cry because I could not spend time with the baby," said a Manhattan piece worker. "I worked in the house but I had no time for the baby. I put the baby in the rocker by my feet and I worked and rocked the baby with my feet."

Women also took in boarders—even if they were already cramped in three-room apartments that could barely accommodate the immediate family. Somewhere between 25 and 50 percent of immigrant families in the late nineteenth century had boarders, which meant the housewife had a secondary occupation as landlady and sometimes as a short-order cook. To make things even worse, the husband sometimes set himself up as a garment industry subcontractor and ran the business out of the home. Those tiny sweatshops, which were very common on New York's Lower East Side, took up the front room of the tenement apartment, where employees ran sewing machines and cut fabric while the presser prepared the garments for delivery in the kitchen. The presser needed to keep his irons heated on the stove, so the fight for space with the housewife, who had to heat water for laundry and feed her children, must have been fierce.

A wife spent a great deal of time running up and down the stairs— tenement houses generally had five floors, with the cheapest apartments on the top. Even if the building provided water and a hall toilet, she had to make several trips to the basement each day for coal. Few apartments had much in the way of refrigeration, so every meal required a run to the store for fresh food. Checking on children, throwing out dirty water, delivering piecework to the contractor—the women, who were frequently pregnant, spent their lives climbing. Cleaning was a constant battle given the city soot and the number of people using every inch of a tenement apartment. But although the public tended to think of immigrants as dirty, many charity workers reported arriving at a home that was devoid of furniture and finding a woman scrubbing the floor.

The dirt outside, however, continually threatened the health of the families. In Chicago, garbage was deposited in wooden boxes attached to the street. "Those swill boxes in the alley used to stay so packed full that the covers were all the time standing up," said Rosa Cavalleri. "Oh my, oh mercy! It was stinking so the poor little children were holding their noses when they ran back the alley to come home. . . . After the wagon passed to shovel the box out—they weren't careful how it was falling—all the alley was full of white worms. . . . The garbage was terrible, terrible! I don't know why everybody in Chicago didn't die." Cavalleri said that even the local settlement house, where she worked as a cleaning woman, had huge rats that ran under the diners' legs during dinner. Lillian Wald, who ran a visiting nurse service at the Henry Street Settlement in New York, wrote that no matter how clean the immigrant family, the old tenements in which they lived were so full of vermin that a nurse who sat up all night with a sick child came back "with face and neck inflamed from bites."

## "SURE, SIX DAYS IS ENOUGH TO WORK"

Many middle-class Americans' first interaction with the new immigrants was in their own homes, where foreign-born servants quickly replaced native-born girls who were heading for the department stores and business offices. For the American housewife, having a servant was the difference between respectability and commonness. Common people answered their own door, and common women were forced to clean their own stoves and wring their own laundry. Respectable people had a "girl" who opened the door and told the caller whether or not her mistress was "in." Servants also served dinner to the family and performed all the sweatier chores around the house. The anonymous author of the guide to economical housekeeping *Six Hundred Dollars a Year* wrote: "Humble as was our position in the great world we had a certain status to maintain. We must live in a respectable house, we must dress genteely at least, and keep a servant, too." In her careful budgeting, she allotted $1.50 a week for the servant's wages.

The live-in domestics' workweek was about 50 percent longer than the factory workers' and they were always on call. They could not entertain visitors in their rooms. "Especially is objection made to the fact that her evenings are not her own," said a report prepared on the subject of the servant shortage. Lucy Salmon of Vassar College interviewed former domestics in 1897 and found that they preferred waitressing, fruit picking, and work in canneries or factories. Reformers generally believed the life of a servant, under the supervision of a middle-class American housewife, provided the most morally secure surroundings for a single woman. They never quite reconciled this with the fact that domestic service was the occupation most likely to make women feel they would prefer life on the streets. A social service investigator interviewed the assistant manager of the Door of Hope Mission, who had received at least 1,000 wayward girls, and noted: "Questioned as to the relative safety of occupations, assigned domestic service as far safer for a girl than store or factory, but admitted that they got very few factory girls and very many domestics. Did not attempt to account for this."

Most of the new generation of domestics were Irish. From the days of the Pilgrims, the women who came to America generally came because a man—a father or spouse—thought it was a good idea, or because they wanted to improve their chances of finding a husband. But the typical Irish immigrant was a single woman, who came with the intention of getting a job and supporting herself. "I am getting along splendid and likes my work," reported a young seamstress in Connecticut to her people back in Ireland. "I will soon have a trade and be more independent. . . . You know it was always what I wanted so I have reached my highest ambition."

Even before the great famines, daughters in Irish families had been encouraged to go off to the cities and find work in a store or as a servant, while the sons stayed home to work on the farm. They were expected to take care of themselves—although the cultural ban on premarital sex was strict, there was no thought that young women would require a chaperone or watchful brother to protect them from trouble. They emigrated eagerly, intending to get a job, save money, and bring over other members of the family.

Although almost no one liked domestic service, Irish women seemed to find the jobs more bearable than many others. They were not troubled by problems with the English language, and since so many of them were on their own, they might have found living in someone else's home more acceptable than girls who had a family in America. They also seem to have adapted to situations in which they were given little chance to meet young men. In Ireland people tended to marry late, and about a quarter of the women never married at all. One sign of the Irish women's priorities was that when they arrived in America, they headed out for the places that offered the best jobs, not the best opportunity for matrimony.

By midcentury, 74 percent of the domestic servants in New York were Irish, and familiarity did not necessarily bring affection. (Edwin Godkin, the editor of *The Nation*, claimed the performance of Irish domestics was a major reason American opinion had swung toward

Ætatis suæ 21. Aᵒ. 1616.

Matoaks als Rebecka daughter to the mighty Prince
Powhatan Emperour of Attanoughkomouck als virginia
converted and baptized in the Christian faith, and
Wife to the worᵗʰ Mʳ Thoᵐ Rolff.

Pocahontas is the Native American whose story we know best, but unfortunately we only know it as told by English males who put themselves in the starring role. She was only about twenty years old when she died, but she had already made the equivalent of a public relations tour of England in which she was painted wearing the fashions of the day. (National Portrait Gallery, Smithsonian Institution/ Art Resource, N.Y.)

Nobody expressed the feelings of strong-minded women during the Revolutionary era better than Abigail Adams. Her letter to her husband, in which she urged him to "Remember the Ladies" when writing the nation's new laws, is famous. Less well-known is his response: "... I cannot but laugh." (Library of Congress, Prints and Photographs Division)

When women from Edenton, North Carolina, pledged to boycott English tea prior to the Revolutionary War, word traveled back across the Atlantic. The cartoon of "A Society of Patriotic Ladies" is a good example of the level of outrage, as well as the shortage of subtlety, in the British media. (Library of Congress, Prints and Photographs Division)

In the eighteenth and early nineteenth century Americans still regarded very small children as very small adults, as this portrait suggests. (Smithsonian American Art Museum, Washington, D.C./Art Resource, N.Y.)

*A DOWNRIGHT GABBLER,*
or a goose that deserves to be hissed—

*Frances Wright was possibly the first woman to speak in public to audiences of both sexes. Her lecture tour in 1829 created a sensation, but when it was over "Fanny Wrightism" was a household term for an extremely impractical radicalism. (Library of Congress, Prints and Photographs Division)*

*Angelina (ABOVE) and Sarah Grimke were much more successful than Frances Wright when they lectured on behalf of the abolitionist cause. Their extreme piety probably had something to do with it. (Library of Congress, Prints and Photographs Division)*

*Harriet Beecher Stowe, here shown surrounded by a group of anti-slavery workers, was a member of the fabled Beecher clan, and two of her sisters mobilized to help her write her first novel,* Uncle Tom's Cabin. *(Hulton Archive/Getty Images)*

*Sarah Josepha Hale, the first woman to edit a magazine for American women, told her readers to ignore fashion while the very popular plates in her Godey's Lady's Book made them yearn for elegant gowns and tightly corseted waists. She shunned the public world for the joys of housekeeping and assured her readers she had only gone to work to support her fatherless children. Cynics might have noticed that her family emergency lasted until she retired at age ninety, when her youngest child was fifty-five. (CORBIS; Library of Congress, Prints and Photographs Division)*

GODEY'S FASHIONS FOR FEBRUARY 1865.

Even within the institution of slavery a few sexual rules continued to hold sway. Although there was little or no difference between the amount of work required of men and women in the field, the women were still expected to do the cooking, laundry, and housekeeping by themselves. *(Bettmann/CORBIS)*

Sojourner Truth, former slave, author, and professional lecturer was seventy years old when she had a series of run-ins with racist Washington streetcar conductors. Although Truth cheerfully said her battle had left the cars integrated and looking "like salt and pepper," she was seriously injured in one of her encounters. *(Schomburg Center for Research in Black Culture, New York Public Library)*

*Magazines, clergy, and doctors decried the binding of women in tight corsets from childhood to old age, but ads and the fashion photos in magazines like Godey's made it clear that the beauty standard of the day required a waist much smaller than anything nature was likely to provide. (Culver Pictures; Bettmann/ CORBIS)*

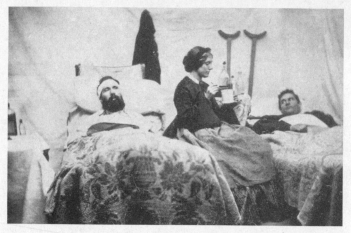

*Dorothea Dix, the superintendent of Union nurses during the Civil War, required all her volunteers to be over thirty and "plain looking." While men on both sides were originally shocked at the idea of allowing middle-class women to treat hospitals full of wounded men, the reduction in fatality rates convinced most to change their minds. (CORBIS)*

*In the 1870s the "whiskey wars" began in Ohio, with local matrons and their daughters singing hymns outside local taverns. The more aggressive protesters knelt in the snow to make their point. Some even convinced the cowed saloon-keepers to let them smash the barrels of whiskey with an ax. (Culver Pictures)*

Friends and comrades in arms for more than fifty years, Elizabeth Cady Stanton (LEFT) and Susan B. Anthony represented the struggle for women's rights from the era before the Civil War until the turn of the century. Neither lived to see the triumph of the suffrage movement in 1920. The fight to get women the right to vote, said Stanton near the end of her life, "like all things too long postponed, now gets on everybody's nerves." (Bettmann/CORBIS)

Post–Civil War Americans loved to watch Wild West shows and read pulp fiction about cowboys, Indians, and daring cowgirls. The most famous by far were Calamity Jane (RIGHT) and Annie Oakley (BELOW)— America's first action heroines.

Oakley combined genteel ladylike behavior with the ability to drill holes in playing cards with her rifle. During the Spanish-American War, she wrote to President McKinley, offering to raise a company of "fifty lady sharpshooters" to serve in Cuba. (CORBIS; Hulton Archive/Getty Images)

*Lillian Russell was one of the pioneers in the "wheeling" craze of the turn of the century. Bicycles gave women a sudden feeling of both freedom and speed, and Susan B. Anthony felt they "did more to emancipate women than anything else in the world." (Culver Pictures)*

*Jane Addams was the ultimate example of the New Woman, everyone's idea of moral perfection— until she began speaking out against World War I. (Underwood & Underwood/CORBIS)*

*At the turn of the century, elaborate hats required so many feathers and even entire stuffed birds that several species were slaughtered into extinction. In 1900, one fashion writer said he eventually expected to see women wearing "life-sized turkeys" on their heads. (Hulton-Deutsch Collection/CORBIS)*

*The labor organizer Mother Jones, shown here with President Coolidge, used her sex and age to embarrass male strikers into action. "I have been in jail more than once and expect to go again. If you are too cowardly to fight, I will fight," she told them. (CORBIS)*

*Most immigrants believed a married woman's place was in the home. But for many, that meant bringing the factory into the tenement, where they sewed piecework in their tiny, dark living rooms while their children either helped or fended for themselves. (George Eastman House/Lewis Hine/Getty Images)*

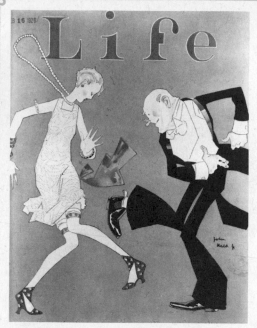

The fashions of the 1920s were all about freedom—suddenly women were baring their arms and their knees, and cutting their hair into light bobs. (Hulton Archive/Getty Images)

The one-piece bathing suit was a shocking revolution for a country that had only recently expected women to cover every possible inch of skin in several layers of clothing when they went into the water. (Culver Pictures)

Ida Wells-Barnett, journalist, public speaker, and activist, was president of a suffrage club for black women in Chicago. When leaders of the great 1913 march in Washington sent her group to the back of the parade, Wells-Barnett waited on the sidewalk and stepped back into the street as the regular Illinois delegation passed, joining her white friends for the rest of the march. (Library of Congress, Prints and Photographs Division)

Frances Perkins (LEFT), the first female cabinet member, usually wore dark and old-fashioned clothing under the theory that men react best to powerful women who remind them of their mothers. Perkins was part of a large circle of activist women in high places during the New Deal. At its center, of course, was Eleanor Roosevelt. (Bettmann/ CORBIS)

U. S. ARMY
OFFICIAL POSTER

SOLDIERS *without guns*

*The government's effort to get women out of the house and into the workforce during World War II was supported by an intense propaganda campaign. (CORBIS)*

*During the war Japanese American women were often rounded up with their children and sent to internment camps while their husbands were being questioned as suspected enemy agents. (Hulton Archive/Getty Images)*

*When Rosa Parks, a quiet middle-aged seamstress in Montgomery, Alabama, was arrested for refusing to give her seat to a white passenger, civil rights leaders knew they had found a case to challenge the segregation laws. (AP/Wide World Photos)*

*One of the most famous photos of the early civil rights movement showed Elizabeth Eckford, one of nine students to integrate Little Rock's Central High School in 1955, surrounded by an angry mob. Hazel Bryan, the white girl behind her, was the only one of her tormenters to apologize. (Bettmann/CORBIS)*

The first time most Americans heard the term "women's liberation" was probably during a demonstration against the Miss America contest in 1968. (AP/Wide World Photos)

Marilyn Monroe was the favorite movie star of the 1950s, but women preferred the new breed of tiny, childlike actresses such as Sandra Dee, who played the title role in Gidget— a word that referred to a half-girl, half-midget. (John Springer Collection/CORBIS)

On the fiftieth anniversary of the ratification of the constitutional amendment giving women the right to vote, Betty Friedan called for women across the country to hold mass marches. (Werner Wolf/Black Star)

the British side on the question of Ireland's independence.) The young women, who came mainly from farm backgrounds, did not all share their middle-class employers' standards for housekeeping, and they were notoriously poor cooks. They also had a reputation for sauciness. However, employers' ideas of what made a rebellious servant were rigid. In the book *Plain Talk and Friendly Advice to Domestics*, under the heading of "evil counsels" the author described an Irish troublemaker named Elizabeth who told the other servants, "Sure, six days is enough to work and the seventh, that belongs to us."

When Irish women married, they immediately quit work. But their husbands had a much more difficult time finding jobs than women did. The *Irish World* examined the work of the Free Labor Bureau in New York in 1870 and found that it had provided jobs to 81 Irish men and 628 Irish women. The men were often forced to take dangerous work no one else would accept. (In the South before the Civil War they were employed on projects on which slave owners did not want to risk their valuable slaves.) Irish women often found themselves widowed by industrial accidents or deserted by husbands who were unable to make a living. Some of the most destitute people in big cities during the late nineteenth century were Irish women who had simply collapsed under the strain of their problems. The population of American almshouses and insane asylums tended to be heavily Irish, and most of them were women.

Those who survived the first generation in America usually engineered a very quick turnaround for their daughters. Second-generation Irish girls had the advantage of education in the parochial schools that sprang up in every large city, and many moved into careers in nursing or teaching—jobs that rewarded women for postponing marriage. None of them went into domestic service.

## "I DIDN'T GO NOPLACE"

Italian-American immigrants put a particularly high value on keeping their women at home. "I didn't go noplace," summarized one woman who arrived as an adult and never learned English. Jane Addams reported that when her Chicago settlement house gave a party for Italian women in the neighborhood, the invitees sent their husbands instead, "and the social extension committee entered the drawing room to find it occupied by rows of Italian workingmen." Rosa Cavalleri said that among her Italian neighbors in Chicago, the height of entertainment for the women was to pull their chairs onto the street during the summer and sit on the sidewalk, drinking a cold can of beer they'd bought together from the saloon. "That's all the pleasure we had—the cool from the beer in summer," she said. Like many of the new arrivals, Italian women had trouble sympathizing with the temperance movement. One member of Addams's Hull-House staff went to see the mother of a kindergarten student who had come to school intoxicated from breakfasting on bread soaked in wine. The mother listened politely to a lecture about the evils of drink, then offered the visitor a glass of her best wine. When the woman refused, the mother reappeared with a glass of whiskey, proudly saying: "See, I have brought you the true American drink." The settlement worker concluded that her visit might have convinced the mother that good American children breakfasted on bread soaked in whiskey.

Addams was struck by the isolation of the Italian women and recalled one moment when an Italian neighbor admired the red roses in a vase at the settlement house. The woman was sure they had been imported all the way from Italy because she had never seen such flowers since she left her native village six years before. "During all that time, of course, the woman had lived within ten blocks of a florist's window; she had not been more than a five-cent car ride away from the public parks, but she had never dreamed of faring forth for herself and no one had taken her," Addams wrote. "Her conception of America had been the untidy street in which she lived and had made her long struggle to adapt herself to American ways."

Italian girls were less likely to work than other immigrant teenagers. When they did get jobs, they were often walked to and from the factory by their brothers. "One girl told me that her mother made a note of the exact time at which she returned every day from work, and that she had to account for every minute of deviation," said a social worker. "Seldom are Italian girls permitted to join clubs or evening classes. . . . When they are allowed this privilege, they are invariably escorted to and from the gathering by a parent or older brother, who must be assured that no mingling of the sexes has been allowed."

The contrast between life in southern Italy, where everything happened outdoors in the sun, and that in a tenement house in a poor urban neighborhood was hard on the newcomers. In Italy, women washed their clothes with their friends at the river. In New York, some tried carrying baskets of clothes to the East River, toting them on their heads as they did at home. But such foreign behavior was impermissible even in a neighborhood full of foreigners. "They were beaten up for doing this, they stoned us," said one immigrant. In Italy, the women had done the cooking, sewing, and spinning outside. Their old houses, with stone floors, had required cleaning only once a month. Now they had wooden floors that looked dirty even after they had been scrubbed. "You have no idea how simple life is over there," one said.

## "WELL, WHAT DID YOU THINK OF THAT YOUNG MAN?"

When Rose Cohen was a teenager, she was sent to buy sugar at a different grocery store than the one her family usually patronized. Two days later, her mother asked, "Well, what did you think of that young man?" The befuddled girl was led to understand that the grocery store clerk with whom she had exchanged a few words was a potential suitor. A "date" was arranged for the next Saturday, and it included all her family as well as the suitor's uncle. The young people were sent for a walk, and the suitor explained in detail his ability to support her. After this brief get-together, the family proposed an alliance and Rose was engaged.

Arranged marriages were common for many immigrant cultures, although how much a girl was bound by her parents' choice varied with the community and the girl. Rose Cohen's parents were upset when she decided she did not want to be the store clerk's wife, but they did not force her to go through with the marriage. Still, an arranged marriage was a way to ensure that daughters stayed within their own ethnic group. It was also an answer to the question of how a girl was supposed to find a husband if her parents did not allow her to talk to young men.

Despite the theory that girls should be kept innocent—or ignorant—about sex until they were married, young women who lived in tenements must have noticed what went on between their parents in the tiny apartments. At work, they were continually subjected to various forms of sexual harassment. Rose Cohen said the first sentence she learned in English was "Keep your hands off, please." When she grew up, she said, "the thought of marriage often filled me with fear, even with disgust. So the sweatshop left its mark."

Hester Vaughn was a cautionary tale of what could happen to a young woman who failed to keep predatory males at bay. She came from England before the Civil War to marry her fiancé, but he deserted her and she became a dairymaid. Her employer raped her and months later, when her pregnancy started to show, he gave her $40 and told her to leave. Hester went to Philadelphia and worked as a seamstress until her money ran out. Then with her last two dollars, in a terrible blizzard, she found and rented an unheated attic room. She had been without food for two days when she went into labor alone. The next day the landlady found her lying on the floor, her dead baby so frozen that a piece of its skin stuck to the floor. Hester was charged with infanticide, tried without a lawyer, convicted, and sentenced to be hung. Her story was so extreme that it attracted national attention, and she became a feminist cause. The governor rejected a plea for clemency by Elizabeth Cady Stanton, saying he was acting on "principle." But after a year of protests she was pardoned, and her supporters raised money to send her back to England.

Jewish wives tended to have fewer children than other immigrant women. One of their secrets may have been the religious rule that forbade couples from having sex while the woman was nursing. This may have been one instance in which the theory that nursing mothers could not get pregnant really worked. Although couples—particularly fathers—were proud of their big families, many women were desperate for ways to keep from having more babies. Emma Goldman, who worked as a midwife to immigrant women around the turn of the century, said that most of the women she knew "lived in continual dread of conception." When they discovered they were pregnant, Goldman said, they often tried to induce miscarriage. "It was incredible what fantastic methods despair could invent: jumping off tables, rolling on the floor, massaging the stomach, drinking nauseating concoctions and using blunt instruments." One Jewish woman from Eastern Europe recalled that when her mother, who was too poor to feed the children she had, got pregnant again, "I heard a funny sound and crept out in the middle of the night. My mother was lifting a heavy barrel full of pickles and dropping it again and again." Her mother's sister, she said, had eight children and fourteen abortions before she reached the age of forty. Abortions, which were illegal, were common but very dangerous—one study estimated one in five was fatal.

The most truly pathetic members of the immigrant community were single women attempting to support children. It was almost impossible for a mother alone to be both breadwinner and caretaker. She could take in piecework to supplement the family income, but that was not a living wage. In 1853, the *Tribune* estimated that a needlewoman who actually maintained full employment might make $91 a year. At the time, a family of four required $600 to sustain themselves at a marginal level. Any job that took a mother out of the home left her young children in peril. Jane Addams said the first three crippled children her settlement house workers encountered in Chicago had all been injured while their mothers were at work. "One had fallen out of a third-story window, another had been burned, and the third had a curved spine due to the fact that for three years he had been tied all day long to the leg of the kitchen table, only released at noon by his older brother who hastily ran in from a neighboring factory to share his lunch with him."

Immigrants nursed their infants on demand and continued breast-feeding for a long time—sometimes eighteen months. But many women were so badly nourished that it was impossible for them to nurse, and they fed their babies milk that they bought out of large buckets and carried home in pails. Because of lack of refrigeration at the stores, and unsanitary conditions in the dairies, the milk was frequently contaminated with bacteria. A third of all babies in immigrant neighborhoods died before their fifth birthday and the milk they drank was one of the reasons. But bad air, bad food, lack of sunlight, and dirty streets made the urban immigrant children vulnerable to almost every conceivable disease. Jane Addams reported bitterly that in one year "six promising pupils out of a class of fifteen developed tuberculosis"—a disease that was, for poor people, a death sentence.

The women were suspicious of doctors, and they believed that hospitals were places where you went to die. The medical community returned the sentiment, treating immigrant parents as if they were too dense to understand their methods. In 1908, doctors swooped down on schools on the Lower East Side bent on removing all the students' adenoids in the name of preventive medicine. Their mothers rioted and marched on the schools to rescue their offspring. The *Tribune* reported that they "stoned the school houses, smashed windows and door panes."

Children were the center of immigrant women's world, but they died so often that many bereaved mothers showed the same kind of fatalism that their middle-class American neighbors had left behind in the eighteenth century. Addams recalled a devoted mother whose five-year-old boy tumbled from the roof while he was helping her hang laundry. "His neck was broken by the fall, and as he lay piteous and limp on a pile of frozen refuse, his mother cheerily called for him to 'climb up again' so confident do overworked mothers become that their children cannot get hurt." At the funeral, the bereaved woman said her one wish was to have a day off work so she could stay at home "and hold the baby," because she had never had time to hold the one she lost.

## "I WANTED A NEW THING—HAPPINESS"

Most immigrants came from rural backgrounds, in which life consisted of work and sleep. But American cities had amusement parks, pleasure steamers, and dance halls, and by the late nineteenth century they were no longer intended just for prostitutes and their escorts. Nice girls could go in a group and meet boys. Once they had paired off, the girls expected their escorts to "treat" them for the rest of the evening. The high point of the summer for New York immigrant girls might be an excursion to Coney Island, where there were eight large dance halls of varying degrees of exclusivity. One of the great pleasures of such outings was the chance to assume a different identity, and factory girls frequently passed themselves off as department store clerks, while the clerks were pretending to be typists or ladies of leisure. "I wanted a new thing—happiness," said a Jewish girl who begged to learn to dance. For some immigrants, happiness consisted of something as simple as a streetcar ride out of the neighborhood with the family. "Oh my God, what a treat it was to go to Central Park," remembered an Italian woman.

Young people of every class and ethnicity shocked their elders with the risqué way they moved to the music. "The Negro race is dancing itself to death," worried the Reverend Adam Clayton Powell in Harlem. "The town is dance mad," announced *Survey* magazine. "Down on the Lower East Side, dancing is cheap. Twenty five cents for a couple is all it costs, and ten cents for the girls." Many parents, particularly the Italians, wouldn't let their daughters go anywhere near the dance halls, and they weren't being entirely unreasonable. In many of the halls, dance instructors were actually pimps on the look-out for new talent. "The pimps were hunters," wrote Mike Gold, a product of the Jewish Lower East Side. "A pretty girl growing up on the East Side was marked by them. They watched her fill out, grow tall, take on the sex bloom. When she was fifteen, they schemed to trap her. . . . Pimps infected the dance halls. Here they picked up the romantic factory girls who came after the day's work. They were smooth story tellers." The dances sponsored by political or ethnic

groups were safer, and many young people discovered untapped interests in causes like Irish independence. Maureen Connelly, who went to
work after the eighth grade, said she and all her friends joined the
Friends of Irish Freedom, although they knew nothing about politics.
The Friday night dance was the draw—"the highlight of our lives."

One of the main reasons immigrant women were attracted to the
labor movement was the hope for shorter workdays. "It was quite
wonderful to get home before it was pitch dark at night and a real
joy to ride on the cars and look out the windows and see something," said a young woman who was a member of a union in New
York City. Although immigrant girls had a great need for labor
unions, few of the unions were interested in them. By the Civil War,
the labor movement had become almost exclusively male, focused on
the idea that men should be able to earn enough to support their
families.

But as the twentieth century approached, unions began to recruit
women, and they found many of them eager listeners. Irish women,
who had regarded politics as a male issue, sometimes decided that
labor unions came more in the line of economics, which was their turf.
Italian girls sometimes ignored their parents' injunctions against making associations outside the family and became union members. But
the biggest and most successful labor movement came in the garment
industry, with Jewish girls taking the leading role. In 1909, the International Ladies Garment Workers Union held a meeting of 2,000
workers, in which speakers droned on in general terms until a young
woman named Clara Lemlich rose and said in Yiddish that she was
tired of the delay. "What we are here for is to decide whether we shall
or shall not strike. I offer a resolution that a general strike be declared
now." The audience rose as one, voted to strike, and took a Jewish
pledge: "If I turn traitor to the cause I now pledge, may the hand
wither with the arm I now raise." Twenty thousand workers went out
on strike, 80 percent of them women.

## "I HAVE IT LIKE HEAVEN"

Americans love the story of the immigrant who comes through Ellis Island with no possessions but struggles to success and happiness. It is the story that most defines us, and we tell it to ourselves over and over. But for the real immigrants, each story was different, and the happiness of the ending changed with every telling. Rose Cohen lived out her youth on the Lower East Side of New York, in three-room tenements and sweatshops. "We liked moving from one place to another," she wrote. "Moving even from one dingy place to another is a change. And then, too, some were less dingy than others." But despite poor health, she learned to read and write in English and attracted the attention of settlement house workers, who helped her find medical treatment and more congenial work. The family became modestly prosperous when Rose's father saved enough money to open a grocery store. Her brother went to Columbia University and Rose, after she married Joseph Cohen and had a daughter, stopped working and went to night school.

A genuine American success story, Rose became comfortable enough writing English that she composed her autobiography, which was published to critical praise. She met and became friends with some of the country's most prominent writers and artists. But her success apparently alienated her from her husband, and she may have fallen into an unhappy relationship with an older married man. She stopped writing and dropped out of history, but a newspaper article in 1922 reported that a forty-year-old Rose Cohen had committed suicide by jumping into the East River from a landing at the New York Yacht Club.

Rosa Cavalleri never learned to write in English. Her story was taken down by social workers at a Chicago settlement house where she was both a cleaning woman and a member who entertained people with her talent for telling stories. When her autobiography was recorded, Rosa was an aging widow in poor health. But she told her friends she had no desire to die. Her youngest son took care of her, and the work at the settlement house gave her some pin money. "I can

go to the picture-show and see the good story. I have it like heaven—
I'm my own boss." Her only wish, she said, was to go back to Italy and
show everyone that a poor peasant girl could learn to hold her head
high and stand up for her rights. "They wouldn't dare hurt me now I
come from America," she said. "Me, that's why I love America. That's
what I learned in America: not to be afraid."

# 13

# Turn of the Century:
# The Arrival of the New Woman

## "TO DEMONSTRATE PUBLICLY
## THAT WOMEN HAVE LEGS"

In 1895, Frances Willard, the longtime head of the Women's Christian Temperance Union, wrote a little book called *How I Learned to Ride the Bicycle.* It recounted how, at age fifty-three, she made herself "master of the most remarkable, ingenious and inspiring [vehicle] ever devised upon the planet." Although written in a friendly, no-nonsense style, the book followed the temperance movement's classic story line of error, enlightenment, and rebirth. Willard confessed to her readers that a decade before she would have found the idea of a woman cyclist "shocking." But she had seen the light, and she urged her millions of female fans: "Go thou and do likewise."

If there's any symbol for the transformation that had occurred in the lives of American women as they approached the twentieth century, it ought to be the bicycle. The pictures of Willard tooling around in her long black skirt and high-necked blouse might remind modern readers of the villainous Margaret Hamilton in *The Wizard of Oz,* pedaling off with Toto in her basket. But women who had spent their lives wrapped in corsets and weighed down by heavy skirts must have been thrilled to be able to go flying down the street on two wheels. "Wheeling" offered independence as well as speed, and it was not only respectable; it was fashionable. Lillian Russell began pedaling through Central Park on a gold-plated bike that Diamond Jim Brady gave her. Susan B. Anthony enthused that bicycling "did more to emancipate women than anything else in the world."

The whole nation was crazy about bicycling. By 1900 more than 10 million bikes were on the road, and every manufacturer offered a "lady's model." The undergarment industry quickly invented a cycling corset, but it never caught on. The Victorian standards of proper dress were not going to survive the wheeling generation. "A few years ago, no woman would dare venture on the street with a skirt that stopped above her ankles," wrote an essayist in *Scribners*. But the bicycle, the writer said, "has given to all American womankind the liberty of dress for which reformers have been sighing for generations." Lillian Russell confided to her fans (she confided just about everything) that her "wheeling costume consists of the regulation skirt and China silk bloomers with a long woolen shirt. I wear no corset while exercising." *Life* noted approvingly in 1897 that "a large proportion of the bicycle girls look exceedingly well in bicycle clothes. . . . Not the least good thing the bicycle has done has been to demonstrate publicly that women have legs."

Americans had entered a world in which drastic social changes could occur in a decade instead of requiring a generation. The bicycling craze took over the nation so quickly that people barely had time to go through the traditional soul-searching over whether cycling would make women nervous or endanger their reproductive systems. The Boston Rescue League, however, did claim that 30 percent of the fallen women who came seeking aid had been "bicycle riders at one time."

## "AGGRESSIVE AS BECAME THEIR SEX"

The media called these free-wheelers of the turn of the century the New Women. The country was fascinated with them, although people didn't always agree on what a New Woman was. (Advertisers, shameless as usual, announced that the New Woman was someone who used Rubifoam tooth powder or a Sweeperette carpet sweeper.) Madame Yale, a popular beauty lecturer of the era, said she was "a hearty playfellow, a good comrade who rides, walks, rows, golfs and wouldn't be guilty of fainting for a kingdom." A New York journalist claimed that although men might enjoy her company, "they rarely marry her," while many men thought—or hoped—that she was sexually liberated.

There were actually all sorts of New Women, but they shared an independent competence that some found rather terrifying. In 1896, *Life* published a tale about the man of the future, who sits darning socks while "two noisy, sturdy girls, as aggressive as became their sex, romped merrily about the sewing room." Meanwhile "their gentle little brother sat quietly by his father's side, studying pictures in an old book" that showed men actually wearing the pants in the family. *Ladies' Home Journal,* which teetered back and forth from shock to sympathy, was in a sympathetic mood when it printed a short story in 1902 about Rebekah, a newly minted college graduate, who sweeps into town and saves her family's farm from bankruptcy. Reminding her cowed stepfather that she is "a girl who . . . can bring to her work the added assistance of higher education, scientifically applied," Rebekah saves the cows by summoning a female college chum who has "studied drainage" and promptly cleans out the stables.

Getting rid of the messes that men had let pile up was one of the New Woman's missions. Except for a few sparsely populated states out west and the occasional school board election, very few American women had the right to vote. But they were still setting the domestic agenda in a way they had never done before and would not do again until the end of the twentieth century. They founded settlement houses to help the urban poor, organized unions, demonstrated for the right to vote, and investigated everything from unsanitary dairies to oil trusts. The New Woman's younger sisters were reading novels about girls who had adventures without the cover of family emergency. The heroine of the Grace Harlow series not only went to college, she got married, had a child, and then, leaving her baby with her husband, went off globetrotting to solve mysteries and run down smugglers. The extremely popular Outdoor Girls were four teenagers who liked to go camping, take long hikes, and drive their own cabin cruiser.

The New Woman was also sometimes old. Throughout the nineteenth century, girls had been taught that their moment in the sun was going to be a brief one that began with courtship and ended with marriage. After that, they would be encouraged to live out their remaining years in quiet dignity at home. But by the turn of the century, when Americans were marching into what historians now call the Progressive Era, stage stars like Lillian Russell were still drawing big crowds in their fifties, and reformers like Elizabeth Cady Stanton and Susan B. Anthony were more popular than they had ever been when they were younger. (Stanton, addressing the men in the audience at a tribute to her eightieth birthday at the Metropolitan Opera House in 1895, assured them: "I fear you think the New Woman is going to wipe you off the planet, but be not afraid. All who have mothers, sisters, wives or sweethearts will be very well looked after.") A middle-aged Annie Oakley wrote to President McKinley, offering to raise a company of "fifty lady sharpshooters" to serve in the Spanish-American War. Frances Willard said she had learned to ride the bicycle for several reasons, "last but not least because a good many people felt I could not do it at my age."

Unlike earlier versions of liberated womanhood, this one seemed to have no downside. "Almost the best reason I know for being a suffragist is that there is so much fun and gladness in it," said Inez Milholland. A skilled equestrian who often rode a horse at the head of political parades, the beautiful Milholland was careful to add that politics was also a "healthy activity," like lawn tennis or bicycling. The newspapers followed this new generation of daring, competent women with the same avidity they pursued stories about captains of industry and sensational murders. Everybody wanted to read about women like Rose Pastor, a Jewish cigar factory worker who married the wealthy and prominent J. G. Phelps Stokes. Hers was a rags-to-riches story with a Progressive Era twist. Rose refused to promise to "obey" during the wedding ceremony and converted her new husband to socialism. The newlyweds became extremely popular on the lecture circuit—even conservative groups like the Daughters of the American Revolution wanted to hear about left-wing politics when it was explained by the central players in "our greatest social romance."

Another very New Woman who fascinated the country was Alva Belmont, a wealthy socialite who embraced almost every conceivable turn-of-the-century trend, from suffrage to social climbing. In 1895, she shocked New York society by divorcing her hyperrich husband, William Vanderbilt, on the grounds of adultery and marrying Oliver Belmont, the son of a fabulously wealthy banker who had himself just divorced his wife. It drove home the fact that divorce was no longer a rarity in American society. In fact, the United States had the highest divorce rate in the world, and the trend was particularly strong in the West—Denver would soon be contemplating the fact that one divorce was filed in the city for every two marriage licenses issued. And Alva Belmont was a watershed in that she went on with her social life, after divorce and remarriage, just as she had before. Society still swooned when she appeared at an over-the-top costume ball in 1897 dressed as Marie Antoinette, on the arm of her second husband, who was wearing a suit of gold-inlaid armor he'd borrowed from a cooperative Metropolitan Museum. Divorce began to seem, if not desirable, at least like a necessary evil that need not leave a woman floating in social limbo ever afterward.

## "LESS ABOUT SOUL AND MORE ABOUT PIMPLES"

The physical ideal of turn-of-the-century American women was the Gibson Girl, the creation of illustrator Charles Dana Gibson, who himself became a celebrity thanks to her popularity. Like the Gilded Age beauties, the Gibson Girl had a full bust and hips, but her body was thinner, firmer, elongated. She was tall, often dressed for sport, and she appeared to be wearing comfortable clothes, although her waist was so tiny, there had to be a corset somewhere. The *New York Herald* admired her "wholesome athletic air that does not smack too much of athletics." The Gibson Girl looked a little like Lillie Langtry, the British blond who was a celebrity in Europe thanks to her affair with the Prince of Wales. When Langtry made her stage debut in America, people were taken aback at first by her athletic figure and her much-publicized fetish for exercise. But by 1900, the fashionable American woman no longer literally resembled an hourglass. "Diet" became a verb for the first time, though women did not become obsessed with counting calories until later. They were encouraged to believe that a beautiful appearance was connected to beautiful thinking. Lillie Langtry claimed her lovely complexion came from the serenity she got studying Buddhism—although once, in need of cash, she gave the credit to Pear's soap. Lillian Russell, who had a popular beauty column in the *Chicago Tribune*, wrote so much about the importance of having a lovely spirit that her editor telegraphed her, begging her to "write less about soul and more about pimples."

## "WHENEVER SHE WAS DISTURBED OR DEPRESSED SHE WOULD MOVE THE FURNITURE"

The most remarkable woman in this remarkable era was Jane Addams, the pioneer of the settlement house movement, reformer, writer, and (much less popularly) peace activist. Addams was the daughter of the wealthiest man in a small Illinois town. Her mother died when she was two years old, and Jane was the pet of both her rather stern father and older siblings. Perhaps it was that combination of being both fussed over and bereaved that gave her the air of cool sympathy that other people, particularly other women, found so attractive. In college, where she was class president and valedictorian, one girl wrote that she relied on Jane "as I do the Sun, as I do on divine help." Jane was daring enough to try opium in an attempt to better understand the fevered writings of the addict Thomas de Quincey, but Victorian enough to take only an ineffectual dose. She was so independent she never wore a corset.

After she graduated from college, Addams wanted to study medicine. The number of female doctors was growing at the turn of the century, and the percentage of women in medicine in 1910 would not be matched again until 1980. But a series of crises, including ill health and the death of her father, plunged her into a depression that lasted eight years. Eventually, she became convinced that her problem was the lack of an occupation—a common dilemma for women who graduated from college and then found no task serious enough to match their skills and ardor. When she visited a London settlement house run by dedicated college men who worked with the poor, she became determined to start a similar institution in Chicago, run by women.

Chicago was full of two populations that helped define American society at the turn of the century—poor immigrants and well-educated women who were looking for something to do with their lives. Addams's genius was in bringing them together. The immigrants may have been drawn to her because she was not judgmental, and she was a good listener, interested in understanding how her neighbors viewed things. When she became a renowned speaker later in life, she was their interpreter. She disapproved of dance halls, but she could tell her audiences why poor girls liked them, why they preferred factory work to domestic service, and the practical reasons why their fathers voted for corrupt ward heelers rather than reform politicians.

Wealthy women saw Addams as one of their own and readily gave her their money. She and her former college classmate, Ellen Starr, quickly became a "fashionable fad" as they went around Chicago raising funds and looking for a place to start their settlement. In 1889, they discovered Hull House, an old mansion that stood in the middle of a poor Italian community. It was owned by Helen Culver, an heiress and real estate dealer. After extensive coaxing, Culver leased the property to the settlement, then eliminated the rent and finally handed over the title. As Addams darted from one meeting to another, she discovered that most of her physical and emotional ailments had disappeared. In describing her work later, she would always say that the settlement house did more to help the young women who worked there than it did their clients.

Moving into Hull House, Addams nested. She put her family's heirloom silver on the sideboard, brought in handsome furniture, hung pictures. She was a homebody with a different kind of home. "Whenever she was disturbed or depressed she would move the furniture in all the rooms," said a friend. The settlement house was a good symbol for the difference between the age of the New Woman and that of the Victorians. Jane Addams was a natural descendant of Clara Barton and Dorothea Dix and Catharine Beecher, whose rootless lives seemed to embody the principle that there would never be a place where such forceful women could permanently fit in. But Addams and her fellow settlement workers had a home. They achieved domesticity, not with a husband and children, but with other women.

Addams and Starr established the first playground in Chicago, on a vacant lot near Hull House. They started a nursery school and organized women's clubs, lecture series, and art exhibits. Within two years the settlement had more than fifty rooms and endless classes that occupied every corner of the house for the twelve hours a day it was open. A thousand people came to its programs every week. Hull House residents organized demonstrations against bad health conditions, and after Addams had protested 700 times in one summer about the same overflowing garbage boxes that had horrified Rosa Cavalleri, she submitted a bid for the garbage removal contract. Although the bid was unsuccessful, the publicity forced the mayor to appoint her garbage inspector, and the nation was both inspired and charmed by the idea of this tiny, well-born woman marching around the slums to make sure the refuse was picked up.

By 1907, Hull House was a complex of thirteen buildings, including a residence for working girls known as the "Jane Club," and Jane herself had become a household name. She wrote for women's magazines, gave speeches everywhere, and in 1912 was chosen to second the nomination of Theodore Roosevelt for president. Thanks to her example, the six settlement houses that existed in the United States in 1892 became nearly 100 by 1900. Like so many great transitional figures in American history, she introduced the public to new ideas while assuring them they were not buying into anything dangerously radical. She was on every list of most admired people in America, and when she won the 1931 Nobel Peace Prize, many felt it was a long overdue honor for work she did before World War I.

## "I FOUGHT THE RATS, INSIDE AND OUT"

Most labor union leaders were still indifferent or hostile to women workers. At best they regarded them as people who should be home with the children. At worst, they saw women as surplus labor who drove down the pay scale for men. In 1930, census takers discovered that while one in nine male workers was a union member, only one in thirty-four women was unionized, mainly those in the garment trade. But one of the more remarkable female union leaders of the era, Mother Jones, was devoted to organizing the all-male mining industry.

Born Mary Harris in Cork, Ireland, the woman who would become Mother Jones had an intimate and recurring knowledge of stupendous tragedy. She spent her early years amid the great Irish famine and went to Canada with her family on one of the infamous "coffin ships" that left so many of their passengers dead from drowning or disease. But her family survived, and Mary was trained to be both a dressmaker and a teacher. She made her way to Memphis, where she married an ironworker named George Jones. She was well on her way to a happy, unremarkable life as wife and mother when yellow fever struck the city in 1867, killing her husband and four children. "I sat alone through nights of grief," she wrote later. "No one came to me. No one could. Other homes were as stricken as mine." She nursed other victims until the disease ran its course, then moved to Chicago where she ran a dressmaking business. When the great Chicago fire broke out in 1871, Mary Jones survived again, although she lost all her belongings.

Trying to find some meaning in her life, she embraced the labor movement—her husband had been an active union member—and the cause of the working poor. She became "Mother Jones," the gray-haired woman in an old-fashioned black dress whose fearlessness inspired men half her age and rallied an unexpected militancy in their wives and daughters.

Mother Jones traveled constantly, carrying everything she owned wrapped up in a black shawl. "She had a complete disregard for danger or hardship," said John Brophy, an official in the miners' union. "She had a lively sense of humor—she could tell wonderful stories, usually at the expense of some boss." She was also a fire-breathing orator—Elizabeth Gurley Flynn, another Irish immigrant who would become a spellbinding speaker for the labor movement, heard Mother Jones describe the bloody labor wars in the mines when she was eighteen years old, and was so overcome she fainted.

Because of her age (which she exaggerated) and her gender, Mother Jones could easily embarrass men into action. "I have been in jail more than once and I expect to go again. If you are too cowardly to fight, I will fight. You ought to be ashamed of yourselves, actually to the Lord you ought, to see one old woman who is not afraid," she told them. In 1913, during the labor wars in the Colorado mines, she repeatedly defied official orders that she leave town, and wound up— at age seventy-six—locked in a jail that had previously been condemned as unfit for habitation. "I had sewer rats . . . to fight, and all I had was a beer bottle; I would get one rat and another would run across the cellar at me," she told the Commission on Industrial Relations later. "I fought the rats inside and out just alike."

Mother Jones was unusual for her era in that she was an equal-opportunity organizer, who welcomed African American workers and brought women and children into the strikes. She organized the wives of miners into teams armed with mops and brooms so they could guard the mines against scabs. She staged pageants where one child was crowned queen of the strikers and parades with children carrying signs that read: "We Want to Go to School and Not to the Mines."

Along with the miners, child workers were her particular concern. During a silk strike in Philadelphia, 100,000 workers, including 16,000 children, left their jobs over a demand that their workweek be cut from sixty to fifty-five hours. Mother Jones organized a children's march of 100 boys and girls from Philadelphia to New York City "to show the New York millionaires our grievances." The march attracted considerable publicity, but national bans on child labor were not successfully passed into law until 1941.

In 1897, the *National Labor Tribune* declared Mother Jones a "New Woman."

## "I AM NOW SURROUNDED BY ALL MY DREAMS COME TRUE"

For all the chances women had to make an impact at the turn of the century, they had far less opportunity to make much money. Only a few women had careers that were lucrative as well as useful. Ida Tarbell was one of them. She was a direct descendant of Rebecca Nurse, the bedridden housewife who became one of the first victims of the Salem witch trials. Tarbell was the star investigative reporter for *McClure's* magazine, known for her obsessive research and willingness to go anywhere to follow a lead. "She could mobilize just as swiftly as any lad in the place—could accept a decision at noon to start for Chicago without turning a hair," said a fellow staff member. (He never knew that Tarbell fought against a fear of strange hotels that caused her hand to shake whenever she signed a register.) Her most famous work, "The History of the Standard Oil Company," was a pathbreaking exposé of corporate greed and collusion that helped prod Theodore Roosevelt into his career as a trustbuster. "Miss Ida Tarbell is the most popular woman in America," announced a profile in *The Reader*. At minimum, the article said, the choice would lie between Tarbell and Jane Addams.

The successful female entrepreneurs of the era often worked in the business of beauty—one of the first parts of the economy where a woman could be investor, owner, and boss. Florence Nightingale Graham, a poor immigrant from England, became a receptionist in a high-toned Manhattan beauty parlor and worked her way up until she had a shop of her own, then her own brand of products, which she marketed under the name Elizabeth Arden. Harriet Hubbard Ayer, a divorced mother, began manufacturing a face cream in 1886 that became such a big success it eventually inspired her ex-husband and daughter to have her committed to an asylum so they could take over the company. The beauty business was also unique in that it offered opportunities to ambitious black women. The most successful was Sarah Breedlove, who became famous as Madam C. J. Walker, with thousands of agents selling her products all over the country.

Walker was the daughter of sharecroppers, the first child in the family to have been born free. She was orphaned at age seven and worked as a laundress in Louisiana when she was still a child, trudging across town bearing bundles of clothes and standing for hours with her swollen hands immersed in hot water and lye or wrestling with irons that had to be heated in the hearth. She married young, had a daughter at seventeen, and was widowed. She moved to St. Louis and joined a church whose congregation included many of the city's black clubwomen. It was under the influence of those helpful ladies that Sarah began to learn middle-class speech and manners while she sent her daughter, Lelia, to college with the money she made over the laundry tub. Meanwhile, she was horrified to discover her hair was starting to fall out. It may have been stress, but hair loss was a common problem for women at that time, possibly because of mercury poisoning from patent medicines. Many of the victims were poor women who had low-protein diets and rarely washed their hair. Scalp diseases were rampant, and pores that became blocked by dirt were a breeding ground for dandruff, eczema, and fungus. Sarah, who was soon to take the name of her third husband, C. J. Walker, developed a lotion that made her hair grow back in. She always claimed it was revealed to her by an African ancestor in a dream. The result was actually not much more than good shampoo, but when used regularly, along with scalp massages and perhaps improved diet, it generally restored lost hair and caused it to grow in more thickly.

Walker's success had to do with her energy and her talent for promotion. She inspired her audiences not only with the story of her recovered beauty, but with her vision of a future for black women that went beyond washing clothes and cleaning houses. Women signed up to learn the Walker hair care technique, to sell the products, and to open Madame C. J. Walker beauty parlors. She traveled endlessly, at first in the hated segregated railroad cars and, later, as her business began to prosper, in her own touring car. When she moved to New York, she and her daughter were as well known for their benevolence as for their expensive lifestyles. During World War I, Walker was a continual subscriber to war bond drives, determined that Harlem would not be outstripped by other neighborhoods when it came to patriotism. Her town house and hair salon on 136th Street in Harlem were as elegant as anything on Fifth Avenue, and her estate on the Hudson, in a neighborhood where the Rockefellers and other magnates had their mansions, was built on her commission by a black architect. "I had a dream, and that dream begot other dreams until I am now surrounded by all my dreams come true," she said shortly before she died.

## "TELL ME, PRETTY MAIDEN, ARE THERE MORE AT HOME LIKE YOU?"

Middle-class girls might have dreamed of becoming a journalist or going off to help the poor, but working-class girls liked to imagine themselves performing on stage. The chorus girl was a New Woman, too—she made her own money, and her public image was one of assertive independence. Her spunk was supposed to be rewarded with fancy dinners, expensive gifts, and ultimately marriage to a wealthy admirer. Most chorus girls, of course, lived the unglamorous lives of traveling theater folk, dragging their meager baggage from one small town venue to the next. Still, the dream had some validity. The ultimate chorines at the turn of the century were the Floradora Girls—six fashionably dressed, minimally talented young women of the same size and coloring who sashayed around the stage twisting parasols while their male partners sang, "Tell me, pretty maiden, are there more at home like you?" All six of the originals married millionaires very soon after *Floradora* opened on Broadway. They were replaced by more pretty brunettes—five feet four inches, 130 pounds—who were not required to do anything but look enticing on stage and be clever about choosing among the suitors who waited outside the stage door after the show.

But the classic training camp for the New Woman was the college campus. The first generation of female college students enrolled around 1870, when there had been the inevitable controversy about whether their delicate systems were up to the challenge. Dr. Edward Clarke, a retired professor at Harvard Medical School, made a big splash when he published *Sex in Education, or, a Fair Chance for Girls*, which warned that women who used up all their vital energies on studies would endanger their "female apparatus." Nevertheless, a decade later 40,000 women were in college—nearly a third of all the students. The idea of higher education for women became so acceptable by 1890 that *Ladies' Home Journal* sponsored a contest in which the girl who sold the most subscriptions won a scholarship to Vassar. By 1910, when 5 percent of all college-age Americans were enrolled in school, 40 percent were female. Nearly half of all college students were coeds in 1920, when the percentage would peak and then begin receding.

The women students tended to be serious. Florence Kelley remembered her freshman year at Cornell as "one of continual joy. . . . No one, as far as I know, read a daily paper. . . . Our current gossip was Froude's *Life of Carlyle*." Some of the elite colleges were alarmed at the number of women flocking in. When the University of Chicago discovered that the proportion of women had risen from 25 to 50 percent, the administration developed a curriculum aimed at attracting more men. At Cornell, women were barred from joining campus organizations. Some large state schools restricted women to home economics and teaching courses. But other schools were far more welcoming. The year the University of Kansas was founded, the classes were almost all preparatory, and only two of the students were taking actual college courses. However, they were both women.

## "SMASHED"

Most women who attended college went to coeducational public schools. But the all-female, private colleges were the ones that provided the parade of young graduates into politics, social work, and academia. While preparing for the outside world, the students at places like Smith and Vassar lived a rather cloistered life, with limited contact with the opposite sex. Even the spring proms at many schools were all-girls affairs. At Smith, the sophomores escorted the freshmen to the annual Freshman Frolic. The *Cosmopolitan* reported in 1901: "Each soph considers herself a cavalier for the freshman to whom she is assigned. She sends her flowers, calls for her, fills her order of dance, introduces her partners, fetches ice and frappes between dances and takes her to supper . . . and if the freshman has taken advantage of the opportunity and made the desired hit, there are dates for future meetings and jollifications, and a good night over the balusters, as lingering and cordial as any freshie has left behind her." In many of these events, the girls playing "cavalier" dressed as men, and the colleges were nervous enough about what this all meant to ban any photo-taking. One former Vassar student explained the concept of "smashes" among undergraduates: "When a Vassar girl takes a shine to another, she straightaway enters upon a regular course of bouquet sendings, interspersed with tinted notes, mysterious packages of 'Ridley's Mixed Candies,' locks of hair perhaps and many other tender tokens, until at last the object of her intention is captured, the two become inseparable, and the aggressor is considered by her circle of acquaintances as—smashed."

The hero worship young women felt for their teachers, mentors, and the stars of the social reform movement also took on sexual over-tones. While Jane Addams was sitting on a window seat at Hull House one afternoon, a volunteer came up and grabbed her ankle, saying, "If you won't let me hold your hand, do let me hold your foot." Addams never had a serious romantic relationship with a man, and the degree to which she understood, or was comfortable with, her own sexuality will never be known. She kept that as closed off as most of her deep feelings. But the only people who penetrated the cool, benevolent sur-face of her personality were Ellen Starr and later Mary Rozet Smith. Smith, the daughter of a wealthy manufacturer, happily devoted her life to supporting Addams and her money to backing the settlement house. Starr may have been thinking about Smith's wealth as well as her love when she told her old friend, near the end of their lives, that she had "for a great many years been thankful that Mary came along to supply what you needed."

## "RACE SUICIDE"

When Jane Addams was asked why most women in her circle had never married, she said that men "did not at first want to marry women of the new type, and women could not fulfill the two functions of pro-fession and homemaking until modern invention had made a new type of housekeeping practicable." But the emergence of the career wife and mother wasn't simply waiting for the invention of the vacuum cleaner; Addams added that women had to be patient "until public opinion tolerated the double role." At the turn of the century, public opinion was definitely not ready. College graduates—the first Ameri-can women who had the luxury of a career crisis—could marry, or they could become "professionals"—teachers, librarians, social workers. Almost no one felt they could do both. Even union leaders and college presidents retired when they became wives. But, fre-quently, educated women opted for jobs over husbands. Nearly half of all female college graduates in the late nineteenth century remained unmarried.

It was the golden age of the American single woman, and magazines routinely published pieces by unmarried professionals, defending their decision to forgo matrimony. The authors assured their readers that they had not been lacking in offers—one essay, which *Ladies' Home Journal* regarded as among the most popular pieces it had ever published, was by a single woman who said she had turned down five suitors. Few of the writers really discussed their careers—they said they had chosen celibacy because the men weren't good enough. "I never married because I never met a man whose love covered the faults in his character which I was sure would make me unhappy," declared "Old Maid." Their choosiness was possible, however, because of the new opportunities for women to work. "My earning powers are no more liable to wane than are those of a man," wrote "A Spinster Who Has Learned to Say No."

The white middle class worried about "race suicide." The best-educated native-born women were failing to reproduce while immigrant families had tons of healthy babies. President Theodore Roosevelt was a particular fretter. "If Americans of the old stock lead lives of celibate selfishness . . . or if the married are afflicted by that base fear of living which . . . forbids them to have more than one or two children, disaster awaits the nation," he proclaimed. G. Stanley Hall, that professional worrier, warned that "if women do not improve," men would have to look for immigrant wives or perhaps undertake "a new rape of the Sabines." *Ladies' Home Journal*, which never seemed to regard consistency as a particular editorial virtue, alternated its essays by happy spinsters with short stories about women who grabbed for matrimonial happiness in the nick of time. "I'm too much a woman to be wasted this way!" proclaimed a college teacher who is inspired by the sight of a happy family at Christmastime and shucks her career to marry the boy back home.

## "LIFE IS TOO SHORT TO SPEND IT DIGESTING PORK"

With the ascension of "professional women," housewives were in need of a Catharine Beecher for a new generation, to reinterpret housekeeping for the twentieth century and give it some of the cachet it had lost. They found her in Ellen Swallow Richards, the founder of the science of home economics.

Swallow was one of those intense female college students who literally walked around campus with a book in front of her face. She loved science, and after graduating from Vassar, she attempted to get an advanced degree in chemistry at MIT, where there were no female students. The faculty reluctantly allowed her to enroll as a special student, making no promises about what kind of degree she might qualify for. In an attempt to win over the professors, she mended their shirts and swept the laboratory floors. "Perhaps the fact that I am not a Radical . . . and that I do not scorn womanly duties but claim it as a privilege to clean up and sort of supervise the room and sew things is winning me stronger allies than anything," she wrote to her parents hopefully. MIT was never grateful enough to give her any degree higher than another B.S., but in the meantime Ellen fell in love and married one of her professors—Robert Hallowell Richards, a specialist in metallurgy. Richards had opposed coeducation at MIT, which he said introduced "feelings, interests foreign to the lecture room." But he respected his wife as a scientist. She acted as a chemist for his experiments while he gave financial support to her efforts to improve scientific education for women.

Ellen Richards equipped an empty laboratory and took on students, most of whom were already teachers, to give them grounding in chemistry. To make the course relevant, she applied the lessons to women's work, analyzing the ingredients in cleaning products and identifying the chemical processes involved in cooking. Boiling a potato was drudgery, she said, "but the cook who can compute the calories of heat which a potato of a given weight will yield is no drudge." In her wake, the Boston Cooking School would offer courses in Bacteriology and the Chemistry of Soap, and home economics would become an academic discipline. It also became a career path in academia for women who didn't want to be home at all. By 1914, more than 250 colleges offered home economics programs, and girls were able to take chemistry and biology and geology under the theory it would help them to become better homemakers.

In the 1890s, anything scientific was regarded as a good thing. Even laypeople understood the germ theory, and cleaning was no longer about neatness, but a way to vanquish contagion. "To keep the world clean, this is one great task for women," cheered *Household Economics*. Turn-of-the-century Americans were in love with the idea of efficiency, "scientific management," and motion study. Lillian Gilbreth, an industrial engineer, suggested that housewives perform time and motion studies of their work by having a child follow Mother around with a ball of string, unwinding it to measure the distance she traveled. (Gilbreth, the heroine of the book *Cheaper by the Dozen*, had two college degrees, but when she married she turned her attention to home and overachieved again by having twelve children. When her husband died suddenly, Gilbreth responded to the emergency and took over his consulting business, becoming an international expert in a growing field while two of her offspring wrote best-selling books about her.)

Nutritionists broke food down into its component parts, and recipes were valued for their efficiency, wholesomeness, and the way they made the plate look tidy. American cuisine, which had never been admired by the rest of the world for anything but the abundance of its ingredients, took another beating from the scientific school of cookery, which emphasized nutrition to the almost total exclusion of anything else. "Cooking has a nobler purpose than the gratification of appetite and the sense of taste," said a speaker at the World's Congress of Women at the Chicago World's Fair. The scientific housewives worshiped the god of protein and the energy-building calorie. (The turn-of-the-century obsession with calories was not about cutting them down, but about finding foods that could deliver the maximum caloric cargo per bite.) Dinners were also supposed to be eye-catching, and experts favored color-coordinated meals with hand-carved vegetables and solids floating in liquids. The early-twentieth-century hostesses particularly liked food that resembled something else. Fish could be pureed and put into a mold to look like anything from a moon to George Washington's profile. A chicken salad could be shaped like a lamb chop, a pear pierced with almond slivers to impersonate a porcupine. Virtually any dish could be improved by covering it with white sauce—a mixture of flour, milk, and butter that muffled taste while improving the "daintiness" of the plate. The scientific cooks also worried endlessly about digestion. Sarah Tyson Rorer, the founder of the Philadelphia Cooking School who once recommended a dish of boiled chicken covered with popcorn and white sauce, harangued against pork because she believed it took five hours to digest. "Life is too short to spend it digesting pork," she said.

Child rearing was also being approached scientifically. The experts demanded that mothers follow a strict schedule and not give in to their wailing infants' demands. John Watson was an enormously influential child-care specialist whose mission was to protect the younger generation from the potentially smothering mother love. "Dress them, bathe them . . . never hug and kiss them, never let them sit in your lap," he advised. "If you must, kiss them once on the forehead when they say good night. Shake hands with them in the morning." The Watsonians regarded the turn-of-the-century child as a little machine that should be oiled and greased regularly, but otherwise let alone. A popular government pamphlet on child care admitted that "the rule that parents should not play with the baby may seem hard, but it is no doubt a safe one."

It's unclear how many women took all this advice to heart. Social workers who tried to preach the gospel of scientific child care despaired when their immigrant clients insisted on nursing their babies whenever they were hungry. Margaret Mead's middle-class mother consulted a book that urged parents not to pick up a crying baby unless it was in pain. "She accepted the admonition . . . but she said her babies were good babies who would cry only if something was wrong, so she picked them up." The best-selling cookbook of the era was actually by Fannie Farmer, who never hesitated to recommend a dish as "tasty." (Farmer, the first writer to provide exact amounts of ingredients with her recipes, was celebrated as "The Mother of Level Measurements.")

Thanks to the obsession with scientific domesticity, people began asking themselves whether keeping house and raising children should become career specialties rather than the vocation of every married woman. *Looking Backward,* a hugely popular novel by Edward Bellamy, told the story of a man who falls asleep and wakes up in the year 2000—when life is just about perfect, and a happy army of industrial workers does everybody's laundry "at excessively cheap rates" and cooks delicious meals in public kitchens. It inspired a raft of other utopian novels, and wherever the heroes woke up, they found that society had abolished household chores. One of the people who picked up on these ideas was Charlotte Perkins Gilman, a grandniece of Catharine and Harriet Beecher. Her book, *Women and Economics,* envisioned a world of cooperative kitchens preparing meals for families who didn't like to cook, and centralized nurseries run by men and women who were talented at child care. "What would shoes be like if every man made his own?" she demanded. For a while, the home economists and theoreticians like Gilman inspired would-be entrepreneurs to invest in equipment that would deliver nutritious meals to the door for housewives who wanted to get out of the kitchen. But the idea never really caught on anywhere but the women's colleges—Inez Milholland said *Women and Economics* was "the Bible of the student body" while she was at Vassar. Perkins, in her later life, said she realized that she was never going to live to see the improvements she envisioned. It's hard to imagine how she would have reacted to fast food.

## "HAS SUCH A THING EVER HAPPENED . . . BEFORE?"

World War I began in Europe in 1914, and long before America entered the fray in 1917, American women were crossing the ocean and volunteering to serve as nurses, canteen hostesses, ambulance drivers, and switchboard operators. An estimated 25,000 women made the trip, often with no idea what they would do when they got to the fighting. The sixty-year-old American writer Margaret Deland, who was herself doing relief work in France, was inspired by their determination. "Has such a thing ever happened in the world before: A passionate desire on the part of the women of one people to go to the help of the men of another people?" Deland wondered if young European women would have gone as readily to the aid of soldiers in a North American war. The answer was probably no, because no other young women in the world enjoyed the independence of American girls in that era.

Relief and medical services in the early years of World War I were so uncoordinated that women who were daring and willing could easily assign themselves to duty. Barnard College sent women overseas as canteen workers after a one-week course that allegedly included instruction in French, cooking, history, customs of the European allied nations, games, and storytelling. Other volunteers found themselves assisting doctors in the French hospitals. "I knew nothing about nursing and had to learn on my patients, a painful process for all concerned," said Juliet Goodrich, who had been a canteen worker until she was recruited to work in a Paris medical facility in 1918. Although the image of the relief worker was a dewy young girl, some of the American women who volunteered were middle-aged or older, like Deland. "I'm too old to fight, but I'm sending my mother," said Florence Kendall's son when she set sail for Europe. Edith Wharton, the American novelist, was fifty-two years old and living in Europe when the war broke out. She started a sewing workroom to employ displaced women, and established clinics, free clothing centers, a cooperative where refugees could buy cheap groceries, a day nursery, an employment agency, vocational training classes, and a tuberculosis clinic. She did it all without fanfare and told a friend she had discovered that "it takes a great deal more time to do good than to have fun."

Sympathy for the overrun Belgians and imperiled French was high in America, and millions of women back home organized committees to roll bandages, raise relief funds, or even send aid to suffering French animals. But the volunteers who crossed the ocean were also in search of adventure. "To be in the front ranks in this most dramatic event that was ever staged, and to be in the first group of women ever called out for duty with the United States Army . . . is all too much good fortune for any one person," enthused Julia Stimson, a nurse. Their derring-do was unflappable. "It isn't exactly an alluring prospect to be exiled in the backwoods of Russia for a couple of months with only two English-speaking people to run an infectious hospital, but it will be rather fun," insisted Ruth Holden.

There were nearly 200,000 black servicemen overseas, and they were often ignored by white female volunteers. Black women eagerly offered to help, but they were almost always rebuffed by white officials. Some Red Cross administrators refused to allow them to do canteen work in the United States because they did not want African Americans wearing their uniform. Two thousand black nurses volunteered and were certified as ready for duty overseas, but American officials preferred not to bother finding them accommodations. Addie Waites Hunton, a college graduate who was on the national board of the YMCA, was turned down when she first requested that the organization send her overseas. Eventually, the Y did agree to send Hunton and two other black women. They attended a three-day conference for YMCA secretaries in France, and when one of the women told the minister who had run the gathering how much she appreciated it, he replied: "I'm glad you enjoyed it, but we don't mix in the States and you must not expect to here." Hunton and her friends wound up as virtually the only African American women serving in Europe. They were overwhelmed by the black soldiers' reaction to their presence, and the men's longing for the women they had left behind. One night when they were showing a newsreel, a Red Cross parade in Manhattan appeared on screen. "When a group of colored women were shown marching the men went wild. They did not want that particular scene to pass and many approached and fondled the screen with the remark 'Just look at them!' "

The canteen work, although hardly as dramatic as nursing, could be a wearing business for all the volunteers, black or white. "We have only twenty girls and there are always two thousand or more men," said Marian Baldwin. The rule was that whenever a whistle blew, soldiers could cut in on dancing couples. "The consequence is that a girl is literally hurled from one man to another while dozens of eager hands try to snatch her away from him. Of course it is all pretty rough and one comes out of it every night with black and blue spots." The women also reported that they never had enough to eat and suffered from the cold. Virtually all the volunteers wanted to get as close as possible to the fighting, although conditions at the front were far worse than most had imagined. Julia Stimson worked at a casualty clearing station and reported that the odor in the operating room from the steam, ether, and filthy soldiers' clothes "was so terrible that it was all that any of them could do to keep from being sick." After fourteen hours in surgery, Stimson said, the nurses went off "with freezing feet to the meal of tea and bread and jam and off to rest if you can in a wet bell tent in a damp bed without sheets." Mary Elderkins and a dozen other nurses shared seven cots underground, to protect them from the shelling. "If we sat erect on our cot our head struck the rough stone above. Water dripped on us all night long. Huge black bugs crawled about, and after we quieted down we could hear the rats." Writing about the soldiers she treated, Elderkins said, "I don't believe one of us had ever imagined men could be so absolutely 'shot to pieces.' " Anna Coleman Ladd, an American sculptor, volunteered to make "portrait masks" for mutilated men to wear so they could go out in public without frightening people.

Some women were appalled by the war even if they never saw it firsthand. Jane Addams lost most of her popularity when she came out strongly against American involvement. Jeanette Rankin of Montana, the first woman to serve in the House of Representatives, voted "no" when Congress authorized U.S. entry into the fighting. She had been elected on a peace platform in a year when most politicians, including President Woodrow Wilson, were vowing to stay out of the conflict, and Rankin felt she could not break her word to her constituents. "I want to stand by my country, but I cannot vote for war," she said. Her vote, only four days after she had taken her seat in the House, was the first cast by any woman in Congress. The final tally was 373–50 and Rankin's action was widely interpreted as a sign that women could not face the hard facts of political life. She was not reelected the following year.

# Reforming the World: Suffrage, Temperance, and Other Causes

In an era when American women were becoming not only typists and teachers but also labor organizers, investigative reporters, and college presidents, it sometimes seemed there was only one thing they couldn't do. "We have got the new woman in everything except the counting of her vote at the ballot box," remarked Susan B. Anthony in 1895. "And that's coming. It's coming sooner than most people think." But actually, success was still a quarter of a century off. When the Wyoming territory gave women the full right to vote in 1869, it was an international breakthrough. But by the time America enacted national suffrage for women in 1920, Great Britain, Canada, Germany, the Soviet Union, Australia, and a number of other countries had gotten there first.

At the turn of the century, the woman suffrage movement revolved around Susan B. Anthony and Elizabeth Cady Stanton, just as it had in the era before the Civil War. They were friends and comrades in arms for more than fifty years, even though they spent relatively little time together and had entirely different personalities. Anthony, the gaunt, selfless reformer who never married, was one of those restless peripatetic women of the Victorian era. Stanton was stout, fond of fancy dresses, and anchored to her responsibilities as a wife and mother. Her childbearing was the despair of Anthony, who tended to regard marriage and maternity as betrayal of the cause. When Stanton became pregnant with her seventh offspring, Anthony was shocked that "for a *moment's pleasure* to herself or her husband, she should thus increase the *load* of *cares* under which she already groans." And Stanton complained that Anthony had no sympathy for her domestic burdens. "I must buy butter and meat, hear youngsters spell and multiply, coax parted threads in stocking heels and toes to meet again . . . and smooth down the ruffled feathers of imperious men or cross chambermaids and cook. Then comes Susan, with the nation on her soul, asking for speeches, resolutions, calls, attendance at conventions." (Stanton was a devoted and famously permissive mother, and her daughter Harriot Stanton Blatch recalled later that the sight of Susan on the doorstep "was not a matter for rejoicing.")

No one knows exactly how Elizabeth Cady Stanton and Susan B. Anthony first became friends, but the community of people who believed in women's rights before the Civil War was so small, they would inevitably have run into each other. In any case, they discovered that the combination of their very different talents produced a virtually unstoppable force. Stanton was the idea person, the writer of speeches and newspaper essays, interested in everything and boldly urging Anthony to expand her reformist impulse to issues like divorce reform and religion. She was unflappable, always speaking her mind, and happy to shock people. (At her eightieth birthday party she told her audience of dignitaries that it was time to rewrite the Bible.) Anthony was the organizer, the worker bee who would take the suffrage message to every corner of the country and rally women behind its banner. Unlike her friend, Anthony second-guessed herself constantly and persevered through force of will rather than self-confidence.

Both were abolitionists who spent the Civil War years pressing for full emancipation of all slaves, speaking out before hostile white mobs, collecting signatures on petitions, campaigning, and lobbying. But they had assumed, perhaps naively, that women would get the vote at the same time as African American men. When that didn't happen, they turned on old friends and aligned themselves with a racist benefactor, arguing for woman suffrage by comparing educated white women like themselves to semiliterate black men who were getting the ballot first. It was a bitter, dark period during which Stanton shocked her friend Frederick Douglass with her denunciation of "Patrick and Sambo and Yung Tung . . . making laws for . . . the daughters of Adams and Jefferson . . . women of wealth and education . . ." The women's movement split, leaving radical feminists like Anthony and Stanton on one side and the more moderate women, like Lucy Stone, on the other. ("Mrs. Stone felt the slaves' wrongs more deeply than her own—my philosophy was more egotistical," said Stanton later.) The breach would not really be healed until the next generation took over.

By the turn of the century, the two great suffrage warriors were resigned to the idea that they would not live to see women vote nationwide. "Logically, our enfranchisement ought to have occurred . . . in Reconstruction days," said Elizabeth Cady Stanton at eighty-six, shortly before her death in 1902. "Our movement is belated, and like all things too long postponed, now gets on everybody's nerves." The cause of woman suffrage had become respectable by then, but the energy had gone out of the fight. The movement had hit a period that suffrage leaders came to call "the doldrums." Women had given up hope that Congress would approve an amendment to the Constitution, and under the leadership of Carrie Chapman Catt, suffrage organizers embarked on a campaign to amend every single state constitution instead. It was a dispiriting business, short on excitement and long on circulating petitions and lobbying uninspiring state legislators. All the horrors of the state-by-state strategy were epitomized by South Dakota, with its summer heat, winter cold, remote towns, thin population, and unreliable political allies. The suffragists staged five different full-bore campaigns to change South Dakota's state constitution and win the vote for its scattered female residents. During one of these efforts, Catt got typhoid and nearly died. After Anthony, then seventy, returned home from a summer of South Dakota campaigning, her sister Mary remarked that for the first time she realized Susan was growing old.

"To get the word 'male' in effect out of the Constitution cost the women of the country fifty-two years of pauseless campaign," said Carrie Chapman Catt when it was all over. "During that time they were forced to conduct 56 campaigns of referenda to male voters, 480 campaigns to get Legislatures to submit suffrage amendments to voters, 47 campaigns to get state constitutional conventions to write woman suffrage into state constitutions; 277 campaigns to get State party conventions to include woman suffrage planks, 30 campaigns to get presidential party campaigns to include woman suffrage planks in party platforms and 19 campaigns with 19 successive Congresses."

On the surface it was hard to understand why politicians were so resistant. True, they still got up and made speeches about the importance of keeping women safe at home. But in reality, most women worked, at least until they married, and when the nation entered World War I, some of them took the place of men in steel foundries, munitions factories, and behind the wheels of tractors and trains. Many states whose legislators opposed national suffrage allowed women to vote in certain elections—school board contests in some states, presidential elections in others. The real opposition was pragmatic. Democrats suspected that women would vote Republican. Urban machine politicians distrusted women voters because they connected them with reform movements. Much of the money to run anti-suffrage campaigns came from the liquor industry, which realized it would be out of business if women got to vote on Prohibition. Perhaps most important of all was the solid resistance from southern politicians. By the end of the nineteenth century they had successfully deprived black men of the right to vote, and the last thing they wanted was pressure to open the door for black women.

It was all very well for Anthony and Stanton to resign themselves to dying before the vote arrived. But it must have been depressing for suffragists when Carrie Catt, who was forty-one years old when she succeeded Anthony as head of the National American Woman Suffrage Association, indicated she didn't expect to get it in her lifetime, either. In 1912, Catt wrote to a friend that she was sure a woman would eventually rise up and lead the suffrage movement to victory. "Some day she'll come. Perhaps she is growing up now . . ." she wrote. While Anthony had assured women that failure was impossible, Catt in her gloomier moods sometimes gave the impression victory wasn't all that likely, either.

A former school superintendent who had worked her way through college, Carrie Catt was totally dedicated to the suffrage cause. Before her marriage, she and her future husband, a wealthy engineer, signed a legal contract which provided that Carrie would have two months off in the spring and two months off in the fall to work for women's right to vote. But some people felt she was too cautious and eager to compromise. Harriot Stanton Blatch, returning to the United States after twenty years in England with her British husband, found the women's movement her mother had started depressing beyond words, and far too identified with the needs of well-to-do clubwomen. "The only method suggested for furthering the cause was the slow process of education," she said. "We were told to organize, organize, organize, to the end of educating, educating, educating."

Blatch wanted to be daring. (When some of the old guard protested her tactics might subject them to ridicule, Blatch, who was definitely her mother's daughter, said: "Ridicule, ridicule. Blessed be ridicule.") She and her friends wanted to bring working women into the movement and encourage them to take a leading public role. They also wanted fun, excitement, and parades. After yellow was adopted as the official suffrage hue, no parade was complete without many variations on the theme of gold—in Louisville, twelve little girls decked out as yellow butterflies led a train of floats and automobiles. In 1912, a parade for women's right to vote in Manhattan attracted 10,000 marchers in a display "the like of which New York never knew before," said the *Times*. It was not just the size of the event that caught the nation's notice, but the way it cut across class lines. Corset makers, nurses, social workers, schoolgirls, writers, society women, laundresses, and teachers walked arm in arm. The wealthy trendsetter Alva Belmont marched with the factory workers. The dressmakers carried a banner showing a sewing machine, and the writers had pictures of Harriet Beecher Stowe.

In California in 1911, western women used the same upbeat tactics in a second try at changing their state constitution. The movement swung into action with all the parades, pageants, plays, and billboards it could muster. Volunteers distributed lapel buttons and suffrage baggage stickers and draped everything in sight in yellow. The advertising industry, never shy about glomming on to a trend with pizzazz, invented a "Suffragette Cracker" and ran "Votes for Women" headlines over the most unlikely copy. In one, a woman appeared to be dropping a cereal biscuit in the ballot box as the ad argued that Shredded Wheat was "a vote for health, happiness and domestic freedom." Despite the liquor industry's best effort to pack the ballot boxes, the women won. The margin was a minscule 3,587 votes, but to the suffrage movement, it was more than enough. Martha Farnsworth, a Kansas housewife, was at a meeting of the Topeka Good Government Club when word came that California had given its women the right to vote. "We all shouted for joy, some hugged and kissed one another, some cried and some jumped up and down for joy and joined most heartily in singing 'Praise God from Whom All Blessings Flow.' O, we were a happy lot," she wrote in her diary.

Western states, however, had always been more open to women's rights and women's votes than the rest of the country. Except for the South, the Northeast, where the suffrage movement was born, turned out to be the most resistant, due to the opposition of urban machine bosses, the liquor industry, and a distinct lack of enthusiasm in the Catholic Church. In 1915, Carrie Chapman Catt led a mammoth effort to win the vote in New York that featured, by her count, 10,300 meetings, 7.5 million leaflets ("or three and a half for every voter"), and a parade of 20,000 people in New York City. But the women lost. "Men too drunk to sign their own name voted all over the state," Catt said later. Nevertheless, everyone was impressed by her organizational drive—not to mention her way with statistics. She was also a newly minted heiress. Mrs. Frank Leslie, a magazine editor, died in 1914 and left the bulk of her estate to Catt for use in the suffrage effort. After the relatives finished contesting the will, it still amounted to more than a million dollars.

## "THERE IS NO ALICE PAUL. THERE IS SUFFRAGE."

Even with their parades and yellow bunting, American women were far more conservative in their tactics than the suffragists in England, who were willing to smash windows, throw rocks, and get arrested. (In the most spectacular act of British militancy, Emily Davison threw herself in front of the king's horse during the running of the English Derby in 1913, achieving instant if gruesome martyrdom for the cause.) Alice Paul, the last great leader of the American movement, spent her political apprenticeship with the English suffragists. Then, like Harriot Blatch, she moved back home and dedicated her life to the cause. When Paul dedicated herself, she went all the way. Although she was a voracious reader who eventually earned three law degrees, for a long time she refused to read anything except tomes on suffrage, lest her attention be diverted. She was another one of those charismatic female leaders who was both powerfully assertive and tantalizingly remote. (A magazine writer, assigned to produce a profile on the "real" Paul, concluded in despair: "There is no Alice Paul. There is suffrage.") Paul seemed uninterested in things as mundane as food and refused to spend more than 30 cents a day on meals. Always small and frail-looking, she was so single-minded that one of her political opponents was convinced her lack of nutrition had drained her sanity, calling her an "anemic fanatic."

Paul hated the state-by-state strategy. She believed women would never win the right to vote without a constitutional amendment, but there was no sign Congress was prepared to pass one. Woodrow Wilson, when asked his opinion on suffrage during the presidential campaign of 1912, dodged grandly: "Ladies, this is a very arguable question and my mind is in the middle of the argument." On the day before his inauguration in 1913, Paul made her national debut with a great suffrage parade in Washington, featuring 8,000 marchers, 26 floats, 10 bands, and 6 chariots. Inez Milholland, the beautiful horse-woman who assured young American womanhood that fighting for suffrage provided good exercise, led the marchers astride a white steed. Over a half million people gathered to watch them, and when the president-elect arrived by train that morning, he was disconcerted to find no crowds assembled to greet him.

In his youth, Woodrow Wilson had once called woman suffrage "the foundation of every evil in this country." He supported the idea that each state should decide the issue for itself—the stance that the South was also pushing, because it would allow southern states to keep the franchise as limited and as white as possible. Alice Paul became one of the banes of his life, but her intransigence began pushing him closer to Carrie Catt and the mainstream suffragists. Wilson had always needed admiring women in his life—while the nation was under the impression he was deep in mourning for his recently deceased wife, the lonely president was already courting a successor. Women like Catt were exactly the kind he found most sympathetic—well-to-do, well educated, and respectful of authority. Catt and her friends seemed to understand his problems and find Alice Paul as trying as he did. He and the second Mrs. Wilson appeared at the annual convention of the National American Woman Suffrage Association during his reelection campaign in 1916, and Wilson hinted as broadly as possible that he was coming around: "We feel the tide; we rejoice in the strength of it and we shall not quarrel in the long run as to the method of it." The next speaker, in response, said: "We have waited so long, Mr. President, for the vote—we had hoped it might come in your administration." Spontaneously, the entire audience stood and silently turned to face their guest of honor. The president, Catt felt certain, was in their corner.

After Wilson's reelection, Alice Paul and her supporters decided to picket the White House. The demonstrations went on for eighteen months and when America entered World War I, Paul resisted other leaders' urging that she abandon the protests until hostilities were over. Instead, the picketers carried banners asking how the country could fight for democracy abroad when women did not enjoy it at home. They were harassed by passersby, and after one rough day of demonstrating, Paul was warned that the women would be arrested if they ever returned to the White House.

"I feel that we will continue," she told the chief of police.

Arrests followed—first perfunctory trips to the police station, then fines, which the protesters refused to pay, and finally increasingly severe prison sentences. Suffragists were shot at and dragged down the street by people attempting to wrest away their banners. They received longer and longer sentences to Occoquam prison, where the cells were small, dank, and heavily populated with rodents and the food was full of worms. In October 1918, Alice Paul, serving a six-month sentence, began a hunger strike to protest the prison conditions. Rose Winslow, a Polish immigrant who fasted along with Paul, smuggled out messages to her husband and friends, reporting that they were being force-fed by prison officials, who poured food into their stomachs via a tube stuck down their throats. "Yesterday was a bad day for me in feeding," she wrote. "I was vomiting continually during the process. The tube has developed an irritation somewhere that is painful. . . . Don't let them tell you we take this well. Miss Paul vomits much . . . we think of the coming feeding all day. It is horrible." As women were released, they toured the country dressed in prison garb, to publicize their comrades' plight. Democrats began to worry they would suffer reprisals in the November elections.

Finally, Wilson threw himself behind the drive to win women the vote. With heavy lobbying from the president, the House took up the Susan B. Anthony amendment: "The rights of citizens of the United States to vote shall be not denied or abridged by the United States or by any state on account of sex." It was a moment some men, as well as women, had been waiting for. One congressman, who had been in the hospital for six months, staggered into the House to cast his vote for suffrage. Representative Thetus Sims of Tennessee, who had broken his arm and shoulder, refused to have it set for fear of missing the vote. Another supporter had himself carried in on a stretcher. Frederick Hicks of New York, who had been home at the bedside of his dying wife, left at her urging and went to Washington to vote for suffrage. The amendment passed by exactly the two-thirds vote necessary and Representative Hicks returned home for his wife's funeral.

The president then took the extraordinary step of going to the Capitol to personally plead with the Senate and remind them that disenfranchised women were at that very moment nursing soldiers overseas and filling in for absent men on the home front. "We have made partners of the women in this war; shall we admit them only to a partnership of suffering and sacrifice and toil and not to a partnership of privilege and right?" he asked. The Senate was unmoved. The vote was 62–34, two votes short of the two-thirds majority needed. It took more than another year to get the Anthony amendment completely through Congress. Meanwhile, a number of states had approved suffrage on their own, including New York and South Dakota, on the fifth try. Catt wryly said she presumed South Dakota voters "had accumulated some education on the subject" by then.

Congressional approval, so long coming, was only the first step. The suffragists still had to get the amendment ratified by thirty-six states, and by late summer 1920, the drive seemed stuck, just one state short of success. Everyone converged on Tennessee, where the legislature was so divided and so heavily lobbied it was impossible to tell what would happen. Lawmakers were alternately threatened and plied with liquor, and by the night before the Senate vote, Carrie Catt reported that "both suffrage and anti-suffrage men were reeling through the hall in an advanced state of intoxication." The Senate voted 25–4 for the amendment. Catt, watching a lifetime of work hang in the balance, must have wondered if that girl she envisioned growing up to lead the suffrage movement to victory was going to turn out to be herself after all. "We are up to the last half of the last state," she wrote.

The struggle for women's right to vote had been filled with high drama and cliffhanger votes from the beginning, and it would have been a shame if the last moments were not equally exciting. The Tennessee House didn't let history down. The Speaker, who had been a suffrage supporter, suddenly changed his mind and ratification seemed to be one vote short. Then Harry Burn, at age twenty-four the youngest state legislator and a presumed opponent, rose to say he had received a letter from his mother, telling him: "Hurrah and vote for suffrage. Don't keep them in doubt. . . . I have been watching how you stood but have not seen anything yet. Don't forget to be a good boy and help Mrs. Catt." Burn voted yes. "I know that a mother's advice is always safest for a boy to follow," he said.

In November 1920, Charlotte Woodward, who had driven as a teenage girl to the famous gathering at Seneca Falls, cast her first vote for president of the United States. She was the only person who had been there at the beginning and lived to see the end.

## "BELIEVE . . . AT LEAST FOR THE TIME BEING, IN THE SYMPATHY OF WOMEN"

In 1913, when Alice Paul decided to steal the thunder from Woodrow Wilson's inauguration with her great parade, Ida Wells-Barnett, the black journalist and activist, arrived in Washington with a sixty-member delegation of African American women from her Alpha Suffrage Club in Chicago. Paul was not thrilled to see them. In an effort to placate southern suffragists, she had announced that there would be no black women in the march. But African Americans were determined this historic moment was not going to be an all-white affair. "If the Illinois women do not take a stand now in this great democratic parade then the colored women are lost," said Wells-Barnett. In the end, Paul reluctantly allowed the black women to walk at the end of the procession. Only Wells-Barnett broke ranks. She vanished into the crowd and then stepped back onto the street as the Illinois delegation passed, joining her white friends for the rest of the march.

This sort of thing happened to black suffragists all the time. Whenever there was a question of choosing between the sensibilities of racist southerners and the feelings of African American women, they

wound up on the outside—or the back of the parade. When the suffrage movement held its first big convention in the South in 1894 in
Atlanta, Susan B. Anthony asked Frederick Douglass to stay away out
of "expediency." When the convention met in New Orleans in 1903,
black women were barred from attending. Anthony paid a visit to one
of the largest black women's clubs in the city in an effort to make
amends. The president, Sylvanie Williams, greeted her politely, then
said pointedly: "When women like you, Miss Anthony, come to see us
and speak to us, it helps us to believe in the Fatherhood of God and the
Brotherhood of man, and at least for the time being, in the sympathy
of women."

Women like Williams and Ida Wells-Barnett wanted very much to
vote, but they had other, more pressing concerns as well. In the North,
African Americans were being confronted with newly rigid segregation rules and urban riots while in the South, the lynchings that had
begun after Reconstruction had turned into a permanent weapon of
political and social intimidation. In 1918 in Georgia, Mary Turner, a
pregnant black woman, tried to intervene when a crowd lynched her
husband. She was tortured, her body slashed open, and the fetus
pulled out before she was burned to death. Members of the National
Association of Colored Women in Savannah sent out telegrams begging for an investigation to everyone from the president to white
women's clubs. Although the Savannah Federated Women sent back a
note of sympathy, the president of the Georgia Federation of White
Women wrote that lynching would not end "until you teach your people not to molest the whites."

All things being equal, most of the white suffrage leaders would
have been happy to march next to Wells-Barnett in the parade or sit
with Sylvanie Williams at a convention. But African American women
had virtually no political power and southern whites had all the power
in the world, at least in their ability to stop a constitutional amendment. So people like Susan Anthony and Alice Paul were constantly
trying to avoid reminding the South that black women were part of
the suffrage movement. When people like Wells-Barnett failed to

appreciate their position, they explained the situation again, as though the only problem was a lack of political sophistication on the part of the African Americans.

## "LIPS THAT TOUCH ALCOHOL"

Despite all the publicity the suffrage movement received, most women who became involved in public affairs between the Civil War and World War I were not all that interested in the right to vote. They were concerned with temperance. The liquor industry was right— many women wanted to vote just so they could use the ballot box to ban the sale of alcohol.

Drinking was the nation's biggest consumer industry, and alcohol consumption was at one of its highest levels in history. Most Americans were actually abstainers, but the others were drinking overtime. The kind of women who joined reform movements did not drink at all, and they often made it uncomfortable for anyone else who did. An American gentleman, a visitor commented, "thinks it ungallant to drink anything stronger than water in a lady's company." One result was the distinct lack of male presence in the drawing room, a solidifying of the separation of the sexes. Temperance represented women's desire to keep their men at home, and their dedication to that great middle-class American virtue of self-control. It also spoke to fear of a changing world populated by foreign people with strange ways. Immigrants—even many immigrant women—drank. Turning them into abstainers made them less threatening and more American. It was the same impulse that compelled early social workers to urge immigrant women to stop cooking strange dishes like pasta and take up patriotic fare like roast meats and potatoes.

Before the Civil War, temperance movements had all been led by men, and the goal was usually to reform drunkards—moderation was the byword, and some reformers simply asked members to drink nothing stronger than wine. But in the 1870s, opposition to liquor emerged as a woman's issue, and the goal became more stark—to shut down saloons and drive all forms of alcoholic beverage out of the country.

In 1873, just before Christmas, about eighty married women marched up to the saloons in Hillsboro, Ohio, demanding that they close forever. The demonstrations went on for months, attracting national attention. A reporter from Cincinnati interviewed a Hillsboro man who said he and his friends walked into a bar and ordered drinks when "the rustle of women's wear attracted their attention, and looking up they saw what they thought was a crowd of a thousand ladies entering." One of the horrified men saw his mother and sister, another his future mother-in-law. Soon, women in small towns all over Ohio were kneeling in the snow before the town tavern, singing hymns and sometimes taking an ax to the bartender's wares. Seemingly spontaneous assaults on saloons—which were in fact frequently urged on by male temperance lecturers—occurred in nearly 1,000 communities, involving tens of thousands of women over a period of about six months. It was the start of an antialcohol crusade by America's middle-class women that would continue until Prohibition became the law of the land in 1919.

Temperance advocates could be mind-bogglingly self-righteous, and they tended to blame alcohol for everything bad except the weather. (Frances Perkins, who would become the secretary of labor in Franklin Roosevelt's administration, recalled that as a student at Mt. Holyoke, she visited a poor mill town and was stunned that some of the impoverished residents didn't drink. It had never occurred to her that anything but alcohol caused poverty.) Nevertheless, they were talking about a genuine social issue that ruined the lives of a great many American women. A drunken husband was an emotional burden, a potential physical danger, and a drain on the family finances. With little control over her property or her children's custody, a woman who had the bad luck to pick a husband with an alcohol problem could do little but watch and worry—unless she came to the end of her rope and grabbed a hatchet and marched to the nearest saloon.

The ultimate symbol of saloon-smashing was Carry Nation, who first drew national attention in 1900 when she walked into the rather elegant bar of the Hotel Carey in Wichita, Kansas, and threw two stones at a huge nude painting of *Cleopatra at the Bath*, ripping the canvas. She shattered a $1,500 mirror, drove the patrons from the room with her cane, and broke all the bottles and glasses on the bar. She was dragged away, shouting at her jailers, "You put me in here a cub, but I will go out a roaring lion and make all hell howl." Nation's first husband had been an alcoholic, and as she grew older and increasingly eccentric, she became obsessed with the evils of alcohol and tobacco. Her second husband left her when she became a celebrity, and she embarked on a career of lecturing, smashing, and publishing magazines like *The Hatchet* and *The Smasher's Mail*. She also inspired imitators like May Sheriff, who organized "The Flying Squadron of Jesus," fifty women who raided bars along the Oklahoma border.

Nation was not a temperance leader—she was part of the lunatic fringe. But millions of mild-mannered American women defended her ends, if not necessarily her means. They distributed literature that chronicled the terrible fate that befell doubters who rebelled in even the smallest way against the antialcohol creed. (In one story, a farmer insisted on using a few barrels of apples to make hard cider. His brilliant son sampled the drink and swiftly turned into a hopeless inebriate.) Women urged their sons to sign temperance pledges and raised their daughters to regard a man who drank as the worst possible candidate for a husband. The discovery that a suitor indulged even occasionally was enough to break off a relationship. "Lips that touch alcohol shall never touch mine" went the mantra of the day.

## "DO EVERYTHING"

The Women's Christian Temperance Union became the biggest mass political organization of American women in history. In the 1890s, ten times as many New York women were in the WCTU as in all the suffrage groups combined. Tampa alone had three different women's temperance organizations (one for blacks, one for whites, and one for Cuban Americans), but Florida's suffrage group had only twenty members in the whole state, eight of them men. However, all those temperance women gradually began to feel that having the vote would be a very good thing because it held the key to the prohibition of liquor. They became critical grassroots soldiers for the suffrage movement, organizing all those petition drives and referenda campaigns and state lobbying efforts that kept the effort going during the doldrums and gradually pushed it forward to success.

The woman who brought these two very different political drives together was Frances Willard, the president of the WCTU for twenty years, and a leader with a far more sweeping vision of how women could reform the country than most of her followers. She was one of the best-known people of her era, and she was certainly the most famous woman of the nineteenth century whose name is virtually unknown today. Willard was the head of the Ladies College at Northwestern University when her former fiancé, whom she had rejected, was named university president. (Although she would hint vaguely about other romances, all of Willard's known close personal relationships throughout her life were with women.) It became clear that she needed to find another life's work. She began making speeches at temperance meetings and then, impelled by what she believed was divine guidance, committed herself to the cause. She toured the country from 1874 to 1883, averaging a lecture a day, staying with local townspeople, attempting to support her mother with the donations she collected. In one eighty-day period, she delivered forty speeches and wrote 2,000 letters.

Willard had a genius for building a mass movement by finding common ground for compromise. She initiated a policy called "Do Everything" in which the members were encouraged to fight for reform in whatever way struck them as best. The national headquarters had dozens of departments, dedicated to everything from world peace to public health, and one of the most active was the section devoted to woman suffrage. In many small towns, the WCTU was the center of all feminine political activity. Everett Hughes, a Chicago sociologist, remembered the WCTU gatherings his mother hosted, in which the women talked about "general sanitation and improving education, about the child labor laws."

Willard became the nation's most prominent orator, but far from the best paid. Her trips were organized in the cheapest way possible, including overnight rides, slow freights, and even trips in the caboose, one of which took five and a half hours to cover thirty-six miles. She was troubled by ill health, and when she collapsed in February 1898, she went into a rapid decline, during which she was politician enough to call in a sympathetic reporter for a final interview. Thirty thousand people walked past her bier in one day. Crowds stood for hours to see her coffin. In 1905, Illinois chose her to represent the state in Statuary Hall in the nation's Capitol, calling her "the first woman of the nineteenth century, the most beloved character of her time."

## "BEAUTIFUL WHITE GIRLS SOLD INTO RUIN"

The Purity Campaign was the third great strand in the women's reform movement, and, like temperance, its bottom line was forcing men to behave. The WCTU started a campaign to get men to wear white ribbons, showing they had taken a pledge to be sexually pure until marriage and faithful to their wives afterward. Some of the organization's other efforts were more dictatorial, from censoring movies to covering up paintings of naked women. "Nude art never helped a soul to belief in the Lord Jesus Christ," opined the WCTU newspaper in support of a protest against the Boston Museum of Fine Arts. Frances Willard supported the WCTU's censorship impulses, but her own priority was more serious—raising the age of sexual consent for girls, which was as low as ten years old in a number of states and seven in Delaware. By 1920, the WCTU had generally succeeded in making it illegal to seduce a girl under eighteen, although it took enormous effort to keep legislators in some states from bolting and bringing the age back down again.

The Purity Campaign, like temperance, was based on the idea that middle-class women were morally superior and therefore had the right to tell everyone else what to do. But also like temperance, it targeted a real social problem that brought its worst evils home to torture innocent housewives. Venereal disease had always been a secret fear of American women. When *Ladies' Home Journal* warned girls that holding a boy's hand could be the first step on a path to "crippling illness and disease," readers understood what that meant. Doctors conspired with their male patients to keep wives from knowing that they had been infected, and in 1904, Dr. Prince Morrow, a New York physician, stunned his audience by estimating "that there is more venereal infection among virtuous wives than among professional prostitutes." (Other physicians felt that was a wild exaggeration, although they agreed the situation was serious.) Morrow claimed that 60 percent of American men had contacted syphilis or gonorrhea, generally from prostitutes, leaving their wives in danger of disease, sterility, and insanity. The American Social Hygiene Association, which he founded, advocated blood tests before marriage for men and sex education for women to warn them what to watch out for.

For the first time, people began considering sex education in the schools. But the classes offered were generally extremely vague—or so chilling in their depiction of the dangers of promiscuity that impressionable girls came out of them wondering if sex was really worthwhile. One psychologist studied the reaction of teenage girls to a class about venereal disease and discovered eleven of the twenty-five students "developed a pronounced repulsion for men." A women's college graduate claimed that "lectures . . . showing lantern slides of the ravages of disease" turned several of her classmates against men and marriage forever. One friend, she said, broke an engagement with "a fine young chap" after he confessed that once, while in college, he had "gone to a party with the boys."

The most common reaction from middle-class women was not a desire for education; when *Ladies' Home Journal* ran a series of articles on venereal disease in 1906, 75,000 readers canceled their subscriptions. And they certainly did not approve of trying to keep venereal disease in check by treating prostitution as a public health issue. In 1870, St. Louis legalized brothels and required licensed prostitutes to pass weekly health inspections, only to have the program killed by opposition from clergymen and female reformers. Even Elizabeth Cady Stanton hated the idea. Their goal was not to have men sleep with prostitutes safely, but to have them stop using women as sex objects altogether.

Ending prostitution had always been a primary goal of women's reform movements. The Sexual Purity Campaign created a panic over the issue of "white slavery," producing books and tracts that described swarms of innocent girls lured away from their small-town homes by pimps and kept prisoner in brothels by brutal gangsters. The idea fit into white women's gut conviction that none of their sex (or at least none of their sex and race) would fall into prostitution voluntarily. One reformer noted wryly that the old middle-class vision of the prostitute as a "ruined and abandoned thing . . . too vile for any contact with the virtuous and respectable" had been replaced by a fantasy of the prostitute as "a shanghaied innocent kept under lock and key."

The white slavery hysteria also played on people's sense that the younger generation of women was spinning out of control, dancing the shimmy and going out to dinner with boys they weren't planning to marry. The same women who lived in terror of their sons taking to drink began to worry about their daughters falling into sexual slavery. Books and movies picked up on the theme, some clearly more interested in titillating their readers than mobilizing them into action. "Beautiful White Girls Sold into Ruin . . . Illustrated with a large number of startling pictures," one promised.

## "CAN THEY NOT USE SELF-CONTROL?"

Sexual Purity crusaders blamed the falling birthrate on the plague of venereal disease, in part because they didn't want to acknowledge that nice women were using birth control. As with alcohol, disapproval of contraception quickly translated into a drive for a national ban. In 1873, Congress passed a law prohibiting the dissemination through the mail of birth control literature, drugs, or devices. It was the work of Anthony Comstock, an antipornography crusader who had accumulated enormous influence while heading the New York Committee for the Suppression of Vice. Comstock, who lost his only daughter as a baby and later adopted a child, may have resented women who limited the size of their families when he and his wife had difficulty conceiving. Or perhaps the fact that Comstock arranged for the adoption without telling his wife suggests that he simply disliked the idea of female control. He supported only "natural" contraception, which meant total or periodic abstention. Once, when a journalist asked if it was all right for a woman to use other means if a pregnancy would endanger her life, he replied: "Can they not use self-control? Or must they sink to the level of the beasts?"

Comstock's Society for the Suppression of Vice, which managed to acquire legal enforcement powers for itself, arrested 105 men and women for birth-control-related offenses. Posing as an impoverished father, Comstock approached the famous abortionist Madame Restell and asked her for birth control devices. When she complied, he had her arrested, and Restell, then a sixty-seven-year-old millionaire, put on a diamond-studded nightgown and cut her throat in the bathroom of her Fifth Avenue mansion. "A bloody ending to a bloody life," Comstock wrote. Another of his targets, Ida Craddock, was a spiritualist who had published a guide to marital sex for women. When she was imprisoned for violating the Comstock law, she, too, committed suicide. When Comstock brought Sarah Chase, a homeopathic physician, before a grand jury for the sale of birth control devices, the all-male jurors declined to charge her, and one demanded to know if Comstock intended to drive Chase to suicide, too. Outraged, Comstock snuck into the grand jury room and persuaded the foreman to sign two bills of indictment he had prepared on his own.

Artificial birth control was not at that point an issue for which women reformers had much sympathy. Women's rights advocates argued for "voluntary motherhood," by which they meant the right to say no to marital sex. The idea that women would want to indulge in intercourse while avoiding pregnancy was strange to many people who still believed that women were too pure to be interested in sex. But the Comstock Act did not necessarily have much effect on private behavior—the size of families continued going down. The fertility rate for white native-born women dropped from 278 live births per 1,000 in 1800 to 124 in 1900.


## "WHAT EVERY GIRL SHOULD KNOW"

Margaret Louise Higgins was the middle child in a family of eleven, the daughter of Irish immigrants in Corning, New York. Her father was a stonemason, better at giving speeches about his radical political theories than keeping a job. Her older sisters helped earn money to send Margaret, the family scholar, to a boarding school. She trained to be a nurse, and in 1902 she married Bill Sanger, a young architect. They plunged into Manhattan's exciting left-wing political community and became regulars at the salon of Mabel Dodge, a wealthy collector of intellectual and artistic celebrities. Even in a permissive circle of friends in a permissive city, Margaret Sanger was apparently well ahead of most women when it came to sexual sophistication. Mabel Dodge called her "the first person I ever knew who was openly an ardent propagandist for the joys of the flesh."

From early on, the Sanger marriage was troubled. While Margaret was giving birth to three children, Bill Sanger switched to an unprofitable career as an artist, and she resented his failure as a breadwinner. To bring in some money, she went to work for Lillian Wald's visiting nurses on the Lower East Side. She quickly became familiar with women who were ruining their health with too many pregnancies, just as her own mother had done. For the rest of her life, she would tell the possibly apocryphal story of Sadie Sachs, a poor woman with a small apartment and several small children. Sanger treated her for complications from a self-induced abortion. When Sadie pleaded with a doctor for reliable contraception, Sanger would say, the doctor laughed and advised her to "tell Jake to sleep on the roof." Three months later she came back to find the woman dying from septicemia from another abortion.

Sanger was asked to write a column on sex education, "What Every Girl Should Know," for *The Call*, a daily newspaper with socialist sympathies. When she tackled the subject of venereal disease, her column was banned by Anthony Comstock, who had acquired censorship as well as prosecutorial powers. The paper ran an empty space with the title: "What Every Girl Should Know. Nothing; by order of the U.S. Post Office." Out of the turmoil of her complicated private and professional lives, Sanger developed a mission—to bring family planning information to American women. Many of her male friends in the labor movement or politics found the crusade either strange or irritating. One night, Sanger and Bill Haywood, the famous labor leader, addressed a group of women strikers. An observer remembered that Sanger spoke of women's right to limit the size of their families and "received a hearty response" from the audience. Haywood then followed, promising the women that in the glorious economy built by union labor in the future, they would be able to have "all the babies they pleased." He was greeted by dead silence.

The birth control devices available to women in the first half of the twentieth century weren't much different from those on sale in the nineteenth, but the information was going to be better. Sanger was the first to evaluate all the available forms of birth control and produce clear explanations of what each one did, and how to use it. Eventually, she fled to Europe to avoid criminal obscenity charges for her work. While she was gone, Bill Sanger was arrested for distributing her pamphlet *Family Limitation.* "If some persons would go around and urge Christian women to bear children instead of wasting their time on woman suffrage, this city and society would be better off," the judge told him.

When Margaret returned to the United States, her husband was in jail and newspaper coverage of his case brought the controversy over contraception into public view for the first time—even though the *New York Times* discreetly refused to tell its readers the exact topic of the pamphlet Sanger was charged with distributing. Two months later the Sangers' little girl Peggy died suddenly, an event that haunted the guilt-ridden Margaret so much that she could never bear to remain in the presence of another mother and daughter. But to the public, the tragedy made both the Sangers martyrs for their cause and Anthony

Comstock their persecutor. In the end, Bill Sanger got thirty days in prison, and Comstock got a chill attending the trial, which led to a fatal case of pneumonia.

Despite their political victory, the Sangers' marriage was over but a new phase of Margaret's public career was about to begin. In 1916, she rented a storefront in Brooklyn and on October 16, she wrote: "I opened the doors of the first birth control clinic in America. . . . Halfway to the corner they were standing in line, at least one hundred and fifty, some shawled, some hatless, their red hands clasping the cold, chapped smaller ones of their children." Margaret and her sister Ethel, a nurse, charged 10 cents for consultations. In the few weeks the clinic was able to operate, the staff saw 464 women. But Margaret and her sister were arrested for selling a sex education pamphlet to an undercover policewoman and carted off to jail. As the police wagon drove them away, some of their clients loyally followed behind, walking down the street with their children in hand.

# The Twenties: All the Liberty You Can Use in the Backseat of a Packard

## "FLAPPERS ARE BRAVE AND GAY AND BEAUTIFUL"

Margaret Mead arrived at DePauw University in Indiana in 1919, expecting to "take part in an intellectual feast." But instead, Mead found the other coeds wearing muskrat coats and sorority pins. They were the first members of their family to go to college, and they were determined to enjoy the experience. "It was a college to which students had come for fraternity life, for football games and for establishing the kind of rapport with other people that would make them . . . good members of the garden club," sniffed Mead. A spiritual daughter of the Jane Addams era, Mead had stumbled into the advance guard of the flapper decade.

American women were transformed after World War I. They seemed to embody the changes going on in the country itself. The United States went from a young industrial state that was accumulating the capital to build factories and railroads to a world power with a consumer economy that relied on its citizens to keep the boom going by borrowing money and buying homes and cars. Meanwhile, the celibate settlement house worker was replaced as a female prototype by the jazz-crazed flapper dancing the Charleston in a speakeasy. Everything that had anything to do with consumption was in style. That included drinking, smoking, and sex—for women as well as men. Anything that reeked of "reform" was out. " 'Feminism' has become a term of opprobrium to the modern young woman," wrote the essayist Dorothy Dunbar Bromley in 1927. "For the word suggests either the old school of fighting feminists who wore flat heels and had very little feminine charm, or the current species who antagonize men with their constant clamor about maiden names, equal rights, woman's place in the world and many another cause . . . ad infinitum."

Not every young woman in America was committing herself to drinking gin and sneering at anyone in flat shoes. Mead transferred from DePauw to Barnard College in Manhattan, where she found "the kind of student life that matched my earlier dreams" and began the studies that would turn her into a world-famous anthropologist. Most girls in America belonged to poor rural or immigrant or African American families, and they had more pressing concerns than whether or not to pledge a sorority. But the educated middle-class women with "causes" who had been setting the national agenda before World War I no longer captured much attention. Their daughters were interested in a different form of liberation—the kind that gave them the right to enjoy themselves in the same ways men did. "Flaming youth had just caught fire," wrote Ernestine and Frank Gilbreth in *Cheaper by the Dozen*. "It was the day of the flapper and the sheik, of petting and necking, of flat chests and dimpled knees. It was yellow slickers with writing on the back. . . . 'Collegiate' was the most complimentary adjective in the American vocabulary. . . . The accepted mode of transportation was the stripped down Model T Ford, preferably inscribed with such witticisms as . . . 'The Mayflower—Many a Little Puritan Has Come Across in It.' "

It was a disturbing time for the older generation who had grown up believing that they had a duty to make the world better. Women professors found themselves out of sympathy with the students they were teaching—Vida Scudder of Wellesley thought the 1920s were the bleakest years of her professional career. Marjorie Nicolson of Columbia looked out over the sleek heads of her female students and decided that her own era had been "the only generation of women which ever found itself." Jane Addams said girls' "astounding emphasis on sex" was disquieting, given the unique social contribution the "educated unmarried woman" had made for the last fifty years. It was exactly the sort of statement that Dorothy Dunbar Bromley found passé.

The younger women returned the disdain. A much-quoted article by "an ex-feminist" entitled "The Harm My Education Did Me" excoriated female academics as withered, bitter man-haters who were warping their charges with "artificial standards of bygone feminists." The idea of finding one's personal satisfaction among a community of women went out the window. As women strove to become comrades and pals with the men in their lives, it sometimes seemed as if they had left no emotional space for anyone else. "I think a woman gets more happiness out of being gay, light-hearted, unconventional, mistress of her own fate than out of a career that calls for hard work, intellectual pessimism and loneliness," said Zelda Fitzgerald, whose husband, F. Scott, turned her into the emblem of the twenties. She expressed the hope that her own infant daughter would not become "a genius."

"I want her to be a flapper, because flappers are brave and gay and beautiful," Zelda said.

## "SKINNY AND FLAT-CHESTED AND POPULAR"

The word *flapper* had been used to describe everything from a gawky preadolescent to unbuckled galoshes, but in America it became the all-purpose designation for the girl of the hour. The flapper was energetic, daring, and self-absorbed. She defined herself by her unrestrained clothing. She did not wear a corset, and she bared her arms. Her skirts went up to her knees, and she sometimes rolled down her sheer stockings, exposing her skin. But she hid her breasts. Her dresses hung straight down from the shoulders, and while she never used tight undergarments to sheathe her slim hips and middle, a flapper who had the bad luck to be amply endowed did bind her breasts so she could have the requisite flat shape. It was a peculiar combination of sexuality and boyishness and every young woman who was not very, very serious wanted to be part of the excitement, no matter what her race, class, or economic status. A survey in Milwaukee in 1927 found only 70 of 1,300 working girls still wearing a corset.

"That's what's the matter with this generation. Nobody thinks about being smart or clever or sweet or even attractive. No sir, they want to be skinny and flat-chested and popular," bellowed Frank Gilbreth, the father of the authors of *Cheaper by the Dozen* when his oldest daughter, Anne, declared: "I'm never going to wear long underwear again." Like parents all over the country, the Gilbreths eventually gave in and allowed their daughters to buy silk stockings and flimsy underwear and bob their hair, although according to the authors, when Anne arrived at the dinner table with her new haircut, her mother dropped the peas and burst into tears. At first, a bobbed head was seen as a sign of dangerous radicalism. When the manager of the Palm Garden in New York rented his hall to a left-wing group whose meeting ended in a riot in 1918, he defended himself by saying the woman who signed the lease was well dressed and drove a nice car. He added: "Had we noticed then, as we do now, that she had short hair, we would have refused."

The underlying impulse was freedom—from the mores of the past that required women to keep themselves in check, physically and emotionally. The woman of the twenties was supposed to be a "pal" to her male friends and later her husband. She was not going to keep the hearth warm while her mate was out carousing. She was out there with him. She needed to be physically free to dance the wild, flapping dances of the moment, play golf, drive a car, and leap up and down at football games. In summer, one commentator of the era noted that men were now wearing "four times as much clothes by weight as women." Rebellion was not just in the wind, it was in the junior section at local department stores. It was intended, in part, to drive the older generation crazy, and it succeeded. The president of the University of Florida predicted: "The low-cut gowns, the rolled hose and short skirts are born of the devil and his angels and are carrying the present and future generations to chaos and destruction." In the Ohio legislature, someone introduced a bill prohibiting any female over fourteen from wearing skirts that did not "reach to that part of the foot known as the instep." The head of a Wisconsin tuberculosis sanatorium announced that short skirts led to TB.

It was a losing battle. Not only did American girls want to look like flappers, they convinced many of their mothers to do the same. "Ten years ago women still had ages. . . . Today mother and daughter may be found . . . supplementing their wardrobe from the same rack," complained the *Chicago Tribune* in 1928. In the past, women regarded aging as inevitable and believed that if they stayed youthful, it was a special blessing from God. Now it was an act of will. Hair could be dyed, cheeks made artificially rosy, and skin moisturized until it sloshed. "Thanks to cosmetics the mother of today is more the big sister and enjoys and appreciates the pleasures of her daughter," explained an analyst for the industry, which had become the fourth biggest business in the United States—behind cars, movies, and bootlegged liquor.

By 1927, a survey found that 50 percent of women wore rouge and 90 percent wore face powder. Everyone from teenagers to middle-aged matrons carried compacts in their purses, and powdering one's nose became a reflexive act, required whenever a woman moved from one activity to another. (Aviatrix Ruth Elder was forced to make an emergency landing while flying across the Atlantic, and when she emerged from her plane, she immediately powdered her nose.) The advertising industry bombarded women with products to make them more beautiful. Many of the ads were written by women who had come of age in the earlier feminist era, and some of their efforts had a strange mixture of the old rhetoric and the new priorities. One Ponds cold cream ad featured an endorsement by Alva Belmont, the socialite-turned-suffragist. "Mrs. Belmont has not only given lavishly to women's causes from her colossal fortune . . . but also is particularly interested in woman's special problem of how to keep her force and charm throughout her life," it enthused. Since Alva refused to let her photograph be used, the ad was illustrated with a picture of her library.

## "A LOT OF LASHING AND LATHER"

The double standard that women reformers had fought against for so long was finally in retreat. But instead of forcing men to follow the same rules of chastity as women, society lowered the bar for girls. The new national pastimes were necking and petting—terms that seemed to cover behavior ranging from nuzzling to everything short of inter-course. "Nice" girls, abetted by the privacy of the automobile, allowed their boyfriends to put their hands and mouths places that previous generations would never have considered—or at least never admitted to. A writer for *Survey* magazine reported in 1925 that when young women came out of work, they were being picked up by "gas hawks" (young men in automobiles) who "pet them even in the street. They have done it outside my window with an enthusiasm which even two large paper bags filled with water and hurled against their windshield . . . failed to cool." In the definitive 1920s novel, *This Side of Paradise,* F. Scott Fitzgerald's hero, the self-absorbed Princetonian Amory Blaine, "saw girls doing things that even in his memory would have been impossible." None of the mothers, Amory was sure, "had any idea how casually their girls were accustomed to be kissed."

The "belle" who had a half-dozen callers every afternoon and never allowed herself to be alone with any one man until she was engaged was succeeded by the "baby vamp" who disappeared with her partner between dances and returned looking rather flushed and rum-pled. Some young women regarded the new norms as rather noble. "The girl with sport in her blood . . . kisses the boys, she smokes with them, she drinks with them, and why? Because the feeling of com-radeship is running rampant," wrote an Ohio State coed. "The girl does not stand aloof. She and the man meet on common ground, and yet can she not retain her moral integrity?"

More women—perhaps a third—were having sex before marriage,

THE TWENTIES    *333*

and surveys of college men indicated they no longer felt it was essential to marry a virgin. Young men were much more likely to be having premarital sex with their girlfriends, and as a result they were only about half as likely as their fathers to visit prostitutes. It was yet another example of how purity reformers should have been careful what they wished for. Nevertheless, the social convention that sexual intercourse should be saved for marriage—or at least engagement—generally held firm. An editor of the Duke University newspaper in 1927 described the sexual activities of most coeds as "a lot of lashing and lather on the surface with miles of unmoved depths below."

Middle-class girls were following the lead of working-class girls, who had been going on "dates" since the 1890s, while their more affluent peers were still receiving callers at home. Obviously, a girl who lived in a small tenement apartment could not receive gentlemen friends in the midst of the crowd of relatives and boarders who lived there, too. There was also a kind of rough justice to the idea of having a boy "treat" for a night at the movies or a dance since boys were generally not required to turn their paychecks over to their parents as the girls did. Perhaps most important, dating was a demonstration of popularity—for girls in college as well as in factories. Dates became the social equivalent of scalps on a girl's belt—the number of dates and the quality of suitors was the way young women defined their desirability. Nevertheless, when calling ended and dating began, girls lost a certain amount of power. The etiquette of the earlier period gave girls the right to decide which young men would be invited to call. With dating, men took the initiative, and the fact that they paid for the evening gave them even more control.

After a century of enforced innocence, women in the 1920s were expected to know all about sex. Sigmund Freud had lectured in America in 1909, and by World War I almost everybody had read magazine articles about his theories. A college friend told Margaret Mead that "the man you marry will certainly have an Oedipal fixation on you, which will be all right if it isn't joined to an incest complex." Another of Fitzgerald's heroines sighed: "I'm hipped on Freud and all that, but it's rotten that every bit of *real* love in the world is ninety-nine percent passion and one little soupçon of jealousy." By 1920, 200 books about Freudianism had been published in America, and if the average student's understanding of the subject was shallow, she picked up enough to be convinced that sex was the center of everything for women as well as men.

The era when even abstention within marriage was regarded as healthy was most definitely over. Everybody wanted a "companionate" marriage, in which husband and wife were both pals and inventive sexual partners. Given the declining birthrate, people were obviously using birth control, and Lysol became a popular douche after its makers started running ads hinting that their product not only cleaned floors, it was useful as protection against "calendar fear." But the most effective protection was a diaphragm and spermicidal jelly. Germany manufactured the best diaphragms, and Margaret Sanger's second husband, Noah Slee, a motor oil magnate, shipped tons of them to his plant in Montreal and smuggled them into the country in Three-in-One Oil drums.

Until World War I, Americans had been so naïve about homosexuality that lesbians could live together without ever raising eyebrows. But in the twenties, women living together were assumed to be having sex even if they weren't, and people began wondering if all-female colleges were unhealthy. At Barnard, Margaret Mead and her friends "worried and thought over affectionate episodes in our past relationships with girls and wondered if they had been incipient examples." In 1926, a play about lesbianism, *The Captive*, became a critical and popular hit on Broadway. (Since it portrayed lesbianism as a terrible, but uncontrollable, curse, the audience could enjoy being titillated while feeling morally superior.) But as time went on, people began to notice that the bulk of the ticket-buyers were young girls. The critic George Jean Nathan withdrew his endorsement when a friend reported that "he and apparently a mere handful of males in the house, felt embarrassingly conspicuous amidst such an overwhelmingly feminine assemblage."

## "SOAP TO MATCH HER BATHROOM'S COLOR SCHEME"

By the 1920s, most American women had completely broken from the pioneer past and the burdens of Victorian domesticity. Martha

Farnsworth, a middle-class Topeka housewife, got indoor plumbing in 1903, took her first automobile ride in 1907, and got a telephone in 1908. By 1920, she had electric lights in her house, an electric iron, a vacuum cleaner, and a record player and was yearning to take an airplane ride. She occasionally recalled, with wonder, that as a child she had been afraid of Indians and wolves and spent her days herding the family oxen.

For the first time, most middle-class Americans had not only running water in their homes, but the full system of sinks and drains and toilets and sewers. By 1927 nearly two-thirds of American homes had electricity, and women were using it to power vacuum cleaners, ranges, refrigerators, toasters, and irons. The washing machine was still a work in progress, but many women sent their clothes to laundries, where business was at an all-time peak. American woman's most celebrated job was that of consumer-in-chief. "Today's woman gets what she wants," enthused an advertisement in the *Chicago Tribune*. "The vote. Slim sheaths of silk to replace voluminous petticoats. Glassware in sapphire blue or glowing amber. The right to a career. Soap to match her bathroom's color scheme." The ad industry begged for her attention; the department stores spoiled her with extra services. Women didn't have to carry packages—all their purchases were sent to a central desk, wrapped together, and turned over to the free and frequent delivery service. Customers sometimes got carried away by the attention and made ridiculous demands, insisting that the bones from their lunch be wrapped and delivered free to their dogs at home, or that a specially altered suit be returned because it arrived at 1:30 instead of 1:00.

Pregnant women were no longer supposed to stay home from the first moment the baby began to show. Ready-to-wear maternity clothes had been in the stores since 1910, and the *New York Herald* printed ads that announced: "It is no longer the fashion or the practice for expectant mothers to stay in seclusion." When it was time to deliver, more women went to the hospital, drawn by the promise that they could sleep through the entire experience: "Two yellow capsules, a jab in the arm, swiftly blot out the scene, time, knowledge and feeling for the woman. . . . When she is not aware, sunlight pierces the drapery. And one of the amiable nurses chirps: 'It's all over. You've got your baby.' " Even though women were less likely to fear the pain, they knew having a baby was still potentially dangerous. During World War I, the number of American women who died from the effects of childbirth was greater than the number of men who died on the battlefield. It was an in-between period in medical progress: Doctors understood about germs and the nation had been introduced to the importance of "vital-amines," but there was still no penicillin and not many vaccines. Children could be healthy one day, and on death's door the next from pneumonia or a common childhood ailment—like Margaret Sanger's little girl. Half a million Americans died in the influenza epidemic after World War I.

The first successful sanitary napkins went on sale in 1921, in what must have been one of the most important unheralded moments in the history of American women. The Kimberly-Clark Company had manufactured bandages made out of wood pulp for army hospitals in World War I. American nurses used them when they had their periods and raved about their absorbency and disposability. After the war, the firm began selling the bandages under the name Kotex in pharmacies and department stores—where they were often marketed in the corset department. An early ad, signed by a registered nurse, praised the product's "Immaculacy" and "clean exquisiteness under circumstances which most women find exceedingly trying." It was the new openness about sexual issues that allowed Kotex to connect with the female population. Other companies had attempted to market "Hygienic Towelettes for Ladies" since the 1890s but found it difficult to get magazines or newspapers to run their ads.

Most women had been using washable pads or rags until then, and one of the reasons women stuck so long to black skirts and multitudinous petticoats may have been the desire to wear several layers of clothes in case of accidents. A "Women's Comfort Sanitary Traveling Set" marketed by Sears in 1914 included washable pads, a belt, a waterproof pouch to carry the used pads in, and an apron made with cloth-covered rubber, which was supposed to hang like the back half of a skirt beneath the petticoats, protecting them from staining. The Kotex ads, in contrast, frequently cheered "Nothing to launder!" and promised an end to "discomfort and uncertainty." The disposability factor also probably encouraged girls to change their napkins more frequently—the turn-of-the-century rule had been once in the morning and once at bedtime.

## "REACH FOR A LUCKY INSTEAD OF A SWEET"

Women took up smoking in the twenties with the same suddenness they cut their hair and raised their skirts. They smoked in restaurants, in speakeasies, in the country clubs where they went to play golf and bridge, and in private homes during that new invention, the cocktail hour. For the younger generation, smoking was another example of "freedom" and women's right to enjoy the same pleasures as men. But they got a prod from the mass media. Magazine ads urged weight-conscious flappers to "reach for a Lucky instead of a sweet." Cigarettes, which had frequently been marketed as a health aid that would cure nervousness or aid indigestion, became a weapon in the war against fat.

Dieting became an obsession in the twenties, as young women struggled to achieve the wraithlike forms necessary to look good in a flapper's outfit, and their mothers tried to stay thin enough to continue shopping in the junior's department. (A child of the era horrified her mother by looking at a picture of Lillian Russell and asking: "Who is that fat lady?") Meat consumption in restaurants dropped 50 percent in the decade. The Victorian breakfast, with its endless array of food, completely gave way to cereal and juice, and lunch became a sandwich. There were strange drugs on the market like Marmola, which was made from the dried thyroid glands of various animals. If you used it, the ads promised, you could abandon "table restraint" and still stay slim.

Restraint was something women were encouraged to exercise only when it came to eating. In the flapper ethos, drinking, even to excess, was no longer considered shocking. "When I was a boy, girls of their upbringing weren't allowed to move a step without chaperones or personal maids, and a spoonful of eggnog on New Year's Day was the extent of their drinking. Now they stand up at the bar and order whiskey sours like seasoned cannoneers," wrote Heywood Broun in *Harper's*. It was fashionable for men and women to swig gin out of the same hip flask.

Prohibition, which went into effect by constitutional amendment in 1919, had not worked out the way the women reformers had expected, although it actually was successful in a limited way. People like Frances Willard had hoped that banning alcohol would reduce the amount of drinking in poor and immigrant homes where women suffered so much from their drunken husbands. To some extent, that happened in neighborhoods where people could not afford bootleg whisky. But the temperance women had never expected their own class to cheerfully flout the law in massive numbers. Some of them lost enthusiasm for Prohibition when they realized that rather than eliminating the danger that their sons would drink, the Eighteenth Amendment had extended the peril to their daughters. Pauline Sabine, a socialite who switched sides to the repeal movement, said: "Many of our members are young mothers—too young to remember the old saloon. But they are working for repeal because they don't want their babies to grow up in the hip flask, speakeasy atmosphere that has polluted their own youth."

## "SPLINTERED INTO A HUNDRED FRAGMENTS"

Giving women the right to vote did not have unanticipated consequences like Prohibition. In fact, the shock for suffragists was that it hardly seemed to have any consequences at all. Most women appeared to vote the way their husbands, brothers, and fathers did—not necessarily because they felt obliged to follow the men's lead, but because they shared the same loyalties to class, ethnic group, and region. Like many newly enfranchised groups, women were also voting less frequently than those who had been at it for a long time. In 1920, when American women went to the polls across the nation for the first time, they made up an estimated one-third of the voters. Mainly, they voted for Warren Harding, who turned out to be one of the worst presidents in American history. He had stuffed his platform with female-friendly promises like equal pay for equal work, an end to child labor, and more women appointees to government positions. But his attraction was probably the same for both sexes—the promise of a return to "normalcy" after the war and the turmoil that followed it.

The most surprising development was the virtual disappearance, almost overnight, of the political movement that had forced the government to approve woman suffrage in the first place. "The American women's movement . . . is splintered into a hundred fragments under as many warring leaders," mourned Frances Kellor, a reformer. The National American Woman Suffrage Association, Carrie Chapman Catt's group, turned itself into the League of Women Voters, and its membership plunged to one-tenth of what it was. But women had their reasons for dropping out of politics. Prohibition was a discouraging lesson in the difficulty of legislating morality. And the twenties were not a good time for anything that smacked of political reform. The nation had been traumatized by race riots and labor violence, and since the war some people had gotten in the habit of responding to any whiff of disturbance by smashing down anyone who looked different. A man in Indiana was shot to death for saying "To hell with the United States," and a jury took only minutes to acquit his killer. The Radcliffe debating team came under fire from the vice president of the United States when the students successfully defended the proposition that collective bargaining for unions was a good thing. In 1924, the first two women were elected governors, and both were uninspiring stand-ins for their husbands. Nellie Tayloe Ross, the widow of the governor of Wyoming, had not even wanted her husband to run for office, and when he died suddenly, the Democrats nominated her to fill out his term without her permission. "Ma" Ferguson of Texas ran for office when her husband was impeached. Her signature achievement as governor was to pardon an average of 100 criminals a month in what critics claimed was a fee-for-freedom scheme.

For a while, the specter of the "women's vote" frightened male politicians, who had no idea what these newly enfranchised females wanted. In 1920, Warren Harding's handlers were worried that women would react badly to rumors that the Republican presidential candidate had black ancestors, and they started publishing glorified versions of the Harding family tree for the edification of puzzled Americans, most of whom hadn't heard the rumor and none of whom appeared to care. On a more elevated plane, in 1921 Congress passed the Sheppard-Towner Maternity Act, the first step toward reformers' dream of a national system of well-baby clinics to improve the health of the poor. But physicians felt it threatened their practices, and by the end of the 1920s, when it became clear that women were not going to vote as a bloc, the program was phased out.

### "TOO MUCH PERSONALITY"

People had always spent much of their lives sitting at home in silence—the ability to play the piano was a feminine accomplishment of great significance because it gave families a chance to listen to something besides the sound of their own voices. Then in 1921, there was radio. "It came with a rush," said Frederick Allen, in a look back at the twenties he published soon after the decade was over. By 1929, a third of all American households were listening to radio, the vast majority every day.

At first, the men did most of the listening. Boys gathered in living rooms or garages with headphones over their ears, carefully manipulating a thin wire and crystal to bring in music and voices from far away. But a lot of women were involved on the other end, producing, writing scripts, booking guests, emceeing the programs, and often serving as the program itself, by delivering book reviews, culture reports, or anything else they concocted to fill the time. It would have been surprising if they hadn't been active, since early radio was exactly the sort of operation—disorganized, badly paid, and in great need of multitasking—that welcomed creative women. In 1925, a journalist named Gwen Wagner reminisced for *Radio Age* about the "days of yore"—1921—when she ran radio station WPO in Memphis. Wagner worked for the newspaper that sponsored the station and, in addition to her regular journalism duties, "wrote all the material for the radio column, engaged the radio artists and arranged the programs. At night I went out to the studio and broadcast." But once radio became a moneymaking success, women stopped being asked to serve as announcers or to deliver the news. Their on-air role was limited mainly to singing or acting in soap operas. Industry executives claimed that female voices did not broadcast well and one much-quoted poll of 5,000 listeners showed men's voices were preferred 100 to 1. The manager of the station that conducted the poll theorized women's voices had "too much personality."

In the movies, where performers were seen and not heard, the biggest early stars were actresses. More than any other decade, the movies of the 1920s stressed plots that appealed to women—romances and melodramas over action adventures and comedies—and many of the most successful early screenwriters were women. (Frances Marion, a Hollywood legend, used her two Academy Awards as doorstops.) Although salary-conscious studios tried hard to keep their actors and actresses anonymous, the public instantly glommed on to a few familiar faces, particularly that of "the girl with the curls." Mary Pickford, who specialized in playing spunky child-heroines, received 500 fan letters a day by 1915. A professional actress since her actual childhood, Pickford had always been her family's meal ticket, and she was a tough contract negotiator who managed to become one of the very few women to get a foothold in the production end of the business, as a founding partner of United Artists. But on-screen the public demanded that she remain a golden-haired girl, and she played children's roles well into her thirties. Her private life was slightly less tidy than her film personas, and though she kept her marriage to fellow actor Owen Moore a secret, she could not really cover up the fact that she had deserted him for the also-married screen star Douglas Fairbanks. (Fairbanks was so nervous about the scandal that he denounced rumors of the romance as German propaganda during World War I.) After they finally divorced their respective mates and ran off to Europe to marry in 1920, Pickford looked out of her London hotel window and saw the streets crammed with "thousands and thousands" of people who had been waiting just to get a glimpse of the girl with the curls and her dashing swashbuckler of a husband. "Come home—all is forgiven," begged *Photoplay* from the other side of the Atlantic. This was the beginning of the era of movie magazines and tabloid movie columns, when most Americans went to the movies at least once a week, and ordinary women around the country would identify with the heroines they saw on the screen, striving to be perky like Pickford, or dangerous like Theda Bara. (In a fairly typical effort, *The Rose of Blood*, Bara played a spy in the Russian Revolution who, as one reviewer explained, "wrecks hearts, railroad trains, slays one after another and concludes the fifth reel by blowing up the peace cabinet, which includes her husband.")

Men and women went to the movies with equal enthusiasm, but women spent much more time reading, thinking, and talking about movie stars. Gossip, for all its destructive potential, had always been an important way for women to bond with one another, affirm their social values, express insights about human character, and experiment with new ideas about what was and was not permissible behavior. In a world where fewer people lived in small towns and shared mutual acquaintances, the film stars created a common national neighborhood that everyone could visit. Mary Pickford was an entire week's worth of coffee chat all by herself. When she bobbed her hair in a desperate attempt to get her fans to accept her as an adult actress, the country was aghast, and things were never the same between the public and Mary again.

### "IF I SHOULD BOP OFF, IT'LL BE DOING THE THING THAT I'VE ALWAYS MOST WANTED"

In the 1920s, most American families acquired cars, and there was no real question whether women would be allowed in the driver's seat—that had been resolved by the previous generation. Women had been getting driver's licenses since 1899, and in 1905, three Los Angeles women made news with a "sensational cross-country run" in which they made the ninety-five-mile drive to Santa Barbara in under ten hours. The Motor Girls series for young readers arrived in bookstores in 1910, quickly followed by The Motor Maids and the Automobile Girls. (The author of one series, a Mrs. Penrose, was said to be both an "able writer" and an "expert automobilist.") The Outdoor Girls added driving to their other accomplishments.

But early automobiles were tough for women, let alone girls, to handle. Getting a car going and keeping it on the road required considerable strength, dexterity, and a willingness to get down in the mud and change the fragile tires, which seldom lasted long between punctures. Starting the early model cars was an arduous process that required the driver to turn a crank on the front of the engine while fiddling with a wire that served as the clutch. Then he or she had to race back to the driver's seat in time to turn on the ignition so it would "catch." Many men found it difficult, especially because the cars stalled out on a regular basis. Woman had the additional burden of long skirts, and one of the first complaints about female drivers was that they tended to wait along the side of the road for a man to stop and help when their car needed restarting. But by the twenties, the crank starter was pretty much obsolete, and women were getting behind the wheel as a matter of course. They ferried children to music lessons or visits to the dentist; they shopped for groceries and picked up their husbands at the train station after work. Ads for the Model T announced that "More than ever—the Ford is a woman's car."

Young readers who got tired of all those heroines in automobiles may have followed the adventures of the Flying Girls, starring Orissa Kane ("self-reliant and full of sparkling good nature"), who flew around with her brother, a more reckless pilot who frequently had to be rescued. Judging by the book's jacket, Orissa's airplane resembled a flimsy glider. Early aviation was another one of those enterprises that was so disorganized it was easy for women to get involved. In the beginning, anybody who had enough nerve could take to the sky. In 1903, Aida de Acosta, a young Cuban American, was vacationing in Paris with her mother when she got a look at some dirigibles. After three lessons of flight instruction, she became the first woman to fly a powered aircraft alone—months before the Wright brothers took off at Kitty Hawk. In 1910, Bessica Raiche built a plane inside her house over a long western winter and then flew it after getting just enough instruction to know how to make it go up and down.

Bessie Coleman, known as "Brave Bessie," was one of the few African Americans in early flight. She heard returning World War I veterans talk about flying while she worked as a manicurist in a Chicago barbershop. When she discovered blacks were barred from American flight schools, she went to Paris. Back in America, she became a stunt pilot in a flying circus, one of a number of women barnstormers who flew from town to town in the twenties. Female daredevils danced the Charleston on an airplane wing as it flew over the crowd, or took the helm to fly loops and take gawking townspeople on rides. All these exploits in extremely primitive aircrafts were obviously very dangerous. Harriet Quimby, the first licensed American female pilot, died in a crash in Boston only three months after she flew across the English channel. Bessie Coleman fell to her death when her plane rolled over in the air while she was not wearing a seat belt. However, Jessie Woods, another pioneer barnstormer and airplane wing-walker, lived to perform her trick again in an air show in 1991, when she was eighty-two.

Amelia Earhart was the most famous woman in flight. A former mechanic, barnstormer, and social worker, she became the first woman to fly across the Atlantic in 1928, then spent the next few years trying to explain that her only role had been to sit as a passenger "like a sack of potatoes." She finally did fly the Atlantic solo in 1932, to international acclaim. The younger generation adored her athleticism, her boyish good looks, and her confident ease in handling the media. Their parents appreciated her social-worker sensibility and refusal to smoke or drink. In 1937, she and her navigator disappeared during an attempted flight around the world, and although they were clearly killed, her fans never stopped theorizing about ways she might have survived on a deserted island or been captured as a spy by the Japanese. "If I should bop off, it'll be doing the thing that I've always most wanted to do," she told a friend before her departure.

## SWIM GIRL, SWIM

Tanned skin became fashionable for the first time in the 1920s, deeply confusing the cosmetic industry, which had always believed that the lighter, the better. But tans no longer meant you were so poor you had to labor outdoors. They suggested leisure, golf games, and tennis. The swimsuit and tennis dress were the defining clothes of the era, and as the decade went along, they got increasingly skimpy. Helen Wills, a popular tennis player known as "Little Miss Poker Face," began wearing short skirts and sleeveless blouses on the court, arguing that they made it easier for her to play. Her fans followed suit, although many of them could not bear to relinquish their silk stockings and simply put socks on over them.

One of the most famous athletes of the twenties was Gertrude Ederle, an Olympic swimmer who astonished the world in 1926 when, at age nineteen, she swam the English Channel—twenty-one miles of freezing water inhabited by jellyfish and the occasional shark. Only five men had ever done it before her, and she did it faster, following a boat filled with her family and supporters, who urged her on by singing "The Star-Spangled Banner" and "Yes, We Have No Bananas." Although Ederle came of age when women were expected to be active, almost no one thought them capable of heroic feats of physical endurance. But when she pulled it off, the world was thrilled, and Americans welcomed the daughter of German immigrants back to New York with a ticker tape parade. She got all the trappings of twentieth-century American celebrity, including a role as herself in the 1927 movie *Swim Girl, Swim* and a vaudeville tour in which she performed in a huge collapsible swimming pool. But water damage to her eardrums during the Channel swim eventually destroyed her hearing, and she suffered a back injury that forced her to spend four years in a cast. In 1928, Ederle had a nervous breakdown, but she recovered her emotional balance and became a swimming coach for deaf children.

Ederle's feat inspired tens of thousands of women to earn Red Cross swimming certificates, and when they went in the water, modesty no longer required that they be weighed down by their clothing. The bathing suit underwent drastic changes. The older generation was still wearing multilayered models that concealed every possible inch of skin, from the neck to the bathing shoes, and a number of towns had ordinances requiring women to keep their arms and legs covered at the beach. But once flappers started baring their arms and legs on downtown streets, they turned up at the swimming pool in sleeveless one-piece suits without skirts. When the first Miss America contest was held in 1921, the audience gasped and applauded when the girls marched onstage in the latest swimwear. The organizers did their best to suggest that the pageant was being conducted in the spirit of athleticism rather than exhibitionism—in 1922, the New York City contingent of entrants arrived in a seaplane, swimming their way to shore. Still, the contest was canceled from 1928 to 1935 because some Atlantic City hotel owners complained that their customers found it immoral.

## "THE REASON NOBODY WILL GIVE"

In 1929, at the end of one of the most incredible runs of prosperity in history, 59 percent of American families still could not make enough money for even a minimal standard of living. A survey of black women workers found that only 13.6 percent worked an eight-hour day or less, while 40 percent worked ten or more hours. African American women of middle age or younger in the North had approximately the same literacy rate as white women their age and were just as likely to send their children to school. But the payoff was much lower for black students. Even those with high school degrees were shut out of clerical and sales jobs in white neighborhoods. Employers refused to hire black women, even though they were better educated and worked for less than the pool of available whites. (Addie Hunter, a graduate of an excellent high school in Boston, fought for years to find a white-collar job but wound up working in a factory. "Color— the reason nobody will give, the reason nobody is required to give, will always be in the way," she concluded.) Part of the reason was the demand by white workers for total segregation, which meant the expense of separate bathrooms and lunchrooms. Inevitably, most black women wound up in domestic service. African Americans were about a fourth of the domestics in 1900 and half by 1930. Employment agencies went through the South offering jobs and transportation to women who were willing to come north and work as servants.

Partly as a result of the demand for female domestic workers, most of the 750,000 blacks who moved north in the 1920s were women. There was a sexual imbalance in many black neighborhoods— in New York City there were 10 women for every 8.5 men. Black women's lives were both very similar and very different from those of white immigrant women who shared their economic class. Black wives were five times more likely to work than any other ethnic group, and they had fewer children than immigrants. Unlike immigrants, black parents allowed their working children to keep the money they made, and they were less likely to expect their sons and daughters to support them in old age.

Black women were very much constrained by the Jim Crow segregation rules of the era and the awareness that most whites regarded them as, in the words of Marita Bonner, a young black writer, "only a gross collection of desires, all uncontrolled." Unlike white women her age, Bonner said, she could not travel alone to another city, lest she give the impression of being a loose woman. Although there continued to be an elite group of black families who had made their fortunes in an earlier, less structured economy, the opportunities of breaking through to the middle class for ambitious newcomers were minimal. Even the black cosmetics business was being taken over by white men, some of whom created fictional black women to serve as the company symbol. Madam Mamie Hightower was supposedly the head of the Golden Brown Beauty Company, but she was actually the wife of the company porter. When Madam C. J. Walker died, her company was run by men, and although they were African American, they began to market the skin lighteners she had always refused to endorse. One much-publicized but very narrow avenue to real all-American success for black women was the world of entertainment, and the one area of entertainment in particular was music. In 1920, Mamie Smith's "Crazy Blues" was selling 8,000 records a week, setting off a craze for black female singers that extended through the decade. Bessie Smith saved Columbia Records in its infancy by selling 6 million records in six years.

## "IF I WERE BORN 100 YEARS FROM NOW, WELL AND GOOD"

The question of whether women should work had been settled as decisively as the one about them driving, and people seemed rather pleased with the notion that the spunky American girl, compact in one hand and automobile wheel in the other, was ready for anything. "Within the space of a single day, one can ride in a taxi driven by a woman, directed by traffic signals designed by a woman, to the office of a woman engineer, there to look out of the window and observe a woman steeplejack at her trade . . ." enthused the *Annals of the American Academy of Political and Social Sciences* in 1929. But the lady steeplejack was more an example of the twenties' love affair with stunts and oddities than the beginning of a trend. The proportion of women in the workforce was actually lower in 1930 than it had been in 1910, and women professionals were concentrated almost entirely in four areas—teaching, nursing, social work, and libraries. Dr. Lillian Walsh, a longtime practitioner, concluded sadly that women doctors had become as fashionable as "a horse and buggy." Any woman ready to announce that she was trading in her law books for a cookbook could find a ready market for her memoirs in the women's magazines.

For most women, work was a brief interlude between school and marriage. They made much less than men; in 1927, the average weekly wage for a man was $29.35 and for a woman it was $17.34. Women were also likely to be overqualified for the work they could get. One writer in the *Atlantic*, surveying the business world, concluded that the boss's secretary was more likely to be a college graduate than he was. Although there were plenty of poor women and single mothers who depended on their paychecks, society generally liked to think of the working girl as a young thing saving money to fill her hope chest. "I pay our women well so they can dress attractively and get married," said Henry Ford.

The idea that women would *not* get married had gone out of style. Girls at Barnard or Vassar might be daring enough to think that they could wait until they were twenty-five or even—perhaps—thirty. But now that Americans had been convinced that women needed sex, the idea that they might march into middle age without husbands began to look either pathetic or sinister. Vassar started offering courses in "Motherhood" and "Husband and Wife." F. Scott Fitzgerald had one of his heroines complain that to attract suitors she has to "descend to their level and let them patronize my intellect." It never occurs to her to drop the boring dunces and support herself: "If I were born 100 years from now, well and good, but now what's in store for me—I have to marry, that goes without saying."

Only about 10 percent of women kept their jobs after marriage, and most were working-class wives who could not afford to quit. Even within the elite women's colleges, attempts to combine family and careers were mostly confined to those who opted for work and childless marriages. But a great many more women were dissatisfied with their choices. They embarked on a discussion about "having it all" that would continue for the rest of the century. "There must be a way out and it is the problem of our generation to find the way," said the *Smith College Weekly*.

# 16

# The Depression:
# Ma Perkins and Eleanor Roosevelt

### "ROMANCE CAN BEGIN AT THIRTY-FIVE"

When NBC radio moved into the vast new Rockefeller Center in 1932, Margaret Cuthbert, the head of the women's division, outlined the "great possibilities" she imagined might be achieved at the new address. Daytime radio, she wrote hopefully, "might become a great national headquarters for women," bringing improving lectures, university extension courses, and cultural programs to the housewives of America. Of course, nothing of the sort happened. The daytime hours were devoted to women, but in the form of soap operas—fifteen-minute daily serials that investigated whether Our Gal Sunday, "a girl from a little mining town in the West," could find happiness "as the wife of a wealthy and titled Englishman." (Not usually.) They followed Mary Noble, *Backstage Wife*, and Helen Trent's attempt to prove "what so many women long to prove, that because a woman is thirty-five, or more, romance in life need not be over, that romance can begin at thirty-five." By 1936, more than half of the daytime programming was made up of long-running melodramas, in which the characters wrestled with domestic woes and occasionally commented on the fine quality of the sponsor's laundry detergent.

That soap operas became a central feature in the lives of millions of

American women so quickly was a tribute to how lonely and boring housework had always been. Mary Knackstedt Dyck, a Kansas farm wife who kept a family diary at her windswept Depression-era home, included the developments in the lives of soap opera characters as faithfully as she did those of her husband, who was always at work, and her children, who had moved away. In October 1936, after recording that she was mending her husband's trousers, she added, "Bob is making plans to get his Marriage Lisense tomorrow"—an apparent reference to a development on *Betty and Bob*, a radio drama about a secretary who marries her boss. Mrs. Dyck knew the characters weren't real (although some women never grasped that and sent wedding gifts or baby presents whenever a soap opera heroine got married or pregnant). But they were a central part of her existence, more reliable company than her grown offspring or preoccupied husband. Though her life in the center of the Depression-era Dust Bowl had plenty of sorrows, nothing seemed to bring Mrs. Dyck down like static on the radio.

Critics were as appalled by the soap operas as they had been by the women's novels of the pre–Civil War period, even though in this case many of the scripts were written by men. (Echoing Nathaniel Hawthorne's complaint about the "scribbling women," William Faulkner wrote crankily from Hollywood: "I seem to be out of touch with the Kotex Age here.") The radio soaps did have some similarities with the weepy fiction of that earlier era, only one of which was a lack of immortal prose. Many soap opera heroines had careers they had begun in response to a crisis—like the ever-wise Ma Perkins, who took over the family lumberyard when her husband died, or Mary Marlin, who assumed her husband's Senate seat when his plane disappeared over Siberia. In the more action-oriented soaps, the emergencies could reach epic proportions. The actress who played Stella Dallas recalled that when Stella's daughter was kidnapped by a sheik, "I had to go to the Sahara Desert and try to save her. On the way I saved a lot of people from a train wreck. Then I was trapped in a submarine at the bottom of the Suez Canal."

Mainly, the soap operas reworked over and over again a single theme—the men had failed to live up to their duties, and women had to pick up the pieces. The heroines were strong in the face of male weakness. The men in their lives were handsome but unreliable. They had affairs—Senator Marlin's itch for philandering was cooled only by his crash into the arctic tundra. They failed in business or made everybody miserable with their irrational jealousy. Or they were left helpless by blindness, amnesia, or some crippling trauma. "The man in the wheelchair has come to be the standard Soapland symbol of the American male's subordination to the female and his dependence on her greater strength of heart and soul," complained James Thurber. Meanwhile, in the real world, the Depression was under way. The men at the top had somehow run the economy into the ground, and the ones at the bottom had lost their jobs and were unable to pay the mortgage. The women had to soldier on, holding the family together and sympathizing with the woes of Helen Trent and Stella Dallas.

## "DOING IT YOURSELF THESE DAYS?"

The Great Depression lasted from the fall of the stock market in October 1929 to America's entry into World War II in December 1941. The country had faced other huge economic crises, but this was the first to arrive since America had developed a large urban middle class, families who were dependent on wage income and who believed that the necessities of life included not only food and shelter, but electricity, indoor plumbing, and an automobile. Few of those people went hungry or homeless during the Depression, but they lived in a constant state of fear and diminished expectation. Diana Morgan, a North Carolina college student, felt "the world was falling apart" when she came home for Christmas vacation and found the phone had been disconnected. Children were shocked by seeing their fathers put on overalls instead of a suit for work, or a mother trying to sell door-to-door products. The writer Caroline Bird said her worst memory was seeing a friend of the family, who she remembered as a proud captain in the U.S. Navy, taking tickets at the neighborhood movie theater.

The average family income dropped 40 percent between 1929 and 1933, and while men took second jobs or searched for better-paying employment in an oversaturated market, most of their wives stayed home and struggled with what Eleanor Roosevelt called "endless little economies and constant anxieties." At the bottom of the middle class, women worried about losing their homes and falling back into the class of renters—in Indianapolis, more than half the families with mortgages had defaulted on them by 1934. Those higher on the economic ladder simply had to figure out how to keep up appearances without the help of servants. (An ad for bleach showed a pair of elegant hands in a tub of dirty laundry and asked: "Doing it yourself these days?")

Of course, there were people on the very top who kept their fortunes intact during the crash, and they didn't always have the good grace to keep a low profile. Sally Rand, a touring ballet dancer stranded in Chicago, was outraged when she read about women spending thousands of dollars to buy gowns for the exclusive Beaux Arts Ball. She hired a horse and rode into the hotel (un)dressed as Lady Godiva, the legendary tax protester who rode naked through the streets of Coventry. She created a sensation and became the star of the Chicago World's Fair, playing peekaboo with the audience behind a set of big fans. (Rand claimed she invented her fan dance—a less naughty version of the striptease—because she couldn't afford a costume.) "I got my first $1,000 a week . . . and the first thing I bought with it was a tractor for my stepfather," she said later.

Looking back on the Depression decades later, some people got nostalgic about the way hard times produced family solidarity. The thirties-era media also claimed to see a silver lining. "Many a family that has lost its car has found its soul," editorialized a paper in Muncie, Indiana. But most women remembered a vague unease or a larger sense of crisis. The marriage rate dropped. The nation declared a truce in its war against spinsterhood, and magazines once again ran articles about women who found happiness in life without a husband. *Live Alone and Like It* was a best-seller. "Do you realize how many people in my generation are not married?" asked Elsa Ponselle, who was working as a teacher when the Chicago school system ran out of money and started paying its staff with IOUs. Her own boyfriend, a commercial artist, vanished when he was laid off from his job. "It hit him like a ton of bricks," she told journalist-historian Studs Terkel.

Society's fight against contraceptives came to a virtual halt as well, partly because of national outcries against women on the dole who continued to have babies. In 1936, the federal court struck down all federal restrictions against birth control, in a case memorably named *U.S. v. One Package of Japanese Pessaries.* By 1940, only Massachusetts and Connecticut completely prohibited the dissemination of birth control. The birthrate plunged so low that for the first time in American history, the nation was not replacing itself. (The birthrate was about 3 million babies a year lower than it had been before the Crash.) In the 1930s, Caroline Bird recalled, the first thing friends asked a newly pregnant woman was "whether she had considered 'doing something about it.' " Studies found high incidences of impotence in unemployed men—an easy metaphor for all those crippled husbands on radio series. The rate of divorce dropped, but abandonment soared. Lillian Wald's visiting nurses in New York discovered a woman, the wife of an unemployed teacher, who had gone to the hospital to give birth to her first child and arrived home to find an eviction notice, no husband, and no furniture. He had emptied out the apartment before decamping.

The people who suffered most during the Depression had generally been poor all along, and now they quickly got poorer. "I have watched fear grip the people in our neighborhood around Hull House," wrote Jane Addams. Of all the terrible signs of the Depression, she felt, "That clutch of cold fear is one of the most hideous aspects." In New York, Meridel LeSueur, writing an article for *New Masses,* said it was "one of the great mysteries of the city where women go when they are out of work and hungry." Few women were actually on the breadlines, she noted, and there were no cheap flophouses for women as there were for men. A single woman, she concluded, "will shut herself up in a room until it is taken away from her, and eat a cracker a day and be as quiet as a mouse so there are no social statistics concerning her." (The *New Masses*, although it printed LeSueur's impassioned essay, added an editor's note criticizing the piece for being "defeatist in attitude, lacking in revolutionary spirit and direction.")

Certainly some single women slept in city parks and even traveled as hoboes on the rails—"dressed in slacks like men, you could hardly tell 'em," one male itinerant said. Bertha Thompson, who called herself "Boxcar Bertha," estimated that 500,000 to 2 million people were hoboes in the 1930s, and that perhaps a tenth of them were women. Most traveled in pairs, Thompson said, either with a man or another woman. "A few women traveled about with a mob or gang of men. These were of the hard-boiled bossy type usually, who had careless sex relations with anyone in their own group." But mainly, the women who took to the road went with their families. Peggy Terry, who traveled as a migrant worker, remembered seeing a "Hooverville" in Oklahoma City. "Here were all these people living in old, rusted-out car bodies. I mean that was their home. There were people living in shacks made of orange crates. One family with a whole lot of kids were living in a piano box. This wasn't just a little section, this was maybe ten miles wide and ten miles long." The sense of solidarity among the poor was often—although certainly not always—strong. Housewives with very little still fed hungry tramps who came to their back doors. Pauline Kael, a teenager during the Depression who grew up to be a famous film critic, remembered her mother vowing: "I'll feed them till the food runs out." One of Lillian Wald's visiting nurses went to teach a young woman how to give her firstborn baby a bath and found not one new mother and baby but two. The other girl had been in the next bed in the maternity ward, and when she confided she had no place to go, she was invited to the tiny tenement, where the husband gave up his half of the bed to the guest. "I can't do much for her, but I can put a roof over her head," said the first mother.

## "THE MOST LIBERATED WOMAN OF THE CENTURY"

For Americans in the 1930s, Franklin and Eleanor Roosevelt loomed over everything. Times had been tough before, but people had never felt such a personal connection to the president who was trying to pull the nation out of its economic spiral. And the closest the country had come to an activist First Lady before Eleanor was probably when Dolly Madison saved the White House furnishings from the British during the War of 1812. Americans generally loved—or hated—the Roosevelts as a team. Eleanor was the most important woman in the Depression era, and possibly in the country's history. During her husband's administration, particularly in the early years before the threat of war, she was the great symbol of the left wing of the New Deal, the side that wanted not only to get the economy moving again, but also to lift up the majority of the population that had never gotten a share of the Roaring Twenties wealth. Eleanor's people wanted to improve the housing of tenant farmers, give black people equal access to government services, and create model communities for impoverished coal mining families. They wanted to bring the ethic of the settlement houses into the federal government.

Eleanor was a member of one of America's great families, niece to Teddy Roosevelt and a distant cousin of her future husband. But she was not raised to be anyone significant. In fact, it's surprising she survived her upbringing at all—one cousin called it "the grimmest childhood I had ever known." Her father was an alcoholic who kept abandoning the family. One of her two brothers died when she was five years old, and her mother, who she remembered as "kindly and indifferent," died when she was eight. Her father, who Eleanor worshiped despite his endless betrayals, died two years later. The orphan was sent to live with her grandmother, a stern woman with two alcoholic adult sons whose advances caused a teenage Eleanor to put three locks on her door. When she met Franklin, he was a student at Harvard and was known in the family as the not particularly impressive only son of a domineering widow. Eleanor got pregnant right after her wedding and spent the next ten years having six children and wriggling under her mother-in-law's thumb. ("I was your real mother; Eleanor merely bore you," Sara Roosevelt told her grandchildren.) During World War I, Eleanor discovered that Franklin had been having an affair with her social secretary. "The bottom dropped out of my own particular world," she later told her friend Joseph Lash. Eleanor had a gift for intense friendships with both men and women, and one of the hallmarks of her confidence was the moment when she would sit down with a new friend and confide the story of Franklin and the social secretary.

Although Eleanor had been growing increasingly active and independent, and showed a surprising taste for politics, she was released to become the woman we know in history when Franklin was stricken with polio in 1921 and crippled from the waist down. From then on, her primary duty, as she would famously explain, was to serve as his legs, to go where he could not go. She was no longer expected to live at home with her unfaithful spouse and his difficult mother and a houseful of children who she loved but never seemed to feel entirely comfortable with. Her job, as a wife and a woman, was to travel around—first through New York, and later through the entire country. She turned out to be one of those peripatetic women, heir to the restless spirit of Catharine Beecher, Clara Barton, and Susan B. Anthony. ("Mrs. Roosevelt Spends Night at White House," jibed one newspaper headline.) She laid the political groundwork for her husband's quick ascent from invalid to governor to president, then became the heart of the Roosevelt administration's assault on the Depression, delivering news to her husband about what was happening around the country, pestering him about the things she had discovered, and introducing him to people she felt he needed to know. She averaged 100,000 pieces of mail a year, most from people who felt they had a personal connection with her from the movie newsreels, the radio, her lectures, her syndicated column, and her myriad articles for the national magazines. She answered up to 100 letters a day, sometimes enclosing personal checks.

She was far ahead of her time when it came to things like civil rights, and she befriended people who were too controversial for her husband to associate with. (The FBI's secret file on her eventually reached 4,000 pages.) But she took the edge off her radicalism by putting everything she did in the context of her role as a loyal wife. She went down into coal mines or flew off to the Pacific to visit American troops because her husband needed her to go on his behalf. She presented herself as the equivalent of the eighteenth-century Yankee merchant's spouse, or the nineteenth-century plantation mistress, running the family business while her husband was far away. When she wrote and spoke, she made constant references to her role as mother and wife.

The people accepted her work as the president's substitute, just as they accepted all those widow-congresswomen who kept going to Washington to fill their husbands' seats. A 1939 Gallup poll showed 67 percent of the public approved of Eleanor's performance as First Lady, more than supported her husband at that time. "Eleanor, I think she's the greatest thing that happened to anybody," said Elsa Ponselle, the Depression-era Chicago schoolteacher. "I think of the way they talked about her, about her looks, about her voice. I used to get rabid." Eleanor was no beauty, as she very well knew herself. "My dear, if you haven't any chin and your front teeth stick out it's going to show on the camera plate," she told a friend who tried to coach her on how to pose for the photographers. And her high, fluty upper-class voice was an eager target for mimics. The gossip about her was vicious. The same people who spread rumors that Franklin was a syphilis-ridden madman locked up in a padded room in the White House claimed that Eleanor had a black lover, or that the Roosevelts were both part of a Jewish conspiracy to take over the American government. But remarkably, her many enemies never seemed to notice the reality of her extremely unconventional personal life. In Eleanor's time the White House was stuffed with her friends of both sexes, and Franklin's friends of both sexes, who sometimes lived with them for months, or even years. Many of these friendships had an intense sexual undertone. Historians have never figured out whether Franklin was able to have sexual relations with anyone after his illness, or whether Eleanor ever had an actual affair with Lorena Hickok, the wire service reporter who gave up her career rather than give up her relationship with the First Lady. But they saved their strongest and most intimate feelings to share with people other than each other.

Eleanor was generally unconcerned about physical comfort, clothes, or good food, much to the dismay of her husband and their dinner guests. (She happily set an example for the nation by serving 7-cent meals in the White House that any Depression-era family could eat, although few would have wanted to.) She never really forgave Franklin for the social secretary, and he often bridled at her nagging about political causes. But she had an extraordinarily fruitful political partnership with the most powerful man on earth. And she had learned how to live the life that suited her. She never let anyone, including the Secret Service, keep her penned up. She went flying with Amelia Earhart. She carried her own bags from the train if no one happened to be around to grab them away from her. She drove by herself and, when her guards protested about the danger, took target practice and carried a gun. One historian called her "the most liberated woman of the century."

## "I DIDN'T LIKE THE IDEA OF BEING IMPEACHED"

Once women got the right to vote, almost every president made it a point to give at least one woman a federal post. But until Franklin Roosevelt those jobs were not very important or very numerous. "Twelve appointments by five presidents in 24 years was not an exhilarating record," said Molly Dewson, an official of the Democratic Party who was the chief lobbyist for female candidates for jobs in the Roosevelt administration. Dewson was very successful. Frances Perkins, who had been Roosevelt's chief labor adviser when he was governor of New York, became the secretary of labor—the first woman ever to hold a Cabinet-level position. Nellie Tayloe Ross, that reluctant governor of Wyoming, resurfaced as director of the Mint. Businesswoman Josephine Roche was named assistant secretary of the Treasury. The Roosevelt appointees were generally middle-aged, overachieving products of the turn-of-the-century woman's culture.

(Florence Allen, who became the first woman federal appeals court judge in 1934, wrote in her autobiography that her earliest memory was sitting on her father's lap while he taught her a sentence in Greek.) The Roosevelt administration women dined together, sent each other notes, and supported each other in times of trial. When the Gridiron Club of Washington journalists invited all the Cabinet members except Frances Perkins to their annual dinner, Eleanor Roosevelt organized a counterevent at the White House for female government officials—and female reporters, who weren't invited to the Gridiron, either.

The women's network was above all Eleanor's network. "When I wanted help on some definite point, Mrs. Roosevelt gave me the opportunity to sit by the President at dinner and the matter was settled before we finished our soup," said Dewson. Mary McLeod Bethune, the Negro Affairs Director for the National Youth Administration, had a medium-level post but she used Eleanor's access to carve out a powerful role as the emissary between black Americans and the White House. Bethune, the founder of a college in Daytona, Florida, was one of the most gifted organizers in American women's history—a Frances Willard with far less money and a needier constituency. While she lobbied for jobs and programs for her people, she gave as well as took, boosting the Roosevelts among black voters, and, later, mobilizing African American support for the war.

Frances Perkins, the labor secretary, was the highest-ranking woman to serve in the federal government and a lightning rod for conservative opponents of the Roosevelt administration. She rarely showed much emotion, having been trained to a certain stolidity by her parents, who made it a point to warn their small daughter that she was not pretty, so she would learn to face unpleasant facts squarely. As she became more influential, she began to wear rather old-fashioned black dresses, under the theory that men responded best to powerful women who reminded them of their mothers. She was singularly unflappable. Early in her career, a Philadelphia brothel owner named Sam Smith decided that Perkins's reform work interfered with his business and followed her home one night with some of his thuglike associates. Perkins ducked down a dark alley, opened her umbrella, and let the men turning the corner walk into it while she screamed "Sam Smith!" as loudly as she could. The men ran away, and Smith was eventually put out of business. When Perkins worked for Roosevelt, she repeatedly calmed down labor crises by getting government officials to withdraw their police and state troopers and let the employers and strikers work out things on their own. On one of those occasions, the grateful workers took her to a house where she watched men emerge from the basement with sacks and suitcases full of dynamite they had been planning to use to blow up their factory. They dumped it into a nearby canal instead.

By the time she became secretary of labor, Perkins was her family's sole support. Her husband, an economist named Paul Wilson, had become mentally ill, with what we would now probably diagnose as a bipolar disorder. "It was always up and down," Perkins said in her usual matter-of-fact tone. "He was sometimes depressed, sometimes excited. . . . There was a great variety in the whole process." When Perkins was honored at a testimonial lunch in 1929, she paid tribute to her husband's "brilliant mind" and to her daughter "who has grown to girlhood without being a troublesome child," but saved her fulsome praise for the family housekeeper and nanny.

Serving as labor secretary during the Great Depression turned out to be an endless crisis, and it was lucky that the first woman to hold the job knew how to keep her emotions in check. "Labor can never be reconciled to the selection," said the president of the AFL, who eventually was. Her predecessor never spoke to her and left her a desk full of cockroaches. The Supreme Court rejected many of her attempts to establish minimum wage laws and maximum workweeks. Conservative congressmen resented Perkins's support for collective bargaining and her lack of enthusiasm for deporting illegal aliens—a job her predecessor had embraced so avidly he sometimes wound up shipping off people who were American citizens. The lightning rod for dissatisfaction was Harry Bridges, a militant leader of the California dockworkers who had been born in Australia. Conservatives wanted Bridges deported because he was a suspected Communist. When Perkins refused, rumors started to float around that she, too, was a Communist, or perhaps even Bridges's secret wife or mistress. (The Supreme Court eventually upheld the Labor Department's ruling that Bridges could not be deported, and he became a U.S. citizen.) In a xenophobic Washington, many people believed Perkins was actually a foreign-born alien named Matilda Watski. In 1938, her opponents began a movement to forcibly remove her from office. "I didn't like the idea of being impeached," she understated. The effort failed, and in the meantime, Perkins had become one of the central figures in the creation of the Social Security Act. FDR rejected all her attempts to quit, and in the end, she served through his entire administration. On April 12, 1945, when the Cabinet learned that the president was dead, Perkins and Eleanor Roosevelt went out in the hall together, and the stolid labor secretary and the First Lady "sat on a bench like two schoolgirls" and cried.

## "A MENACE TO SOCIETY"

In 1932, *Fortune,* in a peculiar burst of public-spiritedness, urged housewives to hire servants instead of buying appliances. The price of 1 million refrigerators sold the prior year, the magazine said, would have employed thousands of maids and paid for "all the minor amenities of extra-clean corners, polished silver, punctiliously served meals. . . ." Housewives still preferred the refrigerators, and working women preferred jobs in the refrigerator-making factories to domestic service. A far more popular plan for increasing employment opportunities was to make all married women stay home. Pollster George Gallup said the opposition to married female workers was a conviction "on which the voters are about as solidly united as on any subject imaginable—including sin and hay fever." (Usually, the issue was couched in terms of women whose husbands made decent salaries, but a 1936 poll asked if a woman should be able to keep a full-time job if her family needed the money, and only 35 percent said yes.) "I think the single girl is entitled to make a living more so than the married woman who has a husband to support her and mostly they work so they can buy a lot of luxuries," a twenty-three-year-old woman wrote to the U.S. Department of Labor. Even Frances Perkins, when she was working for Governor Roosevelt in New York in 1930, joined in the outcry, denouncing any woman who worked merely for "pin money" as "a menace to society, a selfish and short-sighted creature who ought to be ashamed of herself."

Very few women had the luxury of working for pin money—Perkins herself was supporting her unemployable husband and their daughter. But the issue of whether married women should work was chewed over constantly in the newspapers and women's magazines, with the consensus coming down on the side of not. A federal law, passed during the Depression, prohibited the employment of "married persons" whose spouses also worked for the government. Of the people forced to quit, three-quarters were women. (Eleanor Roosevelt called the law "a very bad and foolish thing"—government salaries, she argued, were so low, a family needed two incomes just to get along.) Legislators in twenty-six states introduced laws completely banning the hiring of married women, although only Louisiana actually passed a law, and it was quickly declared unconstitutional. More than three-quarters of the nation's public school districts refused to hire married teachers—unless they were male.

Despite all this, the number of married women who worked continued to increase throughout the decade. Although most of these women struggled to keep poor families above water, a number were middle class and were attempting to preserve the good things they had gotten used to since World War I—like electric lights and gas stoves, and the ability to keep their children in school. It was an important cultural shift that sent married women into the workforce in larger and larger numbers. And for all the endless debating about whether or not it was good for society, the issue was resolved not by social theorists but by the wives themselves, determined that they and their families would not only survive but also move up.

Replacing female workers with men also turned out to be harder than people imagined. The world was too clearly divided between male and female jobs. No man would work as a housekeeper or as a private duty nurse, just as no woman could get a job as a construction worker or airline pilot. (The hopes that female fliers had for becoming commercial pilots had fizzled out when the Commerce Department ruled a woman could not fly a plane carrying passengers in bad weather.) Men did take jobs as teachers and librarians and social workers, reducing the number of women in those professions. And with so many qualified applicants for almost every job, employers set any arbitrary standard they wanted. One hospital rejected an applicant for nursing school because her teeth were crooked. The New York City board of education rejected Rose Freistater for a teaching job because she weighed 182 pounds—arguing that she might have trouble moving fast in a fire drill.

## "NOT A BIT OF DUST FOR THIS GREAT 4TH DAY OF FEB."

A fifth of American families lived on farms in the 1930s, and their lives seemed different from the ones of the pioneer era only in the advantages of automobiles and window screens. In 1935, more than 6 million of America's 6.8 million farms had no electricity. Only 20 percent of farms in Missouri had a kitchen sink with a drain; 7 percent in Kentucky had indoor bathrooms. A researcher visiting white tenant farm wives in the South found the women cooking from before dawn till long after dark on wood-burning stoves and toting water from a well or remote spring to perform the dreaded washing chores, which had to be done at least once a week because they had so few clothes. The wives bore their children at home with the help of a neighborhood "granny" and believed, like their colonial ancestors, that a woman could not conceive unless she had an orgasm. "It's not my fault that I had so many children—I never enjoyed it one bit," one told a visitor.

The New Deal program that had the greatest effect on the most women was probably rural electrification. When the hole-diggers, polemen, and axmen made their way across the Texas hill country, bringing wiring to the isolated farmhouses, the farm wives fed them dinner on their best plates—banquets by local standards, as much food as they could lay their hands on for the men who were bringing them electric power. Electricity split through the long, bleak nights on the farms, where women had sat in the darkness for much of their lives, while their children crowded around the kerosene lamp, squinting at their homework. And though most farm families did not have enough money to buy refrigerators or washing machines, they could often afford a fan, an electric iron, or a radio—a blessed radio bringing music and news and The Romance of Helen Trent.

The farm wives needed all the distraction they could get. They had to cope not only with the Depression but environmental collapse as well, due to years of heavy farming in the thin prairie soil that was never meant to be used for anything but light grazing. A drought that began in 1932 and lasted through the decade turned the broken farmland into dust, and the wind turned it into terrifying dust storms. "Just at noon the air gradually thickened and became almost opaque," said Joan Ostrander, who grew up in a South Dakota farming town. "A thick gritty blanket descended slowly, covered and lay suffocatingly over the land, leaving us in almost total darkness at mid-day—a blackout no light could penetrate. It was a tangible thing—we could feel it between our fingers and teeth and against our faces. . . . Toward the evening the black mass began to lift. . . . The maple, scarlet and splendid that morning, stood withered and ragged. . . . The asters and sunflowers were gray, and so was the whole surrounding world." Housewives stuck oiled cloth under the doors and in the window sashes, but the dust came in anyway. Chickens and wild birds died. Fences and sheds lay buried in dust. Mary Dyck, the Kansas farm wife who kept a family diary during the thirties, recorded nearly 100 days of dust storms during the first six months of 1937. The storms killed her garden and destroyed her orchard and kept her husband working round the clock, digging deep furrows in the land that would catch some of the dirt that otherwise would be blown away. It drove her into depression and a sense of futility. Any day without a storm was worth recounting: "Not a bit of dust for this great 4th day of Feb.," she wrote in 1938.

## "GOODNESS HAD NOTHING TO DO
## WITH IT, DEARIE"

Besides the radio, Depression-era women were fixated on the movies.
Films had learned to talk—clumsily at first, and then obsessively, in
smart repartee between the hero and the sassy heroine. The man
almost always won out over the spunky woman by the last reel—
unless the woman died, which happened rather frequently. It was the
beginning of the "woman's movie," a film that, on the high end, probably starred someone like Bette Davis and focused almost exclusively
on her loves and travails. Women's movies were tearjerkers that distracted the audience from their real sorrows—in the movies people
lost their loves, and sometimes their lives, but very few ever lost their
jobs. (In *Dark Victory*, Davis, having found bliss in marriage to a dedicated doctor, sits in the kitchen of her large Vermont house and
explains the virtues of the simple life to her maid and cook. "Here we
have nothing and yet we have everything," she tells the staff.) The
women in the audience weren't looking for lessons on how to cope
with hard times. They were looking for escape and glamour, and when
the sultry vamps of the 1920s turned into the platinum blonds of the
early talkies, women began to bleach their hair with peroxide and to
cement it into rigid "permanent waves" like Jean Harlow.

Harlow, whose meteoric career began when she was nineteen years
old, specialized in movies about tough, sexy, self-sufficient women. (It
was ironic, since her real life was an archetype of helplessness, including marriage to a man who was probably both impotent and abusive
and an unnecessary death at twenty-six, from untreated uremic poisoning.) She was one of a raft of actresses in the early 1930s playing
characters who used sex to get the better of men rather than becoming
victims of love. *Red-Headed Woman* begins with Harlow trying on a
new dress and asking the saleslady whether she could see through it.
"I'm afraid you can, dear," says the woman, and Harlow promptly
decides to wear it home. After seducing her hitherto happily married
boss, the heroine abandons him for an even richer, older man, who she
cuckolds with the chauffeur. At the end, after her betrayals are

exposed, Harlow drives off in triumph with a new, rich, ancient husband —in a car piloted by her old lover, the chauffer. By 1934, a new Hollywood production code made those kinds of characters extinct. Studio self-censorship ensured that on the big screen even married people slept in separate beds, that Tarzan's chimpanzees wore body stockings for modesty, and that sexual experimentation led to death, disaster, or at least a life of perpetual chastity. The early Depression era was the last time for a long while that girls went to movies to express their rebellion, or sexual curiosity.

Mae West was a sort of marker for the shifting attitudes toward women's sexuality in the country and in Hollywood. She was a product of the tougher side of the New York entertainment industry, where she made her name with a series of plays that she wrote and was repeatedly arrested for starring in. The first was called *Sex*. Another, *Drag,* was about a group of gay female impersonators. Her play *Diamond Lil* was her breakout success, both with the public and critics. People liked its humor and its setting in the 1890s Bowery—an era in which West, with her Lillian Russell–like figure, seemed very much at home. The nostalgic veneer made it easier for people to overlook the fact that West was playing a heroine who is the mistress of a mobster and the leader of a gang of shoplifters, who deals cocaine on the side and who stabs another woman to death in the second act with no serious repercussions.

West went to Hollywood in 1932 when she was already nearly forty, to play a role in a gangster movie starring her old friend George Raft. The part was a flat one, and West rewrote all the lines, including the immortal comeback when a woman said: "Goodness, what beautiful diamonds!" and West retorted, "Goodness had nothing to do with it, dearie." She was enough of a hit that she persuaded Paramount Studios, which was teetering on bankruptcy, to produce a somewhat laundered version of *Diamond Lil* under the new name *She Done Him Wrong*. It was a huge hit—huge enough to save Paramount—and it made West the biggest star in Hollywood, despite the fact that her demeanor and delivery were very much like those of the female impersonators she had worked with in *Drag*. She earned the second-largest salary in the country, after the publisher William Randolph Hearst, whose newspapers were baying in outrage at West's soaring career. Her biggest fans were young women—perhaps because neither sex nor men in general seemed nearly as intimidating when they were in West's hands. One theater in Omaha held special women-only screenings of West's second feature, *I'm No Angel*.

West's ability to put sexual connotations to what seemed like completely innocent lines of dialogue drove the studios' internal censorship system crazy, as well as conservative moral watchdogs in the country at large. She was probably the performer most responsible for the creation of the Legion of Decency, which was formed by the Catholic Church to combat immoral movies. The pressure from the censors eventually forced West into movies that didn't suit her bawdy, ironic style, and her stardom dwindled away. Her successor as the hottest female in Hollywood was, appropriately enough, Shirley Temple, a curly-haired tot who sang, danced, and straightened out the problems of all the adults in her films.

## "I HAD A WIFE ONCE BUT SHE VANISHED INTO THE NBC BUILDING"

The women who captured the public's notice in the thirties were almost always very competent, like Mae West—or even Shirley Temple. They wore fashions that broadcast the fact that they were much sturdier and more mature than the little flapper. (If they were going to carry the world on their shoulders, those shoulders had better be padded ones.) They could take care of themselves at a time when men couldn't be counted on. The ultimate heroine of the decade, Scarlett O'Hara, could do anything except pick the right man—she was, as one critic pointed out, a flapper in reverse, a woman who broke all the rules *except* the ones about sex.

*Gone with the Wind* was perhaps the biggest fictional success story of the twentieth century, just as *Uncle Tom's Cabin* was in the nineteenth. They were both novels that interpreted the greatest crisis in American history—slavery and the Civil War—through women's concerns. Politically, *Gone with the Wind* was the ultimate anti–*Uncle Tom* tract—once again the reader was invited into an antebellum South where every decent black person preferred being a slave. (Margaret Mitchell, the author, was an Atlanta girl who had walked out of a history course at Smith College when an African American student was admitted to the class.) But most readers loved the book not for its politics but for the romance between willful Scarlett and Rhett Butler, and the dramatic saga of Scarlett's fight to preserve her home and family.

The message of *Gone with the Wind* at the time of its release in 1936 was that True Womanhood could no longer hold its own against the emergencies of the modern world. Melanie Wilkes, the yin to Scarlett's yang, was a strong and practical and very, very good woman, but she was stuck in the traditional American pattern. Melanie understood as well as anybody that it would take a newer model, a Scarlett, to bring everyone safely through war and violent social upheaval. *Gone with the Wind* quickly sold a million copies when it was released at the then-astounding price of three dollars. Despite generally unfavorable reviews, the novel sold immediately to the movies, and as production was under way, a poll in 1939 showed that more than 56 million Americans were planning to see the film version.

Depression-era girls who were too young to identify with Scarlett gobbled up Nancy Drew mysteries, the most popular of a horde of girl detective novels that made their appearance in the 1930s. Nancy was about eighteen years old and was free of the constraints of school. She did not have a regular job, although she did assist her father, a wealthy lawyer, when his clients required a mystery solved. She was strong and mind-bogglingly competent. As novelist Bobbie Ann Mason pointed out in a tribute to the "Girl Sleuth," Nancy could, on a moment's notice, perform as a bareback rider in a circus, take over the part of the leading lady in a play, assist a doctor doing brain surgery, and "lie bound and gagged in a dank basement or snowed-in cabin for as much as twenty-four hours without freezing to death or wetting her pants."

One of Hollywood's stock heroines was the girl reporter, tough as nails on the outside but with a secret romantic streak. Perhaps 15,000 women actually worked for newspapers in the era—fewer, possibly, than could be found riding the rails as hoboes. But the reporters were a lot more fun to think about. In 1940, Howard Hawks introduced the ultimate gal reporter, Hildy Johnson of *His Girl Friday*. Hawks took the venerable script of *The Front Page*, a comedy about a manipulative editor and his (male) star reporter and cast Rosalind Russell in the reporter's role. It worked perfectly. Meanwhile, Brenda Starr, ace reporter, took her place on the comic strip, and in the ultimate B-movie fusion, Hollywood made a movie called *Nancy Drew, Reporter*.

Most of the women who worked in journalism were confined to the women's department, or small-town community papers. But reporting was still one of the professions where, early on, a few women had been able to have adventures in full public view. Dorothy Thompson became an incredibly influential columnist in the 1920s after she went to Europe and sold freelance stories on the German political situation. At the time, international reporting was a new field, not particularly prestigious or well paid—fertile territory for ambitious women. Thompson's analysis of what was going on in Germany and Eastern Europe was must-reading in the years before World War II, and when she married novelist Sinclair Lewis she also became half of one of the nation's top celebrity couples. She wrote her three-times-a-week newspaper column out of a New York apartment with nine telephones and three secretaries. She also lectured all around the country and made frequent radio appearances. "I had a wife once but she vanished into the NBC building and has never been heard of since," grumbled Lewis. (The marriage didn't last.)

# 17

# World War II: "She's Making History, Working for Victory"

## "I AM GOING TO ASSIST IN BUILDING A PLANE TO BOMB HITLER"

World War II was an emergency on an epic scale. Although American women weren't shelled and driven from their homes as some were during the Civil War, the country needed their participation more desperately, and in more different ways, than it ever had before. If housewives had paid strict attention to the barrage of demands and warnings from government propaganda machines, they probably would have gone mad with anxiety. They were told that it was their duty to take over for the men who had gone to the front, filling in as bus drivers, bank tellers, and defense workers in the aircraft and munitions factories. They had to support food rationing by shunning the black market, buying only the amounts of meat, sugar, and butter their ration cards allowed. But their meals had to be healthy and tasty—otherwise they and their family might succumb to "hidden hunger" and slow down war production at work, thus endangering the soldiers in combat.

Women who failed to volunteer for a factory job were dogged by pictures of idle equipment that warned a "soldier may die unless you man this machine." If they *did* go to work, every moment counted.

One of the many propaganda films slipped in between the movie features was called *Conquer the Clock,* and it showed a soldier being killed because a female defense worker slipped off for a cigarette, allowing some cartridges to go through the assembly line uninspected. Constance Bowman, a worker assigned to install safety belts at an aircraft factory, was told that if she took a day off, the planes might roll off the assembly line without seat belts, endangering fliers' lives. Copywriters for public service ads came up with so many scenarios for how civilian women could wreak havoc on the casualty rates that an official at the Office of War Information warned his subordinates: "threatening women with the death of a soldier is poor psychology with which to attempt to drive them into the labor market."

Married women, who formed the main target of the propaganda barrage, were supposed to volunteer for defense jobs, save pan drippings and turn them in to the nearest butcher, contribute to metal scrap drives, grow victory gardens and can the harvest, and above all, continue to nurture the family and keep the home fires burning. Those who worked—and wrestled with the painful bus commutes made necessary by gasoline rationing—were still supposed to respect rationing regulations even though they had virtually no time to shop. (In the movie *Tender Comrades,* five soldiers' wives have a spirited argument about what to do when the butcher sends them more meat than their ration stamps permit. The star, Ginger Rogers, takes the position that accepting the bacon could endanger the lives of their husbands overseas.) The government and the media uncovered a host of role models, like Mrs. Chris Laukhug in Defiance County, Ohio, who canned 2,000 quarts of forty different kinds of food, dried bushels of fruit and vegetables, and made her own maple syrup. In Atlanta, Helen Dortch Longstreet, eighty, became a star when she was discovered working in an aircraft plant. Mrs. Longstreet, the widow of a Confederate general (it had been a May-December romance) assured her interviewers, "I am going to assist in building a plane to bomb Hitler . . . to the judgment seat of God."

## "A WOMAN'S ARMY . . .
## THINK OF THE HUMILIATION"

In 1940, Jeanette Rankin, the Montana Republican who had been the first woman ever elected to Congress in 1916, resumed the career that had been derailed when she voted against World War I. Rankin was elected to her old House seat, once again on a pacifist platform. "By voting for me . . . you can express your opposition to sending your sons to foreign lands to fight in a foreign war," she told her audiences. At the time, most Americans shared her antiwar sentiments, but after the Japanese bombed Pearl Harbor on December 7, 1941, national opinion changed overnight. Congresswoman Rankin rushed back to Washington, "driving to my execution," as she remembered it. On December 8, the House voted 388–1 to declare war on Japan. Again, she had been elected just in time to vote against a world war. Police had to escort Rankin back to her office through the angry crowd. "Montana is 100 percent against you," her brother cabled from home. William Allen White, the legendary editor of the *Emporia Gazette* in Kansas, editorialized that his paper "entirely disagrees with the wis-, dom of her position" then added: "But Lord, it was a brave thing." At the end of her term, she would retire, consistent and unrepentant.

Rankin was not the only American woman with limited enthusiasm for armed combat. Two months after Pearl Harbor, a survey found that 57 percent of the male respondents favored war with Japan "even if our cities would be bombed" while only 36 percent of the women were willing to go that far. Still, it was becoming clear that the nation was going to require women not only to support the war effort, but also to join the military itself. The army needed them to do clerical work and other noncombatant jobs, to free up more men for fighting. But most of the top brass was adamant that the women should only be there temporarily and should not receive full military status.

The generals marched headlong into Representative Edith Nourse Rogers, a Massachusetts Republican, who was equally determined that women would get the same rights and protections as other members of the service. Rogers had gotten to Congress by the traditional route, succeeding her husband when he died in office. But unlike most House widows, Rogers won reelection in her own right. (She died in 1960 at the age of seventy-nine, campaigning for her seventeenth term.) She had gone overseas as a Red Cross volunteer during World War I, and she remembered how badly the military had treated the American women who did its clerical and communications work in Europe. Refused military commissions, they "received no compensation of any kind in the event they were sick or injured—and many were," Rogers told her colleagues. After a series of compromises, she managed to pass legislation establishing the Women's Army Corps (WAC). Most of the other military services had smaller women's units. More than 350,000 women wound up enlisting during the war, mainly in the WAC and the nursing corps.

The army still went out of its way to stress that it hoped the WACs' role would last no longer than the hostilities. For a while, the War Department adopted the slogan "The WAC who shares your army life will make a better postwar wife." Officials also stressed how mundane the women's role would be. Assistant Chief of Staff John Hildring echoed a familiar sentiment when he said that "we have found difficulty in getting enlisted men to perform tedious duties anywhere nearly as well as women will do it."

The attention given to women far outweighed their numbers; they were never more than 2 percent of the armed forces. But while they were celebrated in endless newsreels and magazine photos, they were also denigrated. Frieda Schurch, a WAC assigned to Drew Field in Tampa, remembered that the regular army folk did not feel it was appropriate to have women on base "so they put us five miles out, off the base, in a swamp that wasn't drained and had mosquitoes." Although Drew Field had only about 100 WACs, she said, "We always averaged 14 in the hospital for infected mosquito bites." The area was drained only after the women were evacuated and the barracks became housing for prisoners of war.

From the beginning there were rumors that the women were sexually promiscuous, that the WACs in particular were a sort of geisha corps recruited to improve the "morale" of the troops in the most basic way possible. There was a widely reported rumor that thousands of pregnant WACs had been evacuated from North Africa, a story that turned out to have grown out of the evacuation of three women, one who was ill and two others who were married and pregnant. "It raised hell," wrote one company commander. "Long-distance calls from parents began to come in, telling the girls to come home. The girls all came in crying, asking if this disgrace was what they had been asked to join the Army for. . . . It took all the pride and enthusiasm for the Army right out of them." The FBI was called in to determine if this was some sort of enemy disinformation campaign and found that most of the talk originated with male servicemen.

The idea that American men were fighting to protect the women back home was extremely powerful during the war, and many servicemen felt diminished by having women in the military. True, women were restricted to noncombatant duty, but most of the men never saw combat, either. The only thing that identified them as defenders of the homeland was their uniform, and now women wanted to wear that, too. "A woman's Army to defend the United States of America! Think of the humiliation. What has become of the manhood of America that we have to call on our women to do the duty of men?" asked a congressman from New York during the debate over Representative Rogers's bill. Black male soldiers, who had plenty of other assaults on their dignity, were unhappy about the arrival of black women. "The efforts of the women to be supportive of the men was mistaken for competition and patronage," said one African American WAC. Even the idea that women were simply stepping in to free up men for the front lines drew a decidedly mixed reaction, depending on how enthusiastic the soldiers were about getting the chance to risk their lives for their country. A WAC in Birmingham ran into the man whose job processing payrolls she had taken and was told: "Thanks for letting me go." But Evelyn Fraser, a former Indiana reporter who volunteered for the military, said that a lieutenant she had been sent to replace refused to explain how to do the job, for fear that once she learned, he'd be sent overseas.

## "THREE HOLES IN THE TAIL, BOYS,
## THAT'S A LITTLE TOO CLOSE"

The first five WACs flown to Europe had been trained to serve as executive secretaries. They arrived in England and were promptly put on a boat for North Africa, which was sunk. Although all five were rescued, Oveta Culp Hobby, the Texas newspaper publisher who had been appointed head of the WACs, flew to the training center at Daytona Beach to warn the women about the dangers of going into a combat theater. After her speech, the WACs were given a break to eat and were urged to think about whether they still wanted to volunteer for duty overseas. "We didn't go to dinner, we all got in line to sign up," one woman wrote. "The whole battalion, one behind the other. . . . The officers were walking around with tears running down their cheeks, especially Colonel Hobby." Of the 300 women at Daytona Beach, 298 volunteered.

Not all the overseas assignments worked out well. More than 5,000 women wound up in the Southwest Pacific, mainly performing post office duties, like sorting and censoring the soldiers' mail to make sure it didn't reveal military secrets. They went through endless piles of letters from young men to their friends and lovers, much of it obscene. They worked ten hours a day seven days a week, and since no one was willing to give them special permission not to wear their uniforms, their heavy clothing was constantly wet with sweat and gave them skin diseases. The only alternative was light cotton shirts that left them vulnerable to mosquitoes and malaria. Some of the officers were so worried about the women's safety that they kept them virtual prisoners and after a year or more of close confinement, WACs in New Guinea were reported to be guilty of "resentment, disobedience and immature conduct." Other women, who landed after the troops in Italy, North Africa, and Normandy, got better treatment and more meaningful work.

The theory that women should only be asked to do work that was safe and relatively mundane was ignored whenever something risky or difficult actually needed to be done. The Women's Airforce Service Pilots (WASP) was created to free male fliers for service overseas.

The 1,000 women who were accepted flew 60 million miles during the war, in every type of plane manufactured by the military, including experimental jets and the B-29 Superfortress. Male pilots, who often felt they should not have to risk their lives on domestic flights far from the glory of combat, cheerfully turned over dangerous assignments to the women. Originally, the WASPs were supposed to simply fly new planes from the factories to the ports, but they also wound up towing targets so the artillery could practice, flying past long lines of guns being fired by inexperienced trainees. Sometimes when the WASPs returned, their planes were riddled with the bullets that were supposed to be directed at the targets they were towing. The male pilots at Camp Irwin in California refused to tow targets for tank gunners, who tended to fire wildly as they raced their cumbersome vehicles across the desert while attempting to aim and shoot. The next time the tanks were taken out for a drill, they heard a female voice over the radio calmly saying: "Three holes in the tail, boys, that's a little too close." The male pilots also were happy to hand over the job of testing planes that had been grounded for safety reasons and had theoretically been repaired.

Early on, the women pilots had to fight against military attempts to ground them when they had their periods. An army flight surgeon, Nels Monsrud, conducted a rigorous study of the women's performance and produced scientific evidence that menstruation had no effect on their capacity to perform as pilots, putting an end to a legend that had bedeviled women fliers since the days of the Wright brothers. (It wasn't the only theory about female biology circulating in the corridors of power. Men in both the military and Congress still believed that as women approached menopause they lost their reason, and the Surgeon General was called in to beat back an attempt to require women with military commissions to retire before their fortieth birthday.)

Although the WASPs' safety record was better than that of men doing comparable jobs, thirty-eight of them were killed in service. (One of them was crushed when her plane crashed after someone put sugar in the gas tank.) When a WASP died in the line of duty, her friends raised money to send the body home, because their corps was never given official military status. The dead flier was not even eligible to have an American flag placed over her coffin, although the women who accompanied the bodies of their comrades home never had the heart to tell the families that their daughters and sisters could not have that military honor. The WASPs believed that eventually they would get their commissions, but as the war went on, the military developed a surplus of pilots, and male fliers stationed at domestic bases were suddenly faced with the possibility that they might be transferred into the infantry. Jill McCormick, a WASP who once survived a midair explosion of a battered dive bomber she was ferrying to a reclamation center, was sitting in a Raleigh hotel lobby when she was surrounded by men in uniform, calling her a slut and shouting at her to go back home. Under pressure from the male pilots, Congress rejected a bill to militarize the WASPs, and future training classes were canceled. The program was deactivated at the end of 1944, and the women were unceremoniously sent home.

## "LITTLE DID I DREAM THAT WE WOULD BE ALWAYS HUNGRY, ALWAYS FRIGHTENED"

No one questioned what the more than 70,000 women who served in the army and navy nurse corps were doing in the military, although female doctors had to fight tooth and nail to get commissions, just as they had in World War I. (The secretary of war's niece, who was a physician, wound up enlisting in the British medical forces out of frustration.) Toward the end of the war, Congress was actually preparing to draft registered nurses because the need was so great, but hostilities ceased before the plan was put into operation. However, the nurses also suffered from a torrent of rumors that they were promiscuous. There was a mean streak in the national character that presumed women who willingly went to live among thousands of soldiers could be after only one thing. In a letter to Eleanor Roosevelt, one nurse in training explained that few of her classmates were enlisting because they feared their reputations would be ruined. "Everywhere one turns—on trains, streetcars, at social gatherings or the USO—men of our armed forces debase the very organization that protects and heals them in their afflictions," she complained.

Although nurses worked near the lines of battle in North Africa and Italy, and six were killed after the landing at Anzio, they were generally kept well away from the front. Corpsmen attempted to stabilize the wounded on the battlefield and removed them to hospitals in the rear. That policy was inspired, at least in part, by a disaster during the first moments of the war, when nearly 100 army and navy nurses were caught in the Japanese assault on the Philippines; most spent years as prisoners of war. They were not women who had gone to the East for combat duty. Before the war, a posting in Manila was one of the military's cushiest assignments, a world of houseboys and maids, palm groves and orchids, tennis courts and weekly polo matches. "We lived high on the hog," said Minnie Stubbs, one of the nurses.

In the disarray following Pearl Harbor, the army and navy could not hold the Philippines, nor could they rescue their personnel. The Americans decided to retreat to the Bataan peninsula, from which they hoped eventually to be evacuated. The nurses served for months in makeshift hospitals set up in the jungles of Bataan, under constant Japanese bombardment and fear of imminent attack. "Little did I dream that we would be always hungry, always frightened," said one of the nurses later. As Japanese warships shelled American positions, nurse Sally Blaine looked around her and saw patients lying on the jungle floor as far as the eye could see. "I can remember doing dressings, starting right after breakfast and continuing throughout the day," said Hattie Brantley. After a while, she found that her back would not straighten up between patients, "and I'd get down on my knees, finally not even bothering to arise but crawling to the next cot." The officers noticed how uncomplaining the nurses were. "I was continually amazed that anyone living and working under such primitive conditions could remain as calm, pleasant, efficient and impeccably neat and clean as those remarkable nurses," wrote a military surgeon after the war.

A small number of the nurses were evacuated, and when they

arrived back home, they found themselves feted in a peculiar, distancing way. They were either portrayed as superheroes, who drove through enemy fire to deliver vitamins to men on the front, or as fluffy little things intent on keeping their noses powdered. Brunetta Kuehlthau, a physical therapist, managed to send a letter to her family through the blockade at Bataan. She assured them she was "comparatively safe" and mentioned some homey details that she thought would not disturb her mother. The *New York Times* reported on the letter under the headline "Nurse on Corregidor Finds It 'Not Too Bad': Letter Says Hairpin Shortage Causes Women to Cut Hair." Hollywood cranked out a string of movies about the Bataan nurses. In the most famous, *So Proudly We Hail,* Veronica Lake sacrifices herself to save her fellow nurses from a group of rapacious Japanese soldiers by detonating a grenade she had hidden in her breasts.

Thinking of the Bataan nurses as action heroes with thermometers or as coeds on a bad vacation concealed the grim reality of what was actually going on. The soldiers who the nurses tended to in Bataan wound up being driven on a death march during which Japanese guards shot anyone who fell by the wayside from exhaustion and disease. Most of the nurses were taken as prisoners of war and held with 3,000 American and British civilians captured in Manila. They were even kept from taking care of the American soldiers, who were interned separately. When they emerged from their camp three years later—miraculously all alive, although many of their fellow prisoners had died of malnutrition or tropical diseases—the stories about them almost always focused on things like their eagerness to buy cosmetics and investigate the newest hairstyles. Unlike male prisoners of war, they were not treated for the psychological effects of their ordeal—the doctors seemed to assume that the women's clinical training made them invulnerable to posttraumatic stress.

Physicians who had served with Maude Davidson, the crusty head of nurses in the internment camp, urged that she be awarded the Distinguished Service Medal. General Jonathan Wainwright, who had commanded the troops on Bataan, rejected the idea, arguing that her position was not high enough to merit the army's third-highest award.

During the fall of Bataan, Wainwright had told the American people that the nurses' names "must always be hallowed when we speak of American heroes," but after years of grueling imprisonment himself, he had apparently raised the bar on heroism. To add insult to injury, the major general in charge of the awards board concluded that although Davidson must have had to take some independent actions in keeping her nurses together and working through the evacuation, bombardment, and years of internment, "a large share" of the initiative and responsibility "must have been carried by doctors and commanders."

## "SHE'S MAKING HISTORY, WORKING FOR VICTORY"

Meanwhile, back at home, more than 13 million people had left for the service, and the same women who had been told to stay out of the job market during the Depression were now being begged to go to work. About 6 million women did take jobs during the war, joining the 14 million who had already been working and doing everything from paving roads to operating cranes. By the time fighting ended in 1945, women made up more than a third of the national workforce. Although most of them held clerical, sales, and other pink-collar jobs, the idealized female employee of the 1940s was Rosie the Riveter, a mythic creature celebrated by Norman Rockwell on the cover of the *Saturday Evening Post* with a famous portrait that showed her perched on a steel beam, munching a sandwich and displaying her muscles while she casually ground Nazi propaganda under her heel.

"While other girls attend a favorite cocktail bar," went a song of the hour . . .

> *Sipping dry martinis, munching caviar;*
> *There's a girl who's really putting them to shame—*
> *Rosie is her name.*

> *All day long, whether rain or shine*
> *She's part of the assembly line,*

> *She's making history, working for victory,*
> *Rosie, Rosie, Rosie, Rosie, Rosie, Rosie the Riveter.*

The number of women actually munching caviar during the war was hardly extensive, but still, for the first time the country was singing the praises of women who did hard labor. Women's magazines, with a great deal of prodding from the federal government, applauded women who held down jobs in the same way they had always celebrated women who stayed home. *Ladies' Home Journal* ran a story about a female surgeon who called off her engagement when she discovered her fiancé expected her to quit working. On the radio, Stella Dallas and other soap opera heroines signed up for defense jobs. (It was only one of the contributions soap opera heroines made to the war effort. Several lost fictional sons or husbands in combat, and Helen Trent fell over a cliff while trying to save a truckload of war supplies.) In many ways, this was an old story. In the Revolutionary and Civil Wars, women had taken over their husbands' farm duties, and plowing a field was certainly as tough a job as slinging rivets. The difference in World War II—as it had been in World War I on a smaller scale—was that a huge number of women had to be recruited to do jobs that were not part of the family business.

The first women to volunteer for defense jobs had already been working, in low-status, low-paying positions, and they grabbed at the chance to make better salaries. Peggy Terry, who got a job with her mother and sister at a shell-loading plant in Kentucky, was euphoric. "We made the fabulous sum of thirty-two dollars a week," she said. "To us it was just an absolute miracle. Before that, we made nothing." Even when the chemicals they were handling turned the women's faces and hair orange, Terry said, they weren't fazed: "The only thing we worried about was other women thinking we had dyed our hair." As a result of the great migration of women to defense jobs, 600 laundries went out of business in 1942, and in Detroit, a third of the restaurants closed because of the lack of help.

Although most unmarried women were already working when the war started, a number of college students quit school to join the war

effort. Among the other early volunteers were the wives of servicemen. "Darlin, You are now the husband of a career woman—just
call me your Ship Yard Babe!" wrote Polly Crow to her husband overseas. Rose Kaminski of Milwaukee, whose husband served in the navy,
left her young daughter with an elderly neighbor when she learned
that crane operators were needed at an ordnance plant to move the
huge howitzer gun barrels. "Well I was running one in three days,"
she recalled much later. "It just came to me; I loved it." At her old job
at a machine shop, she said dismissively, she had handled "piddly little
pieces" of the guns, whose function she never understood. "This
seemed like part of it. You were doing something."

The shortage of teachers impelled most school boards to drop their
rules against married women, and some actually appealed to married
ex-teachers to return. The Office of War Information suggested articles it would like to see in print to newspapers and magazines, urging,
among other things, "stories showing the advent of women in logging
camps, on the railroads, riding the ranges, and showing them not as
weak sisters but coming through in manly style." For a few women on
the home front, the war opened up opportunities that might otherwise
have been unimaginable. People began dancing to all-girl bands. The
owner of the Chicago Cubs started an All-American Girls League,
which required its players to wear uniforms that featured short skirts
and satin briefs—a combination that led to endless bruises for women
who had to slide into bases barelegged.

By late 1942, unemployment was virtually nonexistent, and the
government projected a need for 3 million more workers in the next
year. Child labor laws were suspended for youngsters over twelve.
Handicapped Americans were given opportunities to enter the workplace, as were black women and older women. But the prime pool of
potential workers was married women. Ads and movie newsreels constantly emphasized how defense work was just like housework:
"instead of cutting the lines of a dress, this woman cuts a pattern of
aircraft parts . . . a lathe holds no more terror than a sewing
machine . . . after a short apprenticeship, this woman can operate a
drill press just as easily as a juice extractor." However, even when the

war was at its height and the need for workers was most desperate, nearly 90 percent of the housewives who had been at home when Pearl Harbor was bombed still ignored the call.

One of the reasons undoubtedly was the lack of child care. Unlike England, where the government provided all sorts of support services for women who worked, the U.S. government left them to their own devices. Congress didn't appropriate money for federal day care centers until 1943, and even then it was used so ineptly that only about 10 percent of the defense workers' children were ever enrolled. And while married women were being criticized as unpatriotic for failing to work, they were being denounced as bad mothers if they did. Agnes Meyer, the wife of the publisher of the *Washington Post*, published a report on latchkey children that was quoted everywhere: "In Los Angeles a social worker counted 45 infants locked in cars at a single parking lot while their mothers were at work in war plants," she wrote. "Older children in many cities sit in the movies, seeing the same film over and over again until mother comes off the evening 'swing' shift and picks them up. Some children of working parents are locked in their homes, others locked out."

But there were other less tangible reasons for the unenthusiastic response to recruitment campaigns. Defense work, although more rewarding than waiting tables, was not all that pleasant. In 1943, two San Diego high school teachers, Constance Bowman and Clara Marie Allen, wrote about their experiences during the summer, when they volunteered for the swing shift at a factory that built the B-24 bombers. At the end of the first shift, Bowman wrote, "I was tireder than I have ever been in my life and also dirtier. My hair was tinseled with tiny shavings of metal, my hands were grimy, and my fingernails were bordered in black. . . . My uniform, my bright blue uniform of yesterday afternoon, had a tear in the knee, a streak of grease across the blouse and a large dusty circle on the seat of the pants where I had sat on the floor." Being forced to wear pants to work instead of skirts made Bowman and Allen feel that they had lost their position in the universe. Men no longer offered them seats on the crowded buses; they were snubbed by clerks and ticket agents and leered at by strange males on the street. "It was a great shock to C.M. and me to find that being a lady depended more upon our clothes than upon ourselves," Bowman wrote. (Though women wore slacks for athletics, they were not yet common for street wear. When four WASPs were grounded by weather in Americus, Georgia, in 1944, they were arrested by local police for violating a rule against women wearing slacks on the street at night.)

Throughout American history, the concept of the woman as a protected homebody went hand in hand with the reality that most women—poor women—were expected to work and were not given any special deference because of their sex. By going off to sling rivets or weld airplane wings, middle-class women lost their status and joined the other part of American womanhood that was expected to fend for itself. "Whether they are dust-bowl mothers buying butter and eggs for the first time, or former dime store clerks making more money than army majors, or war wives who feel they must keep them flying because their husbands are flying them, or school teachers putting in a summer vacation on a war job," Bowman concluded, the defense factory workers had all been leveled: "they are women who wear slacks instead of skirts."

## "VARIETY MEATS: THEY ARE GOOD, ABUNDANT, HIGHLY NUTRITIOUS"

Whether women worked or not, their lives were made infinitely more complicated by rationing, which restricted the availability of sugar, coffee, butter, certain types of meat, and canned goods as well as things like gasoline, tires, and stockings. New appliances were not being manufactured, and children who were promised a bicycle on the eve of World War II were sometimes licensed to drive by the time it became available. Unable to find stockings, women began wearing leg makeup instead. And since the stockings of the 1940s had seams down the back, women's magazines ran guides on how to draw a realistic-looking line down the calf.

American rationing was mainly a matter of inconvenience. By eating less sugar and being forced to walk because of the gasoline shortage, the population was arguably in better shape than it would ever be in again. "Never in the long history of human combat have so many talked so much about sacrifice with so little deprivation as in the United States in World War II," sniped John Kenneth Galbraith, who worked at the Office of Price Administration. But for the American middle class, long accustomed to prime cuts of beef for dinner, the appearance of government-issued recipes for "Tongue Rolls Florentine" or "Tripe à la Maryland" was traumatizing. A government-issued magazine article entitled "Variety Meats: They are Good, Abundant, Highly Nutritious" explained in the most irritating manner possible that the army did not serve things like kidneys, livers, or tripe "because they spoil easily, take time to prepare and the men don't like them. These objections, valid for the Army, make no sense when cited by civilians."

Civilians got stamps every month that gave them the right to buy different products. "My mother and all the neighbors would get together around the dining-room table, and they'd be changing a sugar coupon for a bread or a meat coupon. It was like a giant Monopoly game," said Sheril Cunning, who was a child in Long Beach, California, during the war. The Office of Price Administration raised or lowered point values to encourage people to consume things that were in oversupply, notably eggs. At times, the government's enthusiasm for getting women to buy more eggs was so intense it seemed as if Hitler could be stopped only if everyone ate an omelet a day. Some housewives noted bitterly that if they were given a larger allotment of sugar for baking, they could find plenty of ways to get rid of the eggs that were currently causing rebellion at the dinner table. "Give us housewives more sugar and watch the eggs disappear," wrote Mrs. George Coffey of Montana. "People can only eat so many cooked eggs or they will become nauseated of them. . . ." Commercial bakeries got a much more generous sugar allotment than individual citizens, encouraging the trend away from home-baked goods.

All the wartime propaganda about nutrition gave Americans far more knowledge about the food they ate. Despite the diet-conscious

1920s, most people still did not know the difference between a vitamin and a calorie. It was in World War II that housewives were introduced to the food pyramid and the "basic seven" kinds of food necessary for a healthy diet. It was a fat-friendly listing that gave butter a category all to itself.

## "WE WOULD GO TO DANCES AND GIRLS WOULD DANCE WITH GIRLS"

Even as women were being urged to the factories, they were being warned to remember that this was just for the emergency, and not to get carried away. A Seattle paper told them to avoid going "berserk over the new opportunities for masculine clothing and mannish actions." A *Des Moines Register* cartoon showed a giantess of a woman in overalls, her pocket stuffed with "her own man's size pay envelope" marching off with her toolbox while a tiny husband in apron and broom calls out: "But remember you gotta come back as soon as the war is over!"

"Oh yeah?" sneers the hulking female war worker.

The war actually did a great deal to restore men's Depression-battered position as the most important member of the family. The nation's entire attention was turned to the fate of husbands, brothers, sons, and boyfriends fighting overseas. Meanwhile, the men who remained back home were a rare and valuable commodity—perhaps a little bit like those southern women of the seventeenth century. Dorothy Zmuda of Milwaukee remembered one male coworker in her office who never did his share of work. When she discovered he was making more money than she was, her boss told her: "This is this time of our life that men earn more than women. They are considered more important, and even if you do the same thing he does and even if he doesn't even do it, he gets more money than you do and this is our world today."

Marriage rates jumped. "The pressure to marry a soldier was so great that after a while I didn't question it," said Dellie Hahne of Los Angeles, who wound up unhappily wed to a man in uniform. "That women married soldiers and sent them overseas happy was hammered at us." Single Americans yearned for someone who was waiting for them, or for whom they were waiting. Dorothy Zmuda was casually dating a young man who suddenly offered her a ring when he was drafted. When she told him no, he found another girl who accepted it a couple of weeks later. "The girls that I knew all had boyfriends who were in the service and we didn't date because we were 'tagged' " said Emily Koplin of Milwaukee. "We didn't do any dating—those were the years where we would go to dances and girls would dance with girls." The *Baltimore Sun* noticed that "Women who never ventured out at night without a man sally forth in twos and threes without a qualm. Late movies have a large female audience."

The forties was a time when women rediscovered the community of other women. "It was very important to have somebody to lean on, to have somebody to talk to," said Koplin, who felt that parents "were worried about their sons being overseas, not necessarily the daughter that was left back home." That sense of female solidarity was probably strongest among the women whose husbands were away in the service. Jean Lechnir was pregnant with her third child in Prairie du Chien, Wisconsin, when her husband was drafted. She banded together with nine other women in the neighborhood whose husbands were away at war. They pooled their ration stamps and played cards for a pound of butter or bag of sugar, and once a month, when the serviceman's pay came in, they left their children with relatives and went out to eat. "Maybe a top meal was $2.50 . . . and maybe we could have a cocktail or glass of pop or something for another twenty-five or fifty cents. That was our evening. But we'd extend it long enough to sit and watch other people dance or just sit and reminisce and compare notes of the letters we got from our husbands." The friendships she formed in that group, Lechnir said, extended on for the next half century.

## "WELL, OF COURSE, SO WERE THE JAPANESE"

World War II had a way of cracking open America's tight-knit immigrant communities. While the sons were serving in the military with people from all parts of the country, the daughters, who might normally have dropped out of school to get married, stayed on to graduate and went to work in factories where they made friends with people from different backgrounds. Anne Dinsmore, the daughter of Sicilian immigrants, stayed in the Italian community in Madison, Wisconsin, with her husband's family while he was in service. When the sons went off to war, she noted, "their fathers fell apart . . . Just fell apart. And it was the women who stood very strong and kept the families together." Dinsmore remembered the Italian women worried that the country would turn on them when Italy allied with Germany and became an enemy nation. "And I kept saying 'No, that can't be. You see, your sons, our brothers, are fighting in this war,' " said Dinsmore. "Well, of course, so were the Japanese."

The Japanese were different. Earl Warren, the future Supreme Court Chief Justice, was attorney general in California when 110,000 Japanese Americans were rounded up and taken to live behind barbed wire for the duration of the war. He assured the nation that Italian Americans and German Americans did not need the same treatment. "We believe that when we are dealing with the Caucasian race . . . we can . . . arrive at some fairly sound conclusions because of our knowledge of the way they live in the community," he said. After all, Dwight Eisenhower, who was leading the Allied forces, was of German descent, and some of the most popular American celebrities, like Frank Sinatra and Joe DiMaggio, were Italian. But most Americans had never met someone of Japanese origin.

When the Japanese Americans were interned, they were allowed to bring with them only what they could carry. Many of the men had been taken away first, because they were suspected of being enemy agents. "These poor women whose husbands were rounded up by the FBI, they were all fairly young and they had small children and no one to help them and they had to somehow make ready to leave . . . in forty-eight hours," said Fred Fujikawa. "This was in December so a lot of the families had already brought their Christmas presents, like new phonographs or radios, refrigerators. . . . These guys would come in and offer ten or fifteen dollars and because they had to leave, they'd sell." Jeanne Wakatsuki was seven years old when her father was taken off by FBI agents and her mother was forced to move the family to a camp. When a dealer offered her $15 for the family's heirloom china "blue and white porcelain, almost translucent," her mother lost control and began breaking the plates, sending the dealer racing for the door. "When he was gone she stood there smashing cups and bowls and platters until the whole set lay in scattered blue and white fragments across the wooden floor," her daughter remembered.

Yoshiko Uchida and her sister and parents were sent to a center in California where they were quartered in a stable, each family assigned to one horse stall. "The stall was about ten by twenty feet and empty except for three folded Army cots lying on the floor," she wrote later. "Our stable consisted of twenty-five stalls facing north which were back to back with an equal number facing south, so we were surrounded on three sides." Neighbors not only could hear a family's conversations, they knocked on the wall to ask that someone repeat a comment they failed to catch. The latrines in most of the camps were a line of open toilets and many of the older women were humiliated at the lack of privacy. Some held newspapers over their faces. Others dragged large cardboard cartons to the latrine, and set them around the toilets like a screen.

Once the internees were relocated to permanent camps, the Japanese Americans created lives as best they could. The Department of the Interior boasted that the camp residents, who included some of the West's most successful produce farming families, "are now producing practically all the vegetables needed by the 90,000 people residing at the centers." Meanwhile, 33,000 young Japanese American men were serving in the army, many fighting with great distinction overseas. Japanese American women, eager to prove their patriotism, volunteered for the WACs. But the army did everything it could to downplay their presence. When one of the first groups of Japanese WACs was sworn in at a ceremony in Denver, a reporter covering the event was forbidden to take a picture, and WAC officials later successfully lobbied to kill the story entirely.

## "HITLER WAS THE ONE THAT GOT US OUT
## OF THE WHITE FOLKS' KITCHEN"

In San Francisco, when the call went out for women to fill in for the men who had gone to war, a young Maya Angelou decided that she wanted to be a streetcar conductor. "I'd pictured myself, dressed in a neat blue serge suit, my money changer swinging jauntily at my waist, and a cheery smile for the passengers which would make their own work day brighter," she wrote later. Her mother warned her that although the city was advertising desperately for conductors "they don't accept colored people on the streetcars." Angelou stubbornly determined that she was going to get a job anyway, even though she was systematically ignored whenever she applied. "My trips to the streetcar office were of the frequency of a person on salary," she said. "One day, which was tiresomely like all the others before it, I sat in the Railway office, ostensibly waiting to be interviewed. The receptionist called me to her desk and shuffled a bunch of papers to me. They were job application forms." Thanks to Angelou's persistence, and the city's pressing need for workers, she did become a conductor— although one with some of the worst schedules of shifts in San Francisco. In New York, other black women with a similar stubborn patience finally broke the color barrier in 1944 and got jobs as telephone operators.

For black women, the war years were a combination of opportunity and frustration. The high-paying defense factories were the hardest to crack. In 1943, at the height of the labor shortage, the United Auto Workers surveyed 280 factories that employed women workers and found that only 74 were willing to hire an African American. When light industry went out recruiting, it turned to white women while heavy industry targeted black men. Most employers, when challenged by government or civil rights groups, claimed they could not hire black women because white women refused to work with them. That was often true, although companies that took a firm line and forced their employees to choose between integration and loss of their lucrative jobs generally managed to overcome the problem fairly quickly. White women seemed to have a different reaction to integration on the job than white men. Studies suggest that men were not threatened by the presence of African Americans in the factories, but they reacted angrily if black men were promoted to jobs with higher salaries or more authority. The white women, on the other hand, seemed intent on keeping a physical distance. They sometimes demanded separate bathrooms, claiming black women carried venereal disease.

The war was a complicated matter for black women. When hurtful things happened—like a South Carolina resolution announcing that Americans were overseas "fighting for white supremacy" or the Red Cross's insistence that blood donations be segregated by race, or the Boston USO's rule that black women could serve as hostesses only if they promised not to dance with white soldiers—they must have been tempted to wash their hands of the whole business. But they also understood that although there were plenty of things wrong with America, there were none that Hitler was going to fix. "Despite all the bad things that happened in the country, this was our home. This is where I was born. It was where my father and mother were. So there was a feeling of wanting to do your part," said Gladys Carter, one of the first black WACs to serve overseas.

One way some black women made sense of all this was through a campaign called Double V, in which African Americans pledged to work for both victory overseas and social justice at home. Pauli Murray, a student at Howard University, recalled that when the male students joined the service, those who were left behind targeted a small segregated cafeteria in the heart of a black neighborhood "which had long been a source of mortification for unsuspecting Negroes." While volunteers sat in at the tables, demonstrators carried signs reading "We Die Together, Why Can't We Eat Together?" The owner was forced to close for the day, and eventually the restaurant was integrated. But the administration at Howard University, frightened by all the publicity, forced the students to cease and desist, and the restaurant quickly went back to its old ways. (A decade later, when black college students in the South began sitting in at lunch counters to force integration, Murray realized that she had been a woman ahead of her time.)

It was not until 1944, under heavy pressure from Eleanor Roosevelt, that black women were welcomed into the military. (Elsie Oliver, who unsuccessfully petitioned to be among the African American women assigned overseas, called the First Lady's office and left a message registering her complaint. Mrs. Roosevelt was on the phone within the hour and Oliver was shipped out the same day.) The WAC eventually enlisted 4,000 black recruits. Despite its grave shortage of nurses, the army was reluctant to take black RNs—particularly if they would be treating white soldiers. The corps eventually took 500 and then enraged the black community by assigning some of them to work in prisoner-of-war camps.

The military's policy—articulated as seldom as possible—was to give the black women separate but equal accommodations. Major Harriet West, the highest-ranking black in the WAC, felt that the African American women in the army could have borne the segregation better if people had not insisted on rubbing her soldiers' faces in their status. When the first class of the WAC Officer Candidate School arrived at the reception center at Fort Des Moines, the women were waiting to be assigned quarters when a male officer walked in and ordered "all the colored girls" to move over to one isolated corner of the room. A black journalist traveling with Major West to Fort McClellan in Alabama reported that they were required to travel in "a dirty, segregated coach" where Major West was insulted by a white conductor "whom she had asked to hand her baggage from the train." At Fort Devens, black women who had been trained as medical technicians were assigned to work as orderlies, scrubbing floors and windows. When they complained to the commander of the hospital, he said that they were there to do the dirty work. Nearly sixty black WACs refused to report to work in protest, and though most were persuaded to give up rather quickly, four continued their work stoppage and were court-martialed and sentenced to a year of hard labor. The resultant outcry forced the War Department to reverse the verdict, reinstate the WACs, and transfer them to a new post.

In civilian life, black women moved into whatever slots white women left. They often took over low-paying jobs like elevator operators and car cleaners on railroads, but whatever the job, they saw it as an improvement over domestic work. "My sister always said that Hitler was the one that got us out of the white folks' kitchen," said Tina Hill, a Los Angeles aircraft plant worker. The white housewives who were left scrambling for domestic help blamed the government—particularly the Roosevelts—for encouraging the black women to look for higher-paying opportunities. Rumors were rife, particularly in the South, of secret "Eleanor Clubs" that encouraged former servants to flaunt their new equality by showing up at the grocery store when their ex-mistresses were doing their shopping.

## "IT JUST ENDED OVERNIGHT"

"Ohh, the beautiful celebrations when the war ended," said Peggy Terry, the defense plant worker from Paducah, Kentucky. "Everybody was downtown in the pouring rain and we were dancing. We took off our shoes and put 'em in our purse. We were so happy."

When the war ended, the nation welcomed the men home and began enforcing the promise the women workers had made—or the country had decided they had made—to give up their jobs for the returning soldiers. "They always got priority and they would replace us, one by one," recalled Rose Kaminski. "Finally the fellow that I replaced came, and I remember him coming back and I was laid off. It didn't bother me. . . . I think we kind of looked forward to it." But after a few years of "normal living" and the birth of another daughter, she called her old boss and took a "temporary" job at the factory. It wound up lasting thirty-one years.

Three million women left the workforce in 1946, and many of the younger ones were indeed eager to set up households and get on with the postwar baby boom. But most of the women who had worked during the war were older, with children who no longer needed them at home. They either needed to supplement their husbands' pay or they were the sole support of their families. Surveys showed 70 percent of the female war workers wanted to stay at their jobs, but few were given the choice. "It just ended overnight," said Marye Stumph, a single mother who had made three times her previous salary as an assembler at an aircraft factory. She was on weeklong vacation in New Mexico when the war ended, and by the time she returned to her home in California, a telegram was waiting "saying that the job was over. A ten-word telegram." William Mulcahy, who supervised women at an electric parts assembly factory in Camden, remembered "the day after the war ended. We met the girls at the door, and they were lined up all the way down Market Street to the old movie theater about eight blocks away and we handed them a slip to go over to personnel and get their severance pay. We didn't even allow them in the building, all these women with whom I had become so close, who had worked seven days a week for years and had been commended so many times by the navy for the work they were doing."

It was inevitable that many of the women would lose their jobs—the defense industry was shutting down, and the employees that the heavily unionized factories were going to keep were the most senior, male workers. The enlisted men had been guaranteed their jobs back, and sentiment for hiring the men was so high that new male applicants were given jobs over women with seniority. The public relations machine that had gotten the women into the factory worked double-time getting them out. But as usual, the national theory about a woman's place ignored the fact that many women didn't have husbands to go out and work for them. "I happen to be a widow with a mother and son to support," Ottilie Juliet Gattus wrote to President Truman after she was laid off from a job at Grumman Aircraft. "I am a lathe hand . . . classified as skilled labor, but simply because I happen to be a woman I am not wanted."

If defense work did not lead to a career for most women, it was still a transforming experience for many. Peggy Terry, the Kentucky woman who worked in a shell factory, had so little knowledge of the world that she barely understood what being at war meant. Her horizons expanded when she wound up in Michigan, working at a plant with a large population of Polish workers. "They were the first people

I'd ever known that were any different from me," she told journalist Studs Terkel years later. "A whole new world just opened up. . . . I believe the war was the beginning of my seeing things."

The country thought of itself as far more tolerant after the war, and in many ways it was. The dozens of movies about army squadrons made up of Italian, Irish, Jewish, and Anglo-Saxon soldiers reflected an image of America that society wanted to believe in. It was glorious, but of course only half a picture—blacks, Hispanics, and Asians were generally left out of the new egalitarian view of the American community. Minority women were doubly ignored, but they had been changed by the war, too, and to see the glass as empty would be to dismiss their accomplishments. "We got a chance to go places we had never been able to go before," said Sarah Killingsworth, who had begun the war cleaning ladies' rooms at an aircraft plant, then went on to open her own restaurant in Los Angeles. "For a person that grew up and knew nothing but hard times to get out on my own at eighteen years old and make a decent living and still make a decent person out of myself, I really am proud of me."

Despite the universal desire to return to "normal," things had changed. The old pattern, in which women worked until they married and then never again, was broken. And the women who went back to their homes, never to enter the job market again, were different, too. "They realized that they were capable of doing something more than cook a meal," concluded Dellie Hahne, the music teacher, who remembered decades later when she went to Sunday dinner at an older woman's home and listened while "she and her sister . . . were talking about the best way to keep their drill sharp in the factory. I had never heard anything like this in my life. It was just marvelous. I was tickled."

# 18

# The Fifties:
# Life at the Far End of the Pendulum

## "I DREAMED I STOPPED TRAFFIC
## IN MY MAIDENFORM BRA"

In the era after World War II, American women embraced discomfort in a big way. Their full skirts came to midcalf and were held out with stiff petticoats made of taffeta or some equally itchy fabric. Or they wore equally long formfitting sheathes that constrained the wearer to take only tiny steps as she tottered along in her 4-inch stiletto-heeled shoes. Their hair had to be set on huge rollers, and girls went to sleep wearing what must have felt like a helmet full of tin cans. Hairstyles kept getting bigger and stiffer, requiring tons of spray to keep them in shape. There were legends—possibly invented by exasperated mothers—about girls who died of blood poisoning when insects made nests inside their overly lacquered mounds of hair.

Breasts were supposed to be large, high, and pointy, which for all but the most anatomically gifted meant either a lot of padding or a lot of bra. Women thought quite a lot about bras in the fifties; even undeveloped preteens wanted to wear them, and manufacturers readily complied by inventing the utterly useless but extremely popular "training bra." Strapless evening gowns required strapless bras, an engineering challenge for the well-endowed women who were the fashion ideal. Industrialist Howard Hughes put some of his aircraft engineers to work on a cantilevered bra that lifted and separated the breasts, which his friend actress Jane Russell wore to great effect. Russell became a big star in the fifties, just when the breast was beginning its career as the most important part of the female anatomy. One of the era's most famous ad campaigns showed women clad only in bras from the waist up, engaged in all sorts of activities from bullfighting to dog-walking. "I dreamed I stopped traffic in my Maidenform bra," announced the copy below a picture of a half-clothed policewoman. The bras in question were such formidable foundation garments that the impact was anything but sensual. Nevertheless, students in some Catholic girls schools, under vigorous encouragement from their teachers, started letter-writing campaigns protesting that the Maidenform ads gave teenage boys impure thoughts.

Girdles, which had been in short supply during the war years, came back in force, along with the merry widow, a boned, laced corset. The idea was to be both curvy and armored. "In order to wear the sheath dresses of the fifties without a bulge we sweltered in Playtex tubes and zipped and hooked ourselves into the iron virgins that would have daunted any Victorian maiden," wrote Benita Eisler, who came of age in the fifties and recalled seeing "the red welts and grooves on the willowy torso of my roommate" as she unbound herself after a date.

Looking back, it's easy to see the clothes as a metaphor for everything else that happened to women in postwar America. (The experiences we equate with the fifties actually stretched, for most people, from 1945 to the mid-1960s—a twenty-year decade.) After the eras of the settlement house workers and the flappers, after having survived the Depression and kept the economy running in World War II, women seemed to have been catapulted back in time to the nineteenth century, to the cult of the True Woman and the corset that went with it. They dropped out of college, married early, and read women's magazines that urged them to hold on to their husband's love by pretending to be dumb and helpless. They were isolated in the suburbs, marooned in a world of women and children while their husbands drove off every day to careers in the city. They came down with mysterious ailments, like the ladies in the pre–Civil War period. TV ads warned of a disease called "tired blood," which only a daily dose of Geritol could cure. Women looking for a more modern remedy took to the new wonder drug called tranquilizers.

But plenty of women worked outside the home during the postwar era. Within a few years of the end of hostilities in 1945, employment of women was just about back to its wartime peak, and still climbing. However, the jobs they were holding down were not, for the most part, careers. Women were typists and sales clerks and telephone operators and receptionists, doing the low-paying and unglamorous work no returning veteran would want to snatch. The housewives who moved to the suburbs felt, for the most part, that they were escaping a slavery to the time clock and setting up their own shops in brand-new houses filled with new conveniences. They might have resembled Victorian True Women, but they were also a little like those Pilgrim wives who yearned to get out of the fields and into the kitchen.

The explosive economy, combined with the generous benefits the government doled out to returning veterans, made it possible for very young couples to marry while the husband was still in school, buy a house without any savings, have several babies right away, and continually ratchet up their standard of living, all on the income from a single salary. It was a phenomenon that couldn't be repeated by the generations that followed, whether they wanted to or not. But when people in the fifties said everybody was doing it, they really did mean almost everybody. Until World War II, only a relatively small slice of the population actually had any options except toiling endlessly on a farm or factory. Then suddenly, 60 percent of American families managed to become home-owning members of the middle class. *Ebony* enthused "Goodbye Mammy, Hello Mom" as it celebrated the ability of African American women to stay in their own kitchens rather than cleaning someone else's. It all seemed almost too good to be true; nearly everybody wanted to take advantage of the opportunity to create families fast, before another disaster overtook the country, like the war or the Depression. And if anybody wondered what that new disaster might be, all they had to do was look at the magazine articles that showed how to construct a do-it-yourself bomb shelter.

The pendulum of modern American social history has a tendency to swing wide. In the 1950s, people were reacting against those editorial writers in the 1930s who felt doing without was good for your soul, and the government propagandists in the war years who expected women to work in steel mills and paint lines down the back of their legs instead of wearing stockings. People wanted large cars, large appliances, and large families. The number of couples with four children or more tripled, and the nation's population growth rate was suddenly rivaling India's. The very young wives and mothers of the postwar era flung themselves into homemaking, trading recipes for green bean casserole made with Campbell's cream of mushroom soup, worrying about the whiteness of their laundry and the greenness of their lawns, and consulting Dr. Benjamin Spock's *Common Sense Book of Baby and Child Care* several times a day.

## "I MADE TERRIFIC FRIENDS RIGHT AWAY"

The suburbs were a new phenomenon. Never before, anywhere on the planet, had so many people had the opportunity to buy their own homes, each attached to a little plot of land, averaging a fifth to a tenth of an acre. Everything was new—even the trees looked raw and unfinished, hardly more than gangly twigs sprouting hopefully from newly seeded front lawns. In the early days, the suburbs were nothing but houses, as far as the eye could see, and most families had only one car, which the husbands took to work, leaving the wives stranded in a vast sea of Cape Cods, ranches, or colonials. In an area west of Cincinnati, an entrepreneurial merchant gutted an old school bus, put in shelves, and stocked them with groceries, painted "Art's Rolling Food Store" on the side, and brought the corner deli to the home-bound wives.

The new neighborhoods were generally racially and sometimes religiously homogeneous. That had some terrible social consequences over the long run—African Americans and other minorities were cut off from the chance to buy that first low-cost, low-interest home which formed the basis of the economic fortune of so many white families. But over the short term, the lack of diversity made it easy for the suburban wives to form quick friendships. "Our lives are held closely together because most of us are within the same age bracket, in similar income groups, live in almost identical houses and have common problems," said the first issue of a community newspaper in Levittown, the famous 17,000-home development in Long Island. The basic Levittown house became a model for developments around the country and it was far from opulent—a four-room Cape Cod with one bathroom and about 750 square feet of living space. But it looked like a castle to women who had been stuck living with relatives or struggling to find an apartment in the postwar housing shortage.

The 1950s suburbs gave birth to a new community of women, as rich in its own way as the ones that preceded it during the war, or around the turn of the century. The housewives looked after each other's children, fed each other's dogs, talked endlessly over coffee in the afternoon or highballs at the end of the day, and entertained each other at neighborhood backyard barbecues or more formal cocktail parties. "I made terrific friends right away through the children," said Carol Cornwall, a suburban housewife in the 1950s who was inter-viewed by Benita Eisler. But there were few escape routes for those who failed to fit in. "I was as miserable there as I've ever been in my life," another woman told Eisler. There were few organizations except the PTA and the churches, and it was a dicey time politically, when fear of the Communist menace made it dangerous for people to hold anything but the most pedestrian views about public affairs. For the excluded or unsociable, the enforced sameness of the suburbs could be mind-bending. (In Levittown, outdoor clothes drying was permitted only on specially designed, collapsible racks.) The heroine of Sinclair Lewis's 1922 novel *Main Street* who had been driven over the edge by the lack of stimulation in Gopher Prairie, Minnesota, had nothing on the unhappy housewife who landed in Orange County, California, or Green Township, Ohio, and discovered she didn't fit in.

## "IF MY WIFE HAD HER WAY
## I THINK WE'D ALL BREATHE IN UNISON"

A century had passed since middle-class families needed to work together as a unit to support themselves. But in the 1950s, husbands, wives, and children were urged to do everything together *except* work. People who wanted to see a movie bundled their children into the car and went to the drive-in. Family restaurants specialized in child-friendly menus, and the opening of Disneyland in 1955 drove home the idea that vacations were meant to be taken as a group. "Emphasis on family members' sharing every aspect of one another's lives has risen to an extraordinary pitch in the last year or so," noted Dorothy Barclay, a columnist for the *The New York Times Magazine* in 1956. She quoted one male friend complaining that at his house "we already read, wash dishes, clean the car, paint, go hiking and fix the furnace together. . . . If my wife had her way I think we'd all breathe in unison."

It was what *McCall's* magazine loudly and insistently referred to as "Togetherness." Wives were supposed to take an interest in their husband's work, and the men were also supposed to get involved in household matters that had always before been designated as womanly concerns. The ideal father went shopping for furniture with his wife, and discussed the color schemes of the house and the menu plans for dinner parties. He changed babies' diapers—at least in emergencies—and listened to children's homework lessons. Dr. Bruno Bettelheim, surveying the changing scene in *Parents* magazine, worried that children would get the impression that their fathers didn't have to work hard to bring home the bacon. "When the father comes home and is tacitly expected (or openly asked) to take over the care of the children . . . the impression is conveyed to the child that he has been more or less loafing all day and Mother now expects him to start on the serious tasks."

In reality, few suburban fathers really shared the household duties. Generally the role celebrated for Dad was that of recreation director. "Adventure is a father's meat. Poor mother is so loaded down with seeing that clothes are clean and food is cooked, she doesn't have much head for thinking up exciting things for the family to do. Here's where father can be of help," wrote the director of the Louisiana Society for Mental Health in *The New York Times Magazine*. However illusory the husbands' real contribution was, however, it was a huge shift for men to be expected to get involved at all.

All this was happening at the same time that another big change was under way: Housekeeping was getting easier. Manufacturers had finally perfected the automatic washing machine and the dryer—the long-awaited inventions that would soak and wash and rinse and dry clothing all by themselves. Ever since humans developed an interest in clean clothing, women had been forced to devote at least one full day a week to the laundry. Suddenly, it became less of a project than something you did any old time, sort of with the back of your hand. The washboard, along with the icebox and the handheld eggbeater, were consigned to the farmhouses or to the old urban tenements you might revisit for fun on the *Honeymooners* TV series. Americans spent a disproportionate amount of their disposable income on appliances in the 1950s—everybody wanted the biggest and the best, preferably in the new colors that were suddenly available, like avocado. Betty Furness, who became a celebrity due to her talent for demonstrating refrigerators and dishwashers on television, noticed that the appliances kept getting larger. When she made the much-heralded Westinghouse commercials that ran during coverage of the 1952 presidential conventions—Furness was on the air three times an hour, more than the candidates—the refrigerators only came up to her shoulder. But by the time the Republicans nominated Dwight Eisenhower for a second term in 1956, the new models were looming over her. All of them featured bigger freezers, the better to store all the new frozen foods that could be turned into full dinners with only a bit of reheating.

## "ALL THE GANG HAS STARTED
## THEIR OWN SETS OF STERLING"

In 1950, Elizabeth Taylor, the beautiful child star of the 1940s, married for the first time at age nineteen. Like almost half of the American women of the period, she was a bride before her twentieth birthday—although Taylor had to have her first baby before the movie magazines would decree her "A Woman at Last." People had begun marrying earlier during the war years, but after 1945, the trend really picked up steam. "Not so long ago girls were expelled from college for marrying; now girls feel hopeless if they haven't a marriage at least in sight by commencement time," wrote Sidonie Gruenberg, a psychiatrist, in *The New York Times Magazine.* Citing the postwar shortage of males, Gruenberg added chillingly: "A girl who hasn't a man in sight by the time she is 20 is not altogether wrong in fearing that she may never get married." *Esquire* reported that senior college women "talk about a career but they don't mean it. Let them have six dates with one boy—they'll have him talking about compatibility and the names of their five children." (The undercurrent of male resentment throughout the 1950s was mined most successfully by *Playboy,* which was founded in 1953. Its theme was that women were unproductive leeches plotting to trap unsuspecting men into a life of white-collar servitude and deprive them of their natural right to life as free and swinging bachelors.)

Postwar women broke a century-long American trend toward later marriages and fewer children. The stampede to the altar was so intense that junior high school students had already chosen their silverware pattern. "All the gang has started their own sets of sterling. We're real keen about it," one teenager told a marketing researcher. Suzie Slattery, a seventeen-year-old California girl chosen by *Life* as the typical teen consumer, liked to spend her summer days wandering through department stores with her mother "picking out frocks or furnishings for her room or silver and expensive crockery for the hope chest she has already started." Once married, they usually had their children—an average of 3.2—quickly, completing their family before their thirtieth birthday.

The proportion of women in college plummeted, dwarfed by the arrival of 6 million male veterans whose tuition was paid on the GI bill. Soon, only 35 percent of the college population was female, and many of the girls who arrived as freshmen dropped out before graduating. Those who did finish school generally married before the ink on the diploma was dry—a professor at Smith complained that he had to cancel his final seminar for the senior honors students because it conflicted with too many bridal showers. The major point of attending college, for most white women at least, was not earning a degree or getting a marketable skill, but finding a husband who had a degree or skill. (This wasn't true of black women. Although relatively few went to college, virtually all who went graduated. "The thing you *didn't* do was quit college or quit work. You were not going to raise a family on one black man's salary," said a woman who later became a school principal in New Jersey.) Male students, although intensely focused on preparing for a career, were not particularly interested in intellectual pursuits, either. A survey in 1958 found that 72 percent of college students felt the main purpose of their education was to acquire well-rounded personalities.

Coeds seemed bent on avoiding anything that would interrupt their fast transition from school to matrimony. The wife of a college sociology professor found that when she and her friends urged her husband's female students to get a little life experience before settling down, they were "characterized as bitter, unromantic old witches, in an affectionate kind of way." The female professors who had survived the shock of trying to teach flappers in the 1920s were horrified once again. "I felt increasingly that something had gone wrong with our young women of college age. . . . I noted it with anger and alarm," said a professor of English at the University of Illinois. But college administrators were willing to go with the flow. The male president of Radcliffe greeted freshmen by telling them their years of college "would prepare them to be splendid wives and mothers and their reward might be to marry Harvard men." Lynn White Jr., the president of a women's college in Oakland, California, proposed in 1950 that the curriculum be adapted to reflect the students' new, postwar interests by including courses in clothing, interior decorating, and "the theory and preparation of a Basque paella, a well-marinated shish-kebab and lamb kidneys sautéed in sherry."

## "YOU'RE NOT GOING TO LIKE IT, GEORGE. SHE'S AN OLD MAID."

Just after the war ended, that future Christmas classic *It's a Wonderful Life* was released. It told the story of George Bailey, an average man who ran a small-town savings and loan. He was given the chance to see what life in his hometown would have been like if he had never been born, and everything was terrible. The town was a slum, his old friends were crooks or drunks, and a nice girl he'd befriended had become a prostitute. But the worst fate of all had befallen his wife. "You're not going to like it, George. She's an old maid. She never married," his guardian angel says in tones that suggest, at minimum, leprosy.

The nation went to war against singleness in the postwar era. In one much-quoted survey, less than 10 percent of the public believed an unmarried person could be happy. The 1947 best-seller *Modern Woman: The Lost Sex* urged that spinsters be barred from teaching children on the grounds of "emotional incompetence." It was the ultimate example of the pendulum swinging—instead of prohibiting the employment of married women as teachers, society now wanted marriage to be mandatory. "A great many children have unquestionably been damaged psychologically by the spinster teacher who cannot be an adequate model of a complete woman either for boys or girls," the authors argued. (The National Woman's Party, Alice Paul's old group that was still fighting the good fight for an Equal Rights Amendment, claimed that *Modern Woman* set the movement back ten years.) An editor at *Mademoiselle* told Betty Friedan that the college girls who came to work as guest editors no longer seemed thrilled at the chance to get into publishing. "The girls we bring in now . . . seem almost to pity us," she said. "Because we're career women, I suppose." She added that not one of the twenty recent guest editors had planned to work at all.

The fear of winding up without a man was wildly out of proportion to reality. This was a time, after all, when more than 95 percent of the women who came of age got married—more than any other American generation. "Except for the sick, the badly crippled, the deformed, the emotionally warped and the mentally defective, almost everyone has an opportunity to marry," said the author of a college textbook on marriage. Still, the fear of not being chosen led teenagers to commit to one another—at least temporarily—at a very early age. "All the guys go steady 'cause it wouldn't be right to leave your best girl home on Saturday night," sang the Beach Boys in 1962, when most of America was still deep into the culture of the 1950s. Instead of a long stag line waiting to break in at the dance, or a string of "beaux" hoping for a date, the proof of a girl's popularity was a pin or ring from one desirable teenage boy who was pledged to date her, and only her, and protect her against the horrors of homebound Saturdays. Some girls began going steady as early as twelve years old and started shopping around for a boyfriend much earlier. A study in one Pennsylvania school district in 1961 found that 40 percent of the fifth graders were already dating.

Girls in earlier generations had been able to keep sexual pressure at bay with a fast turnover of boyfriends. But for teenagers in the 1950s, who were engaging in necking and petting every weekend with the same person, the dangers were obvious. There was still a strong cultural bias in favor of girls keeping their virginity—Carol Cornwall, who grew up in the 1950s, recalled constantly being told "If you go all the way with someone, he'll leave you and marry a 'nice' girl." The girl was supposed to keep her boyfriend under control, and adult authorities continued to delude themselves that all she had to do was send out the right signals. "No boy—no matter whether he's Head of the Wolfpack—will persist in affectionate attentions if he gets a *positively negative* response," said *Senior Scholastic* assuredly. But in the real world, girls spent a great deal of their time in an exhausting and dispiriting battle to keep their steadies from going too far. "He'd push, push, push. I'd say stop, stop, stop," said one veteran of the backseat wars. The goal, for many girls, was "technical virginity," in which they managed to avoid penetration while allowing their boyfriends every other imaginable liberty. An obvious answer to the sexual pressures involved in going steady was the altar. In the end, it's hard to say whether the desire for early marriage triggered the going steady or the going steady triggered the need for early marriage.

Women weren't actually following different rules than they had in other recent generations—although the amount of activity the technical virgins put up with may have been a new wrinkle. Alfred Kinsey, a bookish and rather sweetly retiring biologist, had spent the war years conducting surveys on the sexuality of American men and women. In 1953, he released his second groundbreaking study, *Sexual Behavior in the Human Female,* which reported that about half of white American women had sex before they married—mainly with the men who would become their husbands—and that a quarter committed adultery afterward. "It is impossible to estimate the damage this book will do to the already deteriorating morals of America," said the Reverend Billy Graham. The thing that seemed to trouble critics most was that Kinsey reported his findings in dry academic prose without editorial outrage.

Birth control, mainly in the form of diaphragms, was readily available to married women in most states, but few doctors prescribed them for unmarried girls, and few unmarried girls would have asked. "To go out and actually get it would mean that I *planned* to do these things," explained one woman who had been sexually active as a teenager. "Therapeutic" abortions had been reasonably easy to obtain in hospitals in the 1930s, under the theory that a pregnancy was dangerous to the woman's mental health. But after the war, hospitals became much more rigorous in monitoring what their doctors were up to. As a result, an estimated 250,000 to 1 million illegal abortions were performed every year, in everything from doctors' offices to tables in the back room of a mysterious man or woman with no medical training. (The numbers are actually not much more than educated guesses, although the Kinsey report estimated that 24 percent of married women had had an abortion at one time or another.)

## "IT WAS . . . SO OUT OF CONTROL"

The physical ideal for 1950s women was Marilyn Monroe, the ultimate blond bombshell. (Americans developed a weird tendency to connect nuclear explosions with sexy women. A photograph of actress Rita Hayworth was attached to the hydrogen bomb dropped in a test on the Bikini Islands, and a swimsuit designer, inspired by the event, named his new skimpy bathing suit in honor of the site of the blast.) But women did not like Monroe nearly as much as men did. Teenage girls, who were among the most avid moviegoers, preferred actresses who were small and childlike—like Debbie Reynolds in *Tammy and the Bachelor* or Sandra Dee in *Gidget,* the movie in which a "gidget" is defined as part girl, part midget. They played perky young women who the leading man overlooked during the early action, when he lusted after a larger, older, and more aggressive seductress who failed to see his true inner worth. The audience waited for that moment of recognition in which the wealthy bachelor or the handsome fraternity boy suddenly realized that the little bit of a thing in the corner was really the right woman for him. This theme was replayed in the girls' novels of the era, which went from being about sleuthing to being about dating.

In 1956, the average teenager had an income of $10.55 a week, mainly from her allowance and jobs like baby-sitting. It was the equivalent of an entire family's disposable income in 1940, and it gave very young girls an unprecedented power as consumers. Record companies became obsessed with finding young male singers like Elvis Presley, who could cause teenage girls to scream and buy records. Presley was actually far from the first performer to send girls into fits of sexual sublimation. Back in the nineteenth century, when Ignacy Paderewski played the piano, one observer reported, "The women would leave their seats and press forward like a besieging army. They'd tear off their corsage bouquets and fling them, hundreds of bunches of violets, on the stage." During World War II, teenage girls terrified their parents by writhing and screaming over Frank Sinatra; and in the early

1950s, Johnny Ray, a slight young singer who had to wear a large hearing aid because of his partial deafness, became a sensation by weeping hysterically when he sang. (His hits tended to have names like "Cry.") The more parents expressed outrage about these heroes, the more enticing the whole thing became. When Presley was drafted into the army, he was succeeded by a veritable army of housebroken boy singers with names like Ricky and Bobby and Frankie who were selected almost exclusively because of their ability to send young girls into paroxysms. The sixteen-year-old Fabian Forte was discovered while his father was being rushed to the hospital with a heart attack and a record promoter, attracted by the crowd and the ambulance, decided the boy looked like a teenage idol. His handlers produced his records by stitching together bits and pieces of Fabian's singing until they got one recording in which he hit all the right notes. "I could hardly recognize my own voice," he said later. The terrified teenager was transported from one appearance to another, where he lip-synched his current record in front of a room full of shrieking girls. "It was terrible," the middle-aged Fabian recalled years later. "You'd think it would be flattering but it was . . . so out of control."

## "SOME VERY SENSIBLE GIRL FROM A NICE FAMILY"

Television was the single greatest cultural influence of the postwar era, and it invaded the country almost overnight. In 1946, there were only 7,000 TVs in use in the country, but by 1950, there were 4.4 million, and Americans were buying 5 million new sets every year. The great success of early television was *I Love Lucy,* which debuted in 1951 and quickly became such a hit that Marshall Field's, the big Chicago department store, moved its sale night from Monday, when *Lucy* was broadcast. "We love Lucy, too," the announcement conceded. The series starred Lucille Ball, a semisuccessful movie actress with a talent for physical comedy, and her real-life husband, Desi Arnaz, a Cuban American bandleader. Many of the plots turned around Lucy's desire to work—to "be in the show" at Desi's nightclub or to pursue a harebrained plan to make money. "I want a wife who's just a wife," her husband protested in the first episode. Lucy was virtually the only TV wife who didn't seem entirely content at home. But her attempts at working always led to disaster, and by the final curtain she had learned her lesson, at least until next week. A few of the other early TV series involved single women who worked, in jobs like secretary or teacher, although it was always a given that they were hoping to get married, with varying degrees of desperation.

Television in the fifties was famously bland, particularly when it came to situation comedies. Married couples always slept in twin beds, with no suggestion that they ever had sex. When Lucille Ball became pregnant in real life, scriptwriters wrote her condition into the series, although the word *pregnant* was barred from the air. (Lucy was only referred to as "expectant.") CBS got a panel of clergymen to vet the scripts, and in 1953, 44 million people watched the episode when Lucy had her baby—twice as many as watched Dwight Eisenhower's inauguration the next day.

As the decade went on, the comedies all focused on families, and the mother never did much but help her children get out of innocuous jams. In *Leave It to Beaver,* June Cleaver was famous for wearing high heels and pearls while she worked in the kitchen. When her husband asked June what kind of girl she would like to see their older son, Wally, marry someday, June replied: "Oh, some very sensible girl from a nice family . . . who's a good cook and can keep a nice house and see that he's happy." In *Father Knows Best,* Kathy, the tomboy, discovered how to act dependent and helpless after Dad explained: "The worst thing you can do is try to beat a man at his own game." Betty, the older daughter, learned that pretty girls aren't hired for jobs with a future because they'll leave soon to get married. She happily gave up her hopes for a career in marketing to model bridal gowns. The adventure shows hardly had any women in them at all. The great TV craze of the late 1950s was westerns, which were invariably about men who were unmarried or widowed—sometimes with a young son, but never a daughter. The hero occasionally acquired a girlfriend or fiancée, but she generally died suddenly before the final commercial. The near-universal message of television programming was that girls never got to do anything interesting, and then grew up to be women who faded into the woodwork completely.

## "WOMEN CAN STAND THE SHOCK AND STRAIN OF AN ATOMIC EXPLOSION"

Jean Wood Fuller, one of the most enthusiastic members of the federal Civil Defense Administration, arranged to be one of several "female guinea pigs" when the military tested a nuclear bomb in the Nevada desert in 1955. "The normal feminine excitement prevailed amongst us all," reported Fuller, who was sitting in a trench less than two miles from the blast. But the experience, she told reporters, "shows conclusively that women can stand the shock and strain of an atomic explosion just as well as men." She praised the beauty of the mushroom cloud and called the experience "terrific, interesting and exciting." Fuller's mission in life was to carve out a role for women in nuclear preparedness. Church women who were used to putting on big dinners were "just perfect naturals for our mass feeding groups," she theorized. She urged women to learn home nursing, to play civil defense games with their children, and to stock their bomb shelters with home goods like "grandma's pantry."

The Cold War and anti-Communism overshadowed almost every other aspect of public life in the 1950s. During his famous "kitchen debate" with Soviet Premier Nikita Khruschev in 1959, Vice President Richard Nixon equated social progress with kitchen appliances, and J. Edgar Hoover repeatedly reminded American women that the only good female was a domestic female. Partly as a result of the us-versus-them mood of the era, the country developed a very strong, and unpleasant, tendency to regard anything outside the norm as subversive. The national impulse toward marriage and family was coupled with a wild-eyed rejection of any different path. "You all know women who lack warmth, tenderness, delicacy and sweetness. . . . They do not want to be homemakers, they do not want to be mothers. They want to be presiding judges of the Supreme Court," said a psychiatrist lecturing in New York, who went on to warn that such women were in danger of toppling into frigidity, homosexuality, and psychosis.

The worst side of the 1950s, the fear of being different or of anyone else who might look different, was epitomized by Senator Joseph McCarthy, who terrorized the country with his wildly imaginative claims of secret cells of Communists in every branch of the government. The other members of Congress were as frightened of McCarthy as the hapless public servants whose careers he ruined. The first elected official with the spine to stand up to him was Margaret Chase Smith, a Republican from Maine and the only woman in the U.S. Senate. "Freedom of speech is not what it used to be in America," she told the Senate. "It has been so abused by some that it is not exercised by others." Bernard Baruch, an adviser to several generations of national leaders, said if the speech had been made by a man, he would have been the next president.

Smith got into Congress in the normal way, succeeding her late husband in the House. She served during World War II, when the number of women in Congress was in single digits, and the men did most of their business in drinking sessions in the leaders' offices, in the gym, and other places where women weren't invited to go. During meetings of the Naval Affairs Committee, one of the staff members took Smith for a walk after dinner so that the other legislators could have a break from the discomfort of female company. She had to stand in line in the public bathroom on the floor below the Senate because she wasn't allowed in the lounge off the Senate chambers. But she developed a reputation for meticulous preparation and unflappable grit. During a flight home from a fact-finding tour of Europe, when the plane experienced trouble and the legislators were given life jackets and told to prepare for the worst, Smith brought out harmonicas she had purchased for her nieces and nephews and persuaded the other congressmen to start singing. When the Maine newspapers went into raptures over the story of her bravery, Smith told them she had been as frightened as the others. "Only as a woman I couldn't have the luxury of showing my fear."

A widow with no children, Smith managed to soldier on through the fifties, but there was no popular sense that any other women should want to emulate her. The women's magazines embarked on a twenty-year campaign dedicated to the proposition that American women were interested in absolutely nothing except housekeeping, child care, and their marital sex life and that they needed to protect all those good things by following a rule of utter submissiveness. These magazines had never been particularly profound, but never before had they reflected such a narrow view of what women were like. Betty Friedan theorized that they had been transformed when many women writers dropped out to have children after the war ended and were replaced by males who poured their own vision of domestic bliss into the copy. *Ladies' Home Journal*'s celebration of a woman who said she "never tried to enter into a discussion when the men were talking" and "never disputed her husband in anything" echoed those early-nineteenth-century southern women who were taught to repress their own opinions and sit erect on a straight-backed chair in silence while the menfolk talked about crops. The heroine in one 1958 *McCall's* story almost lost her husband to an attractive widow with a genius for looking helpless. The wife saved the day by becoming terrified of a noise in the night, and once she was clinging appropriately, marital harmony was restored. The magazines ran endless short stories about housewives who find themselves momentarily unhappy until they learn once again the lesson of docility, the same way that poor Lucy learned over and over that she was not allowed to be in the show.

## "THEY'VE MESSED WITH THE WRONG ONE NOW"

Black communities that had sent their sons to die in two world wars were losing patience with the rigors of the Jim Crow South, and they started to fight back, with court suits and, later, direct action in which they dared officials to arrest them for exercising their rights as Americans. It was fitting that the first of the civil rights struggles to capture the nation's attention involved a woman on a bus. Ever since the Civil War, the humiliation of boarding a train in one's best clothes, only to be herded off to a dirty and smelly segregated car, and the frustration of having to wait for a "colored-only" trolley while cars for whites sailed by, had caused black women to explode in acts of defiance. Harriet Tubman, Sojourner Truth, Ida Wells-Barnett, and dozens of less famous names had gone to court—or to jail—over their right to equal use of public transit. It was the sorest of sore points, and if there was a perfect example of the way segregated transportation demeaned black patrons, it was the Montgomery, Alabama, bus system. Two-thirds of its patrons were black, and most of them were women who traveled to and from jobs as domestic workers. The first ten rows of seats were reserved for whites. Beyond that, the bus driver made up the rules, backed by the authority of a gun. "Some drivers made black passengers step in the front door and pay their fare, and then we had to get off and go around to the black door and get on," said Rosa Parks. "Often before the black passengers got around to the back door, the bus would take off without them." If the bus was crowded and a white passenger was forced to stand, the drivers made one of the black riders give up a seat, even if an elderly woman was giving way to a white teenager.

The arbitrariness of it all made degrading incidents inevitable. Jo Ann Robinson, a teacher at the local black college, Alabama State, was one of the lucky people who owned a car and never had to ride the bus. But she decided to leave her car home when she went to catch a flight to Cleveland for the 1949 Christmas holidays. She was "happy as I had ever been in my life" when she dragged her two suitcases on the bus, which had only two other passengers, and unthinkingly walked back and took a seat in the fifth row. The driver stopped the bus and screamed at her to get up, sending her, weeping, out the door. The experience haunted her for the rest of her life. Robinson became a member of the Women's Political Council, an organization of middle-class black Montgomery residents that had been pressing the city to end some of its most hated practices. By 1955, the women were ready to take on the bus system, mobilized by the arrest of two black teenage girls who had been dragged off to jail for refusing to obey drivers' dictates. They organized for a bus boycott, preparing fliers and press releases, but Montgomery's black male leaders found the girls too socially downscale to qualify as proper test cases. Then in early December, Rosa Parks, an eminently respectable seamstress, the kind of lady who wore white gloves and rimless glasses, was riding home from work when the white section of the bus filled up and the driver told her to move. She stayed where she was and the driver threatened to have her arrested.

"You may do that," Parks said.

The legend that built up around the incident, which would turn out to be one of the critical events in the American civil rights movement, was that Parks, a simple woman exhausted from a hard day at work, took her stand because she was tired. In truth, she had been moving toward that moment of defiance all her life. "The only tired I was, was tired of giving in," she explained later. Parks was the product of everything that had happened to black women in American history, and one of the results was that she may have had as many white ancestors as black. Her family tree included a Yankee soldier and at least one Indian. Her grandmother's father was a Scotch-Irish indentured servant who married an African American slave. Her grandfather was the son of a white plantation owner and a mixed-blood slave, both of whom died when he was young. The overseer treated the orphan boy with particular brutality, beating and starving him until Parks's grandfather developed an intense resentment of white people, even though he could easily pass for white himself. Under his influence, she chafed at facts of black life in the South that many of her friends simply tried to ignore. Her husband, Raymond Parks, won her by telling her about his efforts to raise money for the Scottsboro Boys, nine black youths who had been sentenced to die in a trumped-up rape case. She began trying to register to vote in 1943, when only a few dozen blacks in Montgomery had managed to overcome the hurdles of shifting office hours, complicated qualification tests, and poll taxes that had been set up for the very purpose of excluding them. She had also attended the Highlander Folk School in Mississippi, where civil rights organizers were trained.

The petite, tidily dressed middle-aged lady on the bus in Montgomery was, in a word, more of a powerhouse than she seemed. Parks said later that she had no intention of challenging the system that day when she started the ride on the Cleveland Avenue bus and wound up in a jail cell, listening to the romantic problems of a cellmate until her husband and friends came to bail her out. But the leaders of the black community knew they had found in her the perfect test case. "My God, look what segregation has put in my hands," said her euphoric lawyer. Jo Ann Robinson and the Women's Political Council began mimeographing 35,000 handbills, calling for a one-day boycott on the day of Parks's court appearance.

The perfect client went to court on Monday, December 5, 1955, wearing a long-sleeved black dress with white cuffs and collar and a small velvet hat with pearls across the top. "They've messed with the wrong one now," trilled a girl in the crowd. At a mass meeting that night, local black residents packed the Holt Street Baptist Church, where a reporter for the city's white daily found a crowd with "almost military discipline combined with emotion" listening passionately to a local minister who the reporter did not recognize, but would learn later was Martin Luther King Jr. They voted to boycott the city bus system indefinitely, sang hymns, and scrambled for the chance to put money in the hats that were being passed around. Rosa Parks was given a standing ovation, but she was not given a chance to speak on a night in which virtually every black man in Montgomery wanted a moment in the spotlight. "You've said enough," one of the leaders assured her.

The boycott lasted for more than a year, as the blacks of Montgomery stunned the nation, and probably themselves, with the depth of their determination. It made Martin Luther King a national name. In later years Reverend King always acknowledged that the boycott was actually organized by other people, although he never went out of his way to identify them. He rose on the shoulders of women like Jo Ann Robinson, who risked losing the university teaching job she loved in order to get the boycott under way, and the thousands and thousands of black women who walked to work rather than break the strike, braving not only the elements but also white motorists who pelted them with water balloons, rotten eggs, and vegetables. King urged one old lady to go back to riding the bus because he felt she was too frail to keep walking, but the woman insisted she would honor the boycott like everyone else. "Yes, my feets is tired, but my soul is rested," she said. Many years later, E. D. Nixon, the black Montgomery lawyer who represented Rosa Parks, met a woman on an airplane who told him she couldn't imagine what would have happened to black people if Martin Luther King had not come to Montgomery. "I said, 'If Mrs. Parks had got up and given that white man her seat you'd never aheard of Rev. King.' "

Although de facto segregation held sway in the entire nation, it had been codified in law and blood in the South—Ruby Hurley, a black New Yorker who moved to Birmingham in 1951, discovered a city ordinance that banned blacks and whites from playing checkers together. After the Supreme Court ruled in 1954 that the concept of segregated school systems was unconstitutional, a few young southern African Americans—mainly women—attempted to enroll in the far superior white schools in their towns. The result was a series of violent images that shocked the rest of the nation. Autherine Lucy, who became the first black student ever to enter the University of Alabama, had to be driven from one class to the next through a crowd of people yelling, "Let's kill her." They shattered the car window and threw things at her when she jumped out to run into the building. She prayed, she said later, "to be able to see the time when I would be able to complete my work on the campus, but if it was not the will of God that I do this, that he give me the courage to accept the fact that I would lose my life there. . . ." Neither came to pass—the university administration suspended her, saying it was for her own safety, and then expelled her for insubordination when her lawyer criticized the suspension.

Daisy Bates, the head of the NAACP in Little Rock, Arkansas, recruited black students to enroll in the city's all-white high school, and in 1955 she and some local ministers escorted five girls and three boys through a howling crowd to the steps of Central High School, where a federal judge had ordered that they be admitted. A ninth student, tiny fifteen-year-old Elizabeth Eckford, came by herself due to a mixup in arrangements. She struggled through a crowd of angry whites waving bats and screaming, "Lynch her!" A photographer caught a picture of Eckford, looking stolid behind her glasses, clasping her books with her thin arms, while behind her a young woman named Hazel Bryan shrieked, "Go back to Africa." The students eventually attended the school under the protection of federal marshals, and when they were not ignored and snubbed, they were assaulted and harassed. Every morning they met at Daisy Bates's home to prepare themselves for the day, and every evening they went back to discuss what had happened. Bates, the daughter of a woman who had been raped and murdered by a group of never-identified white men, was the heroine of the Little Rock story, an integration effort that Harry Ashmore, editor of the *Arkansas Gazette*, said often depended almost entirely on her "raw courage." It cost her the newspaper business that she and her husband had spent sixteen years building. She was jailed and threatened, and the Ku Klux Klan burned an eight-foot cross on her front lawn.

Years later, the country would look back on those battles of the 1950s as a time when people fought for such obvious justice—the right to sit on a public bus or to go to a public school. But neither Rosa Parks nor Autherine Lucy nor Daisy Bates and the Little Rock students knew that the victories they sought against what seemed like almost universal white opposition would be won so completely. Years later, Montgomery officials honored the day a forty-two-year-old seamstress refused to give up her seat on the Cleveland Avenue bus by changing the street's name to Rosa Parks Boulevard. Autherine Lucy would return to the University of Alabama to lecture to a history class, and her presence on campus seemed so natural that the local papers never even noticed it occurred. In 1999, the Little Rock students received congressional medals from President Bill Clinton, a former Arkansas governor. Elizabeth Eckford, who had a career in the army, exchanged salutes with her commander in chief. On the fortieth anniversary of her walk to school through the shrieking crowd, Eckford posed for newspaper photos outside the school with Hazel Bryan Massery, her former tormenter. Massery had called Eckford in 1962 "to apologize for my hateful actions." Later, the two women became friends.

The only person absent from the ceremony was Daisy Bates, who had died a few days earlier at age eighty-two and been buried only a few hours before. Ernest Green, one of the students she had nurtured and counseled, who had grown up to become a managing director at a Washington brokerage firm and a confidant of the president, laid a wreath on behalf of the Little Rock Nine at the foot of her coffin, which lay in state in the Arkansas capitol.

## 19

# The Sixties: The Pendulum
# Swings Back with a Vengeance

### "YOU SHOULD SEE MY LITTLE SIS"

In 1960, Ernest Evans, an aspiring singer who took the stage name Chubby Checker, became famous with his version of the dance tune "The Twist." The song was so popular it hit number one twice—in 1960 when teenagers started twisting, and again in 1962 when adults discovered the pleasures of a dance that you could perform without any lessons or even much sense of rhythm. It also produced a sort of social liberation for American girls because the Twist was the first universally popular dance in which a couple never touched. You rotated your hips, swung your arms, and moved your feet in time to the music. Theoretically your partner was somewhere nearby, but he was not leading, or even necessarily dancing the same steps. "Oh you should see my little sis," Chubby Checker sang. "She really knows how to rock. She knows how to twist." Throughout the twentieth century, girls had been better at dancing than boys, but they had always been trapped by the necessity of following the man. The Twist, which was succeeded by many, many other variations on the same theme, freed girls to enjoy themselves without having to match what they were doing with their partner. They actually didn't even need a partner, and as time went on it became easier and more socially acceptable for a girl who wanted to get up and dance to simply go and do it.

Outside of the dance floor, the cultural revolution everyone associates with the sixties was slow to arrive. A *Ladies' Home Journal* poll in 1962 found that among the young women it surveyed, almost all "expect to be married by 22. Most want four children . . . many want . . . to work until children come; afterward, a resounding no!" The respondents, between sixteen and twenty-one years old, said they felt a "special responsibility" for holding the line when it came to sex.

Girls were being warned in sex education classes that using tampons was the equivalent of a loss of virginity. When they had their periods, most wore rather bulky sanitary napkins that were kept in place with pins or a suspension belt. They were still sleeping on oversized hair rollers, shopping for hope chest linen while they were in braces, and watching TV housewives cook while wearing what appeared to be party dresses. It would be a few more years before Mary Tyler Moore caused a sensation when she showed up on *The Dick Van Dyke Show* as Laura Petri, who wore pants while she ran the vacuum cleaner. But Laura and her husband still slept in twin beds.

When things changed, they changed fast. Only a few years after Mary Tyler Moore's sartorial breakthrough, middle-class audiences were flocking to see *Hair*, the musical that arrived on Broadway in 1968 with its celebration of nudity, draft card burning, and oral and anal sex. White women threw away their curlers and wore their hair long and straight, or cut in a helmetlike bob; African American women competed with the men to see who could adopt the biggest and most natural-looking Afro. Tights, which had always been reserved for dancers, became the most basic item of underwear for many young women, replacing stockings and girdles. Tights were not only more comfortable, they were critical for a modicum of modesty, because the miniskirt had arrived, and kept getting minier by the hour. "Every week the skirts seemed too long again until we had them so high they barely covered our behinds," wrote Sara Davidson in her memoir *Loose Change*. "With our legs swinging loose and exposed to the air, we felt frisky and reckless." It's hard not to keep making comparisons to the 1920s, when rising hemlines were also a bid for freedom and comfort. And in both eras, most women had difficulty getting in the proper shape for those liberating fashions. A fashion article that Davidson read equated the ideal leg with "a round little pole . . . with absolutely no calf. To be stuck with legs and calves is just too crass for words." Even the willowy Davidson found she "had to diet manicly" to look right in the minis. "Twiggy was the standard," she said. Twiggy was Leslie Hornby, a 90-pound British teenager who had been discovered while working as a shampoo girl in a London beauty shop and turned into the world's most famous model by the time she was seventeen. Her sticklike figure (31-22-32), pale skin, and huge eyes defined the sixties look. While American teenagers had been obsessed with dieting long before Twiggy hit the magazine covers, her status as the ideal of the era made it certain that virtually nobody was ever going to be happy with the shape of her body again. (Twiggy wasn't particularly happy with hers, either. Asked once whether she had the figure of the future, the model replied, "It's not really what you call a figure, is it?")

## "GREGORY, CAN'T YOU DEVISE SOME SORT OF PILL FOR THIS PURPOSE?"

Margaret Sanger had traveled quite a route since the days when she got arrested for passing out birth control literature to the working-class housewives of Brooklyn. She had moved to the right, fallen in with the eugenics movement, married a millionaire, and been widowed. But she never lost sight of her consuming goal of giving women the power to decide if and when they wanted to be pregnant. Sanger's passion was finding more efficient forms of birth control, and in 1951 she had a get-acquainted dinner with Gregory Pincus, a brilliant research scientist who shared her interest. They talked about the difficulty of finding a family planning method that could be used effectively in India. "Gregory, can't you devise some sort of pill for this purpose?" Sanger asked.

"I'll try," responded Pincus.

Sanger eventually put Pincus in touch with Katharine McCormick, the widow of the heir to the McCormick reaper fortune. She was a remarkable woman, who had come from a wealthy Boston family but found herself less interested in society than in science. She obtained a B.S. from MIT in 1904, and then married Stanley McCormick, a childhood friend. When her husband began to show signs of schizophrenia, McCormick devoted much of their money and her energy in attempting to find a cure. She was convinced that the problem was medical, and possibly hereditary, and her own decision to avoid having children may have led to her interest in family planning. She became friends with Sanger and helped her smuggle diaphragms from Europe to New York. When Stanley McCormick died and Katharine received control of his vast fortune, she told Sanger she was interested in helping support contraceptive research. She pledged $10,000 a year to underwrite Pincus's work, which quickly grew to hundreds of thousands, and finally a total of $2 million.

Within a few years, with McCormick nagging him all the way, Pincus had developed an oral contraceptive. It was one of the most critical moments in the history of American women, the arrival of a drug that was so important it became known simply as the Pill. ("There's gonna be some changes made right here on Nursery Hill," sang Loretta Lynn. "You've set this chicken your last time, cause now I've got the Pill.") But in 1960 no one knew that. The pharmaceutical company G. D. Searle, which applied for permission from the FDA to market the contraceptive, was edgy. "It was not an easy decision. Open association with 'contraception' and its positive promotion was . . . regarded as unseemly by the vast majority of academicians and the practicing profession itself," recalled Irwin Winter, Searle's medical director. And many men doubted that women would want to take it. One stock analyst who followed pharmaceuticals recalled people arguing that women would never commit to a regimen of daily medication unless they were sick. Others knew better. The staff physician at Georgetown University Medical Center, who was put in charge of assessing the FDA application, pondered buying stock in Searle, but decided it would be unethical. "I knew that birth control pills would be flying out the windows," he said. "Everybody and her sister would be taking it."

That he was right is a tribute to the desperation women felt about avoiding unwanted pregnancies. The early Pill was hard to tolerate— women suffered from headaches and weight gain, and they had to worry about the danger of blood clots. Most of the side effects were due to estrogen, and the amount in the early version turned out to be far more than necessary. The first contraceptive pill released in 1960 had ten times as much as versions that came along later. The sale of C-cup bras increased 50 percent during the sixties, as all that estrogen caused women's breasts to swell.

## "ONE VAST, ALL-PERVADING SEXOLOGICAL SPREE"

Many people were more worried about the effect of the Pill on women's morals than their bodies—*Readers Digest* fretted that an end to the threat of illegitimate children might trigger "one vast, all-pervading sexological spree." They were prescient, in a way. The sixties saw the onset of a real revolution in the way Americans looked at sex, and at its heart was women's rejection of the double standard. "I told a date nice girls don't, but he just laughed, and he's right. Nice girls do," a college student told Gloria Steinem, who wrote all about it in her first magazine article, "The Moral Disarmament of Betty Coed," in 1962. The double standard had been a target of feminist outrage since the eighteenth century, off and on, but reformers thought the answer was to make men accept the same ground rules that women were required to follow. Even in the periods of social upheaval, there had been an almost universal social agreement that women should not have extramarital sex, with possible exceptions for fiancés.

The birth control pill was a critical factor in spurring on women to demand the same sexual freedom men enjoyed. Things still might have moved more slowly if the civil rights movement had not sensitized people to issues of fair play and evenhandedness. But once sexual liberty was added to the agenda of the rebellious younger generation, it was embraced with much more across-the-board enthusiasm than civil rights, women's rights, gay rights, or opposition to the war in Vietnam. Nobody had to organize demonstrations or picket lines on behalf of free love.

Even before the Pill took hold, Hollywood started to do battle against a double standard that, along with its other disadvantages, severely limited the options for film romance plots. Producers started churning out what author Susan Douglas called "pregnancy melodramas"—films like *A Summer Place* and *Susan Slade* and *Blue Denim* in which the heroine goes all the way, gets in trouble just as the unfeeling adults warned her she would, and then winds up getting the guy and living happily ever after anyway. The unforgivable sin in these movies was hypocrisy, not lust. "Are you antipeople and antilife? Must you suffocate every natural instinct in our daughter, too? Must you label young lovemaking as cheap and wanton and indecent? Must you persist in making sex itself a filthy word?" Sandra Dee's sympathetic dad asks his frigid wife in *A Summer Place*. In *Splendor in the Grass*, the moviemakers demonstrated the terrible danger of *not* losing one's virginity when Natalie Wood went stark raving mad out of sexual frustration.

The opening salvos in the sexual revolution had been fired in the early 1960s by people like Helen Gurley Brown. Her book *Sex and the Single Girl* was published in 1962 and quickly became the first mass-market best-seller in American history to urge young women to have affairs with married men. Brown told her single female readers to start demanding the same kind of rewards single males can get, including a satisfying career, a healthy savings account, and lots of lovers. They could sow wild oats and then marry late. Marriage, she told her public, "is insurance for the *worst* years of your life. During your best years you don't need a husband." In a brilliant stroke of packaging, Brown also confided that in her late thirties she had landed a "brainy, charming and sexy" movie producer, with whom she resided in a "house overlooking the Pacific" with "a full-time maid and a good life." Her readers, she suggested, could do exactly the same thing by becoming confident, interesting women who were successes at work and in bed. The single woman, Brown earnestly admonished her readers, "is emerging as the newest glamour girl of our times," someone who "moves in the world of men"—a "far more colorful world than the one of P.T.A., Dr. Spock and the jammed clothes dryer."

It was quite a shift in message, but a good chunk of the country was ready to hear it. The age of marriage had begun to rise again, starting in 1957, and the birthrate had begun to fall. Women were no longer quite as eager to forgo that period of independence between school and marriage. Partly it was because low-cost mortgages and free college tuition for married men were no longer as readily available. But the terror of sterile and possibly unnatural singlehood was also losing its hold. *Sex and the Single Girl* virtually monopolized the cultural debate—until the next year, when Betty Friedan's *The Feminine Mystique* came along and brought a similar, if much more somber, message to the women who had already dedicated the best years of their lives to the very things Brown was now telling their daughters to avoid at all costs.

In the growing political turmoil in the Vietnam War years of the late sixties and early seventies, sexual liberation came to be connected with everything from environmentalism to opposition to the war. "Obscene is not the picture of a naked woman who exposes her pubic hair but that of a fully clad general who exposes his medals, rewarded in a war of aggression," argued Herbert Marcuse, the political theorist and hero of the New Left. Antidraft protesters marched with signs that announced "Girls say yes to men who say no." The younger generation—trailed by the enthusiastic media—was well ahead of the rest of the nation when it came to unleashing their libidos; as late as 1969, 68 percent of the American population was opposed to premarital sex. But the majority caught up pretty fast, and by 1973, the same pollsters reported that most respondents felt sex before marriage was okay. In the same year, a survey of eight colleges determined that 76 percent of female students had had intercourse by their junior year— about the same proportion as the male students. (In his report in 1953, Alfred Kinsey had found about a quarter of women in college were sexually active.) The double standard was, if not completely dead, certainly fading fast. In 1975, TV reporter Morley Safer asked First

Lady Betty Ford what she would do if her unmarried daughter Susan told her she was having an affair. "Well, I wouldn't be surprised. I think she's a normal human being like all young girls," said Mrs. Ford.

## "MOVE ON, LITTLE GIRL"

In the wild swing of the historical pendulum of the 1960s and early 1970s, the sexual liberation movement preceded the women's liberation movement, and many girls felt free to say yes before they figured out that they had the right to say no. Refusing a date's demand for sex had been difficult enough when both parties grudgingly accepted the idea that women should remain virgins until they married. Now, as one conservative intellectual complained, the new morality was giving women "the obligations of an impersonal lust they did not feel but only believed in." Even women who were charter members of the political rebellion felt they were being used; the double standard still seemed to rule when it came to everything but sex. Jane Alpert, a fugitive radical who had helped her lover, Sam Melville, set bombs in eight government and corporate buildings in New York City in 1969, wrote later that when Melville thought the house needed to be cleaned, he wrote "Wash Me" on the side of a dirty refrigerator in black magic marker. During a climactic meeting of New Left leaders in 1968, one of the men patted activist Shulamith Firestone on the head and said, "Move on, little girl; we have more important issues to talk about here than women's liberation." The Yippees, the free-wheeling counterculturists who described utopia as "free grass, free food, free shelter, free chicks" had a saying: "Shake a chick's tit instead of her hand."

Young men seemed much more ready to accept marriages in which each partner could have outside sex than marriages in which each partner did an equal share of the housework. And neither the black leaders of the civil rights movement (like Stokely Carmichael, who said that the proper position for women was "prone") nor the white students who ran the protests against the war were particularly eager to bring women into the decision-making process. While some women got their first taste of leadership in organizing opposition to the war, many of them were identified as the wife or girlfriend of a male leader. In 1965, at a meeting of student radicals in Michigan, one man said that "women made peanut butter, waited on tables, cleaned up, got laid. That was their role."

For young middle-class whites, the core of American political and cultural activity in the later sixties and early seventies was the war in Vietnam. The growing disillusionment with the conflict, even among many people with fairly traditional political outlooks, did more than create bad feeling toward the politicians in Washington. It cast a cloud of illegitimacy over authority in general. If the people in charge could be so wrong about something as important as a war, why should anyone assume that they were right about the necessity of maintaining one's virginity, avoiding drugs, or obeying a school dress code? And if everything was focused on the war, young men were at the center of the war issue. They were the ones, after all, who were in danger of being drafted and sent to die in a jungle in Southeast Asia. They were the ones who had to decide whether to join the service or burn their draft cards or escape to Canada. Women were on the periphery, supporting the men in their great moral and political crisis. The slogan about girls saying yes to men who said no was an echo of those young ladies in the Revolutionary and Civil War eras who were supposed to reject any suitor who failed to enlist. And it seemed to suggest that Stokely Carmichael might have been right about women's position in the movement after all.

## "NOWADAYS, WOMEN WOULDN'T STAND FOR BEING KEPT SO MUCH IN THE BACKGROUND"

The March on Washington took place on August 28, 1963, and is still remembered for Martin Luther King's amazing "I Have a Dream" speech. A quarter million people flooded into the capital to urge Congress to pass the pending Civil Rights Act—college students who had formed the shock troops of the drive for integration and voter registration projects in the South, the black ministers who were the most recognizable leaders of the movement, the white politicians, and movie stars and union leaders who had provided money and publicity and political muscle. Rosa Parks was there, and Pauli Murray, who had staged that first sit-in at a Washington restaurant during World War II, and Daisy Bates from Arkansas. But they were not included on the lengthy speakers' list. Instead of marching with the male leaders, up front where the TV cameras and newspaper reporters were recording every minute of the event, they were directed to walk with those men's wives. There was not a single woman scheduled to speak at the march, and when the lone woman on the nineteen-member planning committee protested, the organizers threw together a last-minute "Tribute to Women" in which A. Philip Randolph introduced Parks and other female dignitaries, like the dancer Josephine Baker and the actress Lena Horne, while they sat there silently. (Randolph, the venerable union leader, had begun the week's activities by giving a speech at the all-male National Press Club luncheon, in which female reporters were consigned to a small balcony, denied the right to ask questions.) "Nowadays, women wouldn't stand for being kept so much in the background, but back then women's rights hadn't become a popular cause yet," said Parks later.

African Americans had always celebrated the virtues of strong women who kept families going under extraordinary political and economic pressures. But they also wanted to see black men take the leadership role they had been systematically denied in American history. Almost as soon as slavery came to the colonies it was established that black women could be more outspoken than their husbands and brothers and fathers. The sharp-tongued Charleston market women of the eighteenth century and the sassy "mammy" of the plantation South were only two of the models for black women who could, under certain circumstances, give white people a piece of their mind. The liberties were greater for older women than younger, and for large, maternal-looking women than pretty girls. But there was no model for a black male being permitted to put white people in their place. It was probably because of that legacy that civil rights workers, who went into the small towns of the Deep South hoping to register black voters, found women more willing to step forward and take risks. "There is always a 'mama,' " said one organizer. "She is usually a militant woman in the community, outspoken, understanding, and willing to catch hell, having already caught her share."

Black men generally could assert themselves only by ordering around black women, and they were not any readier than white men to cede authority to the opposite sex. Even Rosa Parks's lawyer told her that he believed the proper place for women was in the kitchen. At church, the center of black communities, the minister was always a male, and the congregation was mainly female, doing his bidding. "All of the churches depended, in terms of things taking place, on women, not men. Men didn't do the things that had to be done," said Ella Baker, a veteran organizer. Baker was asked by the Southern Christian Leadership Conference to run its voter registration drive and work as the de facto executive director. But for all her skills, she was never considered for the permanent executive director's job, which always went to a man.

Many black women were willing to defer to the men simply because they felt there was a need for strong male role models in their community. "Around 1965 there began to develop a great deal of questioning about what is the role of women in the struggle. Out of it came a concept that black women had to bolster the ego of the male. . . . I personally have never thought of this as being valid." said Baker, who became the guiding spirit of the Student Nonviolent Coordinating Committee, the preeminent civil rights group of the younger generation.

The women often wound up taking the public role of victim—the heroines who were beaten, or arrested, or chased by mobs and were honored for their courage and endurance. In Americus, Georgia, two dozen girls, most of them not yet teenagers, were taken off to jail where they were beaten, burned with cattle prods, and left for weeks in a cell awash in urine and feces. When a rattlesnake slithered into the cell, the girls had to call for half an hour before a guard came in to kill it. In Albany, Georgia, Carolyn Daniels, a black single mother who ran the local beauty shop, gave rooms to several organizers, and as a result Daniels was shot and her house firebombed. Fourteen-year-old

Joanne Christian was arrested thirteen times, beaten, kicked, and dragged by her hair. Her eleven-year-old sister, Dear, was jailed seven times, remaining in prison forty-seven days. In Indianola, Mississippi, Irene Magruder allowed voter registration workers to use her house as an office. It was set on fire, and white firemen stood watching, their hoses turned off, until it burned to the ground, destroying everything she owned.

The most famous example of the brave local "mamas" was Fannie Lou Hamer, the youngest of twenty children of a Mississippi share-cropper. She volunteered to register to vote when the civil rights organizers came to her town of Ruleville, Mississippi. She was rejected because she was unable to correctly interpret a section of the state constitution on de facto laws. But for merely attempting, she and her husband were put off the plantation where they worked. As Hamer continued her civil rights activity they were constantly harassed—the couple once received a $9,000 water bill for a home that had no run-ning water. In 1963, Hamer and some other civil rights workers were arrested at a bus station in Winona, Mississippi, and she was beaten so severely she suffered kidney damage and blood clots for the rest of her life. She told her story at the 1964 Democratic convention, where she was part of a Freedom slate attempting to unseat the all-white regular delegation. "All this on account we want to register, to become first-class citizens," she said, in testimony that was broadcast on television across the country. It was one of the most arresting moments in mod-ern political history, but when the time came for the Freedom slate to negotiate with the party leaders, Hamer was excluded from most of the meetings.

The tension of divided loyalties was not limited to black women. Lesbians found themselves in danger of being frozen out by both the early gay rights movement, which was mainly run by men, and the women's liberation movement, which proved to be surprisingly homophobic. Mexican American women were torn between the desire to fight for Hispanic rights and the need to assert themselves against the paternalistic power structure of the Chicano movement. At the Mexican American National Issues Conference in Sacramento in 1970, the women broke away and formed their own organization, saying they had been excluded from leadership opportunities by both Anglo society and Mexican American males. But they were very conscious that they were leaving themselves open to being branded as "man haters" or traitors to their race. When 600 Chicana activists met in Houston in 1971, arguments immediately broke out between those who defined themselves as "loyalists" and the more feminist majority. In the end, the gathering passed a resolution saying that "traditional roles are, for Chicanas, no longer acceptable," and the loyalists walked out in protest.

## "YOU CAN'T EVEN SAFELY ADVERTISE FOR A WIFE ANY MORE"

When the landmark Civil Rights Act was being debated in 1963, Representative Howard Smith of Virginia, the chairman of the powerful Rules Committee, moved to add "sex" to the part of the bill banning discrimination in the workplace on the basis of race, color, religion, or national origin. Legend had it he was joking, or just trying to kill the bill. It was easy to see how people got that idea, since during the debate, Smith had the male legislators in stitches when he expanded on his theories about sex discrimination by reading a letter from a woman protesting the shortage of prospective husbands. (Emanuel Celler of Brooklyn, the chairman of the Judiciary Committee, volunteered that he always had the last word in all domestic discussions, as long as the words were "Yes, dear.") Actually, Smith was one of those politicians who expressed his opposition to blacks by pointing out that they were about to be treated better than white women. He was an ally of Alice Paul and the National Women's Party, a group that was not so much opposed to black civil rights as simply worried that it might get in the way of the women's agenda. Once again, women and African Americans were both vying to make progress, and bumping up against one another in the process. But this time no one wound up being excluded. Martha Griffiths, a Democratic representative from Michigan, realized that Smith's motion would draw heavy support from conservative southerners who simply wanted to make trouble for the Civil Rights Act. But if she could get 100 northern and western representatives, she calculated, the amendment could actually pass. "If I can't argue enough to get that other hundred, I ought to leave Congress," she told herself. Griffiths was the first woman to be a member of the committee that controlled tax laws, and she had accumulated a substantial number of chits in the legislative favor bank.

Thanks to an unlikely collection of female lawmakers, liberal northern men, and southern segregationists in the House, and with the help of the redoubtable Margaret Chase Smith in the Senate, the Civil Rights bill became law with a clause that made it illegal to discriminate against women in hiring, pay, or promotions. But most people didn't take the idea of ending sex discrimination seriously. Instead, they asked jovially whether the law would require the Playboy clubs to start hiring men as bunnies—those waitresses who dressed up in rabbit ears and skimpy costumes. "Bunny problem, indeed!" editorialized the *New York Times,* which also playfully worried about male Rockettes dancing in the chorus line at Radio City: "This is revolution, chaos. You can't even safely advertise for a wife any more." Actually, the country had already learned in the Depression that there were very few men who regarded any traditionally feminine job as worth having, even the ones that women found relatively desirable. (Gloria Steinem had just written an article about her undercover experiences as a Playboy bunny that made it clear the job wasn't very pleasant even for an attractive woman.) But most critics dismissed the entire idea of women's rights in the job market by raising the specter of hairy male legs on the chorus line. Others had a clearer vision of the real dangers to the status quo. A personnel officer for an airline asked a reporter in horror: "What are we going to do when a gal walks into our office, demands a job as an airline pilot and has the credentials to qualify?"

When the law went into effect, the airline industry was indeed one of the first employers challenged. But it was the stewardesses, not would-be pilots, who filed the complaints. The airlines had originally hired nurses as flight attendants in order to emphasize passenger safety, but they had quickly switched over to glorified waitresses— "girls" who were trained in makeup and grooming and who had their scalps examined to make sure their hair was its natural color and their stomachs poked by supervisors to make sure they were wearing girdles. They were required to retire if they had the bad grace to gain weight, get married, or turn thirty-two. "It's the sex thing," an airlines executive told the head of the stewardesses' union. If the person serving coffee and passing out pillows looks like "a dog," he claimed, "twenty businessmen are sore for a month." When several stewardesses appeared before a House Labor subcommittee to testify, Representative James Scheur of New York asked them to "stand up, so we can see the dimensions of the problem."

The newly created Equal Employment Opportunity Commission, however, was not planning on using its limited resources to advance the cause of stewardesses or any other aggrieved women. The majority on the five-member commission, which included only one woman, felt their primary duty was to help African American workers— though the question of what they planned to do about African American women was never made entirely clear. The commission made its disinterest in the woman's issue evident in 1965, when it ruled that newspaper help-wanted ads could no longer discriminate on the basis of race, religion, or national origin, but that it was okay to continue dividing them into "Male Help Wanted" and "Female Help Wanted" sections. Representative Griffiths angrily took to the floor of the House to remind the EEOC officials that "they took an oath to uphold the law, not just the part of it that they are interested in."

The help-wanted ads were a particularly sore point because they had such a broad effect on women's job opportunities. At a convention of various state commissions on the status of women in 1966, fifteen angry women met in Betty Friedan's hotel room to talk about starting a new organization—a sort of NAACP for women. The meeting degenerated into a fight about tactics. (At one point, Friedan demanded that everyone who disagreed with her leave and locked herself in the bathroom.) But before the conference was over, even the more conservative women had to admit that their efforts to work from the inside had been useless, and the National Organization for Women (NOW) was born. Friedan thought up the name on the spur of the moment and wrote out a statement of purpose on a paper napkin. It was the beginning of the women's liberation movement.

## "SHE IS DISSATISFIED WITH A LOT THAT WOMEN OF OTHER LANDS CAN ONLY DREAM OF"

Betty Friedan had been a celebrity since *The Feminine Mystique* came out in 1963, and she was still being deluged with letters from fans who recognized themselves in the description of bored, frustrated housewives in her book. But Friedan had been writing most of all about herself. She was the prototype of the kind of woman who was doomed to be miserable as a suburban homemaker. Friedan had intended to have a career in psychology, but she turned down the chance for the kind of fellowship that would have put her on the fast track in academia. At the time she thought it was because a man she was interested in felt he could not compete with her success. But later she wondered if she had just been frightened of taking the plunge into the real world. At any rate, she married and gave up her work, and by the late 1950s there she was, rearing three children and trying to balance the family budget by writing freelance articles for women's magazines, on topics such as breastfeeding and what it was like to be married to a millionaire. She was becoming strangely obsessed with her upcoming Smith college reunion, and she got a commission from *McCall's* to write an article refuting that best-seller *Modern Women: The Lost Sex,* which argued that higher education got in the way of women adjusting to their natural role as wives and mothers. Friedan was planning a good-news piece about how college and domesticity went together. But she found her fellow graduates as restless as she was. When the distinctly bad-news article she wrote was rejected by both *McCall's* and *Redbook,* Friedan turned it into a book. "The problem lay buried, unspoken, for many years in the minds of American women. It was a strange stirring, a sense of dissatisfaction, a yearning that women suffered in the middle of the twentieth century in the United States," she began.

*The Feminine Mystique* was both powerful and a good read, full of anecdotes and surprising statistics, although Friedan's conclusion tended to mirror her own experience. Women, she felt, were sticking to home and hearth because they were frightened of taking the plunge into the real world. Her all-purpose solution was for wives to get jobs—something about a third of them already had. But she had hit a nerve—both with the women who had never felt comfortable with suburban domesticity and those who were beginning to feel at loose ends once their children approached adulthood.

The women who got married after World War II usually spaced their babies close together, often telling each other they wanted to compress the exhausting years of caring for infants and toddlers—to "get it over with." By 1963, the first wave of baby-boom children was getting ready for college. Their mothers were over "it," without any clear idea of what came next. For the first time, the nation had a very large population of middle-aged women who had no children left at home, no particular need to work for money, household chores that weren't demanding, and decades of life still ahead of them. "Usually, until very recently, mom folded up and died of hard work somewhere in the middle of her life," wrote Philip Wylie in *Generation of Vipers,* a postwar best-seller that was critical of virtually everything but reserved special rancor for "Momism." To Wylie, the era when mothers seldom survived beyond childbearing years was a kind of Paradise Lost.

Some suburban housewives slid smoothly into volunteer work or jobs. But others ran into empty-nest life crises, made infinitely worse by the new national emphasis on personal happiness and sexual fulfillment that had doubled the divorce rate between the midsixties and midseventies. Although it was hard to tell who was leaving whom, being dumped by one's spouse was certainly more frightening to women, many of whom had never worked or even handled a checkbook. The mass media had noticed the phenomenon of the unhappy housewife, although the general analysis was that women just didn't appreciate how good they had it "She is dissatisfied with a lot that women of other lands can only dream of," said *Newsweek* reprovingly.

## "LADY JUROR BAN ENDED BY COURT"

At the beginning of the 1970s, when the women's liberation movement was getting under way, the *New York Times* printed a story about
a woman attempting to rent an apartment who was forced to get her
husband, a mental hospital patient, to cosign the lease. A wealthy
middle-aged divorcée who wanted to buy a co-op had to get her
father's signature on the contract. Mortgage lenders frequently
refused to count a wife's salary in determining family income under
the theory that she would stop working and have babies—although
some offered to make exceptions for anyone who could prove she'd
had a hysterectomy. Divorced women were regarded as high risks by
insurance companies, and they had trouble getting credit cards. Mary
Tyler Moore, still shattering tradition, wanted to play a divorcée in her
new series, but CBS felt the nation wasn't ready for that and compromised on making her the survivor of an unhappy engagement.

There were ten women in the 435-member House of Representatives in 1970 and one in the U.S. Senate. In North Carolina, only a virgin could charge a man with rape. In Alabama, the idea of women
serving on juries was still something of a novelty—the courts had
only ordered the state to include them in 1966. ("Lady Juror Ban
Ended by Court" announced the *Huntsville Times*. The *Alabama Journal* interviewed local attorneys who felt "women perhaps would be
more sympathetic to a defendant . . . but on the other hand their sympathies could be with the aggrieved party.") In newspaper stories
women were all referred to as Miss or Mrs.; a reporter interviewing a
witness to a traffic accident had to ask if she was married in order to
refer to her by name in print.

In 1970, 3 percent of the nation's lawyers, and 7 percent of the doctors, were women. A woman, on average, had to have a college degree
to outearn a man with an eighth-grade education. There were virtually
no women judges at any but the very lowest level courts. In the mass
media, almost all the top editors were male, even at the women's magazines. At *Newsweek*, one of the fifty-two writers was a woman and one

of the thirty-five researchers was a man, and when the women filed suit under the Civil Rights Act, the editor said the setup was a "news magazine tradition going back almost fifty years." There had been only one more woman in the president's Cabinet since Frances Perkins.

There was obviously plenty to reform. As movements go, women's liberation was going to be both extraordinarily ambitious and extraordinarily successful. And while it forced some women into tortured journeys through abuse and repression in their past, most of the people involved would have agreed with lawyer Flo Kennedy, who emerged from the famous Miss America protest of 1968 saying it was "the best fun I can imagine anyone wanting to have on any single day of her life."

## "DEGRADED MINDLESS BOOB-GIRLIE SYMBOL"

The Miss America demonstration was one of those small, but resonant moments in the national history of dramatic gestures—a twentieth-century successor to the day nine-year-old Susan Boudinot threw her cup of British tea out the governor's window. It was the first time many people realized the women's liberation movement existed, and it would permanently affect their perceptions of it, for good and ill.

Beauty pageants, particularly the one in Atlantic City, had evolved over the twentieth century from a fairly shocking display of female flesh to a wholesome part of Americana—President Nixon said the Miss America contest was the only program he ever allowed his daughters Julie and Tricia to stay up late to watch. Miss America was, as the song said, the national "ideal," a young woman with a sunny personality who could proffer the kind of bland generalities about world peace and healthy children that got generations of middle-class wives through PTA teas and their husbands' business functions. But she was also a person in her own right with a talent, like singing or baton twirling. She had a pretty face and looked good in a bathing suit. The idea that there could be something wrong with all this was new and rather shocking.

A group of women, led by former TV child star Robin Morgan, arrived in the afternoon, when the TV crews waiting for the judging to begin had relatively little to do. They set up a "freedom trash can" on the Atlantic City boardwalk and threw in bras, girdles, high-heeled shoes, and hair curlers. They crowned a sheep, waved placards, and shouted slogans. The *New York Times* story undoubtedly marked the first time the paper ever used the term "degraded mindless boob-girlie symbol" even inside quotation marks. But adhering to its stylebook, the *Times* referred to the demonstration's leader as "Miss Morgan . . . a housewife who uses her maiden name." (Morgan, who had spent her childhood starring in the beloved TV show *I Remember Mama,* was married to a gay man and later wrote a famous diatribe, "Goodbye to All That," in which she announced, "We are the women that men have warned us about.") Although the women virtuously abided by the Atlantic City fire regulations and refrained from setting the freedom trash can on fire, the demonstration saddled the movement forever with the all-purpose put-down "bra-burners." At the end of the real Miss America pageant, as the eighteen-year-old Miss Illinois was walking down the runway, gingerly balancing her new crown, some of the demonstrators who had been smuggled into the auditorium unfurled a sign over the balcony that read "Women's Liberation." It was the first time most of the viewing public had ever heard the term.

But very soon the nation became the audience in a constantly evolving guerrilla theater of women's protests. Demonstrators were swooping down on bridal fairs and marriage license bureaus to protest the imbalance of power in American marriages. They put a hex on the unsympathetic Justice Department and staged a sit-in at *Ladies' Home Journal* and plastered signs that said "This Ad Degrades Women" on particularly sexist advertisements. All around the country, women were spontaneously organizing themselves into "consciousness-raising groups" in which they discussed everything from faked orgasms and concerns about the size of their breasts to long-repressed rapes or black-market abortions. The entire postwar period, from suburbia to New Left communes, had encouraged them to focus on pleasing men, and American women were thrilled to discover the sisterhood of their own sex. Many of them had been as estranged as the unhappy pioneer wife who had sadly discovered "I cannot make a friend like mother out of Henry." By reinventing something very old, they marched together into a new era.

But the challenge of remaking the world so that the sexes could live as real equals was much more daunting, and more painful, than the old strategy of retreating permanently into the community of women. It was probably inevitable that one wing of the early liberation movement decided the answer to all problems was just to get rid of the men entirely. They were the equivalent of the early-twentieth-century saloon-smashers, and they formed groups with names like WITCH or BITCH or SCUM (Society for Cutting Up Men) whose leader, Valerie Solanas, became famous by trying to assassinate the artist Andy Warhol. They wrote pamphlets demanding that all men be killed, or at minimum that women leave their husbands and stop having sex with the enemy. Some of the extremists were reacting rather naturally to their own personal histories as victims of male abuse. Others were more cynical, responding to the media's desire for sensational examples of bra-burning radicalism. Others were just carried away by the excitement.

Most American women obviously didn't relate to the kill-the-men theory of liberation. It was hard sometimes to tell *what* most American women were thinking since things were happening so quickly, and since the publicity about the movement was such a mixture of sympathy and scorn. In the spring of 1970, Betty Friedan, who had become president of NOW, impulsively called for women across the country to demonstrate on August 26, the fiftieth anniversary of Tennessee's final ratification of the Anthony amendment to the Constitution and the arrival of woman suffrage. No one, including Friedan, was sure that with just a few months of organization and publicity women in large numbers would feel compelled to show up to demonstrate on behalf of themselves. The mayor of New York was rather confident they wouldn't, and he denied the women permission to march down Fifth Avenue, the traditional parade route; they were told to keep to the sidewalks.

Friedan herself was worried on the day of the march, and she was almost late rushing to the start-off point in Central Park because traffic was tied up in a manner that was unusual even for Manhattan. "The reality dawned when I rounded the corner into the park and saw not hundreds but *thousands* of women and men and babies and grandmothers beginning to mass," she wrote later. "When the march spilled out of the park onto Fifth Avenue I was in the front row between Judge Dorothy Kenyon, a suffragette veteran in her eighties . . . and one of the young radicals in blue jeans. We kept jumping up to look back at the marchers behind us, but we could never see where the march ended. The mounted police were trying to make us march on the sidewalk, but I saw how many we were. There was no way we were about to walk down Fifth Avenue in a little, thin line. I waved my arms over my head and yelled, *'Take the street!'*

"What a moment that was."

# EPILOGUE

## "DRAGGING THE WORD 'HOUSEWIFE' THROUGH THE MUD"

Alice Paul was still alive and kicking in 1970, when the *New York Times* called her one of "the founding grandmothers and maiden grandaunts who have languished for nearly half a century in the historical garret." At eighty-five, she was still single-minded. Urged to reminisce about how women got the right to vote, Paul said, "I'd rather talk about now." "Now" was the Equal Rights Amendment, which Paul had spent fifty years pursuing—with a short time out to earn three law degrees. The E.R.A. was an extraordinarily simple proposal, a constitutional amendment that would say: "Equality of rights under the law shall not be denied or abridged by the United States on account of sex." Paul had lobbied for it through the Depression and World War II and through the long postwar era when her National Women's Party had shrunk to a few dozen active members and the nation was debating whether it was safe to leave schoolchildren in the care of unmarried teachers. When a new generation of rebellious young women began worrying about the war in Vietnam and the sexual revolution, Paul continued arguing that they would never achieve full legal equality by repealing one discriminatory law after another. They needed a sweeping constitutional amendment, she said, just as they had needed one to secure their right to vote.

The E.R.A. had been bottled up in Congress by a handful of powerful men—one of them, House judiciary chairman Emanuel Celler of Brooklyn, delighted in saying that women were no more the same as men than horses were the same as horse chestnuts, or, when the mood struck him, than lightning was the same as lightning bugs. Then suddenly in the 1970s women's rights became all the rage and Alice Paul's constitutional amendment was pried out of committee. It flew through the House and Senate in March 1972. A half hour after its final passage, the Hawaii state legislature became the first to ratify it. The sponsors predicted it would take only two years to get the necessary 38 states to add the Equal Rights Amendment to the Constitution.

It never happened. While 22 states ratified the amendment in 1972, only 8 more joined in the next year. Momentum flagged and some states attempted to retract their earlier approval. When Alice Paul died in 1977 at the age of ninety-two, the movement had ground to a halt, 3 states short of ratification.

The E.R.A. was meant to endorse women's right to all the chances for careers, adventures, and choice that men had, and to promise that this time the opportunities won today would not be withdrawn tomorrow. It would have nailed down a revolution that was overturning nearly 400 years' worth of ideology about what women's place was supposed to be. But it turned out that many women saw it as a repudiation of everything they had devoted their lives to. "It's time for housewives . . . to pull on the combat boots and battle those dragging the word 'housewife' through the mud," said Jaquie Davison, who announced she was founding a group called Happiness of Womanhood (HOW) to combat the E.R.A. movement.

Much of the fight over the E.R.A. was due to the jockeying of conservative ideologues for a place in the shifting world of American politics. But it was easy for the amendment's backers to forget that for most American women throughout history, the goal had been getting into the house, not out of it. The vast majority never got a chance to reject the limitations of a career as a full-time housewife. Trapped in a world of endless work on the farm or in the factory, they yearned for a chance to exercise more control and creativity as wives and mothers. Susan B. Anthony had said that married women were only allowed to be dolls or drudges, but stay-at-home wives saw themselves as something else entirely—as domestic entrepreneurs whose accomplishments entitled them to some respect. When that status was threatened, both the women who had it and the ones who hoped someday to get it reacted with dismay.

The idea that women—average women, not paragons like Lillian Gilbreth or Elizabeth Cady Stanton—should be able to combine the rewards of domestic and public life was still very new. Most people accepted it in theory and a great many women who would never have considered applying for a job themselves had sweet dreams about the day their daughters might become doctors or attorneys. But the status of traditional homemakers was a sore point. Young wives going to their husband's business parties were at a social disadvantage if they had no occupation outside the house to talk about, and older women were wounded when their daughters behaved as though their domestic achievements were unimportant. The subject had to be approached with tact and sensitivity, and tact was generally not the strong suit of the women's movement of the early 1970s. "Housewives have been called leeches, parasites and even legal prostitutes by some in the liberation movement," said Jaquie Davison.

Both sides in the fight over the role of American women were reacting to one very important fact: the rate of divorce was soaring, undermining everyone's confidence in marriage as a secure harbor. There was only about a fifty-fifty chance that "till death us do part" would really come true. It seemed socially acceptable for men to walk away from their families, and the government wasn't able to force them to support the wives and children they left behind. After divorce, a man's financial situation generally improved, while the ex-wife's plummeted. Obviously, women who weren't able to earn their own living could wind up in a perilous situation. The traditionalists could not change the direction in which society was moving, but they could go down fighting, and take the Equal Rights Amendment with them.

Fortunately, Alice Paul turned out to be wrong about how much the E.R.A. was needed. Even as it was foundering, virtually all the legal barriers that restrained women's opportunities were being eliminated and their real political power was increasing. Congress banned discrimination in credit, and required schools that got public money to treat boys and girls equally. Medical schools and law schools, which often set a flat 5 percent cap on female students, were forced to open their doors. The number of women medical school graduates rose from 7.5 percent in 1969 to nearly 20 percent in 1976.

### "MY WIFE: I THINK I'LL KEEP HER"

The early 1970s were a giddy time of testing possibilities. In 1973, 50 million Americans watched a televised "Battle of the Sexes" at the Houston Astrodome in which tennis star Billie Jean King out-psyched Bobby Riggs, a fifty-five-year-old hustler who had made a new career for himself by claiming he could beat any woman in the game. Riggs arrived in a chariot, wearing his trademark "Sugar Daddy" jacket, but King beat him to the hype, having herself carried in on a divan borne by men dressed as Roman slaves. She also beat him on the court, 6–4, 6–3, 6–3, in an evening that was the making of women's professional tennis, which soon had its own tour sponsored by Virginia Slims. (Virginia Slims was advertised as a cigarette especially for the 1970s version of the New Woman, with a commercial that enthused about the progress women had made, and concluded: "You've got your own cigarette now, baby!" It was one of a number of 1970s promotions that demonstrated how the advertising industry was impressed but somewhat at sea with what was going on with women. Geritol tonic had a huge national campaign starring an invigorated woman whose happy husband announces, "My wife: I think I'll keep her.")

By the middle of the 1970s, however, the country's mood was soured by an economic tailspin that sent unemployment up to an unthinkable 9 percent. The women's liberation movement splintered, the victim in part of its own success, and also crippled by an ideology so egalitarian that anyone who was identified as a leader was instantly pilloried. Radical feminists claimed Gloria Steinem was working for the CIA. Meanwhile, Betty Friedan said that publicity over lesbians in the movement was creating a "lavender herring" that threatened women's progress.

The country was moving toward the 1980s, a very different social, cultural, and political terrain in which feminism was once again consigned to the dust bin of history, women reembraced high-heeled shoes and dress-up clothing, and fear of spinsterhood reemerged as a popular pathology. (In 1986, *Newsweek* warned famously, if inaccurately, that a single forty-year-old woman had a better chance of being killed by a terrorist than finding a husband.) But it all had precious little effect on what was happening on the ground. The economic crash in the 1970s simply encouraged more women to get jobs to help preserve their family's standard of living. The teenage girls of the 1980s might never have met a self-described feminist younger than forty, but they were trotting off to college in their stiletto heels, anticipating careers as routinely as their brothers did. For the first time, most mothers of pre-school children held down jobs. When young lovers built their castles in the air, they planned on two salaries to pay the mortgage.

The nation had, over just two decades, accepted a radical new view of women's place: that it was everywhere. Americans almost universally believed women should have complete financial and legal control of their lives, and that they should be able to do whatever they were capable of doing, even if it was putting out fires or playing Little League baseball or flying 500 passengers from New York to Miami. They felt women should be able to go to a movie alone without feeling self-conscious or have dinner with a male business colleague without anyone regarding it as a prelude to seduction. They believed women should be able to run for Congress without being a congressman's widow. In the 1980s, there were women in space, women in the pulpit, and women in military academies. A woman was appointed to the Supreme Court and a woman was nominated by the Democratic Party for vice president of the United States.

Much of this would never have happened—or it would not have happened nearly as fast—if the economy had not required it. Just as society suddenly embraced women as the ideal teachers and typists when there was nobody else to do the job, the idea of women working through their lives caught on when the information era succeeded the industrial age. The vast number of educated women was too valuable a resource to let go once they began to have children. Meanwhile, the consumer economy developed more and more things that families felt they needed, which they could no longer acquire on the salary of a single breadwinner.

The unanswered question was whether the new economy had created yet another variation on the theme of an emergency. While society's attitude toward women's proper role had changed dramatically, there was a part of the old pattern that remained stubbornly in place: the new challenges and opportunities did not replace the old duties; they were just added on. Any girl had the right to try to become an astronaut or a neurosurgeon, but if she wanted to have a husband and children as well—and most women did—she was expected to figure out on her own how to make it work. Americans did not immediately redefine the obligations of husbands and fathers, and government did not completely rethink its responsibility to provide services like day care or after-school programs.

It was a struggle that had been going on beneath the surface since Elizabeth Cady Stanton had fretted about the household help and Antoinette Brown had fantasized about a pleasant home full of orphans and servants who would greet her when she came off the road. The ability to work for decent wages was the factor most responsible for the change of women's status in America. They were able to pursue marriage, motherhood, and careers with avidity and success, but with a continual rueful feeling that their plates are too full for anybody's good.

In the year 2000, the country was far from having worked out all the issues about gender and sex that had bedeviled it from the beginning. The abortion wars, which feminists thought had ended in the 1970s with the Supreme Court decision in *Roe* v. *Wade*, were still going strong. Although the nation had reached a level of acceptance of homosexuality that would have been unimaginable a few decades before, there were still many places lesbians were put at a disadvantage. And there had been losses with the gains. Neighborhoods missed the nonworking mothers who had time to raise money for the school or run the Brownie troop. Suburban neighborhoods cleared out in the morning when parents went to work, and not many people had time for the kind of chats over coffee in someone's kitchen that once helped women form strong networks of friendship and support. Now that women could be anything they wanted to be, the country suffered because not enough of them wanted to be teachers or nurses. Parents who rejoiced that their little girl didn't have to wait miserably by the phone for a boy to call may not have been thrilled to discover how many young women, barely in their teens, felt empowered not just to pursue the male they fancied but to initiate sexual encounters. ("They have more attitude," a sixteen-year-old boy told Alex Kuczynski in the *New York Times*. "They have more power. And they overpower boys more. I mean, it's scary.") Nobody was happy that while teenage girls in 1900 made resolutions about how to become better people, a century later they almost always fixated on perfecting their bodies rather than their character.

But it's impossible, still, not to cheer. By the year 2000, America's women received 55 percent of the nation's college degrees and made up nearly half of most law and medical school classes. They owned more than a third of the nation's businesses. Among two-income families, more than a quarter of the wives earned more than their husbands. There were sixty women in the House of Representatives and fourteen in the Senate, and the appearance of women candidates for governor or mayor was no longer worthy of much comment. Even the most conservative segments of society believed women should mate out of preference, not necessity, and that they should be able to get as much education as they desired.

The country has been enriched, over the last half century, by the arrival of new generations of immigrants, many of them Latinas. They're writing their own chapter in this story right now. Poor women and women of color struggle against odds middle-class whites have trouble appreciating or even imagining. But their chances in life are not dictated by Y chromosomes. Today, nobody believes being a girl disqualifies you from having adventures. When the hero of the spectacularly successful movie *Titanic* drowned, the heroine went on to have a life full of excitement and romance before being reunited with him after death. It was hard to avoid the impression that she wouldn't have had nearly as much fun if he'd managed to keep his head above water. All those actresses who succumbed pathetically in TV westerns so the hero could continue to ride alone must have been cheering somewhere.

Today, we live on the same continent that Eleanor Dare sailed into in 1587, carrying the child she would only have time to give birth to and name before both of them vanished from sight and history. You want to reach out and warn her to go back, just as you want to tell those tobacco brides who came to the new world in search of husbands and wound up dead in an Indian massacre that there really are worse things in life than failing to get married. There are so many brave and headstrong women who refused to do the prudent thing and died failures in their own time. Now we put their pictures on stamps and name roads and schools in their honor. We stand on their shoulders and tell our children their stories.

# ACKNOWLEDGMENTS

Every error in this book is my own doing, but many of the facts were culled by researchers, particularly Karen Avrich, Daisy Hernandez, Carol Lee, Christina Lem, Sasha Soreff, and Jen Uscher. This book has been only a sidelight in their lives, which otherwise have been full of achievement and adventure. Karen, the only professional researcher in the group, worked with me on my last book, *Scorpion Tongues*, and I was lucky enough to have her assistance again while she divided the rest of her time among other books-in-process and a movie script. Daisy, who undoubtedly learned more about the history of menstruation on this project than she necessarily wanted to know, coedited her own book, *Colonize This*, a collection of essays by young women of color. Sasha, who read and underlined books about everything from the history of waitressing to Amelia Earhart, pursued her career in choreography and teaching dance. One of her pieces, *Tipping the Hourglass*, was recently performed on public television. Christina has almost finished her own book about four generations of her family. Jen, among many other projects, got married and became famous as an expert on wild parrots in Brooklyn. Carol has finished graduate school, published her own journalism, and begun work as the researcher for the *New York Times* editorial department. One of the pleasures of doing this book was getting to share bits and pieces of all their lives. Others who assisted with research included Carolyn Brook, Melissa Henley, Latasha Quinones, Kam ChAn and Dean Cully Clark, and Lisa Daigle at the University of Alabama.

My friends Gail Gregg and Trish Hall were loyal readers and advisers throughout, and I'm grateful for the help of Eleanor Randolph and Maureen Dowd. I'm also lucky to be related to a bunch of extremely smart and supportive women. My sister-in-law, Kathleen Collins, helped with the research and provided constant encouragement. My mother, Rita Gleason, gave me really good suggestions for editing. My father, Roy, and my siblings, in-laws, nieces, and nephew cheered me on and put up with my disorganization and sporadic inattention. Another pleasure of this project was getting to know the world of women's historians. Without implicating them in the product, I want to thank Linda Kerber, Christine Stansell, Elizabeth Brown Pryor, Carol Berkin, Carol Smith-Rosenberg, Katherine Kish Sklar, Kathleen Barry, Mary Beth Norton, and Joan Brumberg for their kindness and courtesy to me or my researchers.

The people who deserve my undying thanks for putting up with me while I was writing this book are too numerous to mention, but they certainly include everyone on the *New York Times* editorial board, particularly Phil Taubman, the deputy editor, whose patience and support were truly above and beyond the call of duty.

Finally, thanks to my agent, Alice Martell, the only person who likes what I write as much as my mother; Henry Ferris of William Morrow, who was the book's first champion and who endured what was probably the worst Christmas of his existence in order to do a terrific last-minute editing job; and, above all, Dan Collins, without whom nothing would have been any fun.

# NOTES

## CHAPTER 1: THE FIRST COLONISTS

### THE EXTREMELY BRIEF STORY OF VIRGINIA DARE

The story of the Roanoke voyage is constantly being reexamined by historians, although the basic facts about who went and how they arrived never change. It was told for the first time by Richard Hakluyt in his reports on voyages to the Virginia colony, and it will never lose its fascination unless, improbably, someone definitively proves what happened to the colonists.

1–2    *The inaptly named* . . . Richard Hofstadter, *America at 1750*, p. 41.

2      *The wife of John Dunton* . . . Paula Treckel, *To Comfort the Heart: Women in Seventeenth-Century America*, p. 47.

       *"overgrown with Melons . . ."* Henry Burrage, *Early English and French Voyages*, p. 288.

2–3    *The Dares and other English* . . . There are almost as many studies on the Native Americans who were living at the time of the first settlements as there were tribes on the eastern seaboard, although few of them focus on the women. For an overview see chapter 3 of Carol Berkin's *First Generations*.

### "FEDD UPON HER TILL HE HAD CLEAN DEVOURED ALL HER PARTES"

3      *Sir Thomas Dale* . . . Karen Ordahl Kupperman, "Apathy and Death in Early Jamestown," *Journal of American History* (June 1979), p. 25.

3–4    *The Jamestown that greeted* . . . Julia Cherry Spruill, *Women's Life and Work in the Southern Colonies*, p. 20 (footnote).

4          *People gnawed on . . .* Spruill, p. 5.
           *Anne Burras:* Virginia Bernhard, "Men, Women and Children at
           Jamestown: Population and Gender in Early Virginia," *Journal of Southern
           History* (November 1992), p. 616.
           *Temperance Flowerdew:* See John Henry Yardley's *Before the Mayflower.*
5–6        *Pocahontas:* My take on this somewhat mysterious figure is based, in main,
           on Paula Treckel's *To Comfort the Heart,* pp. 58–61. For a full treatment of
           everything that's known, or guessed, about Pocahontas, see Grace Steele
           Woodward in *Three American Indian Women.*
6          *The bride-to-be did not confide . . .* David Smits, " 'Abominable Mixture,' "
           *The Virginia Magazine of History and Biography* (April 1987), p. 177.

## "IT IS NOT KNOWEN WHETHER
## MAN OR WOMAN BE THE MOST NECESSARY"

6          *There wasn't much prospect . . .* Roger Thompson, *Women in Stuart En-
           gland and America,* p. 33.
           *"If any Maid or single . . ."* Spruill, p. 15.
           *An even more enthusiastic . . .* Spruill, p. 46.
7          *In 1619, the Virginia House . . .* Spruill, pp. 8–9.
           *"tobacco brides":* David Ransome, "Wives for Virginia," *William and Mary
           Quarterly* (January 1991), pp. 10–18.
8          *In October 1618, a warrant . . .* "Kidnapping Maidens, to Be Sold in Virginia,"
           *Virginia Magazine of History and Biography* (January 1899), pp. 228–33.
           *The danger of being dragged . . .* The information in this section comes
           from William Hart Blumenthal's *Brides from Bridewell,* pp. 58–102.
9          *a study in one Maryland county showed . . .* Lois Green Carr and Lorena
           Walsh, "The Planter's Wife," *William and Mary Quarterly* (October 1977),
           pp. 548–49.
10         *The legislature reasoned . . .* Carol Berkin and Leslie Horowitz, *Women's
           Voices, Women's Lives,* p. 16.
           *The court records reveal . . .* Ralph Semmes, *Crime and Punishment in Early
           Maryland,* pp. 96–108.
10–11      *"What we unfortunat . . ."* Nancy Cott et al., eds., *Root of Bitterness: Doc-
           uments of the Social History of American Women,* p. 41.

## "PERFORM THE MOST MANFUL EXERCISES AS WELL AS MOST MEN"

11         *Alice Proctor:* Spruill, pp. 233–35.
           *"Many of the Women . . ."* Cott et al., *Root of Bitterness,* p. 41.
           *William Byrd described . . .* Thompson, *Women in Stuart England and
           America,* p. 105.
12–14      *Margaret Brent . . .* This section is taken from Mary Beth Norton's *Found-
           ing Mothers and Fathers,* pp. 282–87, Julia Spruill's *Women's Life and Work
           in the Southern Colonies,* pp. 236–41, and Lois Green Carr's "Margaret
           Brent: A Brief History" in the Maryland State Archives.

## "CONTRACTING HERSELF TO . . . SEVERAL MEN AT ONE TIME"

14    *The niece of the novelist . . .* Alice Morse Earle, *Colonial Dames and Good Wives,* p. 11.

*"a nest of the most notorious . . ."* Kirsten Fischer, "Common Disturbers of the Peace," p. 15, in *Beyond Image and Convention,* Janet Lee Coryell et al., eds.

15    *The average union ended . . .* Carr and Walsh, "Planter's Wife," p. 552.

*Women's life expectancy . . .* Berkin, *First Generations,* pp. 10–17.

*One minister sued . . .* Thompson, *Women in Stuart England and America,* p. 39.

*Sarah Offley:* Cynthia Kierner, *Beyond the Household,* pp. 11–12.

16    *In 1624, Eleanor Spragg . . .* Spruill, p. 151.

*In 1687, William Rascow . . .* Thompson, *Women in Stuart England and America,* p. 38.

*The people who colonized . . .* See Mary Beth Norton's "Gender and Defamation in Maryland," *William and Mary Quarterly* (January 1987), pp. 37–38.

*In some areas, a third . . .* Carr and Walsh, "Planter's Wife," p. 551.

17    *Ann Fowler:* Kathleen Brown, *Good Wives, Nasty Wenches and Anxious Patriarchs,* p. 95.

*The Virginia General Assembly . . .* K. Brown, p. 148.

## "WHITE PEOPLE . . . ARE ENTIRELY RUINED AND RENDERED MISERABLE"

17    *Mary Johnson:* Teresa Amott and Julie Matthaei, *Race, Gender and Work,* p. 143.

18    *In Charleston . . .* This section is based on Robert Olwell's "Loose, Idle and Disorderly: Slave Women in the 18th Century Charleston Marketplace," in *More Than Chattel,* David Barry Gaspar and Darlene Clark Hine, eds.

*In Virginia, officials . . .* Amott and Matthaei, p. 143.

## "I FEAR THE POWER OF ENGLAND NO MORE THAN A BROKEN STRAW"

Except where otherwise noted, this section is based on Susan Westbury's "Women in Bacon's Rebellion," in *Southern Women: Histories and Identities,* Virginia Bernhard et al., eds.

19–20  *Sarah Drummond, the wife . . .* K. Brown, p. 166.

20    *Sarah Grendon:* Wilcomb Washburn, *The Governor and the Rebel: A History of Bacon's Rebellion in Virginia,* p. 109.

*The female captives went down . . .* Spruill, pp. 234–35.

21    *Mrs. Grendon then admitted . . .* Washburn, p. 127.

*Sarah Drummond's husband . . .* Spruill, pp. 234–36.

22    *"As I live, the old fool . . ."* Mary Flournoy, *Essays Historical and Critical,* p. 21.

# CHAPTER 2: THE WOMEN OF NEW ENGLAND

"HIS DEAREST CONSORT, ACCIDENTALLY FALLING OVERBOARD"
That little phrase is all Cotton Mather had to say about Dorothy May Bradford in his biography of William Bradford. It's in chapter 1 of the second book of *The Ecclesiastical History of New England, From Its First Planting in the Year 1620, Unto the Year of the Lord, 1698.* Bradford himself wrote a history of the Plymouth Plantation, which tells about the voyage and the early settlement, but mentions Dorothy May not at all.

"NOT SO HUMBLE AND HEAVENLY AS IS DESIRED"
Except where otherwise noted, the information in this section comes from Lyle Koehler's *A Search for Power.*

26      *"Touching our government . . ."* Letter of William Bradford and Isaac Allerton, *American Historical Review* 8 (1903), pp. 294–301.
         *When the residents of Chebacco . . .* Thompson, *Women in Stuart England and America,* p. 106.
         *By the middle of the century . . .* Roger Thompson, *Sex in Middlesex,* pp. 88–89.
27      *Pennsylvania eventually gave women . . .* Berkin and Horowitz, p. 99.

"PREACHES BETTER GOSPELL
THAN ANY OF YOUR BLACK-COATES"
Unless otherwise noted, the part of this section about Anne Hutchinson is based on Mary Beth Norton's *Founding Mothers and Fathers.*

28–29   *Within a year of her arrival . . .* Koehler, *A Search for Power,* p. 219.
29      *"Preaches better Gospell . . ."* Norton, p. 368.
         *"a woman of haughty . . ."* G. J. Barker-Benfield and Catherine Clinton, eds., *Portraits of American Women,* p. 48.
         *Emboldened by her success . . .* Another theory is that Hutchinson's undoing came when she became weak from exhaustion, and stumbled into making the heretical admission that she believed herself to be in direct communication with God.
29–30   *Reverend Cotton urged . . .* Koehler, *A Search for Power,* p. 226.
30      *Once exiled . . .* This paragraph is based on Koehler, *A Search for Power,* pp. 230–32, and *Lying-In,* by Richard and Dorothy Wertz, p. 22.
         *Mary Oliver of Salem:* Koehler, *A Search for Power,* pp. 220–21.
         *Anne Eaton:* Janet Wilson James, "Women in American Religious History: An Overview," in *Women in American Religious History,* p. 32.
         *Lydia Wardell:* Koehler, *A Search for Power,* pp. 251–52.
31      *Susanna Hudson:* Berkin, *First Generations,* pp. 95–96.
31–32   *Anne Bradstreet . . .* Ola Elizabeth Wilson's biography in *Notable American Women,* James and James, eds., vol. 1, p. 223.

## "CHOPPED INTO THE HEAD
## WITH A HATCHET AND STRIPP'D NAKED"

Except when otherwise noted, this section is based on Laurel Ulrich's *Good Wives*, and *Women's Captivity Narratives*, edited by Kathryn Derounian-Stodola.

34    *Elizabeth Tozier* . . . Koehler, *A Search for Power*, p. 429.

*In 1682, Mary Rowlandson* . . . Thompson, *Women in Stuart England and America*, p. 105.

## "BY MY OWN INNOCENCE
## I KNOW YOU ARE IN THE WRONG WAY"

The story of the Salem witch trials, which seems to be of perpetual fascination, has been examined more than any other part of the colonial experience. A good all-around, well-written description of what we know is Frances Hill's *A Delusion of Satan*. Paul Boyer and Stephen Nissenbaum have done some of the most interesting research into the Salem defendants and their accusers, which they published in *Salem Possessed*. Boyer and Nissenbaum have also published a documentary record of the episode, *Salem-Village Witchcraft*. Carol Karlsen approaches the story from a feminist perspective in *The Devil in the Shape of a Woman*. Except when otherwise noted, this section is based on their books. The most recent important revisiting of the Salem legend is Mary Beth Norton's *In the Devil's Snare*. In it, Norton concluded that the trauma of the Indian wars was at the root of the hysteria.

35    *The trouble began during the long winter of 1691–92* . . . This story of Tituba's fortune-telling is the way most histories of the Salem witch-hunt begin. In her book, Mary Beth Norton argues that the evidence it really happened is too shaky to be accepted, and she begins her own account with the affliction of the girls at the Parris house.

*"little sorceries"* . . . This remark, as quoted in Boyer and Nissenbaum's *Salem Possessed* (p. 1), comes from Cotton Mather.

*Tituba* . . . Like most things about the Salem story, Tituba is subject to different interpretations. Most historians have identified her as a slave from the West Indies. Norton believes she was a Native American.

36    *One observer reported* . . . Bryan Le Beau, *The Story of the Salem Witch Trials*, p. 63.

*But others described* . . . Boyer and Nissenbaum, *Salem Possessed*, p. 24.

*Cotton Mather had published a description* . . . Le Beau, p. 42.

38    *There were virtually no witch trials* . . . Le Beau, p. 34.

39    *Ann Hibbens:* Karlsen, and John Demos, *Entertaining Satan*, pp. 87–88.

44    *Sarah Good cried back* . . . Le Beau, p. 171.

*"He lies with the Indian squaws . . ."* Le Beau, p. 141.

45    *Cotton Mather and Margaret Rule:* Le Beau, p. 221.

## CHAPTER 3: DAILY LIFE IN THE COLONIES

### "MY BASON OF WATER FROZE ON THE HEARTH"

48    *Harriet Beecher Stowe described* . . . Jack Larkin, *The Reshaping of Every-day Life*, p. 135.

*Anna Green Winslow:* Alice Morse Earle, *Diary of Anna Green Winslow*, p. xvi.

*"Night and morning were made fearful . . ."* Elisabeth Garrett, *At Home*, p. 111.

*There was at most only one real chair* . . . David Hawke, *Everyday Life in Early America*, p. 56.

49    *"This day is forty years . . ."* Nancy Cott et al., *Root of Bitterness*, pp. 61–62.

*Elizabeth Saltonstall* . . . Ulrich, *Good Wives*, pp. 74–75.

### "FOR SHE HAS BEEN AND IS A GOOD WIFE TO ME"

Alice Morse Earle wrote her histories of everyday life in colonial New England more than a century ago, but they're still in print and well worth reading. I used *Home Life in Colonial Days* as a reference for this section, except when otherwise noted.

50    *the New England General Court ordered* . . . Elaine Crane, *Ebb Tide in New England*, p. 101.

51    *Martha Ballard:* One of the recent classics on the colonial period is Laurel Ulrich's *A Midwife's Tale: The Life of Martha Ballard*.

51–52  *A Maine author* . . . Ulrich, *A Midwife's Tale*, p. 92.

52    *"The women in families . . ."* Elizabeth Buffum Chace, *Two Quaker Sisters*, p. 37.

*In 1664, Elizabeth Perkins* . . . Ulrich, *Good Wives*, p. 98.

53    *When Ensign Hewlett* . . . Ulrich, *Good Wives*, p. 46.

### "WOMEN CHOOSE RATHER TO HAVE A THING DONE WELL THAN HAVE IT OFTEN"

On matters of sexuality in American history, I'll refer again and again to *Intimate Matters: A History of Sexuality in America* by John D'Emilio and Estelle Freedman. Another very readable book on sexuality is *The Empty Cradle: Infertility in America from Colonial Times to the Present*, by Margaret Marsh and Wanda Ronner.

53    *Cotton Mather urged* . . . Koehler, *A Search for Power*, p. 32.

*A third of the accused* . . . Norton, *Founding Mothers*, p. 78.

*New Englanders who survived* . . . Richard Archer, "New England Mosaic," *William and Mary Quarterly* (October 1990), p. 497.

54    *Daniel Ela* . . . Berkin, p. 31.

*One man who had beaten* . . . Koehler, *A Search for Power*, 140–41.

*If a first child* . . . Ulrich, *Good Wives*, p. 31.

*But between 1720 and 1740* . . . John Demos, "Families in Colonial Bristol," *William and Mary Quarterly* (January 1968), p. 56.

*A visitor to New York* . . . Treckel, pp. 109–10.

54–55    *Mary Latham:* D'Emilio and Freedman, p. 12.
55       *New Haven justices dismissed* . . . Norton, *Founding Mothers,* p. 76.
         *Men who read books about sex* . . . Marsh and Ronner, p. 15.
         *Many couples believed* . . . Marsh and Ronner, p. 13.
         *but having sex too often* . . . Koehler, *A Search for Power,* p. 79.

## "THIS MIGHT POSSIBLY BE THE LAST TRIAL OF THIS SORT"

55       *Elizabeth Drinker: The Diary of Elizabeth Drinker,* p. 216.
56       *In the malaria-ridden* . . . David F. Hawke, *Everyday Life in Early America,*
         p. 65.
         *Benjamin Franklin:* Earle, *Child Life in Colonial Days,* pp. 11–12.
         *a visitor to Charlestown* . . . Spruill, *Women's Life and Work in the Southern
         Colonies,* p. 46.
         *Childbirth was a communal affair* . . . My information on childbirth is
         drawn in the main from Laurel Ulrich's *Good Wives* and *A Midwife's
         Tale.*
         *Samuel Sewall:* Sewall, *The Diary and Life of Samuel Sewall,* p. 9.
57       *Midwives were a critical* . . . Claire Elizabeth Fox, "Pregnancy, Childbirth
         and Early Infancy in Anglo-American Culture, 1675–1830," doctoral dis-
         sertation, University of Pennsylvania, 1966.
58       *One popular physician:* Berkin and Horowitz, p. 19.

## "IF I ONLY KNIT MY BROW SHE WILL CRY"

58       *Samuel Sewall:* Sewall, *The Diary and Life of Samuel Sewall,* p. 11.
         *Sewall felt* . . . Sewall, p. 2.
         *In 1740 a virulent* . . . Nancy Dye and Daniel Smith, "Mother Love and
         Infant Death," *Journal of American History* (September 1986), pp. 332–35.
59       *Fanny Kemble:* Frances Anne Kemble, *Journal of a Residence on a Georgian
         Plantation,* p. 99.
         *The Puritan minister John Robinson* . . . Philip Greven, *The Protestant Tem-
         perament,* p. 37.
         *Esther Burr:* Greven, p. 35.
59–60    *Madam Coleman:* Alice Morse Earle, *Child Life in Colonial Days,* pp. 101–3.
60       *Susan Blunt* . . . Larkin, p. 34.
         *There's a pathetic story* . . . Koehler, *A Search for Power,* p. 190.
         *Mrs. Walker:* Koehler, *A Search for Power,* p. 115.
60–61    *Caroline Howard Gilman:* Caroline Gilman, *Reflections of a Southern
         Matron,* p. 56.

## "NOT HAVING BEEN WETT ALL OVER
## ATT ONCE, FOR 28 YEARS PAST"

Some excellent books about everyday life through American history are, fittingly, in
the Everyday Life in America series. *The Reshaping of Everyday Life* by Jack Larkin is
one of the best. This section is deeply indebted to it, as well as "The Early History of

Cleanliness in America" by Richard and Claudia Bushman, published in *The Journal of American History*, March 1988, and a doctoral dissertation by Elizabeth Claire Fox, "Pregnancy, Childbirth and Early Infancy in Anglo-American Culture." Anyone who wants to get better acquainted with Elizabeth Drinker, one of the best journal-keepers of her era, can read *The Diary of Elizabeth Drinker*, edited by Elaine Forman Crane.

61      *In 1798, Elizabeth Drinker* . . . Bushman and Bushman, p. 1214.

         *At the beginning of the nineteenth* . . . Larkin, p. 163.

61–62   *"The women are pitifully . . ."* Hawke, p. 72.

62      *In Northampton* . . . Fox, pp. 55–56.

         *Moreau de St. Mèry* . . . *Moreau de St. Mèry's American Journey*, p. 297.

63      *It was a practice* . . . Fox, pp. 244–47.

64      *Lewis Miller, writing* . . . Larkin, p. 161.


## "STRANGERS ARE SOUGHT AFTER WITH GREEDINESS"

Julia Cherry Spruill is another one of the pioneer women historians, born early enough to have been a supporter of suffrage in her teens. When she was a faculty wife at the University of North Carolina, she enrolled in a graduate history seminar, where she discovered that there had been almost no research on southern women. From this came *Women's Life and Work in the Southern Colonies*, which is still one of the most terrific books on women in the South ever written. This section and a great many sections to come are indebted to it.

64      *"Strangers are sought . . ."* Earle, *Home Life*, p. 396.

         *A circuit judge* . . . Spruill, pp. 109–10.

65      *They were a chance* . . . Larkin, p. 298.

         *Carving became* . . . Spruill, p. 70.


# CHAPTER 4: TOWARD THE REVOLUTIONARY WAR

## "TO SPEND . . . WHAT OTHERS GET"

Except where otherwise noted, this section is based on Jeanne Boydston's *Home and Work: Housework, Wages and the Ideology of Labor in the Early Republic*.

67      *Hetty Shepard:* Koehler, *A Search for Power*, p. 339.

67–68   *While he was traveling* . . . Spruill, p. 41.

68      *Women, Cotton Mather told* . . . Boydston, p. 26.

         *In New Amsterdam* . . . Berkin, pp. 79–87.

69      *A well-known Puritan* . . . William Gouge, as quoted by Ruth Bloch in "American Feminine Ideals in Transition: The Rise of the Moral Mother," *Feminist Studies* (June 1978), p. 107.


## "LEFT TO PONDER ON A STRIP OF CARPET"

Constance Schulz has a good biography of Eliza Pinkney in *Portraits of American Women*, pp. 65–81, edited by Barker-Benfield and Clinton. Eliza's letters are still in print, with an introduction by her descendant, in *The Letterbook of Eliza Lucas Pinckney, 1739–1763*.

71 *"I have frequently seen . . ."* Spruill, p. 71.
Caroline Gilman . . . Gilman, *Recollections of a Southern Matron*, pp. 252–56.

"THEY LACED HER UP, THEY STARVED HER DOWN"

72 *"They braced my aunt . . ."* Earle, *Child Life in Colonial Days*, p. 109.
*When upper-class . . .* Ulrich, p. 115.
*Nicholas Culpepper . . .* Berkin and Horowitz, p. 19.
*Lucinda Lee . . .* Spruill, pp. 105–7.

73 *Dr. William Buchan . . .* Fox, p. 73.
*shoes with very high heels . . .* See Alice Earle's *Two Centuries of Costumes*, chapter 13.

74 *"Some of the ladies . . ."* Carolyn Shine, "Dress for the Ohio Pioneers," in *Dress in American Culture*, edited by Patricia Cunningham and Susan Lab, pp. 43–45.
*a Boston journal in 1755 . . .* Eric John Dingwall, *The American Woman*, p. 51.

74–75 *Cotton Mather, naturally . . .* Koehler, *A Search for Power*, p. 354.

"MISERABLE OLD AGE AND HELPLESS INFANCY"

Except where otherwise noted, this section is based on Gary Nash's "The Failure of Female Factory Labor in Colonial Boston," *Labor History* (Spring 1979).

76 *The maximum weekly rate . . .* Berkin, p. 153.
*Judith Stevens . . .* Berkin and Horowitz, p. 110.

"A VERY EXTRAORDINARY FEMALE SLAVE"

There are several different editions of Phillis Wheatley's poems in print. This section is based on a biography by Charles Scruggs in *Portraits of American Women*, Barker-Benfield and Clinton, eds.; as well as the entries in *Notable American Women*, James and James, eds.; and *Black Women in America*, Darlene Clark Hine, ed.

"WHAT HAVE I TO DO WITH POLITICKS?"

My two favorite books about American women in the Revolutionary War are Linda Kerber's *Women of the Republic* and Mary Beth Norton's *Liberty's Daughters*.

78 *Getting the cooperation . . .* Kerber, p. 37.
*half of all homes had tea sets . . .* Larkin, p. 174.
*Susan Boudinot . . .* Kerber, *Woman of the Republic*, p. 39.

79 *In 1774, fifty-one women . . .* Kierner, pp. 81–82.
*A much-quoted poem . . .* Kerber, *Women of the Republic*, p. 38.
*The* Virginia Gazette *announced . . .* Kierner, p. 83.

79–80 *Eliza Pinckney . . .* Pinckney, p. xxiii.

80 *Some women were raped . . .* Berkin, p. 184.
*A North Carolina man . . .* Kierner, p. 89.
*"We are in no ways . . ."* Abigail Adams to her husband, Sept. 20, 1775. As quoted in Kerber, p. 67.

*"And such is the distress . . ."* Abigail Adams to her husband, Sept. 8, 1775, in Charles Francis Adams, *Familiar Letters of John Adams and His Wife Abigail Adams,* p. 124.

*In November 1775 . . .* Adams, p. 124.

80–81   *In the summer of 1777 . . .* Rosemary Keller, *Patriotism and the Female Sex,* p. 118.

81      *one South Carolina man claimed . . .* Kierner, p. 95.

*Edmund Burke told the British . . .* I found this quote from the Nov. 6, 1776, debate in the House of Commons in Sara Evans's *Born for Liberty.* It was first noted by historian Linda Kerber, but neither Kerber nor anyone else appears to have ever found any other references to the woman who burned down New York. One letter written from New York reported: "The first Incendiary who fell into the Hands of the Troops was a Woman, provided with Matches and Combustibles; but that her Sex availed her little, for without Ceremony she was tossed into the Flames." But other letter-writers named other suspects. (See *The Iconography of Manhattan* by I. N. Phelps Stokes, Vol. 5. pp. 1020–26.)

*Deborah Sampson Gannett:* Elizabeth Evans, *Weathering the Storm,* pp. 303–34.

*"Molly Pitcher":* Holly Mayer, *Belonging to the Army,* p. 21.

81–82   *Margaret Corbin . . .* Mayer, pp. 50, 144.

82      *Letters to husbands . . .* Keller, pp. 108–14.

*Ann Gwinnett . . .* Kerber, *Women of the Republic,* p. 79.

*"Tho a female . . ."* S. Evans, *Born for Liberty,* p. 48.

*Thomas Jefferson wrote . . .* E. Evans, p. 5.

82–83   *One of the era's most quoted . . .* Abigail Adams, March 31, 1776, in L. H. Butterfield et al., eds., *The Book of Abigail and John,* p. 121.

83      *Adams's response . . .* John Adams, April 14, 1776, in Butterfield et al., eds., p. 122.

### "WE MAY SHORTLY EXPECT TO SEE THEM TAKE THE HELM—OF GOVERNMENT"

Except where noted, this section is based on Edward Raymond Turner's "Women's Suffrage in New Jersey, 1790–1807," *Smith College Studies in History* (October 1915).

83      *In 1797, during . . .* Marion Thompson Wright, "The Early Years of the Republic," *Journal of Negro History* (April 1948), p. 173.

### CHAPTER 5: 1800–1860

#### "MAN IS STRONG—WOMAN IS BEAUTIFUL"

One valuable book about this era is *The Feminization of American Culture,* by Ann Douglas.

85      *Sarah Josepha Hale . . .* Nancy Woloch has an excellent section on Hale in *Women and the American Experience.* An interesting biography of Hale was

published by Ruth Finley in 1931. A good shorter biography, by Paul
Boyer, is in *Notable American Women*, Edward James and Janet Wilson
James, eds.

86      *"not to win fame . . ."* Woloch, p. 138.

Harper's Magazine *estimated . . .* Woloch, p. 136.

*Its publisher boasted . . .* Woloch, p. 116.

87      *"Our men are sufficiently . . ."* Douglas, *Feminization of American Culture*,
p. 57.

*When Mrs. Hale noticed . . .* Glenna Matthews, *"Just a Housewife,"* p. 71.

*qualities of the True Woman . . .* In 1966, Barbara Welter published an
essay on "The Cult of True Womanhood" in *American Quarterly*. Her
description of how the early-nineteenth-century mass media—and
middle-class society—viewed women was, and still is, one of the most
influential pieces of writing on this period. In the spring of 2002, the *Journal of Women's History* published a restrospective on it.

*"Man is strong . . ."* Boydston, pp. 142–43.

*"The majority of women . . ."* Woloch, pp. 127–28.

87–88   *"True feminine genius . . ."* Welter, "The Cult of True Womanhood,"
p. 160.

88      *she had to suffer in silence . . .* Douglas, *Feminization of American Culture*,
p. 46.

*In the bust of 1818 . . .* Celia Morris Eckhardt, *Fanny Wright*, p. 46.

*when the panic of 1837 . . .* Sean Wilentz, *Chants Democratic*, p. 294.

*The railroads kept having wrecks . . .* Daniel Boorstin, *The Americans: The
National Experience*, p. 101.

### "IN DANGER OF BECOMING PERFECT RECLUSES"

Anyone interested in this section should read Mary P. Ryan's *Women in Public*. The
observations from Frances Trollope should make it clear that *Domestic Manners of
Americans* is still a great read, almost 200 years after it was written.

89      *Frances Trollope reported from Cincinnati . . .* Trollope, p. 60.

*"Staid in . . ."* Ryan, *Women in Public*, p. 24.

*"She has a head . . ."* Wertz and Wertz, p. 58.

90      *Complaining about the constant presence . . .* Trollope, p. 70.

*"This darkness . . ."* Trollope, p. 210.

*"I hardly know . . ."* Trollope, p. 18.

*A Mrs. Hall . . .* Larkin, p. 168.

*Mrs. Trollope attended . . .* Trollope, pp. 176–77.

### "INITIATED INTO THE ARTS AND MYSTERIES OF THE WASH TUB"

This section, and sections to come, are indebted to three wonderful biographies:
Joan Hedrick's *Harriet Beecher Stowe: A Life*, Carolyn Karcher's *First Woman in the
Republic: A Cultural Biography of Lydia Maria Child*, and Kathryn Kish Sklar's
*Catharine Beecher: A Study in Domesticity*.

91      *"Oh, if we only . . ."* Matthews, p. 23.

        *published as* The American Frugal Housewife . . . Child's housekeeping
        guide is still in print today.

        *"written for the lower . . ."* Karcher, pp. 133–35.

92      *"wandering like a trunk . . ."* Hedrick, p. 390.

        *"initiated into . . ."* Catharine Beecher, *A Treatise on Domestic Economy,*
        p. 55.

"HOW COULD *I* TELL SHE WAS GOING TO BE SO FAMOUS!"

Some of the popular women's novels of the pre–Civil War period are in print today.
They are generally rather heavy going; one of the most accessible to modern
women might be Fanny Fern's *Ruth Hall.* A number of scholars have done the job
of reading them for us, however—most recently Nina Baym in *Women's Fiction,* a
very good guide to both the books and the period.

93      The Lamplighter, *the novel* . . . Nina Baym, in the introduction to *The
        Lamplighter,* p. ix.

        *Harriet Beecher Stowe, whose writings* . . . Hedrick, pp. 239–40.

95      *was estimated to have "245 tear flows"* . . . Fred Lewis Pattee, *The Feminine
        Fifties,* p. 56.

        *Nathaniel Willis:* Pattee, pp. 52–53.

        *"I love everybody"* . . . Douglas, p. 206.

        *"I observe that feminine . . ."* Pattee, p. 70.

        *"My mother, then a loom-tender . . ."* Pattee, p. 53.

"INTEMPERANCE AMONG THE MEN
AND LOVE OF DRESS AMONG THE WOMEN"

Anyone interested in this section should read Lori Ginzberg's *Women and the Work
of Benevolence.*

96      The Advocate of Female Reform *called* . . . Ryan, *Women in Public,* p. 100.

        *When a young man* . . . Barbara Epstein, *The Politics of Domesticity,* p. 94.

97      *Louisa May Alcott:* Ginzberg, p. 58.

        *A refuge for prostitutes* . . . Ryan, *Women in Public,* pp. 101–2.

        *One member of* . . . Anne Boylan, "Women in Groups," *Journal of Ameri-
        can History* (December 1984), p. 504.

        *Maria Burley* . . . Christine Stansell, *City of Women,* p. 71.

98      *"You cannot imagine . . ."* Ginzberg, p. 76.

"STANDING UP WITH BARE-FACED IMPUDENCE"

98      *When Harriet Beecher* . . . Hedrick, p. 238.

        *Mary Ann Duff* . . . Claudia Johnson, *American Actress: Perspectives on the
        Nineteenth Century,* p. 3.

        *William Wood* . . . Johnson, p. 8.

99      *Wood's wife survived not only* . . . Johnson, p. 23.

        *In 1840, when factory girls* . . . Johnson, pp. 54–56.

*Fanny Wright:* Unless otherwise noted, the information on Fanny Wright comes from Celia Morris Eckhardt's *Fanny Wright: Rebel in America.*

100   *Mrs. Trollope said her most outrageous . . .* Trollope, p. 203.
*One of Brown's biographers noted . . .* Elizabeth Cazden's *Antoinette Brown Blackwell,* p. 62.

### "OUR SIS CAME OFF WITH FLYING COLOURS"

100–101 *In Lancaster, Pennsylvania . . .* Wilson, p. 153.
101   *Dorothea Dix:* See Dorothy Clarke Wilson's *Stranger and Traveler: The Story of Dorothea Dix.*
*She was on board . . .* Thomas Brown's *Dorothea Dix: New England Reformer,* p. 136.
*Margaret Fuller:* Bell Gale Chevigny has a biography of Margaret Fuller in Barker-Benfield and Clinton's *Portraits of American Women,* and Ann Douglas has a very good section on Fuller in *The Feminization of American Culture.* Those who want to know more about her should find *The Portable Margaret Fuller,* edited by Mary Kelley.
*"Humanity is divided . . ."* Barker-Benfield and Clinton, eds., p. 193.
102   *Antoinette Brown . . .* See Cazden.
*Elizabeth Blackwell . . .* Blackwell left her own autobiography of sorts, a collection of letters she called *Pioneer Work in Opening the Medical Profession to Women.*
*"The idea of winning . . ."* Malcolm Sanders Johnston, *Elizabeth Blackwell and Her Alma Mater,* p. 10.
103   *"A hush fell over the class . . ."* Jordan Brown, *Elizabeth Blackwell, Physician,* p. 52.
*"Our sis came off . . ."* Johnston, p. 24.
*"Who will ever guess . . ."* Blackwell, p. 198.
*Before she married . . .* Matthews, pp. 58–59.

### "APPEAR TO BE AVERSE TO WHAT SHE INWARDLY DESIRES"

104   *Henry Bedlow:* To read more about the Bedlow trial, see Christine Stansell's *City of Women* and Marybeth Hamilton's essay, "The Life of a Citizen in the Hands of a Woman," in *New York and the Rise of Capitalism,* published by the New-York Historical Society in the spring of 1983.
*"Any woman who is not . . ."* Hamilton, "The Life of a Citizen," p. 233–34.
*"in the hands of a woman . . ."* Hamilton, "The Life of a Citizen," p. 246.
105   *Daniel Sickles . . .* I wrote about the Sickles trial in *Scorpion Tongues: Gossip, Celebrity, and American Politics.*

### "THE CHANCE THAT IN MARRIAGE SHE WILL DRAW A BLOCKHEAD"

106   *Thomas Jefferson . . .* Boorstin, p. 187.
*Sara Hale enthusiastically . . .* Woloch, p. 110.

*In a demonstration of Hale's commitment* . . . Welter, "The Cult of True Womanhood," p. 167.

*Elizabeth Buffum Chace* . . . Chace and Lovell, *Two Quaker Sisters*, pp. 23–24.

107    *Thomas Gallaudet* . . . Keith Melder, *Beginnings of Sisterhood*, pp. 24–25.

*One superintendent wrote* . . . Jackie Blount, *Destined to Rule the Schools*, p. 19.

*In 1838, Connecticut paid* . . . Melder, p. 25.

*In Ohio, the Superintendent* . . . Carl Kaestle, *Pillars of the Republic*, p. 123.

*By 1870* . . . Catherine Clinton, *The Other Civil War*, p. 46.

*"They are the natural . . ."* Melder, p. 24.

*"They'll be educating the cows . . ."* Douglas, *Feminization of American Culture*, p. 59.

108    *Although there have been* . . . Barbara Welter, "Anti-Intellectualism and the American Woman," *Mid-America* (October 1966), p. 264.

*Margaret Fuller* . . . Douglas, *Feminization of American Culture*, p. 58.

*In Petersburg* . . . Suzanne Lebsock, *The Free Women of Petersburg*, p. 173.

*Catharine Beecher's first* . . . Vivian Hopkins, *Prodigal Puritan: A Life of Delia Bacon*, p. 20.

*"Dear Madam"* . . . Bernard Wishy, *The Child and the Republic*, p. 14.

## "THEY WEAR OUT FASTER THAN ANY OTHER CLASS OF PEOPLE"

109    *A quarter of the native-born women* . . . Maris Vinovskis, "The Female School-Teacher in Ante-Bellum Massachusetts," *Journal of Social History* (March 1977), p. 333.

*Maria Waterbury* . . . Susan Cayleff, *Wash and Be Healed*, p. 82.

*A special commission in Connecticut* . . . Boorstin, p. 44.

*"Went over to make . . ."* Many of these anecdotes are taken from Polly Welts Kaufman's very interesting *Women Teachers on the Frontier*, p. 140.

*"Teaching before dependence . . ."* Mary Elizabeth Massey, *Women in the Civil War*, p. 113.

110    *A would-be teacher* . . . Kaufman, pp. 12–34.

*Elizabeth Blackwell* . . . Blackwell, p. 17.

*Augusta Hubbell* . . . Kaufman, pp. 158–59.

*In the South during* . . . Massey, p. 114.

## "I AM LIVING ON NO ONE"

111    *By the 1820s, New England* . . . Mary Ryan, *Womanhood in America*, p. 105.

*"Don't I feel independent!"* . . . Woloch, pp. 142–43.

*Harriet Hanson* . . . Claudia Bushman, *A Good Poor Man's Wife*, pp. 13–14.

*In 1833, when President Jackson* . . . Harriet Jane Hanson Robinson, *Loom and Spindle*, p. 50.

111–12 *A third of the female workers* . . . Bushman, p. 41.

112    *Eliza Hemingway:* Rosalyn Baxandall and Linda Gordon, *America's Working Women*, p. 65.
       *Some women kept . . .* Edwin Burrows and Mike Wallace, *Gotham*, p. 406.
       *In 1845, the New York . . .* Alice Kessler-Harris, *Out to Work*, p. 65.
       *Millworker Mary Paul . . .* Thomas Dublin, *Farm to Factory*, p. 136.
113    *Elizabeth Sullivan Stuart . . .* Faye Dudden, *Serving Women*, p. 66.

### "OH LIZZIE! THOU WILL MAKE US RIDICULOUS!"

This section is based on Elizabeth Cady Stanton's autobiography, *Eighty Years and More*, and Elisabeth Griffith's biography of Stanton, *In Her Own Right*.

113    *"As Mrs. Mott and I . . ."* Stanton, pp. 82–83.
       *"There is such a struggle . . ."* Stanton, p. 137.
       *"with such vehemence . . ."* Stanton, p. 148.
114    *"Oh Lizzie! . . ."* Alma Lutz, *Created Equal*, p. 46.
       *"My only excuse . . ."* E. Griffith, p. 59.

## CHAPTER 6: LIFE BEFORE THE CIVIL WAR

### "A TERRIBLE DECAY OF FEMALE HEALTH ALL OVER THE LAND"

My favorite essay on this subject is Ann Douglas's "The Fashionable Diseases" in *Clio's Consciousness Raised*, edited by Mary Hartman and Lois Banner.

115    *Catharine Beecher . . .* Woloch, p. 129; Page Smith, *Daughters of the Promised Land*, pp. 133–35.
115–16 *by 1840, their life expectancy . . .* Carl Degler's *At Odds: Women and the Family in America from the Revolution to the Present*, p. 28.
116    *The nineteenth century was the first time . . .* Ann Dally makes this point about the "chronic sufferer" in her book *Women Under the Knife.*
       *The number of doctors increased . . .* Larkin, p. 87.
       *"Let the reader imagine . . ."* Caroll Smith-Rosenberg's *Disorderly Conduct*, p. 200.
117    *One professor of medicine thought . . .* Douglas in Hartman and Banner, p. 3.
       *Tuberculosis, or consumption:* Anyone interested in this subject should read Sheila Rothman's *Living in the Shadow of Death*. The quote from Dr. Sweetser is on p. 16; Mrs. Fiske, p. 120.
117–18 *In* The Young Lady's Friend . . . Welter, "The Cult of True Womanhood," p. 164.
118    *one was so large . . .* Dally, p. 130.
       *Johann Friedrich Dieffenbach . . .* Dally, pp. 23–24.
119    *J. Marion Sims:* The saga of Dr. Sims is told in his own autobiography and from a different perspective in Dally's *Women Under the Knife*. For a third view, see Diana Scully's "From Natural to Surgical Event" in Pamela Eakins's *The American Way of Birth*.

119–20  *Jane Todd Crawford* . . . Dally, pp. 8–19.
120     *Both Harriet Beecher Stowe* . . . Hedrick, p. 175.
        *A famous English gynecologist* . . . Hartman and Banner, p. 4.
        *Salmon P. Chase* . . . Wertz and Wertz, p. 68.
121     *It's no wonder that* . . . A brief overview of the health reformers of the era
        can be found in the introduction to Susan Cayleff's *Wash and Be Healed.*
        *Sylvester Graham claimed* . . . Mary P. Ryan's *The Empire of the Mother,*
        p. 28.
        *Harriet Beecher Stowe spent* . . . Cayleff, pp. 143–44.


"AFRAID OF NOTHING SO MUCH AS GROWING STOUT"
On the issue of women's body image throughout history, I've relied on Lois Banner's *American Beauty* more than any other book.
122     *William Baxter* . . . Banner, p. 54.
        *Harriet Beecher Stowe theorized* . . . Banner, p. 54.
        *the corset:* Anyone who wants to know a great deal more about the history
        of corsets should consult Valerie Steele's *The Corset.*
123     *A southern woman wrote* . . . Catherine Clinton, *The Plantation Mistress,*
        p. 99.
        *"We in America* . . ." Banner, p. 47.
        *"They never wear* . . ." Trollope, p. 234.
124     *"Remember* . . . *not to go out* . . ." Clinton, *The Plantation Mistress,* p. 100.
        *Elizabeth Cady Stanton* . . . Stanton describes her love affair with the
        bloomer outfit in chapter 13 of her autobiography.
        *Cady Stanton, whose figure* . . . Banner, p. 97.


"ONE OF THE BEST OBSTETRICIANS OF HIS TIME . . . WAS BLIND"
There are a lot of excellent studies of the history of childbirth in America, but my favorite is *Lying-In* by Richard and Dorothy Wertz. This section relies heavily on their research, along with the works cited below
125     *In Philadelphia, twenty-one women* . . . Catherine Scholten's "On the
        Importance of the Obstetrick Art" in *William and Mary Quarterly* (July
        1977), p. 434.
        *in 1840 at Bellevue* . . . Janet Carlisle Bogdan's "Aggressive Intervention
        and Mortality" in Eakins, p. 83.
        *William Dewees* . . . Judith Walzer Leavitt, " 'Science' Enters the Birthing
        Room," *Journal of American History* (September 1983), p. 286.
        *In 1833 in Boston* . . . Wertz and Wertz, pp. 68–69.
126     *A Virginia doctor* . . . Wertz and Wertz, p. 97.
        *Dr. Thomas Denman* . . . Scholten, p. 443.
        *"I confess* . . ." Wertz and Wertz, p. 33.
127     *When Dr. Oliver Wendell Holmes* . . . Finley, p. 103.

## "MARRIED PERSONS WILL READILY UNDERSTAND THE NATURE OF THE TOPICS"

Except where noted, this section is based on Janet Farrell Brodie's fascinating *Contraception and Abortion in Nineteenth-Century America*.

127     *by the end of the nineteenth century* . . . Linda Gordon, *Woman's Body, Woman's Right*, p. 48.

        *In 1840, Priscilla Cooper Tyler* . . . Brodie, p. 31.

128     *But early American recipe books* . . . Baxandall and Gordon, p. 13.

        *"The Portuguese . . ."* Gordon, pp. 53–54.

        *One New York firm advertised* . . . Brodie, p. 70.

        *Frederick Hollick* . . . Brodie, pp. 112–17.

129     *Lester and Lizzie Ward* . . . James Reed, *From Private Vice to Public Virtue*, pp. 30–31.

        *"Female Physician in the two . . ."* Gordon, p. 54.

130     *In real life, Madame Restell* . . . Seymour Mandelbaum's biography of Ann Lohman in *Notable American Women*, James and James, eds., vol. 2, pp. 424–45.

## "TOO SPARING IN THEIR USE OF WATER"

The two main sources of information about eighteenth- and nineteenth-century cleanliness in this book are the Bushmans' "The Early History of Cleanliness" and Suellen Hoy's *Chasing Dirt*. The best analysis of how American women handled the problem of menstruation through history is Joan Jacobs Brumberg's *The Body Project*.

130     *Lucy Larcom* . . . Larcom, *A New England Girlhood*, p. 168.

        *William Alcott* . . . Hoy, p. 24.

        *The girls at the Euphradian Academy* . . . Clinton, *The Plantation Mistress*, p. 133.

131     *By 1860 there were only about 4,000* . . . Bushman and Bushman, pp. 1225–26.

        *"Females, with all . . ."* *The American Lady's Medical Pocket-Book*, p. 43.

        *The idea of washing* . . . Cayleff, p. 37.

        *"The loss of my teeth . . ."* Elizabeth Fox-Genovese, *Within the Plantation Household*, pp. 4, 12, 27.

131–32     *The most important function* . . . Brumberg, p. 37.

132     *At the very end of the nineteenth* . . . Brumberg, p. xxvii.

## "BEAT IT THREE QUARTERS OF AN HOUR"

This section and other pieces of this book that deal with housekeeping rely heavily on Ruth Schwartz Cowan's *More Work for Mother*.

132     *"To be sweet, nutritious . . ."* Priscilla Brewer, *From Fireplace to Cookstove*, p. 98.

133     *In her recipe book* . . . Ellen Plante, *Women at Home in Victorian America*, p. 114.

        *In 1850, a Philadelphia* . . . Matthews, p. 12.

"*Take eight eggs . . .*"  Cowan, pp. 52–53.

*Martha Coffin Wright* . . .  Boydston, p. 107.

134      *By 1830, about a quarter* . . .  Larkin, pp. 139–44.

"*Who has not* . . ."  Gilman, *Recollections of a Housekeeper,* pp. 62–63.

"*It is all shoreless* . . ."  Hedrick, p. 186.

135      *Writing to her sister-in-law* . . .  Hoy, p. 10.

*The first brooms* . . .  Larkin, p. 131.

*In Chicago in 1844* . . .  Boorstin, pp. 145–46.

### "CHILDREN ARE KILLED BY THE MANNER IN WHICH THEY ARE DRESSED"

135–36   *When she was five, Helen Hunt* . . .  Rothman, p. 94.

136      *One physician announced that* . . .  Dye and Smith, p. 344.

*The influential Dr. William Dewees* . . .  Wishy, p. 40.

*An 1833 guide used by* . . .  Clinton, *The Plantation Mistress,* p. 145.

### "FADED AT TWENTY-THREE"

137      *A Spaniard, Domingo Sarmiento* . . .  Banner, p. 80.

138      *Alexis De Toqueville* . . .  De Toqueville, *Democracy in America,* pp. 233–35.

*Another visitor* . . .  P. Smith, pp. 87–88.

*In the 1840s, the Young Ladies* . . ."  Lee Virginia Chambers-Schiller, *Liberty, a Better Husband,* pp. 15–28.

*An estimated 40 percent* . . .  Chambers-Schiller, pp. 27–28.

138–39   *In 1850, the governor* . . .  Chambers-Schiller, pp. 32–33.

## CHAPTER 7: AFRICAN AMERICAN WOMEN

For much of our history, when black Americans were interviewed by social scientists or historians, their answers were transcribed phonetically, complete with the dropping of the *g* in words like *something* and the *t* in words like *don't.* The idea was to give a feeling for the rhythms of their speech, but I've always found it distracting. Since whites arc generally given the benefit of having their words recorded in regular English, I've treated the quotes from African Americans the same way throughout this book. No words were changed in the process.

Anyone interested in the history of women in slavery should read two books that actually aren't about women in particular: Herbert Gutman's *The Black Family in Slavery and Freedom* and Eugene Genovese's *Roll, Jordan, Roll.* However, the one book I've relied on most for the entire history of African American women is Jacqueline Jones's *Labor of Love, Labor of Sorrow.*

### "THE WOMEN WERE THE PLUCKIEST"

140      "*They are the ones who work* . . ."  John Thornton, "Slave Trade and Family Structures," in *Women and Slavery in Africa,* Claire Robertson and Martin Klein, eds., p. 44.

*"Women are scarce . . ."* Robin Law, *The Slave Coast of West Africa*, p. 167.

*One ship, acquiring . . . Black Voyage*, Thomas Howard, ed., pp. 135–36.

141 *In 1721, an African woman . . .* Deborah Gray White, *Ar'n't I a Woman? Female Slaves in the Plantation South*, pp. 63–64.

*Edward Manning . . .* Howard, ed., p. 166.

*Samuel Hall . . .* John Blassingame, *The Slave Community*, p. 25.

## "I NEVER SEE HOW MY MAMMY STAND SUCH HARD WORK"

During the Depression one of the many public works projects underwritten by the federal government, the Federal Writers Project, dispatched workers through seventeen states to interview former slaves. Those interviews, added to ones conducted earlier by researchers from black colleges, saved the voices of an entire people and era. Everyone who cares about American history should bless that project. Those interviews are now included in dozens of books, a number of which are noted below. Others can be found in the bibliography. My own particular favorite is *Remembering Slavery*, edited by Ira Berlin et al.

141 *Katy Ferguson: Black Women in White America*, Gerda Lerner, ed., p. 76.

142 *At a time when a reasonably productive . . .* Jones, *Labor of Love, Labor of Sorrow*, p. 15.

*"The women plowed . . ."* John Blassingame, *Slave Testimony*, p. 656.

*Bob Ellis . . .* Jones, p. 31.

143 *"A child raised . . ."* Wilma King, "Suffer With Them Till Death," in *More Than Chattel*, David Gaspar and Darlene Clark Hine, eds., p. 147.

*The* Plantation Manual *advised . . .* White, p. 100.

## "I WANT TO BE IN HEAVEN SITTING DOWN"

143 *Angelina Grimke . . . Black Women in White America*, Gerda Lerner, ed., p. 21.

143–44 *The image of the slave . . . Bullwhip Days*, James Mellon, ed., p. 42.

144 *"If Marse catch . . ."* Mellon, ed., p. 383.

*Milla Granson . . .* Darlene Clark Hine and Kathleen Thompson, *A Shining Thread of Hope*, p. 74.

## "IT WAS FREEDOM BEFORE SHE COME OUT OF THAT CAVE"

144 *"They'd dig a hole . . ."* Remembering Slavery, Ira Berlin et al., eds., p. 91.

*"Husbands always went . . ."* Berlin et al., eds., p. 140.

145 *Leah Garrett . . .* Berlin et al., eds., pp. 23–24.

*Salomon Oliver . . .* Berlin et al., eds., p. 49.

## "WE MADE THE GALS HOOPS OUT OF GRAPEVINES"

145 *In the 1930s, Violet Guntharpe . . . Before Freedom When I Can Just Remember*, Belinda Hurmence, ed., pp. 5–6.

146 *When Fanny Kemble urged . . .* Kemble, p. 100.

*A white Georgian ... To Toil the Livelong Day,* Carol Groneman and Mary Beth Norton, eds., pp. 79–80.

147    *"Sunday clothes was dyed ..."* Genovese, p. 555.

      *"That sure was hard living ..."* Fox-Genovese, p. 165.

      *A former slave in Nashville ...* Tera Hunter, *To 'Joy My Freedom,* p. 12.

      *Katie Phoenix ...* Berlin et al., eds., p. 214.

147–48  *"Slaves lived just ..."* *Weevils in the Wheat,* Charles Perdue et al., eds., p. 49.

148    *"All week they wear ..."* Fox-Genovese, p. 219.

      *"Couldn't spring up ..."* Jones, p. 34.


"A CHANCE HERE THAT WOMEN HAVE NOWHERE ELSE"

148    *Slave women, the well-to-do ...* Gutman, pp. 63–64.

149    *Priscilla McCullough ...* Gutman, p. 70.

      *One black preacher in Kentucky ...* Steven Mintz and Susan Kellogg, *Domestic Revolutions: A Social History of American Family Life,* p. 72.

      *"We was married ..."* Berlin et al., eds., pp. 123–25.

150    *"Didn't have to ask ..."* Berlin et al., eds., p. 126.

      *Hannah Chapman ...* Jones, p. 37.

      *Mattie Jackson ...* Gutman, p. 287.

150–51  *Charles Ingram ...* Joan Cashin, *A Family Venture,* p. 50.


"THE GREATEST ORATOR I EVER HEARD WAS A WOMAN"

151    *Cornelius Garner ...* Gutman, p. 148.

      *One historian estimated ...* Mintz and Kellogg, p. 70.

      *"Oh, my mother! ..."* Mary Ryan, *Six Women's Slave Narratives,* p. 5.

      *Sojourner Truth's parents ...* Nell Irvin Painter, *Sojourner Truth: A Life, a Symbol,* pp. 12–13, 39.

151–52  *John Randolph ...* Genovese, p. 456.

152    *When Delcia Patterson ...* Berlin et al., eds., pp. 42–43.

      *William Massie ...* Genovese, p. 453.

152–53  *"One morning we is ..."* Berlin et al., eds., p. 157.

153    *Laura Clark:* Cashin, p. 55.

      *nearly 20 percent said ...* Mintz and Kellogg, pp. 69–70.

      *"I love you just as well ..."* Gutman, pp. 6–7.

      *In 1863, an ex-slave ...* Gutman, p. 149.


"I WAS TOO YOUNG TO UNDERSTAND RIGHTLY MY CONDITION"

153    *But their infants died ...* King in Gaspar and Hine, eds., p. 150.

      *More than a third died ...* Mintz, p. 72.

153–54  *Octavia George ...* Berlin et al., eds., p. 114.

154    *"This was the happiest ..."* Ryan, *Six Women's Slave Narratives,* p. 1.

      *Ellen Betts ...* Mellon, p. 381.

      *Leah Garrett ...* Berlin et al., eds., p. 23.

*Angelina Grimke . . . Black Women in White America*, Lerner, ed., p. 20.

154–55    *Young Henrietta King's . . .* Berlin et al., eds., pp. 20–21.

"A SAD EPOCH IN THE LIFE OF A SLAVE GIRL"

155    *Fannie Berry treasured . . .* King in Gaspar and Hine, eds., pp. 171–72.

*Harriet Jacobs . . .* Harriet Jacobs, *Incidents in the Life of a Slave Girl*, p. 26.

156    *Anne Broome . . .* Genovese, pp. 462–63.

*One ex-slave told . . . In Joy and Sorrow*, Carol Bleser, ed., p. 64.

*Annie Burton . . . Black Women in Nineteenth-Century American Life*, Bert James Lowenberg and Ruth Bogin, eds., p. 98.

*Thomas Foster . . .* Bleser, ed., p. 61.

*When Senator Richard Johnson . . .* Collins, pp. 53–54.

156–57    *In Mississippi shortly before . . .* Bleser, ed., pp. 63–64.

157    *New Orleans had a "fancy girl" . . . Black Women in White America*, Lerner, ed., pp. 10–12.

"IT'S ME, HARRIET. IT'S TIME TO GO NORTH."

This section is based on John Hope Franklin's short biography of Tubman in *Notable American Women*, James and James, eds., and Darlene Clark Hine's in *Black Women in America*.

158    *"Col. Montgomery and his gallant . . ."* Hine and Thompson, p. 132.

"STOMP DOWN FREEDOM TODAY"

159    *"The news went . . ."* Berlin et al., eds., p. 234.

159–60    *"I remember the first Sunday . . ."* Berlin et al., eds., p. 267.

## CHAPTER 8: WOMEN AND ABOLITION

"THEN LET IT SINK. I WILL NOT DISMISS HER."

Except when otherwise noted, this section relies on the work in *Three Who Dared*, by Philip Foner and Josephine Pacheco, and *A Whole-Souled Woman*, by Susan Strane.

162    *"Then let it sink . . ."* This version of Prudence's famous quote comes from Strane. Foner uses another version "Then it might sink then, for I should not turn her out."

163    *One was dumped . . .* Strane, pp. 70–72.

164    *"would not let me . . ."* Thomas Drake in *Notable American Women*, James and James, eds., vol. 1, p. 400.

"WE ABOLITION WOMEN ARE TURNING
THE WORLD UPSIDE DOWN"

Except when noted, the information on the Grimke sisters is taken from Gerda Lerner's biography, *The Grimke Sisters from South Carolina*. More recently, Mark

Perry has written a study of both the sisters and their half-black nephews, *Lift Up Thy Voice: The Grimke Family's Journey from Slaveholders to Civil Rights Leaders.*

165    *Between 1834 and 1837 . . .* Julie Roy Jeffrey's *Great Silent Army of Abolition,* p. 49.

    *Ellen Smith . . .* Jeffrey, *Great Silent Army,* p. 198.

    *"If this is the last bulwark . . ."* Alma Lutz's biography of Maria Chapman in *Notable American Women,* James and James, eds., vol. 1, p. 324.

    *One Boston volunteer . . .* Jeffrey, *Great Silent Army,* p. 51.

166    *"Confusion has seized . . ."* Lerner, *The Grimke Sisters,* p. 145.

## "PUTTING THEM ON AN EQUALITY WITH OURSELVES"

For this section, and much else in this chapter, I'm indebted to Julie Roy Jeffrey's *The Great Silent Army of Abolition.*

170    *"Her fine genius . . ."* Michael Goldberg's "An Unfinished Battle" in *No Small Courage,* Nancy Cott, ed., p. 228.

    *In Fall River . . .* Jeffrey, *Great Silent Army,* pp. 43–44.

    *The Buffum sisters . . .* Chace and Lovell, pp. 31–32.

170–71    *Hannah Austin . . .* Jeffrey, *Great Silent Army,* p. 45.

## "THE MOST ODIOUS OF TASKS"

171    *"How can you eat . . ."* Jeffrey, *Great Silent Army,* p. 19.

    *"almost everything good" . . .* Jeffrey, *Great Silent Army,* p. 48.

    *The Dover Anti-Slavery . . .* Jeffrey, *Great Silent Army,* p. 79.

172    *Even the unstoppable . . .* Jeffrey, *Great Silent Army,* p. 90.

    *In 1836, 20 percent . . .* Edward Magdol, *The Anti-Slavery Rank and File,* p. 102.

    *Embroidered linens . . .* Ronald Walters, *The Antislavery Appeal,* p. 24.

    *Lewis Tappen, Garrison's opponent . . .* Ginzberg, p. 64.

    *"How heretical, harsh . . ."* Catherine Clinton's biography of Chapman in *Portraits of American Women,* Barker-Benfield and Clinton, eds., pp. 150–53.

173    *Julia Lovejoy . . .* Ginzberg, pp. 115–16.

## "I AM TRYING TO GET UNCLE TOM OUT OF THE WAY"

Except where noted, this section is based on information in Joan Hedrick's *Harriet Beecher Stowe.*

173    *"Many families who . . ."* Jacobs, pp. 14–15.

173–74    *"Why I have felt almost choked . . ."* Hedrick, pp. 204–7.

174    *"I am trying . . ."* Hedrick, p. 221.

175    *the crowd chanted . . .* Hedrick, p. 306.

## "I CRAWLED ABOUT MY DEN FOR EXERCISE"

175    *The real Eliza . . .* Henrietta Buckmaster, *Let My People Go,* pp. 121–22.

175–76    *Ellen Craft:* Lerner, *Black Women in America,* pp. 65–72; Buckmaster, pp. 157–58.

176      *"The garret was . . ."* Jacobs, pp. 128–29.
         *Child, the editor . . .* Jacobs, p. xx.
176–77  *Not every writer . . .* Hedrick, pp. 248–49.

## "WHY CAN'T SHE HAVE HER LITTLE PINT FULL?"
Except when otherwise noted, this section is based on Nell Irvin Painter's *Sojourner Truth: A Life, a Symbol.*
177      *"See if Im not . . ."* Ginzberg, p. 105.
178      *"If colored men . . ."* Painter, *Sojourner Truth*, p. 220.
         *Frances Watkins Harper decided . . .* Painter, *Sojourner Truth*, p. 225.

## "DOES SHE BELONG TO YOU?"
179      *Elizabeth Jennings:* This information is taken from "The Search for Elizabeth Jennings" by John Hewitt, *New York History* 71, no. 4, pp. 387–415.
180      *Frances Watkins Harper had . . .* Jeffrey, *Great Silent Army*, p. 208.
         *Sarah Walker Fossett . . .* Jeffrey, *Great Silent Army*, pp. 127–28.
         *In 1865, Harriet Tubman . . .* Massey, p. 269.
         *Sojourner Truth . . .* Painter, *Sojourner Truth*, p. 211.

## "IT IS PLEASANT TO LOOK AT—ALTHOUGH IT IS BLACK"
181      *Charlotte Forten, a member . . .* Jeffrey, *Great Silent Army*, p. 196.
         *Forten's story . . .* Unless otherwise noted, Brenda Stevenson's biography of Forten in *Portraits of American Women*, Barker-Benfield and Clenton, eds., was the source of information for this section.
182      *When she traveled . . . We Are Your Sisters*, Dorothy Sterling, ed., pp. 280–83.

## "KEPT MOIST AND BRIGHT WITH THE OIL OF KINDNESS"
183      *"Mrs. Stowe betrays . . ."* Hedrick, p. 232.
         *Caroline Lee Hentz . . .* Helen Papashvily, *All the Happy Endings*, pp. 83–86.
         *Mary Hamilton Campbell . . .* Fox-Genovese, p. 134.
         *A Southern slave owner . . .* D. White, p. 58.

## "THERE IS MANY THINGS TO DO ABOUT A PLACE THAT YOU MEN DON'T THINK OF"
The classic work about white women on Southern plantations before the war is Catherine Clinton's *The Plantation Mistress.* For the relation between these women and their servants, see *Within the Plantation Household* by Elizabeth Fox-Genovese.
184      *When Anne Nichols . . .* Kierner, p. 177.
         *"It is quite out of . . ."* Clinton, *The Plantation Mistress*, p. 176.
         *John Steele . . .* Clinton, *The Plantation Mistress*, p. 75.
         *"I would willingly . . ."* Clinton, *The Plantation Mistress*, p. 29.
         *Southern men went to spas . . .* Clinton, *The Plantation Mistress*, p. 151.

### "I WOULD NOT CARE IF THEY ALL DID GO"

185     *Charles Eliot Norton* . . . Ann Firor Scott, *The Southern Lady*, p. 50.
         *"In all my life . . ."* C. Vann Woodward, *Mary Chesnut's Civil War*, p. 255.
         *A New Orleans slave* . . . Larry Gara, *The Liberty Line: The Legend of the Underground Railroad*, p. 58.
185–86  *Susan Davis Hutchinson* . . . Fox-Genovese, pp. 144–45.
186     *"I sometimes think . . ."* Scott, *The Southern Lady*, p. 47.
         *Sarah Gayle* . . . Fox-Genovese, pp. 144–45.
         *Caroline Merrick* . . . Fox-Genovese, pp. 144–45.
187     *"Slavery degrades . . ."* Virginia Burr, *The Secret Eye*, p. 169.
         *Catherine Hammond* . . . *The Hammonds of Redcliffe*, Carol Bleser, ed., pp. 10–11.
         *"God forgive us . . ."* Woodward, p. 29.

## CHAPTER 9: THE CIVIL WAR

Although there are a disproportionate number of good books about white Southern women during the Civil War, the one I kept going back to while writing this chapter was *Mothers of Invention* by Drew Gilpin Faust. Two other books I relied on heavily were Victoria Bynum's *Unruly Women: The Politics of Social and Sexual Control in the Old South* and Mary Elizabeth Massey's *Women in the Civil War*—an early book by women's history standards but still extremely useful. They're all very readable.

### "MY STATE IS OUT OF THE UNION"
This section, like many to come, draws particularly on the work of Drew Gilpin Faust.

188     *"Politics engrosses . . ."* Faust, pp. 11–14.
189     *According to the* Southern Illustrated News . . . Faust p. 46.

### "DOES SHE MEAN TO TAKE CARE OF ME—OR TO MURDER ME?"
One of the reasons there are so many good histories of Southern women may be that they were such gifted diarists. The most famous is that of Mary Chesnut, a well-to-do wife of a Confederate politician. It's a great read in C. Vann Woodward's *Mary Chesnut's Civil War*.

189     *Keziah Brevard* . . . Faust, p. 57.
         *Lewis B. Norwood* . . . Bynum, p. 115.
         *The wealthy Mary Chesnut* . . . Woodward, p. 199.
190     *"I dread . . ."* Faust, p. 76.
         *One Georgia slave-owning family* . . . Hunter, p. 19.
         *Kate Foster* . . . Faust, p. 78.

### "THE WOMEN ARE AS BAD AS MEN DOWN HERE"
A book I relied on for much of this section was Bynum's *Unruly Women*.

191     *In New Bern* . . . Faust, p. 31.
         *A soldier's pay* . . . Bynum, p. 134.

*"I do not like . . ."* Faust, p. 47.

*"The women are . . ."* Bynum, p. 133.

*"The self-sacrifice has vanished . . ."* Faust, pp. 243–45.

## "WATCH OVER THEIR DAUGHTERS AS WELL AS THEIR SONS"

192    *Although men still . . .* Ginzberg, pp. 157–58.

*The necessary supplies . . .* Alfred Bloor, "Letter to Senator Sumner," *Women's Work in the War.*

*In 1863, when Irish . . .* Ryan, *Women in Public,* pp. 148–51.

## "WERE THEY THE SAME SCHOOL GIRLS OF 1861?"

193    *Amy Clarke . . .* Massey, pp. 79–81.

*Rose O'Neal Greenhow . . .* Ishbel Ross's biographical sketch in *Notable American Women,* James and James, eds., vol. 2, pp. 89–90.

193–94  *Belle Boyd:* Thomas Robson Hay in James and James, eds., vol. 1, pp. 215–17.

194    *More than 250,000 people . . .* Massey, p. 291.

*As the Union forces . . .* Faust, pp. 43–44.

*In Vicksburg . . .* Massey, p. 225.

*An Atlanta resident . . .* Scott, *The Southern Lady,* p. 86.

*While marching to Savannah . . .* Hunter, p. 20.

194–95  *Emma Steward . . .* Sterling, p. 241.

## "THE BEST THING THAT COULD HAVE TAKEN PLACE FOR ME"

195    *"Nothing looks funnier . . ."* Faust, pp. 224–27.

*Southern women began . . .* Faust, pp. 88–91.

196    *In 1864, when the note signers . . .* Massey, pp. 140–42.

196–97  *In the North . . .* Massey, pp. 132–38.

## "ALMOST WILD ON THE SUBJECT OF HOSPITAL NURSING"

197    *At least 3,000 women . . .* Clinton, *The Other Civil War,* p. 182.

197–98  *"Our women appear . . ."* Baxandall and Gordon, eds., pp. 76–77.

198    *"I will not agree . . ."* Faust, p. 97.

*Dorothea Dix . . .* Mary Gardner Holland, *Our Army Nurses,* p. iii.

*One young woman . . .* Massey, pp. 45–47.

*Elida Rumsey Fowle . . .* Massey, p. 82.

## "I AM A U.S. SOLDIER . . . AND THEREFORE NOT SUPPOSED TO BE SUSCEPTIBLE TO FEAR"

Except where otherwise noted, this section is based on information in Elizabeth Brown Pryor's *Clara Barton, Professional Angel.*

200    *Katherine Wormeley:* Judith Ann Giesberg, "Katherine Wormeley and the U.S. Sanitary Commission," *Nursing History Review* 3 (1955), pp. 43–53.

201    *An army surgeon . . .* Massey, pp. 48–49.

## "A HOSPITAL HAS NONE OF THE COMFORTS OF HOME"

Anyone interested in nursing during the Civil War—from the Union perspective at least—should read *Our Army Nurses: Stories from Women in the Civil War* by Mary Gardner Holland.

201     *Phoebe Yates Pember* . . . Massey, p. 56.

202     *Mary Rutledge Fogg* . . . Faust, pp. 94–95.

        *"Nobody chided me* . . ." Lee Ann White, "The Civil War as a Crisis of Gender," in Catherine Clinton's *Divided Houses*, p. 17.

        *"Are the women of the South* . . ." Faust, pp. 101–2.

        *"I have had men die* . . ." Holland, pp. 84–94.

203     *Anna McMahon* . . . Holland, p. 132.

        *Rebecca Wiswell* . . . Holland, p. 295.

        *"We all know* . . ." Kristie Ross, "Arranging a Doll's House," in Clinton's *Divided Houses*, p. 102.

        *Francis Bacon* . . . Ginzberg, p. 145.

        *Doctors on both sides* . . . Barbara Mann Wall, "Called to a Mission of Charity," *Nursing History Review* 6 (1998), pp. 85–113.

## "GIRLS HAVE MARRIED MEN THEY WOULD NEVER HAVE GIVEN A THOUGHT OF"

203–4   *"My happy life!* . . ." *The Civil War Diary of Sarah Morgan*, Charles East, ed., p. 29.

204     *In what the whole South came* . . . Massey, p. 257.

        *There were 80,000 widows* . . . Scott, *The Southern Lady*, p. 92.

        *"Girls have married* . . ." Massey, p. 257.

        *Sarah Morgan wrote* . . . East, ed., p. 62.

        *One newspaper concluded* . . . White in Clinton, *Divided Houses*, p. 19.

204–5   *Jefferson Davis* . . . See Joan Cashin's essay on Varina Davis in *Portraits of American Women*, Barker-Benfield and Clinton, eds., pp. 259–77.

205     *"I will not be a dependent* . . ." Massey, p. 110.

        *By 1883, an Alabama* . . . Scott, *The Southern Lady*, p. 111.

## "IF I STAY HERE I'LL NEVER KNOW I'M FREE"

Like the preceding chapter, most stories about slavery in America stop on the happy ending. Tera Hunter's *To 'Joy My Freedom* is a good antidote for that. Except where otherwise noted, this section is based on pp. 29–50 of that book.

205     *Patience, an ex-slave* . . . Jones, p. 51.

206     *In South Carolina an ex-slave named Sue* . . . D. White, pp. 170–71.

206–7   *"Slavery to our Islanders* . . ." Jones, pp. 69–70.

207     *"When I married my wife* . . ." D. White, p. 184.

        *The white community, however* . . . Jones, pp. 58–60.

# CHAPTER 10: WOMEN GO WEST

Perhaps because they were so lonely for home, pioneer women were very generous in leaving behind piles of letters and journals. As a result, tons of books are available on the subject of women settlers in the West. My overall favorite book on this period is *Frontier Women,* by Julie Roy Jeffrey.

### "I THOUGHT WHERE HE COULD GO I COULD GO"

Anyone interested in the story of the migration west should begin with the classic *Women and Men on the Overland Trail,* by John Mack Faragher.

208–9  *Nancy Kelsey:* Jo Ann Chartier and Chris Enss, *With Great Hope: Women of the California Gold Rush,* pp. 13–22.

209  *The* Daily Missouri Republican *advised* . . . Faragher, *Women and Men on the Overland Trail,* p. 7.

"*I would not be left* . . ." Luzena Wilson, *Luzena Stanley Wilson, 49er,* p. 1.

210  *Bethenia Owens-Adair* . . . B. Owens-Adair, *Dr. Owens Adair,* p. 493.

"*Some women have very little help* . . ." Robert Munkres, "Wives, Mothers, Daughters: Women's Life on the Road West," *Annals of Wyoming* (October 1970), pp. 189–224.

*One pioneer recounted* . . . Lillian Schlissel, *Women's Diaries of the Western Journey,* p. 57.

211  *James Clyman* . . . Dee Brown, *The Gentle Tamers,* p. 104.

211–12  *Frances Grummond* . . . Dee Brown, pp. 39–40.

### "WE SAW LONG BRAIDS OF GOLDEN HAIR"

212  "*Very dusty roads*" . . . *Covered Wagon Women,* Kenneth Holmes, ed., pp. 131, 142–43.

212–13  "*Boxes and trunks* . . ." Holmes, ed., pp. 257–58.

213  "*Days passed before* . . ." Dee Brown, p. 209.

*Juliette Brier* . . . Jo Ann Levy, *They Saw the Elephant,* pp. 26–29.

*Mrs. Samuel Young* . . . Schlissel, p. 46.

"*If there were any graves* . . ." Martha Gay Masterson, *One Woman's West,* Lois Barton, ed., pp. 40–41.

*One pioneer remembered* . . . Dee Brown, p. 37.

213–14  *Janette Riker* . . . Dee Brown, pp. 40–41.

### "HE WAS IN GREAT HASTE TO MARRY
### TO SAVE A HALF SECTION OF LAND"

214  "*Even I have* . . ." B. Wilson, p. 32.

*Irwin, Colorado, had* . . . Anne Butler, *Daughters of Joy, Sisters of Misery,* p. 53.

*The wife of an army officer* . . . Dee Brown, p. 222.

*Martha Gay Masterson* . . . Barton, ed., pp. 54–55.

215    *When Elizabeth Gunn* . . . Jeffrey, *Frontier Women*, p. 156.
       *"In the short space . . ."* Louise Amelia Clappe, *The Shirley Letters*, p. 133.
       *"I* like *this wild . . ."* Clappe, pp. 177–78.

"MORE ACTIVE AND INDUSTRIOUS THAN THE MEN"
Just as we're blessed with a bounty of studies about white women in the West,
we're starved for information about Mexican Americans. My single greatest regret
in doing this book was my inability to follow their trail further. But new studies are
coming in every day, and for those interested in the subject, I'd recommend beginning with Douglas Monroy's *Thrown Among Strangers: The Making of Mexican
Culture in Frontier California* and Richard Griswold del Castillo's *La Familia: Chicano Families in the Urban Southwest.*

215    *"Their manners toward . . ."* Del Castillo, p. 44.
       *"Riding on horseback . . ."* Monroy, p. 151.
216    *Indian women, wrote* . . . Monroy, p. 9.
       *"She never let them . . ."* Virginia Marie Bouvier, *Women and the Conquest
       of California,* p. 84.
       *Mexican soldiers had no* . . . Monroy, p. 29.
       *After the women were raped* . . . Monroy, p. 83.
216–17 *Narcissa Prentiss Whitman* . . . See Michael Goldberg's "Breaking New
       Ground" in Nancy Cotted, *No Small Courage,* pp. 209–12.

"I WENT INTO THE SPORTING LIFE FOR BUSINESS REASONS"
If you're interested in this perpetually interesting subject, start with *Daughters of
Joy, Sisters of Misery,* by Anne Butler.

217    The Home Missionary . . . Dee Brown, p. 89.
       *"I went into . . ."* Brandon Marie Miller, *Buffalo Gals,* pp. 35–36.
       *A Frenchman named Albert Bernard* . . . Levy, *They Saw the Elephant,* p. 163.
218    *On paydays* . . . Anne Seagraves, *Soiled Doves,* pp. 60–61.
       *The most desperate stories involved Chinese women* . . . Many Chinese Ameri-
       can women in the nineteenth-century West weren't prostitutes, and the
       attempt to portray every Asian woman as a brothel worker was one of the tac-
       tics used to keep the door locked against female immigration. For the story of
       all those other women, see George Anthony Peffer's excellent *If They Don't
       Bring Their Women Here.* For a brief survey of Chinese immigrant women in
       the nineteenth century, see Lucie Cheng Hirata in *Women of America: A His-
       tory,* edited by Carol Berkin and Mary Beth Norton, pp. 224–44.
       *Lilac Chen* . . . Jeffrey, *Frontier Women,* p. 149.
       *Toward the end of the century* . . . Seagraves, pp. 135–42.

"A SMART WOMAN CAN DO VERY WELL IN THIS COUNTRY"
One of the most entertaining and interesting books on the women of early California settlements is *They Saw the Elephant: Women in the California Gold Rush,* by Jo Ann Levy.

219     *Luzena Wilson* . . . Levy, pp. 91–107.

        *A woman wrote from California* . . . Dee Brown, p. 253.

        *One pioneer recalled* . . . Levy, p. 93.

219–20  *Martha Gay Masterson* . . . Barton, ed., p. xii.

220     *One woman was troubled* . . . Levy, p. 45.

220     *Nellie Pooler Chapman* . . . Chartier and Enss, pp. 79–83.

        *"A smart woman . . ."* Jeffrey, *Frontier Women*, p. 154.

        *Charley Parkhurst* . . . Levy, pp. 122–23.

        *Lotta Crabtree* . . . There's a portrait of Lotta in Chartier and Enss's *With Great Hope.*

221     *Legend has it* . . . Dee Brown, pp. 168–69.


"STANDING ERECT UPON THE BACK OF HER UNSADDLED HORSE"
This section is based on Glenda Riley's *The Life and Legacy of Annie Oakley*, and *Calamity Jane* by Roberta Beed Sollid.

223–24  *But the real creator* . . . Doris Faber, *Calamity Jane, Her Life and Legend*, pp. 38–40.


"SHE PUT HER ARMS AROUND A TREE AND HUGGED IT"
It's either something about the kind of women who go to Kansas or the kind of things Kansas did to the women, but the most amazing books about women farmers on the plains all seem to be about that particular state. My favorite is *Pioneer Women: Voices from the Kansas Frontier*, by Joanna Stratton.

224–25  *Julia Lovejoy* . . . Michael Fellman, "Julia Lovejoy Goes West," *Western Humanities Review* (Summer 1977), p. 236.

225     *One girl who lived* . . Stratton, p. 53.

        *Julia Lovejoy found* . . . Fellman, p. 233.

225–26  *One female pioneer* . . . Dee Brown, p. 192.

226     *"The wind whistled . . ."* Stratton, p. 52.

        *"When our covered wagon . . ."* B. Miller, p. 24.

        *Another woman begged* . . . Stratton, p. 80.

        *"Many a time my mother . . ."* Stratton, p. 82.

        *"They commenced on a . . ."* Dee Brown, p. 208.

226–27  *Another woman remembered* . . . Stratton, p. 103.

227     *A visitor to frontier Illinois* . . . John Mack Faragher, *Sugar Creek*, p. 90.

        *Matilda Lockhart, who was taken* . . . Dee Brown, pp. 19–20.

        *George Custer* . . . Elizabeth Custer, *Boots and Saddles*, pp. 56–57.

        *Susan Parrish* . . . Schlissel, p. 69.

228     *The Lakota called 1844* . . . Jeffrey, *Frontier Women*, p. 37.

        *Pretty Shield* . . . Linda Peavy and Ursula Smith, *Pioneer Women*, p. 66.

228–29  *"If women could go . . ."* Sarah Winnemucca Hopkins, *Life Among the Piutes*, p. 53.

229     *A Mrs. Miller* . . . Jeffrey, *Frontier Women*, p. 72.

## "I CANNOT MAKE A FRIEND LIKE MOTHER OUT OF HENRY"

Although it isn't specifically about women, one book that anyone interested in the history of plains farmers has to read is *Bad Land: An American Romance* by Jonathan Raban.

229    *In Topeka . . . Plains Woman: The Diary of Martha Farnsworth*, Marlene and Haskell Springer, eds., p. xiii.

        *A Texas woman . . .* James Featon, "Women on the Staked Plains," in *At Home on the Range*, John Wunder, ed., p. 241.

        *"I have been very blue" . . .* Jeffrey, *Frontier Women*, p. 73.

        *Margaret Armstrong . . .* Harriette Andreadis, "True Womanhood Revisited: Women's Private Writing in Nineteenth Century Texas," *Journal of the Southwest* (Summer 1989), p. 185.

229–30  *Annette Botkin . . .* Stratton, pp. 86–87.

230    *Jessie Hill Rowland . . .* Stratton, pp. 135–36.

        *Susanna Townsend . . .* Levy, p. 62.

231    *Bertha Anderson . . .* Peavy and Smith, p. 30.

        *At a luncheon . . .* Dee Brown, p. 48.

        *Louise Clappe's remote . . .* Clappe, p. 90.

231–32  *"Someone had said that . . ."* Stratton, p. 68.

## "BESIEGED BY A CROWD OF MEN, ALL ANXIOUS TO EMPLOY HER"

232    *They were called Exodusters . . . Exodusters*, by Nell Irvin Painter, covers this little-known piece of African American history.

        *"These sable workwomen . . ."* Painter, *Exodusters*, p. 55.

232–33  *"The scenery to me . . ."* William Katz, *Black Women of the Old West*, p. 60.

233    *"In the earliest days . . ."* B. Miller, p. 26.

        *"I ain't got . . ."* Katz, p. 73.

        *Mary Ann Pleasant . . .* A full portrait of Mary Ann Pleasant by Quintard Taylor is included in *By Grit and Grace: Eleven Women Who Shaped the American West*, Glenda Riley and Richard Etulain, eds.

        *Clara Brown:* Except when noted, information on Clara Brown comes from Kathleen Bruyn's *"Aunt" Clara Brown: Story of a Black Pioneer*.

        *in the words of a local paper . . .* Katz, p. 25.

234    *When she died in 1885 . . .* Katz, p. 26.

## "WE NOW EXPECT QUITE AN IMMIGRATION OF LADIES TO WYOMING"

234    *Anna Dickinson:* The story of Anna Dickinson and Wyoming is told in T. A. Larson's *History of Wyoming*, pp. 80–82.

234–35  *Esther McQuigg Morris:* See the profile by Gene Gressley in *Notable American Women*, James and James, eds., vol. 2, p. 583.

235    *William Bright . . .* Larson, *History of Wyoming*, pp. 91–92.

        *"We now expect . . ."* Larson, *History of Wyoming*, p. 80.

235–36    *Esther Morris's son* . . . Michael Massie, "Reform Is Where You Find It: The Roots of Woman Suffrage in Wyoming," *Annals of Wyoming* (Spring 1990).

236    *"Won't the irrepressible . . ."* Larson, *History of Wyoming*, p. 83.
*"Many ladies have voted . . ."* Dee Brown, p. 245.
*"There was plenty of drinking . . ."* Larson, *History of Wyoming*, p. 85.
*"We will remain out of the union . . ."* T. A. Larson, "Petticoats at the Polls," *Pacific Northwest Quarterly* (April 1953), p. 79.
*On July 23, 1890 . . .* Larson, *History of Wyoming*, pp. 260–61.

237    *"Neither is handsome". . . .* Larson, *History of Wyoming*, p. 87.
*Grace Greenwood . . .* Dee Brown, p. 248.
*When the California legislature . . .* Sidney Howell Fleming, "Solving the Jigsaw Puzzle: One Suffrage Story at a Time," *Annals of Wyoming* (Spring 1990), pp. 33–73.
Frank Leslie's Illustrated Newspaper *reported . . .* Larson, *History of Wyoming*, p. 86.
*Discussing her service . . .* James and James, eds., p. 584.

## CHAPTER 11: THE GILDED AGE

### "THERE WAS PLENTY OF HER TO SEE"

The first part of this section, and much else in this chapter, relies heavily on Lois Banner's *American Beauty*, particularly the chapter on "The Voluptuous Woman." This is also my opportunity to recommend two books by Kathy Peiss: *Hope in a Jar: The Making of America's Beauty Culture*, and *Cheap Amusements: Working Women and Leisure in Turn-of-the-Century New York*.

238    *An Englishman reported . . .* David Macrae, *The Americans at Home*, p. 40.
*Lillian Russell:* There are a number of biographies of Russell. I used one by Armond Fields.

239    *"There was plenty . . ."* Banner, pp. 135–36.
*In the 1890s,* Metropolitan Magazine *claimed . . .* Banner, p. 151.
*Helen Hunt . . .* Banner, p. 114.
*one photographer complained . . .* Peiss, *Hope in a Jar*, p. 47.
*"She is a compound . . ."* Peiss, *Hope in a Jar*, p. 27.

239–40    *They wore elaborate hats . . .* Jennifer Price, *Flight Maps*, p. 59.

240    *The slaughter of wild birds . . .* Price, p. 99.
*"I went down and saw . . ."* Daniel Sutherland, *The Expansion of Everyday Life*, p. 256.

240–41    *In New York, one Coney Island . . .* Peiss, *Cheap Amusements*, pp. 127–32.

241    *The single most important new public amenity . . .* To learn more about early department stores, try *Counter Cultures*, by Susan Porter Benson.
*Mary Antin . . .* Antin's story of her experiences as a young immigrant, *The Promised Land*, is one of the best memoirs of turn-of-the-century immigrant life.

*Nathaniel Fowler* ... Douglas, *The Feminization of American Culture*, p. 67.

### "QUALITIES WHICH ALL SOUND-HEARTED MEN AND WOMEN ADMIRE"

242    *Nellie Bly* ... The definitive biography of Bly and an excellent history of women in turn-of-the-century journalism is Brooke Kroeger's *Nellie Bly*.
*In 1870, the country had only five female lawyers* ... Anyone wondering why there weren't more can read the biography of Myra Bradwell, *America's First Woman Lawyer*, by Jane Friedman.

242–43    *In 1869, a few women* ... Theodora Penny Martin, *The Sound of Our Own Voices*, p. 44.

243    *Thanks in large part* ... Thomas Schlereth, *Victorian America: Transformations in Everyday Life*, p. 74.
*An in-house newspaper* ... Peiss, *Cheap Amusements*, p. 49.
*The men in the mail-order* ... Peiss, *Cheap Amusements*, p. 62.
*As the federal bureaucracy* ... Schlereth, p. 75.

243–44    *Women were making rapid* ... Dee Garrison, "The Tender Technicians," in Hartman and Banner, eds., p. 164.

244    *The typewriter was a new* ... My information about typists comes, except when otherwise noted, from Margery Davies's *Woman's Place Is at the Typewriter*.

244–45    *when Mrs L. V. Longley* ... Bruce Bliven, *The Wonderful Writing Machine*, p. 112.

245    *Marion Harland, in an essay* ... Davies, pp. 81–82.
*At the turn of the century* ... Bliven, pp. 12–13.
*In 1904, the organizer of the first* ... Bliven, p. 76.

### "WE HAD A LOVELY PICTURE OF HER WE GOT WITH COFFEE WRAPPERS"

246    *The American public fell madly* ... The best portrait of Mrs. Cleveland is in Carl Anthony's *First Ladies*.

246–47    *Far away in Colorado* ... Anne Ellis, *The Life of an Ordinary Woman*, p. 128.

### "LURED WOMEN FROM THEIR DUTIES AS HOMEMAKERS"

This section is based on Theodora Penny Martin's great book about the study club movement, *The Sound of Our Own Voice*.

248    *Josephine Ruffin* ... Anne Firor Scott presented a paper, "Most Invisible of All," on black women's voluntary associations that was published in *The Journal of Southern History* in February 1990. Elizabeth Fortson Arroyo has a profile on Josephine Ruffin in *Black Women in America*, Hine, ed., vol. 2, pp. 994–97.

## "WAS THAT CROQUET?"

249    *In 1883, the travel writer* . . . Kenneth Jackson, *Crabgrass Frontier*, p. 25.

249–50  *"I saw the scamp . . ."* Sutherland, p. 76.

## "ZINC COFFINS"

This section includes information from one of my favorite housekeeping books: Susan Strasser's *Never Done: A History of American Housework*.

250    *A study by the Boston* . . . Strasser, p. 41.

       *All in all, sweeping* . . . Schlereth, p. 131.

251    *Some experts decried the idea of bodily* . . . Sutherland, p. 60.

       *Even in houses with bathtubs* . . . Maureen Ogle, *All the Modern Conveniences*, p. 114.

       *Catharine Beecher* . . . Schlereth, p. 128.

251–52  *In 1893 in New York, far and* . . . Goldsmith, p. 424.

## "OH, DOCTOR, SHOOT ME, QUICK!"

252    *When the reformer* . . . Goldsmith, p. 424. Although this book is, alas, not going into Victoria Woodhull's career, or the Beecher sex trial that she precipitated, I would urge everybody to take a stroll down that path. Barbara Goldsmith's *Other Powers* is the best guide.

       *Removing the clitoris* . . . G. J. Barker-Benfield writes about this in *The Horrors of the Half-Known Life*. Except when noted, my information is from her book.

       *The founders of Woman's Hospital* . . . Barbara Ehrenreich and Diedre English, *For Her Own Good*, pp. 123–24.

253    *A report from the American Phamaceutical* . . . David Courtwright, *Dark Paradise: A History of Opiate Addiction in America*, p. 51.

       *Somewhere between 200,000* . . . David Musto, *The American Disease*, pp. 16, 50–51, 253–54.

254    *A traveler who spent time* . . . Nathaniel Philbrick, *In the Heart of the Sea*, p. 16.

       *Laudanum, an opium* . . . Clinton, *The Plantation Mistress*, p. 70.

       *In 1897, the Sears* . . . James Inciardi, *The War on Drugs*, pp. 5–6.

       *"No name is signed . . ."* H. Wayne Morgan, *Drugs in America*, p. 101.

       *"Young women cannot go . . ."* Dick Griffin, "Opium Addiction in Chicago," *Chicago History* (Summer 1977), p. 108.

       *A North Carolina doctor* . . . Morgan, p. 27.

255    *The most famous was Lydia Pinkham's* . . . *Female Complaints* by Sarah Stage is a fascinating book about both the Pinkhams and the patent medicine industry.

       *"I do wish . . ."* Stage, p. 126.

       *Colonel Hoestetters* . . . Maud Banfield, "About Patent Medicine," *Ladies' Home Journal* (May 1903), p. 26.

"THAT SO LITTLE SHOULD BE SAID ABOUT THEM
SURPRISES ME FOR THEY ARE EVERYWHERE"

255    *The post–Civil War* . . . Woloch, pp. 279–80.
256    *"If only you were here . . ."* Cazden, p. 75.
257    *"The loves of women . . ."* Woloch, p. 281.


CHAPTER 12: IMMIGRANTS

Tons of books are available on the immigrant experience, and this is one part of
American history where women's voices are well represented. The two books to
which this section is particularly indebted are Elizabeth Ewan's *Immigrant Women in
the Land of Dollars* and Christine Stansell's wonderful *City of Women*.

"AS YOU SEE, I AM NOT STAYING FAR BEHIND"

258    *"They say in this country . . ."* Peiss, *Cheap Amusements*, p. 63.
       *"In the old country . . ."* Ewan, p. 198.
       *Rose Cohen:* Cohen, *Out of the Shadow*, pp. 153–54.
259    *Marie Prisland . . . Immigrant Women*, Maxine Schwartz Seller, ed., p. 1.
       *Although some social workers . . .* Ewan, p. 126.
259–60 *Two of the few who did . . .* Rose Cohen published her memoir: *Out of the
       Shadow: A Russian Jewish Girlhood on the Lower East Side*. Rosa Cavalleri's
       story was recorded by settlement house worker Maria Hall Ets: *Rosa: The
       Life of an Italian Immigrant*.
261    *"When they learned . . ."* Roger Daniels, *Coming to America*, p. 274.
       *The terrors and heartbreak . . .* Judy Yung, *Unbound Feet*, pp. 63–66.

"AMERICA IS A WOMAN'S COUNTRY"

This chapter makes use of another one of those great *Everyday Life* books, Thomas
Schlereth's *Victorian America: Transformations of Everyday Life*.

261    *The Irish were the only . . .* Daniels, p. 225.
262    *Overall, one in three . . .* Schlereth, p. 11.
       *Ukrainian men told an interviewer . . .* Ewan, p. 101.
       *An Italian immigrant . . .* Ewan, p. 65.
       *A social worker described . . .* Ewan, pp. 103–4.
       *Jane Addams surveyed . . .* Addams, *Twenty Years at Hull-House*, p. 164.
263    *Handling the finances . . .* For more about this point, see Stansell's *City of
       Women*.
       *The classic first home . . .* Anyone who happens to be in New York City and
       wants to see how immigrants lived should visit the Tenement Museum on
       the Lower East Side of Manhattan.
       *"Water . . . to my mother . . ."* Ewan, pp. 65–66.
       *Men and women regularly fell . . .* Doris Weatherford, *Foreign and Female*,
       p. 148.

263–64   *One tenement described by* . . . Fon Boardman, *America and the Gilded Age,*
         pp. 107–9.

264      *"It was nothing unusual . . ."* Cohen, p. 292.
         *"A kind of obligation . . ."* Peiss, *Cheap Amusements,* p. 21.

264–65   *"The walls are hung . . ."* Schlereth, p. 120.

## "I WORKED AND ROCKED THE BABY WITH MY FEET"

265      *"The boss said that a woman . . ."* Rose Laub Coser, et al., *Women of
         Courage: Jewish and Italian Immigrant Women in New York,* p. 110.
         *That allowed them to stay* . . . Stansell, *City of Women,* p. 114.
         *"I used to cry . . ."* Coser et al., p. 102.
         *Somewhere between 25 and 50 percent* . . . Evans, *Born for Liberty,* p. 131.

266      *But although the public* . . . Stansell, *City of Women,* p. 48.
         *"Those swill boxes . . ."* Ets, pp. 222–25.
         *Lillian Wald* . . . Wald, *The House on Henry Street,* pp. 40–41.

## "SURE, SIX DAYS IS ENOUGH TO WORK"

The sections in this book about the Irish are based on Hasia Diner's fascinating
*Erin's Daughters in America;* unless otherwise noted, the information about domestic service comes from another great book, Faye Dudden's *Serving Women.*

267      *The anonymous author of* . . . Dudden, p. 112.
         *The live-in domestics' workweek* . . . Woloch, p. 238.
         *"Especially is objection . . ."* Peiss, *Cheap Amusements,* p. 40.
         *Lucy Salmon* . . . Schlereth, pp. 73–74.

267–68   *A social service investigator* . . . Sarah Deutsch, *Women and the City: Gen-
         der, Space and Power in Boston, 1870–1940,* p. 59.

268      *"I am getting along splendid . . ."* Diner, p. 71.
         *By midcentury, 74 percent* . . . Stansell, *City of Women,* p. 156.

268–69   *Edwin Godkin* . . . Diner, p. 88.

269      *In the book* Plain Talk . . . Dudden, pp. 180–81.
         *The* Irish World *examined* . . . Diner, p. 84.
         *In the South before* . . . Daniels, p. 137.
         *Irish women often found* . . . See Diner, chapter 5.
         *Second-generation Irish* . . . Schlereth, pp. 73–74.

## "I DIDN'T GO NOPLACE"

269      *"I didn't go noplace . . ."* Coser, p. 41.

269–70   *Jane Addams reported* . . . Addams, p. 234.

270      *Rosa Cavalleri* . . . Ets, p. 222.
         *One member of Addams's* . . . Addams, pp. 67–68.
         *Addams was struck* . . . Addams, pp. 72–73.
         *"One girl told me . . ."* Weatherford, *Foreign and Female,* p. 84.

271      *In New York, some tried* . . . Ewan, pp. 149–50.

## "WELL, WHAT DID YOU THINK OF THAT YOUNG MAN?"

271    *When Rose Cohen* . . . R. Cohen, pp. 199–207.

272    *Rose Cohen said* . . . R. Cohen, p. 85.

    *When she grew up* . . . R. Cohen, p. 297.

    *Hester Vaughn* . . . Goldsmith, pp. 172–73.

273    *Emma Goldman* . . . Ryan, *Womanhood in America*, p. 216.

    *One Jewish woman* . . . Seller, ed., p. 132.

    *Abortions, which were illegal* . . . Weatherford, *Foreign and Female*, p. 11.

    *In 1853, the* Tribune *estimated* . . . Stansell, *City of Women*, p. 111.

    *Jane Addams said the first* . . . Addams, p. 112.

274    *A third of all babies* . . . Ewan, p. 137.

    *Jane Addams reported bitterly* . . . Addams, p. 250.

    *In 1908, doctors swooped* . . . Ewan, p. 143.

    *Addams recalled a devoted* . . . Addams, p. 116.

## "I WANTED A NEW THING—HAPPINESS"

275    *"I wanted a new thing* . . ." Ewan, p. 195.

    *"Oh my God* . . ." Ewan, p. 215.

    *"The Negro race* . . ." D'Emilio and Freedman, p. 196.

    *"The town is dance mad"* . . . Ewan, p. 209.

    *"The pimps* . . ." Michael Gold, *Jews Without Money*, p. 33.

276    *Maureen Connelly* . . . Peiss, *Cheap Amusements*, p. 61.

    *"It was quite wonderful* . . ." Peiss, *Cheap Amusements*, pp. 43–44.

    *In 1909, the International Ladies* . . . Ryan, *Womanhood in America*, p. 223.

## "I HAVE IT LIKE HEAVEN"

277    *"We liked moving* . . ." R. Cohen, p. 186.

    *But her success* . . . Thomas Dublin in the introduction to Cohen's *Out of the Shadow*, p. xv.

278    *"They wouldn't dare* . . ." Ets, p. 254.

## CHAPTER 13: TURN OF THE CENTURY

### "TO DEMONSTRATE PUBLICLY THAT WOMEN HAVE LEGS"

279    *In 1895* . . . Frances Willard, *How I Learned to Ride the Bicycle*, pp. 19, 51.

280    *Lillian Russell began pedaling* . . . Albert Auster, *Actresses and Suffragists*, p. 108.

    *Susan B. Anthony enthused* . . . Lisa Larabee in Willard, pp. 84–90.

    *"A few years ago* . . ." Dulles, p. 267.

    *Lillian Russell confided* . . . Auster, p. 108.

    Life *noted approvingly* . . . Patricia Marks, *Bicycles, Bangs and Bloomers*, p. 193.

    *The Boston Rescue League* . . . Somers, pp. 142–43.

"AGGRESSIVE AS BECAME THEIR SEX"

This section marks the first reference to two books I really enjoyed, Naomi Braun Rosenthal's very short but very valuable *Spinster Tales and Womanly Possibilities*, and Sandra Adickes's *To Be Young Was Very Heaven*.

281    *Madame Yale* . . . Peiss, *Hope in a Jar*, pp. 85–87.

       *In 1896, Life published* . . . Marks, pp. 162–63.

       Ladies' Home Journal, *which teetered* . . . Rosenthal, pp. 19–30.

281–82 *The heroine of the Grace Harlow series* . . . Gwen Athene Tarbox, *The Club-women's Daughters*, pp. 67–70.

282    *Stanton, addressing the men* . . . Geoffrey Ward, *Not for Ourselves Alone*, p. 7.

       *A middle-aged Annie Oakley* . . . Glenda Riley, *The Life and Legacy of Annie Oakley*, p. 142.

       *Frances Willard said* . . . Willard, p. 75.

       *"Almost the best . . ."* Adickes, pp. 72–73.

282–83 *Rose Pastor* . . . Adickes, pp. 61–62.

283    *Alva Belmont:* Christopher Lasch has a short biography of Mrs. Belmont in *Notable American Women*, James and James, eds., pp. 126–28. The story about the costume ball is in Alex Gregory's *Families of Fortune in the Gilded Age*, p. 194.

       *the United States had the highest* . . . Schlereth, p. 281.

       *Denver would soon* . . . Lynn Dumeril, *Modern Temper*, p. 130.


"LESS ABOUT SOUL AND MORE ABOUT PIMPLES"

284    *The* New York Herald *admired* . . . Banner, p. 157.

       *Lillian Russell* . . . Albert Auster, *Actresses and Suffragists*, p. 96.


"WHENEVER SHE WAS DISTURBED OR DEPRESSED
SHE WOULD MOVE THE FURNITURE"

Anyone who wants to get acquainted with Jane Addams should start with her own *Twenty Years at Hull-House*. The two biographies I've relied most on are *American Heroine* by Allen Davis, and the very readable *A Useful Woman* by Gioia Diliberto.

285    *"fashionable fad"* . . . Diliberto, p. 146.

286    *"Whenever she was disturbed . . ."* Diliberto, p. 173.

287    *Thanks to her example* . . . Evans, *Born for Liberty*, p. 148.


"I FOUGHT THE RATS, INSIDE AND OUT"

This section is based on Elliott Gorn's very thorough biography, *Mother Jones*.

287    *In 1930* . . . Dorothy Brown, *Setting a Course: American Women in the 1920s*, p. 90.

       *"I sat alone . . ."* Gorn, p. 41.

288    *"She had a complete . . ."* Gorn, p. 74.

       *Elizabeth Gurley Flynn* . . . Gorn, p. 143.

"*I have been in jail . . .*" Gorn, p. 178.
"*I had sewer rats . . .*" Gorn, p. 210.
289     *Mother Jones organized* . . . Gorn, p. 134.
        *In 1897, the* National Labor Tribune *declared* . . . Gorn, p. 119.


"I AM NOW SURROUNDED BY ALL MY DREAMS COME TRUE"
My information on Ida Tarbell comes from Katherine Brady's *Ida Tarbell: Portrait of a Muckraker.* Madame C. J. Walker's great-great-granddaughter, A'Lelia Bundles, has written a very interesting biography, *On Her Own Ground,* on which much of this section is based.
289     "*She could mobilize . . .*" Brady, p. 95.
        "*Miss Ida Tarbell . . .*" Brady, p. 150.
290     *Harriet Hubbard Ayer* . . . Peiss, *Hope in a Jar,* pp. 64–71.
291     "*I had a dream . . .*" Bundles, p. 277.


"TELL ME, PRETTY MAIDEN,
ARE THERE MORE AT HOME LIKE YOU?"
292     *Floradora Girls:* Banner, pp. 181–82.
        *Dr. Edward Clarke* . . . Solomon, p. 56.
        *Nevertheless, a decade later* . . . Evans, *Born for Liberty,* p. 147.
        *The idea of higher education* . . . Rosenthal, p. 46.
        *By 1910* . . . Woloch, p. 281.
        *Nearly half of all* . . . Rosenthal, pp. 73–74.
        *Florence Kelley remembered* . . . A. Davis, p. 12.
        *When the University of Chicago* . . . Woloch, p. 288.
293     *The year the University of Kansas* . . . Jeffrey, *Frontier Women,* pp. 233–34.


"SMASHED"
293     *The* Cosmopolitan *reported* . . . Helen Lefkowitz Horowitz, *Alma Mater,* pp. 162–63.
        *One former Vassar student* . . . Tarbox, p. 63.
294     *While Jane Addams* . . . Diliberto, p. 243.
        *Smith, the daughter* . . . Diliberto, p. 191.


"RACE SUICIDE"
294     *When Jane Addams was asked* . . . Diliberto, p. 244.
        *Nearly half* . . . Evans, *Born for Liberty,* p. 147.
294–95  *It was the golden age* . . . Rosenthal, pp. 48–50.
295     "*If Americans of the old stock . . .*" Ehrenreich and English, p. 135.
        Ladies' Home Journal, *which never* . . . Rosenthal, p. 68.

"LIFE IS TOO SHORT TO SPEND IT DIGESTING PORK"
A great deal of the information in this section comes from one of my favorite
books, Laura Shapiro's *Perfection Salad.*

296     *"Perhaps the fact . . ."* Janet Wilson James's profile in *Notable American
        Women,* James and James, eds., p. 143.
        *Richards had opposed* . . . Ehrenreich and English, p. 151.
        *Boiling a potato* . . . Shapiro, p. 40.
        *By 1914* . . . Shapiro, p. 175.
297     *"To keep the world clean . . ."* Ehrenreich and English, pp. 158–59.
        *Lillian Gilbreth* . . . Strasser, p. 213.
        *"Cooking has a nobler purpose . . ."* Shapiro, p. 67.
298     *Sarah Tyson Rorer* . . . Shapiro, p. 75.
        *"Dress them, bathe them . . ."* Dorothy Brown, p. 120.
        *A popular government pamphlet* . . . Ehrenreich and English, p. 201.
        *Margaret Mead's* . . . Mead, *Blackberry Winter,* pp. 25–26.
299     *Charlotte Perkins Gilman* . . . Gilman told her own story in *The Living of
        Charlotte Perkins Gilman.* Also see chapter 5 of Dolores Hayden's *The
        Grand Domestic Revolution.*
        *Inez Milholland* . . . Paul Boyer's profile of Milholland in *Notable American
        Women,* James and James, eds., vol. 1, p. 189.


"HAS SUCH A THING EVER HAPPENED . . . BEFORE?"
Except where otherwise noted, the information in this section is drawn from Dorothy
and Carl Schneider's *Into the Breach: American Women Overseas in World War I.*

301     *Two thousand black nurses* . . . Lettie Gavin, *American Women in World
        War I,* p. 59.
        *Addie Waites Hunton* . . . "Two Colored Women with the AEF," in *Beyond
        the Homefront,* Yvonne Klein, ed.
        *"I'm glad you . . ."* Schneider and Schneider, pp. 170–73.
        *"When a group of colored . . ."* Hunton in Klein, ed., pp. 103–7.
301–2   *"We have only . . ."* Schneider and Schneider, p. 128.
302     *Julia Stimson worked* . . . Schneider and Schneider, p. 111.
        *Mary Elderkins* . . . Schneider and Schneider, pp. 113, 116.
302–3   *Jeanette Rankin of Montana* . . . Norma Smith has written a biography of
        Rankin, *Jeanette Rankin: America's Conscience.*


## CHAPTER 14: REFORMING THE WORLD

"LIKE ALL THINGS TOO LONG POSTPONED,
NOW GETS ON EVERYBODY'S NERVES"
Eleanor Flexner and Ellen Fitzpatrick's *Century of Struggle* was a groundbreaker
when it was first published in 1959, and it's still one of the best and most readable

books about the suffrage movement. For Stanton, read her autobiography and Elisabeth Griffith's *In Her Own Right*. To go directly to the source on Anthony, see Lynn Sherr's *Failure Is Impossible: Susan B. Anthony in Her Own Words*. Geoffrey Ward has put together a lavishly illustrated book about the two women's friendship, *Not for Ourselves Alone*.

304     *"We have got . . ."* Sherr, p. 298.

305     *When Stanton became pregnant . . .* Sherr, p. 4.

        *And Stanton complained . . .* Goldsmith, p. 118.

        *the sight of Susan on the doorstep . . .* Ellen Carol DuBois, *Harriot Stanton Blatch and the Winning of Woman Suffrage*, p. 20.

        *At her eightieth birthday . . .* E. Griffith, p. 210.

306     *It was a bitter . . .* Goldsmith, p. 181.

        *"Mrs. Stone felt . . ."* E. Griffith, p. 111.

        *"Logically, our enfranchisement . . ."* Goldsmith, p. 435.

        *All the horrors . . .* Flexner and Fitzpatrick, p. 214.

307     *"To get the word . . ."* Janet Zillinger Giele, *Two Paths to Women's Equality*, pp. 112–13.

308     *In 1912, Catt wrote to a friend . . .* Flexner and Fitzpatrick, p. 264.

        *A former school . . .* Eleanor Flexner has a profile of Catt in *Notable American Women*, James and James, ed., vol. 1, pp. 309–12. For a more lengthy study, see Robert Booth Fowler's *Carrie Catt: Feminist and Politician*.

        *Harriot Stanton Blatch . . .* See DuBois's *Harriot Stanton Blatch*, also Flexner and Fitzpatrick, p. 243.

        *"Ridicule, ridicule . . ."* Ward, p. 221.

        *In 1912, a parade . . .* Adickes, pp. 6–7.

309     *Volunteers distributed . . .* I found these particular pieces of memorabilia at an exhibit by the Huntington Library in San Marino, CA.

        *Martha Farnsworth . . .* Springer and Springer, eds., p. 209.

        *In 1915, Carrie Chapmen Catt . . .* Anne Firor Scott and Andrew M. Scott, *One Half the People*, pp. 112–13.

310     *Mrs. Frank Leslie . . .* Flexner and Fitzpatrick, p. 265.


"THERE IS NO ALICE PAUL. THERE IS SUFFRAGE."

Except where otherwise noted, the information on Paul comes from Christine Lunardini's *From Equal Suffrage to Equal Rights: Alice Paul and the National Woman's Party*. Lunardini also has a profile of Paul in *Portraits of American Women*, G. J. Barker-Benfield and Catherine Clinton, eds.

310     *A magazine writer . . .* Lunardini in Barker-Benfield and Clinton, p. 432.

        *Always small and frail-looking . . .* Lunardini in Barker-Benfield and Clinton, p. 432.

311     *He and the second . . .* Flexner and Fitzpatrick, pp. 271–72.

312     *"Yesterday was a bad . . ."* Seller, p. 284.

        *It was a moment some men. . .* Flexner and Fitzpatrick, p. 283.

313     *The president then took* . . . This section is based on Flexner and Fitz-
        patrick, pp. 302–15.

313–14  *The Tennessee House* . . . Flexner has a good account of the drama in Ten-
        nessee, and there's an entire book on the story, *The Perfect 36* by Carol
        Lynn Yellin and Janann Sherman.

## "BELIEVE . . . AT LEAST FOR THE TIME BEING,
## IN THE SYMPATHY OF WOMEN"

The story of the fight for suffrage from the African American woman's point of
view is recounted in Rosalyn Terborg-Penn's *African American Women in the
Struggle for the Vote, 1850–1920.* This section is based on the information in her
book.

314     *"If the Illinois women* . . ." Terborg-Penn, p. 122.

315     *When the suffrage movement held its first* . . . Terborg-Penn, p. 111.
        *"When women like you* . . ." Terborg-Penn, p. 116.
        *Mary Turner:* Terborg-Penn, p. 96.

## "LIPS THAT TOUCH ALCOHOL"

316     *An American gentleman* . . . Andrew Barr, *Drink: A Social History of Amer-
        ica,* p. 127.

317     *A reporter from Cincinnati* . . . Evans, *Born for Liberty,* p. 126.

317–18  *The ultimate symbol* . . . Paul Messbarger has a good profile of Nation in
        *Notable American Women,* James and James, eds., pp. 609–11.

318     *In one story, a farmer* . . . Giele, pp. 70–71.

## "DO EVERYTHING"

Except where noted, this section is based on Ruth Bordin's biography, *Frances
Willard.*

318     *In the 1890s, ten times* . . . Degler, *At Odds,* p. 317.
        *Tampa alone had three* . . . Nancy Hewitt, *Southern Discomfort, Women's
        Activism in Tampa, Florida, 1880s–1920s,* p. 63.

319     *In one eighty-day period* . . . Bordin, p. 80.
        *Everett Hughes* . . . Giele, p. 89.

320     *In 1905* . . . Bordin, p. 6.

## "BEAUTIFUL WHITE GIRLS SOLD INTO RUIN"

The classic book on the way Americans have handled sex throughout the country's
history is *Intimate Matters,* by John D'Emilio and Estelle Freedman. I've relied on it
throughout this book, including this section.

320     *raising the age of sexual consent* . . . Giele, pp. 100–106.

321     *Dr. Prince Morrow* . . . D'Emilio and Freedman, pp. 204–5.
        *One psychologist studied* . . . Allan Brandt, *No Magic Bullet: A Social His-
        tory of Venereal Disease in the United States Since 1880,* p. 38.

*A women's college graduate* . . . Anonymous, "The Harm My Education Did Me," *The Outlook* (November 30, 1927), pp. 396–405.

*when* Ladies' Home Journal *ran* . . . Brandt, p. 24.

321–22 *In 1870, St. Louis* . . . D'Emilio and Freedman, p. 149.

322 *One reformer noted wryly* . . . Reed, p. 58.

"*Beautiful White Girls* . . ." D'Emilio and Freedman, p. 209.

### "CAN THEY NOT USE SELF-CONTROL?"

Birth control in America is the topic of a number of good books, including James Reed's *From Private Vice to Public Virtue*. My favorite book on the 1800s is Jane Farrell Brodie's *Contraception and Abortion in Nineteenth-Century America*. For the twentieth century, my choice would be Andrea Tone's *Devices and Desires: A History of Contraception in America*, which you'll be seeing a lot of in notes to come.

323 *Comstock arranged for the adoption* . . . Brodie, p. 274.

*Once, when a journalist asked* . . . Tone, p. 16.

"*A bloody ending* . . ." Tone, p. 34.

*Another of his targets* . . . D'Emilio and Freedman, p. 161.

*When Comstock brought* . . . Tone, p. 34.

323–24 *But the Comstock Act did not* . . . Schlereth, p. 274.

### "WHAT EVERY GIRL SHOULD KNOW"

Margaret Sanger wrote her autobiography and there is a good biography currently available, Ellen Chesler's *Woman of Valor*. This section is based on it unless otherwise noted.

324 *Mabel Dodge called her* . . . Chesler, p. 96.

325 *An observer remembered that Sanger spoke* . . . Reed, p. 78.

"*If some persons would* . . ." Chesler, p. 127.

*The* New York Times *discreetly refused* . . . Chesler, p. 129.

326 "*I opened the doors* . . ." Margaret Sanger, *An Autobiography*, p. 216.

## CHAPTER 15: THE TWENTIES

### "FLAPPERS ARE BRAVE AND GAY AND BEAUTIFUL"

The survey book I found most useful when studying the twenties was Dorothy Brown's *Setting the Course*.

327 *Margaret Mead arrived* . . . Mead, p. 90.

328 " '*Feminism' has become a term* . . ." Dorothy Dunbar Bromley, "Feminist—New Style," *Harper's* (October 1927).

*Mead transferred* . . . Mead, p. 102.

"*Flaming youth* . . ." Frank Gilbreth and Ernestine Gilbreth Carey, *Cheaper by the Dozen*, pp. 175–76.

329 *Jane Addams said* . . . Mary Ryan, *Womanhood in America*, p. 256.

*A much-quoted article* . . . *The Outlook* (November 30, 1927), p. 405.

"*I think a woman* . . ." Evans, *Born for Liberty*, pp. 175–76.

## "SKINNY AND FLAT-CHESTED AND POPULAR"

330     *A survey in Milwaukee* . . . Gerald Leinwand, *1927,* p. 174.

        *"That's what's the matter* . . ." Gilbreth and Carey, *Cheaper by the Dozen,*
        pp. 177–79.

        *When the manager* . . . Frederick Lewis Allen, *Only Yesterday: An Informal
        History of the 1920's,* p. 2.

        *In summer* . . . *The American Sexual Dilemma,* William O'Neill, ed., p. 39.

330–31  *The president of the University of Florida* . . . Barr, p. 150.

331     *"Ten years ago* . . ." Jenna Weisman Joselit, *A Perfect Fit,* p. 60.

        *"Thanks to cosmetics* . . ." Peiss, *Hope in a Jar,* p. 141.

        *By 1927, a survey found* . . . Leinwand, p. 174.

        *Aviatrix Ruth Elder* . . . Peiss, *Hope in a Jar,* p. 186.

331–32  *One Ponds cold cream ad* . . . Peiss, *Hope in a Jar,* pp. 137–38.

## "A LOT OF LASHING AND LATHER"

332     *A writer for* . . . Virginia Scharff, *Taking the Wheel,* p. 139.

        *"The girl with sport* . . ." Paula Fass, *The Damned and the Beautiful,* p. 307.

        *More women—perhaps* . . . Reed, p. 61.

333     *surveys of college men* . . . Fass, p. 277.

        *they were only about half* . . . Reed, p. 61.

        *An editor of* . . . Woloch, p. 413.

        *Middle-class girls* . . . For more about this switch in the concept of court-
        ing, see Beth Bailey's *From the Front Porch to the Back Seat.*

        *A college friend told* . . . Mead, p. 103.

333–34  *Another of Fitzgerald's* . . . Fitzgerald, *This Side of Paradise,* p. 238.

334     *By 1920, 200 books* . . . Dorothy Brown, p. 18.

        *Lysol became a popular* . . . Harvey Green, *The Uncertainty of Everyday Life,*
        p. 132.

        *Germany manufactured the best* . . . Tone, p. 126.

        *At Barnard, Margaret Mead* . . . Mead, p. 104.

        *In 1926, a play about* . . . Marybeth Hamilton, *When I'm Bad, I'm Better,*
        p. 98. This biography of Mae West also has some fascinating information on
        the way sex and gender were treated in popular entertainment during the
        early part of the century.

## "SOAP TO MATCH HER BATHROOM'S COLOR SCHEME"

334–35  *Martha Farnsworth* . . . See *Plains Woman: The Diary of Martha
        Farnsworth,* Marlene and Haskell Springer, eds.

335     *For the first time* . . . Cowan, p. 87.

        *many women sent their clothes* . . . Green, p. 64.

        *"Today's woman gets* . . ." Dumeril, p. 129.

        *the department stores spoiled* . . . Benson, pp. 88–94.

        *Ready-to-wear maternity* . . . Reed, p. 59.

335–36  *"Two yellow capsules* . . ." Dorothy Brown, p. 111.

336     *During World War I* . . . Weatherford, *Foreign and Female*, p. 26.

*An early ad* . . . The Ad Access Project, funded by the Duke Endowment Library 2000 Fund, has a collection of ads for feminine hygiene products over the years. You can access it on the Internet.

*Other companies had attempted* . . . This is from another good source of information on what women did when they got their period over history: the Museum of Menstruation.

## "REACH FOR A LUCKY INSTEAD OF A SWEET"

337     *A child of the era* . . . Banner, p. 153.

*Marmola:* Leinwand, p. 223.

337–38  *"When I was a boy* . . ." Barr, p. 151.

338     *Pauline Sabine* . . . Barr, p. 152.

## "SPLINTERED INTO A HUNDRED FRAGMENTS"

339     *"The American women's movement* . . ." Dorothy Brown, p. 50.

*The National American Woman Suffrage Association* . . . Ryan, *Womanhood in America*, p. 254.

*A man in Indiana* . . . Allen, *Only Yesterday*, p. 39.

340     *In 1920, Warren Harding's* . . . Collins, pp. 125–27.

## "TOO MUCH PERSONALITY"

340     *"It came with a rush"* . . . Allen, *Only Yesterday*, p. 65.

*By 1929, a third* . . . Green, p. 188.

340–41  *In 1925, a journalist named* . . . Michelle Hilmes, *Radio Voices*, p. 130.

341     *one much-quoted poll* . . . Hilmes, pp. 142–43.

*More than any other decade* . . . Haskell, p. 49. Anyone interested in the period might start with Cari Beauchamp's *Without Lying Down: Frances Marion and the Powerful Women of Early Hollywood.*

*Mary Pickford:* My information comes from Scott Eyman's *Mary Pickford.*

342     *Theda Bara:* See Eva Golden's *Vamp: The Rise and Fall of Theda Bara.*

## "IF I SHOULD BOP OFF, IT'LL BE DOING THE THING THAT I'VE ALWAYS MOST WANTED"

342     *Women had been getting* . . . Scharff, p. 25.

342–43  *"sensational cross-country run"* . . . Scharff, p. 51.

343     *The Motor Girls* . . . Bobbie Ann Mason, *The Girl Sleuth*, p. 11. This is my chance to recommend this book, one of my all-time favorites.

*Starting the early model cars* . . . This is all based on information in Scharff.

*the Flying Girls* . . . Mason, p. 14.

343–44  *Early aviation was another* . . . The rest of this section is indebted to Gene Nora Jessen's *The Powder Puff Derby*, a very readable book about women's role in early American aviation.

344     *Bessie Coleman* ... There's a profile of Bessie Coleman by Elizabeth
        Hadley Freydberg in *Black Women in America*, Hine, ed.
344–45  *Amelia Earhart* ... Katherine Brick has an essay on Earhart in *Notable
        American Women*. For a full biography, see Susan Butler's *East to the Dawn*.

### SWIM GIRL, SWIM

345–46  *Gertrude Ederle:* Kelli Anderson, "The Young Woman and the Sea," *Sports,
        Illustrated* (November 29, 1999), p. 90, and Paul Gallico's *The Golden People*, pp. 49–65.
346     *The older generation* ... The two books by Frank Gilbreth and Ernestine
        Gilbreth Carey are a really pleasant way to get a picture of family life in
        the early part of the century. Chapter 5 of *Belles on their Toes* has a won-
        derful portrait of the generational divide on bathing suits.
        *When the first Miss America* ... Banner, pp. 267–69.

### "THE REASON NOBODY WILL GIVE"

This section is indebted to Jacqueline Jones's *Labor of Love, Labor of Sorrow*, one
of the very best books on African American women in this country's history.
346     *In 1929* ... Cowan, p. 182.
        *A survey of black* ... Dorothy Brown, p. 94.
        *African American women of middle age* ... Jones, p. 193.
346–47  *Addie Hunter* ... Jones, p. 179.
347     *There was a sexual imbalance* ... Jones, p. 156.
        *Black wives were five times* ... Jones, p. 162.
        *Unlike immigrants, black parents* ... John Bodnar et al., *Lives of Their
        Own: Blacks, Italians and Poles in Pittsburgh, 1900–1960*, p. 92.
        *Marita Bonner* ... Cheryl Wall, *Women in the Harlem Renaissance*, p. 4.
        *Madame Mamie Hightower* ... Piess, *Hope in a Jar*, pp. 112–13, 117.
348     *In 1920, Mamie Smith's* ... Susan Douglas, *Listening In*, p. 90.

### "IF I WERE BORN 100 YEARS FROM NOW, WELL AND GOOD"

350     *"Within the space ..."* Leinwand, p. 49.
        *The proportion* ... William Leuchtenburg, *The Perils of Prosperity*, p. 159.
        *They made much less than men* ... Leinwand, p. 51.
349     *"I pay our women ..."* Scharff, p. 54.
        *F. Scott Fitzgerald* ... Fitzgerald, p. 237.
        *Only about 10 percent* ... Dumeril, p. 113.
        *"There must be a way ..."* Solomon, p. 174.

## CHAPTER 16: THE DEPRESSION

### "ROMANCE CAN BEGIN AT THIRTY-FIVE"

350     *When NBC radio moved* ... Hilmes, *Radio Voices*, pp. 150–51. This is my
        favorite book about radio in the pre-TV days.

*Helen Trent's attempt* . . . Robert LaGuardia, *From Ma Perkins to Mary Hartman: The Illustrated History of Soap Operas*, p. 7.

351    *Mary Knackstedt Dyck* . . . Mrs. Dyck's journals can be found in *Waiting on the Bounty*, Pamela Riney-Kehrberg, ed.

*In October 1936* . . . Riney-Kehrberg, ed., p. 26.

*Echoing Nathaniel Hawthorne's* . . . Joseph Blótner, *Faulkner*, p. 938.

*The actress who played* . . . LaGuardia, p. 9.

352    *"The man in the wheelchair . . ."* James Thurber, *The Beast in Me and Other Animals*, p. 221.

## "DOING IT YOURSELF THESE DAYS?"

Many of the voices of women in this chapter come from Studs Terkel's great oral history, *Hard Times*. This is also an opportunity to put in a plug for a longtime favorite book, *Domestic Revolutions: A Social History of American Family Life* by Steven Mintz and Susan Kellogg.

352    *Diana Morgan* . . . Terkel, *Hard Times*, p. 181.

*The writer Caroline Bird* . . . Bird, *The Invisible Scar*, p. 273.

353    *The average family income* . . . Mintz and Kellogg, p. 134.

*"endless little economies . . ."* Susan Ware, *Holding Their Own: American Women in the 1930s*, p. 2.

*in Indianapolis, more than half* . . . Mintz and Kellogg, p. 135.

*An ad for bleach* . . . Cowan, p. 176.

*Sally Rand* . . . Terkel, *Hard Times*, pp. 198–205.

*"Many a family . . ."* Mintz and Kellogg, p. 136.

353–54  *"Do you realize how . . ."* Terkel, *Hard Times*, p. 447.

354    *The birthrate plunged* . . . Mintz and Kellogg, p. 137.

*The birthrate was about* . . . Green, p. 78.

*In the 1930s, Caroline Bird* . . . Bird, p. 289.

*Lillian Wald's* . . . A section of Wald's book *Windows on Henry Street* appears in *Women of Valor*, Bernard Sternsher and Judith Sealander, eds., p. 39.

*"I have watched . . ."* Woloch, p. 451.

*In New York, Meridel* . . . Meridel LeSueur, "Women on the Breadlines," *New Masses* (January 1932).

355    *"dressed in slacks . . ."* Green, p. 79.

*"A few women . . ."* Ben Reitman, *Boxcar Bertha*, p. 69.

*Peggy Terry* . . . Terkel, *Hard Times*, pp. 67–68.

*Pauline Kael* . . . Terkel, *Hard Times*, p. 51.

*One of Lillian Wald's* . . . Sternsher and Sealander, eds., p. 38.

## "THE MOST LIBERATED WOMAN OF THE CENTURY"

There is a library's worth of biographical work on Eleanor Roosevelt; a reader with plenty of time might want to start with Blanche Wiesen Cook's two wonderful volumes on Mrs. Roosevelt's life up to World War II, move on to Doris

---

Kearn Goodwin's *No Ordinary Time* for the war years, and then to Joseph Lash's *Eleanor—The Years Alone*. For a very quick first immersion, try the essay in Susan Ware's *Letter to the World: Seven Women Who Shaped the American Century*.

356   *one cousin called it . . .* William Chafe's profile in Barbara Sicherman and Carol Green, *Notable American Women, The Modern Period*, p. 595.

357   *"I was your real . . ."* Ware, *Letter to the World*, p. 10.
      *"The bottom dropped . . ."* Joseph Lash, *Eleanor and Franklin*, p. 220.

358   *"Eleanor, I think she's . . ."* Terkel, *Hard Times*, p. 448.
      *"My dear, if . . ."* Ware, *Letter to the World*, p. 5.
      *The gossip about her was vicious . . .* Collins, pp. 148–50.

359   *One historian . . .* Joseph Lash, "Eleanor Roosevelt's Role in Women's History," in *Clio Was a Woman: Studies in the History of American Women*, Mabel Deutrich and Virginia Purdy, eds., p. 244.

## "I DIDN'T LIKE THE IDEA OF BEING IMPEACHED"

359   *"Twelve appointments . . ."* Ware, *Beyond Suffrage: Women in the New Deal*, pp. 89–90.

360   *Florence Allen . . .* See her autobiography, *To Do Justly*.
      *"When I wanted help . . ."* Ware, *Beyond Suffrage*, p. 10.
      *Mary McLeod Bethune . . .* See Elaine Smith's "Mary McLeod Bethune and the National Youth Administration" in Deutrich and Purdy, eds.
      *Frances Perkins:* This section is based on information from *Frances Perkins: Champion of the New Deal* by Naomi Pasachoff.

361   *"It was always up and down . . ."* Pasachoff, p. 39.
      *When Perkins was honored . . .* Ware, *Beyond Suffrage*, p. 28.

362   *On April 12 . . .* Ware, *Beyond Suffrage*, p. 131.

## "A MENACE TO SOCIETY"

362   *In 1932, Fortune, in a peculiar . . .* Bird, p. 279.
      *Pollster George Gallup . . .* Ware, *Holding Their Own*, p. 27.
      *Usually, the issue . . .* Mary Hargreaves, "Darkness Before the Dawn: The Status of Working Women in the Depression Years," in Deutrich and Purdy, eds., p. 181.

362–63 *"I think the single girl . . ."* Gerald Moskowitz and David Rosner, *Slaves of the Depression*, p. 154.

363   *Even Frances Perkins . . .* Woloch, p. 452.
      *Eleanor Roosevelt called the law . . .* Lash in Deutrich and Purdy, eds., p. 249.
      *More than three-quarters . . .* Penny Colman, *Rosie the Riveter*, pp. 24–25.
      *Despite all this . . .* Winifred Bolin makes this point in "The Economics of Middle-Income Family Life: Working Women During the Great Depression," *Journal of American History* (June 1978).

364   *The hopes that female fliers . . .* Ware, *Holding Their Own*, p. 177.
      *The New York City board . . .* Bird, p. 53.

"NOT A BIT OF DUST FOR THIS GREAT 4TH DAY OF FEB."

364    *In 1935, more than* . . . Robert Caro, *Lyndon Johnson: The Path to Power*,
       p. 516.
       *Only 20 percent* . . . Green, p. 101.
       *A researcher visiting* . . . This is drawn from Margaret Jarman Hagood,
       *Mothers of the South: Portraiture of the White Tenant Farm Woman*.
       *The New Deal program* . . . Robert Caro has a riveting description of
       the coming of electricity to the Texas hill country in his first Johnson
       book, pp. 502–15.
365    *"Just at noon . . ."* Joan Ostrander, *Bits and Pieces of Way Back When*,
       pp. 36–37.
       *"Not a bit of dust . . ."* Riney-Kehrberg, p. 117.

"GOODNESS HAD NOTHING TO DO WITH IT, DEARIE"
This section is based on Marybeth Hamilton's *When I'm Bad, I'm Better*.

"I HAD A WIFE ONCE BUT SHE VANISHED
INTO THE NBC BUILDING"

368    *she was, as one critic pointed out* . . . Haskell, p. 125.
369    *Margaret Mitchell, the author* . . . Pierpont, p. 93.
       *As novelist Bobbie Ann Mason* . . . Mason, pp. 52, 67.
370    *Dorothy Thompson* . . . This section is based on Susan Ware's portrait in
       *Letter to the World: Seven Women Who Shaped the American Century*.

## CHAPTER 17: WORLD WAR II

"I AM GOING TO ASSIST IN BUILDING A PLANE TO BOMB HITLER"

371    *But their meals* . . . This note introduces one of my all-time favorite books
       on life on the home front during World War II—Amy Bentley's *Eating for
       Victory*.
       *Women who failed* . . . Leila Rupp, *Mobilizing Women for War*, p. 156.
371–72 *One of the many* . . . Rupp, *Mobilizing Women*, p. 157.
372    *Constance Bowman* . . . Bowman and Allen, *Slacks and Calluses*, p. 31.
       *Copywriters for public* . . . Straub in Deutrich and Purdy, eds., p. 215.
       *The government and the media* . . . Bentley, p. 137.
       *In Atlanta, Helen Dortch Longstreet* . . . Paul Casdorph, *Let the Good Times
       Roll*, p. 137.

"A WOMAN'S ARMY . . . THINK OF THE HUMILIATION"
American historians are obviously doing a good job of preserving the oral histories
of women who took part in World War II, either in the military or on the home
front. One of my favorites, done by the State Historical Society of Wisconsin, is
*Women Remember the War*, Michael Stevens, ed., and as a result the voices of women
from Wisconsin get what is probably more than their share of space in this book.

373     *"By voting for me . . ."* N. Smith, p. 176.

        *Congresswoman Rankin rushed* . . . Smith, pp. 183–85.

        *Two months after* . . . D'Ann Campbell, *Women at War with America*, p. 7.

374     *She had gone overseas* . . . Lisa Meyer, *Creating G.I. Jane*, p. 11.

        *For a while, the War Department* . . . Meyer, p. 55.

        *Officials also stressed* . . . Susan Hartman, "Women in the Military Service," in Deutrich and Purdy, eds., p. 196.

        *Frieda Schurch* . . . Stevens, ed., pp. 56–57.

375     *There was a widely reported* . . . Helen Rogan, *Mixed Company*, p. 142.

        *The FBI was called* . . . Campbell, p. 37.

        *"A woman's Army . . ."* Meyer, p. 13.

        *"The efforts of . . ."* Meyer, p. 40.

        *A WAC in Birmingham* . . . Stevens, ed., p. 53.

        *But Evelyn Fraser* . . . Studs Terkel, *The Good War: An Oral History of World War II*, p. 123.

## "THREE HOLES IN THE TAIL, BOYS, THAT'S A LITTLE TOO CLOSE"

My single best source of information on women who served overseas during the war was Helen Rogan's *Mixed Company*, which is, alas, out of print. If you want to read more about the WASPs, try Sally Van Wagenen Keil's *Those Wonderful Women in their Flying Machines*. The part of this section on the WASPs is based on that book unless otherwise noted.

376     *The first five WACs* . . . Rogan, p. 133.

        *More than 5,000 women* . . . Rogan, p. 143.

377     *"Three holes . . ."* Keil, p. 269.

        *An army flight surgeon* . . . Keil, p. 169.

        *It wasn't the only theory* . . . Campbell, p. 28.

378     *Jill McCormick* . . . Keil, p. 303.

## "LITTLE DID I DREAM THAT WE WOULD BE ALWAYS HUNGRY, ALWAYS FRIGHTENED"

A very thorough recounting of the story of the Bataan nurses is *We Band of Angels*, by Elizabeth Norman. Helen Rogan also has interviews with a number of the survivors in *Mixed Company*.

378     *Toward the end of the war* . . . Doris Weatherford, *American Women and World War II*, pp. 19–20.

378–79  *one nurse in training* . . . Campbell, p. 57.

379     *"We lived high . . ."* Rogan, p. 260.

        *"Little did I dream . . ."* Weatherford, *American Women and World War II*, p. 3.

        *As Japanese warships* . . . Norman, p. 43.

        *"I can remember . . ."* Rogan, p. 262.

        *"I was continually amazed . . ."* Weatherford, *American Women and World War II*, p. 63.

380       *Brunetta Kuehlthau* . . . Norman, p. 55.
          *Most of the nurses* . . . Thousands of American civilian women and chil-
          dren were interned in Japanese camps in the South Pacific, including mis-
          sionaries, wives of businessmen, and teachers. Theresa Kaminski collected
          information about them for her book *Prisoners in Paradise: American
          Women in the Wartime South Pacific.*
380–81    *General Jonathan Wainwright* . . . Norman, p. 238.


"SHE'S MAKING HISTORY, WORKING FOR VICTORY"

381–82    *"While other girls . . ."* Colman, pp. 15–16.
382       Ladies' Home Journal *ran a story* . . . Rosenthal, p. 127.
          *Peggy Terry* . . . Terkel, *The Good War,* pp. 105–6.
          *As a result of the great migration* . . . Colman, pp. 42–43.
383       *"Darlin, You are . . ."* Judy Barrett Litoff and David Smith, *Since You
          Went Away,* p. 146.
          *Rose Kaminski* . . . Stevens, ed., pp. 11–12.
          *The Office of War Information* . . . Colman, p. 51.
          *The owner of the Chicago Cubs* . . . The story of the All-American Girls
          League is told in Sue Macy's *A Whole New Ballgame.*
          *Ads and movie newsreels* . . . Colman, p. 10.
384       *nearly 90 percent of the housewives* . . . William Tuttle, *Daddy's Gone to
          War: The Second World War in the Lives of America's Children,* p. 71.
          *Congress didn't appropriate money* . . . Woloch, p. 474.
          *Agnes Meyer* . . . Tuttle, p. 74.
          *In 1943, two San Diego high school* . . . Constance Bowman and Clara
          Marie Allen, *Slacks and Calluses: Our Summer in a Bomber Factory.* This lit-
          tle book, which is still in print, gives you a very good feel for what defense
          work was like for two middle-class women.
          *"I was tireder . . ."* Bowman and Allen, p. 42.
385       *"It was a great shock . . ."* Bowman and Allen, p. 69.
          *When four WASPs* . . . Keil, p. 259.
          *"Whether they are . . ."* Bowman and Allen, p. 67.


"VARIETY MEATS: THEY ARE GOOD,
ABUNDANT, HIGHLY NUTRITIOUS"

Except where otherwise noted, the information in this section comes from Amy
Bentley's *Eating for Victory.*
386       *"Never in the long . . ."* Bentley, p. 3.
          *A government-issued* . . . Bentley, p. 97.
          *"My mother and all . . ."* Terkel, *The Good War,* p. 234.
          *"Give us housewives . . ."* Bentley, pp. 106–7.
387       *It was in World War II* . . . Bentley, pp. 67–68.

### "WE WOULD GO TO DANCES
### AND GIRLS WOULD DANCE WITH GIRLS"

387   *A Seattle paper* . . . There's a reproduction of this cartoon on p. 98 of Colman's *Rosie the Riveter.*
      *Dorothy Zmuda of Milwaukee* . . . Stevens, ed., p. 47.
      *"The pressure to marry . . ."* Terkel, *The Good War,* p. 114.
388   *Dorothy Zmuda was casually* . . . Stevens, ed., p. 45.
      *"The girls that I knew . . ."* Stevens, ed., p. 35.
      *The* Baltimore Sun *noticed* . . . Bentley, p. 44.
      *"It was very important . . ."* Stevens, ed., p. 36.
      *Jean Lechnir* . . . Stevens, ed., p. 84.


### "WELL OF COURSE, SO WERE THE JAPANESE"

One good memoir of life in the relocation camps is *Farewell to Manzanar,* by Jeanne
Wakatsuki Houston and James D. Houston.
389   *Anne Dinsmore* . . . Stevens, ed., pp. 92–94.
      *Earl Warren* . . . Casdorph, pp. 27–28.
      *"These poor women . . ."* Lawson Fusao Inada, *Only What We Could Carry,*
      p. 61.
389–90 *Jeanne Wakatsuki was seven* . . . Wakatsuki Houston and Houston, pp. 14–15.
390   *Yoshiko Uchida* . . . Inada, pp. 69–80.
      *The Department of the Interior* . . . Bentley, p. 121.
      *When one of the first groups* . . . Meyer, p. 67.


### "HITLER WAS THE ONE THAT GOT US OUT
### OF THE WHITE FOLKS' KITCHEN"

391   *a young Maya Angelou* . . . Angelou, *I Know Why the Caged Bird Sings,*
      pp. 265–69.
      *In New York, other black women* . . . Karen Anderson, *Wartime Women,* p. 84.
      *In 1943, at the height* . . . See Karen Anderson, "Last Hired, First Fired:
      Black Women Workers During World War II," *Journal of American History* (June 1982).
392   *"Despite all . . ."* Brenda L. Moore, *To Serve My Country, to Serve My Race:
      The Story of the Only African American WACs Stationed Overseas During
      World War II,* p. 19.
      *Pauli Murray* . . . *Bitter Fruit: African American Women in World War II,*
      Maureen Honey, ed., pp. 277–79.
393   *Elsie Oliver* . . . Moore, p. 18.
      *Despite its grave* . . . Campbell, p. 64.
      *Major Harriet West* . . . Meyer, pp. 90–93.
      *At Fort Devens* . . . Meyer, pp. 97–99.
394   *"My sister always . . ."* Sherna Berger Gluck, *Rosie the Riveter Revisited,* p. 23.

## "IT JUST ENDED OVERNIGHT"

394     *"Ohh, the beautiful . . ."* Terkel, *The Good War,* p. 109.
        *"They always got priority . . ."* Stevens, ed., pp. 23–24.
395     *"It just ended . . ."* Gluck, p. 65.
        *William Mulcahy . . .* Colman, pp. 21–22.
        *"I happen to be a widow . . ."* Colman, pp. 97–98.
        *Peggy Terry, the Kentucky woman . . .* Terkel, *The Good War,* p. 107.
396     *"We got a chance . . ."* Terkel, *The Good War,* p. 112.
        *"They realized that they were . . ."* Terkel, *The Good War,* p. 119.

## CHAPTER 18: THE FIFTIES

### "I DREAMED I STOPPED TRAFFIC IN MY MAIDENFORM BRA"

My two favorite books on women in the 1950s are Stephanie Coontz's *The Way We Never Were: American Families and the Nostalgia Trap,* and Jessica Weiss's *To Have and to Hold: Marriage, the Baby Boom and Social Change.*

398     *"In order to wear . . ."* Benita Eisler, *Private Lives: Men and Women of the Fifties,* p. 120.
399     *Women looking for a more modern . . .* William Chafe, *The Unfinished Journey: America Since World War II,* p. 126.
        *But plenty of women worked . . .* Coontz, *The Way We Never Were,* p. 31.
        *Then suddenly, 60 percent . . .* Coontz, p. 24.
399–400 Ebony *enthused . . .* "Hello Mammy, Good-bye Mother," *Ebony* (March 1947), p. 36.

### "I MADE TERRIFIC FRIENDS RIGHT AWAY"

401     *"Our lives are held . . ."* K. Jackson, p. 235.
        *"I made terrific . . ."* Eisler, pp. 212–16.
401–2   *In Levittown, outdoor . . .* K. Jackson, p. 236.

### "IF MY WIFE HAD HER WAY I THINK WE'D ALL BREATHE IN UNISON"

402     *"Emphasis on family . . ."* Dorothy Barclay, "Family Palship—With an Escape Clause," *The New York Times Magazine,* November 18, 1956, p. 48.
        *Dr. Bruno Bettelheim . . .* Bettelheim, "Fathers Shouldn't Try to Be Mothers," *Parents* (October 1956), p. 40.
403     *"Adventure is a father's . . ."* Weiss, p. 90.
        *Betty Furness . . .* David Halberstam, *The Fifties,* pp. 498–500.

### "ALL THE GANG HAS STARTED THEIR OWN SETS OF STERLING"

404     *Like almost half . . .* Brett Harvey, *The Fifties,* p. 70.
        *"Not so long ago . . ."* Weiss, p. 123.
        *"All the gang has . . ."* Betty Friedan, *The Feminine Mystique,* p. 220.

*Suzie Slattery* . . . Eisler, p. 104.

*Once married* . . . Harvey, p. 70.

405　*The proportion of women* . . . Harvey, p. 70.

*a professor at Smith complained* . . . Friedan, *The Feminine Mystique*, p. 152.

*"The thing you* didn't *do* . . ." Harvey, p. 61.

*A survey in 1958* . . . Bailey, p. 132.

*The wife of a college* . . . Elaine Tyler May, *Homeward Bound: American Families in the Cold War Era*, p. 71.

*"I felt increasingly* . . ." May, *Homeward Bound*, p. 71.

*The male president* . . . Harvey, pp. 46–47.

### "YOU'RE NOT GOING TO LIKE IT, GEORGE. SHE'S AN OLD MAID."

406　*In one much-quoted* . . . Coontz, p. 25.

*The 1947 best-seller* . . . Ferdinand Lunberg and Marynia Fannham, *Modern Woman, the Lost Sex*, pp. 364–65.

*The National Woman's Party* . . . Leila Rupp, *Survival in the Doldrums*, p. 19.

*An editor at* Mademoiselle *told* . . . Friedan, *The Feminine Mystique*, p. 56.

407　*"Except for the sick* . . ." Douglas Miller and Marion Nowak, *The Fifties: The Way We Really Were*, p. 152.

*A study in one Pennsylvania* . . . Bailey, p. 48.

*Carol Cornwall* . . . Eisler, p. 129.

*"No boy—no matter* . . ." Bailey, p. 90.

408　*In 1953, he released* . . . Kinsey et al., *Sexual Behavior in the Human Female*, pp. 287, 416.

*"It is impossible* . . ." Halberstam, p. 280.

*"To go out and actually* . . ." Harvey, pp. 11–12.

*As a result, an estimated* . . . May, *Homeward Bound*, p. 136.

### "IT WAS . . . SO OUT OF CONTROL"

409　*In 1956, the average teenager* . . . Stuart Kallen, *The 1950s*, p. 61.

*Back in the nineteenth century* . . . Banner, p. 179.

410　*The sixteen-year-old Fabian* . . . John Jackson, *American Bandstand*, pp. 137–38, 145.

### "SOME VERY SENSIBLE GIRL FROM A NICE FAMILY"

A great book on the media's view of young women in the fifties and sixties is Susan Douglas's *Where the Girls Are*.

410　*In 1946, there were only* . . . May, *Homeward Bound*, p. 153.

I Love Lucy: Halberstam, pp. 196–20.

411　*When her husband asked* . . . Halberstam, p. 509.

Father Knows Best: Douglas, *Where the Girls Are*, pp. 37–38.

"WOMEN CAN STAND THE SHOCK AND STRAIN
OF AN ATOMIC EXPLOSION"

A great book about women and the Cold War is *Homeward Bound*, by Elaine Tyler May.

412     *Jean Wood Fuller* . . . Fuller, "L.A. Woman in Trench at A-Blast," *Los Angeles Times*, May 6, 1955, p. 2.
        *Fuller's mission in life* . . . May, *Homeward Bound*, p. 91.
        *"You all know women . . ."* Shapiro, pp. 214–15.
413     *The first elected official* . . . The information on Senator Smith comes from Janaan Sherman's *No Place for a Woman: The Life of Senator Margaret Chase Smith*.
414     *Betty Friedan theorized* . . . Friedan, *The Feminine Mystique*, p. 54.
        *The heroine in one* . . . Josephine Bentham, "I Didn't Want to Tell You," *McCall's*, January 1958.

"THEY'VE MESSED WITH THE WRONG ONE NOW"

Anyone interested in the role of women, black and white, in the civil rights movement in the South should read Lynne Olson's *Freedom's Daughters*.

415     *it was the Montgomery, Alabama, bus system* . . . The two women most centrally involved in the Montgomery bus boycott have written their accounts of what happened: Rosa Parks's *My Story* and Jo Ann Robinson's *The Montgomery Bus Boycott and the Women Who Started It*.
        *"Some drivers made . . ."* Parks, p. 77.
        *She was "happy as I . . ."* J. Robinson, pp. 15–16.
416     *"The only tired . . ."* Parks, p. 116.
417     *"My God, look . . ."* Parks, p. 125.
        *"They've messed . . ."* Parks, p. 133.
        *"You've said enough . . ."* Parks, p. 130.
417–18  *King urged one old lady* . . . Howell Raines, *My Soul Is Rested*, p. 61.
418     *Many years later* . . . Raines, p. 57.
        *Ruby Hurley* . . . Raines, p. 131.
        *Autherine Lucy, who became* . . . Raines, p. 326.
419     *Bates, the daughter* . . . Olson, p. 136.
        *Autherine Lucy would return* . . . Raines, p. 327.
419–20  *On the fortieth anniversary* . . . Jack Schneider, "British Film to Revisit Crisis at Central High," *Arkansas Democrat-Gazette*, May 17, 1999.

## CHAPTER 19: THE SIXTIES

"YOU SHOULD SEE MY LITTLE SIS"

422     *A* Ladies' Home Journal *poll* . . . Barbara Ehrenreich (with Elizabeth Hess and Gloria Jacobs), *Re-Making Love*, pp. 24–25.
        *"Every week the skirts . . ."* Sara Davidson, *Loose Change*, p. 150.

## "GREGORY, CAN'T YOU DEVISE SOME SORT OF PILL FOR THIS PURPOSE?"

This section, all the way down to the Loretta Lynn song, is based on information in chapter 9 of Andrea Tone's history of contraceptives in America, *Devices and Desires*. *Notable American Women*, James and James, eds., has a good portrait of Katharine McCormick by James Reed.

## "ONE VAST, ALL-PERVADING SEXOLOGICAL SPREE"

425     *Reader's Digest fretted* . . . Douglas, *Where the Girls Are*, p. 61.
       *"I told a date . . ."* Gloria Steinem, "The Moral Disarmament of Betty Coed," *Esquire*, September 1962, p. 156.

426     *Producers started churning* . . . Douglas, *Where the Girls Are*, pp. 73–80.

426–27    *Marriage, she told her public* . . . Helen Gurley Brown, *Sex and the Single Girl*, pp. 2–4.

427     *"Obscene is not . . ."* D'Emilio and Freedman, p. 306.
       *as late as 1969* . . . May, *Homeward Bound*, pp. 198–99.

427–28    *In 1975, TV reporter* . . . Weiss, *To Have and to Hold*, pp. 170–71.

## "MOVE ON, LITTLE GIRL"

Most of the memoirs of women in the New Left are interesting, and actually getting more so as the era becomes more and more distant. But the best all-purpose book on this subject I've found is Sara Evans's *Personal Politics: The Roots of Women's Liberation in the Civil Rights Movement and the New Left*.

428     *Jane Alpert* . . . Alpert, *Growing Up Underground*, p. 344.
       *During a climactic* . . . Evans, *Personal Politics*, pp. 198–99.
       *The Yippees* . . . Robin Morgan, *Saturday's Child*, p. 237.
       *like Stokely Carmichael* . . . Carmichael defended himself by saying he was joking, but he made the comment so often, he obviously enjoyed the joke. See Jones, *Labor of Love*, p. 283.

429     *In 1965, at a meeting* . . . Evans, *Personal Politics*, p. 160.

## "NOWADAYS, WOMEN WOULDN'T STAND FOR BEING KEPT SO MUCH IN THE BACKGROUND"

429     *The March on* . . . This account is based on Lynne Olson's *Freedom's Daughters*, pp. 284–90.

430     *"Nowadays, women wouldn't . . ."* Parks, p. 166.

430–31    *"There is always . . ."* Jones, pp. 279–80.

431     *Even Rosa Parks's lawyer* . . . Parks, p. 82.
       *"All of the churches . . ."* Olson, p. 143.
       *"Around 1965 there began . . ."* Joanne Grant, *Ella Baker*, p. 229.
       *In Americus, Georgia* . . . Olson, pp 279–80.
       *In Albany, Georgia* . . . Olson, pp. 244–45.

432     *In Indianola* . . . Olson, p. 301.

*The most famous example* ... This information on Fannie Lou Hamer comes from Kay Mills's biography, *This Little Light of Mine: The Life of Fannie Lou Hamer.*

432–33 *Mexican American women were torn* ... Sara Evans, *Tidal Wave: How Women Changed America at Century's End,* pp. 33–34.


"YOU CAN'T EVEN SAFELY ADVERTISE FOR A WIFE ANY MORE"
For an extremely thorough history of the woman's movement, see Flora Davis's *Moving the Mountain: The Women's Movement in America Since 1960.*

433      *When the landmark* ... See F. Davis, pp. 38–45, and Jo Freeman, "How 'Sex' Got into Title VII," which is available on her website, www. jofreeman.com.

434      *"Bunny problem indeed!* ... "De-Sexing the Job Market," *New York Times,* August 21, 1965, p. 20.

         *Gloria Steinem had just written* ... "A Bunny's Tale," *Show,* 1963, reprinted in *Outrageous Acts and Everyday Rebellions* as "I Was a Playboy Bunny."

         *A personnel officer for an* ... "New Hiring Law Seen Bringing More Jobs, Benefits for Women," *Wall Street Journal,* June 22, 1965, p. 1.

435      *"It's the sex thing"* ... F. Davis, p. 21.

         *Representative Griffiths angrily* ... Ruth Rosen, *The World Split Open,* p. 73.

         *At one point, Friedan* ... Marcia Cohen, *The Sisterhood,* p. 135.

436      *Friedan thought up* ... Betty Friedan, *Life So Far,* p. 174.


"SHE IS DISSATISFIED WITH A LOT THAT
WOMEN OF OTHER LANDS CAN ONLY DREAM OF"
Any study of the women's liberation movement ought to begin with reading *The Feminine Mystique.* Except where otherwise noted, this section is based on that book and Betty Friedan's autobiography, *Life So Far.*

437      *"Usually, until very* ..." Philip Wylie, *Generation of Vipers,* p. 199.

         *"She is dissatisfied* ..." Sandie North, "Reporting the Movement," *Atlantic Monthly* (March 1970), pp. 105–6.


"LADY JUROR BAN ENDED BY COURT"
438      *the* New York Times *printed* ... Elizabeth Fowler, "Some Women Find Discrimination When Trying to Establish Credit," May 15, 1972, pp. 53, 55; Georgia Dullea, "Women Demanding Equal Treatment in Mortgage Loans," October 29, 1972, pp. R1, 10.

         *In North Carolina* ... D'Emilio and Freedman, p. 314.

         *In Alabama, the idea* ... "Lady Juror Ban Ended," *Huntsville Times,* February 8, 1966, p. 1; Helms, "Reaction on Jury Ruling," *Alabama Journal,* February 8, 1966, p. 9.

         *In 1970, 3 percent* ... "Who's Come a Long Way, Baby," *Time,* August 31, 1970, pp. 16–21.

438–39   *At* Newsweek *one of the fifty-two* . . . F. Davis, pp. 110–11.
439      *Flo Kennedy* . . . M. Cohen, p. 152.

### "DEGRADED MINDLESS BOOB-GIRLIE SYMBOL"

439      *President Nixon said* . . . M. Cohen, p. 150.
440      *A group of women* . . . There are many stories recounting this protest.
         Robin Morgan, the leader, tells her version in *Going Too Far*, pp. 62–77,
         and in her autobiography, *Saturday's Child*, pp. 259–63.
         *The* New York Times *story* . . . Charlotte Curtis, "Miss America Pageant
         Is Picketed by 100 Women," September 8, 1968, p. 81.
441      *In the spring of 1970* . . . Friedan, *Life So Far*, pp. 238–39.

## EPILOGUE

### "DRAGGING THE WORD 'HOUSEWIFE' THROUGH THE MUD"

443      *Alice Paul was still alive* . . . Marylin Bender, "Liberation Yesterday—the
         Roots of the Feminist Movement," *New York Times*, August 21, 1970, p. 41.
444      *"It's time for housewives* . . .*"* "They're Housewives and Proud of It," *New
         York Times*, April 3, 1972, p. 44.
445      *"Housewives have been called* . . .*"* *New York Times*, April 3, 1972.
446      *The number of women medical school graduates* . . . S. Evans, *Tidal Wave*,
         p. 82. This is virtually the only good survey of the history of American
         women since the epochal 1970s.

### "MY WIFE: I THINK I'LL KEEP HER"

447      *Radical feminists claimed* . . . S. Evans, *Tidal Wave*, p. 109.
         *In 1986*, Newsweek *warned* . . . "Too Late for Prince Charming?"
         *Newsweek*, June 2, 1986, p. 54.
449      *"They have more attitude"* . . . Alex Kuczynski, "She's Got to Be a Macho
         Girl," *New York Times*, November 1, 2002, sec. 9, p. 1.
         *Nobody was happy that while* . . . Joan Brumberg makes this point in the
         introduction to *Girl Culture*, by Lauren Greenfield.

# BIBLIOGRAPHY

In order to make it easier for readers to find other books and periodicals on subjects they're interested in, this bibliography is divided into sections: The early years (chapters 1–4), the first half of the nineteenth century (chapters 5–6), the Civil War (chapters 7–9), post–Civil War (chapters 10–12), the turn of the century and 1920s (chapters 13–15), and the Depression to the present (chapters 16–19).

## CHAPTERS 1 TO 4

### BOOKS

Adams, Charles Francis. *Familiar Letters of John Adams and His Wife, Abigail Adams, During the Revolution.* New York: Hurd & Houghton, 1876.

Allestree, Richard. *The Ladies Calling.* Oxford, England, 1673.

Amott, Teresa, and Julie Matthaei. *Race, Gender and Work.* Boston: South End Press, 1996.

Arber, Edward, ed. *The Story of the Pilgrim Fathers, 1606–1623 A.D.* New York: Kraus Reprint, 1969.

Barker-Benfield, G. J., and Catherine Clinton, eds. *Portraits of American Women.* New York: Oxford University Press, 1998.

Berkin, Carol. *First Generations: Women in Colonial America.* New York: Hill & Wang, 1996.

Berkin, Carol, and Leslie Horowitz, eds. *Women's Voices, Women's Lives: Documents in Early American History.* Boston: Northeastern University Press, 1998.

Blumenthal, Walter Hart. *Brides from Bridewell: Female Felons Sent to Colonial America.* Rutland, Vt.: Charles E. Tuttle, 1962.

Boorstin, Daniel J. *The Americans: The Colonial Experience*. New York: Vintage, 1958.

———. *The Americans: The National Experience*. New York: Vintage, 1965.

Boydston, Jeanne. *Home and Work: Housework, Wages and the Ideology of Labor in the Early Republic*. New York: Oxford University Press, 1990.

Boyer, Paul, and Stephen Nissenbaum, eds. *Salem Possessed: The Social Origins of Witchcraft*. Cambridge, Mass.: Harvard University Press, 1974.

———. *Salem-Village Witchcraft*. Boston: Northeastern University Press, 1993.

Brekus, Catherine. *Strangers and Pilgrims: Female Preaching in America.*. Chapel Hill: University of North Carolina Press, 1998.

Brown, Kathleen. *Good Wives, Nasty Wenches and Anxious Patriarchs*. Chapel Hill: University of North Carolina Press, 1996.

Burr, Esther. *Esther Burr's Journal*. Washington: Woodward & Lothorp, 1903.

Burrage, Henry. *Early English and French Voyages, Chiefly from Hakluyt*. New York: Scribner's, 1930.

Butterfield, L.H., Marc Friedlaender, and Mary-Jo Kline. *The Book of Abigail and John: Selected Letters of the Adams Family, 1762–1784*. Cambridge, Mass.: Harvard University Press, 1975.

Chace, Elizabeth Buffum, and Lucy Buffum Lovell. *Two Quaker Sisters*. New York: Liveright Publishing, 1937.

Clinton, Catherine, and Michele Gillespie, eds. *The Devil's Lane: Sex and Race in the Early South*. New York: Oxford University Press, 1997.

Coryell, Janet Lee, Martha Swain, Sandra Treadway, and Elizabeth Hays Turner, eds. *Beyond Image and Convention*. Columbia, Mo.: University of Missouri Press, 1998.

Cott, Nancy F., Jeanne Boydston, Ann Braude, Lori Ginzberg, and Molly Ladd-Taylor, eds. *Root of Bitterness: Documents of the Social History of American Women*. Boston: Northeastern University Press, 1996.

Crane, Elaine Forman. *Ebb Tide in New England: Women, Seaports and Social Change: 1630–1800*. Boston: Northeastern University Press, 1998.

Cunningham, Patricia, and Susan Voso Lab, eds. *Dress in American Culture*. Bowling Green, Ohio: Bowling Green State University Popular Press, 1993.

De Marly, Diana. *Dress in North America*. New York: Holmes & Meier, 1990.

D'Emilio, John, and Estelle Freedman. *Intimate Matters: A History of Sexuality in America*. Chicago: University of Chicago Press, 1997.

Demos, John. *Entertaining Satan*. New York: Oxford University Press, 1982.

———. *A Little Commonwealth: Family Life in Plymouth Colony*. New York: Oxford University Press, 1970.

Derounian-Stodola, Kathryn Zabelle. *Women's Indian Captivity Narratives*. New York: Penguin Books, 1998.

De St. Mèry, Moreau. *Moreau de St-Mèry's American Journey, 1793–1798*. Garden City, N.Y.: Doubleday, 1947.

Dingwall, Eric John. *The American Woman: A Historical Study.* New York: Rinehart, 1956.

Earle, Alice Morse. *Child Life in Colonial Days.* Stockbridge, Mass.: Berkshire House, 1993.

———. *Colonial Dames and Good Wives.* Boston: Houghton Mifflin, 1895.

———. *Diary of Anna Green Winslow.* Bedford, Mass.: Applewood Books, 1996.

———. *Home Life in Colonial Days.* Stockbridge, Mass.: Berkshire House, 1993.

———. *Two Centuries of Costume.* New York: Macmillan, 1903.

Evans, Elizabeth. *Weathering the Storm: Women of the American Revolution.* New York: Charles Scribner's & Sons, 1975.

Evans, Sara. *Born for Liberty: A History of Women in America.* New York: Free Press Paperbacks, 1997.

Flournoy, Mary. *Essays Historical and Critical.* Freeport, N.Y.: Books for Libraries Press, 1967.

Garrett, Elisabeth Donaghy. *At Home: The American Family, 1750–1870.* New York: Harry N. Abrams, 1990.

Gaspar, David, and Darlene Clark Hine, eds. *More Than Chattel: Black Women and Slavery in the Americas.* Bloomington: Indiana University Press, 1996.

Geller, I. D., ed. *They Knew They Were Pilgrims.* New York: Poseidon Books, 1971.

Gilman, Caroline. *Recollections of a Southern Matron.* New York: Harper & Bros., 1838.

Godbeer, Richard. *Sexual Revolution in Early America.* Baltimore: Johns Hopkins University Press, 2002.

Gregory, John. *A Father's Legacy to His Daughters.* London: W. Strahan, 1781.

Greven, Philip. *The Protestant Temperament.* Chicago: University of Chicago Press, 1978.

Hawke, David Freeman. *Everyday Life in Early America.* New York: Harper & Row, 1988.

Hill, Frances. *A Delusion of Satan.* New York: Da Capo Press, 1997.

Hine, Darlene Clark, ed. *Black Women in America: An Historical Encyclopedia.* Brooklyn, N.Y.: Carlson, 1993.

Hofstadter, Richard. *America at 1750: A Social Portrait.* New York: Vintage Books, 1973.

James, Edward, and Janet Wilson James, eds. *Notable American Women, 1607–1950: A Biographical Dictionary.* Cambridge: Harvard University Press, 1971.

James, Janet Wilson. "Women in American Religious History: An Overview." *Women in American Religion.* Philadelphia: University of Pennsylvania Press, 1980.

Jensen, Joan. *Loosening the Bonds: Mid-Atlantic Farm Women, 1750–1850.* New Haven, Conn.: Yale University Press, 1986.

Karlsen, Carol. *The Devil in the Shape of a Woman.* New York: Norton, 1998.

Keller, Rosemary Skinner. *Patriotism and the Female Sex: Abigail Adams and the American Revolution.* Brooklyn, N.Y.: Carlson, 1994.

Kemble, Frances Anne. *Journal of a Residence on a Georgian Plantation in 1838–1839.* Athens Ga.: University of Georgia Press, 1984.

Kerber, Linda. *No Constitutional Right to Be Ladies.* New York: Hill & Wang, 1998.

―――. *Women of the Republic.* Chapel Hill: University of North Carolina Press, 1980.

Kierner, Cynthia. *Beyond the Household: Women's Place in the Early South, 1700–1835.* Ithaca, N.Y.: Cornell University Press, 1998.

Knight, Sarah Kemble. *The Journal of Madam Knight.* New York: Garrett Press, 1970.

Koehler, Lyle. *A Search for Power: The "Weaker Sex" in Seventeenth-Century New England.* Urbana: University of Illinois Press, 1980.

Larcom, Lucy. *A New England Girlhood.* Gloucester, Mass.: Peter Smith, 1973.

Larkin, Jack. *The Reshaping of Everyday Life: 1790–1840.* New York: Harper & Row, 1989.

Le Beau, Bryan. *The Story of the Salem Witch Trials.* Upper Saddle River, N.J.: Prentice Hall, 1998.

Marble, Annie Russell. *The Women Who Came in the Mayflower.* Boston: Pilgrim Press, 1920.

Marsh, Margaret, and Wanda Ronner. *The Empty Cradle: Infertility in America from Colonial Times to the Present.* Baltimore: Johns Hopkins University Press, 1996.

Mayer, Holly. *Belonging to the Army: Camp Followers and Community During the American Revolution.* Columbia: University of South Carolina Press, 1996.

Morello, Karen Berger. *The Invisible Bar: The Woman Lawyer in America, 1638 to the Present.* New York: Random House, 1986.

Norton, Mary Beth. *Founding Mothers and Fathers: Gendered Power and the Forming of American Society.* New York: Knopf, 1996.

―――. *In the Devil's Snare.* New York: Knopf, 2002.

―――. *Liberty's Daughters.* Ithaca, N.Y.: Cornell University Press, 1980.

Pinckney, Eliza Lucas. *The Letterbook of Eliza Lucas Pinckney, 1739–1763.* Columbia University of South Carolina Press, 1997.

Reis, Elizabeth. *Damned Women: Sinners and Witches in Puritan New England.* Ithaca, N.Y.: Cornell University Press, 1997.

Rogers, Horatio. *Mary Dyer of Rhode Island: The Quaker Martyr That Was Hanged on Boston Common, June 1, 1660.* Providence, R.I.: Preston & Rounds, 1896.

Semmes, Raphael. *Crime and Punishment in Early Maryland.* Baltimore: Johns Hopkins Press, 1938.

Sewall, Samuel. *The Diary and Life of Samuel Sewall.* Boston: Bedford Books, 1998.

Spruill, Julia Cherry. *Women's Life and Work in the Southern Colonies.* New York: W. W. Norton, 1998.

Stiles, Henry Reed. *Bundling.* Sandwich, Mass.: Chapman Billies, 1999.

Stokes, I. N. Phelps. *The Iconography of Manhattan Island* (vol. 5). New York: The Lawbook Exchange, 1998.

Thompson, Roger. *Sex in Middlesex.* Amherst: University of Massachusetts, 1986.

―――. *Women in Stuart England and America.* London: Routledge & Kegan Paul, 1974.

Treckel, Paula A. *To Comfort the Heart: Women in Seventeenth-Century America.* New York: Twayne, 1996.

Ulrich, Laurel Thatcher. *Good Wives: Image and Reality in the Lives of Women in Northern New England, 1650–1750.* New York: Vintage Books, 1991.

————. *A Midwife's Tale: The Life of Martha Ballard, Based on Her Diary, 1785–1812.* New York: Knopf, 1990.

Vuilleumier, Marion. *Indians on Olde Cape Cod.* Taunton, Mass.: William S. Sullwood, 1970.

Washburn, Wilcomb. *The Governor and the Rebel: A History of Bacon's Rebellion in Virginia.* Chapel Hill: University of North Carolina Press, 1957.

Webb, Stephen Saunders. *1676: The End of American Independence.* Syracuse, N.Y.: Syracuse University Press, 1984.

Wertz, Richard, and Dorothy Wertz. *Lying-In: A History of Childbirth.* New Haven, Conn.: Yale University Press, 1977.

Westbury, Susan. "Women in Bacon's Rebellion." In *Southern Women: Histories and Identities,* edited by Virginia Bernhard et al. Columbia: University of Missouri Press, 1992.

White, Elizabeth Wade. *Anne Bradstreet: The Tenth Muse.* New York: Oxford University Press, 1971.

Woodward, Grace Steele, et al. *Three American Indian Women.* New York: MJF Books, 1997.

Yardley, John Henry. *Before the Mayflower.* New York: Doubleday, 1931.

## PERIODICALS

Archer, Richard. "New England Mosaic: A Demographic Analysis for the Seventeenth Century." *William and Mary Quarterly* (October 1990), pp. 477–502.

Baker, Beth. "First Lady of the Bar." *Washington Post,* Dec. 9, 1998, p. H01.

Bernhard, Virginia. "Men, Women and Children at Jamestown: Population and Gender in Early Virginia, 1607–1610." *Journal of Southern History,* (November 1992).

Bloch, Ruth. "American Feminine Ideals in Transition: The Rise of the Moral Mother." *Feminist Studies* 4, no. 2 (June 1978), pp. 101–26.

Bradford, William. Letter to Isaac Allerton. *American Historical Review* 8 (1903), pp. 294–301.

Bushman, Richard, and Claudia Bushman. "The Early History of Cleanliness in America." *Journal of American History* 74, no. 4 (March 1988), pp. 1213–28.

Carr, Lois Green. "Margaret Brent: A Brief History." Maryland State Archives.

Carr, Lois Green, and Lorena Walsh. "The Planter's Wife." *William and Mary Quarterly* (October 1977), pp. 542–71.

Child, Lydia Maria. *The American Frugal Housewife.* Mineola. N.Y.: Dover Publications, 1999.

Cook, Mrs. Henry Lowell. "Maids for Wives." *Virginia Magazine of History and Biography* (December 1942), pp. 300–19.

Demos, John. "Families in Colonial Bristol, Rhode Island: An Exercise in Historical Demography." *William and Mary Quarterly* (January 1968), pp. 40–57.

Duffy, John. "The Passage to the Colonies." *The Mississippi Valley Historical Review* 38, no. 1 (June 1951), pp. 21–38.

Dunn, Mary Maples. "Saints and Sisters: Congregational and Quaker Women in the Early Colonial Period." *American Quarterly* 30, no. 5 (Special Issue: Women and Religion) (Winter 1978), pp. 582–601.

Dye, Nancy Schrom, and Daniel Blake Smith. "Mother Love and Infant Death, 1750–1920." *Journal of American History* (September 1986), pp. 329–53.

Fox, Claire Elizabeth. "Pregnancy, Childbirth and Early Infancy in Anglo-American Culture, 1675–1830." Ph.D. dissertation, University of Pennsylvania, 1966.

"Kidnapping Maidens, to Be Sold in Virginia. *Virginia Magazine of History and Biography* (January 1899), pp. 228–33.

Koehler, Lyle. "The Case of the American Jezebels: Anne Hutchinson and Female Agitation During the Years of Antinomian Turmoil, 1636–1640." *William and Mary Quarterly* (January 1974), pp. 55–78.

Kupperman, Karen Ordahl. "Apathy and Death in Early Jamestown." *Journal of American History* 66, no. 1 (June 1979), pp. 24–40.

Nash, Gary. "The Failure of Female Factory Labor in Colonial Boston." *Labor History* (Spring 1979), pp. 165–86.

Norton, Mary Beth. "The Evolution of White Women's Experience in Early America." *American Historical Review* 89, no. 3 (June 1984), pp. 593–619.

————. "Gender and Defamation in 17th Century Maryland." *William and Mary Quarterly* 44, no. 1 (January 1987), pp. 3–39.

Pearce, Haywood. "New Light on the Roanoke Colony." *Journal of Southern History* (May 1938), pp. 148–63.

Ransome, David. "Wives for Virginia." *William and Mary Quarterly* 48, no.1 (January 1991), pp. 3–18.

Smits, David. "'Abominable Mixture': Toward the Repudiation of Anglo-Indian Intermarriage in Seventeenth Century Virginia." *Virginia Magazine of History and Biography* 95, no. 2 (April 1987), p. 177.

Turner, Edward Raymond. "Women's Suffrage in New Jersey: 1790–1807." *Smith College Studies in History* 1, no. 1 (October 1915), pp. 165–87.

Ulrich, Laurel Thatcher. "A Friendly Neighbor: Social Dimensions of Daily Work in Northern Colonial New England." *Feminist Studies* 6, no. 2 (Summer 1980), pp. 392–405.

Wells, Robert. "Family Size and Fertility Control in Eighteenth-Century America: A Study of Quaker Families." *Population Studies* 25, no. 1 (March 1971), pp. 73–82.

Wright, Marion Thompson. "The Early Years of the Republic." *Journal of Negro History* 33, no. 2 (April 1948), pp. 171–77.

## CHAPTERS 5 TO 6

### BOOKS

*The American Lady's Medical Pocket-Book and Nursery-Adviser.* Philadelphia: James Kay Jr., 1833.

Banner, Lois. *American Beauty,* New York: Knopf, 1983.

Barker-Benfield, G. J., and Catherine Clinton, eds. *Portraits of American Women.*

Baxandall, Rosalyn, and Linda Gordon, eds. *America's Working Women: A Documentary History, 1600 to the Present.* New York: W. W. Norton, 1995.

Baym, Nina. *Woman's Fiction: A Guide to Novels by and About Women in America, 1820–70.* Urbana: University of Illinois Press, 1993.

Beecher, Catharine. *A Treatise on Domestic Economy.* New York: Harper & Brothers, 1856.

Blackwell, Elizabeth. *Pioneer Work in Opening the Medical Profession to Women.* London: Longmans, Green, 1895.

Bleser, Carol, ed. *The Hammonds of Redcliffe.* Columbia: University of South Carolina Press, 1981.

———. *In Joy and In Sorrow: Women, Family and Marriage in the Victorian South.* New York: Oxford University Press, 1991.

Blount, Jackie. *Destined to Rule the Schools.* Albany: State University of New York Press, 1998.

Boorstin, Daniel. *The Americans: The National Experience.*

Boydston, Jeanne. *Home and Work.*

Brewer, Priscilla. *From Fireplace to Cookstove: Technology and the Domestic Ideal in America.* Syracuse, N.Y.: Syracuse University Press, 2000.

Brodie, Janet Farrell. *Contraception and Abortion in Nineteenth-Century America.* Ithaca, N.Y.: Cornell University Press, 1994.

Brown, Jordan. *Elizabeth Blackwell, Physician.* New York: Chelsea House, 1989.

Brown, Thomas. *Dorothea Dix: New England Reformer.* Cambridge, Mass.: Harvard University Press, 1998.

Brumberg, Joan Jacobs. *The Body Project: An Intimate History of American Girls.* New York: Vintage Books, 1997.

Burr, Virginia Ingraham, ed. *The Secret Eye: The Journal of Ella Gertrude Clanton Thomas.* Chapel Hill: University of North Carolina Press, 1990.

Burrows, Edwin, and Mike Wallace. *Gotham: A History of New York City to 1898.* New York: Oxford University Press, 1999.

Bushman, Claudia. *A Good Poor Man's Wife.* Hanover, N.H.: University Press of New England, 1981.

Carter, Alison. *Underwear: The Fashion History.* New York: Drama Book, 1992.

Cashin, Joan. *A Family Venture: Men and Women on the Southern Frontier.* New York: Oxford University Press, 1991.

Cayleff, Susan. *Wash and Be Healed: The Water-Cure Movement and Women's Health.* Philadelphia: Temple University Press, 1987.

Cazden, Elizabeth. *Antoinette Brown Blackwell.* Old Westbury, N.Y.: The Feminist Press, 1983.

Chace, Elizabeth Buffum, and Lucy Buffum Lovell. *Two Quaker Sisters.*

Chambers-Schiller, Lee Virginia. *Liberty, a Better Husband: Single Women in America.* New Haven, Conn.: Yale University Press, 1984.

Clifford, Deborah Pickman. *Crusader for Freedom: A Life of Lydia Maria Child.* Boston: Beacon Press, 1992.

Clinton, Catherine. *The Other Civil War: American Women in the Nineteenth Century.* New York: Hill & Wang, 1984.

————. *The Plantation Mistress: Woman's World in the Old South.* New York: Pantheon Books, 1982.

Collins, Gail. *Scorpion Tongues: Gossip, Celebrity, and American Politics.* New York: Morrow, 1998.

Cowan, Ruth Schwartz. *More Work for Mother.* New York: Basic Books, 1983.

Cummins, Maria Susanna. *The Lamplighter.* New Brunswick, N.J.: Rutgers University Press, 1995.

Dally, Ann. *Women Under the Knife.* London: Hutchinson Radius, 1991.

Degler, Carl. *At Odds: Women and the Family in America from the Revolution to the Present.* New York: Oxford University Press, 1980.

D'Emilio, John, and Estelle Freedman. *Intimate Matters.*

De St. Mèry, Moreau. *American Journey.*

De Tocqueville, Alexis. *Democracy in America.* New York: Mentor, 1956.

Douglas, Ann. *The Feminization of American Culture.* New York: Noonday Press, 1977.

Dublin, Thomas, ed. *Farm to Factory, Women's Letters, 1830–1860.* New York: Columbia University Press, 1993.

Dudden, Faye. *Serving Women: Household Service in Nineteenth-Century America.* Middletown, Conn.: Wesleyan University Press, 1983.

Eakins, Pamela, ed. *The American Way of Birth.* Philadelphia: Temple University Press, 1986.

Eckhardt, Celia Morris. *Fanny Wright: Rebel in America.* Cambridge, Mass.: Harvard University Press, 1984.

Epstein, Barbara Leslie. *The Politics of Domesticity: Women, Evangelism and Temperance in Nineteenth-Century America.* Middletown, Conn.: Wesleyan University Press, 1981.

Evans, Augusta J. *Beulah.* New York: Derby & Jackson, 1860.

Ewing, Elizabeth. *Dress and Undress: A History of Women's Underwear.* London: B. T. Batsford, 1989.

Fern, Fanny. *Ruth Hall.* New York: Penguin Books, 1997.

Finley, Ruth. *The Lady of Godey's: Sarah Josepha Hale.* Philadelphia: J. B. Lippincott, 1931.

Foster, Margaret. *Significant Sisters: The Grassroots of Active Feminism, 1839–1939.* London: Secker & Warburg, 1984.

Fox-Genovese, Elizabeth. *Within the Plantation Household: Black and White Women in the Old South.* Chapel Hill: University of North Carolina Press, 1988.

Gilman, Caroline Howard. *Recollections of a Housekeeper. By Mrs. Clarissa Packard.* New York: Harper & Bros., 1834.

Ginzberg, Lori. *Women and the Work of Benevolence.* New Haven, Conn.: Yale University Press, 1990.

Gordon, Linda. *Woman's Body, Woman's Right: A Social History of Birth Control in America.* New York: Grossman, 1976.

Griffith, Elisabeth. *In Her Own Right: The Life of Elizabeth Cady Stanton*. New York: Oxford University Press, 1984.

Hartman, Mary, and Lois Banner, eds. *Clio's Consciousness Raised: New Perspectives on the History of Women*. New York: Harper & Row, 1974.

Hedrick, Joan. *Harriet Beecher Stowe: A Life*. New York: Oxford University Press, 1994.

Hoffman, Nancy. *Woman's "True" Profession: Voices from the History of Teaching*. Old Westbury, N.Y.: The Feminist Press, 1981.

Hopkins, Vivian Constance. *Prodigal Puritan: A Life of Delia Bacon*. Cambridge, Mass.: Belknap Press of Harvard University Press, 1959.

Hoy, Suellen. *Chasing Dirt: The American Pursuit of Cleanliness*. New York: Oxford University Press, 1995.

Hunt, Gaillard. *As We Were: Life in America, 1814*. Stockbridge, Mass.: Berkshire House, 1993.

Isenberg, Nancy. *Sex and Citizenship in Antebellum America*. Chapel Hill: University of North Carolina Press, 1998.

James, Edward, and Janet Wilson James, eds. *Notable American Women*.

Johnson, Claudia. *American Actress: Perspectives on the Nineteenth Century*. Chicago: Nelson-Hall, 1984.

Johnston, Malcolm Sanders. *Elizabeth Blackwell and Her Alma Mater*. Geneva, N.Y.: W. F. Humphrey Press, 1947.

Kaestle, Carl. *Pillars of the Republic*. New York: Hill & Wang, 1983.

Karcher, Carolyn. *The First Woman in the Republic: A Cultural Biography of Lydia Maria Child*. Durham, N.C.: Duke University Press, 1994.

Kaufman, Polly Welts. *Women Teachers on the Frontier*. New Haven, Conn.: Yale University Press, 1984.

Kelley, Mary. *The Portable Margaret Fuller*. New York: Penguin Books.

———. *The Power of Her Sympathy: The Autobiography and Journal of Catharine Maria Sedgwick*. Boston: Massachusetts Historical Society, distributed by Northeastern University Press, 1993.

Kemble, Frances Anne. *Journal of a Residence on a Georgian Plantation in 1838–1839*.

Kessler-Harris, Alice. *Out to Work: A History of Wage-Earning Women in the United States*. New York: Oxford University Press, 1982.

Kierner, Cynthia. *Beyond the Household*.

Larcom, Lucy. *A New England Girlhood*.

Larkin, Jack. *The Reshaping of Everyday Life, 1790–1840*.

Lebsock, Suzanne. *The Free Women of Petersburg*. New York: W.W. Norton, 1984.

Lerner, Gerda. *The Grimke Sisters from South Carolina*. New York: Oxford University Press, 1998.

Lutz, Alma. *Created Equal: A Biography of Elizabeth Cady Stanton*. New York: The John Day Company, 1940.

Marsh, Margaret, and Wanda Ronner. *The Empty Cradle*.

Massey, Mary Elizabeth. *Women in the Civil War*. Lincoln: University of Nebraska Press, 1994.

Matthews, Glenna. *"Just a Housewife": The Rise and Fall of Domesticity in America*. New York: Oxford University Press, 1987.

Melder, Keith. *Beginnings of Sisterhood: The American Woman's Rights Movement, 1800–1850*. New York: Schocken Books, 1977.

Minnigerode, Meade. *The Fabulous Forties*. New York: G. P. Putnam's, 1924.

Papashvily, Helen Waite. *All the Happy Endings*. New York: Harper & Bros., 1956.

Pattee, Fred Lewis. *The Feminine Fifties*. New York: D. Appleton-Century, 1940.

Plante, Ellen. *Women at Home in Victorian America: A Social History*. New York: Facts on File, 1997.

Reed, James. *From Private Vice to Public Virtue: The Birth Control Movement and American Society Since 1830*. New York: Basic Books, 1978.

Ricketson, Shadrach. *Means of Preserving Health and Preventing Disease*. New York: Collins, Perkins, 1806.

Robinson, Harriet Jane Hanson. *Loom and Spindle*. Kailua, Hawaii: Press Pacifica, 1976.

Rothman, Sheila. *Living in the Shadow of Death: Tuberculosis and the Social Experience of Illness in American History*. Baltimore: Johns Hopkins University Press, 1994.

Ryan, Mary P. *The Empire of the Mother*. New York: Harrington Park Press, 1985.

————. *Womanhood in America from Colonial Times to the Present*. New York: New Viewpoints, 1975.

————. *Women in Public*. Baltimore: Johns Hopkins University Press, 1990.

Scott, Anne Firor. *The Southern Lady: From Pedestal to Politics*. Chicago: University of Chicago Press, 1970.

Sims, J. Marion. *The Story of My Life*. New York: D. Appleton, 1884.

Sklar, Kathryn Kish. *Catharine Beecher: A Study in American Domesticity*. New York: Norton, 1976.

Smith, Page. *Daughters of the Promised Land*. Boston: Little, Brown, 1970.

Smith-Rosenberg, Carroll. *Disorderly Conduct: Visions of Gender in Victorian America*. New York: Knopf, 1985.

Southworth, Emma. *The Deserted Wife*. New York: Street & Smith, 1855.

Stansell, Christine. *City of Women. Sex and Class in New York, 1789–1860*. Urbana: University of Illinois Press, 1987.

Stanton, Elizabeth Cady. *Eighty Years and More: Reminiscences, 1815–1897*. Boston: Northeastern University Press, 1993.

Steele, Valerie. *The Corset: A Cultural History*. New Haven, Conn.: Yale University Press, 2001.

Stowe, Harriet Beecher. *Uncle Tom's Cabin*. New York: Bantam Books, 1981.

Trollope, Frances. *Domestic Manners of the Americans*. London: Penguin Books, 1997.

Warner, Susan. *The Wide, Wide World*. New York: The Feminist Press, 1986.

Wertz, Richard W., and Dorothy C. Wertz. *Lying-In*.

Wilentz, Sean. *Chants Democratic: New York City and the Rise of the American Working Class, 1788–1850*. New York: Oxford University Press, 1984.

Wilson, Dorothy Clarke. *Stranger and Traveler: The Story of Dorothea Dix, American Reformer.* Boston: Little, Brown, 1975.

Wishy, Bernard. *The Child and the Republic.* Philadelphia: University of Pennsylvania Press, 1968.

Wolfe, Margaret Ripley. *Daughters of Canaan: A Saga of Southern Women.* Lexington: University Press of Kentucky, 1995.

Woloch, Nancy. *Women and the American Experience.* New York: McGraw-Hill, 2000.

Woodward, C. Vann, ed. *Mary Chesnut's Civil War.* New Haven, Conn.: Yale University Press, 1981.

### PERIODICALS

Boylan, Anne. "Women in Groups: An Analysis of Women's Benevolent Organizations in New York and Boston, 1797–1840." *Journal of American History* 71, no. 3 (December 1984), pp. 497–523.

Bushman, Richard, and Claudia Bushman. "The Early History of Cleanliness."

Cott, Nancy. "Passionlessness: An Interpretation of Victorian Sexual Ideology, 1790–1850." *Signs* 4, no. 2 (1978), pp. 219–36.

Dye, Nancy Schrom, and Daniel Blake Smith. "Mother Love and Infant Death, 1750–1920."

Glen, Myra. "School Discipline and Punishment in Antebellum America." *Journal of the Early Republic* 1, no. 4 (Winter 1981), pp. 395–408.

Hamilton, Marybeth. "The Life of a Citizen in the Hands of a Woman: Sexual Assault in New York City, 1790–1820." In *New York and the Rise of American Capitalism.* New York Historical Society (Spring 1983).

Leavitt, Judith Walzer. " 'Science' Enters the Birthing Room: Obstetrics in America Since the Eighteenth Century." *Journal of American History* 70, no. 2 (September 1983), pp. 281–304.

Murray, Gail S. "Charity Within the Bounds of Race and Class: Female Benevolence in the Old South." *South Carolina Historical Magazine* 96, no. 1 (January 1995), pp. 54–70.

Rosenberg, Charles. "Sexuality, Class and Role in 19th-Century America." *American Quarterly* 25, no. 2 (May 1973), pp. 131–53.

Scholten, Catherine. "On the Importance of the Obstetrick Art: Changing Customs of Childbirth in America, 1760 to 1825." *William and Mary Quarterly* 34, no. 3 (July 1977), pp. 426–45.

Smith-Rosenberg, Caroll. "The Female World of Love and Ritual: Relations Between Women in Nineteenth-Century America." *Signs* I, no. 1 (1975), pp. 1–29.

Smith-Rosenberg, Caroll, and Charles Smith-Rosenberg. "The Female Animal: Medical and Biological Views of Woman and Her Role in Nineteenth-Century America." *Journal of American History* 60, no. 2 (September 1973), pp. 332–56.

Stearns, Bertha-Monica. "Reform Periodicals and Female Reformers." *American Historical Review* 37, no. 4 (July 1932), pp. 678–99.

Ulrich, Laurel Thatcher. "The Living Mother of a Living Child: Midwifery and Mortality in Post-Revolutionary New England." *William and Mary Quarterly* 46, no. 1 (January 1989), pp. 27–48.

Vinovskis, Maris. "The Female School Teacher in Ante-Bellum Massachusetts." *Journal of Social History* 10, no. 3 (March 1977), pp. 332–45.

Vinovskis, Maris, and Richard Bernard. "Beyond Catharine Beecher: Female Education in the Antebellum Period." *Signs* 3, no. 4 (1978), pp. 856–69.

Welter, Barbara. "Anti-Intellectualism and the American Woman, 1800–1860." *Mid-America* (October 1966), pp. 258–70.

———. "The Cult of True Womanhood: 1820–1860." *American Quarterly* 18, no. 2 (Summer 1966), pp. 151–74.

## CHAPTERS 7 TO 9

### BOOKS

Amott, Teresa, and Julie Matthaei. *Race, Gender and Work.*

Barker-Benfield, G. J., and Catherine Clinton, eds., *Portraits of American Women.*

Baxandall, Rosalyn, and Linda Gordon, eds. *America's Working Women.*

Berkin, Carol. *First Generations.*

Berlin, Ira, Marc Favreav, and Steven Miller, eds., *Remembering Slavery.* New York: New Press, 1998.

Blackwell, Elizabeth. *Pioneer Work in Opening the Medical Profession.*

Blassingame, John W. *The Slave Community: Plantation Life in the Antebellum South.* New York: Oxford University Press, 1972.

———. *Slave Testimony.* Baton Rouge: Louisiana State University Press, 1977.

Bleser, Carol, ed. *The Hammonds of Redcliffe.*

———. *In Joy and in Sorrow.*

Buckmaster, Henrietta. *Let My People Go.* Columbia: University of South Carolina Press, 1992.

Burr, Virginia Ingraham. *The Secret Eye.*

Bynum, Victoria. *Unruly Women: The Politics of Social and Sexual Control in the Old South.* Chapel Hill: University of North Carolina Press, 1992.

Carnegie, Mary Elizabeth. *The Path We Tread: Blacks in Nursing Worldwide, 1854–1994.* New York: National League for Nursing Press, 1986.

Cashin, Joan. *A Family Venture.*

Chace, Elizabeth Buffum, and Lucy Buffum Lovell. *Two Quaker Sisters.*

Clinton, Catherine. *Divided Houses: Gender and the Civil War.* New York: Oxford University Press, 1992.

———. *The Other Civil War.*

———. *The Plantation Mistress.*

Collins, Gail. *Scorpion Tongues.*

Cott, Nancy, ed. *No Small Courage: A History of Women in the United States.* New York: Oxford University Press, 2000.

East, Charles, ed. *The Civil War Diary of Sarah Morgan*. Athens: University of Georgia Press, 1991.

Fage, J. D. *An Introduction to the History of West Africa*. Cambridge, England: Cambridge University Press, 1955.

Faust, Drew Gilpin. *Mothers of Invention*. New York: Vintage Books, 1997.

Finley, Ruth. *The Lady of Godey's*.

Foner, Philip, and Josephine Pacheco. *Three Who Dared: Prudence Crandall, Margaret Douglass, Myrtilla Miner*. Westport, Conn.: Greenwood Press, 1984.

Fox-Genovese, Elizabeth. *Within the Plantation Household*.

Gara, Larry. *The Liberty Line: The Legend of the Underground Railroad*. Lexington: University of Kentucky Press, 1996.

Gaspar, David, and Darlene Clark Hine, eds. *More Than Chattel*. Bloomington: Indiana University Press, 1996.

Genovese, Eugene. *Roll, Jordan, Roll: The World the Slaves Made*. New York: Random House, 1974.

Ginzberg, Lori. *Women and the Work of Benevolence*.

Goldsmith, Barbara. *Other Powers: The Age of Suffrage, Spiritualism and the Scandalous Victoria Woodhull*. New York: Knopf, 1998.

Griffith, Mattie. *Autobiography of a Female Slave*. Jackson: University Press of Mississippi, 1998.

Groneman, Carol, and Mary Beth Norton, eds. *To Toil the Livelong Day: America's Women at Work, 1780–1980*. Ithaca, N.Y.: Cornell University Press, 1987.

Gutman, Herbert. *The Black Family in Slavery and Freedom*. New York: Vintage Books, 1976.

Hall, Margaret Hunter. *The Aristocratic Journey: Being the Outspoken Letters of Mrs. Basil Hall*. Edited by Una Pope-Hennessy. New York: G. P. Putnam's, 1931.

Hedrick, Joan. *Harriet Beecher Stowe*.

Hine, Darlene Clark, ed. *Black Women in America*.

Hine, Darlene Clark, and Kathleen Thompson. *A Shining Thread of Hope*. New York: Broadway Books, 1998.

Hodes, Martha. *White Women, Black Men: Illicit Sex in the Nineteenth-Century South*. New Haven, Conn.: Yale University Press, 1997.

Holland, Mary Gardner. *Our Army Nurses*. Roseville, Minn.: Edinborough Press, 1998.

Howard, Thomas, ed. *Black Voyage: Eyewitness Accounts of the Atlantic Slave Trade*. Boston: Little, Brown. 1971.

Hunter, Tera. *To 'Joy My Freedom: Southern Black Women's Lives and Labors After the Civil War*. Cambridge, Mass.: Harvard University Press, 1997.

Hurmence, Belinda, ed. *Before Freedom, When I Just Can Remember*. Winston-Salem, N.C.: John F. Blair, 2000.

Jacobs, Harriet. *Incidents in the Life of a Slave Girl*. New York: Signet, 2000.

James, Edward T., and Janet Wilson James, eds. *Notable American Women*.

Jeffrey, Julie Roy. *The Great Silent Army of Abolitionism*. Chapel Hill: University of North Carolina Press, 1998.

Jones, Jacqueline. *Labor of Love, Labor of Sorrow: Black Women, Work and the Family from Slavery to the Present*. New York: Vintage Books, 1995.

Kaplan, Sidney, and Emma Nogrady. *The Black Presence in the Era of the American Revolution*. Amherst: University of Massachusetts Press, 1989.

Karcher, Carolyn. *First Woman in the Republic*.

Kemble, Frances Ann. *Journal*.

Kierner, Cynthia. *Beyond the Household*.

Law, Robin. *The Slave Coast of West Africa, 1550–1750*. Oxford, England: Clarendon Press, 1991.

Lebsock, Suzanne. *The Free Women of Petersburg*.

Lerner, Gerda, ed. *Black Women in White America: A Documentary History*. New York: Vintage Books, 1992.

————. *The Grimke Sisters from South Carolina*.

Lowenberg, Bert James, and Ruth Bogin, eds. *Black Women in Nineteenth-Century American Life*. University Park: Pennsylvania State University Press, 1996.

Magdol, Edward. *The Anti-Slavery Rank and File*. New York: Greenwood Press, 1986.

Massey, Mary Elizabeth. *Women in the Civil War*.

Melder, Keith. *Beginnings of Sisterhood*.

Mellon, James, ed. *Bullwhip Days: The Slaves Remember*. New York: Avon, 1988.

Mintz, Steven, and Susan Kellogg. *Domestic Revolutions: A Social History of American Family Life*. New York: The Free Press, 1988.

Painter, Nell Irvin. *Sojourner Truth: A Life, a Symbol*. New York: W. W. Norton, 1996.

Papashvily, Helen. *All the Happy Endings*.

Parker, Mary. *Rights and Wrongs in Boston*. Boston: Female Anti-Slavery Society, 1837.

Perdue, Charles, Thomas Barden, and Robert Phillips, eds. *Weevils in the Wheat: Interviews with Virginia Ex-Slaves*. Charlottesville: University Press of Virginia, 1992.

Perry, Mark. *Lift Up Thy Voice: The Grimke Family's Journey from Slaveholders to Civil Rights Leaders*. New York: Viking, 2001.

Pryor, Elizabeth Brown. *Clara Barton, Professional Angel*. Philadelphia: University of Pennsylvania Press, 1987.

Rable, George. *Civil Wars: Women and the Crisis of Southern Nationalism*. Urbana: University of Illinois Press, 1989.

Reverby, Susan. *Ordered to Care: The Dilemma of American Nursing, 1850–1945*. New York: Cambridge University Press, 1987.

Robertson, Claire, and Martin Klein, eds. *Women and Slavery in Africa*. Madison: University of Wisconsin Press, 1983.

Ryan, Mary. *Women in Public*.

Scott, Anne Firor. *The Southern Lady*.

*Six Women's Slave Narratives*. New York: Oxford University Press, 1988.

Stanton, Elizabeth Cady. *Eighty Years and More.*

Sterling, Dorothy, ed. *We Are Your Sisters: Black Women in the Nineteenth Century.* New York: W. W. Norton, 1997.

Strane, Susan, *A Whole-Souled Woman: Prudence Crandall and the Education of Black Women.* New York: W. W. Norton, 1990.

Treckel, Paula. *To Comfort the Heart.*

Walters, Ronald G. *The Antislavery Appeal: American Abolitionism After 1830.* Baltimore: Johns Hopkins University Press, 1976.

Waugh, Charles, and Martin Greenberg, eds. *The Women's War in the South.* Nashville: Cumberland House, 1999.

White, Deborah Gray. *Ar'n't I a Woman? Female Slaves in the Plantation South.* New York: W. W. Norton, 1985.

Wolfe, Margaret Ripley. *Daughters of Canaan.*

Woodward, C. Vann. *Mary Chesnut's Civil War.*

Yellin, Jean Fagan, and John C. Van Horne, eds. *The Abolitionist Sisterhood.* Ithaca, N.Y.: Cornell University Press, 1994.

### PERIODICALS

Bloor, Alfred. "Letter to Senator Sumner." *Women's Work in the War,* New York: s.n., 1866.

Giesberg, Judith Ann. "Katherine Wormeley and the U.S. Sanitary Commission." *Nursing History Review* 3 (1995), pp. 43–53.

Hewitt, John. "The Search for Elizabeth Jennings, Heroine of a Sunday Afternoon in New York City." *New York History* 71, no. 4 (October 1990), pp. 387–415.

Horton, James Oliver. "Flight to Freedom: One Family and the Story of the Underground Railroad." *The Magazine of History, Bloomington* 15, no. 4 (Summer 2001), pp. 42–45.

Ritter, Kera. "A Stark Reminder." *Boston Globe,* November 2, 1999, p. B1.

Schweninger, Loren. "Prosperous Blacks in the South, 1790–1880." *American Historical Review* 95, no. 1 (February 1990), pp. 31–56.

Smith-Rosenberg, Carroll. "Dis-Covering the Subject of the 'Great Constitutional Discussion,' 1786–1789." *Journal of American History* 79, no. 3 (December 1992), pp. 841–73.

Stewart, James Brewer. "Modernizing 'Difference': The Political Meaning of Color in the Free States, 1776–1840." *Journal of the Early Republic* 19, no. 4 (Winter 1999), pp. 692–712.

Wall, Barbra Mann. "Called to a Mission of Charity: The Sisters of St. Joseph in the Civil War. *Nursing History Review* 6 (1998), pp. 85–113.

Wood, Kirsten. "Broken Reeds and Competent Farmers: Slaveholding Widows in the Southeastern United States, 1783–1861. *Journal of Women's History* 13, no. 2 (2001), pp. 34–57.

## CHAPTERS 10 TO 12

BOOKS

Addams, Jane. *Twenty Years at Hull-House.* New York: Signet, 1961.

Anthony, Carl Sferrazza. *First Ladies.* New York: Morrow, 1990.

Aron, Cindy. *Working at Play: A History of Vacations in the United States.* New York: Oxford University Press, 1999.

Banner, Lois. *American Beauty.*

Barker-Benfield, G. J. *The Horrors of the Half-Known Life.* New York: Routledge, 2000.

Barton, Lois, ed. *One Woman's West: Recollections of the Oregon Trail by Martha Gay Masterson, 1838–1916.* Eugene, Ore.: Spencer Butte Press, 1990.

Benson, Susan Porter. *Counter Cultures.* Urbana: University of Illinois Press, 1988.

Berkin, Carol, and Mary Beth Norton. *Women in America: A History.* Boston: Houghton Mifflin, 1979.

Bliven, Bruce. *The Wonderful Writing Machine.* New York: Random House, 1954.

Boardman, Fon. *America and the Gilded Age, 1876–1900.* New York: Henry Z. Walck, 1972.

Bouvier, Virginia Marie. *Women and the Conquest of California, 1542–1840.* Tucson: University of Arizona Press, 2001.

Brodie, Janet Farrell. *Contraception and Abortion in Nineteenth-Century America.*

Brown, Dee. *The Gentle Tamers: Women of the Old Wild West.* Lincoln: University of Nebraska Press, 1958.

Bruyn, Kathleen. *'Aunt' Clara Brown: Story of a Black Pioneer.* Boulder, Colo.: Pruett Publishing, 1970.

Burke, John. *Duet in Diamonds.* New York: G. P. Putnam's, 1972.

Butler, Anne. *Daughters of Joy, Sisters of Misery.* Urbana: University of Illinois Press, 1987.

Butruille, Susan. *Women's Voices from the Oregon Trail.* Boise: Tamarack Books, 1993.

Cazden, Elizabeth. *Antoinette Brown Blackwell.*

Chace, Elizabeth Buffum, and Lucy Buffum Lovell, *Two Quaker Sisters.*

Chartier, JoAnn, and Chris Enss. *With Great Hope: Women of the California Gold Rush.* Helena, Mont.: Falcon, 2000.

Clappe, Louise Amelia. *The Shirley Letters.* Santa Clara, Calif.: Santa Clara University Press, 2001.

Clinton, Catherine. *The Plantation Mistress.*

Cohen, Rose. *Out of the Shadow.* Ithaca, N.Y.: Cornell University Press, 1995.

Coser, Rose Laub, et al. *Women of Courage: Jewish and Italian Immigrant Women in New York.* Westport, Conn.: Greenwood Press, 1999.

Cott, Nancy, ed. *No Small Courage: A History of Women in the United States.* New York: Oxford University Press, 2000.

Courtwright, David. *Dark Paradise: A History of Opiate Addiction in America.* Cambridge, Mass.: Harvard University Press, 2001.

Cowan, Ruth Schwartz. *More Work for Mother.*

Custer, Elizabeth. *Boots and Saddles; or, Life in Dakota with General Custer.* Norman: University of Oklahoma Press, 1961.

Daniels, Roger. *Coming to America.* New York: HarperCollins, 1990.

Davies, Margery. *Woman's Place Is at the Typewriter.* Philadelphia: Temple University Press, 1982.

Davis, Allen. *American Heroine: The Life and Legend of Jane Addams.* Chicago: Ivan R. Dee, 2000.

Degler, Carl. *At Odds.*

D'Emilio, John, and Estelle Freedman. *Intimate Matters.*

Deutsch, Sarah. *Women and the City: Gender, Space and Power in Boston, 1870–1940.* New York: Oxford University Press, 2000.

Diner, Hasia. *Erin's Daughters in America.* Baltimore: Johns Hopkins University Press, 1983.

Douglas, Ann. *The Feminization of American Culture.*

Dudden, Faye. *Serving Women.*

Dulles, Foster Rhea. *A History of Recreation.* New York: Appleton-Century-Crofts, 1965.

Dunlap, Patricia Riley. *Riding Astride: The Frontier in Women's History.* Denver: Arden Press, 1995.

Ehrenreich, Barbara, and Deirdre English. *For Her Own Good.* Garden City, N.Y.: Anchor Press, 1978.

Ellis, Anne. *The Life of an Ordinary Woman.* Boston: Houghton Mifflin, 1999.

Ets, Marie Hall. *Rosa: The Life of an Italian Immigrant.* Madison: University of Wisconsin Press, 1970.

Evans, Sara. *Born for Liberty.*

Ewan, Elizabeth. *Immigrant Women in the Land of Dollars.* New York: Monthly Review Press, 1985.

Faber, Doris. *Calamity Jane: Her Life and Her Legend.* Boston: Houghton Mifflin, 1992.

Faragher, John Mack. *Sugar Creek.* New Haven: Yale University Press, 1986.

————. *Women and Men on the Overland Trail.* New Haven: Yale University Press, 2001.

Fields, Armond. *Lillian Russell.* Jefferson, N.C.: McFarland & Co., 1999.

Friedman, Jane. *America's First Woman Lawyer.* Buffalo, N.Y.: Prometheus Books, 1993.

Gilfoyle, Timothy. *City of Eros.* New York: W. W. Norton, 1992.

Gold, Michael. *Jews Without Money.* New York: Carroll & Graf, 1996.

Goldsmith, Barbara. *Other Powers.*

Gregory, Alexis. *Families of Fortune in the Gilded Age.* New York: Vendome Press, 1993.

Griswold del Castillo, Richard. *La Familia: Chicano Families in the Urban Southwest, 1848 to the Present.* Notre Dame, Ind.: University of Notre Dame Press, 1984.

Hartman, Mary, and Lois Banner, eds. *Clio's Consciousness Raised.*

Hine, Darlene Clark, ed. *Black Women in America.*

Holmes, Kenneth, ed. *Covered Wagon Women.* Lincoln: University of Nebraska Press, 1983.

Hoy, Suellen. *Chasing Dirt.*

Inciardi, James. *The War on Drugs.* Palo Alto, Calif.: Mayfield Publishing, 1986.

Jackson, Kenneth. *Crabgrass Frontier.* New York: Oxford University Press, 1985.

Jeffrey, Julie Roy. *Frontier Women.* New York: Hill & Wang, 1998.

Joselit, Jenna Weissman. *A Perfect Fit.* New York: Henry Holt, 2001.

Katz, William. *Black Women of the Old West.* New York: Atheneum Books, 1995.

Kroeger, Brooke. *Nellie Bly.* New York: Times Books, 1994.

Larson, T. A. *History of Wyoming.* Lincoln: University of Nebraska Press, 1965.

Laxton, Edward. *The Famine Ships.* New York: Henry Holt, 1998.

Levy, Jo Ann. *They Saw the Elephant.* Norman: University of Oklahoma Press, 1992.

Lindgren, H. Elaine. *Land in Her Own Name.* Norman: University of Oklahoma Press, 1996.

Macrae, David. *The Americans at Home.* Edinburgh: Edmonston & Douglas, 1870.

Maines, Rachel. *The Technology of Orgasm.* Baltimore: Johns Hopkins University Press, 1999.

Martin, Theodora Penny. *The Sound of Our Own Voices.* Boston: Beacon Press, 1987.

Miller, Brandon Marie. *Buffalo Gals.* Minneapolis: Lerner Publications, 1995.

Mintz, Steven, and Susan Kellogg. *Domestic Revolutions.*

Monroy, Douglas. *Thrown Among Strangers: The Making of Mexican Culture in Frontier California.* Berkeley: University of California Press, 1990.

Morantz-Sanchez, Regina. *Conduct Unbecoming a Woman,* New York: Oxford University Press, 1999.

Morgan, H. Wayne. *Drugs in America: A Social History.* Syracuse, N.Y.: Syracuse University Press, 1981.

Musto, David. *The American Disease.* New Haven, Conn.: Yale University Press, 1973.

Ogle, Maureen. *All the Modern Conveniences.* Baltimore: Johns Hopkins University Press, 1996.

Owens-Adair, Bethenia. *Dr. Owens Adair: Some of Her Life Experiences.* Portland, Ore.: Mann & Beach, 1906.

Painter, Nell Irvin. *Exodusters: Black Migration to Kansas after Reconstruction.* Lawrence: University of Kansas Press, 1986.

Peavy, Linda, and Ursula Smith. *Pioneer Women.* Norman: University of Oklahoma Press, 1996.

Peffer, George Anthony. *If They Don't Bring Their Women Here.* Urbana: University of Illinois Press, 1999.

Peiss, Kathy. *Cheap Amusements.* Philadelphia: Temple University Press, 1986.

———. *Hope in a Jar.* New York: Henry Holt, 1998.

Philbrick, Nathaniel. *In the Heart of the Sea.* New York: Viking, 2000

Poling-Kempes, Lesley. *The Harvey Girls.* New York: Marlowe, 1991.

Price, Jennifer. *Flight Maps.* New York: Basic Books, 1999.

Raban, Jonathan. *Bad Land.* New York: Vintage Books, 1996.

Richardson, Dorothy. *The Long Day: The Story of a New York Working Girl*. Charlottesville: University Press of Virginia, 1996.

Riley, Glenda. *The Life and Legacy of Annie Oakley*. Norman: University of Oklahoma Press, 1994.

Riley, Glenda, and Richard Etulain, eds. *By Grit and Grace: Eleven Women Who Shaped the American West*. Golden, Colo.: Fulcrum, 1997.

Ryan, Mary. *Civic Wars: Democracy and Public Life in the American City During the Nineteenth Century*. Berkeley: University of California Press, 1997.

———. *Womanhood in America from Colonial Times to the Present*.

———. *Women in Public*.

Schlereth, Thomas. *Victorian America: Transformations in Everyday Life*. New York: Harper Perennial, 1992.

Schlissel, Lillian. *Women's Diaries of the Western Journey*. New York: Schocken Books, 1992.

Seagraves, Anne. *Soiled Doves: Prostitution in the Early West*. Hayden, Idaho: Wesanne Publications, 1994.

Seller, Maxine Schwartz, ed. *Immigrant Women*. Albany: State University of New York Press, 1994.

Shapiro, Laura. *Perfection Salad: Women and Cooking at the Turn of the Century*. New York: The Modern Library, 2001.

Sollid, Roberta Reed. *Calamity Jane: A Study in Historical Criticism*. Helena: Montana Historical Press, 1995.

Solomon, Barbara Miller. *In the Company of Educated Women*. New Haven, Conn.: Yale University Press, 1985.

Springer, Marlene, and Haskell Springer, eds. *Plains Woman: The Diary of Martha Farnsworth*. Bloomington: Indiana University Press, 1986.

Stage, Sarah. *Female Complaints*. New York: W.W. Norton, 1979.

Stansell, Christine. *City of Women*.

Strasser, Susan. *Never Done: A History of American Housework*. New York: Henry Holt, 1982.

Stratton, Joanna. *Pioneer Women: Voices from the Kansas Frontier*. New York: Simon & Schuster, 1981.

Sutherland, Daniel. *The Expansion of Everyday Life, 1860–1876*. Fayetteville: University of Arkansas Press, 2000.

Tone, Andrea. *Devices and Desires: A History of Contraceptives in America*. New York: Hill & Wang, 2001.

Wald, Lillian. *The House on Henry Street*. New York: Henry Holt, 1915.

Wang, Holman. *Bathroom Stuff*. Naperville, Ill.: Sourcebooks, 2001.

Weatherford, Doris. *Foreign and Female*. New York: Facts on File, 1995.

Wilcox, R. Turner. *Mode in Hats and Headdress*. New York: Scribner's, 1945.

Wilson, Luzena. *Luzena Stanley Wilson 49er*. Mills College, Calif.: Eucalyptus Press, 1937.

Winnemucca Hopkins, Sarah. *Life Among the Piutes*. Bishop, Calif.: Califant Press, 1969.

Woloch, Nancy. *Women and the American Experience.*

Wunder, John, ed. *At Home on the Range: Essays on the History of Western Social and Domestic Life.* Westport, Conn.: Greenwood Press, 1985.

Yung, Judy. *Unbound Feet.* Berkeley: University of California Press, 1995.

Zanjani, Sally. *Sarah Winnemucca.* Lincoln: University of Nebraska Press, 2001.

## Periodicals

Andreadis, Harriette. "True Womanhood Revisited: Women's Private Writing in Nineteenth-Century Texas." *Journal of the Southwest* 31, no. 2 (Summer 1989), pp. 179–202.

Banfield, Maud. "About Patent Medicine." *Ladies' Home Journal* (May 1903), p. 26.

Degler, Carl. "What Ought to Be and What Was: Women's Sexuality in the Nineteenth Century." *The American Historical Review* 79, no. 5 (December 1974), pp. 1467–90.

Faragher, John Mack, and Christine Stansell. "Women and Their Families on the Overland Trail to California and Oregon, 1842–1867." *Feminist Studies* 2 (1975), pp. 150–66.

Fellman, Michael. "Julia Lovejoy Goes West." *Western Humanities Review* 31, no. 3 (Summer 1977), pp. 227–41.

Fleming, Sidney Howell. "Solving the Jigsaw Puzzle: One Suffrage Story at a Time." *Annals of Wyoming* 62, no. 1 (Spring 1990), pp. 33–73.

Graham, Patricia Albjerg. "Expansion and Exclusion: A History of Women in American Higher Education." *Signs* 3, no. 4 (Summer 1978), pp. 759–73.

Griffin, Dick. "Opium Addiction in Chicago." *Chicago History* 6, no. 2 (1977), pp. 107–16.

Hogan, William Ransom. "Pamela Mann: Texas Frontierswoman." *Southwest Review* 20, no. 4 (July 1935), pp. 360–70.

Kroll, Helen. "The Books that Enlightened the Emigrants." *Oregon Historical Quarterly* 45, no. 2, (June 1944), pp. 103–23.

Larson, T.A. "Petticoats at the Polls: Woman Suffrage in Territorial Wyoming." *Pacific Northwest Quarterly* 44, no. 4 (April 1953), pp. 74–79.

Lerner, Gerda. "Early Community Work of Black Club Women." *Journal of Negro History* 59, no. 2 (April 1974), pp. 158–67.

Massie, Michael. "Reform Is Where You Find It: The Roots of Woman Suffrage in Wyoming." *Annals of Wyoming* 62, no. 1 (Spring 1990), pp. 2–21.

Munkres, Robert. "Wives, Mothers, Daughters: Women's Life on the Road West." *Annals of Wyoming* 42, no. 2 (October 1970), pp. 189–224.

Read, Georgia Willis. "Women and Children on the Oregon-California Trail in the Gold Rush Years." *Missouri Historical Review* 39, no. 1 (October 1944), pp. 1–23.

Riley, Glenda. "Women's Responses to the Challenges of Plains Living." *Great Plains Quarterly* 9, no. 3 (Summer 1989), pp. 174–84.

Rosenberg, Charles. "Sexuality, Class and Role in 19th-Century America."

Scott, Anne Firor. "Most Invisible of All: Black Women's Voluntary Associations." *Journal of Southern History* (February 1990), pp. 3–22.

Somers, Dale. "The Leisure Revolution: Recreation in the American City, 1820–1920." *Journal of Popular Culture* 5, no. 1 (Summer 1971), pp. 125–45.

Stansell, Christine. "Women on the Great Plains, 1865–1890." *Women's Studies* 4 (1976), pp. 87–98.

Ueda, Reed. "The High School and Social Mobility in a Streetcar Suburb: Somerville, Massachusetts, 1870–1910." *Journal of Interdisciplinary History* 14, no. 4 (Spring 1984), pp. 751–71.


# CHAPTERS 13 TO 15

## BOOKS

Addams, Jane. *Twenty Years at Hull-House.*

Adickes, Sandra. *To Be Young Was Very Heaven.* New York: St. Martin's Press, 1997.

Allen, Frederick Lewis. *Only Yesterday: An Informal History of the 1920's.* New York: Harper & Row, 1964.

Auster, Albert. *Actresses and Suffragists.* New York: Praeger, 1984.

Bailey, Beth. *From Front Porch to Back Seat.* Baltimore: Johns Hopkins University Press, 1989.

Banner, Lois. *American Beauty.*

Barker-Benfield, G. J., and Catherine Clinton, eds., *Portraits of American Women.*

Barr, Andrews. *Drink: A Social History of America.* New York: Carroll & Graf, 1999.

Beauchamp, Cari. *Without Lying Down: Frances Marion and the Powerful Women of Early Hollywood.* Berkeley: University of California Press, 1997.

Bellamy, Edward. *Looking Backward.* New York: Signet Classic, 2000.

Benson, Susan. *Counter Cultures.*

Blocker, Jack. *American Temperance Movements: Cycles of Reform.* Boston: Twayne, 1988.

Bodnar, John, Roger Simon, and Michael Weber. *Lives of Their Own: Blacks, Italians and Poles in Pittsburgh, 1900–1960.* Urbana: University of Illinois Press, 1982.

Bordin, Ruth. *Frances Willard.* Chapel Hill: University of North Carolina Press, 1986.

Brady, Kathleen. *Ida Tarbell.* Pittsburgh: University of Pittsburgh Press, 1989.

Brandt, Allan. *No Magic Bullet: A Social History of Venereal Disease in the United States Since 1880.* New York: Oxford University Press, 1987.

Brodie, Janet Farrell. *Contraception and Abortion in Nineteenth-Century America.*

Brown, Dorothy. *Setting a Course: American Women in the 1920s.* Boston: Twayne, 1987.

Bundles, A'Lelia. *On Her Own Ground: The Life and Times of Madam C. J. Walker.* New York: Scribner's, 2001.

Burnham, John. *Bad Habits.* New York: New York University Press, 1993.

Chesler, Ellen. *Woman of Valor: Margaret Sanger and the Birth Control Movement.* New York: Simon & Schuster, 1992.

Cowan, Ruth. *More Work for Mother.*

Damon-Moore, Helen. *Magazines for the Millions.* Albany: State University of New York, 1994.

Davies, Margery. *Woman's Place Is at the Typewriter.*

Davis, Allen. *American Heroine.*

Degler, Carl. *At Odds.*

D'Emilio, John, and Estelle Freedman. *Intimate Matters.*

Deutsch, Sarah. *Women and the City.*

Diliberto, Gioia. *A Useful Woman.* New York: Scribner's, 1999.

Douglas, Ann. *Terrible Honesty.* New York: Farrar, Straus & Giroux, 1995.

Douglas, Susan. *Listening In.* New York: Times Books, 1999.

DuBois, Ellen Carol. *Harriot Stanton Blatch and the Winning of Woman Suffrage.* New Haven, Conn.: Yale University Press, 1997.

Dudden, Faye. *Serving Women.*

Dulles, Foster Rhea. *A History of Recreation.*

Dumeril, Lynn. *Modern Temper.* New York: Hill & Wang, 1995.

Ehrenreich, Barbara, and Deirdre English. *For Her Own Good.*

Ellis, Anne. *The Life of an Ordinary Woman.*

Eyman, Scott. *Mary Pickford.* New York: Donald Fine, 1990.

Evans, Sara. *Born for Liberty.*

Faderman, Lillian. *Odd Girls and Twilight Lovers.* New York: Penguin, 1992.

Fass, Paula. *The Damned and the Beautiful.* New York: Oxford University Press, 1977.

Fitzgerald, F. Scott. *This Side of Paradise.* New York: Scribner's, 1960.

Flexner, Eleanor, and Ellen Fitzpatrick. *Century of Struggle.* Cambridge, Mass.: Belknap Press, 1996.

Fowler, Robert. *Carrie Catt: Feminist Politician.* Boston: Northeastern University Press, 1986.

Gavin, Lettie. *American Women in World War I.* Niwot: University of Colorado Press, 1997.

Giele, Janet Zollinger. *Two Paths to Women's Equality.* New York: Twayne, 1995.

Gilbreth, Frank, and Ernestine Gilbreth Carey. *Belles on Their Toes.* New York: Bantam Books, 1984.

———. *Cheaper by the Dozen.* New York: Bantam Books, 1975.

Gilfoyle, Timothy. *City of Eros.*

Gilman, Charlotte Perkins. *The Living of Charlotte Perkins Gilman.* Madison: University of Wisconsin Press, 1990.

Goldberg, Michael Lewis. *An Army of Women: Gender and Politics in Gilded Age Kansas.* Baltimore: Johns Hopkins University Press, 1997.

Golden, Eva. *Vamp: The Rise and Fall of Theda Bara.* Vestal, N.Y.: Emprise Publishing, 1996.

Goldsmith, Barbara. *Other Powers.*

Gorn, Elliott. *Mother Jones.* New York: Hill & Wang, 2001.

Green, Harvey. *The Uncertainty of Everyday Life, 1915–1945.* Fayetteville: University of Arkansas Press, 2000.

Griffith, Elisabeth. *In Her Own Right.*

Hall, Radclyffe. *The Well of Loneliness.* New York: Anchor Books, 1990.

Hamilton, Marybeth. *When I'm Bad, I'm Better.* Berkeley: University of California Press, 1997.

Hartman, Mary, and Lois Banner, eds. *Clio's Consciousness Raised.*

Haskell, Molly. *From Reverence to Rape: The Treatment of Women in Movies.* New York: Holt, Rinehart & Winston, 1974.

Hayden, Dolores. *The Grand Domestic Revolution.* Cambridge, Mass.: MIT Press, 1995.

Hewitt, Nancy. *Southern Discomfort: Women's Activism in Tampa, Florida, 1880s–1920s.* Urbana: University of Illinois Press, 2001.

Higonnet, Margaret, ed. *Lines of Fire: Women Writers of World War I.* New York: Plume, 1999.

———. *Nurses at the Front.* Boston: Northeastern University Press, 2001.

Hilmes, Michele. *Radio Voices.* Minneapolis: University of Minnesota Press, 1997.

Hine, Darlene Clark, ed. *Black Women in America.*

Horowitz, Helen Lefkowitz. *Alma Mater.* Amherst: University of Massachusetts Press, 1993.

———. *Campus Life.* Chicago: University of Chicago Press, 1988.

James, Edward T., and Janet Wilson James, eds. *Notable American Women.*

Jeffrey, Julie Roy. *Frontier Women.*

Jessen, Gene Nora. *The Powder Puff Derby of 1929.* Naperville, Ill.: Sourcebooks, 2002.

Jones, Jacqueline. *Labor of Love, Labor of Sorrow.*

Joselit, Jenna Weissman. *A Perfect Fit.*

Klein, Yvonne, ed. *Beyond the Home Front: Women's Autobiographical Writing in Two World Wars.* New York: New York University Press, 1997.

Kroeger, Brooke. *Fannie.* New York: Times Books, 1999.

Lash, Joseph. *Eleanor: The Years Alone.* New York: W. W. Norton, 1972.

Leinwand, Gerald. *1927.* New York: Four Walls Eight Windows, 2001.

Lender, Mark, and James Martin. *Drinking in America.* New York: The Free Press, 1987.

Leuchtenburg, William. *The Perils of Prosperity.* Chicago: University of Chicago Press, 1993.

Lunardini, Christine. *From Equal Suffrage to Equal Rights.* Lincoln, Nebr.: toExcel, 2000.

Marks, Patricia. *Bicycles, Bangs and Bloomers: The New Woman in the Popular Press.* Lexington: University of Kentucky Press, 1990.

Mason, Bobbie Ann. *The Girl Sleuth.* Athens: University of Georgia Press, 1995.

May, Elaine Tyler. *Barren in the Promised Land.* Cambridge, Mass.: Harvard University Press, 1995.

———. *Great Expectations.*

Mead, Margaret. *Blackberry Winter.* New York: Kodansha America, 1995.

Merz, Charles. *The Dry Decade.* Garden City, N.Y.: Doubleday, 1931.

Mulvey, Kate, and Melissa Richards. *Decades of Beauty.* New York: Facts on File, 1998.

Nasaw, David. *Going Out: The Rise and Fall of Public Amusements.* Cambridge, Mass.: Harvard University Press, 1993.

Odem, Mary. *Delinquent Daughters*. Chapel Hill: University of North Carolina Press, 1995.

O'Neill, William, ed. *The American Sexual Dilemma*. New York: Holt, Rinehart & Winston, 1972.

Parker, Alison. *Purifying America*. Urbana: University of Illinois Press, 1997.

Peiss, Kathy. *Cheap Amusements*.

———. *Hope in a Jar*.

Reed, James. *From Private Vice to Public Virtue*.

Riley, Glenda. *The Life and Legacy of Annie Oakley*.

Rosen, Marjorie. *Popcorn Venus: Women, Movies and the American Dream*. New York: Coward, McCann & Geoghegan, 1973.

Rosenthal, Naomi Braun. *Spinster Tales and Womanly Possibilities*. Albany: State University of New York Press, 2002.

Ryan, Mary. *Womanhood in America*.

Sanger, Margaret. *An Autobiography*. New York: W.W. Norton, 1938.

Scharff, Virginia. *Taking the Wheel*. New York: The Free Press, 1991.

Schlereth, Thomas. *Transformations in Everyday Life*.

Schmalhausen, Samuel, and V. F. Calverton, eds. *Woman's Coming of Age: A Symposium*. New York: Horace Liveright, 1931.

Schneider, Dorothy, and Carl Schneider. *Into the Breach: American Women Overseas in World War I*. Lincoln, Nebr.: toExcel, 2000.

Scott, Anne Firor, and Andrew MacKay Scott. *One Half the People*. Urbana: University of Illinois Press, 1982.

Seller, Maxine, ed. *Immigrant Women*.

Shapiro, Laura. *Perfection Salad*.

Sherr, Lynn. *Failure Is Impossible: Susan B. Anthony in Her Own Words*. New York: Times Books, 1995.

Smith, Norma. *Jeanette Rankin: America's Conscience*. Helena: Montana Historical Society Press, 2002.

Solomon, Barbara Miller. *In the Company of Educated Women*.

Springer, Marlene, and Haskell Springer, eds., *Plains Woman*.

Stanton, Elizabeth Cady. *Eighty Years and More*.

Stearns, Peter. *Fat History*. New York: New York University Press, 1997.

Strasser, Susan. *Never Done*.

Tarbox, Gwen Athene. *The Clubwomen's Daughters*. New York: Garland, 2000.

Terborg-Penn, Rosalyn. *African American Women in the Struggle for the Vote, 1850–1920*. Bloomington: Indiana University Press, 1998.

Tone, Andrea. *Devices and Desires*.

Wall, Cheryl. *Women of the Harlem Renaissance*. Bloomington: Indiana University Press, 1995.

Ward, Geoffrey. *Not for Ourselves Alone*. New York: Knopf, 1999.

Ware, Susan. *Beyond Suffrage: Women in the New Deal*. Cambridge, Mass.: Harvard University Press, 1981.

————. *Letter to the World: Seven Women Who Shaped the American Century.* Cambridge, Mass.: Harvard University Press, 1998.

Weatherford, Doris. *Foreign and Female.*

Willard, Frances. *How I Learned to Ride the Bicycle.* Sunnyvale, Calif.: Fair Oaks Publishing, 1991.

Woloch, Nancy. *Women and the American Experience.*

Yellin, Carol Lynn, and Janann Sherman. *The Perfect 36: Tennessee Delivers Woman Suffrage.* Oak Ridge, Tenn.: Iris Press, 1998.

## PERIODICALS

Anonymous. "The Harm My Education Did Me." *The Outlook,* November 30, 1927, pp. 396–405.

Armstrong, Anne. "Seven Deadly Sins of Women in Business," *Harper's* (August 1926), pp. 295–303.

Bok, Edward. "At Home with the Editor." *Ladies' Home Journal* (April 1893), p. 18.

Breen, William J. "Black Women and the Great War: Mobilization and Reform in the South." *Journal of Southern History* 44, no. 3 (August 1978), pp. 421–40.

Bromley, Dorothy Dunbar. "Feminist—New Style." *Harper's* (October 1927), pp. 552–60.

Carey, Henry R. "Career or Maternity?" *North American Review* 228 (July 1929), pp. 737–44.

Cookingham, Mary. "Combining Marriage, Motherhood and Jobs Before World War II: Women College Graduates, Classes 1905–1935." *Journal of Family History* 9, no. 2 (Summer 1984), pp. 178–95.

Deegan, Mary Jo. "Dear Love, Dear Love: Feminist Pragmatism and the Chicago Female World of Love and Ritual." *Gender & Society* 10, no. 5 (October 1996), pp. 590–607.

DeVoto, Bernard. "The Co-Ed: The Hope of Liberal Education. *Harper's Magazine* (September 1927), pp. 452–59.

Fletcher, Grace Nies. "Bringing Up Fathers," *Ladies' Home Journal* (September 1927), pp. 35, 199–201.

Scott, Anne Firor. "After Suffrage: Southern Women in the Twenties." *Journal of Southern History* (August 1964), pp. 298–318.

Somers, Dale. "Leisure Revolution."

Stricker, Frank. "Cookbooks and Law Books: The Hidden History of Career Women in Twentieth-Century America." *Journal of Social History* 10, no. 1 (Fall 1976), pp. 1–19.

Ticknor, Caroline. "The Steel-Engraving Lady and the Gibson Girl." *Atlantic Monthly* (July 1901), pp. 105–8.

Tunis, Lucy. "I Gave Up My Law Books for a Cook Book." *American Magazine* (July 1927), pp. 172–77.

Wolfson, Theresa. "Trade Union Activities of Women." *Annals of the American Academy of Political and Social Sciences* (May 1929), p. 120.

## CHAPTERS 16 TO 19

### BOOKS

Aaron, Daniel, and Robert Bendiner, eds. *The Strenuous Decade*. Garden City, N.Y.: Anchor Books, 1970.

Allen, Florence. *To Do Justly*. Cleveland: Press of Western Reserve University, 1965.

Allen, Frederick Lewis. *Since Yesterday: The 1930s in America*. New York: Perennial Library, 1972.

Alpert, Jane. *Growing Up Underground*. New York: William Morrow, 1981.

Anderson, Karen. *Wartime Women*. Westport, Conn.: Greenwood Press, 1981.

Angelou, Maya. *I Know Why the Caged Bird Sings*. New York: Bantam Books, 1992.

Bailey, Beth. *From Front Porch to Back Seat*.

Bentley, Amy. *Eating for Victory*. Urbana: University of Illinois Press, 1998.

Bird, Caroline. *The Invisible Scar*. New York: David McKay, 1966.

Blackwelder, Julia Kirk. *Women of the Depression: Caste and Culture in San Antonio, 1929–1939*. College Station: Texas A&M University Press, 1984.

Blótner, Joseph. *Faulkner: A Biography* (Vol. 2). New York: Random House, 1974.

Bowman, Constance, and Clara Marie Allen. *Slacks and Calluses*. Washington, D.C.: Smithsonian Institution Press, 1999.

Brown, Helen Gurley. *Sex and the Single Girl*. New York: Pocket Books, 1962.

Brumberg, Joan Jacobs. *The Body Project*. New York: Vintage, 1997.

Butler, Susan. *East to the Dawn: The Life of Amelia Earhart*. Reading, Mass.: Addison-Wesley, 1977.

Campbell, D'Ann. *Women at War with America*. Cambridge, Mass.: Harvard University Press, 1984.

Caro, Robert. *Lyndon Johnson: The Path to Power*. New York: Knopf, 1982.

Casdorph, Paul. *Let the Good Times Roll*. New York: Paragon House, 1989.

Chafe, William. *The Unfinished Journey: America Since World War II*. New York: Oxford University Press, 1999.

Cohen, Marcia. *The Sisterhood*. New York: Fawcett Columbine, 1988.

Collins, Gail. *Scorpion Tongues*.

Colman, Penny. *Rosie the Riveter: Working Women on the Home Front in World War II*. New York: Crown, 1995.

Cook, Blanche Wiesen. *Eleanor Roosevelt, Vols. 1 and 2*. New York: Viking, 1992, 1999.

Coontz, Stephanie. *The Way We Never Were*. New York: Basic Books, 1992.

Cowan, Ruth Schwartz. *More Work for Mother*.

Davidson, Sara. *Loose Change*. Berkeley: University of California Press, 1977.

Davis, Flora. *Moving the Mountain: The Women's Movement in America Since 1960*. Urbana: University of Illinois Press, 1999.

D'Emilio, John, and Estelle Freedman. *Intimate Matters*.

Deutrich, Mabel, and Virginia Purdy, eds. *Clio Was a Woman: Studies in the History of American Women*. Washington, D.C.: Howard University Press, 1980.

Douglas, Susan. *Where the Girls Are.* New York: Times Books, 1995.

Ehrenreich, Barbara. *The Hearts of Men.* New York: Random House, 1983.

———. *Re-Making Love* (with Elizabeth Hess and Gloria Jacobs). New York: Anchor, 1986.

Eisler, Benita. *Private Lives: Men and Women of the Fifties.* New York: Franklin Watts, 1986.

Evans, Sara. *Born for Liberty.*

———. *Personal Politics.* New York: Vintage, 1979.

———. *Tidal Wave: How Women Changed America at Century's End.* New York: The Free Press, 2003.

Friedan, Betty. *The Feminine Mystique.* New York: W.W. Norton, 1997.

———. *Life So Far.* New York: Simon & Schuster, 2000.

Furman, Bess. *Washington By-Line.* New York: Knopf, 1949.

Gallico, Paul. *The Golden People.* Garden City, N.Y.: Doubleday, 1965.

Gluck, Sherna Berger. *Rosie the Riveter Revisited.* New York: New American Library, 1987.

Goodwin, Doris Kearns *No Ordinary Time.* New York: Simon & Schuster, 1994.

Grant, Joanne. *Ella Baker.* New York: John Wiley & Sons, 1998.

Green, Harvey. *The Uncertainty of Everyday Life, 1915–1945.*

Greenfield, Lauren. *Girl Culture.* San Francisco: Chronicle Books, 2002.

Hagood, Margaret Jarman. *Mothers of the South: Portraiture of the White Tenant Farm Woman.* Charlottesville: University Press of Virginia, 1977.

Halberstam, David. *The Fifties.* New York: Ballantine Books, 1993.

Hamilton, Marybeth. *When I'm Bad, I'm Better.*

Harris, Mark Jonathan, Franklin Mitchell, and Steven Schechter. *The Homefront.* New York: G. P. Putnam's, 1984.

Harvey, Brett. *The Fifties: A Woman's Oral History.* New York: HarperCollins, 1993.

Haskell, Molly. *From Reverence to Rape.*

Hilmes, Michele. *Radio Voices.*

Honey, Maureen, ed. *Bitter Fruit: African-American Women in World War II.* Columbia: University of Missouri Press, 1999.

Houston, Jeanne Wakatsuki, and James Houston. *Farewell to Manzanar.* New York: Random House, 1973.

Inada, Lawson Fusao. *Only What We Could Carry: The Japanese American Internment Experience.* Berkeley, Calif.: Heyday Books, 2000.

Jackson, John. *American Bandstand.* New York: Oxford University Press, 1997.

Jackson, Kenneth. *Crabgrass Frontier.*

Jones, Jacqueline. *Labor of Love, Labor of Sorrow.*

Kallen, Stuart. *The 1950s.* San Diego: Lucent Books, 1999.

Kaminski, Theresa. *Prisoners in Paradise.* Lawrence: University of Kansas Press, 2000.

Keil, Sally Van Wagenen. *Those Wonderful Women in Their Flying Machines.* New York: Four Directions Press, 1990.

Kinsey, Alfred, et al. *Sexual Behavior in the Human Female.* Philadelphia: W. B. Saunders, 1953.

LaGuardia, Robert. *From Ma Perkins to Mary Hartman: The Illustrated History of Soap Operas*. New York: Ballantine Books, 1977.

Lash, Joseph. *Eleanor and Franklin*. New York: W.W. Norton, 1971.

———. *Eleanor: The Years Alone*.

Litoff, Judy Barrett, and David Smith. *Since You Went Away*. Lawrence: University Press of Kansas, 1991.

Lundberg, Ferdinand, and Marynia Farnham. *Modern Woman: The Lost Sex*. New York: Harper & Bros., 1947.

Lynd, Robert, and Helen Merrell Lynd. *Middletown in Transition*. New York: Harcourt, Brace, 1937.

Macy, Sue. *A Whole New Ballgame*. New York: Henry Holt, 1993.

Mason, Bobbie Ann. *The Girl Sleuth*.

May, Elaine Tyler. *Homeward Bound: American Families in the Cold War Era*. New York: Basic Books, 1999.

Meyer, Leisa. *Creating G.I. Jane*. New York: Columbia University Press, 1996.

Miller, Douglas, and Marion Nowak. *The Fifties: The Way We Really Were*. New York: Doubleday, 1975.

Mills, Kay. *This Little Light of Mine: The Life of Fannie Lou Hamer*. New York: Plume, 1993.

Mintz, Steven, and Susan Kellogg. *Domestic Revolutions*.

Moore, Brenda. *To Serve My Country, to Serve My Race*. New York: New York University Press, 1996.

Morgan, Robin. *Going Too Far*. New York: Vintage, 1978.

———. *Saturday's Child*. New York: W. W. Norton, 2001.

Moskowitz, Gerald, and David Rosner. *Slaves of the Depression*. Ithaca, N.Y.: Cornell University Press, 1987.

Norman, Elizabeth. *We Band of Angels*. New York: Pocket Books, 1999.

Olson, Lynne. *Freedom's Daughters*. New York: Scribner's, 2001.

Ostrander, Joan. *Bits and Pieces of Way Back When*. Lincoln, Nebr.: Writers Club Press, 2000.

Palladino, Grace. *Teenagers: An American History*. New York: Basic Books, 1996.

Parks, Rosa. *My Story*. New York: Puffin Books, 1992.

Pasachoff, Naomi. *Frances Perkins: Champion of the New Deal*. New York: Oxford University Press, 1999.

Raines, Howell. *My Soul Is Rested*. New York: Viking Penguin, 1983.

Reitman, Ben. *Boxcar Bertha*. New York: Amok Press, 1988.

Riney-Kehrberg, Pamela. *Waiting on the Bounty: The Dust Bowl Diary of Mary Knackstedt Dyck*. Iowa City: University of Iowa Press, 1999.

Robinson, Jo Ann. *The Montgomery Bus Boycott and the Women Who Started It*. Knoxville: University of Tennessee Press, 1987.

Rogan, Helen. *Mixed Company*. Boston: Beacon Press, 1981.

Roosevelt, Eleanor. *It's Up to the Women*. New York: Frederick A. Stokes, 1933.

Rosen, Ruth. *The World Split Open*. New York: Viking, 2000.

Rosenthal, Naomi. *Spinster Tales*.

Ruiz, Vicki. *From Out of the Shadows.* New York: Oxford University Press, 1998.

Rupp, Leila. *Mobilizing Women for War.* Princeton, N.J.: Princeton University Press, 1978.

———. *Survival in the Doldrums* (with Verta Taylor). New York: Oxford University Press, 1987.

Shapiro, Laura. *Perfection Salad.*

Sherman, Janann. *No Place for a Woman: A Life of Senator Margaret Chase Smith.* New Brunswick, N.J.: Rutgers University Press, 2001.

Sicherman, Barbara, and Carol Green. *Notable American Women: The Modern Period.* Cambridge, Mass.: Belknap Press, 1980.

Smith, Norma. *Jeanette Rankin: America's Conscience.*

Steinem, Gloria. *Outrageous Acts and Everyday Rebellions.*

Sternsher, Bernard, and Judith Sealander, eds. *Women of Valor.* Chicago: Ivan R. Dee, 1990.

Stevens, Michael, ed. *Women Remember the War: Voices of the Wisconsin Past.* Madison: State Historical Society of Wisconsin, 1993.

Terkel, Studs. *The Good War: An Oral History of World War II.* New York: Ballantine Books, 1984.

———. *Hard Times: An Oral History of the Great Depression.* New York: Washington Square Press, 1970.

Thurber, James. *The Beast in Me and Other Animals.* New York: Harcourt Brace Jovanovich, 1973.

Tone, Andrea. *Devices and Desires.*

Tuttle, William. *Daddy's Gone to War.* New York: Oxford University Press, 1993.

Van Amber, Rita. *Stories and Recipes of the Great Depression, Vol. 2.* Menomonie, Wis: Van Amber, 1993.

Ware, Susan. *Beyond Suffrage.*

———. *Holding Their Own: American Women in the 1930s,* Boston: Twayne, 1982.

———. *Letter to the World.*

Weatherford, Doris. *American Women and World War II.* New York: Facts on File, 1990.

Weiss, Jessica. *To Have and to Hold,* Chicago: University of Chicago Press, 2000.

Woloch, Nancy. *Women and the American Experience.*

Wylie, Philip. *Generation of Vipers.* Normal, Ill.: Dalkey Archive Press, 1996.

## PERIODICALS

Anderson, Karen Tucker. "Last Hired, First Fired: Black Women Workers During World War II." *Journal of American History* (June 1982), pp. 82–97.

Anderson, Kelli. "The Young Woman and the Sea," *Sports Illustrated* (November 29, 1999), p. 90.

Barclay, Dorothy. "Family Palship—With an Escape Clause." *The New York Times Magazine,* November 18, 1956, p. 48.

Bender, Marylin. "Liberation Yesterday—The Roots of the Feminist Movement." *New York Times,* August 21, 1970, p. 41.

Bentham, Josephine. "I Didn't Want to Tell You." *McCall's* (January 1958).

Bethune, Mary McLeod. "My Secret Talks with President Roosevelt." *Ebony* (April 1949), pp. 43–51.

Bolin, Winifred Wandersee. "The Economics of Middle-Income Family Life: Working Women During the Great Depression." *Journal of American History* 65 (June 1978), pp. 60–74.

Curtis, Charlotte. "Miss America Pageant Is Picketed by 100 Women." *New York Times,* September 8, 1968, p. 81.

Dullea, Georgia. "Women Demanding Equal Treatment in Mortgage Loans." *New York Times,* October 29, 1972, p. R1.

Fowler, Elizabeth. "Some Women Find Discrimination When Trying to Establish Credit." *New York Times,* May 15, 1972, pp. 53, 55.

"Good-bye Mammy, Hello Mom." *Ebony* (March 1947), p. 36.

Gruenberg, Sidonie. "Why They Are Marrying Younger." *The New York Times Magazine,* January 30, 1955, pp. 17, 38.

Helms, Judith. "Reaction on Jury Ruling." *Alabama Journal* (February 8, 1966), p. 9.

Kuczynski, Alex. "She's Got to Be a Macho Girl." *New York Times,* November 3, 2002, sec. 9, p. 1.

"Lady Juror Ban Ended." *Huntsville Times,* February 8, 1966, p. 1.

LeSueur, Meridel. "Women on the Breadlines." *New Masses* (January 1932), pp. 5–7.

Miller, Frieda. "What's Become of Rosie the Riveter?" *The New York Times Magazine,* May 5, 1946, pp. 21, 48.

"New Hiring Law Seen Bringing More Jobs, Benefits for Women." *Wall Street Journal,* June 22, 1965, p. 1.

North, Sandie. "Reporting the Movement." *Atlantic Monthly* (March 1970), pp. 105–6.

Pierpont, Claudia Roth. "A Study in Scarlett." *The New Yorker* (August 3, 1992), pp. 87–103.

Schneider, Jack. "British Film to Revisit Crisis at Central High." *Arkansas Democrat-Gazette,* May 17, 1999.

Steinem, Gloria. "The Moral Disarmament of Betty Coed." *Esquire* (September 1962), pp. 97, 157.

Strecker, Edward. "What's Wrong with American Mothers?" *Saturday Evening Post* (October 16, 1946), pp. 14, 103.

"Their Sheltered Honeymoon." *Life* (August 10, 1959), p. 51.

"They're Housewives and Proud of It." *New York Times,* April 3, 1972.

# INDEX